MODERN CANADIAN PLAYS

volume two

fourth edition

edited by Jerry Wasserman

D1441648

TALONBOOKS

2001

Talonbooks
P.O. Box 2076
Vancouver, British Columbia, Canada V6B 3S3
Tel.: (604) 444-4889; Fax: (604) 444-4119
Internet: www.talonbooks.com

Typeset in Optima and printed and bound in Canada by AGMV Marquis.

Fourth Edition, First Printing: July 2001

National Library of Canada Cataloguing in Publication Data

Main entry under title:

Modern Canadian plays

Includes bibliographical references.
ISBN 0-88922-436-6 (vol. 1) — ISBN 0-88922-437-4 (vol. 2)

1. Canadian drama (English)—20th century.* I. Wasserman, Jerry, 1945-
PS8315.M63 2001   C812'.5408   C00-910760-6
PR9196.6.M63 2001

The publisher gratefully acknowledges the financial support of the Canada Council for the Arts; the Government of Canada through the Book Publishing Industry Development Program; and the Province of British Columbia through the British Columbia Arts Council for our publishing activities.

Modern Canadian Plays

volume two

fourth edition

CONTENTS

INTRODUCTION

Volume One of this fourth edition of *Modern Canadian Plays* contains a dozen seminal plays from the first two decades of modern Canadian theatre, dating from the watershed year of 1967. The plays in this Volume Two span the third decade, beginning in 1987. At that time neo-conservatism was firmly entrenched in the power centres of the Western democracies, including Canada. The North American Free Trade Agreement was on the horizon, as was the collapse of the Soviet empire. And the megamusical had begun what looked like a blitzkrieg to conquer Canadian theatre. By the time this volume closes in 1997, the IT revolution appears triumphant and with it the dominant ideology of globalism, apparently erasing national borders. Right-of-centre, fiscally conservative neo-liberals hold office everywhere and proclaim "the end of history." The stock market bubble grows ever larger. The megamusical bubble is about to burst. Millennium approaches.

In choosing the twelve plays for this volume I looked for the entertaining and the provocative, plays that have made a mark on audiences and critics, in most cases plays by writers who have impacted Canadian theatre with a substantial body of work. I did not consciously seek out dramatic barometers, material measuring the direct effects of the changing cultural and historical atmosphere. Unlike Canadian drama from the late 1960s and '70s that very often responds overtly to the countercultural and nationalist agenda of that period, the plays of the late 1980s and '90s suggest nothing resembling a master narrative. Nevertheless, *fin de siècle* Canadian theatrical consciousness registers whatever moves and shakes the world both within and beyond Canadian borders.

The concerns of the era resonate in these plays in a range of ways. The Berlin Wall, civil war in El Salvador, O.J. Simpson and Oprah make offstage appearances. Socio-economic and political issues also find expression in anxieties about crime, violence and poverty, personal responsibility and the anomie of modern life. The plays are full of attempts to determine and re-define family and gender roles, personal, national and ethnic identities, the significance of race and class. Implicitly or otherwise, they challenge the multinational concept of a world without borders, the brand-name, market-driven universe manifested theatrically in the Nineties by shows like *Cats* and *Phantom of the Opera*: mass-produced companies, identically directed and choreographed, performing in corporately identified theatres (Ford Centres and others) right across the continent. In fact *borders* may be the most significant trope linking these plays. As a determinant of difference, borders are deconstructed and reconstructed, blurred and sharply etched again as the plays explore the relationship between the (Canadian) self and the world outside it. In their metatheatricality, many of the plays investigate the border between the theatre and the world, the nature and meaning of the performing self on and off the stage.

Only three of the plays in this volume carry over from the third edition. Robert Lepage has cemented his reputation as one of the world's most exciting playwrights and directors, certainly Canada's most famous theatrical export. *Polygraph*, written with actress Marie Brassard, remains one of his most enticing creations, a play that involves the crossing of many borders. Sally Clark's problematic feminist(?) comedy *Moo* and Tomson Highway's *Dry Lips Oughta Move to Kapuskasing*, still the most powerful work to come out of the First Nations' theatrical renaissance, round out the holdovers. The other nine plays are new to this anthology. Kelly Rebar's prairie comedy *Bordertown Café* and Guillermo Verdecchia's solo tour de force, *Fronteras Americanas*, confront the issue of national and geographical borders from very different perspectives. Michel Marc Bouchard's *The Orphan Muses* and Joan MacLeod's *Amigo's Blue Guitar* look at two families, one in rural Quebec, the other in coastal B.C., struggling to find ways of imagining and making sense of loss. Life in the city gets disparate treatments in Morris Panych's existential comedy *7 Stories*, Djanet Sears' complex examination of love and race, *Harlem Duet*, and *Lion in the Streets*, perhaps the most extraordinary play by one of Canada's consistently most amazing playwrights, Judith Thompson. Among the other superstars of English-Canadian theatre, Daniel MacIvor is represented by the high theatricality of *Never Swim Alone* and George F. Walker closes the volume with the brutally intense, darkly comic *Problem Child*.

Although each of these plays makes sense individually, they all make better sense within the larger contexts of Canadian theatre history. Since many readers will be using Volume Two without Volume One, we have reprinted the parts of the Introduction from Volume One that trace the evolution of modern Canadian theatre to 1986. Then the story continues through to the turn of the new millennium. So if you have read the Introduction to Volume One, you can skip sections I to III that follow and go straight to section IV. You won't find out how it ends, but the characters and plot are pretty exciting.

I.

Taking into account the ritual activities of the future nation's aboriginal inhabitants, the long and fascinating theatrical history of Canada reaches back beyond the previous millennium. But even Canadian plays by European settlers date from as early as 1606 when Marc Lescarbot wrote *Le Théâtre de Neptune en la Nouvelle-France* and staged it in Indian war canoes to honour the arrival of French dignitaries at Port Royal. Playwriting in Canada in English dates back to the eighteenth century, and in the nineteenth century Canadian playhouses sprang up in substantial numbers, though mainly to accommodate American and British touring companies. The first half of the twentieth century saw the development of a thriving amateur theatre movement and the best radio drama on the continent, as well as the emergence of a handful of noteworthy playwrights.[1] But as late as 1945 there were no Canadian professional theatre companies. As late as 1959 the foremost theatre critic in the country could write, "there is not in Canada a single person who earns a living as a playwright, or who has any practical hope of doing so."[2] Even as late as 1965 a report on "Trends in Canadian Theatre" could omit any mention of the role of Canadian plays or playwrights.[3]

The remarkable fact is that Canadian theatre as an indigenous professional institution dates only as far back as the end of World War II. And English-Canadian *drama*, in the sense of a body of dramatic work by Canadian playwrights written for performance in professional theatres, is a more recent development still. Modern drama in Quebec had its inception with Gratien Gélinas' *Tit-Coq* in 1948. For English Canada the key date was 1967: Centennial Year, the year of Expo and of the first (and last) all-Canadian Dominion Drama Festival. Over the course of that year amateur companies presented sixty-two Canadian plays in French and English in the Dominion Drama Festival competitions, twenty-nine of which were performed for the first time. (Not surprisingly, a play from the already more mature Quebec theatre, Robert Gurik's *Le Pendu*, took home all the major awards.)[4] More important was the success of the new plays given professional productions literally from coast to coast as part of the Centennial celebrations: Gélinas' *Yesterday the Children Were Dancing* in English translation at the Charlottetown Festival, James Reaney's *Colours in the Dark* at Stratford, Ann Henry's *Lulu Street* in Winnipeg, John Coulter's *The Trial of Louis Riel* in Regina, George Ryga's *The Ecstasy of Rita Joe* in Vancouver. Right across the country audiences and critics, buoyed by a new national self-consciousness and pride, were taking note of this latest cultural phenomenon—plays written by Canadian playwrights, performed by Canadian actors in Canadian theatres. And in New York, Toronto's John Herbert had a major hit with *Fortune and Men's Eyes*.

These events and the subsequent explosion of Canadian drama over the next decade seem in retrospect products of a particular historical moment, like the new European theatre that appeared in the 1870s, the new American theatre of the 1920s and the British theatrical renaissance of the mid-1950s. Yet all these movements were culminations of social and cultural forces that had been gathering momentum for many years. In the case of Canadian theatre the revolution of 1967 was rooted in an evolutionary process that began to take shape clearly around the time of the First World War.[5]

II.

The Canadian stage at the turn of the century was, in Alan Filewod's words, "a branch-plant extension of the novel American discovery that if theatre was business, then it could be big business ... By 1910 almost every playhouse in Canada was owned directly [by] or contractually locked into the American theatrical syndicates ... "[6] Those syndicates offered Canadian playgoers a predictable commercial product delivered by imported talent—American plays with American players. As an alternative, and an antidote to the Americanism with which many Canadians still attached to the British Empire felt uncomfortable, Canada's theatrical pioneers turned to trans-Atlantic models. In the first decade of the century Toronto's Arts and Letters Club Players devoted themselves to performing contemporary works from the world repertoire. They were inspired by the vogue of European art theatres, especially the Irish Abbey Theatre which would be cited time and again as a positive model for Canadians. Others, like industrialist and future cultural mandarin Vincent Massey, looked to the British model of high art infused with the ideal of a National Theatre. One thing that became clear in the midst of these first stirrings was that a genuine Canadian theatre would need its own dramatists. "There are no signs as yet upon our literary horizon of the arrival of our dramatist," a writer for *The Canadian Magazine* concluded poignantly in 1914, "but we are waiting expectantly, for we feel that he should soon come now."[7] At about the same time Vincent Massey wrote that "if we are to have a Canadian drama we must have a Canadian theatre in which to produce it."[8]

Under Massey's auspices both these ideals began to take form with the founding of Hart House Theatre in 1919. This was a well-equipped building as well as a company of the most talented actors, designers and directors in Toronto, dedicated to doing plays which would otherwise have gone unproduced in that city, including plays written by Canadians. Encouraged by this policy dramatists did arrive, enough to fill two modest volumes of *Canadian Plays from Hart House Theatre* by 1927. The most interesting was Merrill Denison. His Hart House successes, especially the satirical comedy "Brothers in Arms," and his 1923 published collection, *The Unheroic North*, established him as Canada's first playwright of note. Unable to make a living writing for the stage in Canada, Denison eventually moved to the United States in 1931 to write for American radio. Also included in Massey's collection was a play by Carroll Aikins, who would take over the running of Hart House Theatre in the late 1920s. Aikins' own experimental Home Theatre, set up in the middle of an apple orchard in B.C.'s Okanagan Valley, lasted from 1920–22.

Throughout the 1920s and into the '30s amateur theatre flourished under the umbrella of the Little Theatre movement, a burgeoning of homegrown playmaking in large and small communities on both sides of the Canada-U.S. border. Those obsessed with the idea of a National Theatre found new hope even in such humble companies, "because they build the foundation for more mature creative theatres and develop an audience for the Ultimate National Canadian theatre."[9] That imperial goal seemed to move a large step closer to realization with the establishment in 1932 of the Dominion Drama Festival, a nationwide competition organized by the new Governor General, Lord Bessborough, and chaired by Vincent Massey. The Festival was to consist of an annual series of regional playoffs climaxing in a final (held in a different city each year) at which various awards would be given for production and performance. Community theatres, school and university drama groups and such established amateur companies as Hart House would all be eligible, and adjudicators would provide helpful comments as well as determining the winners. The aim of the Festival was to showcase theatre in Canada and at the same time upgrade the quality of Canada's theatrical arts and crafts through competition and cross-fertilization.

During the years of its existence (1933–70, with a hiatus from 1940–46 due to the war), the DDF helped institutionalize amateur theatre in Canada. Whether it accomplished much more than that has been a matter of some debate. It certainly provided a proving ground for Canadian talent which often went on to New York, London, Hollywood, or by the 1950s to Stratford or other areas of the nascent Canadian professional theatre. Through special trophies and cash prizes the DDF also encouraged the writing and production of Canadian plays, an encouragement which proved at least statistically impressive. In 1934 the Festival organizers could come up with just nine Canadian titles for inclusion on its list of suggested plays sent out to participating groups; by 1966 the list contained 240 Canadian titles in English alone. But the quality and adventurousness of the work the Festival inspired were often questionable. Even as late as 1967, the DDF would refuse to allow Michel Tremblay's contentious *Les Belles-Soeurs* to be produced as part of its all-Canadian celebrations.

An earlier indictment of the limitations of the DDF was its inability to contend with the multi-media expressionism of Herman Voaden's plays, which consistently failed to advance beyond regional competitions in the 1930s because the adjudicators did not know what to make of them.[10] Voaden was an ardent nationalist and theatrical innovator who desired a Canadian dramatic art as distinctive as the paintings of the Group of Seven. To that end he sponsored a playwriting competition in Toronto in 1929 which required that each play be set in the Canadian North and suggested that the play's subject or mood be based on the writer's favourite Canadian painting. Voaden himself combined an obsession with the Canadian landscape and such disparate theatrical influences as modern dance, Wagnerian opera and symbolist drama to create a synaesthetic form he called "symphonic expressionism" in plays with titles like *Rocks, Earth Song* and *Hill-Land*. The Play Workshop he ran from 1934 to 1936 with the aim of encouraging Canadian playwriting and an indigenous theatrical style resulted in the production of twenty-five new works as well as continued experiments in total theatre. For all his eccentric and often striking work as playwright, producer, director and educator, Voaden probably made his greatest impact on the development of Canadian drama as a persistent lobbyist for increased government support for the theatre, leading to his election as the first president of the new Canadian Arts Council in 1945.

The Play Workshop and Hart House were not the only centres of Canadian playwriting activity. A group of women journalists organized the Playwrights' Studio Group in Toronto in 1932 and by the end of the decade they had produced more than fifty new plays, mainly society comedies. At the other end of the spectrum were the Progressive Arts Clubs in Toronto, Montreal, Winnipeg and Vancouver, leftist workers' theatre groups that created and performed agitprop and social protest plays throughout the Depression years. In Alberta the Banff School of the Theatre was founded in 1933, later evolving into the Banff School of Fine Arts which is still an important centre for theatre training and workshop production. Associated with Banff from the beginning was Gwen Pharis Ringwood, whose stark prairie tragedies "Still Stands the House" and *Dark Harvest* were among the strongest Canadian plays of the 1930s and '40s. (Later she would teach playwriting at Banff to George Ryga among others.) Ringwood remained a prolific and popular dramatist (in amateur circles) until her death in 1984, but her residence in northern B.C. left her out of the mainstream of the new Canadian professional theatre that grew up during the last thirty years of her life.

Probably the most significant development for Canadian drama in the 1930s and '40s was the rise of radio. The CBC had been established in 1932, and in 1936 it began broadcasting radio plays for which it actually paid writers, producers, directors, actors, musicians and technicians. What came to be known as "The Golden Age" of Canadian radio began when Andrew Allan became Supervisor of Drama for CBC and producer of its weekly *Stage* series. Under Allan from 1944 to 1955 *Stage* and *Wednesday Night* created consistently bold and imaginative drama that maintained high standards of excellence while proving broadly popular—at one time only *Hockey Night in Canada* drew more listeners than *Stage*. The stable of writers and actors that Allan assembled was "far and away the most exciting repertory group that can be heard," *The New York Times* proclaimed in 1946,[11] and it became Canada's equivalent of a national professional theatre. Hundreds of original scripts by Allan's house writers such as Lister Sinclair and Len Peterson were produced for broadcast. Even though radio's golden age faded with the coming of television in the

1950s, and CBC has been slowly eviscerated by budget cuts since the 1980s, radio drama still pays some of the bills for Canadian playwrights who might not otherwise be able to afford the luxury of writing for the chronically impecunious live stage.

In spite of the varied successes of the DDF and the CBC, neither amateur theatricals nor radio drama could satisfy the need for a vibrant, professional domestic stage culture. John Coulter, who quickly became an award-winning DDF playwright and one of the most frequently produced CBC dramatists after emigrating to Canada from Ireland in 1936, was a vocal critic of the Canadian theatre scene. In "Canadian Theatre and the Irish Exemplar," an article published in 1938, he passionately held up Dublin's Abbey Theatre as a model for Canadians, a theatre "showing the Irish to themselves … Irish mugs in Irish mirrors." Canadians too, he argued, could find dramatic subject matter in indigenous situations: "in prairie droughts and crop-failure, in mining disasters, in the poverty of the slum dwellers of city streets or country shacks," although he warned against what he saw as the Canadian propensity for excessive gloom, depression and disillusion.[12] After a series of plays set in Ireland, Coulter took his own advice and turned to Canadian history (about which he had already written for radio), achieving his greatest success with a trilogy of stage plays about Louis Riel. First produced in 1950, *Riel* would serve as a paradigm for the history plays of James Reaney and the Theatre Passe Muraille dramatists of the 1970s: revisionist Canadian history with the rebel or underdog as hero, presented as a synthesis of documentary and myth.

Coulter was fortunate that by the time *Riel* was ready for production there was a professional company to do it: the New Play Society, founded by Dora Mavor Moore in 1946. From 1950 it also included a drama school, one of whose students would be John Herbert (who later went on to act, design and stage manage for the company). Though the New Play Society remained active until 1971, its prime years were 1946–50 when its full seasons of plays in the Royal Ontario Museum Theatre proved to many skeptics the viability of a professional Canadian stage. Its most substantial success was *Spring Thaw*, a musical revue satirizing all things topical in the Great White North, first staged in 1948 and remounted with increased popularity annually for the next twenty years.

In 1954 Toronto found itself with a second homegrown professional theatre, the Crest, which soon superceded the New Play Society in importance, presenting quality work in continuous repertory for thirteen seasons until its demise in 1966. The major Canadian playwright associated with the Crest was Robertson Davies, whose *A Jig for the Gypsy* and *Hunting Stuart* premiered there in 1954–55. Davies had already become English Canada's foremost playwright on the amateur circuit with "Eros at Breakfast," "Overlaid" and *Fortune, My Foe* in 1948–49, satires of Canadian philistinism and what he considered the national disease, "emotional understimulation." Like the Crest itself, Davies remained a significant force in Canadian theatre until the mid-60s when his playwriting career gave way to his work as a novelist.

Aside from his playwriting, Davies' journalism made a strong contribution to the developing Canadian theatre in the 1940s and '50s. Both in his own name and under the pseudonym of Samuel Marchbanks, he raised his voice in protest like Voaden and Coulter against the conditions under which would-be Canadian theatre professionals had to labour—what he called in 1952 "the seedy amateurism which has afflicted the arts here for so long."[13] With fond reminiscences of his experience as a young actor in England, Davies reacted with enthusiasm to the idea of a world-class Shakespearean festival theatre in Stratford, Ontario. Along with Dora Mavor Moore and Festival organizer Tom Patterson, he was instrumental in arranging for the innovative British producer-director Tyrone Guthrie to head the venture, which held its first season of two plays under a tent in the summer of 1953. Guthrie imported British stars Alec Guinness and Irene Worth to play the leads and fleshed out the rest of the company with Canadian actors, a policy that by and large remained standard for Stratford well into the 1980s. Reviewing that first season, Davies concluded that it had given Canadians "a new vision of the theatre":

> This cannot help but have its effect on work everywhere in the country. For one thing, many of our best Canadian actors are working at Stratford … Are these

actors, who have tasted the wine of true theatre, ever again to be satisfied with the sour slops of under-rehearsed, under-dressed, under-mounted, under-paid, and frequently ill-considered and ill-financed theatre projects? ... The Stratford Festival is an artistic bombshell, exploded just at the time when Canadian theatre is most ready for a break with the dead past and a leap into the future.[14]

There is no doubt that the Stratford Festival did have an enormous impact on theatre and the *idea* of theatre in Canada. It became an event of international importance and influence (its new non-proscenium thrust stage designed by Guthrie and Tanya Moisiewitsch made waves in theatres worldwide). Thus it raised the profile of theatre in Canada as nothing else had been able to do and served as a focus of national cultural pride. Stratford also became a training ground for many of the best actors who emerged in Canada over the next three decades, making stars of Christopher Plummer, Frances Hyland and others. Moreover, it was argued,

Stratford created a model for indigenous Canadian theatre: a non-profit organization, unconcerned with the values of New York, unashamedly using imported personnel where Canadian expertise was lacking, equally unashamedly welcoming subsidy support in return for placing its destiny—at a policy-making level—in the hands of a volunteer citizen Board of Governors, and representatives of the community in which it found itself.[15]

But Stratford did little to effect or support the development of Canadian playwriting. Writers like Herbert and Reaney would receive workshop and small-scale public performances of their plays there in the late 1960s. In 1971 a Third Stage was added, in part to produce Canadian work. But by that time Stratford was no longer an adequate model. With its huge financial operation it became in many eyes a cultural dinosaur, devouring large subsidies at the expense of the smaller theatres whose productions of Canadian plays, often on shoestring budgets, were perceived as being more central to an emerging national drama than was a theatre devoted to Shakespeare. Ironically, while Stratford feasted, Canadian drama came of age in the early 1970s as a kind of poor theatre nourished on just those "sour slops" that Davies had complained of in 1953. Today, a half-century after its creation the Stratford Festival continues to thrive. And even with a fully Canadian contingent of lead actors, directors and designers, and a Canadian artistic director, it continues to occupy a controversial place in the Canadian theatrical pantheon.

In any case by 1956 there was good reason for the feeling that "the Canadian theatre ... like the stock market, is bullish these days ... "[16] The success of Stratford and the other new professional theatres was being augmented by CBC television, which from its inception in 1952 gave starts to a number of important dramatists who would later go on to write for the stage, including George Ryga, David French and Michel Tremblay. On the horizon as well was the Canada Council, whose founding in 1957 would change the nature of theatre in Canada more than any other single development, providing a sudden massive influx of government funding for buildings, companies and individuals engaged in the arts.

The Canada Council was the most concrete manifestation of the Royal Commission on National Development in the Arts, Letters and Sciences appointed by Prime Minister Louis St. Laurent in 1949 with Vincent Massey as chairman. Its mandate was to examine how government could contribute to the development of those areas of endeavour "which express national feeling, promote common understanding and add to the variety and richness of Canadian life."[17] Even if, as Alan Filewod, Denis Salter and others have argued, the Massey Commission proceeded from certain British-imported, elitist cultural biases, its 1951 *Report* proved a tremendously valuable national consciousness-raiser. It found that Canadian culture was being stifled by the omnipresence of American influences and the lack of support and facilities for artists in Canada. Its major recommendation was the formation of the Canada Council for the Encouragement of the Arts, Letters, Humanities and Social Sciences to support Canadian culture at home and abroad. From an initial outlay of $2.6 million in arts grants in 1957, the Council's investment in individuals and groups totalled more than $60 million by 1970, a quantum leap in the funds available to fuel the engine of Canadian cultural nationalism.

Money wasn't the only catalyst for change, though. In 1958 in Winnipeg, with virtually no capital but their missionary commitment to convert a whole province to the ideal of a regional professional theatre, Tom Hendry and John Hirsch merged their amateur Theatre 77 with the Winnipeg Little Theatre to create the Manitoba Theatre Centre, with Hirsch as its first artistic director. From the start the MTC "was meant to be more than a theatre, something that could in fact become a focus for all theatrical energy and resources in one community."[18] Combining mainstage productions in Winnipeg with a touring company, children's theatre, and a school, the MTC succeeded so well in galvanizing the support and resources of its constituency that it became the basis for a new concept: a Canadian national theatre that would be decentralized and regional—a professional theatre version of the ostensible Canadian mosaic. With support and encouragement from the Canada Council a network of regional theatres spread across the country: Vancouver's Playhouse and Halifax's Neptune in 1963, Edmonton's Citadel in 1965 and Regina's Globe in 1966. By 1970 Montreal, Calgary, Fredericton and Toronto also had theatres catering in principle to regional communities.

Canada, it seemed, had indeed become bullish on theatre. The building boom didn't stop with the regionals, either. To train and supply actors for the new national theatre network, the National Theatre School was opened in Montreal in 1960 with separate French and English programs. At Niagara-on-the-Lake the Shaw Festival began operation in 1962, and P.E.I.'s Charlottetown Festival was inaugurated in 1964 specializing in Canadian musical theatre. St. John's got its Arts and Culture Centre in 1967. Finally, in 1969–70 the completion of three major Centennial construction projects—Ottawa's National Arts Centre, Toronto's St. Lawrence Centre, and a new building for the MTC—rounded out a decade of extraordinary growth for the Canadian theatre.

III.

With the superstructure finally intact the question now was, where were the plays that might crystallize the new drama in English Canada, implanting it at the heart of the nation's cultural life the way John Osborne's *Look Back in Anger* had done in Britain and Gélinas' *Tit-Coq* in Quebec (and the way Tremblay's *Les Belles-Soeurs* would do again in Quebec, in a different way, in 1968)? Those plays had had in common vernacular speech, anti-establishment anger, and characters, settings and situations that were definitively of their own time and place. So too had the play that finally touched the nerve of English Canada. *The Ecstasy of Rita Joe* premiered at the Vancouver Playhouse on November 23, 1967, in a landmark production that was remounted for the opening of the National Arts Centre in 1969. That year the play was also broadcast on CBC-TV and produced in a French translation by Gratien Gélinas in Montreal, as *Rita Joe* reverberated through the nation's collective consciousness. In a review of a later production, Jamie Portman recalled that "*Rita Joe* happened during Centennial year when Canadians were anxious to look at themselves. But the look that this play provided was an unsettling one. It punctured the euphoria and the smug complacency of Canada's birthday celebrations and declared unequivocally that all was not well. with this country and its institutions." Its implications for Canadian playwriting were equally dramatic:

> This was an indigenous Canadian drama that surfaced and succeeded at a time when indigenous Canadian drama was generally considered to be an aberration. It was a play of merit, worthy of production in any Canadian theatre. It prompted an awareness of the existence of other plays potentially worthy of production. It provided resounding evidence that it was not necessary for any Canadian theatre to rely solely on imported fare. With the arrival of *The Ecstasy of Rita Joe*, Canadian plays ceased to be a rarity in English-speaking Canada. Companies dedicated to the production of new Canadian drama sprang up, and in so doing

nurtured the further growth of playwriting activity. Canada's regional theatres—some of them grudgingly—found themselves forced to take the Canadian playwright seriously for the first time.[19]

Yet the battle for credibility was not quite so easily won. Just how grudgingly the theatre establishment came to accept the Canadian playwright was vividly registered by a 1971 study that found that in the previous year, the seven major regional theatres had produced the work of a total of two Canadian dramatists, and paid them less than $5000 out of combined budgets of more than $2 million.[20] Consider the case of the once pioneering Manitoba Theatre Centre. Despite its success with Winnipeg writer Ann Henry's *Lulu Street*, more than a decade would pass before the MTC presented another new play by a local playwright. The flurry of Canadian play production in 1967 had obviously been in some respects no more than Centennial Year tokenism.

The stage history of John Herbert's *Fortune and Men's Eyes* is especially revealing of the difficulties faced by Canadian playwrights. *Fortune* had been workshopped at Stratford in 1965. But denied a full production there or anywhere else in Canada, the play opened in New York in 1967 and ran for a year off-Broadway. By the end of 1968 it had had a long run in London and become a full-scale international hit. By 1969 it was already being revived in New York. The play's impact on other Canadian dramatists was immediate and inspirational: "the ice-breaker in the channel," George Ryga called it.[21] But for all that, professional productions of *Fortune and Men's Eyes* in Canada to 1970 consisted of a week at the Vancouver Playhouse's "experimental" Stage 2 and a brief run in the MTC's Studio Theatre. Not a mainstage production was to be seen. Herbert's hometown of Toronto would have to wait until 1975 to see the play at all.

What had gone wrong? The expectations and struggles of a half-century had resulted in a Canadian theatre that by the late 1960s had already become entrenched and conservative. Rather than living up to the original promise of the regionals to create new models adapted to the distinctive needs of their communities, which surely should have meant presenting plays written about those communities from within them, the large subsidized theatres mostly tried to emulate Broadway and London's West End. When artistic directors were asked about Canadian plays and playwrights, their responses were often remarkably similar:

I don't see how a play can be Canadian.

I don't think there are any plays that you could call strictly Canadian.

But if you start to define what is a Canadian and what is a Canadian playwright, what do you end up with?

What does the phrase mean?[22]

With few exceptions the regionals served up homogenized theatre: safe, commercial seasons of British and American hits plus a smattering of world classics. Moreover, it was theatre as Cultural Event, like the opera or the symphony, the kind of thing you got dressed up for.

But in the late '60s, the Age of Aquarius and the Generation Gap, many theatre artists and much of the potential audience were evolving in a different direction. The Canadian Centennial just happened to coincide with the most radical cultural upheaval of the century in the Western world. There was a sexual revolution, a musical revolution, a drug revolution; long hair, peace marches and a Summer of Love. By 1968 in Chicago, Paris and Prague the revolution would spill over into the streets. Canada wasn't immune to these forces nor could its theatre be, no matter how stubbornly it tried to remain middle-aged and middle-class.

That the most significant Canadian plays of the decade should have appeared in 1967–68 was not coincidental. *The Ecstasy of Rita Joe*, *Fortune and Men's Eyes* and *Les Belles-Soeurs* are plays very much of their age, marked by strong social consciousness and critical, anti-establishment perspectives. The playwrights too, by virtue of their alienation from the mainstream, were in sync with the temper of the times. Herbert and Tremblay were gay men. Ryga and Herbert were outspoken and uncompromising in their social, artistic and political views. It was characteristic of their outsider status that neither was initially allowed entry into the United States to see his own play in production; characteristic that Herbert refused the DDF's Massey Award (and its $1000 cash prize) for Best Play for *Fortune* in 1968; characteristic that the politics of Ryga's 1970 play *Captives of the Faceless Drummer* would so upset the Board of the Vancouver Playhouse, which had commissioned it, that they would refuse it production. It was ironic but perhaps also inevitable that the two writers whose plays brought modern English-Canadian drama into existence would eventually find themselves virtually unproduced by the major Canadian theatres.

Modern Canadian drama was born out of an amalgam of the new consciousness of the age— social, political and aesthetic—with the new Canadian self-consciousness. Since the larger theatres were generally unsympathetic and unaccommodating to both these forces, an even newer Canadian theatre had to be invented, an alternate theatre. One of its prime movers in Toronto was Martin Kinch, who describes those first heady days as having little to do with nationalism:

> The real influences were Fritz Perls and Timothy Leary, Peter Brook and Jerzy Grotowski, Tom O'Horgan, Café La Mama, Julian Beck, Judith Malina, and the ensemble of the Living Theatre; in short, a host of European and American artists, most of them primarily dedicated to the ethic and the aesthetic of "doing your own thing" ... It was an exciting time, a time of experiment and exploration ... expressionism, hallucination, confrontation, and audience participation flourished. Perhaps most important, however, there existed a definite bond between the theatres and their audience; an audience that was characterized by long hair, beards, bells, and babies in the front rows of the most outrageous plays. Its concerns were the concerns of "the sixties": the breaking of sexual taboo, the problems of individual freedom, and the yearning for community.[23]

In 1969 Kinch became a co-director of Toronto's Theatre Passe Muraille, founded the previous year by Jim Garrard. As its name suggests, Passe Muraille was to be a theatre without walls: neither the traditional fourth wall between actors and audience nor necessarily even the walls of a theatre building. Garrard envisioned "a guerrilla theatre": "Theatre in the subways, get a truck and do theatre in small towns, real circuses, grab people in the streets ... I'd like to make theatre as popular as bowling."[24] A milestone for the new alternate theatre movement was Passe Muraille's production of Rochelle Owen's *Futz* in February 1969. An American play about a man in love with a pig (!), in both style and content it established the parameters of the alternate theatre's self-conscious anti-conventionality. The sex, obscenity and nudity it featured would become almost obligatory. When the show was closed by the morality squad, and the company charged and subsequently acquitted, the new movement had its red badge of courage.

By the summer of 1970 alternate theatre in Toronto had developed to the point where it could celebrate itself with a Festival of Underground Theatre. When the smoke from the festival cleared, the emphasis of the alternates could be seen to have undergone something of a shift from sensationalism to nationalism. Central to the new emphasis were Ken Gass and his Factory Theatre Lab, and the new artistic director of Theatre Passe Muraille, Paul Thompson.

Gass, who had been helping run John Herbert's tiny Garret Theatre, set out to prove that there was no lack of Canadian playwrights; they were just waiting to be discovered and encouraged. His theatre would be both a factory and a laboratory, presenting polished new works as well as works-in-progress, fragments, staged ideas. Most importantly it would be "The Home of the Canadian Playwright." His concept paid off almost immediately with a string of notable new plays: David Freeman's *Creeps*, Herschel Hardin's *Esker Mike and His Wife, Agiluk* and George Walker's *Prince of Naples* all in 1971; most of Walker's other plays over the next dozen years; and exciting (though not necessarily enduring) work by Hrant Alianak, Larry Fineberg, Bryan Wade and Gass himself. Gass remained artistic director of the Factory until 1979, then returned to the post again in 1996 to save the company from what seemed like its imminent demise.

Paul Thompson came to Passe Muraille after working in France with Roger Planchon, whose process-oriented, political brand of theatre was in direct contrast with Thompson's experiences during a brief apprenticeship at Stratford. Rejecting the Stratford model, Thompson steered his company towards a focus on local subject matter and collective creation, involving his actors in first-hand research, improvisation and continual revision, and utilizing their particular skills as key elements in the play wherever possible. When Thompson took over Passe Muraille there was already a precedent for this kind of theatre in Toronto. George Luscombe had been involved with Joan Littlewood's Theatre Workshops in England in the mid-1950s and had put together Toronto Workshop Productions in 1959 based on Littlewood's political and stylistic principles: left-wing politics and an eclectic style that integrated improvs, documentary, *commedia* and often collective scripting. In the late 1960s and early '70s TWP was creating potent socio-political theatre with agit-prop pieces like *Mister Bones* and *Chicago '70* on race and politics in America, and its bittersweet evocation of the Canadian Depression, *Ten Lost Years*. The partnership of Luscombe and Toronto Workshop Productions lasted for thirty years, finally collapsing in 1989 with the company's folding and its building passing on to Sky Gilbert's Buddies in Bad Times Theatre.

But it was Passe Muraille under Paul Thompson's stewardship that became the most important theatre in Canada in the early 1970s. Creations like *Doukhobors*, *The Farm Show* (first performed in a Clinton, Ontario barn), *Under the Greywacke* and *The Adventures of an Immigrant* (performed in Toronto streetcars among other venues) made often stirring theatrical poetry out of material that was sometimes mundane and always local. Docudrama with a high degree of theatricality became the Passe Muraille trademark: a small company of actors using little but their own bodies and voices to create ingenious stage metaphors. They inspired countless imitators across the country, though in less talented hands the deceptively rigorous demands of collective scripting and Passe Muraille's presentational style sometimes had unfortunate results. Among the best of their offshoots was Twenty-Fifth Street House Theatre in Saskatoon, whose *Paper Wheat* was in the finest Passe Muraille tradition, and Newfoundland's CODCO. In addition the company specialized in resurrecting, popularizing, dramatizing and often mythicizing Canadian history in collective scripts or in conjunction with a writer. *Buffalo Jump* with Carol Bolt, *1837: The Farmers' Revolt* with Rick Salutin, *Them Donnellys* with Frank MacEnany and *Far as the Eye Can See* with Rudy Wiebe were some of the best of the collaborations. Later in the decade two Passe Muraille alumni would create *Billy Bishop Goes to War*, and Linda Griffiths (with Paul Thompson) would let loose *Maggie & Pierre* upon the country. Perhaps the most exciting Canadian playwright to emerge in the 1980s, Judith Thompson, also came out of Passe Muraille with her extraordinary first play, *The Crackwalker*. Passe Muraille remains to the present day one of the primary loci of Canadian theatrical production and development.

Not everything was happening in Toronto. In Vancouver, where Sidney Risk had pioneered post-war professional touring with his Everyman Theatre (1946–53), and where John Juliani's experimental Savage God project had been operating since 1966, John Gray, Larry Lillo and a group of other UBC graduates formed Tamahnous Theatre in 1971, a collective that would remain Vancouver's most original and progressive company for the next ten years. Its most enduring legacy may prove to be the special brand of small-cast musical best represented by Gray's *Billy Bishop* and Morris Panych's "post-nuclear cabaret," *Last Call!* Meanwhile the New Play Centre had come into being in 1970 dedicated to developing new scripts by local writers with production as only a secondary priority. Under the direction of Pamela Hawthorn from 1972 until 1989, the New Play Centre had a hand in most of the drama to come out of B.C., including the work of Margaret Hollingsworth, Tom Walmsley, Ted Galay, John Lazarus, Sheldon Rosen, Betty Lambert, Eric Nicol and Sherman Snukal. In the late 1990s the NPC metamorphosed into Playwrights Theatre Centre, which continues its predecessor's work.

Seeded by government grants from Local Initiatives Programs (LIP) and Opportunities for Youth (OFY), new companies doing indigenous theatre sprouted everywhere in 1971–72: Edmonton's

Theatre 3, Calgary's Alberta Theatre Projects, Pier One in Halifax, the Mummers Troupe in St. John's. Lennoxville, Quebec even provided a kind of "alternate" festival theatre. Festival Lennoxville presented all-Canadian summer seasons of plays by the likes of Michael Cook, Herschel Hardin and Sharon Pollock from 1972 until its demise in 1982, a victim of poor demographics and Parti Québécois cultural policy.

Toronto, though, was where most of the action was, and nothing did more to cement its position at the centre of the new movement than Tarragon Theatre. Founded in 1971 by Bill Glassco, who had directed *Creeps* at the Factory Lab earlier in the year, Tarragon opened with a revised version of *Creeps* that proved even more successful than the original. The first Tarragon season ended with a new work which was to become probably the single most influential Canadian play of the 1970s, David French's *Leaving Home*. Its story of generational conflict and a singularly Canadian form of immigrant alienation (ex-Newfoundlanders spiritually adrift in Toronto) elicited strong audience identification, and its straightforward, accessible style had a broad appeal. *Leaving Home* created a vogue for domestic realism that some have argued was a debilitating counterforce to the more adventurous directions that Canadian drama seemed to be taking at the time. Tarragon soon became identified with that particular style, especially in light of Glassco's productions of subsequent plays by Freeman and French that were stylistically tame. But it wasn't really a fair reputation. Tarragon also introduced English Canada to the plays of Michel Tremblay with Glassco as director and co-translator—plays that are domestic in setting but hardly realistic in style. Moreover, from 1973–75 Tarragon produced James Reaney's Donnelly trilogy, which is about as far removed from stylistic realism or naturalism as plays can get. Unlike the great majority of companies devoted to Canadian works Tarragon managed both to combine artistic and commercial success and to sustain it over a number of years. More than any other theatre it succeeded in bringing Canadian drama into the mainstream. Since Glassco left Tarragon in 1985, its status has been maintained under the artistic directorship of former theatre critic Urjo Kareda. The many playwrights in *Modern Canadian Plays* whose work is associated with Tarragon testify to the continued influence, importance and adventurousness of the company.

The great wave of new alternate theatres in Toronto crested in 1972 with the founding of Toronto Free Theatre by Tom Hendry, Martin Kinch and John Palmer. Subsidized by LIP grants, performances were literally free until 1974 when the impossible economics of that policy led to gradually increasing admissions. But Toronto Free's cultivation of an excellent ensemble of actors and a distinctive taste for the psychologically bizarre in plays and production remained constant until (and even after) its merger with Centrestage in 1988 to create the Canadian Stage Company. Many of its early successes were plays by its in-house triumvirate—especially Hendry and Palmer— along with Carol Bolt. George F. Walker and Erika Ritter were among the most noteworthy later additions to Toronto Free's playwriting corps.

Notwithstanding the dynamism of the alternate theatres, drama in Canada in the early 1970s was in danger of falling victim to an insidious form of ghettoization. Canadian plays were relegated to small, low-budget theatres that lacked the financial and technical resources available to the heavily subsidized festivals and regionals. While non-Canadian works had access to lush productions, large casts and relatively highly paid actors, Canadian plays were doomed to what George Ryga called "beggars theatre."[25] Concurrently, of course, Canadian playwrights were denied the financial opportunities that might allow them to make a living by practicing their craft. In an attempt to remedy this situation a group of playwrights met in the summer of 1971 to consider "The Dilemma of the Playwright in Canada." What ensued was a series of strongly worded recommendations, the most contentious of which called for a 50% Canadian content quota for all theatres receiving government funding. Most artistic directors and editorialists were predictably outraged. ("If it ever happened, then critics should also get Canada Council grants for sitting through the plays," was one wit's response.[26]) Though no formal quota system was ever adopted, the controversy led to a full public airing of the situation and, more importantly, to an informal policy decision by the Canada

Council to "appeal" to its client theatres to do more Canadian plays. The results were startling. By the 1972–73 season nearly 50% of the plays produced by subsidized theatres in both English and French were in fact Canadian.

Among the most tangible consequences of this new policy was a return to one of the original precepts of the "regional" ideal, the commissioning of new plays by regional theatres from playwrights with local roots and interests. These arrangements proved mutually fruitful for playwrights and theatres alike, especially Sharon Pollock's work for the Vancouver Playhouse and Theatre Calgary, John Murrell and W.O. Mitchell also at Theatre Calgary, Ken Mitchell and especially Rex Deverell with Regina's Globe, and David Fennario with the Centaur in Montreal. The Blyth and Kawartha Summer Festivals, in their cultivation of Anne Chislett, proved the value of a homegrown product even in the traditionally more commercial milieu of summer theatre. In each of these cases plays written with very specific associations for local audiences made their way into theatres across the country with no lack of success. Maybe Canadian writers and producers had finally learned what John Coulter had called, back in 1938, "the paradoxical truth that the most effective way to keep an eye on Broadway is to keep on looking attentively at the life passing under your own nose in your own home town."[27]

Another way "to keep an eye on Broadway" and the West End was to continue to strengthen and in a sense nationalize the organizational infrastructure of Canadian theatre. 1976 saw the formation of both the Professional Association of Canadian Theatres (PACT) and the Association for Canadian Theatre History, a national academic organization. That same year Canadian Actors' Equity Association declared its independence from U.S. Actors' Equity. Yet a certain amount of retrenchment was also inevitable given the tremendous expansion Canadian theatre had undergone since 1967. Tougher economic times and a general trend towards conservatism put additional strains on an endeavour that is economically marginal even under the best conditions. Theatres as widely divergent as Stratford and Twenty-Fifth Street House had to weather financial and artistic crises that threatened their survival. Some went under: Vancouver's Westcoast Actors, Edmonton's Theatre 3, Montreal's Saidye Bronfman. Facing new audience expectations and a changing ideological climate, the major "alternate" theatres (a term no longer really accurate) in Toronto and Vancouver all underwent structural reorganization and found new artistic directors.

But by the mid-1980s, near the end of its second decade, modern Canadian theatre clearly stood on firm footing and still had some major momentum. Passe Muraille, Tarragon, Factory Theatre (minus the "Lab"), Toronto Free and Tamahnous remained in operation (though Toronto Free would soon disappear in a merger and Tamahnous was no longer the force it had been). Those companies along with the resurgent regionals and successful middle-of-the-road theatres like Vancouver's Arts Club continued to provide a springboard for Canadian plays. Across the country a new generation of neo-alternates arose to take the place of those that fell by the wayside or moved into the mainstream. These included Prairie Theatre Exchange in Winnipeg, Rising Tide Theatre in St. John's, and Nova Scotia's Mulgrave Road Co-op and Ship's Company. Nakai Theatre Ensemble in Whitehorse and Tunooniq in the Arctic ensured the exposure of lively theatrical voices in the Canadian North. In Vancouver Touchstone joined the scene along with Green Thumb, which set the pattern for hard-hitting young people's theatre.

Per capita, probably the most activity was taking place in Edmonton, rapidly becoming Canada's most important centre for English-language theatre after Toronto. Theatre Network, Northern Light, Catalyst, Workshop West and Phoenix Theatre all came on stream before 1982, the year the Edmonton Fringe Festival was born. Modelled on the Edinburgh Fringe, Edmonton's festival has become a hugely successful affair with annual attendance in the quarter-million range, and a prototype for the many other Canadian Fringes which have sprung up in its wake. Meanwhile, Toronto continued its theatrical expansion to the point where it could soon lay claim to being second only to New York as a mecca for theatre in North America. Among its most innovative and important new companies were Necessary Angel, Nightwood (which became Canada's foremost feminist theatre), Buddies in Bad Times (soon the country's most important gay company as well as a key centre for new play development with its spinoff Rhubarb! Festival), Theatre Columbus (clown-based theatre), Cahoots (multicultural), and Native Earth Performing Arts, which led the renaissance of Native theatre in Canada. The Toronto International Theatre Festival in 1981, and its later successor, the Harbourfront, showcased Canadian plays and productions alongside some of the best theatre companies in the world.

Canadian theatre's growing cultural prominence was also signified by the establishment of a series of new awards. Joining the prestigious Chalmers, given by the Toronto Drama Bench since 1972 for best new Canadian play produced each year in Toronto, were the Canadian Authors' Association Award for Drama (est. 1975) and, in 1981, the Governor General's Award in Drama honouring the best new Canadian play in publication in French and the best in English. All offer substantial cash prizes. The Doras in Toronto (after Dora Mavor Moore), the Jessies in Vancouver (after Jessie Richardson), the Sterlings in Edmonton (after Elizabeth Sterling Haynes) and the Bettys in Calgary (after Betty Mitchell) celebrate the best work done on those cities' stages in the name of a local theatrical pioneer. Add to those the Mecca awards, instituted in 2000 to honour English-language theatre production in Montreal, a counterpart of sorts to the Masque awards (est. 1994) given for French-language theatre in Quebec. Just as these prizes have raised the cultural profile of theatre in Canada, so too did the 1984–85 publication of three anthologies of Canadian drama in English, including the first version of this one. As a result Canadian plays became more accessible to high school and post-secondary students, more entrenched in curricula, more academically reputable.

Some things had notably changed by the mid-1980s. The nationalism that had largely inspired and in some ways kick-started the new Canadian theatre had pretty much gone out of vogue. Free trade and globalism were soon to become the new keywords. Even the old keywords had new meanings. As Alan Filewod points out, "in 1974 the terms 'native' and 'indigenous' meant 'Canadian' as opposed to British or American; by 1984 they had acquired a much more specific value (pertaining to aboriginal peoples) which challenged the very meaning of 'Canadian' as it was understood only a decade earlier."[28]

IV.

Nevertheless, the next few years were marked by an unprecedented series of theatrical coups led by what John Gray calls, in his introduction to Billy Bishop Goes to War, the Old Warriors of Canadian Nationalism. Tarragon pioneer Bill Glassco became artistic director of southern Ontario's major regional theatre, CentreStage, in 1985, then engineered a merger with Guy Sprung and Toronto Free Theatre, one of the keystone alternative companies of the 1970s, to create the Canadian Stage Company in 1988. That same year, Tamahnous co-founder and west coast alter-nate-theatre icon Larry Lillo made a triumphant return to Vancouver to run B.C.'s flagship regional theatre, the Playhouse, and Sharon Pollock took over her home-town regional, Theatre New Brunswick. The Stratford Festival's controversial attempt to hire a non-Canadian artistic director in 1980 was resolved in favour of the appointment of John Hirsch, who had co-founded the Manitoba Theatre Centre back in 1958. Canadian actor Richard Monette, who had once played Hosanna at the Tarragon, took over the Festival's reins in 1992. With such apparent victories, along with the broader ideological shifts of the 1980s, the nationalist agenda and overt issues of cultural identity receded in importance. In relative terms this was the case even in Quebec.

But as economic issues superceded nationalism on the larger political landscape, so too did economics assume greater political and artistic impact in the theatre. Canada's non-profit, publicly subsidized theatre system had to deal with shrinking government support in the face of growing deficits and an unsympathetic Conservative regime under Brian Mulroney. Theatre was increasingly perceived as just another commercial commodity, having to find its niche in a competitive and fragmented cultural marketplace battered by two major recessions and dominated by home videos.

Theatre boards run by businessmen assumed more and more power, and corporate sponsorships to replace lost government funding became the norm. Conflicts between the artistic and corporate agendas led to a series of crises. If 1988 had seen the apparent victory of the cultural nationalists, 1989 showed just how fragile the new theatrical order really was. The original and longest-lived of the alternative theatres, Toronto Workshop Productions, shut down in a struggle between its artists and its board. The Canadian Stage Company's board forcibly removed artistic director Guy Sprung, and Sharon Pollock resigned from Theatre New Brunswick in frustration.[29] *Canadian Theatre Review* titled its Summer 1990 issue, "Surviving the Nineties." (A 1996 issue would be titled "Survivors of the Ice Age.")

For a few writers the commercialization of Canadian theatre meant not just surviving but thriving, as hit plays from small non-profit stages got remounted in large, long-run commercial venues. Toronto led the way in this regard with George F. Walker's *Love and Anger* and Brad Fraser's *Unidentified Human Remains and the True Nature of Love* crossing over into commercial production in 1990, and Tomson Highway's *Dry Lips Oughta Move to Kapuskasing* in 1991.[30] But by far the most significant development of the commercial theatre was the appearance of the megamusical. A building and renovation boom accompanied the phenomenon. In 1985, to accommodate Andrew Lloyd Webber's *Cats*, Toronto's old Elgin Theatre/Winter Garden complex was restored to its former glories, and *Cats* ran for two years. In 1989 entertainment mogul Garth Drabinsky renovated another magnificent old vaudeville house, the Pantages, for Lloyd Webber's *Phantom of the Opera*, which ended up running there for ten years and selling over seven million tickets. Meanwhile, producers Ed and David Mirvish had opened *Les Miserables* at their Royal Alexandra Theatre. The extraordinary success of these huge imported shows, not just in Toronto but in their spin-off tours across Canada, led to more of the same. In the early '90s the Mirvishes built the Princess of Wales theatre to house *Miss Saigon*. Drabinsky's Livent Inc. became the largest theatrical production company in North America. They developed the North York Performing Arts Centre which opened with their production of *Show Boat*. In exchange for big dollars they renamed it the Ford Centre for the Performing Arts, and built an identically named complex in downtown Vancouver. While still importing shows, the megamusical producers also began creating their own new versions of musical theatre classics for export (*Show Boat, Joseph and His Amazing Technicolor Dreamcoat*), as well as commissioning and producing new shows like Drabinsky's *Kiss of the Spider Woman* and *Ragtime*, and an all-Canadian *Napoleon*.

The megamusical boom had the virtue of generally fueling the theatrical economy, creating international stars of Canadian actors like Brent Carver and Jeff Hyslop, and spin-off opportunities for a few Canadian non-musical plays. (Drabinsky was responsible for the commercial remount of *Love and Anger*, and the Mirvishes for *Dry Lips*.) But on the whole it posed severe challenges for the Canadian non-profit theatre. Rather than benefitting from a trickle-down of the new audiences created and abetted by the megas, low-budget companies found themselves in a difficult competition for the theatre-going dollar. More insidiously, the success of these shows shaped a certain kind of audience expectation and demand, and fostered pressures, subtle and unsubtle (from boards, funding agencies and others), to conform to the megamusical aesthetic—high on spectacle, low on content, lacking in Canadian reference and empty of political challenge.[31] "Megamusicals can kill intelligent theatre," Sky Gilbert complained, then went even further: "Megamusicals actually make you stupid."[32]

If Gilbert was right, intelligence triumphed. In 1998, with the novelty and popularity of the genre waning, his overextended empire straining, and Drabinsky himself accused of fraudulently cooking the books, Livent collapsed. The Canadian theatrical clock was not turned back a hundred years. The smaller, non-profit theatres where most Canadian plays are born and performed survived the challenge and the debacle. Yet in 2001 Disney's spectacular stage musical of *The Lion King* continued to be one of the hottest tickets in Toronto. And in Vancouver the Ford Centre stood dark and empty for the third year, a reminder of what can happen when the business of theatre becomes business rather than theatre.

Theatre-as-economics and theatre-as-spectacle remained significant issues at the dawn of the new millennium. The news wasn't all bad. On the one hand a series of rich new cash prizes became available to artists and producers: a $25,000 playwriting prize offered by the University of British Columbia, the $50,000 Alcan Arts Award to a producing company in B.C., and the $100,000 Siminovitch Prize for a Canadian theatre artist in mid-career. But at the same time deficit-cutting federal and provincial governments had reduced their grants. Then the prohibition of tobacco advertising led du Maurier to threaten to withdraw many of its sponsorships. The result was a chronic funding crisis. Calgary's Alberta Theatre Projects nearly folded. Toronto's Theatre Plus did. Many in the Canadian theatre community echoed the sentiments of the *Los Angeles Times* critic who lamented how even in the United States, the economic squeeze of the 1990s created a "survival mentality" whereby artistic directors tended to minimize risk and opt for safe programming. In Canada "the poorly funded non-profits embrace facile populism," complained Kate Taylor in the *Globe and Mail*.[33] And what could be safer or more facile than simply putting pretty pictures on stage?

Yet ironically, one of the real strengths of the Canadian theatre as it entered the twenty-first century was its development of a complex visual vocabulary, from the neo-baroque *mise en scène* favoured by many Québécois playwrights and directors to image-based physical theatre, clown, mime, movement, dance and puppetry. Artistic Fraud of Newfoundland (whose *Under Wraps* is performed by 19 actors, 17 totally covered by a sheet), Montreal's Carbone 14 and The Other Theatre, Toronto's Theatre Smith-Gilmour, Winnipeg's Primus (until its demise in 1998), and Calgary's One Yellow Rabbit are just some of the companies that subordinate the spoken word in favour of sharply detailed, carefully choreographed visual effects. Among the most popular acts on the fringe circuit is the duo of Mump and Smoot, Toronto's "clowns of horror," whose only vocalisms are gibberish; and the brilliant marionette shows of Calgary's Ronnie Burkett have been seen and honoured around the world.[34] The first national success of the year 2000 was Morris Panych's triumphant Vancouver Playhouse production and subsequent Canadian tour of Gogol's *The Overcoat*, performed without a single word. Robert Lepage not only writes, performs and directs, but also designs many of the visually stunning plays that have made him an international phenomenon. No doubt Canada's greatest economic success on the world stage, and one of its genuine artistic triumphs, is the spectacle theatre of Cirque du Soleil. Since its founding in 1984, the Montreal-based company has redefined the circus and established a global empire, including two shows permanently running in Las Vegas. One of them, *O*, is the most spectacular piece of theatre I have ever seen.

"Canada on the World Stage" has become an increasingly meaningful phrase. It headlines *Canadian Theatre Review*'s Winter 2001 issue examining the export of Canadian drama to the U.K., the U.S., Italy, Belgium, India and Australia. That issue appeared around the same time as plays by Michel Tremblay, Morris Panych, Daniel MacIvor and George F. Walker, as well as the new Cirque du Soleil show, were running in Washington, D.C., leading the *Washington Post* to declare some-what hyperbolically, "Suddenly ... Canada is hot." Attesting to the "wealth of writing talent in Canada," Washington's artistic directors also hailed the virtues of Canadian government support, including grants to bring American theatre professionals to Canada to see our plays. "One way to fight the dreaded northward creep of American taste is to bring Americans up, inoculate them with some Canadian culture and let them return to spread artistic fever."[35] Though Canada is certainly still a net theatrical importer, the attractiveness of Canadian work outside the country does say something about the relative health of the domestic product. Playwrights like Walker (*Nothing Sacred*), John Krizanc (*Tamara*) and Brad Fraser (*Unidentified Human Remains* and *Poor Super Man*) have had major international hits since the late 1980s. The growing interest in postcolonial studies has also brought added attention to Canadian theatre at international conferences and in collections of plays and essays published abroad.

Another border being crossed more often than before is the one dividing Quebec's French-language culture from the theatre of English Canada. Until recently, only a few francophone playwrights from Quebec had had any impact in English—notably Gratien Gélinas and Michel Tremblay—though their impact was substantial. Now we can add to that list Robert Lepage and Michel Marc Bouchard. But they are hardly alone. The 1998 catalogue of *Québec Plays in Translation* from Montreal's Centre des auteurs dramatiques (CEAD) lists 186 plays in English translation by 62 different Québécois playwrights, many of them produced in English-Canadian theatres. The bridging of the solitudes from the English side to the French has been less dramatic, but the progress has been measurable. Marianne Ackerman's bilingual Theatre 1774 lasted from 1988–97. Canadian theatrical icon Bill Glassco launched the Montreal Young Company in 2000 to appeal to the city's growing bilingual audience. Major anglophone writers given French-language productions in Montreal since 1991 include Brad Fraser, Judith Thompson, Wendy Lill, Sally Clark and Colleen Wagner. Perhaps most significantly, Théâtre de Quat'Sous, the little theatre most closely associated with Tremblay's cultural nationalism in the 1960s and '70s, produced four of George Walker's *Suburban Motel* plays in translation in its 1998–99 season, along with Daniel MacIvor's *Monster*, its first play ever in English.

In so far as cultural diversity is a sign of theatrical well-being, Canadian theatre is looking better. The last decade has seen the publication of new anthologies of plays from Newfoundland, the Maritimes, the North and the "new ethnic West," from women and gays, First Nations and African Canadians, as well as special *CTR* issues on Native, Black, South Asian and Italian Canadian theatre. Gay playwrights have had a relatively high profile in modern Canadian theatre since its beginnings with Tremblay and John Herbert. (Lesbians much less so.) This edition of *Modern Canadian Plays* includes no fewer than seven gay writers. Women have come to be represented, at least in the playwriting ranks, much more fully than before, thanks in part to feminist theatre organizations such as Vancouver's Women in View (1988–97) and Toronto's Nightwood, founded as a collective in 1979. Institutional support has been even more crucial in the development of Native theatre. Native Earth Performing Arts (est. 1982) was the fertile ground from which sprang Tomson Highway's *The Rez Sisters* and *Dry Lips Oughta Move to Kapuskasing*. Under Highway's artistic directorship from 1986-90, and subsequently under Floyd Favel, Drew Hayden Taylor and others, Native Earth has fostered the work of a whole generation of playwrights, partly through its annual new play festival, Weesageechik Begins to Dance, inaugurated in 1988.[36] New Native companies such as Nova Scotia's Two Planks and a Passion and Alberta's Crazy Horse Theatre continue its work.

New theatre companies and festivals have come on stream on a regular basis since the mid-1980s. Montreal's Festival de théâtre des Amériques (1985) and Toronto's du Maurier World Stage (1986) have been important showcases for innovative theatre from Canada and around the world. Two important Calgary festivals, Alberta Theatre Projects' New PlayRites (1986) and One Yellow Rabbit's experimental High Performance Rodeo (1987), joined established new play development organizations like the Banff Centre, Playwrights' Workshop of Montreal, Vancouver's New Play Centre / Playwrights Theatre Centre and the Rhubarb! Festival. Nova Scotia has gotten a wealth of new companies: Festival Antigonish (1988); Eastern Front Theatre in Dartmouth (1993), co-founded by playwright Wendy Lill and director Mary Vingoe to produce new Atlantic-Canadian plays; Halifax's Shakespeare-by-the-Sea (1994) and Wolfville's Atlantic Theatre Festival (1995).

The latter two companies, devoted to classical work, denote an interesting trend in recent Canadian theatre. Toronto's acclaimed Soulpepper company (1998) produces only classical plays and modern classics, and Shakespearean festivals seem to be everywhere. Since Shakespeare-on-the-Saskatchewan set up shop in Saskatoon in 1985, we've had the highly successful Repercussion Theatre in Montreal (1988) and Bard on the Beach in Vancouver (1991), Edmonton's Shakespeare-in-the-Park (1989), Shakespeare-by-the-Sea in St. John's (1993), and Toronto's Shakespeare in the Rough (1994). Meanwhile, the Stratford and Shaw festivals have enjoyed unprecedented box office success in the past few years. That this kind of foundational theatre can thrive alongside theatres devoted to new Canadian plays is a sign of stability and maturity. The continued emergence of exciting young companies creating their own new work, like Vancouver's Electric Company, and the rebirth of Ottawa's National Arts Centre as a vital link in the regional system, co-producing new and established Canadian plays, can only be cause for further optimism.

But since theatre is always and everywhere a tenuous enterprise, optimism within its various component worlds tends to wax and wane. Canadian play publishing, in perennial crisis, took a hard hit in the mid-1990s with the collapse of one of its pillars, Coach House Press. Fortunately, Talonbooks and Playwrights Canada Press, along with Scirocco, Blizzard, NeWest and a few others, remained solvent and took up the slack, ensuring that new plays continue to take material (book) form, and that anthologies like this one become and remain available to students and teachers, producers, directors, actors and scholars.[37] (A related development equally worthy of celebration is the extraordinary archive of Canadian theatre materials accumulated at the University of Guelph.) But in a rhythm much like that of the megamusicals, the Chapters bookstore chain swamped the smaller independents, then, overreaching itself, crashed and burned, leaving the most vulnerable Canadian publishers on the verge of ruin. As I write this in the early spring of 2001, the situation is desperate but, as always, hopeful.

When the going gets tough, there are none tougher than Talon's Karl and Christy Siegler, whom I'd like to thank again, along with Shyla Seller at Talon and all their colleagues engaged in the noble endeavour of publishing Canadian plays. I also want to acknowledge once more all the people I thanked in Volume One, plus the playwrights in this volume who so generously shared their stories with me and ensured that I got things straight. All erroneous facts and ignorant opinions are mine alone. Special thanks to Guillermo Verdecchia for helping me make the hard choices. This volume is dedicated to my mother, Mollie Scher Wasserman (1924–1988).

NOTES

1. The story of the pre-modern period of Canadian theatre has been told in bits and pieces in a variety of books and articles. For a general overview see Eugene Benson and L.W. Conolly, *English-Canadian Theatre* (Toronto: Oxford Univ. Press, 1987). Unfortunately out of print, Anton Wagner, ed., *Canada's Lost Plays* (Toronto: Canadian Theatre Review, 1978–81) is an excellent anthology in four volumes (Richard Plant co-edits Volume One) presenting plays from the nineteenth through the mid-twentieth century with extensive historical introductions.

2. Nathan Cohen, "Theatre Today: English Canada," *Tamarack Review* 13 (Autumn 1959): 28.

3. Thomas B. Hendry, "Trends in Canadian Theatre," *Tulane Drama Review* 10 (Fall 1965): 62–70. That same year Michael Tait concluded his survey of "the grey wastes of Canadian drama" from 1920–60 by noting "perhaps the most depressing feature of theatre in Canada: the lack of any vital and continuing relationship between theatrical activity and the work of the Canadian playwright." See "Drama and Theatre," *Literary History of Canada*, ed. Carl F. Klinck, 2nd ed. (Toronto: Univ. of Toronto Press, 1976), Vol. II, 159, 167.

4. Betty Lee, *Love and Whisky: The Story of the Dominion Drama Festival* (Toronto: McClelland and Stewart, 1973), 296.

5. For a useful collection of articles documenting twentieth century Canadian theatre, see Don Rubin, ed., *Canadian Theatre History: Selected Readings* (Toronto: Copp Clark, 1996).

6. Alan Filewod, "National Theatre/National Obsession," *Canadian Theatre Review* 62 (Spring 1990): 6.

7. Fred Jacobs, "Waiting for a Dramatist," *The Canadian Magazine* 43 (June 1914): 146. On the relationship between Canada's theatre critics and Canadian theatrical development from the nineteenth century to the

present, see Anton Wagner, ed., *Establishing Our Boundaries: English-Canadian Theatre Criticism* (Toronto: Univ. of Toronto Press, 1999).

8. Vincent Massey, "The Prospects of a Canadian Drama," *Queen's Quarterly* 30 (October 1922): 200.

9. Rupert Caplan, "The Ultimate National Theatre," *Canadian Forum* 9 (January 1929): 143–44.

10. See Anton Wagner, "The Developing Mosaic: English Canadian Drama to Mid-Century," in *Canada's Lost Plays, Volume Three,* ed. Anton Wagner (Toronto: CTR Productions, 1980), 19–21.

11. Jack Gould, "Canada Shows Us How," *New York Times* 1 Sept. 1946, Sec. II: 7.

12. John Coulter, "The Canadian Theatre and the Irish Exemplar," in Rubin, ed., *Canadian Theatre History: Selected Readings,* 125.

13. Robertson Davies, *The Well-Tempered Critic: One Man's View of Theatre and Letters in Canada,* ed. Judith Skelton Grant (Toronto: McClelland and Stewart, 1981), 66.

14. Davies, 74.

15. Hendry, "Trends in Canadian Theatre," 64–65.

16. Mavor Moore, "A Theatre for Canada," *University of Toronto Quarterly* 26 (October 1956): 2.

17. *Report of the Royal Commission on National Development in the Arts, Letters and Sciences* (Ottawa: Edmond Cloutier, 1951), xi. Quoted in Don Rubin, "Creeping Toward a Culture: The Theatre in English Canada Since 1945," *Canadian Theatre Review* 1 (Winter 1974): 8.

18. Tom Hendry, "MTC: A View from the Beginning," *Canadian Theatre Review* 4 (Fall 1974): 16.

19. Jamie Portman, "*Ecstasy of Rita Joe* Still Manages to Shock and Scourge," *Vancouver Province* 12 April 1976, 10. Cf. Neil Carson, "Towards a Popular Theatre in English Canada," *Canadian Literature* 85 (Summer 1980): 64–65.

20. David Gustafson, "Let's Really Hear It for Canadian Theatre," *Maclean's* 84 (October 1971): 84.

21. George Ryga, "Contemporary Theatre and Its Language," *Canadian Theatre Review* 14 (Spring 1977): 8.

22. Quoted verbatim from a series of interviews with artistic directors of regional theatres in *The Stage in Canada*: Edward Gilbert (MTC), 3 (May 1967), 14; Robert Glenn (Citadel), 3 (June 1967), 7; Joy Coghill Playhouse), 3 (Sept. 1967), 10; Kurt Reis (MTC), 5 (Nov. 1969), 13.

23. Martin Kinch, "The Canadian Theatre: In for the Long Haul," *This Magazine* 10 (Nov.–Dec. 1976): 4–5.

24. Quoted in Robert Wallace, "Growing Pains: Toronto Theatre in the 1970s," *Canadian Literature* 85 (Summer 1980): 77.

25. George Ryga, "Theatre in Canada: A Viewpoint on Its Development and Future," *Canadian Theatre Review* 1 (Winter 1974): 30.

26. Bill Thomas in the *Victoria Colonist,* quoted in "Playwrights," *The Stage in Canada* 6 (January 1972): 17.

27. Coulter, 125.

28. Alan Filewod, "Between Empires: Post-Imperialism and Canadian Theatre," *Essays in Theatre* 11 (November 1992): 11.

29. See Ray Conlogue, "Reactionary Voice Takes Centre Stage," *Globe and Mail,* 30 December 1989, C6; Guy Sprung, "Getting Our Act Together," *Theatrum* 23 (April/May 1991): 14–16; and Edward Mullaly, "The Return of the Native: Sharon Pollock at Theatre New Brunswick," *Canadian Theatre Review* 63 (Summer 1990): 20–24.

30. John Bemrose, "Hitting the Big Time: Canadian Plays Aim For Commercial Success," *Maclean's* 103 (14 May 1990): 64.

31. The *Globe and Mail* marked the opening of *Miss Saigon* with an editorial lauding commercial musicals and attacking Canadian subsidized theatre. For the spirited retorts of two of its columnists, see Rick Salutin, "An Industrial Strategy for the Arts," *Globe and Mail,* 4 June 1993, A13; and Ray Conlogue, "Success Doesn't Diminish Subsidized Theatre," *Globe and Mail,* 5 June 1993, C2.

32. Sky Gilbert, "Gotta Sing, Gotta Dance, Gotta Cry," *Globe and Mail,* 3 November 1997, A11–12.

33. Michael Phillips, "21st Century Theater: Calling All Risk Takers," *Los Angeles Times*, 28 November 1999, Calendar 46–47; and Kate Taylor, "The Play's the Thing," *Globe and Mail*, 26 December 2000, R1. See also Jason Sherman, "S.O.S: A Message in a Bottleneck," *Globe and Mail*, 17 August 1998, A9.

34. See Liz Nicholls, "World on a String," and Cheryl Cashman, "Clown Noir," *Canadian Theatre Review* 95 (Summer 1998): 31–37, 70–78.

35. Lloyd Rose, "Onstage, Works with a Distinct Canadian Accent," *Washington Post*, 10 September 2000, G24; and Pat Donnelly, "Canadians Are Invading Washington with Great Success," *Montreal Gazette*, 23 September 2000, D1–2.

36. See Jennifer Preston, "Weesageechik Begins to Dance: Native Earth Performing Arts, Inc.," *TDR/The Drama Review* 36 (Spring 1992): 135–59.

37. The Kafkaesque experience of trying to publish a book of Canadian theatre criticism is vividly described by Robert Lecker in "Would You Publish This Book? Material Production, Canadian Criticism, and The Theatre of Form," *Studies in Canadian Literature* 25.1 (2000): 15–36. For the Talonbooks story, see Ginny Ratsoy, "Dramatic Discourse at Talonbooks: Narratives on the Publisher-Author Relationship," *Canadian Theatre Review* 101 (Winter 2000): 25–28; and Kathleen Scherf, "A Legacy of Canadian Cultural Tradition and the Small Press: The Case of Talonbooks," *Studies in Canadian Literature* 25.1 (2000): 131–49.

KELLY REBAR

(b. 1956)

Though "the world's longest undefended border" has become a national cliché, it nevertheless remains an elemental component of Canadian political and psychological geography. Canada's complex love-hate relationship with the American behemoth next door involves a passive-aggressive ambivalence about its powerful seductions. How do we—can we ever—measure up to American standards and achievements? How can we—should we bother trying to—resist American wealth and glamour, the smug but enviable self-confidence and infuriatingly effective self-promotion next to which Canadian values and institutions such as politeness, public health care and hockey pale in comparison? Literally straddling the Canada-U.S. border along the Alberta prairie, the characters of Kelly Rebar's *Bordertown Café* struggle with these issues in the context of a poignant and often hilarious family drama that has become a favourite of Canadian theatre-goers.

Rebar was born in Lethbridge and grew up there and in Calgary, where her first play, *Chatters* (1974), a comedy, was produced at Factory Theatre West when she was just seventeen. After attaining a degree in Film Studies at York University (1978), she returned to Alberta and was offered a commission by Edmonton's Northern Light Theatre. The result, *Checkin' Out* (1981), was a solid hit, with subsequent productions in Ottawa, Vancouver, Thunder Bay and at Winnipeg's Prairie Theatre Exchange (PTE), where it became that company's most successful production to date. An offbeat comedy about young, small-town Albertans struggling with low self-esteem and thwarted personal ambition, it established Rebar's trademark naturalism and colloquial dialogue, a kind of rough prairie poetry. Its characters' fear of change and ambivalence about leaving home also anticipate the themes of *Bordertown Café*. Edmonton's Theatre Network produced *First Snowfall*, a family drama set in Saskatchewan, in 1984. That year Rebar also became playwright-in-residence at PTE, which toured Manitoba with her children's play, *All Over the Map*.

Having married and temporarily moved with her new husband to Washington, D.C. in 1985, she became inspired to write something about Canada–U.S. relations. The result, co-commissioned by Ontario's Blyth Festival and PTE, was *Bordertown Café*. Opening at Blyth in 1987 to less than rave reviews, the play was substantially rewritten for its PTE premiere the same year, and it proved a major success. Productions in Montreal, Regina, Calgary, Vancouver and London followed; it was remounted at Blyth in 1988 and toured Ontario. *Bordertown Café* won the 1990 Canadian Authors' Association Award for Drama, and was made into a feature film, written by Rebar and directed by Norma Bailey, in 1993. The play's popularity endures well into its second decade, especially outside big-city Canada, as indicated by numerous productions in places such as Guelph, Port Stanley and Richmond Hill, Ontario, and Summerland and Terrace, B.C.

In 1991 Rebar was resident playwright at the Banff Centre, and the Blyth Festival produced her *Cornflower Blue*, a memory play about the prairies. She has written scripts for the National Film Board on subjects such as bio-ethics and teenage alienation, as well as adaptations of Alice Munro stories and her own plays *Checkin' Out*, *First Snowfall* and *Bordertown Café*. Since the early '90s she has worked mostly in television, writing episodes of the series *Jake and the Kid* and a TV adaptation of Munro's *Lives of Girls and Women* (1994). Rebar currently makes her home in Nelson, B.C.

In his own way young Jimmy in *Bordertown Café* faces the archetypal Canadian dilemma: stay home in Canada with all its obvious flaws or join the brain drain, the talent drain, south to the Land of Opportunity. His father is the powerfully encoded Western hero of American popular myth—the cowboy as trucker, living his freedom, riding the roads of Wyoming "in a truck higher'n any ole building we got around here," his mythic status enhanced by his never actually appearing on stage. As an added attraction Dad offers Jimmy what appears to be the stability and prosperity of his new American home, a big, modern house fully equipped, including a capable new wife. In contrast

Marlene is a weak, tentative mother. The home she has made for Jimmy on "the Canadian side of nowhere" is provisional and shabby: half-finished, ill-equipped, badly decorated. The café itself is neither here nor there, neither truck stop nor restaurant, an economically marginal relic that doesn't even hold the attractions of nostalgia for Jimmy.

Dad, however, drives a harder bargain than at first appears. His cavalier attitude and flexible scheduling make Jimmy's choices a little more difficult. And Jimmy has other concerns that are not so easily left behind. He has his hockey, his desire to help his grandfather get in the harvest, and a powerful emotional connection with Marlene that all the play's comedy cannot finally hide. Woven in and out of Jimmy's self-deprecating self-consciousness, the sweet adolescent gawkiness for which he constantly beats himself up, is a genuine concern for his mother's emotional welfare and quality of life. His most secret fantasies involve making his mother happy. (This boy is almost too good to be true!) She is, after all, barely older than he, and her own horizons are rapidly receding. We watch her struggling with maternal guilt and inadequacy, trying as hard as her son to figure things out. Coping as a single mother in her circumstances is difficult enough, but she also has to operate within an unorthodox family structure where, as she says, "we're none of us what we're supposed to be … Mom's like my daughter half the time, Jimmy's more of a brother." (Compare this to the more traditional scenario within which, for example, David French's young men consider their options in *Leaving Home*.)

Mom, for Marlene, is Maxine, chauvinistic stage American and designated scene-stealer, larger (and louder and funnier) than life. She supplies a good deal of the play's energy and much of its cultural comedy. As she and the others continually talk over one another, her American inflections merge with their Canadian rural idiom in a rich verbal cacophony and tangled emotional grid that mark this delicately balanced familial détente. Maxine's laconic Canadian husband, Jim, contributes his own verbal revelations at the end, helping to effect his namesake grandson's passage into manhood. Although the feel-good emotional finale may mask the fact that not much substantial has really changed, the play's setting remains fertile ground for the characters to negotiate personal and cultural identity. As postcolonial critic Homi Bhabha writes in his book *The Location of Culture*, the "in-between space" of the borderland provides "the terrain for elaborating strategies of selfhood."

Bordertown Café premiered at the Blyth Festival in Blyth, Ontario on June 23, 1987 with the following cast:

JIMMY   Kevin Bundy
MARLENE   Laurel Paetz
MAXINE   Lorna Wilson
JIM   Jerry Franken

Directed by Katherine Kaszas
Set and Costume Design by Allan Stitchbury
Lighting Design by Kevin Fraser

BORDERTOWN CAFÉ

CHARACTERS

JIMMY, *17*
MARLENE, *34, Jimmy's mother*
MAXINE, *57, Marlene's mother*
JIM, *62, Marlene's father*

SCENE

A café on the Canadian side of the Alberta/ Montana border. The present [late 1980s.]

SET

The kitchen of the café. It is a kitchen which bridges public and private use. In addition to the trays of dishes and cups, ketchup bottles and relish jars, the lard can, the grill and work area, there are indications that this kitchen is a family centre. There is a small kitchen table with chairs, magazines, bills, a paperback or two. The café is old but very clean, organized in its own way. There is an order window and a swinging door to the front of the café. There is a screen door leading outside. There is a door or passageway to the back suite. JIMMY's bedroom either introduces the back suite and one must pass through his room to get to the back, or it is in some way shown to be a room without privacy. The single bed takes up most of the space. Typical teenage boy things are about and, again, there is a tidiness. The closed, tight space of the café is contrasted by a sense of overwhelming prairie sky that surrounds the set.

ACT ONE

The sound of a combine approaching. The sun begins to rise. JIMMY is asleep in his bed. Light enters the kitchen and lends a photographic quality to the place, as if things have been caught in time. The sound of the combine reaches a point, then begins to fade away. As the sound fades, the sunrise approaches its peak. Just as the light seems to hold still, the sound of the combine ceases. JIMMY snaps awake. He gets out of bed and goes into the kitchen to look out through the
screen door. The sun carries on, the kitchen loses its quality, and things appear functional. JIMMY goes back to his room, and goes back to bed. The sound of a meadowlark is heard. The phone rings. It rings again.

JIMMY: Am I getting that Mum?

MARLENE enters from the back suite, doing up her robe. She crosses to the phone in the kitchen.

MARLENE: (*answering*) We're awake, Mum. (*realizing her error*) Oh, hi. You comin' up? Yeah, 'cept for he's got school startin' today, eh.

JIMMY: (*immediately*) No, I don't, Friday's just registration.

MARLENE: What about?

JIMMY: What about what about?

MARLENE: Oh.

Pause.

JIMMY: Oh what Mum?

MARLENE: If that's what he wants.

JIMMY: If he's pickin' me up for a haul, I can't go with him, Grandad and me got a crop to get off.

MARLENE: Just sec. (*to JIMMY*) Am I tryna talk?

JIMMY: There's certain considerations.

MARLENE: (*back to the phone*) Up to him.

JIMMY: (*throwing the covers back*) Wait—wait—

MARLENE: 'Kay then bye.

JIMMY freezes, then falls back to bed. MARLENE hangs up, keeping her hand on the receiver a spell. She crosses to the little kitchen table and lights a cigarette. A tanker can be heard gearing by and fading away. MARLENE waits for it to go. The light makes another transition.

MARLENE: Get up, Jimmy.

JIMMY: Where's he at?

MARLENE crosses to the door to look out. Pause.

JIMMY: Well, if he's just leaving Wyoming now he won't reach the border 'til way past—

MARLENE: Bring me out my curling iron.

MARLENE goes back to the table to place her cigarette down in the ashtray.

JIMMY: Is my dad just leaving Wyoming now, I says.

MARLENE: I'm not beatin' around the bush. I'm gettin' right to the point. Your dad's—just leaving Wyoming now. (*MARLENE takes a quarter from the tip jar and looks toward Jimmy's room.*) And not only that he got married. (*She starts to exit to the front, stopping briefly.*) Make your bed.

She exits. JIMMY jumps out of bed and throws on his jeans. A song comes on the jukebox from out front. JIMMY goes to the kitchen to wait for MARLENE to re-enter.

JIMMY: (*hollering to the front*) And *here* I didn't even know he was goin' with her! (*He realizes the give-away of his lie and hollers louder to cover it.*) He say who to?!

MARLENE comes back in, heading for the back suite.

MARLENE: (*as if it is all one word*) No he never Linda Somebody.

MARLENE sets to making Jimmy's bed. JIMMY follows her into his room to take over from her, but MARLENE finishes any job she starts and JIMMY is forced to watch, guilt-ridden and idle.

JIMMY: Well, it don't matter to me, does it matter to you? He got married?

MARLENE: (*disguised*) Does it look like it matters to me? (*continues with the bed*)

JIMMY: (*watching*) Well, that's great.

MARLENE: Colour hair she got?

JIMMY starts to answer but doesn't finish. He watches MARLENE fuss with the bed. He exits back to the suite and returns with a shaving kit and towel. He watches MARLENE fuss with the bedspread. Finally:

JIMMY: Quit makin' that bed!

MARLENE: I knew it! Every time your dad comes up to Canada, I end up gettin' yelled at! And I know I shoulda got you a new bedspread four, five years ago, but I didn't!

JIMMY: What!

MARLENE: Didn't, Jimmy, didn't. Should change it to my name, Marlene Didn't. Didn't wanna fix this place up 'cause why would a person wanna sock a bunch of money into a back suite when she's gonna buy the Mathison place when it comes up for sale? Mathison place comes up for sale, did I buy it—? No, I *didn't*. I don't have the Mathison place and I don't have the fixed-up back suite and now you're—and he's—and this is for a little boy, this bedspread, it's for a little boy.

Pause.

JIMMY: Did Dad say what time he was gettin' here?

MARLENE: Four!

JIMMY: Four?

MARLENE: And you're standing there tellin' me she's got me beat all to heck, this gal.

JIMMY: I got conditioning at four.

MARLENE: I know that without ever layin' eyes on her.

JIMMY: No, Mum.

MARLENE: Eh?

JIMMY: Don't think that.

MARLENE: Well, this is it. How does he think he could do better'n me with the kinda girls he 'sociates with? Answer me that. Oh, those American girls, don't tell me about American girls, I lived down there, I know exactly what they're capable of down there.

JIMMY: This is mattering, Dad getting married.

MARLENE: No it isn't mattering and I'll tell you why it is. (*pause*) See Jimmy, uh.

JIMMY: What?

MARLENE: I—I—I'm not sayin' it's any great shakes livin' here, but there's a lot o' kids out there without a pillow to call their own, they'd think your room there's a palace. (*She has exited back.*)

JIMMY: I got no problems with it neither.

MARLENE: (*off*) And you can stay out the farm any night the week you want.

She enters carrying her curling iron, which she takes to the outlet nearest the table.

JIMMY: I know—I—oh, I was gonna get that.

MARLENE: Gonna, that's another one—Jimmy Gonna and Marlene Didn't, we should move to Nashville and break into an act—speakin' of which I'm not going through the day with Mum song and dancing about your dad to me, not today.

JIMMY: I won't say nothing but—

MARLENE: I'm countin' on it.

JIMMY: I have a complication I'd like to air.

MARLENE: Yeah, well, he said he'd be here at four.

JIMMY: Coach isn't caring if you're in harvest or not, he said if you wanna play hockey this year you can't miss conditioning. So if he's not carin' about harvest he'll care even less about Dad showin' up—

MARLENE: Just be on that school bus.

JIMMY: But Mum.

MARLENE: (exiting back) And get washed.

JIMMY: I'm cut before I even make the team? (pause) Mum.

MARLENE: (off) What?

JIMMY: This is kind of inconvenient. I can't be takin' off on no haul, I got a crop to get off. I got conditioning. Dad shoulda bin informed. (pause) Mum.

MARLENE: (off) What?

JIMMY: He won't even be here on time, he never is—the guy don't operate on Mountain Standard. But that's okay, Jimmy can count the trucks passin', waitin' on him. (He takes his kit and towel and starts to head to the front, but stops, wheels around, and addresses the back suite.) I wanted to start my last year off like a normal human hockey player. The plan was set. The whole time I'm out in that field I'm thinking, Jimmy?—I know you wrecked your truck, I know it's not exactly smooth in that café but you bin around Grandad all summer long—just take after him and eat your Puff' Wheat like there's nothing the matter. I figgered today, oh, I'd show up at school, say hi to the guys, register, give the girls a quick once-over to see if there's any changes, and then saunter down to the Doughnut Hole—yes,

me, Jimmy—saunter, huck a few bottle caps at the garbage can. Uh huh. Well shall we scrap that plan, Mum?—Number one, I'm up at the crack of dawn filled to the gills with guilt already for not bein' out in that field.

MARLENE: (off) You're gettin' washed up, eh.

JIMMY: "Hey Jimmy," the guys'll say. "Comin' down to the Hole?" "Sorry guys, can't." Carve it into my tombstone. "Sorry guys, can't." (pause) Mum?

MARLENE: (off) Sorry guys, can't.

JIMMY: The Hawks' game, a prime example. Game's over, we won, whole team come truckin' in here for Cokes and burgers and who do they find sittin' in that till? Mr. Humiliation, still waitin' on his off-and-on dad to turn up, take him on a haul. Not only could I a' played, I coulda come back and gone to sleep for five hours before his rig pulled up. Oh, but hockey games, they don't matter, sleep? Who needs it?—Hop on up, kid. If I wanna see the guy, it's in his rig.

MARLENE enters, wearing her uniform. She has her make-up kit and a small, stand-up mirror. She sets up at the kitchen table to do her hair and make-up.

MARLENE: Well, you didn't have to go on those hauls if you didn't want to. Is how I see it.

JIMMY looks to MARLENE until she glances his way.

JIMMY: Didn't want to? Didn't want to, Marlene? A guy would have to be a fool not to wanna go on those hauls—those hauls are the highlight of my life! (pause) Okay, sure the man tends to run behind from time to time and I have to miss the odd hockey game—but how many of my friends get to ride in a truck higher'n any ole building we got around here? You know there's not a truck stop here to California don't know my dad? The kinda life that guy has lived?—well, it's no use even tryna explain it to you, not gonna understand, no girl could, but the life of a trucker, and I mean I bin there and I know, it's better education than anything you learn in school.

MARLENE: Now who is that I'm hearin' talkin', your dad all over again.

JIMMY: (looking out the back door) Gives me a chance to get outta here, see for myself there's somethin' besides *nothin'* out some people's windows. Nothin', that's what I gotta look at. We live smack dab in the middle of nowhere—correction, the Canadian side of nowhere. Houses 'at were here're long gone, fillin' station's history, and us?—we're sittin' in this café like we're stuck in the muck.

MARLENE: Your shirt's ironed, it's on the back of my doorknob.

JIMMY: We should get one of those big tractor-trailers and haul this unit outta here, straight into town. Where we can at least be part of life. This—*this* is the last thing a Canadian sees when he leaves home and the first thing an American sees when he arrives.

MARLENE: Hey. Never mind. Gonna be changes. Big ones. Just soon's I get the money.

JIMMY: Gonna Scotch-tape the rips in the leatherette out there, is that it?

MARLENE: Gonna put a decent bathroom in there. (*motioning to the back suite*) Gonna have a bathtub *and* a shower, and I'm gonna do it all up in pink. And that's gonna be the end of goin' out to the farm for a bath. Or standin' in that aluminum box we got now. Gonna get chiffon curtains. Priscillas. Gonna have it lookin' just like the magazines, so just you wait.

Pause.

JIMMY: Mum, I got the money. I'll do it for ya. I got the money in my account right now, I saved a lot this summer, we can getcha a pink bathtub—

MARLENE: Don't want a pink bathtub, want a white one, want pink *accessories*, I want floral design, I want wallpaper, I want it exactly how I got it in my mind and I'm not lettin' you pay for it, I can afford it, I'm just waitin' 'til—

JIMMY: Oh waitin', waitin', waitin'—for what?!—*him* to come back to you? (*He freezes. He shoves the screen door open, and stands out back.*) How could I say that to her? How?

MARLENE: Yeah, well I got somethin' to say to you, too.

JIMMY: (*re-enters*) I'll tell you how—it's—it's *him* comin' out in me, it's my dad, just like you said.

MARLENE: Nice try but no go.

JIMMY: I know you wouldn't take him back, I know that—even if he come crawlin'.

MARLENE: Which he did more'n once.

JIMMY: He's nothin' but a good ole boy, never be no more.

MARLENE: That's right.

JIMMY: Even if he just got married.

Pause. The sound of the combine. JIMMY looks outside.

MARLENE: Jimmy.

JIMMY: *Why* does he always have to have a haul up to Canada when Grandad needs me the most? Talk about inconsideration. People, they got no respect for the farmer in this world.

MARLENE: Never mind the world, just let me say.

JIMMY: I should be allowed to have your car today, or Maxine's truck, roar into school, register like a madman, then race my tail back out to the field. Stay at 'er 'til I drop, like Grandad does. But no, me, I sleep in, mouth off, and let Grandad talk me into *havin' Friday off.* Frost is gonna nail our crop but good and I was gonna kick around the Doughnut Hole all day? (*The combine fades.*) Which now I can't do 'cause my dad's comin' up?

The sound of a pick-up truck stopping.

MARLENE: Now here's your grandma's truck, act normal.

JIMMY: Well how 'bout tellin' me if I'm comin' or goin' Marlene?

MARLENE: And you can quit callin' me Marlene.

JIMMY: I call Maxine Maxine.

MARLENE: Maxine's Maxine, I'm me.

JIMMY: *You* call her Maxine.

MARLENE: She's my mother.

JIMMY: And you're my mother.

MARLENE: Way you talk to me I'd never know it.

JIMMY: Just tell me what to do.

MARLENE: Fine.

JIMMY: Fine I tell Dad I got the crop to get off?

MARLENE: Well, you could.

JIMMY: Or fine I tell Grandad my dad's—

MARLENE: Get a move on, you're seventeen and you shouldn't have to be told—

JIMMY: Told what?

MARLENE: And when I was seventeen I had *you*.

JIMMY: Yeah? Well, now I'm seventeen and I got you.

MARLENE: You got me?—I wish I had me when I was your age, I wish I had a mother tellin' me not to go—

JIMMY: On a haul?

MARLENE: It's not a haul he was callin' about, it's not a haul he's got in mind.

JIMMY: Well what?

MARLENE: He wants you to go live down there! With him! And her! In a brand new house! Happy?

JIMMY: Huh?

MARLENE: Now go get washed for school!

JIMMY: School?

MARLENE: If you're goin'!

JIMMY: Goin'!

MARLENE: I mean it!

JIMMY: What?

MAXINE flings open the back door. She's wearing a windbreaker over her uniform. She throws her purse down.

MAXINE: Hey! Shut your battletraps! Can hear ya all in the parkin' lot.

JIMMY exits to the front.

MARLENE: Jimmy—

MAXINE: Never mind the parkin' lot, they can hear ya in Missoura. And way up in Yellowknife, for that matter—suppose the coffee's not bin turned on? Wait for Maxine to do it, why not. (*MAXINE prepares the drip machine. MARLENE starts to follow JIMMY, then stops.*) After she's listened to the "Rock of Ages" all night long. Comin' a-outta your dad's nasal passages—spent half the night on the sofa—then he wonders why

I sleep over here so much—gimme one your cigarettes, I'm a-out.

MARLENE: Just got Canadian. Coupla Lucky's in the junk drawer.

MAXINE opens the drawer, gets a cigarette, takes the lighter out of her brassiere, and lights up. MARLENE lights up another of hers.

MAXINE: Well, I'll tell ya.

MARLENE: That couldn't've bin handled worse.

MAXINE: Those people in Oklahoma never cease to amaze me.

MARLENE: Is Dad comin' in for breakfast?

MAXINE: Yeah, this one of 'em got herself on *Good Mornin' America* for winnin' too many toaster ovens, huh.

MARLENE: (*looking out the back*) I should go runnin' out there.

MAXINE: Give a guess how many.

MARLENE: Nine.

MAXINE: Nine nothin', that squirrel won seven hundred and eighty-three.

MARLENE: What's this we're talkin'?

MAXINE: Those deals your Aunt Thelma uses for that asparagus effort she shoves atcha and calls a meal. "When's the last time you folks sat down together *nice* like this?"—far as I'm concerned that woman as good as killed your Uncle Carl with too many minced baloney sandwiches.

MARLENE: Jimmy! (*to MAXINE*) I don't know how you can be so like that to Dad's family and sweet as pie to any stranger't come in here.

JIMMY: (*comes to the order window*) What?

MARLENE: I—I forget now, never mind.

MAXINE: I had a fourth cousin from Oklahoma.

MARLENE: (*to JIMMY*) Our own's free back there, why you usin' the Men's?

JIMMY: Just like that, up and go?

MAXINE: He was so fat when he died they had to knock a-out the livin' room window to get his casket a-out.

JIMMY: Mum.

MARLENE: All I need now is that fat casket story.

MAXINE: That's no lie, his name was Dalton Dooey.

JIMMY: Mum.

MAXINE: Or not Dalton neither, Barney.

MARLENE: (to JIMMY) What?

MAXINE: Barney Dalton.

JIMMY: Just like that, I said.

MARLENE: If that's what you want.

MAXINE: I got a black and white snapshot o' that casket comin' a-out the window, don't ask me where.

JIMMY: You weren't even gonna let me in on it, it just come out by chance.

MARLENE: I was tellin' you all along.

JIMMY: You weren't tellin' me anything but to get washed.

MAXINE: My aunt Marietta was there in full force and she weighed a good three hundred herself.

MARLENE: Didn't I say our own's free, why you usin' the Men's?

JIMMY: You were in it when I started out goin' and I'd like to know why you called me out here in the first place.

MARLENE: I didn't mean to.

MAXINE: You kids don't care but that cousin holds the State record down there. He sure does.

JIMMY: For what, Maxine?

MAXINE: Fat.

MARLENE: Mum.

MAXINE: State o' Oklahoma!—Look it up.

MARLENE: Where's a person look that up?

MAXINE: This is it.

JIMMY exits from the order window. MAXINE has begun her morning preparations—getting the food out and ready, garnishes arranged, etc. She continues speaking through the order window.

MAXINE: Put Waylon on!

MARLENE: Never mind Waylon, is your grill on?

MAXINE: (singing) "I'd rather be an Okie from Muskokie—"

MARLENE: That's Merle *Haggard's* song, Maxine.

MAXINE: He did time, Merle did.

MARLENE: I'm askin' you not to sing.

MAXINE: (singing) "Where they still fly Old Glory down on Main Street."

MARLENE: I'll pay ya to stop. In American funds.

The sound of the combine. MARLENE looks out back. She goes out the door, she comes back in.

MARLENE: Why aren't I knowin' what to do?

MAXINE: (still with her preparations) 'Course the farther south you go the fatter people get.

MARLENE: Mum, can you please just not say nothin' for awhile?

MAXINE: How come? And why aren't I being let in on it?

Pause.

MARLENE: On what?

MAXINE: On round number nine hundred and forty-two you were havin' with that kid.

MARLENE: Don't make it sound like I've done nothin' but fight with him—

MAXINE: These walls tell the story, I'm not sayin' anything original—and as far as that other goes, call me a liar but people from, say, Kansas south, are nine out of ten of 'em that come in here full-fledged porkers. It's the way they eat down there, solid lard casseroles. My mother? She looked like a size four knittin' needle towards the end, sure, but she was a pudgeball when she was young, she didn't lose that weight 'til she left Texas. Minnesota thinned my mother right down. What you havin' for breakfast, I'm gonna go for a bacon sandwich.

The sound of a tanker. MAXINE throws a slab of bacon onto the grill.

MARLENE: I'll eat with Dad, I guess.

MAXINE: So I tried to call over to wake yas up but you were on the line.

MARLENE: Who was I talkin' to, Mum?

MAXINE: Not me, I couldn't get through.

MARLENE: How long you listen in on that party line?

MAXINE: Hey, I got no time for sweet talk before my mornin' coffee. Which don't pose a threat to your dad. Last time anything nice found its way outta his mouth was when you were born. "Well done," he says, like I just baked a cake.

MARLENE: So you don't know what Don said?

MAXINE: What does he ever say? Comin' to get the kid for a haul, isn't he?—Only boy in the world hasn't seen the left hand side of his father, just the right—steering. Oh yeah, speakin' o' steering—I think Jimmy should have your car today, first day and all.

MARLENE: Wrecked his truck, should have my car?

MAXINE: Okay, how 'bout my truck then?

MARLENE: Mum, I already said no to him.

MAXINE: You're takin' this little tumble in the ditch too far. So the kid had a bottle o' beer and hit the only vertical object in a hundred mile radius. As if you never done nothin' dumb when you were that age.

MARLENE: Never wrecked a truck, I'll tell ya.

MAXINE: That's 'cause you left home before you were old enough to reach the gas pedal. You put me through my paces, don't kid yourself. Fifteen years old and that sonovagun strolls in here like Johnny Cash, charms the daylights outta you and me both.

MARLENE: Okay, fine, never mind.

MAXINE: Gets herself married and taken down to Wyoming, set up in the trailer park, starin' at those narrow walls six outta seven.

MARLENE: Don't tell me about that seventh day, Mum.

MAXINE: Which was all it took.

MARLENE: And now we're into the grilled cheese.

MAXINE: I'm standin' at my grill slappin' my cheese together and who pulls up but Don and Marlene in that ole rig—dumps her off here like a sac' o' potatoes and she's showin' this far a-out.

MARLENE: I wasn't that far "a-out" and I don't appreciate talk like that in this café, I just don't this mornin'.

MAXINE: And you can't blame me because your dad tried to warn you, he seen through Don right from the time that blizzard holed Don up here.

MARLENE: Finished?

MAXINE: Point is you weren't an easy kid to raise, I think Jimmy should take my truck.

MARLENE gathers her make-up and mirror and curling iron and heads to the back.

MARLENE: Jimmy does somethin' wrong it's me who puts her through her paces.

MAXINE: He works hard, Mar.

MARLENE: You're sayin' I've been too strict? Well, that's on my conscience from now 'til Kingdom Come 'cept for everyone tells me I'm not strict enough and just 'cause I—I say no doesn't mean I always mean it. Bad enough I ground the kid and then pretend I didn't every time he wants to go out—who ever heard of groundin' a kid only when he's home?—okay, so to make up for it I should let him take your truck to school, he's suffered enough.

MAXINE: Well, he has.

MARLENE: What's it matter now anyway?

MAXINE: These are my sin'imen's exactly. (*watches MARLENE*) Com'ere, honey. (*MARLENE doesn't move. MAXINE goes to her.*) Kids, you know, they want a firm hand when it comes right down to it. They know what's good for 'em. Me, I raised you not knowin' half the time if I was doin' the right thing. Far as that-all goes my mum barely looked up from her gin-rummy the day I set the prairie on fire. Scooter and me burnt away half the state o' Minnesota smokin' roll-me-owns and you wanna know what Mum did?—sent us to the movies. I fixed her, I went ahead and turned a-out normal. Which boils down to the same thing—you're a darn good mother, quit worryin'.

MARLENE: Was I really, Mum?

MAXINE: (*going to the grill*) Sure, why not?

MARLENE: 'Cause I really need to—to hear that right now.

MAXINE: (*coming back*) Why?—I say somethin' wrong again?—I did, darn it—well, I didn't mean nothin' about all that other, runnin' off to Wyoming, you were a good kid, prat'ly raised yourself, don't pay Maxine any mind, this is just me and my dumb self.

MARLENE: No Mum, it's me—I'm touchy today, that's all.

MAXINE: (*taking her into her arms*) Aw, honey. What else is new?

MARLENE: Pardon?

MAXINE: You kinda got the market cornered on bein' touchy, let's face it but how 'bout some ham an' eggs, huh?

MARLENE: You think I'm touchy? Well, I'm not touchy, I'm not the least bit touchy. (*re-gathers her things to take into the back*) Every time Don calls he's comin' up I get my life dragged up and made out like all I had with him was bad times—well, Max?—there was plenny o' good times down in Wyoming that you don't know about, neither of you two, Jimmy or you. And I'd definitely appreciate it if you'd—because my marriage wasn't a total joke even though my life *is* right now for the very simple reason that I darn well know how to have a good time and I'm gonna start one o' these days and *boy*. Okay? Well, I got pictures in this back suite in four different photo albums, *provin'* I had good times in Wyoming.

MAXINE: Oh, hey!—Jimmy!—You gotta get your pitcher taken, first day o' school!

MARLENE: (*exiting to the back and returning*) Wanna know a good time, I'll tell you a good time and it was downright—it was—we had a gas. Well, Don took me for example to a county fair down there, I was thinkin' this here not too long—yest—other day and he won every teddy bear that fella had. Tossin' baseballs in a basket. I was sixteen. Well, those darn bears filled the back seat o' that Chevrolet and that is no exaggeration. It was a—good time.

MAXINE: Oh, there's no doubt in my mind, back home in Minnesota we had fairs bigger'n anything you'd ever find up here.

MARLENE: I left forty, fifty bears back in Wyoming.

MAXINE: (*doing her garnishes*) Bigger'n the ones in Wyoming, our fairs.

MARLENE: Mum, you never bin to Wyoming, least of all a fair. All those teddy bears and enough *Screen Gem* magazines to sink a ship, I lef' back there.

MAXINE: Jimmy-Jim!

MARLENE: I only brung one o' those bears back home—shoved it into that ole trunk at the las' minute—'member you gimme that old trunk to take down?—well, that bear? That bear become Jimmy's Floppy.

JIMMY: (*entering from the front*) What year have we time lapsed into now?

MAXINE: (*to JIMMY*) That trunk weren't mine to give if the truth were known.

MARLENE: Nothin', get dressed.

MAXINE: I snafoofled that trunk off my Aunt Lizzie and she come up the Mississippi River on nothin' but charm.

JIMMY: You mean that old bear I used to practice my slaps with?

MAXINE: She was from Baton Rouge, Louisiana, Lizzie was.

MARLENE: Well, your dad won me that bear.

MAXINE: She dyed her hair red and it turned green.

JIMMY: Dad did?

MARLENE: Your dad could throw a ball.

MAXINE: All Americans can, they're the best baseball players in the United States, 'er the world—I was lead pitcher for my team, that's how good I was.

JIMMY: Geez, Mum, I—

MAXINE: I played for a soda jerk league.

MARLENE: (*to JIMMY*) You what?

MAXINE: Me and eighteen soda jerks.

MARLENE: No, Mum—

MAXINE: *I* wasn't ever a soda jerk, I just played with 'em.

MARLENE: Jimmy's tryna talk.

MAXINE: But the café I waitressed was right across the street from the drugstore and me and this jerk got talkin' one day and before he knew it I was on his team.

JIMMY: No, I was just gonna say I wouldn'na minded seein' Dad—well, seein' him win you that … bear. (*exits to the back suite*)

MARLENE: Yeah?

MAXINE: Oh yeah, we had a ball, and as I say, that trunk has a bit o' history all right. (*pause*) 'Course so do Lizzie.

MARLENE: Mum.

MAXINE: Why do you think she headed north?—the weather?

MARLENE: Jimmy wishes he coulda seen his dad and me at that fair.

MAXINE: Oh, it was somethin' all right.

MARLENE: Mum, you weren't there.

MAXINE: I weren't there?

MARLENE: You were standin' right here slappin' your cheese together waitin' for me to show up pregnant, remember.

MAXINE: Yeah, well, you got that right.

MARLENE: And he didn't drop me off like a "sac' o' potatoes," either—it was my choice to come back up here, to have my baby north o' that border.

MAXINE: I don't know how I always end up touchin' off these Canadian nerves.

MARLENE: And things would be a whole lot smoother around here if you'd quit callin' anything out the ordinary Canadian.

MAXINE: Well, fine, but where's the camera?

MARLENE: And Don come by quite a bit at first, we had a normal marriage off'n on those few times—

MAXINE: First one in the family to get his grade twelve, I'm capturin' it on Kodak.

MARLENE: Okay, so maybe I wasn't a perfect mother, sue me.

MAXINE: It's not in here.

MARLENE: But I—and Don was always showin' up with somethin' for that kid—

MAXINE: Hey, Jimmy!

MARLENE: Droppin' fifty dollars just like that—

MAXINE: It was in this drawer.

MARLENE: That dirt bike alone and top o' the line tanker toys, those don't come cheap and Mum if I go over there and find that camera?

MAXINE: Jimmy, run a-out to the farm and look for the Instamatic!

MARLENE: I know I haven't—I'm not—and Don's not either but when you're not together it's hard to be alone raisin' a kid and Mum it's right here starin' you in the face.

MAXINE: I can't see for lookin', never could.

MARLENE: That's because you don't keep things in order, I clean this drawer out one day and you're messin' it up the next and I happen to have a bone to pick with you about this very sort o' thing—you were in my unicorn collection yesterday, it was not how I lef' it and you better come clean right now, Max.

MAXINE: (*exiting back*) Found it, Jimmy—never mind!

MARLENE: Right now, Maxine—I mean it, you come marching back right here and you—and—Dad—!

JIM has entered from outside. He takes off his hat. MARLENE turns quickly around to face him.

JIM: Uh huh.

MARLENE: Dad, I—Don called!

JIM: Oh yeah.

MARLENE: He—wants Jimmy, he wants him to go live down in Wyoming—this is what he says to me on that phone.

Pause.

JIM: In Wyoming, eh.

MARLENE: Live with him and his new wife. (*pause*) Linda.

JIM: Oh yeah.

MARLENE: *Why* didn't I just grab the Mathison place when it was offered?—I *had* the down payment. But *no*, *I* raise the kid *here*—raise? I didn't even raise him, he just all of a sudden got big and now he's leavin'—he's leavin', Dad.

JIM: All right, simmer down.

MARLENE: Don'll be here at four.

JIM: Number one, he won't be on time. Number two, Jimmy's not moving into that old trailer house o' Don's.

MARLENE: Oh no Dad, a trailer's not good enough for this gal—Don bought her a brand new house.

Pause.

JIM: Have you told Jimmy yet?

MARLENE: Sets her up nice—second wife gets what the first wife wants, it's a fact o' life, it's in all the magazines.

JIM: Jimmy, he know yet Marlene?

MARLENE: Oh, you know me Dad, I decide to turn the jukebox on, I make his bed like my life depends on it, I end up yellin' it out to him like it was all his fault.

JIM: Oh Marlene.

MARLENE: I know. Dad, please—please will you—so that he knows and everything like that?

Pause.

JIM: Well, I will Marlene, I'll talk to him for you. But don't you think he'd—

MARLENE: Yes, I do think he'd rather hear it from me. But I can't talk to that kid, I never could, and you know that.

JIM: Yes, I do.

Pause.

MARLENE: What're you gonna say, so I know?

JIM: Why don't we all three of us sit down here at the table and more or less iron this out together?

MARLENE: Okay, that'd be good I guess.

JIM: I take it you haven't told your mother.

MARLENE: No.

JIM: Let's do ourselves a favour and keep it that way.

JIM heads to the back, rolling up his sleeves to wash.

MARLENE: Dad?

JIM: Eh?

MAXINE: (*enters carrying the camera*) Yeah, you get washed Jim and you can be in the pitcher.

JIM: You're not takin' my picture.

JIMMY: (*entering*) Grandad.

JIM: (*as he exits*) Jimmy.

JIMMY looks after JIM.

MAXINE: Isn't he handsome in that shirt, he's gonna have a swarm o' girls around him today.

JIMMY: Swarm. Right. (*He allows himself to be shuffled out the back door by MAXINE. She barely aims the camera in the right direction before snapping. JIMMY comes inside to sit at the table.*) Only guy in the hemisphere has to have little snaps of his first days of school pinned up over the till for everyone to gawk at.

MAXINE: Never you mind, you get your grade twelve and you and me are gonna get in my pick-up and head 'er south.

JIMMY: Mum?

MARLENE: Yeah?

MAXINE: (*going to pour coffee*) We'll see every state in the union.

The sound of the door opening and closing out front. MARLENE glances towards it.

MARLENE: I said, yeah.

MAXINE: And get a souvenir spoon.

JIMMY: Forget it.

MARLENE takes the coffee pot and menus and heads to the front. MAXINE looks to JIMMY. He gets up and goes toward the front, stopping. He goes back to the table.

MAXINE: Hey Sport.

JIMMY: Yeah?

MAXINE: Tell your Max what's wrong.

JIMMY: Can't.

MAXINE: Yes you can, you can tell your Max everything.

JIMMY: She don't care.

MAXINE: About what? Don't she care. Huh?

Pause.

JIMMY: I get in her way around here, okay. I'm far too large. For my body. That kinda thing. Not only that but I'm a total clutz-act on the farm, I'm a zero-winner, an A-one loser—Grandad's always havin' to come bail me out, make me feel small. Does he ever *say* anything? No. He just … stares. If he'd only haul off and lose his temper, just once. Why can't he yell at me or throw the hammer down or spit even? *Why* Max?

MAXINE: He's weird. They both of 'em are, your mother and him. It's that side o' the family, somethin' in the blood—which if you were to ask her royal highness mother-in-law over there she'd claim was blue. Take your Aunt Thelma and that washtub of curdled jello she tries to peddle off as dessert for those goldarn picnics of hers—with that strain of perversion floatin' around in the family?—well you're bound to be a little backward Jimmy—but hey, you and me, we'll show 'em—we're gonna leave the whole silly lot of 'em up here huddled around their hot water bottles and we're gonna see America—from L.A. to New York, zig-zaggin' our way down to the South—the Virginias, the Carolinas—oh, you name it—we'll go see where President Kennedy was buried and Bobby o' course and up to Yankee Stadium—

JIMMY: Yeah, and I wanna see the Yankees and the Mets and the Islanders and the Rangers—

MAXINE: You ain't just a-whistlin' Dixie, kid—we'll see it all and sidestep over to Minnesota so you can see where your Max was born and where she'll be laid to rest when she cashes a-out for the last time.

JIMMY: You're gettin' buried up here, aren't you?

MAXINE: I'm gettin' buried in American soil!

JIMMY: But what about Grandad?

MAXINE: He can darn well come down there—if you think I'm gonna be a hop, skip and a jump from her majesty and all this crew up here—*if* any of 'em ever do us the favour of passin' away—

JIMMY: Wait a minute Max, you and Grandad aren't hardly together now—don't you at least wanna be together in the end?

MAXINE: Only one in the family I took a half-likin' to was the old man and he had to be the first one to go. Mind you, it took eleven operations—and your grandad and I are together now, what're you talkin' about?

JIMMY: You're not, Max. Last night was the first time in over a week you didn't sleep here.

MAXINE: You don't like your Max stayin' overnight?

JIMMY: No, I do—I do Max, but Grandad needs you over there.

MAXINE: Oh, he don't need no one.

JIM comes in from the back suite but JIMMY has his back to him and cannot see.

JIMMY: Yeah, he does. 'Cause ya see, a man like Grandad—well, any man—they like to have someone, Max. It's time you understood that about men. That's how we are—they are—they need the security. The emotional security.

MAXINE: That right, Jim?

JIMMY: (*jumping up*) Grandad!—*Geez*, Max—you coulda said somethin'—

JIM takes his place at the table.

MAXINE: Yeah, but uh, a woman—you figger she don't need this here security, is that it?

JIM: Leave the boy.

MAXINE: Huh Jimmy?

Pause.

JIMMY: Women got it built-in as far as I can tell. So if he needs it and she's got it, she should provide him with it, and stay put.

JIM: Pass the milk.

MAXINE: (*going to the grill*) Grandad wouldn't touch that one with a ten-foot pole, huh Jim?

JIM: Right.

MAXINE: He may be slow but he's not stupid.

JIM: (*to JIMMY*) Time you get to bed?

JIMMY: Not sure.

JIM: Told you to come in off the field by 11:30. It was nowhere near 11:30 time you done all that.

JIMMY: I—I don't need sleep today, it's just Registration.

MAXINE: I never slep' when I was his age, I partied all night and worked a double-shift to boot—kid's got my stamina, don'tcha Jimmy?

JIMMY: Yep.

MAXINE: What's the capital of Tennessee?

JIM: Not now, Maxine.

MAXINE: We're goin' to Nashville next year, do that place up right, huh Jimmy-Jim?

JIM: Can your mother see you a minute when her order's done?

MAXINE: Where was Lincoln hung?

JIMMY: He wasn't hung, he was shot.

MAXINE: That's what I meant, shot.

JIMMY: (to JIM) See me about what, she tell ya?

JIM: She told me. And I understand she told you, too.

MAXINE: Where was Lincoln shot then?

JIM: Though not in the best way, perhaps. See Jimmy, your mother—

MAXINE: Where was Lincoln shot!

JIM: (to JIMMY) Just tell your grandmother where Lincoln was shot.

JIMMY: Oh—he was shot—uh, was it Edmonton they got ole Lincoln?

Pause. JIMMY signals to JIM to play along.

JIM: Butte, Montana. Custard nailed him.

JIMMY: Was it Custard Grandad?—or Louis Riel?

MAXINE: Who?

JIM: Got me there, Jimmy.

JIMMY: We give up, Max—where was Lincoln shot?

MAXINE: (pointing outside) Out by that burnin' barrel for all you two care. Well fine, but it's a cryin' shame these kids don't know their American history. Sittin' on the most powerful nation in the world and all they wanna do is play hockey.

JIMMY: We know more about you than you know about us.

MAXINE: We?—us?—Hey!—you're more American than you are Canadian!—and I know my Canadian history!—what there is of it. But I don't forget my American ruts, and you don't neither.

MARLENE: (entering from the front) A daily over.

MAXINE: If it wasn't for me you'd know zip about your ruts—capital Zee-I-P.

JIMMY: My what?

MAXINE: Ruts, ruts, where ya come from.

JIMMY: I think she means roots, doesn't she Grandad?

MAXINE: I said ruts.

JIMMY: Spell that zip again, Max—was that Zed-I-P?

MARLENE: Daily over, eh Mum.

MAXINE: (to MARLENE) And as for you, that ole trunk o' Lizzie's? It was a darn sight more full up when you took it down to Wyoming than it was when I brung it up from Minnesota, wasn't it Jim. Yes, it was. I come up to this country with what the little boy shot at and missed, that's how I started a-out my married life—didn't I Jim? Yes I did.

JIM: Sit down, Marlene.

MAXINE: And I packed that ole trunk in half an hour.

MARLENE: Daily over.

MAXINE: Kid has to come to me, an American, to find a-out how this half of him ended up up here—(to JIMMY) What's Grandad talk to you about when you're milkin' those cows every night, huh?

MARLENE: Mum, a daily.

MAXINE: Huh?

JIMMY: I don't know.

MARLENE: Daily, Mum, daily.

JIM: Usually got the radio on durin' chores.

MAXINE: The CBC on in the *barn*. Most educated cows in the county.

JIMMY: District.

MAXINE has finally retreated to the grill area to prepare the order. MARLENE, seated at the table, glances to JIMMY. Then to her dad.

JIM: Jimmy?

JIMMY: Yeah?

JIM: There's a lot o' people tend to think of life as, well, as a road you go down.

MAXINE: (*singing*) "Zippity-do-dah, zippity-day."

JIM: And in that road, there's sometimes the odd fork that comes up.

MAXINE: "My oh my what a wonderful day."

JIM: Well today, you've reached one of those forks and your mother here wants you to consider—

MAXINE: "Plenny o' sunshine, plenny all day—"

JIM: Maxine?

MAXINE: "Zippity-do-dah, zippity-day!"—What?

JIM: A person can't have a decent say.

MAXINE: Huh?

MARLENE: Leave her, Dad.

JIMMY: Leave her.

MAXINE: (*coming from around the grill*) What? (*Pause. She slithers over to JIM, singing.*) I'm … in the mood for love. Simply because you're neeeaaarrr me—(*She wraps her arms around JIM, kissing him on the head. He remains motionless.*) Isn't he just the best-lookin', heart-thumpin', sexiest man in this great big bowlin' ball called Earth? Huh Jim?—You handsome brute—huh?—That trip up here with that old trunk on the train?—huh?—'member? (*to MARLENE*) Four pillow slips is about all I had.

MARLENE: Mum, that fellow looked in a hurry.

MAXINE: I was nineteen and you think you were dumb when you got married, Marlene?—I was dumb—I was waitin' tables in this coffee shop and as I say, in walks Jim and his buddy—well, I give a look to Margaret—she's since died—and I says to her, "Kiddo?—I'll give ya my foursome if you gimme that deuce!"—and didn't Jim and his

buddy end up draggin' that order on for the better part of an afternoon, huh Jim?

JIM: Unlike the fellow out front here that wants *his* filled now so he can be on his way.

MAXINE: They were down in Minnesota for a big auction huh, well, it weren't often you met a fella with manners so I married him.

JIM: (*to MARLENE*) Tell the gentleman it won't be long.

MARLENE doesn't. She knows JIM is just embarrassed.

MAXINE: I took him home to meet my folks and my mum was sold on him before he hit the livin' room—took his shoes off at the door! Didn't you, Jim?

JIM: May have.

MAXINE: He did.

MARLENE: The daily over, Mum.

MAXINE: Well, my dad he'd just as soon get rid o' me as have me stay on account of the fact me and Mum fought so terrible and her with that horrible accent, I mean she never shut up from mornin' 'til night, you talk about a screen door in a wind storm, that woman never quit. Pop, he says,—I can hear him to this day—"Well"—he was from down Iowa way—"They-all up in Canada, they *did* join the War before we did"—hands us sixteen dollars and we were married by four o'clock. Right, Jim?

JIM: It seemed like longer. (*pause*) If I were that gentleman out there I'd have second thoughts about returning to this place with the service so slow.

MAXINE: (*to MARLENE*) That slop pail there's got more romance in him than your dad does. (*getting to work*) Prob'ly doesn't even remember meetin' me. Then he has the nerve to take exception if some fella in here pays attention to me.

JIM: I pay attention to you every time you wanted me to I wouldn't have the crop in, never mind off.

MAXINE goes to fill the order—bacon, eggs, hash browns, toast—as JIM takes a serviette, and MARLENE begins to clear the table.

JIM: And it's not that *they* pay attention to her, it's that *she* pays attention to them. Marlene, leave the *dishes*.

MARLENE sits down. A tanker is heard going by.

JIM: As I was saying.

Pause.

JIMMY: (*jumping up*) I know the crop's not off, I know I'm holdin' you up.

JIM stares at JIMMY for a long time. JIMMY sits down.

JIM: Let's just put our cards on the table. Now Don, he tells us he's got a—a wife now, a house, and he's ready to have a son. Well, that's handy, considering his son is soon celebrating his eighteenth birthday.

JIMMY: Why is it *my* fault I'm eighteen too soon?—I can't help it he wasn't ready 'til now—

MARLENE: You're sayin' it's *my* fault?

JIM: Wait a second—

JIMMY: Did I say it was yours, Marlene?

MARLENE: Well, I know that bedspread's for a little boy, I so much as said it was already.

JIM: Bedspread?

MARLENE: I see those plaid spreads every time I flip through that Sears catalogue, but do I order one?

JIM: Let's keep our eye on the ball.

MARLENE: Red and black, green and black, yellow and black, I can't decide, I don't order one.

JIMMY: I don't want a bedspread.

MARLENE: I shoulda got him a VCR.

JIMMY: VCR?

JIM: Now how would that have solved a darn thing?

JIMMY: I got my own money.

MARLENE: I know I made you work till soon's you were old enough to reach it, I know I made you save your money.

JIMMY: I didn't *mind* working till.

MARLENE: Yes, you did.

JIMMY: No, I didn't.

MARLENE: You hated working till.

JIMMY: I loved working till.

MARLENE: Hated.

JIMMY: Loved. (*exits into the back*)

MARLENE: (*looks to JIM*) Dad—I—go after him.

MAXINE: (*through the order window*) So where ya from, buddy?

JIM: Jimmy?

MAXINE: Texas!—My *mother* was from Texas!

JIM: *Why* couldn't he've bin from Saskatchewan?

MAXINE: Lubbock!—You're from Lubbock? (*heading around to the front*) Well, my mother was from Amarillo!

MARLENE: You saw what happened, Dad—you saw what I did—I'm gettin' outta here, I'm headin' down that highway, I'm not bein' heard from again.

JIM: Marlene.

MARLENE: I'm thirty-four and I'm *nowhere*. (*pause*) My life's over, my kid's leavin'. I got nothin' keepin' me here.

JIM: You got a café to run for starters.

MARLENE: What I got it burns down? I got grade nine. Jimmy's gone farther'n me and in more ways'n one. What's he want from me when *he's* the one bin carted all over the western part o' the United States? Knows Texas like the back' his hand—me, I bin to a trailer park in Wyoming and the Woolco Mall in Lethbridge—*I'm* the one should be askin' *him* what to do.

JIM: When it come right down to it you're still his mother.

MARLENE: I know that and it's about time he grew up and realized it. He's seventeen and—oh, what am I sayin', seventeen isn't very old, it just isn't old enough to leave home.

JIM: No. I know. Neither was fifteen.

MARLENE freezes. Pause. She slowly turns around to look at JIM.

MAXINE: (*off*) Flip those eggs, Mar!

Automatically MARLENE moves to the grill to attend to the order.

JIM: Seemed like one day you were gettin' underfoot in here or beggin' for a ride in the tractor and the next day, it was you that character was comin' to take across the line.

MARLENE: You can't 'member that.

JIM: Eh?

MARLENE: You were combinin'. You didn't come in off the field to say—say good-bye.

JIM: You knew why that was.

Pause.

MARLENE: Had an idea. Guess I got a better one right now. (*as she sets the order up on the ledge*) Wanna know the first thing to come to me when I hung up that phone this morning?—It was like Jimmy was eleven years old comin' in the door there. All summer long I figgered I was teachin' him how to earn a dollar—oh, he had to have those Cooperalls and me I couldn't see shellin' out a hundert bucks for hockey pants when his last year's still had wear. I make him work till his whole summer in addition to the—the farm—his dad shows up end o' August and takes him down to Texas like it were across the road—I'm supposed to compete with that? Kid comes back full of himself, goes into town with that Cooperall money—

JIM: Okay now.

MARLENE: Here, what's he do but end up at Regency Jewelers—Margie, she tells me after, she says, "Marlene, your son put that $97.50 down on my counter like he was layin' out his life for you." *Why'd* he have to see me lookin' in the window at those diamond chip earrings? And what I do when he comes through this door with that velvet box in his hand?

JIM: He knows—he knows you liked the earrings.

MARLENE: Not from me showin' it he don't, Dad. (*She looks to the order.*) That order's up and gettin' cold.

MAXINE enters talking. She starts to finish the order, realizes that it is up, takes it and is more liberal with the serving and garnishes.

MAXINE: (*directing her voice to the front*) Well, if it's your first time up this way, buddy, you better get ready to not know how fast you're driving, how hot it is a-outside, how hard the wind's blowin' or how much gas you're gettin' for your so-called dollar. As for readin' directions on any box or carton—it's all in the wrist action—you'll see a lot a mode da emploi's—means flip it over to English—wrist action—Canadians got real strong wrists, prepares 'em for hockey careers. (*turning to MARLENE*) Mar, take this to my buddy from Texas—I gotta do my garnishes—(*looking out*) Who me? (*MARLENE takes the order out front.*) No, I'm married. (*MAXINE looks ever so assuredly to JIM for an extended pause. Then she looks back out front through the window as she chops her tomatoes, etc.*) I come up in '49. I was nineteen and dumber 'an a dawg, I married a Canadian boy. He farms just over there. I had about a month o' goin' batty in that farmhouse with Miss High and Mighty mother-in-law and got myself on here—we owned it prat'ly ever since and believe me, buddy, it owns us. My grandson Jimmy? He's an exceptional boy. He could grill a sandwich age o' eight.

MARLENE: (*entering*) Mum.

JIM: Leave her.

MARLENE: She's gonna start in on Jimmy's hockey.

MAXINE: He's quite the hockey player—scored a hat trick last year.

MARLENE: Watch, she'll show him the puck over the till.

MAXINE: We kep' the puck, it's over the till, if you care to take a look.

MARLENE: Guess who he sees carryin' on in those stands? Mum. Every goal that kid has scored he has to ask me if I seen it, if I seen the puck go in the net.

MAXINE: No, that's not his *sister* in the picture, that's his mother!—Now *she's* not married?—Her, she's had her dad wrapped round her little finger since the day I brung her into the world which was in the state o' North Dakota. I didn't wanna have my baby up here, *you* know what I mean— we were aimin' for Minnesota but we stopped off for coffee in Dakota and I got laughin' so hard I went into labour—didn't I Jim?

JIM: I don't think laughing actually brought the baby on.

MARLENE: Mum, this fellow I don't know from Sunday now knows how I come into the world.

MAXINE: Uh huh. (*pause*) You know who you look like standin' there, don't you? Thelma.

MARLENE: Thelma. Thelma, Dad!

MAXINE: With a touch of her majesty mixed in there too, huh Jim?

MARLENE: She winked! She thinks it's funny!

JIM: Let's just bring Jimmy out here.

MAXINE: Well, I can't understand it—I teach my daughter her presidents age o' nine, I breathe on her, I spit on my Kleenex and wipe the Hershey Bar off her face and what does she turn around and do on me. End up Canadian.

JIM: Maybe we should shoot her.

MARLENE: I don't appreciate bein' told I'm like Aunt Thelma.

MAXINE: Well, no, why would you, it's not a compliment.

JIM: Girls.

MARLENE: And you were in my unicorns yesterday, I know you were Mum—they were all moved around on that dresser and you were in them, weren't you. (*looks to JIM*) Dad?

JIM: (*slowly looks to MAXINE*) Were ... you in Marlene's unicorns by any chance?

MAXINE: No I wasn't. Just that liver and onions was.

MARLENE: That big fat guy was pawin' through my unicorns?

MAXINE: Not *that* liver and onions. The other one with the bad bleach job, her.

MARLENE: She brings the bad bleach job into my *bedroom.*

MAXINE: She's from Arkansas.

MARLENE: I don't wanna hear about Arkansas.

MAXINE: She's bin bottle jobbin' her hair since Marilyn died.

MARLENE: I don't wanna hear about Marilyn.

MAXINE: I wasn't gonna say nothin' but you asked.

The sound of the front door.

MARLENE: Mum? Can ... you take that new table? And can you top off that Texan's coffee while you're at it?

MAXINE: It's 'cause I showed the bad bleach job her unicorns.

MARLENE: No, it's not.

MAXINE: Her luck was down, that gal. Thought I'd perk her up.

MARLENE: Fine, Mum.

MAXINE: Her poodle died. (*MARLENE says nothing. MAXINE has taken the menus and moved to the exit.*) Mind you it died in 1964 but are you ... mad at your mum?

MARLENE: Mad at myself, Max.

MAXINE: (*exiting*) Get over it.

JIMMY comes in from the back.

JIMMY: Mum?

MARLENE: What?

JIMMY: Never mind.

MARLENE: (*starting to clean*) Got no time for never minds.

JIMMY: Okay, I need the keys to your car.

MARLENE: Pardon?

JIMMY: I gotta go to school one way or the other. If I'm movin' down there I gotta let 'em *know,* don't I? If I'm stayin' here, I gotta *register.* So hand 'em over. (*pause*) Hey, no grade twelve will be on that bus. I want you to know that. Just Jimmy. No one else. I'll be the only one. Apart from girls.

MARLENE: I'm not the one wrecked my truck.

JIMMY: I have to ride the *bus* home at four to sit around *here* and wait for him, eh?—That's what you want?—Me to sit around *here* my only day off?

MARLENE: No, I—

JIMMY: Not able to go to hockey conditioning, not able to even have the *dignity* of drivin' to school on my first day o' grade twelve, *if* I decide to get it?

MARLENE: Okay, I—

JIMMY: I'm sorry Grandad!—I know I'm actin' like a brat! So keep not sayin' nothin', you're warranted.

MARLENE: Hey, you want a firm hand, you quit makin' it be Dad and just—just *go* live down there.

JIM: Oh Marlene—

MARLENE: I didn't want him to have that dirt bike, I didn't want him to grow up spoiled, but his dad shows up here with a top o' the line model and *I'm* supposed to make him take it back?

JIM: Marlene, sit down.

JIMMY: *Dirt* bike?

MARLENE: And if you're not gettin' your Canadian grade twelve you better darn well get your American!

JIMMY: I'm not gettin' my American grade twelve, I'm gonna drive truck!

MARLENE: You're doin' what I tell you to!

JIMMY: Well, if I could figger out what that is we'll *both* know!

MARLENE: Keep your voice down in this café!— Look how I'm talkin' to him, Dad—(*glancing to the front at the sound of the door*) There, another table just walked in, satisfied?—and Mum's tellin' my life history to the other one, and that daily over from Texas is takin' it all in.

JIMMY: Grandad—

MARLENE: Not a whole lot I can do about it either.

JIMMY: She needs a holiday.

MARLENE: She? Who's she? The cat's mother— this is how that kid talks to me, like we're not even related, like we're brother and sister, you heard the man.

MAXINE: (*entering*) The Mormon Tabernacle Choir looks like it just walked in and that couple? They're from Edmonton, they seen Wayne Gretzky buyin' a pair o' shoes. In 1984. (*pause*) Grey ones. They both want one my cin'min buns. (*goes to the grill*) So don't mind me, I just work here.

The sound of the school bus is heard. MARLENE hears it first.

MARLENE: There's the bus here. (*JIMMY goes to grab his jean jacket from his room.*) What do you care if the bus is here if you're takin' Max's truck?

JIMMY stops. MAXINE comes from behind the grill.

JIMMY: I'm takin' Max's truck?

MARLENE: I never said that.

JIMMY: Yes, you did.

MARLENE: I did not.

JIMMY: Yes, you did.

MARLENE: I did not.

JIMMY: I think you did.

MARLENE: I said *if*.

MAXINE: Hey, get while the gettin's good—(*She takes the keys out of her bra and tosses them to JIMMY.*)—and keep your tail outta the ditch, huh.

MARLENE: I didn't say he could have it, I said *if*.

JIMMY: Well, then do I?

MARLENE: You roll your truck and get handed over Max's keys?

JIMMY: I didn't expect to.

MARLENE: What I say don't count.

JIMMY: What *did* you say?

MARLENE: I said *if* I said.

JIMMY: Let's just get that straight.

MARLENE: *If* you're takin' Max's truck, I said!

JIMMY: So now I can't?

MARLENE: I didn't say that.

JIMMY: Yes, you did.

MARLENE: No I didn't.

JIMMY: Yes, you did.

MARLENE: No, I didn't.

The sound of the bus honking.

MAXINE: Well, this is just like last year.

JIMMY: Am I takin' the bus?

MAXINE: I think he deserves my truck.

JIMMY: Or am I takin' Max's truck?

MAXINE: I think he should.

JIMMY: Mum?

MARLENE: Dad?

MAXINE: That's right Jim, step in.

MARLENE: I'm not sayin' that, Mum.

JIMMY: What *are* you sayin' for the second time!

MARLENE: I'm askin' you, Dad.

MAXINE: She's askin' you, Jim.

MARLENE: I am not Mum.

JIMMY: Do I or don't I?

MARLENE: Well, take it or leave it—

JIMMY: The bus or the truck?

MARLENE: See what I care—

JIMMY: The bus?

MARLENE: The truck.

MAXINE: How 'bout her car?

JIM: Maxine—

MAXINE: What!

JIM: (*to JIMMY*) Go wave, you won't ride today.

JIMMY: But I rolled my truck!

MARLENE: He's right, Dad.

MAXINE: Hey, we all end up in the ditch sooner or later.

JIM: Just go.

JIMMY: I had those beers!—I don't *deserve* the truck! I don't *want* the truck, don't *give* me the truck!

JIM: *Go!*

JIMMY takes a step back. Everyone freezes. JIMMY tears out through the back door.

MAXINE: Yeah ... so we get talkin' this West Edmonton Mall, huh, and I said to this couple, I said, "You know that shoppin' cenner don't hold a candle to Disneyland," and that Texan he was quick to agree. Though he hasn't *seen* the Mall yet but then again, neither have I.

She has taken the two cinnamon buns and put them on plates. She heads out, taking more menus. JIMMY comes racing back in.

JIMMY: Okay, this is the kinda total jerk I am. I knew Dad was gonna marry Linda, I knew since July, I kep' it to myself. Day Mum gets clued into it I be this complete dolt to her, make her feel like sludge for not lettin' me take Max's truck.

Pause.

JIM: Jimmy, it's understandable you didn't want to say anything to your mother.

JIMMY: No, it isn't, is it?

JIM: It is.

JIMMY: Eh?

JIM: Yes, Jimmy.

JIMMY: Oh.

MARLENE: It's—it's fine you didn't tell me, Jimmy. It's fine.

JIMMY: Thanks.

MARLENE: Thanks?

JIMMY: Fine.

MARLENE: How old she, this gal?

Pause.

JIMMY: Beg your pardon?

MARLENE: Old.

JIMMY: I don't really know, any girl over sixteen is old to me.

JIM: Is she a responsible person, your mother means.

MARLENE: If she's just some chick—

JIMMY: Linda? She ... isn't much.

JIM: Jimmy, sit down.

They all take a seat at the table. A long pause.

JIMMY: Actually no, Linda's all right. I can't help it, she is. And she keeps *him* in line anyway—he even shows up on time for her and everything. We're headin' over to her place and Dad sees this tavern?—Automatically the guy just navigates into the parking lot. Looks over to me, shakes his head, says, "Second thought I don't really need that Budweiser—not if I know what's good for me"—slips it into reverse and we're outta there before we're even in. "Who *is* this girl got you so turned around?" I says and he turns beet-red, my own dad. I give him this cuff, eh, and he says, "You're pretty damn cocky kid," and o' course he knows I come by that naturally so that ended that. (*pause*) But so, this Linda, she's really worked wonders—(to JIM) Should I 'a said all this. I shouldn't've said all this, should I have?

MARLENE: No Jimmy, it's … fine. It's good your dad's like that to her, it's … good.

JIMMY: Well, I figgered it was.

MARLENE: Then maybe you know about the house too?

JIMMY: That, I didn't know.

MARLENE: It's in a modern development, it's a big split-level, bedrooms galore, full-sized bathroom, prob'ly two even, top o' the line furniture, colonial style he's decked this gal out with.

JIM: Marlene, do you *know* these details?

MARLENE: No, I don't, but I can put two and two together as good as anyone, even *if* I only got junior high.

JIMMY: Did he *say* it was a split-level?

MARLENE: It's nothin' shabby.

JIMMY: Well, no, it wouldn't be, Linda goes in for quality, she had a great apartment, then see, she's been handling all their finances, Dad he signs his paycheques over to her and she put him on this allowance. 'Course with him not drinkin' so much he didn't spend so much and, well, Linda makes a darn good wage herself—

JIM: Quiet, Jimmy.

JIMMY: Pardon?

MARLENE: Well what's this gal *do*, bank teller?

JIMMY: She—I—it's slipped right from my mind.

MARLENE: Slip it back.

Pause.

JIMMY: She's … nothin' but a second-rate secretary, prob'ly pours coffee all day, eh. (*JIMMY jumps up as he realizes what he has said. MARLENE goes to get the coffee pot, and her order pad, and exits to the front.*) I mean!—not

that there's anything wrong with pourin' coffee—Grandad, I didn't mean—look at what we do, think starin' into the north end of a south bound cow's anything to write home about? Huh? Go tell her we're nothin' neither.

JIM: You haven't had an honest breakfast today, have you?

JIMMY: Breakfast? Yes … no—I don't know.

JIM: Well, sit down and put a decent meal in you.

JIMMY: Sit down?—On what?—This gibbled chair, bent cigarette pack underneath its leg? My thighs are so tense they're gonna take off on their own—look, they're puffin' in an' out—my dad's comin', the crop's not off, you're losin' time like sixty bears and I'm supposed to be a normal human Albertan and eat breakfast?—Well, sorry Grandad, but Puff' Wheat is just *not* gonna do it right now, not for this cowboy.

JIM: It's a heckuva way for a guy to grow up, you're right.

JIMMY: It's just *total* stress in here, all the time.

JIM: I've noticed that too.

JIMMY: Grandad, it's not funny, this is my life.

JIM: I know that, Jimmy.

JIMMY: American, Canadian—back, forth—like it *mattered* what a guy was—why couldn't I've bin born in Australia, nowhere *near* the American border?—I go over to Nedchuk's place and *he's* got this complete dream situation—furniture?—totally matches. Sit down to eat and everybody's got their own place?—little doo-dads on the window sill. His dad's got a complete Black and Decker lifestyle down that basement and his mum's all a'fluff her new living-room curtains are a quarter-inch off. (*pause*) That greaseball Nedchuk sits there beefin' a gripe about how he can't blast his stereo. Me, I'm driving home in my truck and I'm thinkin' *what* I wouldn't give for a living-room window—never mind the quarter-inch-off curtains. (*pause*) Okay, I know, I can stay out the farm anytime I want but Max doesn't care about curtains, she's never even over there—Mum cares, but she's afraid to spend a dollar. She's "waitin'."

JIM: Well, that's true.

JIMMY: We should pour cement in this back suite, seal it off.

JIM: Bulldoze the whole café.

JIMMY: Nuke it right off the face of the earth. I'll tell you one thing, I'm not *ever* gettin' married—you can bet the rent on that. I'm gonna build a house. And it's gonna be bought and paid for before I put my wife into it. There's gonna be no make-do, half-done, wait-see about it.

JIM: The girl you're not gettin' married to is sure gonna be set up right.

JIMMY: And it's gonna have a reg'lar kitchen. With appliances rigged up from here to—to—to nowhere. Who am I tryna kid? (*The sound of a tanker going by.*) Let's face it, Grandad, there's … something seriously the matter with me.

JIM: You figger?

JIMMY: I swear to God if people knew the kindsa things find their way into this brain?—they'd have me committed. I cause myself embarrassment, it's no joke.

JIM: Yeah, well, I'll admit I've had my suspicions about you.

JIMMY: Eh?

JIM: Sure. Time you were sittin' out in the middle o' the field there for'n hour'n a half. Now what's that kid up to? I thought. Out I go and your mouth was hangin' open and all the rest—you says, "Gonna be a fight tonight, Grandad." Well, the sun was goin' down on this side and the moon was comin' up on this side and you says to me, "A fight which one's prettier." Well, I knew then you didn't think too reg'lar.

JIMMY: Yeah, but Grandad, it's gotten way worse than that.

JIM: Worse you say.

JIMMY: I start out okay but then before I know it I'm right off the tracks. Like when it's a house I'm gonna build, I get the spot all picked out and settle on a nice little bungalow. But it always happens I'm buildin' the house for Mum instead. And I'll be ridin' along in the combine, or … drivin' my truck, and well, pretty soon that house has something real feasible like eighteen bathrooms—just this ignorant sprawl of a spread that people have to come from miles around just to gawk at. With binoculars. Holidays—I'd take Mum down to L.A. and deck her out with all these clothes—like Dad was always gonna—and she wouldn't have to serve nobody—we'd eat in fancy restaurants and—and Grandad, there's somethin' awful I gotta tell you.

JIM: What Jimmy?

JIMMY: I—I didn't have anything to drink the night I rolled my truck. I just *said* I had those three Canadians to gimme an excuse to do such a fried thing. I couldn't just roll it, not me, I had to smack into the telephone pole to boot. Look up and see fifty head o' cattle standin' there starin' at me like I'm dumber'n they are. I was buildin' the eighteen bathrooms when I rolled my truck, I was takin' Mum to classy restaurants—my mind was wandering, okay? All over the road. And so was the truck. That's the kinda bigshot I am. Bigshot like my old man. Can't even stay on the road.

JIM: Well, Jimmy, I … don't know *what* to say.

JIMMY: Please don't tell no one.

JIM: That you'd bin grounded all summer 'cause you were stone cold sober?

JIMMY: Uh, yeah. (*long pause*) Ya know Grandad, no offence. But you got a way about you that … just seems to narrow in on the idiot side of my personality. Only time I ever feel like I'm on the ball at *all* is when—well, is when I'm with my dad. I can bounce back and forth about goin' on those hauls but I know the minute I hear his rig pull up, I'll just all a' sudden wanna go. I forget everything when I get in that rig. Him and me, we cut-up somethin' terrible. I'm sorry but he's just this hilarious guy, Grandad. And *I'm* pretty funny myself when I'm with him, figger that one out.

JIM: There's nothing wrong with having a good time with your father.

JIMMY: No? Then why do I gotta feel like sludge the minute I come back and see you? You, you're just this perfect human type-guy, never caused no one no trouble when you were a kid—ask anyone in this district, no one'll say a bad word about you—well try livin' up to that, Grandad.

JIM: Oh, Jimmy, where you got such a silly notion of me—

JIMMY: But no, I can't be your clone, I gotta have a father doesn't even know it's harvest—I can't just up and move with the crop not off. (*pause*) Can I?

JIM: We're almost done. I can get Quint.

JIMMY: Quint?

JIM: Not gonna lie to you. You know I'm no fan of your father's. And it's not my belief that a boy should have to decide something like this in a day's time but that's Don.

JIMMY: I'm not a boy, okay.

JIM: Well, no, but I guess he figures it's better now than not at all.

JIMMY: The fact that he wants me at all is pretty strange—I always thought the most my Dad could take o' me was four, five times a year, eh.

Pause.

JIM: Maybe it'll be good for you to get away from all this haywire here. Enjoy yourself for awhile. The farm, well, it'll always be here.

JIMMY: Geez, you sound like—aren't you—

JIM: See Jimmy, when I was about your age—

MAXINE bursts through the door.

MAXINE: I think that couple's Communist.

JIM puts his hat on and exits outside. JIMMY follows him as far as the door. MAXINE starts preparing orders.

MAXINE: Me and that Texan got talkin' politics and how it's such a joke up here with three parties and how was I to know they'd belong to the third—well, her chin got that Thelma look and him, he started twitchin' his neck—they're prob'ly so left o' cenner they gotta hold onto the rails to keep from fallin' off. And to think they're headin' into America. Trust Russia to drop 'em down through Edmonton.

JIMMY has moved to his room.

JIMMY: (*to himself*) Well Grandad's real tore up over all this, isn't he. Mum, she was down on her knees, beggin' me to stay. Guess I'll just have to *pry* myself away from them, break their hearts and move. Aw, there's no way, what am I talkin' about, it's just too late, the damage is done, I've already grown up. Canadian. Am I supposed to just pack up and move?—into that big ... split-level? Be a guy that hangs "a-out." Play their kinda football. I mean, there's no reason for me to—to go, there's just—there's ... *gorgeous* babes down there. American girls. And they're gonna be fallin' at my Canadian feet. Yeah right, Jimmy, you'll be a wipe-out down there just like you are up here. I could ... fake it though.

MAXINE has come towards JIMMY's room.

MAXINE: Fake what?

JIMMY: (*wheels around*) Whataya think of—of America, Max? (*pause*) I might move there, eh.

MAXINE: Sure you might and you can take your Aunt Thelma and Her Majesty with ya—do 'em good to find out what real life is all about—instead o' sittin' up here with milk in their tea, makin' judgements.

JIMMY: I might move there tonight, like.

MAXINE: Huh?

JIMMY: With my dad. Gonna have to say good-bye to this place, isn't that a shame?—Tell a guy—tell a guy why he'd wanna stay *here* when he can move into some swank place down the States. (*MAXINE is stunned. JIMMY looks at her.*) Say somethin', Max. Max.

MARLENE enters from the front.

MARLENE: Two dailies, one ranchman no onions, two ones, one denver and a side o' browns. (*MARLENE looks to MAXINE. MAXINE looks back.*) Side ... o' browns, Mum. (*pause*) Mum.

MAXINE moves to the junk drawer and fumbles for a Lucky. She lights it, having to keep her hand steady. She moves to the kitchen table and sits down. MARLENE looks to JIMMY. He takes the keys out of his pocket and goes out the back door, letting it flap shut. MARLENE goes to the coffee pot and pours MAXINE a cup. Music comes on the jukebox out front to end the act.

ACT TWO

The front of the café. We are now on the other side of the order window and swinging door, and can see into the kitchen. There is a till booth area with rows of Lifesavers and chocolate bars. There is a phone by the cash register. Trophies, postcards and Canadian and American flags are about. Along the counter clusters of serviette canisters, salt and pepper shakers and sugar containers are evenly placed. Red leatherette stools are up to it. Behind it there is a milkshake-maker, pop machine, and coffeemaker, etc. There is a booth and a number of tables with a suggestion of the café existing beyond our view. We are looking through the wall and window of the café so that when the characters look toward us they are seeing the highway and prairie.

As another song comes to an end we can hear the sound of the combine fading in and out. The sun is starting to set, and will reach its peak at the close of the play.

A duffle bag, small suitcase, and hockey stick are placed together near the till. JIMMY, his hat on, is sitting sideways on a booth seat. Chocolate bar wrappers and potato chips are on the table. A tanker can be heard gearing up. JIMMY raises himself up slightly to listen. He slouches back down as the tanker gears by.

MAXINE enters from the kitchen. She is in jeans and a sweatshirt, and carrying Marlene's cigarettes. She places the pack on the counter, puts a coffee mug out, takes the coffee pot from the machine, and pours. She puts the pot back, staring heavily into it.

MAXINE: Readin' this article, oh where was it. *Readers' Digest. (She heads around the counter to sit on a stool, keeping her back to JIMMY.)* Yeah, according to this article ... nine a-outta ten Americans ... carry guns. *(takes her lighter out and lights a cigarette)* Run across the line and get your Max a package o' Lucky's before I affixicate myself on these of your mother's—I'll handle it if your dad shows up while you're gone.

JIMMY: *(not moving)* I bet you will.

MAXINE: Believe it was in the state of Wyoming, speakin' of Wyoming, that this here nutcase done away with was it sixteen families?—on their way to church. He was prob'ly a Vietnam vet, 'course America had no business even *goin'* to Vietnam. Or to any of these other trouble spot countries, in my opinion. *(takes a drink of coffee)* Not to mention the moon. The moon, in my mind, should remain neutral. We got no business puttin' a claim on it. But violence in America is

somethin' the Russians don't have. *(glances over her shoulder to see if JIMMY is paying attention)* Now you know I loved John Fitzgerald more than the brother I didn't have. The day that news come on the air from Dallas?—I was standin' in there makin' a grilled cheese sandwich. Yes. You think a Canadian would ever take a shot at their—I mean our prime minister? No. 'Course there were many that wrestled with the idea more'n they should've when Trudeau was in power. *(takes a drag off her cigarette and butts it in disgust)* Now you take television. The stuff they put on down there? Trash. You wanna know the name of a good program on TV and it's been on for twenty, thirty years and it's *Canadian*, it's not American, it's on the CBC and it's—the—the—it's bin on the years—it's—oh, what the hell's the name o' that show? Well, you know what one I mean, that one. Or how 'bout their national sport, that's a sport?—spittin', chewin' and scratchin' with the odd baseball tossed—and I don't know why you're takin' all this hockey equipment. Hockey isn't nothin' down there, it's not even played.

JIMMY: They play hockey down there.

MAXINE: Well, they *shouldn't!* They're gonna be beatin' yas at your own game before much longer, and then sellin' it back to you, that's the way these people operate, I was raised down there, I know how they think—*me*, us, we're first, we're best, gimme that—you wanna buy it? *(pause)* Jimmy, America is just not the place you think it is. It's not the place it used to be.

JIMMY: Yeah, it seems to've changed an awful lot since this morning even.

MAXINE: What—what happens this girl sees the light like your mother done and walks a-out on your dad. Then who's gonna look after you?

JIMMY: I don't need anyone to look after me. I can look after myself, if you haven't noticed.

MAXINE: Everyone needs someone to look after 'em—or I mean, women don't, they got it built-in, but men, they do.

JIMMY has gone to his gear and picked up his hockey stick.

JIMMY: *I* don't. Any chick who gets serious with me is gonna have a few disappointments. *(fakes a slap shot)* 'Cause I'm not the kind to be held down, okay. *(puts the stick down)* Furthermore—

MAXINE: Oh good, I like these furthermores.

JIMMY: I'm takin' her out normal. To the show, to parties, dances—I'm givin' her everything she wants, we're gonna go out for a long, long time—years—and really get to know each other and *then* she's gettin' a proper ring, the whole bit—church, reception in the Elks Hall, and a two-week honeymoon. And it will be *decades* before any baby is born to wreck our happiness.

MAXINE: Jimmy.

JIMMY: I'm not rushin' into anything, got the picture?

MAXINE: I guess you're kinda like Grandad when it comes right down to it, huh?

JIMMY: You got it.

MAXINE: Yeah, he knew me a day and a half before we got married.

JIMMY: Well, fine, but that's another thing—I'm marrying someone same side o' the *border*.

MAXINE: What side would this be?

The sound of a tanker. JIMMY looks out, seeing if it stops. It gears right on by.

JIMMY: No side.

MARLENE enters. She is wearing jeans and a light sweater. Her appearance changes quite radically when not wearing her uniform. JIMMY wheels around at the sound of the tanker, and sees her enter.

JIMMY: Super, Dad's now five hours late, Marlene.

MAXINE: Is it after nine? (*to MARLENE*) You watchin' *Dallas*?

MARLENE: You … go ahead and watch it, Mum.

MAXINE: Huh?—oh. (*takes her coffee and heads toward the kitchen*)

JIMMY: I *only* tell my coach I'm not gonna be around this year, I *only* tell all the guys, I *only* been holed up in this café since four lookin' out the window every—(*picks up his hockey stick and sets it back down*)—time a truck goes by.

MAXINE: (*at the door*) You go back to that school on Monday and tell everyone you changed your mind. They'll be so happy they'll throw a party for you.

JIMMY: Max, you seem to have this big idea that I'm someone at that school. I'm no one.

MAXINE: You're more'n your mother was.

JIMMY: Well, I maybe am but I'm not no hero.

MARLENE: I didn't have time for friends when I was rushin' back home to work dinner shift, but never mind, I—

MAXINE: You tell your coach you wanna try a-out for the team, he'll letcha, star player like you were last year. Huh, Mar?

JIMMY: Star.

MAXINE: You were the best player on the team last year, the *league*—ask your grandad.

JIMMY: Grandad?—All Grandad said was my coordination was improving. I didn't even know my coordination was bad.

MAXINE: It's not, it's excellent, it's cleared right up. I could catch a pop-fly when I was a kid, back home in Minnesota—I played with a soda jerk team, that's how good I was—you get your athaletic ability from my side.

MARLENE: Mum, you don't *have* a side when it comes to Jimmy.

MAXINE: Huh?

MARLENE: He's got my side, and his dad's side.

MAXINE: My side's your side.

MARLENE: Your side's back home in Minnesota—and—and if you're gonna say I'm every inch Aunt Thelma—

MAXINE: Oh, you never forget nothin' do you—

MARLENE: —even though you wiped your American spit all over my face then don't try to inch me out of my own kid's half.

JIMMY looks to MARLENE, then abruptly away.

MAXINE: Whataya pickin' on Maxine for?—I'm tryna talk the kid a-outta goin'. You don't see your dad in here, do ya?

MARLENE: Dad's got a crop to get off.

MAXINE: I know all about the crop, I bin playin' second fiddle to it since I come up here. And to you, Thelma, and her majesty mother-in-law over there with the tea-stained teeth. Ninety years old and not even a *hint* of poor health. Tellin' me I don't know how to put a meal on the table. Bin doin' it for a livin' all my life, which is somethin' neither of those two know sweet tweet about—living, or makin' one. Sittin' on their royal haunches all their narrow lives—criticizin'. (*exits to the back*)

MARLENE and JIMMY exchange a look.

MARLENE: She's right, you know.

JIMMY: That you take after them?

MARLENE: No, that they're like that—*do* I take after them? I do, don't I—no, I don't.

JIMMY: How should I know and who cares?

MARLENE: Well, fine, but I'm not turnin' out like Thelma.

JIMMY: You think Dad's had himself a wreck?

MARLENE: No, I—I don't, Jimmy. Your dad's fine, he's just runnin' a little behind. He hasn't had himself a wreck.

JIMMY: But what if he jack-knifed in his rush to get here?

MARLENE: Well, that much I doubt for the very simple reason that your dad is a professional from the word go. And say it's a shifted load or somethin', well, that's gettin' fixed right this second, they service those big trucks reg'lar on that innerstate. And if it's not that, well, he coulda got away late.

JIMMY: You said he'd be here at four.

MARLENE: I shouldn't've said four, it's my fault. I shoulda just said I don't know. That's what—

JIMMY: What?

MARLENE: Well, that's what I used to do when you were a kid.

JIMMY: You did?

MARLENE: Sure. Or if he'd call when you were out I wouldn't tell you so you wouldn't wait, or if he didn't show up, well you'd be none the wiser. Then if he did, see, then you got a nice surprise. But I'd like to know why it is you think this is all you'll need down there, this tiny suitcase and that gear.

JIMMY: (*looks to it*) Well, whataya think I should do? Just rip out the whole suite of every bit of evidence I ever lived here? Take all I own so I never have to show my face in here again?

MARLENE: She's gonna think you don't have nothin'!—this is all I ever give ya. Take—take the ghetto blaster at least?—just take it and—oh, what am I sayin', they'll prolly have one, they'll have stereo equipment from here to—(*looking outside*)—that old gas pump.

MARLENE has gone to the window to look out. JIMMY stares out in the direction of the pump as well.

JIMMY: That pump should be bulldozed.

MARLENE: The pump stays. And so does my ole Texaco star.

JIMMY: *Your* ole Texaco star, that's *my* ole Texaco star.

MARLENE: Used to tell folks, I'd say, you wanna find your way back here, all you gotta do is look for the star.

JIMMY: I never heard you say anything so stunned in your life to *anyone*.

MARLENE: When I was a *kid*. Life was goin' on a little bit before *you* were born, you know. I was the kid around here at one time.

JIMMY: I can't help I was born.

MARLENE: I used to watch those little coloured balls hop around when the gas was pourin'—and if I had my way we'd still have that pop machine out front, that Orange Crush.

JIMMY: It wasn't good for anything but slappin' shots against, and you got no right to put a claim on the pump, or the star. They aren't even ours. We never owned that g'rage.

MARLENE: You see anyone around here care a darn? You see anyone wantin' to buy us out and put up a big Voyajer? It's never gonna be a big draw in here.

JIMMY: You wanna turn a profit, you gotta go one way or the other. Which no one in this family can ever do.

MARLENE: What're you talkin' about?

JIMMY: Turn it back into a truck stop. Or upgrade into a restaurant. Who ever heard of a café on the bald-headed prairie with no place to gas up?

MARLENE: We got those that remember us keepin' us afloat, we got a good clientele—and people make a point of stopping back—thanks to Mum.

JIMMY: A place like this doesn't have a clientele, it's got reg'lars.

MARLENE: That's right, Jimmy. But not everyone wants 'a go to a place 'its build around a salad bar they gotta feel guilty about. Get served parsley with a bran muffin by a waitress named Tom. Like the places up in Calgary. Nice way to bring up a kid. You coulda done worse. There's nothin' fancy about the Bordertown but you'll think more of it when you're gone. Think I liked it before I left? Gang from high school used to pile into their dads' Meteors and come in here for something to do. Well, I had to serve those boys. I was thirteen, fourteen years old. Jack Jaffrey would walk like me, talk like me, act the smart aleck in fronna all his friends? I'd say to Mum, I'm not goin' out there, I'm not no more—then I'd run out to the farm. (*This strikes her funny all of a sudden.*)

JIMMY: Why you laughin'?—I'd like to beat the snot outta that guy.

MARLENE: Well, never mind, poor Mum had to cook, serve, clear and do till all on her own—that's how rotten I was to her—I'd take off just like that, I'd go down the coulees sometimes and Dad would have to get me. Bring me back. That Jack Jaffrey ended up on drugs, went the hippie route—grew his hair down to his rear-end and hitch-hiked down to California.

JIMMY: So, Dad, you don't think he's had a wreck?

MARLENE: No, me, I was still poofin' my hair and wearin' stove pipe pants when I got married.

JIMMY: Yeah, well, fine.

MARLENE: Fine what?

JIMMY: Open up a museum in here. Keep the star, keep the pump, plug a Canadian quarter into the jukebox and an American quarter into Maxine and let her pour forth with a few million stories about her fat cousins in Oklahoma. Or how she come up here in '49. Nineteen and dumber 'an a dawg.

MARLENE: Oh crumb, you said it.

JIMMY: Grandad and me are the only ones know it's the present.

MARLENE: Yeah? That farmhouse don't look too modern.

JIMMY: There's nothin' wrong with that farmhouse, it's got a good foundation.

MARLENE: Got four kinds o' linoleum showin' through on the floor, should put indoor-outdoor down in there.

JIMMY: Grandad's dad built that house, you don't rip that linoleum up, I *like* those other floors showin' through. I suppose I'll come back and you'll've talked Grandad into soakin' every last cent into somethin' him and me don't want.

MARLENE: Whata you care? You're goin' to wall-to-wall plush carpet!

JIMMY: Don't change nothin'!

MARLENE: I won't! I won't get nothin' for myself, I won't get my bathroom—

JIMMY: Never said nothin' 'bout in here!

MARLENE: You want me to bulldoze the pump and star!

The sound of a tanker. They watch for it to gear down. It goes right on by.

JIMMY: Great. Prob'ly chattin' up some chick.

MARLENE: And another thing. Don't you—you—you get what I'm sayin'?

JIMMY: Huh?

MARLENE: Don't you start bein' the—the smart aleck down there, like.

Pause.

JIMMY: I already am one. I'm a chip off the ole block.

MARLENE: You just—if the two of you? I mean it. Are somewhere and what have you. Okay? You think of that—you think of that Linda girl and you … (*taps her finger on the counter*) you make sure things stay right for her.

JIMMY: How?

MARLENE: Well.

JIMMY: Huh?

MARLENE: No, but I'm sayin' *you* just be responsible when you meet a girl, and what-all.

JIMMY: Meetin' 'ems one thing, gettin' 'em to go out with you's another.

MARLENE: Jimmy?

JIMMY: What?

MARLENE: Don't be … in a hurry.

Pause.

JIMMY: (*moving away*) Where *is* he, Mum?

MARLENE: Get your grade twelve and you do … good and do … good.

JIMMY is looking outside. MARLENE starts to go to him, to touch him, but he turns around and she moves away.

JIMMY: Why isn't Grandad comin' in off the field to say goodbye?

MARLENE: He said so at supper and he's—he's stayin' out there.

JIMMY: He didn't say nothin', I was doin' till—he stayed in there. (*toward the kitchen*) He figures I should be out there workin' 'steada sittin' on my lazy butt in here.

MARLENE: You had to go to school, you had to tell people, the bank.

JIMMY: So I'm here since four afraid to bring the cows in or do my milkin' 'case Dad shows up, sees I'm not chompin' at the bit to hop on up. Grandad has to ask Quint. *Quint.* Pickin' up my slack.

MARLENE: You know what I'm gonna miss? I'm gonna miss, uh, seein' the hockey games, and what-all.

JIMMY: You're kidding?

MARLENE: That hat trick you scored, type-thing, eh. (*pause*) Last year.

JIMMY: Well what about it?

MARLENE: I'm just sayin'.

JIMMY: Yeah, that was quite the fluke, that night.

MARLENE: Really? Oh. Well, did you want something to eat?

JIMMY: *Eat?*

MARLENE: Eat.

JIMMY: Like what?

MARLENE: Well, food or somethin', whatja have for supper?

JIMMY: Hot beef san'wich.

MARLENE: This gal cook?

JIMMY: Whata you all a' sudden care if I get a balanced diet or not?

MARLENE: You eat reg'lar.

JIMMY: Yeah, I eat *with* 'em too, I'm just reg'lar around here, like Wally and Quint—that's how *I* eat reg'lar.

MARLENE: Well, what do you *want?*

JIMMY: A salad bar.

MAXINE enters, drinking a Coke.

MAXINE: I seen that one.

MARLENE: Mum, Jimmy wants a salad bar in here.

MAXINE: Why didn'tcha say?—We'll haul that jukebox a-out and set 'er up there.

MARLENE: I don't want that jukebox hauled out.

MAXINE: Let's knock a-out a wall.

JIMMY: I don't want a wall knocked out.

MARLENE: He's sayin' I don't feed him reg'lar meals.

MAXINE: We get goin' on this it could be done by Monday.

JIMMY: My dad's had a wreck, she's knockin' out walls.

MARLENE: He hasn't had a wreck and look in that fridge.

JIMMY: Well, it would be just my loser-luck if he *did* have a wreck.

MARLENE: There's a tub o' coleslaw in there day in and day out.

JIMMY: Okay, never mind the coleslaw, never mind the walls.

MAXINE: Your grandad and me nearly had a divorce over that wallpaper—see that buckin' bronc there with the twisted leg?—I took

Marlene's brown crayon and coloured that in—when Jim come in from coolin' off over me handin' him the one strip upside down, he took one look at my artwork and—see this roof? (*points up*) He hit it. He was always horrible to live with, even then.

MARLENE: (*leaving to the back*) He doesn't care about the roof, the wallpaper—thirty years old and still holdin'—he doesn't care about anything—*I* didn't feed him reg'lar meals.

JIMMY: (*watches her leave and goes after her*) I do so care!

MAXINE: (*looks to the back, then to JIMMY*) Yeah!

JIMMY: Yeah, *what* Max?

MAXINE: What about the time you fired the hardball through the window there?

JIMMY: If *I* was gonna be five hours late I'd call a guy and *she's* the one that don't care.

MAXINE: Your mother was ready to sell you to the Hutterites for a nickel that day. I'm the one stuck you under the counter 'til she seen the humour. It was me that risked an early death every Christmas climbin' onto the roof to put Sanny Claus up there with his nose blinkin' off and on in thirty below weather. It was me that shovelled the ditch so the kid could play hockey when he come home from school, not his Canadian grandad out in that field.

JIMMY: Grandad said goodbye at supper.

MAXINE: (*grabbing him*) Tell your Max you're not goin' down there, tell her you wanna stay home. (*hugs him*)

JIMMY: (*moving away*) Yeah well, "home."

MAXINE: What about—

JIMMY: (*wheeling around*) What about that Cuisanart I boughtcha?—Eh? Think that come cheap? I sprung two hunderd Canadian for that rig and you haven't even touched it. It sits over at the farm collectin' dust.

MAXINE: I don't do enough cookin' here I gotta cook there?

JIMMY: And come winter, I wancha to start spendin' more time in that curling rink. Grandad likes that.

MAXINE: I am *not* sittin' … in *no* curlin' rink with a bunch o' whiny *wives* drinkin' coffee outta a styrofoam cup.

JIMMY: Oh sure, yet you sit in the hockey rink other side the buildin' watchin' *me* play.

MAXINE: He wants someone to watch him he's got Marlene.

JIMMY: She liked my hat trick.

MAXINE: She wasn't even there—oh yeah, that's right, she was. (*pause*) Oh boy, that was somethin', that hat trick.

JIMMY: Eh?

MAXINE: You deserved your steak dinner that night, I'll tell ya.

JIMMY: (*picks up his stick and does a shot in slow motion*) You know, I can't even think about that night without feelin' goosebumps. It's almost like it wasn't supposed to happen. I mean, lotsa guys score hat tricks. But, oh, if you woulda known how much I wanted to have a three goal game, all my life, just please God, let me score a hat trick. Me, I'm the kinda guy gets the odd goal if the other team's lousy. Or if their goalie's got the flu. My mind wanders. I think about my skating, I forget I got a stick. But *that* night, we were *even* playin' against an okay team. And it was one, two, three in the net before I knew what was happening.

MAXINE: You musta had horseshoes up your patooie that night! Huh?

A tanker goes by. JIMMY looks to it.

JIMMY: Yeah. That's all it was. Luck. A fluke.

MAXINE: Huh?

JIMMY: But my dad wouldna known luck from skill, he's never even been to a hockey game. He woulda thought I was great. Had he been there. (*pause*) Max?

MAXINE: Yeah?

JIMMY: I thought he was. He said he was gonna, and I kep' lookin' over by the entrance there thinkin' this man was him, same jacket, eh. You can't see worth a darn on that ice.

MAXINE: You mean *that's* why you played so—

JIMMY: But it's these darn dispatchers, eh. They hold a trucker up somethin' terrible.

MAXINE: Yeah. I heard that one before.

JIMMY: It's true.

MAXINE: No, I know, you're right.

JIMMY: He tried, he tried real hard to make that game, I know for a fact he did. Linda even said when I was down in July, she told me lotsa stuff. When she first met him, he took out his wallet and showed her my picture. He didn't pretend like he didn't have a son. Like he coulda done. Only thing is the picture was from grade five or somethin', but so—it's a shifted load is all it is right now, and they're servicin' it right this—this minute.

MAXINE: That's probably it.

JIMMY: No, it isn't. (pause) Don't take five hours to fix a load. If he's—Max, if—he hasn't even bin married to her a month.

MAXINE: Oh, Jimmy, your dad's—

JIMMY: What Max?—what's my dad?—a saint? Huh? No. Well, I clicked in to that a long time ago, okay. First time he took me down to Texas it kinda sunk in. Boy oh boy, he was takin' me to the lonestar state, I was gonna have somethin' to brag about to the guys when I come back. Mum had me workin' till all summer to save up for those Cooperalls but Dad shows up end o' August—well, somehow his sweet talk to the ladies down there started seemin' a little more'n friendly, put it that way. And the more he talks the more it hits me—math's not my favourite subject but I'm addin' up the years I'm alive with the years he's bin "seeing" this one and that one and it's equalling the same thing—he was two-timin' on Mum before I was even born. After. And probably during. Well, I just couldn't wait to get back here, take out my savings and—(pause) Somehow those dumb little diamond earrings Mum wanted were more important that a pair of Cooperalls. You figger that out. (MARLENE comes in from the back, but JIMMY cannot see her.) All day dumb junk like that keeps comin' to me—like my whole life just decides to show up in my head, in Panavision. And still—still Max, I can't help thinkin' how hard Dad's tryin' now and he's got Linda—she's just a way better wife for him than Mum ever was—she's really neat, so easy to

talk to eh, like I can say whatever I want to her, she's a little like you—when she's got somethin' to say? she just says it—

MAXINE: (noticing MARLENE) Oh geez Jimmy—

JIMMY: No Max, lemme tell you—Linda's got a real way about her. (MARLENE exits.) I don't know how Dad managed to get her. Or Mum, for that matter. Women are just like that, they're stupid when it comes to men. But Max, can you see what I mean?—my dad's finally givin' me somethin' I want. Not some bike or toy that I—I used to leave out in the parkin' lot for some Oldsmobile to back up over. Grandad can say I got no value for the dollar—yeah, Grandad, that's why I saved every penny I ever earned just so I could blow it on—(pause) My dad's bin promisin' me this all my life. Okay, it's a little late. And Mum's not gonna be a part of it. But I quit dreamin' that one a long time ago. And I know I gotta leave the guys, hockey, the farm, Grandad and Mum but—

MAXINE: What about your Max, gonna miss her?

MARLENE: (re-entering before JIMMY can answer) I'll see ya then Jimmy, I'm goin' out to the farm, eh.

JIMMY: Pardon?

MAXINE: The farm?

MARLENE: Yeah, so—

JIMMY: What for?

MARLENE: Whataya think, my bath. (a tanker goes by) There he is.

JIMMY: (wheels around, willing it to be his dad) That's not him, Marlene. Did ya hear the rig gear down? No. Is there an engine purrin' out there? No. 'Cause he's not here, he might never get here and you'll be stuck with me. He mighta changed his mind—he don't phone me, I'm just supposed to know. He maybe decided he doesn't want the kid after all—I miss school, miss hockey, miss everything so I can wait. Wait for him like you used to, like you wait for some wonderful thing to happen with your life—some fairy tale ending—yeah, the unicorn collection is all she thinks about, well, isn't that right on the money, she's never gonna get outta here, she just stays in this café mornin', noon and night.

MAXINE: Jimmy, your mum goes a-out.

JIMMY: She doesn't go "a-out." You can't even get her to go to a dance.

MAXINE: She'll come around.

JIMMY: *When?* The woman's only been divorced since I was twelve.

MAXINE: Yeah, well, when you were twelve you weren't too keen on your mother even talkin' to a man in here, never mind goin' a-out with one.

MARLENE: Thank-you, Mum.

MARLENE goes to the till area. JIMMY heads to the door, but wheels around.

JIMMY: *How* could I *say* that to her? How? I can't believe I got so little goin' for me I actually say that-all to her the day I'm leavin'—I don't deserve no father, I don't deserve a home, that's why Dad's not showin' up, he's thinkin' twice about havin' a smart-mouth like me screw up his life again.

MAXINE: Again—you listen here kid, you didn't screw up his life. *He* screwed up ours, the day she run off with him.

MARLENE: "She" didn't run off with no one. *You're* the one figgered the sun rose and set on Don, he was an American—he was gonna just "have to drop on back next time he was up this way."

MAXINE: I say that to everyone! And I can't help it if you were too shy to talk to him yourself.

MARLENE: Mum, I was fifteen.

MAXINE: You were the *oldest* fifteen-year-old I ever come across. I didn't know what to do with her from the time she was this high. (*pause*) Yes, I liked Don. No, I don't see through people. And I didn't listen to Jim. Like I shoulda. But I seen my girl's eyes light up for the first time the day Don walked in this café. (*looks to JIMMY*) And now he's comin' to take *you* across that border and all you tell your Max is how *she* liked your hat trick. (*JIMMY looks abruptly away from MARLENE.*) How you'll miss Grandad. Am I always gonna be alone in this family?

JIMMY: *Alone?*

The sound of the back door.

MARLENE: Here Dad is now, so you just quit talkin' nuts, Mum, I mean it.

MAXINE: Not talkin' nuts, all this kid thinks to say to me is go sit in the curlin' rink, pay attention to Grandad. Does Grandad ever pay attention to *me?*

JIM walks in, stopping at the door. He is exhausted and dusty.

MAXINE: Huh?

JIM: What's goin' on?

MAXINE: Brings me up here after a day and a half and puts me in that farmhouse with his ditzy mother, gotta change her dress to say hello. Well, my folks didn't *have* sit-down meals. I not only had to raise myself, I had to raise my mum in the bargain. 'Cause my mother was useless. And my dad was no screamin' hell either—*when* he was there. So don't expect me to walk in that farmhouse and balance a china teacup on my knee, too nervous to know what to do but talk. They all in that family were just too good for me, you none o' ya involve me like I count, never have.

JIM: What she on about this for?

MAXINE: "She"—"leave her"—like I'm some kinda spoiled brat you have to put up with. Husband don't talk to me, doesn't think I'm bright enough. Maxine, she's just a dumb American. S'what you-all think deep down, I know you do.

JIM: Jimmy, what in the hell is goin' on in here?

JIMMY: I hurt Max's feelings real bad, it's all my fault.

MAXINE: *Kid's leavin'*, Jim. *Care?* I'm the only one showin' I do only to find a-out I'm the only one he's not gonna have a hard time leavin'.

JIMMY: Max, that's not true.

MAXINE: (*to JIM*) You, you're just so afraid all the time o' what I'm gonna do or say if I'm let in on anything. Ever stop to think while you're a-out in that field that I bin here pushin' forty years and I haven't done nothin' yet?

JIMMY: Max, you done plenny, you're my Max.

MARLENE: Shush, Jimmy.

JIMMY: You shush.

JIM: Memory serves me correct, day I brung you up here you turned around and went right back.

MARLENE looks to JIMMY. JIMMY looks to JIM.

JIMMY: No way.

JIM: Yes, she did. I think walkin' out on me is how you'd put it. Because that's what she did—straight through that field there. Across the border. She had no trouble leaving me.

Pause.

MAXINE: I wouldn't say that. I run my nylon on the barb-wire.

JIM: That's right, you did. I was married to her three days, I'd known her five.

MAXINE: Two of which were spent on the train waiting for Saskatchewan to end.

JIM: We got picked up at the station in Lethbridge and—

MAXINE: His dad didn't say one word to us the whole time home. Side by side in that old truck. Me in the middle, a carbon copy on either side, lookin' straight ahead. Walk into that farmhouse expectin' I don't know what and *what* does the woman do but *warm* the teapot. Hands me her best English china just *hopin'* I'd break it, which I did.

JIM: It wasn't her best, it was just some cup I got at the show.

MAXINE: Yeah, but I didn't know that.

JIM: You didn't have to take off.

JIMMY: I can't believe this on the day I'm leavin'.

MAXINE: You didn't have to come after me.

JIM: Well, I did.

Pause.

MAXINE: That's right you did and I'd like to know what for—you-all get along just fine without me.

JIM: I don't know about that.

MAXINE: Huh.

JIM: Said I don't know whereas we would, in fact, get along without you. Maxine.

Pause.

JIMMY: Told ya Max, the man needs ya—it's emotional security.

JIM slowly looks at JIMMY.

JIM: (*to MAXINE*) Speaking of tea.

MAXINE heads to the kitchen to prepare it. Pause.

JIM: Much of a dinner crowd?

MARLENE: Yes.

JIMMY: No. Yes, I mean.

JIM walks over to the gear and case and stares at it. He goes to the window and takes a look out. He takes a deep breath. He takes his hat off and wipes his brow.

JIMMY: I know I shoulda bin out there! I know I didn't even do my chores! You don't have to stand there not tellin' me!

JIM: Well, I didn't expect you to today.

JIMMY: No sooner would I leave he'd show up and how'd he take that? Huh?

MARLENE: Jimmy, don't snap at Grandad, he's gonna wish he never come in.

JIMMY: You snap at Maxine lef', right, and cenner, look how you talk to your own mother, Marlene.

JIM: Here you kids.

MARLENE: My mother is my mother.

JIMMY: Oh, good one, Mum, and who're you?—Way you talk to Max is just pathetic.

JIM: Jimmy, *listen* to yourself son.

JIMMY: Son?—I'm not your son. I never will be, okay? So quit tyin' my stomach up in knots when he's not here yet and I shoulda bin out in that *field* all along. (*pause*) Good one, Jimmy. Insult Grandad now.

JIM: Never mind.

MARLENE: We're none of us what we're supposed to be in this family. Mum's like my daughter half the time, Jimmy's more of a brother. Guess it's no wonder he's itchin' to go south, eh Dad? He's got a new and improved father and a perky little secretary real eager to take my place. Gee, you know Dad, this gal?—she's got a real way about her.

JIMMY: You heard me.

MARLENE: Jimmy can say whatever he wants to her, isn't that great? Wonder if he'll lip her off like he does me. 'Course I'm no one. I pour coffee all day. Raised in the back suite of the Bordertown Café like I had no choice but to tie on an apron, work till, cash out and close up. Time I was fifteen I could run this place. So what? Is that what I wanted? Who cares what I want—he can show me up all he wants to his dad and her, packin' this piddly little amount like it's *all* I could afford.

JIM: Marlene.

MARLENE: Well, Dad, I give him more'n a hockey stick to show them off.

JIMMY: I don't want her to show them off, I don't want *nothin'* from her, Grandad.

MARLENE: Yes, you do. You want something I just don't *have*. And never will. Because I'm not—I just—when I got somethin' to say, I *can't* just say it to you. I'm not her, I'm not the kinda wife your dad needed. I'm not my mother, I'm not Aunt Thelma, I'm no one. Just myself. I—well, I got a few dollars in the Bank o' Montreal, I got a car, I'm thirty-four years old with fallen arches and sore back. But you know what? I *like* this place. And any changes I make I wanna make in my own good time. But first, I'm gonna … tra—travel.

Pause.

JIMMY: *Travel?*

JIM: Travel—?

MARLENE: Booked my flight today. To Hawaii. And I'm goin'. Come Christmas. Two weeks accommodation. Wardair. You said I needed a holiday. Well, I'm takin' one.

JIMMY: Whataya mean you're goin' to Hawaii? By *yourself?*

MARLENE: Well, this is it.

MAXINE enters with a small pot of tea. She sets it on the counter.

JIMMY: Max, Mum's goin' to Hawaii!

MAXINE: Huh!—How?

MARLENE: Gonna dog-paddle, Mum.

MAXINE: Hawaii?—Hawaii's part o' the United States.

JIMMY: *I'm* not spendin' Christmas with my dad and her. I don't even know them for nothin'. Aren'tcha even gonna invite me home?

MAXINE: I'll get Sanny Claus up and bakes my turkey and we'll have all the reg'lars in—it'll be just the same without her.

JIMMY: You mean we aren't gonna be together ever again? You mean this is it? The guy calls and I'm booted out the door?

MARLENE: Max'll give you a Christmas.

A tanker goes by. JIMMY ignores it.

JIMMY: Mum, listen to reason, you can't go off single like that. There's jerks out there. And—and you're easy prey, especially when you get dressed up.

MARLENE: I won't get dressed up. I'll wear my uniform over there and carry a coffee pot.

MAXINE: Thought you said your mother could do with a good time for a change?

JIMMY: Oh, yeah, but don't you think someone should go with her?

JIM: Jimmy should go with you, Marlene. He's right.

JIMMY: No!—I didn't mean *me*.

MARLENE: Well, he could if he … wants.

Pause.

JIMMY: Want me to?

MARLENE: (*looks to him, then away*) She'll prob'ly have somethin' planned for you down there, a real Christmas, nice homey stuff, fix that place up like you wouldn't believe—your dad'll have so many presents for you under that tree—

JIMMY: Yeah, he's prob'ly planning it all right now, which is why he's so late—but fine, I won't go with you, who cares? I only bin waitin' in this café for the man since I was four—I mean, I mean since *four*—but I'll keep waitin', because it's what you want, I'll just—just—(*takes out his wallet and fumbles for a piece of paper*)—give you this now and take my gear and go stand out on the highway, I'll get outta your sight, Mum—(*throwing the paper at her*)—so here, have it, okay?—It's your pink bathroom. It's all paid for, it's looked after, it's what you wanted, it's what you got—white bathtub, pink curtains, flower wallpaper, just like the magazines. You tell the man when he comes Monday, clean, new, modern—exactly how you got it in your head.

Pause.

MAXINE: Kid bought a bathroom. When what she got is fine.

MARLENE: No, it's not fine. A person can hardly turn around in there. There's no place to put my make-up on.

MAXINE: Oh. You're right. The whole suite should be gutted.

MARLENE: No, it shouldn't, just the bathroom.

MAXINE: Just the … bathroom.

MARLENE: I didn't wanna buy the Mathison house, I wanted to stay *here*. I—I try to teach the kid the value of the dollar, I make him work till, I look in the window at those diamond chip earrings, I—and now he's put the mon—the money down on a bathroom.

Pause.

JIMMY: I didn't even *know* you wanted Hawaii though. I figgered it was just the bathroom you wanted, eh.

MARLENE breaks down completely. JIMMY looks to JIM, to MAXINE, back to MARLENE.

JIMMY: I can't *believe* I didn't think of Hawaii.

MAXINE gets a serviette from the canister and hands it to JIMMY. JIMMY goes to MARLENE to give it to her. She reaches out to get it but grabs onto JIMMY's hand instead. She keeps a distance from him, but brings his hand to her face and holds it there.

JIMMY: You never even *mentioned* Hawaii.

MARLENE comes away and rushes to the back suite.

JIM: Go after her, Maxine.

MAXINE exits.

JIMMY: Trust me to come up with a *bathroom*.

JIM: Sit down, Jimmy.

JIMMY sits on one of the stools up to the counter. JIM goes around the counter and reaches under it to a hiding spot. He pulls out a bottle of Canadian

Club whiskey. JIMMY is floored. He watches as JIM takes two glasses and pours two shots.

JIMMY: Grandad. I … are you really doin' this?

JIM hands JIMMY a drink. JIMMY takes it.

JIM: I'm a degenerate, there's no gettin' around it.

JIM comes around the counter and sits beside JIMMY. He clinks his glass with JIMMY's. They drink.

JIMMY: Grandad?

JIM: Yep.

JIMMY: Just tell me if I'm doin' the right thing, goin' down there. That's all I wanna know.

JIM: Can't tell you that.

JIMMY: Maxine tells me.

JIM: Do you listen? No. You still pack your kit.

JIMMY: You don't *like* my dad though. That's sayin' something.

JIM: He's not all bad.

JIMMY: You don't like him, just say you don't like him.

JIM: Not for me to say.

JIMMY: Okay, now *what* don't you like about him?—that he doesn't show up on time, fine. He's not reliable. Now you see where I get it from.

Pause.

JIM: Expecting an answer to that?

JIMMY: Yeah.

JIM: It's a load o' horseshit. (*takes a drink*) Blood only goes so far. It depends what a person sees around him. Some people, like your dad, they for whatever reason think they need the nonsense in life. That's not your problem.

JIMMY: But Linda, she won't stand for it.

JIM: So you tell me. However, who's to say how long her dent will last. Other hand, to be fair, maybe your dad is ready to quit playin' the man, and start bein' one. Before his son beats him to it. (*pause*) Which by God I think you already have.

JIMMY gets up to hide his reaction. He goes to the window to look out across the prairie. The sun is very low now and the light in the café is turning gold and pink.

JIM: You … do a good day's work, Jimmy. I—well, I want you to know I'm proud of you.

JIMMY: (*closes his eyes*) Yeah? (*pause*) How come I lip off my mum so bad?

Pause.

JIM: You get that from your grandmother. Don't worry about your mum. She's had the misfortune of taking after me. So give her time.

JIMMY: I'm runnin' outta time.

JIM: Jimmy, get yourself in the driver's seat. You're lettin' your dad take the reins, take control of your life, waitin' on him like this. You want somethin' outta this bargain, but don't you think he does too? Eh? If he calls, you give him a time and if he doesn't meet it, well, that's his loss. He'll meet it.

JIMMY: He won't meet it, that's just it.

JIM: Prepare yourself for that. But Jimmy, don't chase after somethin' unless it's worth having.

JIMMY: That why you chased after Max? You knew?

A long pause.

JIM: I didn't know. I was just turned twenty.

JIMMY: You *didn't* know?—And yet you went and married her?

JIM: Okay.

JIMMY: And then you went after her over that border when she caught her nylon? It just doesn't sound like you, Grandad. I never stopped to think of it before, but marryin' Max so fast and chasin' her across the field, I just thought, boy, *Grandad?*

JIM: I wasn't called Grandad in those days. (*pause*) I was called Jimmy.

JIMMY: Your whole family prob'ly starin' at you out the window.

JIM sits down. JIMMY sits down beside him. They both look out.

JIM: It was rainin'.

JIMMY: You get all muddy?

JIM: My dad was ready to carve my ass for supper.

JIMMY: Why?

JIM: Well, I hadn't phoned home from Minnesota to say I was bringin' home a wife. He, of course, didn't even approve of me goin' in the first place.

JIMMY: Down the States?

JIM: Actually they thought I was in Manitoba.

JIMMY: What?

JIM: And we were right in the middle of seeding.

JIMMY: You lef' him stranded? *You* left him—

JIM: I wasn't all that keen on work back then.

JIMMY: Huh?

JIM: Chap I met in the Army, from Winnipeg, he had his eye on this Minnesota girl, see. Made the mistake of showin' me her picture. I got it in my head I'd go to Winnipeg, get him to take me down there, introduce us, eh.

JIMMY: You didn't go down for an auction?

JIM: Well, no, that was just the line.

JIMMY: But Grandad—*Max* still thinks it was just chance, an auction you happened to go down for—didn't you *tell* her—after you were married and stuff?

Pause.

JIM: Well, I've been meaning to. But it's not the sort of thing a person likes to admit to. Especially knowin' it'd be general knowledge to anyone who happened to drop in here for coffee. Goin' all the way to Minnesota on the basis of a two-inch photograph your buddy happens to show you in Halifax?

JIMMY: Halifax? You were in Halifax?

JIM: I was there when the war ended.

JIMMY: Wait a sec', wait a sec'—you mean to say—this is just hittin' me—you bin off the prairies?

Pause.

JIM: Drink up, Kid. (*They drink.*) The prairies may be dry, but it was a different kind o' dry in Halifax, when the war ended. We could've done with a little of this then. We couldn't get a bottle o' beer, never mind this.

JIMMY: Why not?

JIM: Banned.

JIMMY: You mean you couldn't celebrate?—What'd you do?

JIM: Well. Not that I was instrumental, but we—we rioted.

JIMMY: *You* rioted?

JIM: Until they threw me in the clinker.

The phone rings. JIMMY jumps.

JIMMY: My dad! (*The phone rings again. JIMMY looks to the back suite.*) I'm gettin' it in here! (*He goes to the phone and stares at it.*)

JIM: Answer it.

JIMMY: (*to himself*) Grandad rioted.

JIM: Pick up the phone.

JIMMY: (*picking up*) Bordertown Café. Hi Dad.

MAXINE and MARLENE enter.

MARLENE: Where's he at?

JIMMY: (*into phone*) Where you at, Dad? (*cupping the phone*) Hasn't left. Yeah? Oh, is that it, eh?—uh huh. Yeah, well, that happens. Tie you up all day like that. (*cupping the phone*) Truck's just gettin' loaded now.

MARLENE moves to the booth to sit down. MAXINE stays behind the counter. JIM sits as he was. They all stare out, as the sun continues to change.

JIMMY: So I guess you … never thought to give us a call? No I know you're callin' now but it's late now—well, never mind, it—it doesn't matter. Eh? Yeah, well this is what Mum was sayin' you said. Pardon? Yeah, I know Linda likes me, why shouldn't she like me, I'm a good guy, eh. Chip off the ole block, right? Eh? Boy, that sounds pretty snazzy Dad. Twelve hunderd square feet, eh. How many? Boy. *Two* bathrooms? Wow, that's a lot. Uh huh. Yeah, well, I'd like to come down, sure—how big's the living-room? Is that right? Is *that* right? (*cups the phone*) Gotta buy more furniture to fill it up. Family room off the kitchen. (*goes back to the phone*) Dad, it sounds just great, I can hardly wait to see it, I'm all

packed and—and what was the reason you said you didn't call? Call, Dad, call. Whataya mean why?—because I bin waitin', I had to—to miss hockey, I couldn't do chores for fear of missin' you, and it turns out you weren't even gonna phone to let a guy know? When I got a crop to get off? That wasn't fair, Dad, it just wasn't and I'm thinkin' maybe I'll take a pass on movin' down there actually. But, uh, uh how be it I come see you at Christmas? Oh heck, hold on, Christmas is no good, I've already told Mum I'd take her to Hawaii. Yeah, well, I checked around and found a deal with Wardair, figgered she'd like to see the place—you know how it is, we're not caught up in spending a lot o' money on houses, we'd rather … travel. Grandad was just tellin' me about Halifax, it's got quite the history, he was there not too long ago—anyhooo—(*cups the phone*) Can you believe what I'm sayin'? (*goes back to the phone*) Tell you what I'm gonna do for ya, Dad. Why don't you just think about droppin' in on me *next* haul so I can know when to be in the café. Like you sayin' next Friday, well, Friday's a twenty-four hour day and I can't sit around here waitin' for you to show up. Guess my point is in a few weeks I'll be eighteen and—and what it boils down to is you're eighteen years too late, Dad. I gotta be up at four-thirty tomorrow, so I'll say good night, you keep in touch, bye. (*He hangs up abruptly. He stares at the phone. He looks up.*) That's *not* what I was gonna say.

MAXINE: We shoulda put booze in that kid's bottle when he was a baby and saved ourselves a lot o' trouble.

MARLENE: It wasn't the liquor, Mum.

JIMMY: Now I'll never see my dad.

JIM: I suspect you'll see more of him.

JIMMY: Mum, I blew it.

MARLENE: Put your stuff in the back suite.

JIMMY: Maybe I should phone back and apologize.

MARLENE: And maybe you shouldn't. (*She holds a look with him. Then she goes to pick up some of his gear.*)

JIM: Listen to your mother. (*JIMMY heads to his things. He picks up the remainder. He looks to JIM.*) I'll finish up tonight, you start in the morning.

MARLENE exits to the back. JIMMY follows her, looking back to him.

JIMMY: That is definitely *not* what I was gonna say. (*exits*)

JIM looks out at the sun setting.

MAXINE: Jim.

JIM: What.

MAXINE: Did you hear that kid talk to his dad?

JIM: Yep.

MAXINE: That's the *American* finally comin' a- out in him. (*JIM looks to her.*) Huh?—Good ole American gumption.

JIM: (*puts on his hat*) Yeah, I guess that's what it is all right.

Pause.

MAXINE: Well, are you just gonna sit there?

JIM: No. (*gets up and heads to the door*) Gonna get back out to the field.

He goes out, letting the screen door flap behind him. MAXINE looks after him, then goes out through the kitchen.

END

ROBERT LEPAGE
(b. 1957)
and MARIE BRASSARD
(b. 1961)

"Using dialogue, mime, dance, music and lighting as means of frustrating and then illuminating the linear, the narrative and the rational, it captures the greatness of what theatre—and only theatre—can do." *Globe and Mail* critic Stephen Godfrey's comment on *Polygraph* typifies the extravagant praise gleaned by the work of Robert Lepage. It also points to the complex theatricality that is the essence of Lepage's dramatic art. In much the same way that Michel Tremblay's concern with language helped define Québécois theatre a generation earlier, Lepage's vivid baroque style with its emphasis on the visual, physical and sonic elements of the stage captures the shape of that theatre since the mid-1980s. At the same time Lepage has not shied away from the theatre of words, or words and music, establishing himself as a director of international stature with his productions of Shakespeare, opera, rock concerts and film. As writer, director, performer and often designer of his own plays, he has pushed the boundaries of the theatrical text farther than nearly any other Canadian dramatist writing in English or French. Of his work with Quebec's Théâtre Repère he says, "We try to eliminate text by replacing it with another form of language." In fact all his plays are resolutely multilingual, transnational in scope and sensibility, incorporating English and French and at least one other tongue as well as the non-verbal languages of performance. In *Polygraph*, Lepage collaborated with actress Marie Brassard to create what its title etymologically suggests: a kind of multiple writing. In the guise of a murder mystery, the play explores questions of truth and falsehood, examining the nature of technology and art, criminology, politics and the human heart.

Lepage was born into a bicultural home in Quebec City: his adopted older brother and sister were anglophones who continued attending English-language schools while Robert and another sister were raised francophone. His early theatrical influences included the elaborate rock concerts of the band Genesis under lead singer Peter Gabriel, whose 1993 North American solo tour Lepage would eventually stage. After graduating in 1978 from the Conservatoire d'art dramatique de Québec (also attended by Marie Brassard), he studied in Paris with Swiss director Alain Knapp, who taught actors to become *acteurs-créateurs* by combining writing and directing with their performance skills. Returning to Quebec, Lepage played improvisational theatresports with the Ligue Nationale d'Improvisation, winning its Most Popular Player award for 1980. In 1981 he joined Théâtre Repère, a Quebec company which based its work on the "RSVP cycles" of the San Francisco Dancers' Workshop. Beginning with a *Resource* (a concrete object or image rather than a theme), they arrange a *Score*, which is then analyzed (*Valuaction*) and ultimately *Performed*. (In French, *REssources*, *Partition*, *Evaluation* and *REpresentation* = REPÈRE.) Most of Lepage's shows in the 1980s evolved and were produced under the auspices of Théâtre Repère. Lepage served as co-artistic director from 1986 to 1989. Marie Brassard joined the company in 1985 and has been an important collaborator in Lepage's work ever since.

Lepage has compiled an impressive international resumé since his first two plays, *Vinci* and *The Dragons' Trilogy*, premiered in 1985–86. A one-man show based on the attempted suicide of an artist friend and on Leonardo da Vinci's paintings, *Vinci* features Lepage as a blind Italian tour guide, a cathedral and the Mona Lisa, among other things. *The Dragons' Trilogy* grew from a ninety-minute piece in Quebec City in 1985 to a three-hour Toronto production in 1986 to a six-hour epic for Montreal's Festival de Théâtre des Ameriques in 1987. An archeological tour (and *tour de force*) through three Canadian Chinatowns during three different eras in three different languages, the trilogy has played across North America, Europe and Australia to enormous critical praise.

His next two major works, *Polygraph* and *Tectonic Plates*, appeared in 1988, the latter a vision of shifting continents and cultures colliding and metamorphosing across centuries on a stage dominated by two grand pianos suspended in the air above a pool of water. Since premiering in Toronto, *Tectonic Plates* has played to great acclaim in England, Scotland and the United States, and in French and English versions at the National Arts Centre where Lepage served from 1989-93 as artistic director of French theatre. In 1991 it was made into a feature film. His second one-man show, *Needles and Opium* (1991), a brilliant theatrical meditation on Miles Davis, Jean Cocteau, drugs and art, consolidated Lepage's reputation at home and abroad. *Alanienouidet* (1992), written (partly in Mohawk) with Marianne Ackerman, continued Lepage's exploration of colliding cultures in its examination of English actor Edmund Kean's fascination with the Hurons during his Canadian tours in the early nineteenth century.

Even as his career became increasingly international, Lepage insisted that his work "remains profoundly Québécois ... It's from Quebec that I want to make contact with the rest of the world." Consequently, when he founded the multidisciplinary company Ex Machina in 1994 to develop and produce his work, he based it in Quebec City where he also built an elaborate multimedia production centre, La Caserne, to house the company. Ex Machina's first production was *The Seven Streams of the River Ota*, a seven-hour epic about Hiroshima, the Holocaust and their aftermaths that evolved in three parts from 1994–96. Typically, the first part premiered in Edinburgh, the second in Vienna, and the third in Quebec City with subsequent tours of the U.K., Europe, Japan and North America. Also touring internationally after its debut in Montreal was *Elsinore* (1995), Lepage's adaptation of *Hamlet* in which he played all the roles himself. Well, not *all* the roles: Rosenkrantz and Guildenstern were represented by two surveillance cameras. Co-produced by Ex Machina and Austria's Salzburg Festival, *The Geometry of Miracles* (1997) chronicles the life of architect Frank Lloyd Wright, though Wright himself is only ever seen from behind in a play that incorporates French, English, Russian and Serbo-Croatian. *Zulu Time* (1999), which premiered in Zurich, is a meditation on air travel featuring dance, mime, electronic music and robots.

In addition to directing all his own plays, Lepage has exercised his multifaceted talents in a variety of arenas. As a film actor he made notable appearances as Pontius Pilate in Denys Arcand's *Jesus of Montreal* (1988) and in Arcand's *Stardom* (2000). His career as a freelance director has been meteoric. Beginning with a bilingual *Romeo et Juliette* (1989) in Saskatoon, co-directed by Gordon McCall and set on the Trans-Canada Highway, he has rapidly become one of the world's foremost interpreters of Shakespeare. His productions of *Coriolanus*, *Macbeth* and *The Tempest* (with Marie Brassard as Puck) in Paris and Montreal (1992–93) were "the first really imaginative Shakespeare we've seen in Canada," according to critic Ray Conlogue. And his 1992 *Midsummer Night's Dream* at London's National Theatre—set in a pool of mud—elicited comparisons to the great Peter Brook's touchstone production of twenty years before. In 1993 the Canadian Opera Company's double-bill of Bartók and Schönberg operas, directed by Lepage, won the $100,000 Scotsman Festival Prize at the Edinburgh Festival. In 1994 he directed an adaptation of *The Tempest* in Tokyo with Japanese actors, and a production of Strindberg's *A Dream Play* in Stockholm at the invitation of Ingmar Bergman.

Lepage has also expanded his career to include moviemaking. He wrote and directed his first feature, *Le Confessional* (1992), a byzantine family drama set against the backdrop of an Alfred Hitchcock film shoot in Quebec City. Marie Brassard stars in the film adaptation of *Le Polygraphe* (1997) for which she wrote the screenplay. *Nô* (1998) is Lepage's own adaptation of *The Seven Streams of the River Ota*, and *Possible Worlds* (2000) is his first feature in English, adapted from the play by Toronto's John Mighton. Lepage's films, like his plays, have won numerous awards. He himself was granted an honorary degree by the University of Toronto in 1997.

Polygraph was first produced by Théâtre Repère in French as *Le Polygraphe* in Quebec City in 1988, developed through improvisation by Lepage, Brassard and Pierre Phillipe Guay, with contributions from Gyllian Raby. A revised version, co-produced by Montreal's Théâtre de Quat'Sous later that year, was translated into English for a 1989 production in London, which won Lepage the *Time Out* award for his direction. The script continued to evolve during 1990–92 as it played Toronto (winning the Chalmers Award), six European summer festivals (including Barcelona, where Marie Brassard won the Best Foreign Actress award), New York, Ottawa, Edmonton and

Vancouver (the first place a Lepage play was directed by anyone other than himself). In 2000 *Polygraphe* toured Spain and Italy in a co-production between Lepage's Ex Machina and three Spanish and Italian theatre companies. Always "a work in progress," the script of the play has continued to evolve. The version printed here is the production script from 1993, substantially different from the script first published in *Canadian Theatre Review* in 1990, and no doubt different from the scripts developed for subsequent productions.

Lepage and Brassard have called *Polygraph* "a metaphysical detective story." A London critic called it "a play disguised as a film." Loosely based on the actual murder of a friend for which Lepage was interrogated by the police, the play invokes the cinematic traditions of the murder mystery with its use of film-style titles, credits, stage directions and music, as well as various *film noir* devices, at the same time as it questions the ability of cinema to embody artistic truth. Structurally, we are presented with a film-and-play-within-a-play. Lucie acts the part of the murdered woman for the exploitational film version of the "real" story in which she, her neighbour François, and her lover David are, in their lives, still inextricably bound up. She is also involved, as an actress, in another murder plot, playing the title role in a stage production of *Hamlet*. Does the theatrical art approach truth any more closely than the cinematic? Is Yorick's prop skull any less a contrivance than the movie's fake tears or the three takes of Lucie's nude death scene? And are the multiple deceptions and manufactured emotions of the characters' lives any more or less authentic than the representations of screen or stage? In a more complicated way than the Russian doll that David gives Lucie, which stands, as he says, for "one truth which is hiding another truth and another one and another one ... ," *Polygraph* presents a reality in which truths are layered within lies, mirroring and distorting one another in the deceptions that make up life, art and the technologies we use to help structure them both.

Along with the movie camera, the polygraph machine is the play's primary technology, a device intended to distinguish truth from falsehood by recording physiological responses to questions. In an earlier draft of the play David says: "The body never lies." Yet the polygraph itself is subject to manipulation and falsification. François' test established his innocence in the murder of Marie-Claude Légaré, but David and the police have kept this information from him, driving him eventually to suicide. In fact the play is full of lying bodies: Lucie's for the movie camera; David's at the end of scene eleven as he checks his watch while making love to Lucie, betraying her no less than he has his girlfriend in Berlin; François' in his "soul-weary," masochistic sexual encounters, his body lying to itself that pain is pleasure.

Physically and metaphorically, the stage is dominated by the wall through which François' naked body crashes in the play's spectacular climax. It stands variously for François' garden wall, the wall between his and Lucie's apartments, the ramparts of Quebec City, and perhaps the "fourth wall" of naturalistic theatre itself, smashed to pieces by the raw presence of the actor in Lepage's meta-theatrical dramaturgy. Characters clamber over the wall and slide down it. At one point it bleeds. The opening scene equates it to both the Berlin Wall and the septum bisecting the human heart. If the heart is indeed divided, if wall-building as a tactic to defend an ideology of lies merely reflects some kind of biological imperative, then the lies with which we practice our art, politics, crime, criminology and love should come as no surprise. But the constant theatrical surprises of Lepage and Brassard's script continue to jolt us into fresh experiences of the world and whatever truth there is in it.

Polygraph was first performed in French as *Le Polygraphe*, produced by Théâtre Repère at Implantheatre in Quebec City on May 6, 1988, with the following cast:

LUCIE CHAMPAGNE	Marie Brassard
DAVID HAUSSMANN	Robert Lepage
FRANÇOIS	Pierre Phillipe Guay

Directed and Designed by Robert Lepage

Polygraph was first performed in English, translated by Gyllian Raby, at the Almeida Theatre in London, England, on February 21, 1989, with the same cast, director and designer.

POLYGRAPH
Translated by Gyllian Raby

CHARACTERS

LUCIE CHAMPAGNE, *an actress*
DAVID HAUSSMANN, *a criminologist*
FRANÇOIS, *a waiter*

SCENE

Montreal, Quebec City and Berlin, 1992.

TRANSLATOR'S NOTE

I first translated *Polygraph* as it was being created, with the odd result that an English text existed before the authors considered their French production to be complete. Through the major revisions since then, I have been more distant from the creation process, but it seems to me that the ideas under exploration have mostly remained the same (along with the majority of the words), even though characters, time-frame and situations have altered—and in our separate reality the Berlin Wall has fallen. The living performance script has been allowed to meta-morphose to reflect the authors' deepening perception of and relationship with their material; while the present version has been stable for eighteen months now, if the world continues to change while the authors are engaged with this work, it will also continue to regenerate.

Punctuation in the fast-moving dialogue section is coded as follows: Where speeches intersect, as in The Filter, "—" indicates that the speech is sus-pended in mid-breath; " ... " indicates that the breath is trailing away.

PROLOGUE

A brick wall runs right across the playing area, behind a shallow platform forestage. Music plays in a film-style introduction, while slides flash the play title and actors' credits in a large format that completely covers the wall. Then, stage right, a projection titles the scene. The film-script style introduction of each scene in this way will continue throughout the play. Dialogue and action begin during the projection of the credits.

Projection:

1. The Filter

Stage left, in a "flashback" performance at an inquest six years prior to the action of the play, DAVID reads a pathologist's report about a murder victim. He demonstrates his points by pointing at the anatomy of a skeleton which lies on the stage floor near his feet. Stage right, behind and above the wall, FRANÇOIS is in a political science class at the university, delivering a presentation on the Berlin Wall.

DAVID: The autopsy has revealed that the stab wounds were caused by a sharp, pointed instru-ment which penetrated the skin and underlying tissues—

FRANÇOIS: After the fall of the Third Reich, little remained of its capital, Berlin, except a pile of ruins and a demoralised people—

DAVID: The body wounds are extremely large considering the small size of the inflicting instrument: I would surmise that the shape, depth and width of the wounds were enlarged during the struggle—

FRANÇOIS: The triumphant Allies enforced a new statute—

DAVID: —by the slicing action of the knife—

FRANÇOIS: —which split the city into inter-national sectors: American, French, British—

DAVID: —as the victim attempted to defend herself.

FRANÇOIS: —and to define their sector, the Soviets built a wall over forty kilometres in length, cutting the city in two.

DAVID: The victim received cuts to the left hand, the right upper arm, and was pierced through the rib-cage and the right lung, to the stomach. We have determined that the fatal cut was given here—

DAVID and FRANÇOIS: —Right through the heart—

FRANÇOIS: of the city.

DAVID: —between the fifth and sixth ribs.

FRANÇOIS: The "Wall of Shame," as the West Germans called it, was built to stop the human—

DAVID and FRANÇOIS: Haemorrhage—

FRANÇOIS: of Berliners leaving the East for the West—

DAVID: —was caused by the laceration of the septum.

FRANÇOIS: —symbolic of the division between the communist and capitalist worlds.

DAVID: The septum functions like a wall bisecting the heart; it controls the filtration of blood—

FRANÇOIS: For almost three decades, visitors from the West have been permitted to enter the Eastern Bloc—

DAVID: —from the right ventricle to the left,

DAVID and FRANÇOIS: —but the passage is one way only. A sophisticated system of alternating doors open and close to allow the flow of—

FRANÇOIS: visitors from the West—

DAVID: —de-oxygenated blood—

DAVID and FRANÇOIS: —and to impede—

FRANÇOIS: —inhabitants of the East—

DAVID: —oxygenated blood—

DAVID and FRANÇOIS: —from circulating the "wrong" way.

As if a continuous loop, the tempo of The Filter dialogue increases with the volume and drive of the music. As it is repeated, the naked body of LUCIE rises stage left behind the wall, lit by anatomical slide projections: muscles, veins, organs and bones superimposed on her flesh, so that she seems transparent. The scene ends on a musical crescendo, and a brief blackout.

Projection:

2. Institut médico-légal, Parthenais,[1] **Montreal Interior, night.**

In the blackout, more meditative music plays. Lights reveal first the skeleton, which slowly rises to its feet, then the rest of the scene. Stage right, DAVID is at work, note-taking as he watches intently the bleeping, whirring polygraph machine. He turns off the polygraph, puts on his coat, and takes a letter from the pocket. He reads a few lines to himself, then replaces it. Thoughtfully, he lights a cigarette. He approaches the skeleton and slowly takes its head in his hand, assuming the clichéd pose of Hamlet with Yorick's skull. Lights crossfade to the next scene as LUCIE's voice is heard.

Projection:

3. Hamlet Exterior, night.

LUCIE appears above and behind the wall, stage left, reciting in profile Hamlet's speech to Yorick (Act 5, Scene 1). She wears black, and holds a skull.

LUCIE: Hélas … pauvre Yorick.
Je l'ai connu Horatio …
Un amuseur infatiguable, d'une fantasie extra-ordinaire:
Il m'a mille fois porté sur son dos.
Et maintenant, que de dégout ne m'inspire-t-il pas …
J'en ai des hauts-le-coeur …
Ici étaient attachées les lèvres où j'ai déposé je ne sais combien de baisers …
Où sont vos malices maintenant, vos pirouettes, vos chansons, vos éclats de joie?
Nul maintenant n'imite vos grimaces …
Vous avez comme perdu la face, non?
Tenez, allez dire cela à ma belle dans sa chambre:
Qu'elle peut s'enduire de fards, mais que c'est à cela qu'elle doit en arriver …

---

1 *Parthenais*—the colloquial name for Le Centre de prévention de Montréal, a remand centre located on the Parthenais. For the purposes of this play it is to be understood as a medico-legal forensic institute.

Lights crossfade into the next scene. A change in soundscore now suggests the hubbub of a busy restaurant.

Projection:

4. François
Interior, night.

FRANÇOIS enters stage left with a table for two over his shoulder. This he swings down in an easy movement. Quickly setting it with plates and cutlery, he then positions two chairs either side. When the table is "set" he immediately unmakes it, swings it over his shoulder, and repeats the whole sequence in a different space, all the while talking rapidly to invisible customers. During the course of the scene he covers the whole stage, suggesting a room full of tables, and he never stops talking.

FRANÇOIS: Vous avez bien mangé? Je vous apporte la facture monsieur. Par ici s'il vous plaît. Vous avez regardé le menu du jour sur le tableau? Oui. C'est pour combien de personnes? Par ici s'il vous plaît. Prendriez-vous un digestif? Deux cafés cognac … toute de suite … Ça sera pas long monsieur … Oui bonjour. Non, mal-heureusement, on a plus de rôti à l'échalotte. À la place, le chef vous suggère son poulet rôti, un poulet au citron, c'est délicieux. Alors deux fois. Allez-vous prendre un dessert? Aujourd'hui, c'est la tarte à l'orange maison. C'est excellent, je vous le recommande … Oui. Une personne. Par ici s'il vous plaît. For two? … I'm sorry we don't 'ave any English menu … I'll translate for you. Deux places? Par ici s'il vous plaît. Pardon? Vous auriez dû me le dire, je vous l'aurait changé sans problèmes. Oui, la prochaine fois, d'accord. Par ici s'il vous plaît.

(*The food was good? I'll bring you the bill, sir. Would you please follow me? Have you noticed today's specials on the board? Yes. You'd like a table for … ? Please, follow me. Something to drink, perhaps? You would like to see the wine list? Two coffees with cognac … It's coming in a minute sir! Good evening. No, unfortunately we're all out of rôti à l'échalotte. The chef suggests the roast chicken in lemon as a substi-tute, it's really delicious. So … two chickens. Would you care for dessert? Today's special is Homemade Orange Pie; it's excellent … So, a* place for one … Would you please follow me? … For two? … I'm sorry we don't have any English menu … I'll be happy to translate for you. For two … I have one table over there … Sorry? Oh … You should have told me before, I could have changed it, no problem … Okay … Next time … This way please; a table for … ?)

LUCIE: (*enters and sits at the table, talking rapidly to keep pace with his non-stop work*) Salut François! Aie, ça l'air que toé pis ton chum, vous êtes venus voir mon show hier … Vous êtes pas venus me voir après, c'est tu parce que vous avez pas aimé ça?

(*Hi François! How're you doing? … Hey, I heard that you and your boyfriend came to see my show yesterday? How come you didn't come backstage to see me—didn't you like it?*)

FRANÇOIS: Ah non! C'était magnifique … On a beaucoup aimé l'idée de faire jouer Hamlet par une femme … De nos jours, c'est beaucoup plus percutant que ce soit une femme que tienne ces propos-là plutôt qu'un homme.

(*Oh no! It was great! We really liked the idea of a woman playing Hamlet. Especially these days, it's more appropriate to have a woman say all that stuff—much more than a man.*)

LUCIE: Ben en fait à l'origine, c'tait pas prévu. Parce que moi je faisais le régie du show mais le gars qui jouait Hamlet y'é tombé malade pis vu qu'y avait juste moi qui savait le texte par coeur, y m'ont coupé les cheveux pis asteur, c'est moi qui le fait … Aie François, j'ai entendu dire … ça d'l'air qu'à CKRL, y cherchent un annonceur pour lire le bulletin de nouvelle le soir … t'as une belle voix … y m'semble que tu serais bon là d'dans.

(*In fact, it wasn't exactly planned … I was stage managing the show, but the guy playing Hamlet got sick, and so me being the only one who knew the script by heart, they cut my hair, and now I do it! Hey François, I heard that radio station CKRL is looking for a guy to read the late night news. You've got such a nice voice, you should apply. You'd be great!*)

FRANÇOIS: C'est gentil d'avoir pensé à moi, mais ces temps-ci c'est pas possible, j'ai trop d'ouvrage au restaurant.

(It's very nice of you to think of me, but right now it wouldn't be possible. There's too much work at the restaurant.)

LUCIE: Aie, j'ai croisé Alain dans l'escalier tantôt, y m'a même pas dit bonjour … c'tu parce qu'yé choqué contre moi?

(François, is Alain angry at me? I met him going down the stairs at home, and he didn't even say hello … Is there a problem?)

FRANÇOIS: Fais-toi en avec ça … c'est à moi qu'y en veut. (Don't worry. It's me he's mad at. We had a fight …)

LUCIE: En tout cas, j'te remercie beaucoup, c'était très bon. (Well … Thank you very much. It was very good.)

LUCIE exits; FRANÇOIS continues at the same pace.

FRANÇOIS: A bientôt Lucie. (See you soon!)

FRANÇOIS goes out with the table settings, returns and sits at the table. Change in lights and music indicates that it is now the end of the day, and he is exhausted. He taps out three lines of coke and snorts it. DAVID enters the restaurant over the wall, sliding down with his back to it, his arms and his suit jacket spread like a giant, ominous spider. DAVID lands smoothly in the empty seat across the table from FRANÇOIS.

DAVID: François, can you hear me properly?
But you can't actually see me, can you?
François, we are going to conduct a little test.
Are we in Canada?
Is it summertime?
Was it you who killed Marie-Claude Légaré?

FRANÇOIS shakes his head, as if to dislodge these disturbing thoughts. DAVID disappears in a slow reversal of the way he came. Lights cross-fade to a spotlight stage right.

Projection:

**5/6. The Audition /
Sauvé metro station
Interior, day.**

LUCIE walks diffidently into the bright spotlight. She squints nervously at the light as she begins her audition, talking to unseen interviewers positioned in the audience. Her English is good, but sometimes hesitant and a bit convoluted.

LUCIE: Hi. My name is Lucie Champagne … My hair is shorter than on the photograph because I'm doing a show right now where I play a guy and so, they cut them a bit … First, I should tell you right off—I've never … What? To the camera! … okay …

She turns slightly to face it.

Yes, I've never worked on a movie but I've done lots of videos … mainly comedies, but I like doing drama just as much … I did lots of videos for the government social services … Let's see … What would be an example … ? Oh yes! they gave me the part of this woman whose money was stolen by her brother-in-law … Between you and I, that might seem a pretty tame crisis but for this woman it is something very dramatic and completely devastating because … it's her money … and … it's her brother-in-law … And so I had to play this part with as much emotion as I possibly could.

Oh yes! One thing I loved to work on while I was still at the theatre school was this play by Tennessee Williams called "Talk to Me Like the Rain and Let Me Listen." The title is very long but the play is actually very short. It is the story of a couple, and I played the woman, and my character, she was anorexic. But not by choice— I mean, she was anorexic because she hadn't eaten for four days, because she didn't have any money, because her boyfriend took off with the welfare cheque … I just loved playing that role …

My first experience? Well, I'll tell you: you are going to laugh!

It was for the priest's birthday when I was in grade one. Everyone in my class was in it, the other kids all lined up in front of the wall behind me, and they sang: "Where are you going little Bo-Peep, where are you going Bo-Peep … ?" And there I was, out in front and wearing this little white dress, and I sang back: "I am following this beauteous star and all my sheeps are saying baaa … "! My God, I loved it! I was a kid who liked telling lies you know—I was not a liar but … I used to be fascinated that I could say things which weren't true but do it so convincingly that people would believe me. So I used to make up all these stories … Maybe the fact I always wanted to be an actress comes from there …

Oh! Yes … For my audition, I brought a soliloquy from Shakespeare's *Hamlet* … No, no, not the part of Ophelia, the part of Hamlet.

Oh … you would prefer an improv. Euh …

She looks around.

Should I improvise here? … What would you like me to improvise? … To imagine myself in a tragic situation … Is that so you can see if I can cry? Because, I mean … I can't cry just like that … Well, no, I mean … Put me in a movie where there is a sad scene where I have to cry, I'd concentrate to the point where tears would well up, but I can't cry just like that …

To imagine myself in an absolute state of panic … Don't you think I'm panicking enough here?

Okay, okay, I'll do it.

Projection of a Metro station logo on the wall, with the sign of Sauvé Metro station. The soundscape evokes a large, hollow-echoing underground. LUCIE focuses on the front edge of the stage, an expression of absolute horror on her face; she backs up to lean against the wall with an inarticulate scream. DAVID enters. He kneels solemnly beside the "tracks" at the edge of the stage. In his hand he holds a bloody t-shirt, which he places in a zip-lock plastic bag. He takes out a notebook and writes. LUCIE, meantime, is going into shock, shouting and crying in semi-hysteria. DAVID assesses her state, contemplates his notes, puts his notebook away carefully, then goes to her. As she sobs for breath, he pulls her away from the wall to lean against him, and smooths her shoulders, rhythmically. Gradually, she is able to control her breathing. He checks her pulse, her heartbeat, and takes some pills from a bottle in his pocket, which he offers to her. When he speaks, it is with a German accent.

DAVID: Take this, it's a mild tranquiliser.

LUCIE: The guy … was he killed on impact?

DAVID: Yes. Can I give you a lift somewhere?

LUCIE: Yes.

DAVID: Where do you live?

LUCIE: In Quebec City.

DAVID is momentarily alarmed as it is three hours drive to Quebec City from Montreal.

LUCIE: I was on my way to get the bus.

DAVID: I'll walk you to the bus terminal then.

DAVID puts his arm around her shoulders and they move off towards stage left. LUCIE breaks away, runs back to look at the tracks, and then returns to her starting position against the wall in her audition spotlight. As DAVID exits, this is now the only light on stage.

LUCIE: (*back in her audition*) Was that enough?

Blackout. A metallic, driving music accompanies a red light that shines from behind the wall.

Projection:

7. The Flesh
Interior, night.

FRANÇOIS enters over the top of the wall into a gay bar. He drinks a beer, watching bodies on the dance floor. Soon he realises that he's been assessed by one of the crowd, and he agrees to follow the man stage right to a back room for sex. A change in light and baffling of sound indicates they are now private. In a very sensual scene, FRANÇOIS takes off his shirt, and then his belt, which he gives to his companion. Their relationship is one where they "play" at coercion. FRANÇOIS unzips his pants and kneels facing the wall, supported by the wall. We hear the sounds of whiplashes; FRANÇOIS's body physically recoils against the wall with each blow. As he comes, as his body shudders, the wall bleeds, gushing blood. FRANÇOIS meets the eyes of his lover. He gives a cursory wave as the other man leaves. With an air of soul-weary satisfaction, FRANÇOIS gathers his clothes, and returns to the bar. As lights fade to black, he drinks another beer and watches the dance floor.

In the blackout, a two-way mirror drops from the ceiling to hang above the wall stage right. It is the make-up mirror of LUCIE's dressing room at the theatre. The audience watches the scene from "behind" the mirror.

Projection:

8. The Tears
Interior, night.

DAVID is waiting in the dressing room with a bunch of carnations, a flower associated with funerals and said by Québécois actors to bring bad luck to a show. LUCIE enters, having finished her performance of Hamlet; she holds the skull of Yorick.

DAVID: Good evening.

LUCIE: David, my God, it's you! Did you come all the way from Montreal just to see the show?

DAVID: Well, in fact, I had some business this week in Quebec City, and I promised myself I was going to see you act one day, so here I am!

LUCIE: We were not exactly sold out tonight …

DAVID: Well, that just makes it more intimate theatre.

LUCIE: So, what did you think? Did you like it?

DAVID: Well, I thought it was quite interesting. Oh … here! (*He presents her with the carnations.*)

LUCIE: Oh my God! Carnations!—Thank you …

DAVID: (*examines the skull on the dressing room table*) Is this Yorick?

LUCIE: You recognize him?

DAVID: Of course … He is the only character who isn't killed at the end of the play!

LUCIE: I like the way you call him by his name. Everyone around here just calls him "the skull." But he was more than that once … whoever he was …

DAVID: What is written on his forehead? (*reading*) … *Hélas pauvre Yorick* …

LUCIE: My lines! Since I didn't have time to learn them properly, I just wrote them down … Would you mind waiting for me, just a second? I have to get changed and I'll come back. (*exits*)

DAVID: "To be or not to be, that is the question … " It must be very difficult for an actress to say things like "To be or not to be" and to deal with the fundamental things in life like love, honour …

DAVID and LUCIE: (*simultaneously, as she re-enters*) Death …

LUCIE: It's on my mind … more than ever now, after seeing that guy throw himself under the train in Montreal. You know … I want to thank you for driving me all the way back to Quebec City … you didn't have to do that!

DAVID: Let's just say I was not acting purely out of duty; it also gave me the opportunity to get to know you a little better and to make a new friend! So … What about the movie? Did you get the part?

LUCIE: Not yet … In fact, next week, we are going to do some screen tests. It makes me very nervous because they want to shoot a scene where I will have to cry and it's not so easy to do … They gave me this. (*She takes a tube from the dressing room table.*) You'll never guess what this is made for. It is a special product they use in movies to help actors cry.

DAVID: Really! Why?

LUCIE: Well … Imagine re-doing the same sad scene twelve times? It's hard to cry every time, right? So, they put it into the actor's eyes and the tears flow all by themselves.

DAVID: Wait a minute. Are you trying to tell me that when an actress like, let's see … Jane Fonda … when she cries … it's all fake?

LUCIE: Sometimes, yes.

DAVID: What a deception! I truly believed that, for an actor at least, tears were the ultimate proof of true emotion!

LUCIE: This is another of the misconceptions people have about acting! D'you want to try it?

DAVID: Surely you don't want to make me cry!

LUCIE: Yes! You'll see, it won't hurt … It will be funny!

DAVID: Well … All right then! What should I do here?

LUCIE: First … I'll ask you to take off your glasses. And now, since we are making a movie, I'll ask you to think about something sad, so the scene will be truthful.

DAVID: Something sad … Something recent?

LUCIE: Whatever you want! And now I say: "Quiet on the set ... sound ... camera ... action!"

As DAVID remembers, there is a musical theme reminiscent of his past in East Berlin. LUCIE freezes, still holding his glasses. Like a statue, she slowly recedes from the playing area, as if flying away. The set of the dressing room disappears simultaneously, and a projection of the Brandenburg Gate fills the cyclorama. DAVID, in another time, brings out a letter from his pocket. A woman's voice is heard, reading the letter in German. In a slow-motion, fearful escape, DAVID acts out his crossing of the Berlin Wall. He swings his upper body over, out and down, head first, holding his legs vertical above him. Gripping the wall, he swivels his legs down into a standing position, but remains suspended against the wall. English subtitles, projected on the wall, translate the letter.

DAVID: Ich weiss, dass man niemanden zur Liebe zwingen kann. Aber ich möchte, dass Sie wissen, das ich das Gefühl habe, Sie sind ein Stück von mir. An dem Morgen, als Sie Ostberlin verliessen, zitterte ich am ganzen Körper. Sie sagen: "Ich bin bald wieder zurück," aber ich wuste sofort, obwohl ich es nicht sagte. Was nicht von Herzen kommt, geht nicht zu Herzen. Ich kann in Ihren Augen lesen. Wenn ich hier nicht gefangen wäre, wäre ich nah bei Ihnen. Sie fehlen mir. Anna.

(I know that it is impossible to force someone into loving ... But I want you to know that I feel you are a part of me. The morning you left East Berlin, I was quite shaken. When I asked "When will you return?" you replied, "Soon." I did not let on, but at that instant, I knew you were lying. What does not come from the heart is not taken to heart ... I can see it in your eyes. If I could leave this city, I would be with you. I miss you deeply. Anna.)

As the letter ends, DAVID reverses his movement, until he is standing where he began the memory, in the dressing room, behind the mirror, talking to LUCIE. But now DAVID is crying. He wipes his eyes.

DAVID: This stuff really burns ... It's like getting soap in your eyes.

LUCIE: It won't hurt for long ... I guess that sometimes you have to suffer if you want it to look like you are suffering ...

Gently, she wipes his eyes. The lights fade as they start to kiss.

Projection:

9. Apartment #7
Interior, night.

Stage left, a washbasin set into the wall, with a mirror above it, indicates the bathroom in FRANÇOIS's apartment. FRANÇOIS enters, drunk, limping and sore. He puts his ear against the wall to listen if anyone is home next door. He calls through the wall.

FRANÇOIS: Lucie! ... Lucie ...

FRANÇOIS puts a glass against the wall to listen for any sounds from next door. Silence: there is no one home. He drops his leather jacket on the floor and peels off his t-shirt. His back is marked with whiplash weals. He soaks the shirt in water and lays it across his back with a sigh of relief.

LUCIE: (*entering his apartment suddenly*) François?

FRANÇOIS: Oui ... entre. (Come in.)

LUCIE: Qu'est-ce qu t'as ... Es-tu malade? (What is the matter ... Are you sick?)

FRANÇOIS: Oui ... J'me sens pas bien ... J'pense que j'ai trop bu ... Ça te tentes-tu de rester prendre un café?

(Yes ... I don't feel very good ... I think I drank too much ... Would you like to stay and have a coffee with me?)

LUCIE: Ben ... J'aimerais ça mais ... (*pointing at the silhouette of a man waiting at the door*) c'est parce que j'suis pas toute seule ...

(Well ... I'd like to but ... I am not alone.)

FRANÇOIS: Ah ... Y a quelqu'un qui t'attend ... (Ah ... Someone's waiting for you ...)

LUCIE: Oui. On se reprendra ... Excuses-moi de te déranger à cette heure là ... C'est parce que je viens d'arriver chez nous pis j'peux pas rentrer, j'ai pas mes clés.

(Yes ... well ... I'll take a raincheck ... Sorry to bug you so late, but I only just got home, and I can't get in. I must have lost my keys.)

FRANÇOIS: Ah ... (*He digs for LUCIE's key inside his jeans pocket and gives it to her.*)

LUCIE: Merci ... Prends soin de toi là ... (Thank you. Well, take care ...)

As she goes to kiss him on both cheeks, she inadvertently touches his back; FRANÇOIS winces. LUCIE tries to look at his back.

LUCIE: Qu'est-ce que t'as, j't'ai-tu fait mal? (What's the matter, did I hurt you?)

DAVID: (*His voice comes from behind the wall.*) Lucie? ...

FRANÇOIS: Non, non ... Laisse faire. (No, no ... It's nothing.)

LUCIE: (*tries again to see his back*) Ben voyons ... Qu'est-ce que t'as? (Come on ... What's the matter?)

FRANÇOIS: Laisse faire j'te dis ... c'est rien. (Leave me—I said it's nothing!)

LUCIE: Okay, okay! ...

DAVID: Lucie, are you alright?

LUCIE: Yeah, yeah ... (*awkwardly, as she exits*) Merci.

FRANÇOIS is now very much alone. Lights cross-fade to the expanse of the cyclorama, above the wall.

Projection:

10. The Snow
Exterior, night.

Above the wall the moonlit night sky glows, and snow falls gently. Music accompanies this. FRANÇOIS appears, as if walking on the ramparts of Quebec City's wall. He wears no shirt, only his leather jacket, which he holds together against the cold. At one point, he stops, climbs on to the edge of the wall, and stares down as if he's considering a suicide jump. He cries silently.

Projection:

11. Apartment #8
Interior, day.

Stage right, a washbasin full of water is set into the wall, with a mirror above it to indicate the bathroom of LUCIE's apartment. DAVID is shaving when he hears violent and lamenting cries from the other side of the wall. The voice belongs to FRANÇOIS. He checks to see if LUCIE is still sleeping, then puts his ear against the wall to listen. The cries get louder. DAVID knocks on the wall a couple of times. The lamentation stops. LUCIE enters, surprising him. She is still sleepy, and goes to embrace him, but he politely fends her off.

LUCIE: David, what are you doing?

DAVID: Good morning! ... Lucie listen ... I really have to go! I promised my secretary I'd be in Montreal at ten o'clock ... It's now eight-thirty and I haven't even left Quebec City yet ... So, you can imagine how impossibly behind I am!

LUCIE: That's too bad, I thought we would have breakfast together. I could put some coffee on—

DAVID: That's very nice of you, but I really must go ...

LUCIE: Will we see each other again?

DAVID: Soon.

LUCIE: When?

DAVID: In fact, next week I have some business in Quebec City. Perhaps we could arrange a rendezvous? I'll be at the morgue.

LUCIE: At the morgue? I would prefer a restaurant!

She walks towards him, allowing her robe to slide from her shoulders to the ground.

DAVID: That's what I meant ...

As they move into a kiss, the cries from FRANÇOIS's apartment begin again. LUCIE stops and turns her head to listen, but DAVID pulls her passionately against him. As they embrace, DAVID checks his watch behind her back, and figuring he has enough time, he gives in to the love scene, and lifts her up on him, turning so that she stretches out her arms to grip the wall for support as he caresses her body with his lips, and lights fade ...

Projection:

12. Travelling backward.[2]
Interior, day.

Thriller music begins in the blackout. Stage right, in shadow, FRANÇOIS prepares the restaurant table for the following scene. Stage left, LUCIE stands naked, her back to the wall. Suddenly, she contracts as though she has been stabbed. She staggers forward, and to the left, clawing at the air, then swivels as she falls: her back is covered with blood from the wall. Her movement is closely tracked by a camera on a panasonic pee-wee dolly that zooms maniacally in and out on her face and body with the tension-rhythm of the music. LUCIE falls, dead, to the floor. The music stops abruptly and she gets to her feet, appearing to listen to instructions from a director. She performs three "takes" of the death scene, After the last one, she receives the thumbs up signal. She speaks to the director.

LUCIE: Can I go now?

LUCIE covers herself with a towel and exits.

Projection:

13. The Wound
Interior, night.

At FRANÇOIS's restaurant. DAVID enters.

FRANÇOIS: Bonsoir monsieur. Ce sera pour combien de personnes?

DAVID: I'm sorry, euh ... (*He doesn't speak French.*)

FRANÇOIS: Excuse me. You would like a table for how many?

DAVID: For two please.

FRANÇOIS: Does this one suits you?

DAVID: Yes, that's fine ... oh ... excuse me ... could you take my coat please?

FRANÇOIS: Sure.

FRANÇOIS leaves with the coat. As he waits, DAVID hides a small gift bag under his chair.

---

2 *Travelling* is Québécois film parlance for a "dolly": smooth lateral movement of a film camera.

LUCIE: (*enters in a rush*) Oh ... David, I'm sorry, I'm late ...

DAVID: That's alright.

LUCIE: I hope you haven't been waiting for too long ...

DAVID: I just walked in this minute ... It's nice to see you.

LUCIE: It was longer than I expected ... We were supposed to finish shooting at three o'clock, but we had a very complicated technical scene.

DAVID: You look tired ...

LUCIE: Playing a victim is tiring!

FRANÇOIS: (*enters to serve them*) Bonjour Lucie.

LUCIE: Ah. Bonjour François ... Tiens, je te presente un ami (Let me introduce you to a friend), David Haussmann, François Tremblay ... He's my next-door neighbour ...

DAVID: Oh ... you're the one in apartment number eight!

FRANÇOIS: Yes.

DAVID: (*shaking his hand*) I heard ... so much about you!

LUCIE: David is the one who drove me back to Quebec City after I saw the guy throw himself in front of the train in Montreal.

FRANÇOIS: Strange circumstances to meet someone.

DAVID: Yes indeed ... Metro stations in Montreal seem to be used more often now to commit suicide than for commuting ...

LUCIE: Why's that?

FRANÇOIS: C'est la façon la plus cheap de se suicider ... (It's the cheapest way to kill yourself.)

DAVID: What?

FRANÇOIS: ... Do you want to order something to drink before your meal?

DAVID: Well ... I think I'll avoid hard liquor—

LUCIE: —Me too—

DAVID: —But ... would you like to drink some wine with the meal?

LUCIE: Yes … sure.

FRANÇOIS: I'll leave you to look at the wine list. (*He gives it to LUCIE, who passes it to DAVID.*)

DAVID: What kind of wine do you prefer?

LUCIE: Well … red or white.

DAVID: That's what I meant … Red or white?

LUCIE: I like both.

DAVID: How about red?

LUCIE: Red! Perfect!

DAVID: What kind of red do you like … Bourgogne, Bordeaux, Beaujolais …

LUCIE: I like all of them.

DAVID: Beaujolais?

LUCIE: Beaujolais … great!

DAVID: What kind of Beaujolais would you prefer?

LUCIE: Euh … It's up to you!

DAVID: How about a bottle of Brouilly?

LUCIE: Good idea!

DAVID: Do you like Brouilly?

LUCIE: I love it! You know … it's a very good restaurant here, they serve a kind of "mixed genre" cuisine … A little of this … a little of that … French, Hindu, vegetarian …

FRANÇOIS: (*re-enters for their order*) Have you decided on the wine?

LUCIE: (*scans the wine list*) Yes, we will have a bottle of … Brouilly.

FRANÇOIS: Brouilly … Okay. (*exits for their order*)

DAVID: So! How does it feel to be a movie star?

LUCIE: My God, give me a chance! … It's my first day of filming! I think I felt a bit … silly … ! I found the director quite aggressive with his camera … He wanted to shoot a scene from above, you know, as if you're looking through the eyes of a murderer who's watching his victim through a skylight But during the shooting, I felt more observed by the crew, and the director himself, than by the voyeur in the scenario.

DAVID: But aren't you used to being watched?

LUCIE: In theatre it's very different. When you perform, the audience is watching the whole you … But today, I felt that they were taking me apart.

DAVID: Taking you apart …

LUCIE: Yes … Close up of one eye, middle shot of the knife in the back, my right hand scratching at the floor.

FRANÇOIS comes back with the bottle and shows it to LUCIE who simply reads the label.

LUCIE: Brouilly.

DAVID: What were you filming exactly? Indoor scenes, outdoor scenes?

LUCIE: We were taking the interiors first, because the film is set in spring … So we have to wait for the end of winter.

DAVID: What will you do if it rains all the time?

LUCIE: It's a thriller! They want it to rain, because all the scenes *happen* in the rain!

DAVID: What if it never rains?

LUCIE: Well … I suppose they'll make it rain!

DAVID: Of course … It's like for tears … As far as they are concerned, making it is not the problem, it's just a question of water quantity!

LUCIE: (*trying to make a pun, just as FRANÇOIS appears with the wine*) Well, in fact, yeah. For "making it," it's the size of the equipment that counts!

She laughs, joined by FRANÇOIS who pours a little wine into her glass so she can taste it. LUCIE is surprised not to get more.

LUCIE: Merci!

FRANÇOIS: Ben … Goûtes-y.

DAVID: Taste it.

LUCIE: Oh … yes, sure. Hum … it's very good … (*as FRANÇOIS pours the rest*) It's even a little bouchonné!

FRANÇOIS: Oh—I'll get you another bottle …

LUCIE: No, no, it's very good … It is *bouchonné* … Bouchonné.

FRANÇOIS: Yes, but … if it's bouchonné—

DAVID: Isn't that supposed to mean that it tastes like cork?

LUCIE: Well … in this case, it can't possibly be bouchonné because it tastes great!

DAVID: Maybe I should double-check … It's a very good bottle!

DAVID does so, religiously. As he looks at FRANÇOIS, he seems to recognize him.

FRANÇOIS: Something wrong?

DAVID: No, no … It's an excellent wine!

LUCIE: Like I said.

FRANÇOIS: Are you ready to order?

DAVID: Go for it Lucie.

LUCIE: No, no … You go first David, you are the guest!

DAVID: What do you mean, I am the guest? I thought I was the one inviting you to dinner!

LUCIE: No, no … I mean … you are the foreigner!

DAVID: (*He does not respond. To FRANÇOIS:*) Is this soup?

FRANÇOIS: Yes … Potage Crécy.

DAVID: Well. I'll have that please, and the filet de boeuf Brisanne. I'd like that done rare but please in the French understanding of the word rare … not the Canadian.[3]

LUCIE: I'll have the same as him, but with the Canadian rare!

FRANÇOIS leaves with the order.

DAVID: Well … Here's to your film! (*They toast. DAVID takes the package from under his chair.*) I'm not very good at this … but here! (*He puts it on the table, offering it to her.*) This is for you.

LUCIE: What is it?

DAVID: What do you think it is? … It is a present!

LUCIE: But it's not my birthday.

DAVID: It's a present just the same.

LUCIE: No … I mean … there is no need for you to be buying me presents, David.

DAVID: Well … I'm sorry then.

A very awkward pause, which LUCIE breaks.

---

3 In France, the expression "à point" means quite red and bloody meat.

LUCIE: No … No … I'm sorry … I'm the one acting weird here … Let me open it! Oh! … a Russian doll!

DAVID: Yes … the real thing.

LUCIE: These come in all different sizes and people collect them!

DAVID: In fact … you won't have to collect them … They are all there, included one inside the other.

LUCIE: What do you mean?

DAVID: Open it!

LUCIE: Oh … it's beautiful …

DAVID: It's called a Matruska.

LUCIE: A Matruska.

LUCIE opens up the dolls and lines them up on the table top so that they form a wall between herself and DAVID.

DAVID: I bought it in Eastern Europe but you find them everywhere now. It's a traditional doll. Representing generations … So, this big one here is the mother of this one and also the grandmother of this one because she is the mother of this one and this one is the mother of that one and that one … and … to infinity I suppose! But … I like to think it may stand for other things like … hidden feelings … One truth which is hiding another truth and another one and another one …

LUCIE: I'm very moved … Thank you.

DAVID: I'm glad you like it.

A marked "slow" change in lights and sound indicates a time warp: time is rapidly passing. LUCIE and DAVID reach for their coffee cups in slow motion, their eyes locked together. FRANÇOIS glides in to take away the empty dishes and glasses. As he takes the bottle of wine, he slowly lays it across the middle of the table, tipping its contents so that the red wine stains the white tablecloth, and drops to the floor.

DAVID: (*back to real time*) … And at one point in the film, the angel turns to him and says: "Beware death … She comes and goes through mirrors … Gaze upon yourself all your life in the looking glass and you will see death at work."

LUCIE: That's beautiful.

DAVID: That's Cocteau.

Another time passage, marked in the same way with lights, sound and slow motion as LUCIE and DAVID stir their coffee, the sounds of the spoons making an evocative late-night rhythm on their china cups. FRANÇOIS comes in, looking at his watch. The meal has been over for a long time.

FRANÇOIS: I'm sorry but I am going to have to close now.

DAVID: What time is it?

FRANÇOIS: A quarter past three.

DAVID: A quarter past three!

LUCIE: My God! ... We didn't notice the time pass!

DAVID: I'm very sorry ... We were completely engrossed in our conversation while digesting this excellent meal!

LUCIE: Oui. Merci beaucoup ... C'était très bon.

DAVID: Can you tell me where I could find my coat please!

FRANÇOIS: It's in the cloakroom ... I'll get it for you.

DAVID: Lucie ... You are forgetting your Matruska!

LUCIE: Oh ... my Matruska ... (*showing it to FRANÇOIS*) Regarde François ce que David m'a donné ... C't'une poupée Russe ... un Matruska. Y l'a acheté a l'Est. (Look at what David gave me. It's a Russian doll; a Matruska. He bought it in the East.)

FRANÇOIS: C'est beau. (It's nice.)

They move towards the exit of the restaurant. LUCIE stands against the wall with the men on each side of her. FRANÇOIS addresses DAVID.

FRANÇOIS: You're from Europe?

DAVID: Yes. I'm from East Berlin. But I have been a Canadian citizen for many years now.

FRANÇOIS: And what do you do here?

DAVID: I am a criminologist. I work for a criminal institute in Montreal.

FRANÇOIS: Parthenais?

DAVID: Yes, Parthenais.

LUCIE: Tu connais ça? (You know this place?)

FRANÇOIS: Oui ... J'ai déjà eu affaire là. (Yes, I had to go there once.)

LUCIE: Comment ça? (Why?)

FRANÇOIS: Pas en prison ... (Not to prison ...) I went there to undergo a polygraph test.

LUCIE: A what?

FRANÇOIS: Un test de polygraphe.

DAVID: A lie detector ... For what?

FRANÇOIS: Because six years ago one of my best friends was murdered here in Quebec City. I was the last one to see her alive, so I was a suspect. In fact, it was me who found her dead in her apartment. She had been tied up, raped and stabbed many times.

DAVID: Did they find the murderer?

FRANÇOIS: No. They never tracked him down.

DAVID: What was your friend's name?

FRANÇOIS: Marie-Claude Légaré.

LUCIE reacts to the name. As if "flashing back" to the previous film-shoot scene, she turns to face the wall, as though she's been stabbed. Her back is covered with blood. She falls to the ground between the two men who, without acknowledging her fall, continue to face each other in conversation.

DAVID: Yes ... I think I remember ... Don't worry, they'll track him down. Nobody is able to go through life with a murder on their conscience ...

As DAVID continues to talk to where FRANÇOIS was standing, FRANÇOIS "relives" finding his friend's corpse, kneels down by her, silently enacts his grief.

DAVID: Well, thank you once again and my compliments to the chef; the food was indeed excellent. And the service, impeccable! Have you been a waiter for long?

FRANÇOIS stands again to continue the conversation normally. He speaks to DAVID's original position as DAVID in turn kneels by LUCIE and performs an "autopsy" on her, ripping her shirt with a scalpel.

FRANÇOIS: Long enough … three years now. Before this, I was at school, university, studying political science—and I worked part time in a Yugoslavian restaurant.

DAVID: Yugoslavian …

FRANÇOIS: Yes. I like it better here though, it's more friendly.

DAVID: Do you intend to do this for long? I mean … waiting tables! I know how transient things are in the restaurant business.

FRANÇOIS: I don't know. If I could find work related to my studies, I'd move on for sure.

DAVID: Well … it's better than no work at all. You know, when I lived in East Berlin, I thought the West was full of "golden opportunities"—but I see now how hard it is to succeed here. Over there, the jobs are trivial sometimes, but at least everybody has the right to work.

LUCIE uncoils from the floor to take the same position against the wall; simultaneously, the two men each put one foot on the wall, turning their bodies horizontally so they appear to be in the classic cinematic "top shot" of a corpse. FRANÇOIS and DAVID shake hands "over" her body.

DAVID: Sure was a pleasure meeting you, François.

The scene returns to "real" time and space.

DAVID: Well … if we want to exercise our own right to work tomorrow, maybe we should be moving along.

LUCIE: (*kissing him*) Salut François.

FRANÇOIS: A bientôt Lucie.

LUCIE walks slowly towards DAVID, looking at her hand.

DAVID: What's the matter Lucie? (*He takes her hand.*) You're bleeding!

LUCIE: It's nothing … I must have cut myself with a knife.

DAVID: Come … we'll take care of it.

As soon as they are gone, FRANÇOIS pulls out a bag of coke and prepares himself a few lines.

Projection:

**14. The Ramparts
Exterior, night.**

A projection of the Quebec City skyscape covers the cyclorama of the theatre. LUCIE and DAVID enter. She is withdrawn and quiet.

DAVID: What an exquisite city.

LUCIE: I come walking here very often but in summer generally, not winter.

DAVID: I greatly prefer the winter. I don't know why really, but I find I like the cold … anything cold. Perhaps it's because I was born in December. You know, usually, when people talk about the cold, it's always in pejorative terms. But for me, the cold evokes a kind of objective calm, wisdom and above all, a great gentleness … like these snowflakes slowly falling … Leaning against the ramparts like that, you remind me of someone I once knew …

LUCIE: Really? Who was she?

DAVID: Someone whom I loved deeply and to whom I did a great wrong … A German woman.

LUCIE: I am too nosy, aren't I?

DAVID: It was a long time ago … What's wrong Lucie? … Since we've left the restaurant you seem preoccupied somehow.

LUCIE: Well … I am. It is because—you know the story François just told us in the restaurant? The story of the film in which I'm playing is identical. It's based on the real murder—but I didn't know François was connected to it. It gave me a shock … And now, I feel uneasy about being a part of it, and I'm wondering if there's still time for them to find someone else.

DAVID: They have lousy taste … to base a film script on an unresolved murder case … How do they end the movie?

LUCIE: Well … after the girl's been killed, they set everything up to look as if it was one of her close friends who did it and at the end … we discover …

DAVID: At the end, we discover that it was the police who did it.

LUCIE: How did you know?

DAVID: It's a classic. When you don't know how to end a who-done-it, you always blame it on the cops. It's easy … When I was a student of criminology, I feared that the people developing investigative techniques were violent brutes: a product of their line of work. But I needn't have worried about becoming a brute. No, they are much more dangerous than that. The men leading the field of criminal research are very, very intelligent; a fact you will never see in a thriller. It's too frightening perhaps. Poor François … At Parthenais they know he is innocent, but he'll probably never be told.

LUCIE: Why?

DAVID: In a police inquiry where the guilty party hasn't been identified, it's strategy to keep everyone in ignorance.

LUCIE: How do you know François is innocent?

DAVID: … François does not know, but I was the one who conducted his polygraph test. This must remain between us, Lucie; it's a confidence.

LUCIE: But—how can I meet his eyes and not tell him?

DAVID: Stop seeing him for a while.

He tries to hold her, but she gently pushes him away, and continues walking along the ramparts. He follows her off stage.

Projection:

15. The Call
Exterior, night.

FRANÇOIS enters, stage right, takes change from his pocket and crosses to stand at a "phone kiosk" in the stage left wing. Noises, as of dialing a pay-phone, are heard. FRANÇOIS is lit so that his shadow is a huge projection across the entire wall, in such a way that every movement of his dialing and speaking on the phone registers. Over the phone line, we hear LUCIE's answering machine.

LUCIE: Bonjour, vous êtes bien chez Lucie Champagne … Malheureusement, je ne peut pas vous répondre pour le moment mais si vous voulez bien laisser votre nom et votre numéro de téléphone, je vous rappelle dans les plus bref délais.

FRANÇOIS lets the phone drop as the message continues. He comes back on stage, kicks the wall, then leans against it, pressing his face and body into it. As lights fade to black, we hear the tone of the answering machine.

Projection:

16. The Line-up
Interior, night.

The line-up is a re-cap scene which shows the most telling moments in the play so far. It begins with a matrix projected on the wall, reminiscent of the "Man in Motion" photographs by Edward Muybridge. The scene is played nude by the actors. Choreographic images of FRANÇOIS working in the restaurant, LUCIE in shock in the subway, FRANÇOIS being whipped, DAVID's meeting with LUCIE, DAVID and LUCIE embracing against the wall, the "film noir top shot" of the handshake in the restaurant. The scene and movement fragments are repeated, overlaid, dissected and recombined at a pace of increasing frenzy. Blackout.

Projection:

17. The Spring
Exterior, day.

FRANÇOIS has a bucket of water with which he sluices the wall. With a brush, he starts to scrub it. DAVID enters, with sunglasses and a travel bag.

DAVID: Hello François. Have you seen Lucie?

FRANÇOIS: Not for a month, at least. She must be busy shooting her movie.

DAVID: I came to say goodbye, but if she is off on location …

FRANÇOIS: You're going away?

DAVID: I'm going back to East Berlin. The government is sending me there for a series of conferences in investigative techniques. Now that the Wall has disappeared, there's this sudden demand for up-to-date technologies. But to tell the truth, my motivation is more personal than professional.

FRANÇOIS: But what's the government's motivation: to share knowledge or sell free enterprise?

DAVID: To share knowledge. Well ... if you see Lucie, tell her I was here ... (*He makes as if to leave, then stops.*) What the hell are you doing, François?

FRANÇOIS: I'm washing the wall.

DAVID: Yes, I can see, but why?

FRANÇOIS: The landlord told me to strip my graffiti off the garden wall before I move out, or else he'll prosecute.

DAVID: Prosecute ... for graffiti! ... What did it say?

FRANÇOIS: L'histoire s'écrit avec le sang.

DAVID: Which means?

FRANÇOIS: History is written with blood. It means that we write history through war, fascism and murder.

DAVID: Murder ... you mean political assassinations.

FRANÇOIS: No. I mean murders. The smallest little killing, of some totally unimportant person ... In a way that's still a political act, don't you think?

DAVID: Is that what you learned in political science?

FRANÇOIS: (*loses his temper*) Why do you ask me so many questions? You sound like an interrogator in a bad detective movie!

Defiantly, FRANÇOIS gathers up his bucket and brush, and exits.

Projection:

18. Travelling forwards[4]
Exterior, night.

LUCIE appears in profile, stage left, behind and above the wall. She's lit from behind by the light of a movie projector positioned in the stage left wing. The rushes of the movie are projected onto the stage right wall, but are not visible to the

---

4 *Travelling forwards*—a film term: dollying in, or tracking forward.

audience while she is watching. The projector stops.

LUCIE: (*addresses the director offstage*) Were these shot yesterday? And what we will shoot tomorrow will be linked with it—? (*She starts to cry silently.*) Excuse me ... (*She pulls herself together.*) May I see it again please?

Blackout.

Projection:

19. Apartment #8
Interior, day.

FRANÇOIS is packing boxes in the washroom of his apartment. The washbasin is set into the wall as before. LUCIE enters with books. The scene is translated by subtitles that are projected with slides on the wall.

LUCIE: Salut François, je t'ai rapporté les livres que tu m'avais prêté ... *L'orgasme au masculin*, j'ai trouvé ça ben intéressant.

(Hi François ... I brought back the books you lent me ... I found the *The Male Orgasm* pretty interesting.)

FRANÇOIS: Tu peux les garder encores si t'en a pas fini. (You can keep them if you're not finished.)

LUCIE: Non non ... j'sais c'que j'voulais savoir ... (No, no. I found out everything I wanted to know!)

LUCIE examines the cosmetics strewn in the washbasin.

LUCIE: Ouan ... t'en a des affaires pour un gars ... (You got a lot of stuff for a guy ...)

She starts to poke around in one of his boxes as he puts the books in.

LUCIE: Tu marque pas ce que tu mets dans tes boites? (You don't write what you put into the boxes?)

FRANÇOIS: C'est pas necessaire ... Pour ce que j'ai ... (It's not necessary. I don't have so many things.)

LUCIE: Marque où c'est que ça va toujours, sinon tu vas être mêlé quand tu vas arriver. (You should at least write where it goes, so you won't be mixed up when you move to your new place.)

She points to a box.

LUCIE: Ça c'est quoi? Des cosmétiques? J'vas écrire pharmacie dessus. Pis celle-là? (What is in there? Cosmetics? I'll write "personal things" on the side. And what's in this one?)

FRANÇOIS: Là dedans … des couvertures, serviettes des débarbouillettes, des livres, des vieux journaux … (… blankets, facecloths, books, old newspapers …)

LUCIE: J'pourrais écrire divers … (I could write … "miscellaneous.")

Inside the box, LUCIE finds a long leather strap with a strange fastening at the end.

LUCIE: Ça … ça sert a quoi? (And … what is this used for?)

FRANÇOIS: (*he puts the strap around his neck and demonstrates*) Quand je me masturbe, j'me sers de ça. J'tire—pis j'lâche, j'tire—pis j'lâche. Pis juste avant de venir, j'tire de plus en plus fort … Mais un moment donné, y faut qu'tu lâche, si tu veux pas venir pour la dernière fois … (When I masturbate, I use it. I pull then release, pull and release and just before I come, I pull harder and harder … But at a certain point, you have to stop unless you want it to be the last time you come.)

LUCIE: Ca sert-tu juste à ça? (Is that all you use it for?)

FRANÇOIS takes the strap from around his neck and goes to the washbasin.

FRANÇOIS: Viens ici. (Come here.) (*She hesitates.*) Viens ici! (*She goes.*) Assis-toi, donnes-moi ta main. (Sit down … give me your hand.)

He ties the belt around LUCIE's hand, takes it through the u-bend pipe on the washbasin and wraps it round her neck before tying it up.

In a simultaneous scene, DAVID gives a lecture about the polygraph machine in East Berlin. He stands upstage of the wall, but not above it. He is visible to the audience only as a reflection in the two-way mirror which is positioned at such an angle as to reveal him.

DAVID: … Firstly, the lie registers on the *cardiograph*, with an accelerated heartbeat. At the *temple*, we monitor for an increase or, in the case of some subjects, a decrease of arterial pressure—

FRANÇOIS: Là m'a serrer un peu … (I'm going to tighten it a bit …)

DAVID: *Respiration* has a direct effect on the person responding to questions: this contributes yet another reading of the physical response. Lastly, we measure the subject's *perspiration*. The polygraph machine detects the most minute psychophysical variations occurring during interrogation.

FRANÇOIS: (*He puts a blindfold on her eyes, rendering her completely helpless.*) Comme ça, t'as vraiment l'impression d'être vulnérable … (This gets you feeling really vulnerable …)

DAVID: The fear and mystique which surrounds the polygraph machine makes it a useful pressure tactic in obtaining a confession. But such strategies, I believe, should be used only with great care and compassion. Sometimes, the psychological response we trigger is so violent as to effect a lasting disorder in the mind of a totally innocent suspect.

LUCIE: Pis après? (And then?)

DAVID: Let me tell you about a polygraph test undertaken in the context of an unresolved murder case. The questioning of a particular suspect went something like this:

FRANÇOIS: Des fois, quand on se ramasse une gang de gars … (Sometimes, when I get together with a gang of friends …)

DAVID: François, we are going to conduct a little test.

FRANÇOIS: Y'en a un qui se fait attacher comme ça … (One of us gets tied up like this …)

DAVID: Can you hear me properly?

FRANÇOIS: … Pis au hasard y'en a un qui est choisi pour aller le rejoindre … (… then someone is picked at random to go in and join him …)

DAVID: But you cannot actually see me, can you?

FRANÇOIS: … celui qui est attaché, y peut rien faire … (… the one who's all tied up can't do anything …)

DAVID: François, are we in Canada?

FRANÇOIS: … Y peut rien voir … (… he can't see anything …)

DAVID: Is it summertime?

FRANÇOIS: … pis l'autre y fait ce qui veut avec … (… and the other one does whatever he wants with him.)

DAVID: Was it you who killed Marie-Claude Légaré?

FRANÇOIS: (reliving, in his memory, the polygraph test) Non.

DAVID: Is it 1986?

FRANÇOIS: Oui.

DAVID: Are we in the month of August?

FRANÇOIS: Non.

DAVID: Are we in the month of July?

FRANÇOIS: Oui.

DAVID: Are you responsible for the death of Marie-Claude Légaré?

FRANÇOIS: Non.

DAVID: Now, the result of this polygraph test gave evidence that this witness was actually telling the truth. But the person conducting the test told him afterwards that the machine had established that he was lying. The spontaneous reaction of the witness could be considered the ultimate proof of his innocence …

FRANÇOIS: (a complete emotional breakdown) Allez-vous me lâcher tabarnak! C'est pas moé qui l'a tuée!! C'est pas moé!! Vous voulez me rendre fou, c'est ça!! Y vont me rendre fou ostie …

(Let me fucking go! I didn't kill her!! It wasn't me! It wasn't me! You want to drive me crazy, is that it? You're driving me out of my goddamn mind …)

LUCIE is frozen, blindfolded and terrified.

LUCIE: François … ? François … ? François … ?

FRANÇOIS gives her no response.

DAVID: But the police never told him he was released from suspicion … He was never let off the hook.

FRANÇOIS: (He slowly recovers, goes to her and takes off the blindfold.) Tu veux-tu que je te détache? (Do you want me to untie you?)

He does so, then silently puts the belt and blindfold in a box.

LUCIE: C'est tu toi que l'a tuée? (Was it you killed her?)

FRANÇOIS: … J'pense pas non … (I don't think so …)

LUCIE: Pourquoi tu dis "J'pense" pas? (Why do you say … you don't "think" so?)

FRANÇOIS: Parce que des fois … je l'sais … pu … (Because sometimes … I don't know … anymore.)

He starts to cry, an emotion from deep inside. LUCIE goes to him, takes him in her arms.

LUCIE: Moi, je l'sais … que tu serais pas capable de faire mal à une mouche. (Listen … I know that you couldn't hurt a fly.)

She holds him, fiercely comforting and reassuring him. She touches his face, and the comfort becomes passion. Lights fade as they start to embrace.

Projection:

20. The Rain
Exterior, day.

Rain falls from the ceiling behind the wall. Above the wall the camera appears, covered with an umbrella. Just the camera: no one else is around.

Projection:

21. Apartment #7
Interior, night.

An eerie dream sequence. LUCIE leans against the wall with a hidden light strapped to her back. It shines at the wall, creating a strange halo around her body, and placing her in silhouette. She walks slowly to the front of the stage.

DAVID: (enters stage left) Lucie! I'm back!

FRANÇOIS enters from LUCIE's bedroom, without a shirt. DAVID is shocked. He appears *not to see LUCIE downstage, and speaks to FRANÇOIS behind her back.*

What are you doing here? Where's Lucie?

FRANÇOIS: She's in the room.

DAVID goes into the room, then comes back in anger.

DAVID: (*pointing to the exit*) Get out!

FRANÇOIS: Maybe we could talk ...

DAVID: Get out!

FRANÇOIS: Wait ...

DAVID seizes FRANÇOIS to throw him out, and they fight violently. FRANÇOIS's head is knocked against the wall. Slowly, LUCIE walks backwards to her original place, and the lighting changes. She leans against the wall, lost in her thoughts. FRANÇOIS enters from the bedroom. He stands against the wall beside LUCIE. He is restless and anxious. They smile gently at one another, and FRANÇOIS takes her hand, as if unable to speak the things in his heart. He holds her like a frightened child—which then becomes a passionate kiss. As in the previous scene, DAVID's voice is heard offstage. FRANÇOIS immediately bids farewell to LUCIE.

DAVID: Lucie! I'm back! (*As FRANÇOIS goes out, they meet.*) Hi!

FRANÇOIS: Hi! (*exits*)

DAVID: How are you?

LUCIE: I'm fine ...

DAVID: (*He takes his bag into the bedroom, then comes back and starts to wash his face in the washbasin.*) Weren't you supposed to be shooting today?

LUCIE: Yes ... I was scheduled, but I decided not to go ...

DAVID: Why?

LUCIE: Because we were supposed to shoot the death sequence, and I think that I don't have the right to do that.

DAVID: That is very courageous of you.

LUCIE: François just left for Montreal ... David ... While you were away—I slept with François.

DAVID stops washing, abruptly. He holds very still.

LUCIE: I've spent the whole week with him because he needed someone. And I told him everything you told me on the ramparts ... He told you the truth, but you lied to him.

LUCIE looks at DAVID, who has straightened to regard her, without expression.

LUCIE: David, react! Feel something!

DAVID: (*calmly turns to her*) What do you want me to "feel"? You want me to be jealous of a fucking homosexual?

LUCIE: If that's the truth, yes! If you want to cry, cry!

The lights fade on them.

Projection:

22. Death
Interior, night.

Behind the wall, FRANÇOIS arrives at the Metro station and paces impatiently, waiting for the train. We can't see him but he is lit so that his silhouette is projected upon the cyclorama behind the wall. We hear the sound of the train coming. FRANÇOIS takes off his leather jacket and lets it fall to the floor behind him; without hesitation, he throws himself in front of the arriving train. As his silhouette dives out of sight, the brick wall suddenly falls and a piercing light shines through as FRANÇOIS's naked body comes hurtling through the falling bricks to land on a hospital gurney. There he lies, amidst the broken bricks, dead, and awaiting an autopsy. DAVID pushes the gurney stage right, so that it is positioned beneath the mirror, which is hung at an angle to reflect FRANÇOIS's body.

LUCY appears above and behind the wall, stage left, in the theatre. She holds a knife, as she recites the famous Hamlet soliloquy.

LUCIE: Être ou ne pas être.
C'est la question.
Est-il plus noble pour une âme de souffrir les flèches et les coups d'un sort atroce, ou de s'armer contre le flot qui monte, et de lui faire face, et de l'arrêter?
Mourir, dormir ... rien de plus.

Terminer par du sommeil la souffrance du coeur
et les mille blessures qui sont le lot de la chair.
C'est bien le dénouement que l'on voudrat ... et
de quelle ardeur!
Mourir, dormir ...
Dormir ... peut-être rêver.
C'est l'obstacle ...
Car l'anxieté des rêves qui viendront dans ce
sommeil des morts, quand nous aurons chassé
de nous le tumulte de vivre, est là pour nous
retenir ...
Et c'est la pensée qui fait que le malheur à si
longue vie.

*The lights on her fade slowly. FRANÇOIS's corpse
is all that is illumined. But now, the reflection in
the mirror over him changes so that we no longer
see his body, but a skeleton which lies in the
same position, as if the mirror sees through his
flesh. Above the wall, across the cyclorama,
clouds are running in a vast sky.*

END

SALLY CLARK

(b. 1953)

In an emblematic scene near the beginning of Sally Clark's *Moo*, the title character speaks to us from an insane asylum, strapped into a straitjacket, having been committed on false pretences by her husband and kept there through the unwitting connivance of a male doctor. In many ways this scene typifies Clark's drama. Her plays nearly all feature a woman judged mad or guilty by men and the patriarchal systems they administer with nightmarish illogic. Engaged in power struggles they almost always lose, Clark's women endure abuses of various kinds, and most end up suffering violent death. Yet the plays are very funny and the women almost all extraordinary, strong and out-spoken. Somewhere in the spectrum between classic victims and feminist rebels lies the fascinating and disturbing paradox of Sally Clark's black comedy.

Born and raised in Vancouver, Clark went to Toronto to pursue a career as a painter. She received her B.A. in Fine Arts from York University in 1973, continued studying painting at the New School of Art, and showed her work at a number of galleries. Meanwhile, she also began writing plays, earning honourable mention in a 1976 competition run by Playwrights' Co-op.

Soon she turned her attention to playwriting in earnest. Her one-act *Ten Ways to Abuse an Old Woman* was first produced in 1983 by Toronto's Buddies in Bad Times at its Rhubarb! Festival of new theatre. A powerful, very black little comedy about an addled old woman abused by her middle-aged daughter and son-in-law, the play sports the quintessential Sally Clark title and a protagonist whose pursuit of her own reality drives others to distraction. Theatre Passe Muraille produced Clark's first major effort, *Lost Souls and Missing Persons*, in 1984. The middle-class heroine of this sprawling comedy wanders away from her empty marriage while on a trip to New York, ending up bereft of her language, her identity, and eventually her life. Both plays suggest that a woman can be happy only if she loses her mind.

Vancouver's Tamahnous Theatre produced *Trial* in 1985, Clark's adaptation of Kafka's nightmare novel of paranoia and bureaucracy. It was restaged with major revisions as *The Trial of Judith K.* by Toronto's Canadian Stage Company in 1989. Judith Kaye, a sexually repressed corporate loans officer, stands in for Joseph K. in an updated, sometimes silly version of Kafka's tale that nevertheless moves inexorably to the same chilling conclusion. *Moo* premiered in Calgary in 1988, and the next year Clark was back in Toronto with *Jehanne of the Witches*, produced by Tarragon. In Clark's complex and confusing retelling of the Joan of Arc story, Jehanne is associated with the matriarchal paganism of pre-Christian Europe. She's also friends with Gilles de Rais, the infamous Bluebeard, aristocratic pederast and reputed mass-murderer of children, played in the original production by Sky Gilbert. In fact the play we're watching turns out to be Gilles' production, with one of his boys in the role of Jehanne.

Life without Instruction, commissioned by Toronto's Nightwood Theatre and first produced by Theatre Plus in 1991, reaches back to history again. Like *Jehanne* and *Judith K.* it also has a trial as its centrepiece. Termed by Clark "a revenge comedy," the play tells the true story of seventeenth-century Italian painter Artemisia Gentileschi, who was raped by the man her father hired to teach her perspective. A Québécois translation played Montreal's La Licorne under the title *La Vie sans mode d'emploi* (1993). More recent history serves as the basis of *Saint Frances of Hollywood*, Clark's take on the twisted life of actress Frances Farmer, which premiered at Calgary's Alberta Theatre Projects in 1994. *Wasps*, a sex farce about a librarian, opened in Toronto in 1996 and was subsequently directed by Clark herself in Vancouver. In *The Widow Judith* (1998) Clark developed the biblical story which had been the subject of Artemisia's painting in *Life Without Instruction*.

Clark has been playwright-in-residence at Buddies in Bad Times (1983–84), Theatre Passe Muraille (1985–86), Nightwood (1987), the Shaw Festival (1988), the University of Cincinnati (1996) and Berton House in the Yukon (2000). She spent 1991 in residence at the Canadian Centre for Advanced Film Studies where she directed her own screenplay of *Ten Ways to Abuse an Old Woman.* Currently she divides her home between Toronto and Vancouver.

Moo had its genesis in 1983 at the Banff Centre, where Clark claims she wrote it in two weeks while workshopping *Lost Souls and Missing Persons.* The script made the rounds for a few years after a 1984 workshop at Toronto's Factory Theatre. It premiered at NovaPlayRites '88, Alberta Theatre Projects' festival of new plays, in a co-production by ATP and Victoria's Belfry Theatre, where it subsequently ran. For its 1989 production at the Factory, *Moo* won the Chalmers new play award.

In *Moo* Clark traces the story of an extraordinary woman over the course of half a century. But does Moragh MacDowell ultimately live a life of value in the intensity of her all-consuming passion for Harry Parker, or simply waste her life in obsessive pursuit of an unworthy man? Moo is strong, capable, smart and independent. In contrast to the comic banality of her conformist sisters and repressed, conventional parents, she explodes with energy and spirit. Pursuing Harry with relentless vigour, she scandalizes her family (to our great delight), and even in her sixties inspires her grand-niece Susan as a role-model of female liberation. But what does she have to show for it all? Six years in an insane asylum, a collection of taunting postcards from exotic South Sea locales, and a missing son whose happiness she sacrificed to her own obsession. Even Susan turns on her in the end. Moo spends much of the play effectively imprisoned, either in the asylum or the nursing home. The thirty-five years the play jumps in the intermission between acts one and two are a huge black hole where the prime of her life should have been. Looking back near the end of the play, she herself concludes that her life was little more than a series of "self-deceits."

Moo is in many ways reminiscent of the women in British playwright Caryl Churchill's *Top Girls,* women whose achievements in a world defined by men come only at enormous personal cost. We might also see her as a comic version of Bob in Sharon Pollock's *Doc.* (See *Modern Canadian Plays, Volume I.*) As young women, both take pride in being able to do well what men can do—in Moo's case, sharpshooting. Both women are disempowered by the men they marry, living the rest of their lives, in effect, on the man's terms: the gunshots that open and close the play, defining Moo's life, are fired by Harry. Unlike Bob, Moo never becomes passive or pathetic. In fact for most of her life she remains the aggressor in her relationship. (Note which character occupies the title in Pollock's play and in Clark's.) It would be tempting to say that she gives as good as she gets, and that Harry, like the "rotter" on which Clark based him, "got more than he bargained for" (Author's Preface). But as Moo points out, the romantic idea that the two of them together form a single magnificent organism has this drawback: "Harry [always] comes out on top and I wind up getting the shit kicked out of me."

Harry himself is a fascinating mass of contradictions: charmer, rotter, part textbook abusive male, part comic Iago, driven, it sometimes appears, by motiveless malignancy. At times he seems to want to tame Moo, just as her sisters do; at other times he leads her on a merry chase, the adventurous soul-mate. He is as obsessed with her as she is with him, but in a different way. He sees her as the archetypal devouring female: eating him alive, prying at his soul, "suck[ing] the very life out of me." And he always chooses women he can victimize: Moo, the aptly named Patsy, and Maude Gormley, whom he casually throws down the stairs.

In making comedy of all this, Sally Clark appears to embrace the politically incorrect. She dedicates the play "to cads, rotters and bounders," and says in an interview in *Fair Play* that she was trying to write "the story of a woman who drove the man to do these things"—what some would call blaming the victim. But she insists that Moo is never truly a victim, that only her family tries to make her out to be one. Certainly, Moo never thinks of herself that way. A warrior in what Clark calls "the old-fashioned battle of the sexes," she asks no quarter and gives none. And in the end she goes out with a bang.

Moo was first performed on February 2. 1988, at Alberta Theatre Projects in Calgary as part of NovaPlayRites '88 and the Olympic Arts Festival. A co-production of Alberta Theatre Projects and the Belfry Theatre, Victoria, *Moo* featured the following cast:

MOO	Wendy Noel
HARRY	Weston McMillan
SARAH	Pat Armstrong
DITTY	Jane Logie
MAUDE GORMLEY/SUSAN/NURSE	Jan Wood
MR. MACDOWELL/WALLY/DOUGALL	Brian Linds
MRS. MACDOWELL/NURSE/JANE/PATSY	Susan Johnston
DOCTOR/CHARLIE/CLERK	Ray Hunt

Directed by Glynis Leyshon
Set and Lighting Design by Warren Carrie
Costume Design by Pamela Lampkin

MOO

CHARACTERS

MOO
HARRY PARKER, *Moo's husband*
SARAH MACDOWELL, *Moo's oldest sister*
DITTY MACDOWELL, *Moo's sister*
MR. MACDOWELL, *Moo's father*
MRS. MACDOWELL, *Moo's mother*
MAUDE GORMLEY, *Harry's second wife*
NURSE/RECEPTIONIST
DOCTOR
DOUGALL, *Moo's son*
PATSY, *Harry's third wife*
CHARLIE, *Sarah's husband*
JANE, *Sarah's daughter*
SUSAN, *Jane's daughter*
WALLY, *Moo's boyfriend*
HOTEL CLERK
ORDERLY

This play can be performed by eight actors: 5 women and 3 men. Suggested casting:
Ditty
Harry
Moo
Doctor/Charlie/Hotel Clerk
Mr. MacDowell/Wally/Dougall/Orderly
Maude Gormley/Susan
Nurse/Mrs. MacDowell/Patsy/Jane
Sarah

SCENE

Vancouver, Seattle, and the "tropical paradises"of Montserrat and Banyu Wangi: 1919–1970.

PREFACE

My grandmother used to tell me stories of women whose lives were ruined by anonymous evil men known as "rotters." Rotters seduced wealthy women and then deserted them, making them the butt of family consolation for years to come (a far more dire fate than the actual desertion).

According to family lore, one of my great-aunts had the misfortune to fall in love with a rotter who, in the grand rotter tradition, ruined her life. I could never quite piece together the tragic image of the betrayed lover with my garrulous aunt who shocked and confronted everyone within range. I began to wonder about the rotter and whether in fact, when he seduced my great-aunt, he got more than he bargained for.

ACT ONE

Scene One

A man, standing, is holding a gun. A woman enters, stops, stares at the man. The man raises the gun, points it at the woman and fires. Blackout.

Scene Two

Seattle, 1925. Insane asylum. Front desk.

HARRY: (*to DOCTOR*) As I've said, I've been worried about her. We've tried consultations with Dr. Swan and he and I both think she'd be better off here for a month or so on a trial basis.

MOO: (*to RECEPTIONIST*) We're visiting his sister. I've never met her. Harry's never wanted me to meet her. He thinks it would upset me.

DOCTOR: If you'll sign right here, Mr. Parker.

MOO: What are you signing, Harry? Is she coming out? She can't stay with us, Harry. (*to RECEPTIONIST*) She can't stay with us. I said I'd meet her but I don't want to bring her home with us.

HARRY: (*laughs uneasily*) Delusions.

MOO: Does she look like you, Harry? (*to RECEPTIONIST*) Isn't it a shame when people go like that?

DOCTOR: Come along, Miss Parker. I'm sure you'll feel right at home here in no time flat. (*guides her away*)

MOO: What are you doing? Harry, what's he doing?

HARRY: He's taking you away.

MOO: Aren't you coming? I don't want to meet her all by myself. What'll I say to her?

HARRY: Goodbye, Moo.

MOO: HARRY! (*to DOCTOR*) Stop grabbing me. (*rushes up to HARRY*) Harry! What's going on?

DOCTOR: I was afraid this was going to be difficult. You should have prepared her.

HARRY: Moo, you're going to stay here for a while.

MOO: WHAT!

RECEPTIONIST: Now now, Miss Parker.

MOO: Mrs. Parker.

DOCTOR: Now, Mrs. Parker, we understand you need a little rest. You remember Dr. Swan?

MOO: Of course, I remember Dr. Swan.

DOCTOR: Did you like Dr. Swan?

MOO: He was all right, I guess. What's all this about?

DOCTOR: Dr. Swan has advised that you rest here for a short time and your brother has agreed.

MOO: My brother.

DOCTOR: Mr. Parker.

MOO: That's my husband. HARRY!

HARRY: Crazy.

MOO: HARRY WHAT THE HELL IS GOING ON!

HARRY: Mad as a hatter.

MOO: HARRY!

HARRY: I've tried everything.

DOCTOR: Please Miss Parker, your brother feels that—

MOO: My brother is dead.

HARRY: There's no reasoning with her.

MOO: He's dead, goddammit. He was killed in the war. Harry fought in the same company with him.

DOCTOR: I see. Displacement personae.

RECEPTIONIST: Quite.

DOCTOR: Now, Miss Parker, come along.

MOO: Harry. This isn't funny, Harry. Tell them who you are.

HARRY: I'm afraid I can't do that, Moo. I am not your husband. I am your brother.

MOO: Harry.

HARRY: I am your brother. Goodbye, Moo.

MOO: (*screams*) H-A-A-R-R-R-Y!!!

Scene Three

HARRY: She always had a vivid imagination. Of course, she liked me when we were young, but I wasn't always her favourite. I mean, she never expressly selected me as such. Not when we were young. No, that happened later. Much later. After George died. I suppose when George was killed, I was all she had left so she became dependent on me. And later, obsessed with me. Moo's a lot younger than George and me. Do you think that has any bearing on it? Her being the youngest. The youngest are usually strange, aren't they? Sibling birth order. I remember reading something along those lines. It's just that, Doctor, may I be frank?

DOCTOR: Of course.

HARRY: I am sick to death of being her love object.

DOCTOR: Yes, I can see it would get tiresome.

HARRY: And now this whole business of our being married.

DOCTOR: She wears a wedding ring.

HARRY: She bought it herself.

DOCTOR: It's quite an expensive ring.

HARRY: She has good taste.

DOCTOR: She mentions sisters.

HARRY: Oh God, the sisters. I thought she'd forgotten about them.

DOCTOR: No. She's quite specific. She wants me to get in touch with them. She's quite insistent about it.

HARRY: The sisters. I'm trying to remember when they entered the picture. When she was very little, she had a friend who was the eldest of a whole family of sisters. Yes. That's right. But Moo hadn't started talking about sisters until just after George was called away. I was called shortly after so I'm not really familiar with that whole side of her madness. In fact, when I returned, I was willing to let the whole thing slide. I thought: so, she has a crush on me, so, she'll outgrow it, but it began to affect my life. I couldn't go anywhere without her calling me. Following me. And women! Out of the question. The minute she got wind of any female involvement, she'd call them up, badger them. That was when the husband business entered into it. (*pause*) Is there nothing we can do?

DOCTOR: Nothing. She is utterly convinced you are her husband.

HARRY: It's hopeless.

DOCTOR: Can you think of anything which might have triggered it?

HARRY: When she was nineteen, she was shot in the head.

DOCTOR: Aaaah.

Scene Four

Moo: (*alone on stage*) And he tried to kill me. He tried to gun me down. No. I'm not getting hysterical. Have you ever had someone try to gun you down. Well, it makes you think. This isn't a laughing matter. I don't know what you're laughing about. You're not laughing. Oh, sorry. I thought you were. I'm a little confused. But it's true. Dammit. It's true. He tried to kill me. Why? How should I know!

Scene Five

Moo: The first day, Harry came to our house to tell us the news about George—

DOCTOR: George.

MOO: My brother.

DOCTOR: You have another brother.

MOO: No. Just one. George.

DOCTOR: And are you married to George as well?

MOO: No. He's dead.

DOCTOR: Were you ever married to George?

MOO: He was my brother.

DOCTOR: But you are married to Harry.

MOO: Harry is not my brother. George is. But he's dead.

DOCTOR: I think we have a little problem here.

MOO: Look, Harry is lying, I don't know why he's lying but he's lying. Call my sisters.

DOCTOR: You have sisters?

MOO: Yes.

DOCTOR: How many sisters?

MOO: Two.

DOCTOR: Do you like your sisters?

MOO: Would you just call them, please?

DOCTOR: Do you like your sisters?

MOO: They're all right.

DOCTOR: Don't you like them?

MOO: I like them. But they drive me crazy. My whole family drives me crazy. Sorry. I didn't mean that. They don't drive me crazy. I just wanted to get away from them so I ran off with Harry.

DOCTOR: Don't you like your family?

MOO: Forget it.

Pause.

DOCTOR: What possible motivation would Harry have for pretending to be your brother?

MOO: I don't know. I don't know why he signed me in here. I have no idea why—

DOCTOR: But you, on the other hand, have any number of reasons for imagining Harry to be your husband.

MOO: What!

DOCTOR: Fear of men, dislike of women—

MOO: I want to go home!

DOCTOR: Now, don't get upset, Miss Parker.

MOO: MRS. PARKER. DAMMIT. MRS. PARKER, MRS. PARKER, MRS. PARKER!

DOCTOR: I see.

Scene Six

In a hospital room. MOO is in a straitjacket, lounging about.

HARRY: (*enters, stares at her*) Don't you think you're carrying this thing a bit far?

MOO: I thought I'd dress for the occasion.

HARRY: You're overdoing it.

MOO: Am I? Why don't you untie me, then.

HARRY: (*unties her*) How did you get this thing? They don't usually put people in these.

MOO: I've been very naughty. I didn't eat my vegetables.

HARRY: There. It's undone.

MOO: Are you sure?

HARRY: Yes.

MOO flings straps around HARRY and ties him to her.

HARRY: Hey!

MOO: I'd just like to take a good look at my brother. It's been so long since I've seen him.

HARRY: You don't have to be two inches from my face. (*tries to untie straps*)

MOO: (*giggles*) What's the matter, Harry?

She trips him. They fall on the floor.

HARRY: Jesus! CHRIST! GET OFF ME, YOU BITCH!

MOO: My own sweet little brother. (*kicks him*)

HARRY: OW!

MOO: You goddamn prick! I'll kill you! (*kicks him furiously*)

HARRY: NURSE!

Scene Seven

MAUDE: You're thinking of her again, aren't you?

HARRY: No. I'm not thinking about her.

MAUDE: Yes. You are. I can tell.

HARRY: Well—stop staring at me then. If you'd stop watching for signs and just relax, maybe we might be able to enjoy ourselves.

MAUDE: We did before.

HARRY: You did.

MAUDE: You said you loved me.

HARRY: I did. I just don't like being watched.

MAUDE: Why can't you talk about her?

HARRY: There's nothing to say. She was crazy.

MAUDE: If she wasn't crazy, would you love her still?

HARRY: Goddamn it, Maude, I'm with you, aren't I? Isn't that enough for you. I've left her and I'm with you.

MAUDE: You only left her because she was crazy. If she was sane, you probably would have stayed.

HARRY: How do you know I didn't drive her crazy?

MAUDE: Did you?

HARRY: No. I don't think so. I think she had a head start on me.

MAUDE: Was she born crazy?

HARRY: Who knows. I don't want to talk about it.

MAUDE: What sort of things did she do? You know. Crazy things.

HARRY: Maude, do we have to talk about her?

MAUDE: I'm interested.

HARRY: You're nosey.

MAUDE: I want to know all about you.

HARRY: You don't give a damn about me. You want to know all about her.

MAUDE: I guess I do.

HARRY: It's morbid.

MAUDE: This is strange, Harry. I don't know how to say this exactly, but—

HARRY: But.

MAUDE: I liked you a lot better before.

HARRY: You did.

MAUDE: Yeah. And I've been thinking about it. Maybe, when I was madly in love with you, it's only because you were with her and you had, like, "assumed" some of her traits. People do that, don't they, Harry?

HARRY: What?

MAUDE: Take on the other person's character. So, I loved you because you were living with her and that must mean that I was actually in love with the two of you. Or, oh Harry, this is awful—

HARRY: What.

MAUDE: Or, maybe, I was actually in love with her. Just her. Not you at all. Does that make me a lesbian, Harry? Do you think I'm a lesbian?

HARRY gets up and walks backwards out of the room, staring at MAUDE cautiously.

MAUDE: Harry?

Scene Eight

MOO: (*in a straitjacket*) I suppose, these days, it's all in one's credibility. If you are short, you have less credibility than a tall person. If you are a woman, you have less credibility than a man. If you are short, a woman and wearing a straitjacket—well, forget it, you have no credibility at all. I go to the mirror and I stand and look at myself wearing this stupid get-up and I think—"Can I believe this woman?" And the answer is of course, "No." And I look and tell myself who I am, where I'm from and how I came to be here and the answer is again, "No." In theory, if I did have sisters and family, they should eventually start looking for me. I don't see anyone except Harry and then, only once a week. Harry, the man I love to hate. I look forward to his visits. For the week, I rage against him; I beat myself against padded walls. I plot and plan all the nasty things I'm going to say to him. Yet, when he shows up, I'm so bloody grateful it's ridiculous. I'm even starting to believe he's my brother. The thing I can't fathom is, if Harry isn't my brother, why is he doing this to me? That's what doesn't make sense. That's what makes me think I must be crazy. Then, it all clicks neatly into place. It all makes sense, then. I'm getting very tired again. I don't know whether it's drugs, bad food or just fatigue, but I sleep all day. I wake up for meals, read the odd book. But mainly I sleep. And await rescue.

Scene Nine

Vancouver, 1919. Grounds of the MacDowell house. MOO is shooting cans. She throws a can up in the air, shoots, hits it. Her sister SARAH walks up behind her.

MOO: Hello, Sarah.

SARAH: Getting out your frustrations?

MOO: At least I have an outlet.

SARAH: Why do you shoot?

MOO: Practice. I want to be good.

SARAH: Why, though?

MOO: Something to do.

SARAH: I worry about you, Moo.

MOO: Why? What's wrong with wanting to be good?

SARAH: Nothing. But this will never get you anywhere.

MOO: By anywhere, you mean marriage.

SARAH: No. I didn't mean that at all.

MOO: I tell you what, Sarah. I'll marry the first man who can outshoot me.

SARAH: I wasn't talking about marriage, Moo. I simply meant if you're going to be good at something, you should find an occupation. Shooting is useless.

MOO: I enjoy it.

SARAH: Since you're not going to get married, you should—

MOO: Who says I'm not going to get married.

SARAH: You did.

MOO: No, I didn't.

SARAH: It's hopeless trying to have a conversation with you. I don't know why I bother.

MOO: You look very nice today. Charlie still lurking about?

SARAH: It's Charles. He doesn't lurk. And yes, he is coming by.

MOO: You're going to marry him, aren't you?

SARAH: Why do you dislike men?

MOO: I don't dislike men, Sarah. I simply dislike Charlie—sorry—Charles. If having an aversion to the little scum implies a general dislike of the male species, forgive me—Mea Culpa.

SARAH: Charles is going to be very successful.

MOO: Single-minded men usually are. He'd have to be successful. He doesn't have any choice. There isn't enough room in his brain to admit any other possibility.

SARAH: I don't know why you dislike him. What is wrong with Charles? Tell me that.

MOO: He's boring.

SARAH: Boring. What's boring?

MOO: Charlie is boring. Oh, you want me to be more specific. Charlie is boring because: one, he has no imagination; two, he likes cars—always distrust a man who likes cars; and three, he plays golf! Golf is a boring man's game.

SARAH: My God, you talk a lot of drivel.

MOO: They get the little matching hats and matching gloves with the knuckles cut out and the cute little shoes that match the gloves and the cute little clubs that have little hats to match the hat the golfer's wearing. And it's all cute as hell.

SARAH: Lots of interesting men play golf.

MOO: I'm sure that's possible. But interesting men don't look like two-toned Christmas trees.

SARAH: Charles loves me.

MOO: And that's why you're marrying him. When George gets back you'll see what a bore Charlie is.

SARAH: You don't understand, Moo. He's a good man and he adores me.

MOO: And that's enough.

SARAH: For me it is. I will love him in time. When a man adores you, he makes it impossible to do otherwise.

MOO: I think it could be a real nuisance after a while.

SARAH: Charles is restrained. He won't overdo it.

MOO: It's your life.

SARAH: Yes. It is. (*stalks off*)

MOO starts shooting. She throws a can up, shoots, hits it. Throws up another can, hits it. HARRY approaches and watches her.

HARRY: Ah, excuse me.

MOO: (*sees him, stops shooting*) Who are you?

HARRY: Harry Parker. (*stretches out a hand*)

MOO: (*does not take it*) What are you doing here?

HARRY: I'm sorry to disturb you, but I'm looking for Mr. MacDowell.

MOO: An odd place to look, don't you think?

HARRY: I couldn't find the house.

MOO: The house is back there.

HARRY: You have a fair amount of ground.

MOO: Is my father expecting you?

HARRY: No. He isn't.

MOO: What business do you have?

HARRY: I'd rather not say, right now. I'd like to speak to him personally.

MOO: He's in the house.

HARRY: Yes. Well. Pleased to meet you. (*waits for MOO to give her name*) Right. Well, I suppose I should go to the house. (*starts to head off, stops*) You were shooting just now.

MOO: Yes.

HARRY: I hate to ask you but can I have a go?

MOO: Ah …

HARRY: Just for a moment?

MOO: Oh. All right.

HARRY: You had a tin can around here.

MOO: You're very observant.

HARRY: (*finds it*) Something I used to do. You try and keep the can up in the air for as long as possible.

MOO: Pardon?

HARRY: You just keep hitting it so it stays up there.

He throws the can up, shoots, keeps the can up for a long time. MOO stares, dumbfounded. HARRY stops, hands the rifle back to her.

HARRY: Thanks. I needed that.

HARRY leaves. MOO stares at him. She throws the can up, tries to shoot it, misses. She stares back at HARRY.

Scene Ten

MacDowell living room.

MR. MACDOWELL: I am indebted to you, Mr., er—

HARRY: Parker.

MR. MACDOWELL: Parker. Quite. It slipped my mind. All the confusion.

HARRY: I understand, sir.

MRS. MACDOWELL: A glass of sherry, Mr. Parker?

HARRY: No thank you, Ma'am.

MRS. MACDOWELL: You must.

HARRY: If you insist, thank you. (*takes glass*)

MRS. MACDOWELL: Did he know he was going to die?

HARRY: I think so, Ma'am.

MRS. MACDOWELL: Did he have a vision?

SARAH: Mother!

MRS. MACDOWELL: I hope he had a vision. When I die, I want to have one.

MOO: You have them all the time, anyway.

MRS. MACDOWELL: You're a very selfish girl, Moragh. You can't live for yourself, you know.

MOO: What does that have to do with it?

SARAH: Moo's just being funny, Mother.

MRS. MACDOWELL: How can she make jokes at a time like this. I don't believe she even cares.

SARAH: Mother, we have company.

MRS. MACDOWELL: Quite. Excuse me, Mr. Parker. I often have these tête-à-têtes with my girls.

MR. MACDOWELL: Jesus, it's awful.

MRS. MACDOWELL: What, dear?

GIRLS: What, Daddy?

MR. MACDOWELL: Oh sorry, I was just thinking.

MRS. MACDOWELL: It's going to be very sad without him.

MR. MACDOWELL: It's going to be unbearable.

SARAH: Pardon, Daddy?

DITTY: Pardon, Daddy?

MR. MACDOWELL: Bloody unbearable.

HARRY: I'm sorry, Mr. MacDowell. I don't know what to say.

MR. MACDOWELL: There's nothing to say. Nothing to do. He was close to you, was he?

HARRY: Yes sir. I'd say so.

MR. MACDOWELL: What are your plans now? Going to see your family?

HARRY: Well—ah—

MR. MACDOWELL: You're welcome to stay here, if you like.

HARRY: Oh now, Mr. MacDowell. I really couldn't inconvenience you. You don't even know me—

MR. MACDOWELL: So, it's settled. You're staying here. Jean!

MRS. MACDOWELL: Yes, dear.

MR. MACDOWELL: Mr. Parker is staying here.

MRS. MACDOWELL: That's nice, dear.

MR. MACDOWELL: We need another man in the place.

MRS. MACDOWELL: Yes, dear.

MR. MACDOWELL: Brighten things up.

MRS. MACDOWELL: Yes, dear.

Scene Eleven

MOO and HARRY, 1919.

HARRY: Self-deceit. That's what the cause of it all is.

MOO: The cause of what?

HARRY: Old age. Ill health. TB. Senility. Our bodies are designed for perfection. Our brain is meant to function logically. But because we are indoctrinated from birth with a particular brand of ethics, morality—all of them, utterly illogical—we are lost. The brain realizes this. But it tries to make sense out of it anyway. Consequently, it jams, malfunctions, and twenty years later, the person dies of tuberculosis.

MOO: Just like that.

HARRY: Sometimes it takes ten years, sometimes fifty, sometimes it happens overnight. The person just snaps.

MOO: So, one must always tell the truth.

HARRY: Only to oneself. You can lie as much as you like to other people.

MOO: Why would I want to lie to other people?

HARRY: Why not. You, Moragh, are a wallower in self-deceit. It will catch up to you.

MOO: Do you lie to people, Harry?

HARRY: Of course.

MOO: To me?

HARRY: To you more than anyone else.

MOO: Why?

HARRY: Because you're special. And because you need it.

MOO: You're an odd man.

HARRY: Yes. Convince yourself.

MOO: If you could do anything at all, what would you like to do?

HARRY: I'd like to live by myself on a desert island.

MOO: Don't you like people, Harry?

HARRY: Not particularly. (*pause*) You don't agree with me.

MOO: About what?

HARRY: Self-deceit.

MOO: I'll think about it.

HARRY: No. You won't.

Scene Twelve

MOO: I knew the moment I laid my eyes on Harry Parker that he was mine. I wanted him and nothing was going to stop me from getting him. The strange thing is, when I think about it rationally, there wasn't really much to want about Harry. He wasn't particularly good-looking, although people said he was; I didn't find him handsome. But he had a certain look in his eyes. A depth and a wildness. The look of a man just slightly out of control. And I knew I had to have that. When I think about it, Harry wasn't even particularly good company. He spoke rarely but he always led you to believe that he possessed information that went far beyond what he said. And he was a good shot. He was a very good shot.

Scene Thirteen

SARAH: I warned Moo about him. Right from the beginning. I said stick with the good men and you can't go wrong. But do you think she'd listen. She was determined to do it her way. That's the way she's been all her life. Everything had to be her way. And Harry—well, what can one say? He was insignificant, really, I mean, he ruined Moo's life but in the grand scheme of things, he was insignificant. Pity, she never saw it that way.

Scene Fourteen

DITTY: The only thing anyone will ever tell you about Harry Parker was that he was very handsome. That's all anyone really knew about him. I knew he was a rotter the moment I laid eyes on him. And of course, I stayed away from him. Couldn't stand the man. Can't say why. I just loathed him. That's all. (*pause*) And that's all I can say on the subject. He was very handsome.

Scene Fifteen

HARRY is shooting. MOO stands at a distance, tossing tin cans in the air.

DITTY: (*enters*) Hello, Harry.

HARRY: (*stops shooting*) Hello, Dorothy.

DITTY: I like it when you call me Dorothy.

HARRY: It's a very nice name.

DITTY: Oh? Do you think so?

MOO: H-A-A-R-R-Y!

HARRY: Yes. I do.

MOO: H-A-A-A-R-R-Y!! Are you going to hit the can or not?

HARRY: Just a minute, Moo.

DITTY: I wish I could learn to shoot.

HARRY: Didn't Moo ever teach you?

DITTY: Oh—no—she never had time.

HARRY: Well, it's quite simple.

DITTY: Oh, would you show me?

HARRY: Of course.

MOO: H-A-A-R-R-Y!

HARRY: I'll show you right now.

MOO: (*marches up to HARRY and DITTY*) Harry, what do you think you're doing? I'm waiting for you. Hello, Ditty.

HARRY: Dorothy wants to learn how to shoot.

MOO: Dorothy?

DITTY: Yes. Harry's going to teach me.

MOO: You never wanted to shoot before.

DITTY: Well, I do now.

MOO: I'll bet.

DITTY: Harry, would you be good enough to show me.

HARRY: Oh yeah. Well, you hold it like so. (*shows her, then hands rifle to DITTY*)

DITTY: (*picks it up*) Oooooh—it's heavy.

HARRY: We need a target. Moo, would you mind?

MOO: Mind what.

HARRY: Tossing some cans in the air.

MOO: She'll never hit those.

HARRY: I'll guide her the first time.

MOO glares at him and walks off at a distance.

DITTY: Thank you, Moo.

HARRY: (*behind DITTY*) Now, you hold the gun so.

HARRY picks it up so he is behind her. Holding the shotgun, he places DITTY's hand on it.

DITTY: (*giggles*) Ooooh it's so heavy.

HARRY: You'll get used to it.

DITTY: Will I?

HARRY: And you—um—put your hand there. No, don't pull the trigger.

DITTY: Trigger?

HARRY: Yeah, that thing there. Keep your hand steady. I'll keep my hand on yours. The gun has a recoil so be careful. Now, you look down the barrel.

DITTY: The barrel?

HARRY: Yeah—um—there's a little sight there—see it!

DITTY: Oh yes.

HARRY has his face pressed near DITTY's.

HARRY: Well, you use that to sight the target. So, you ... ah—(*kisses her neck*)

DITTY: (*squeals*) Eeee!

The gun goes off. HARRY and DITTY are thrown backward. They sit up and look in the direction of MOO.

DITTY: Moo? Moo? MOO! Oh my God, you've killed her!! MOOOO!

DITTY runs to MOO, whose head is bleeding copiously.

Scene Sixteen

Moo's head is bandaged.

HARRY: You don't think I tried to gun you down, do you, Moo?

MOO: Of course not, Harry.

HARRY: Your sister. She's mad, you know.

MOO: Which one?

HARRY: Right. They're both crazy.

MOO: Are they?

HARRY: I brought you something. How is your head?

MOO: It's all right. You just grazed it.

HARRY: Good. (*pause*) I'll probably have to leave soon.

MOO: I guess you will.

HARRY: I didn't do it, Moo. It just went off. That's all.

MOO: I know. What did you bring me?

HARRY: Oh sorry. Here. (*hands her a package*)

MOO: (*opens it*) Perfume. Oh Harry, perfume. (*looks at it*) "My Sin." What sort of perfume is that?

HARRY: French.

MOO: I've never worn perfume before.

HARRY: Wear it now.

MOO: (*sniffs it*) It smells awful.

HARRY: (*sniffs it*) No, it doesn't. Smells like you. (*smells her neck*) Run off with me.

MOO: Elope?

HARRY: No. Run off.

MOO: Harry, you want to marry me?

HARRY: Have it your way. (*kisses her*)

Scene Seventeen

HARRY and MOO's bedroom, 4:30 a.m. HARRY tries to sneak into bed.

MOO: (*in bed*) Where have you been?

HARRY: Oh, hi dear.

MOO: (*sits up, turns on light*) Where have you been?

HARRY: Oh, out and about.

MOO: It's 4:30 in the morning.

HARRY: Is it that late? I had no idea—

MOO: Where were you, Harry?

HARRY: I was out.

MOO: But you go out all the time. You're out all day.

HARRY: Business.

MOO: You come home for dinner. Stay for a few hours, then you're out again.

HARRY: I've got to get myself sorted out. I have to get started again. You'll just have to be patient.

MOO: You never had so much business before.

HARRY: It fell through.

MOO: What sort of business do you do anyway, Harry?

HARRY: It's too complicated, Moo. You wouldn't be interested.

MOO: I want to know.

HARRY: Look, Moo, I'm tired. Things aren't going too well for me and I don't really want to talk about it when I get home.

MOO: But I want to know.

HARRY: You'll just have to wait. I don't know myself what I'm doing.

MOO: Why do you have to hide things from me?

HARRY: I'm not hiding anything from you, I just don't want to talk about it.

MOO: What am I supposed to do while you're out all day?

HARRY: Do what most women do.

MOO: And what is that?

HARRY: How should I know. I'm not a woman. Other women stay home while their husbands do their business. Can't you be like most women? Ask me if I have a nice day at the office, kiss me on the cheek and leave it at that.

MOO: You don't have an office, Harry.

HARRY: How do you know that.

MOO: I've tried to find it, Harry.

HARRY: So now you're spying on me.

MOO: I just want to know who I'm married to. I want to know what you do all day.

HARRY: You want to control me.

MOO: I don't want to control you. It's a simple question.

HARRY: I don't know what you do all day.

MOO: Do you want to know?

HARRY: Not particularly.

MOO: Harry, we're married.

HARRY: Yeah.

MOO: We're supposed to share things.

HARRY: Yeah.

MOO: We're supposed to talk to each other.

HARRY: I'm not a very talkative man, Moo. You knew that.

MOO: Couldn't you at least try?

HARRY: I'm trying to get my business sorted out and I just don't feel like talking about it. It's as simple as that. You don't have to make a god-damn issue out of it.

MOO: Where were you tonight?

HARRY: Jesus Christ! Give me some room. All I want is some room.

MOO: Harry, I love you.

HARRY: (*wearily*) I know that, Moo.

MOO: Do you love me?

Pause.

HARRY: Yes, Moo.

MOO: Say it, Harry. I need to hear you say it.

HARRY: I love you, Moo.

MOO: Do you mean it, Harry?

HARRY: (*no response*)

MOO: Do you mean it?

Scene Eighteen

The asylum.

MOO: They're right, of course. I should be in here. Not for the reasons they think but for the simple reason that I want to see Harry. Wanting to see Harry is a disease. Not yet categorized, but it is a disease. I have every reason in the world not to want to see Harry. He tried to gun me down. Oh yes, he tried to do it. He married me—abducted me, more to the point. He stole all my money and he put me in a loony bin. And I still want to see him. To scream at him? Hurl abuse at him? Get revenge? Oh probably—but mainly to see him. It's almost as though Harry and I, together, form this single magnificent organism. The only drawback being that Harry comes out on top and I wind up getting the shit kicked out of me. Maybe Harry does this to women. That's what I'm not sure about. If he does this to all women, then I'd be an even greater fool than thought I was. There'd be nothing special in it. I'd simply be another one of his victims. In which case, I'd make a severe attempt to cure myself and forget about him. But I think he just does it to me. Harry has this compulsive desire to screw me around and I have this compulsive desire to be screwed. But not just by anyone. Any other Tom or Dick would not do. It has to be Harry.

Scene Nineteen

Hospital room.

NURSE: We have a surprise for you, Miss Parker.

MOO: Mrs. Parker.

NURSE: Yes, well, whatever.

MOO: Mrs. Parker. It's not whatever. It's Mrs. Parker.

NURSE: (*to door*) I don't think she should see you. Not after last time.

HARRY: (*enters*) Hello, Moo.

MOO glares at him.

HARRY: (*to NURSE*) It's all right. You don't need to stay. We'll be just fine.

NURSE: Are you sure?

HARRY: Yes.

NURSE: All right. I'll be outside if you need me. Just call. (*leaves*)

HARRY: Well, Moo, and how have you been? (*MOO glares at him.*) Not too chatty today, are we? (*MOO continues to stare. HARRY shifts uncomfortably.*) Well, dear, the nurses tell me you seem to be much better.

MOO removes her slippers slowly, and performs a partial strip tease, removing her clothes piece by piece.

HARRY: (*pretends not to notice*) Of course, they did say you have bouts of depression. Now, are you unhappy today? You don't seem unhappy. (*pause*) Is there any particular reason that you're removing your clothes? (*MOO continues.*) Is this supposed to be significant? (*MOO advances toward him.*) Well, you could at least say something.

MOO: (*seductively*) Hello, Harry.

HARRY: Hello, Moo.

MOO: (*puts her hand on HARRY's groin*) And how are you today?

HARRY: (*removes her hand*) Fine, thank you.

MOO: That's good. You seem fine. You seem very well, in fact.

HARRY: I'm worried about you, Moo.

MOO: Don't worry, Harry. You worry too much. (*She kisses him. HARRY responds reluctantly.*) Now, tell me you're my brother.

HARRY: I'm your brother.

MOO kisses him again.

Scene Twenty

MAUDE: Do you think I should get a nose job? (*no response from HARRY*) Well—do you?

HARRY: (*looks up*) No. I don't.

MAUDE: Why not?

HARRY: Your nose is fine the way it is.

MAUDE: I don't know, Harry. It's all bent over to one side. See.

HARRY: Looks okay to me.

MAUDE: Nah. It's all twisted. I think I should get a nose job.

HARRY: Okay. Get a nose job.

MAUDE: But will you love me?

HARRY: Pardon?

MAUDE: I'll look different then. Will you still love me with a nose job?

HARRY: I hadn't thought about it.

MAUDE: Do you really think my nose looks funny?

HARRY: No. I think it looks fine.

MAUDE: Really?

HARRY: Yes.

MAUDE: Not too bent?

HARRY: No.

Pause.

MAUDE: I wonder how much a nose job would cost. (*HARRY looks up.*) What if it's expensive? Could you afford it?

HARRY: Probably.

MAUDE: Maybe, I'll get one done. I really don't like my nose, Harry.

HARRY: Mmmmmmmmmhmmmmm.

MAUDE: I think it's ugly. It's a blot upon my face. You know. A real blot.

HARRY: Mmmmmmmmm.

Pause.

MAUDE: Have you always thought my nose was ugly?

HARRY gets up, walks over to MAUDE, picks her up and throws her down the stairs.

Scene Twenty-one

Hospital room.

DOCTOR: I'm terribly sorry, Mrs. Parker. I don't know how to say this. I'm afraid I must apologize.

MOO: What?

DOCTOR: I said I'm sorry. Really very terribly sorry.

MOO: Sorry.

DOCTOR: Yes. Sorry.

MOO: Oh. (*pause*) Why?

DOCTOR: It's all been a terrible mistake. We're very sorry, aren't we, Nurse?

NURSE: Oh yes, we are.

DOCTOR: You see and oh, it's some embarrassment to us.

NURSE: Yes—it is.

DOCTOR: Well, we have discovered that you have two sisters. And I must apologize for not believing your story. That you really do have sisters.

MOO: Sisters?

DOCTOR: Yes. I thought that Mr. Parker's prolonged absence was suspicious, and so decided to look up the names you'd given us in the telephone book and I called Mrs. MacDowell and she said yes, indeed, she was your mother and they'd been looking for you for the last five years. They didn't look too hard, apparently, because you'd run off with Mr. Parker and told them not to come looking for you. Still, it was a long time. Is your family often like that?

MOO: Who?

DOCTOR: So, your sister, Sarah, is coming to pick you up.

MOO: My sister.

DOCTOR: Yes.

MOO: You're sure I have a sister.

DOCTOR: Yes.

MOO: And Harry is not my brother.

DOCTOR: No, of course not.

MOO: Harry is my husband.

DOCTOR Yes. So, it's all settled. We'll get your things. (*motions for NURSE to leave*)

MOO: Where is Harry?

DOCTOR: Oh. Well. Now, that's another problem which I didn't really want to broach quite yet.

MOO: Where is Harry?

DOCTOR: Well, we received this in the mail last week. We didn't show it to you because we thought it might upset you.

MOO: What is it?

DOCTOR: It's a postcard.

MOO: Let's see it. (*DOCTOR hands it to her.*) It's a desert island.

DOCTOR: Yes, pretty isn't it? Now, let's have it back.

MOO: (*turns it over and reads*)
"On the black sands of Montserrat,
People live and die,
How 'bout that.
Harry."

DOCTOR: Your sister will come for you tomorrow.

MOO: Where is Montserrat?

DOCTOR: We'll get your clothes.

MOO: (*stares at postcard*) I'll have to find him.

DOCTOR: Yes. He owes us money.

Scene Twenty-two

SARAH: Oh Moo, you poor dear!

DITTY: I think it's absolutely dreadful. Don't you agree, Father?

MR. MACDOWELL: Oh yes. Dreadful.

MOO: Do we have an atlas?

MRS. MACDOWELL: Yes, dear, it's on the shelf.

MOO goes to shelf, gets atlas and leafs through it while everyone else is talking.

MRS. MACDOWELL: He was a R-E-A-A-L RRRotter.

SARAH: I knew he was a rotter the moment I laid eyes on him.

DITTY: So did I.

SARAH: No, you didn't. You would have done just what Mooley did.

DITTY: Would not.

SARAH: Would too.

MRS. MACDOWELL: I never liked him. He had shifty black eyes.

MOO: They were large and blue, Mother.

MRS. MACDOWELL: Still, they were shifty. don't care how large they were. They moved around a lot. I didn't trust him as far as I could spit. None of us liked him.

MOO: Father liked him.

SARAH: That doesn't count. Father likes everyone.

MR. MACDOWELL: I think it's dreadful.

DITTY: Poor Moo.

SARAH: Poor Moo.

MRS. MACDOWELL: He was a real rotter.

MR. MACDOWELL: Handsome bastard.

SARAH: Oh, did you think he was handsome. I suppose so if you like that type.

MRS. MACDOWELL: He must have hypnotized you, Moo. That's all I can say.

MOO: Mother, why is it when anything untoward happens, it means someone's been hypnotized.

MRS. MACDOWELL: It's the only rational explanation for it. Otherwise, I can't account for why you ran off with that dreadful man.

MOO: Maybe I loved him.

MRS. MACDOWELL: That's just it. You couldn't possibly have loved such a man. He must have hypnotized you.

MOO: I don't want to discuss it.

MRS. MACDOWELL: We're not discussing it. We're sympathizing. Stop flipping through that atlas.

DITTY: Poor Moo.

MOO: Will you stop saying that?

MRS. MACDOWELL: Well, it's all right now, Mooley. You're back home where you belong. We won't say another word about it. (long pause) It's unbelievable that anyone could do such a thing. Why would he sign you away like that?

MOO: Maybe he thought I had money.

MRS. MACDOWELL: Yes. But we have money. You don't have money. He must have realized that.

MOO: I don't know why then.

MR. MACDOWELL: I think it's dreadful.

DITTY: Poor Moo.

SARAH: What a rotter.

MOO: Where is Montserrat?

MRS. MACDOWELL: Pardon?

MR. MACDOWELL: Pardon?

MOO: Where is Montserrat?

MRS. MACDOWELL: Oh, I don't know.

MOO: Do you know where it is, Father?

MR. MACDOWELL: What?

MOO: Forget it.

MRS. MACDOWELL: Africa, I think.

MOO: Are you sure?

MRS. MACDOWELL: I think it's off Africa. Or is it South America? Oh well, it's down there somewhere. Why?

MOO: I think I'd like to get away for a while.

MRS. MACDOWELL: You've just been away.

MOO: I was locked up. It's not quite the same thing.

MRS. MACDOWELL: I suppose you could use a vacation. (to MR. MACDOWELL) What do you think, dear?

MR. MACDOWELL: Mmmm?

MRS. MACDOWELL: Moo wants to go away. What do you think?

MR. MACDOWELL: She's been away.

MRS. MACDOWELL: Yes, yes, dear, we've been through all that. She wants to go—where do you want to go, dear?

MOO: I'm not sure.

MRS. MACDOWELL: I think you better take Ditty. I don't want you travelling by yourself. You're not well.

DITTY: If she's going to Montserrat, I'm not going.

MRS. MACDOWELL: Why not, dear?

DITTY: In the first place, we don't know where it is. In the second—

MOO: DAMMIT!!! IT'S NOT IN HERE! IT'S NOT IN HERE!!! (slams book)

Scene Twenty-three

HARRY, in tropical paradise.

HARRY: Some people eat you alive. They'll consume you utterly if you let them. They'll pick you up, take you in, give you a good mulching over and then spit you out, till there's nothing left but little bones. And then they wonder why they don't want you anymore. And the worst of it is you don't know this is going to happen when you meet them. A sign should be there. Bells should ring. An angel of mercy should shoot down from the sky and wave flags and banners. But no, nothing happens. You blithely saunter into your doom because at that particular moment, you have nothing better to do.

Moo. Sweet, demure when I first met her. Well, as demure as you can get when you're brandishing a .22 calibre rifle. That should have tipped me off. But no, I was feeling rather cocky that day. Sure of myself. So, there it was, that sweet, small little woman gets hold of a small part of my soul and, before I know it, she's in there with an oyster knife, trying to pry the whole thing out. I'm sorry. Sometimes it all comes down to a question of pure, simple survival. Dammit. I wish I didn't love her. I'd give my soul not to love her. I'm fed to the teeth with loving her.

Scene Twenty-four

Montserrat. Hotel room. HARRY, in bed. There is a knock at the door.

HARRY: Who's there?

VOICE: Room service.

HARRY: (*goes to answer door*) I didn't ask for room service.

MOO: (*stands in doorway*) Hello, Harry.

HARRY: Jesus.

MOO: Aren't you going to invite me in?

HARRY: Oh—well—ah—(*grabs her, drags her in, frisks her*)

MOO: What are you doing?

HARRY: Sorry—it's just that—

MOO: Did you think I had a gun or something?

HARRY: It crossed my mind.

MOO: I'm not angry with you, Harry.

HARRY: You should be, Moo.

MOO: I forgive you, Harry.

HARRY: I don't want to be forgiven.

MOO: It's all right, Harry. I forgive you. We can start all over again.

HARRY: I don't want to start over again. I want you to forget about me. Hate me. Anything. Just stay away from me.

MOO: I don't hate you, Harry.

HARRY: I had you committed, Moo. I put you in a loony bin. You might still be there.

MOO: I got out.

HARRY: I should have figured that.

MOO: And I've come back to you.

HARRY: Christ. Where's your pride? Don't you have any dignity? Can't you muster up some self-respect?

MOO: Harry, you know you love me.

HARRY: I don't, Moo.

MOO: You're just saying that.

HARRY: I married you for your money.

MOO: And you're welcome to it.

HARRY: I don't want don't want it anymore. I don't want you!

MOO: You just don't want to admit it. It frightens you, doesn't it? I have a power over you and—

HARRY: You don't have any power over me, Moo.

MOO: It frightens you.

HARRY: I was unfaithful to you, Moo. Those nights when I came home at 4:30, I was screwing Maude Gormley.

MOO: It was just your way, Harry.

HARRY: What!

MOO: You had to prove to yourself that you didn't love me.

HARRY: I succeeded.

MOO: So, you had trivial affairs.

HARRY: They weren't trivial, Moo. Maude was a great screw.

MOO: A screw, though. That's all she was.

HARRY: I wouldn't say that, exactly.

MOO: Why do I frighten you, Harry? (*starts to unbutton blouse*)

HARRY: You don't frighten me. Ah, what are you doing?

MOO: I'm unbuttoning my blouse.

HARRY: Stop it.

MOO: Why, Harry? You're not attracted to me. You just said so.

HARRY: Yes—

MOO: So, it shouldn't make any difference to you if I unbutton my blouse. It's not going to affect you. Not Harry.

She removes a shoe, puts her leg up on the chair close to HARRY, and slowly removes her stocking.

HARRY: I would like you to stop.

MOO: It's very hot in here, Harry. You shouldn't have come to Montserrat in the off-season. (*removes other stocking*)

HARRY: Jesus.

MOO: What's the matter, Harry? Am I affecting you?

She performs a slow strip tease.

HARRY: No. You're not!

MOO: Good. I'm glad. That's a load off my mind.

MOO is stripped to bra and panties. She approaches HARRY.

HARRY: Get away from me.

MOO: Why are you afraid of me?

HARRY: Dammit. I am not afraid of you.

MOO: Prove it.

HARRY: DAMN YOU, WHAT DOES IT TAKE TO CONVINCE YOU!!

HARRY grabs MOO by the shoulders and shakes her. MOO interrupts him by putting her arms around him and kissing him. HARRY resists at first, then responds. They embrace passionately.

MOO: You love me, Harry. You know that.

HARRY: (*wearily*) Yes, Moo. I love you.

MOO: Good.

Scene Twenty-five

Early morning. HARRY and MOO are in bed. He wakes up and glances at her. She is sleeping soundly. He sneaks out of bed, starts to pack clothes. She moans. He freezes, waits for a movement from her. She goes back to sleep. He hurries, finishes packing and steals out the door.

MOO: Mmmmm (*reaches*) Mmmmmm Harry? Harry? (*sits up*) HAAAAAAAAAAARRRRRY!!!!!!!

ACT TWO

Scene One

1960. HARRY and his third wife, PATSY, sitting in front of the television set. He is about 60 years old. She is slightly younger.

HARRY: You know, I was a heartbreaker in my youth.

PATSY: You?

HARRY: Don't act so surprised. Yes, I was a cad.

PATSY: Gowan.

HARRY: I was. A real heartbreaker.

PATSY: AAAW come off it, Harry, you're a real sweet guy.

HARRY: Now, maybe. But not then. I've been married twice, you know.

PATSY: I'm sure you didn't mean it, dear.

HARRY: Yes. I did. Both times. For a year there, I was a bigamist. Saw both of them. Did a lot of commuting.

PATSY: You're a kidder, Harry.

HARRY: I threw my second wife down the stairs.

PATSY: Did she upset you?

HARRY: Well, yeah. I guess so. I guess that's why I threw her down the stairs. Can't really remember why. Curious, isn't it? I could always call her up and ask her. She'd remember.

PATSY: You must have had a reason, Harry.

HARRY: I think I was mad at her.

PATSY: There you are.

HARRY: You're a wonderful woman, Patsy.

PATSY: Harry.

Pause.

HARRY: I put my first wife in an insane asylum.

PATSY: Why was that, dear?

HARRY: She was crazy. I was mad at her. Something to do at the time.

PATSY: I'm sure you weren't thinking, dear.

HARRY: I knew what I was doing.

PATSY: Harry.

HARRY: You don't believe me, do you? I threw her in, locked the door and threw away the key.

PATSY: Did she get out?

HARRY: Oh yeah.

PATSY: Well, no harm done then, is there?

HARRY: No. No harm done. (*pause*) She's mad as a hatter now, though.

PATSY: Have you seen her recently?

HARRY: No.

PATSY: How do you know then?

HARRY: She was crazy when I last saw her.

PATSY: When was that?

HARRY: Oh. Let's see now. Twenty years ago.

PATSY: You don't know then, do you? She might not be mad. She might be dead for all you know.

HARRY: That's true. She might be dead.

PATSY: And if she's dead, then it's all over and done with and you've nothing to worry about.

HARRY: That's true, Patsy. That's very true. (*pause*) What if she's alive?

PATSY: You should send her a Christmas card and let her know you're thinking of her.

HARRY: I don't think so.

PATSY: Huh.

HARRY: I don't think I want to send her a Christmas card.

PATSY: Suit yourself. Everyone likes to get cards though.

Pause.

HARRY: Did anyone ever put a bullet through your brain, Patsy?

PATSY: You're a kidder, Harry.

Scene Two

HARRY: (*alone on stage*) I dream about her. Not all the time, of course. But she's a constant in my life. Years pass and I'm not even aware of it. She's still right where I left her. Raging at me. Loving me. Cursing me for my lack of faith. Faith—coming from her, that's a good one. Most suspicious woman I ever met. Why did I not have faith, she said. I couldn't. I knew she would suck the very life out of me. It's safer this way. Safer to seek shelter. In someone else's flaccid heart.

Scene Three

Moo's sixtieth birthday party. There is one main table with MOO, WALLY, DITTY, SARAH and CHARLIE, SARAH's husband, JANE, SARAH's daughter, and SUSAN, JANE's daughter. The other relatives are at other tables in the room.

CROWD: SPEECH SPEECH! COME ON, CHARLIE!!

CHARLIE: (*rises*) Hhhhhhhmph Hmmmm. Today, erhem, erhem we are celebrating the, erhem, sixtieth birthday …

MOO: You don't have to say which birthday, Charlie.

CHARLIE: Right. Hemm, hemm. Right. The birthday of a most venerable woman …

MOO: I'm not a Chinese ancestor, Charlie.

CHARLIE: Right.

SARAH: Let him get on with it, Mooley.

CHARLIE: Woman, erhem, er, er, a woman—uh—(*pause*) who stands on her own, of course, not simply an—

WALLY is pawing MOO.

MOO: Hooooooh! Wally! (*giggles*)

CHARLIE: Yes, yes, of course, a woman of many diverse talents.

MOO: Stop it, Wally! (*giggles*)

WALLY: (*snorting laugh*) Ooooooooh Mooley …

CHARLIE: Painter. Many of you young people might not realize that your great-aunt Moo was a student of Emily Carr.

SUSAN: Who's Emily Carr?

JANE: Ssssh. Susan.

CHARLIE: Pardon? Did someone say something?

JANE: You shouldn't interrupt your grandfather when he's making a speech.

SUSAN: But Mummy, who's Emily Carr?

JANE: She painted trees. Now shut up.

CHARLIE: Now where was I?

SUSAN: Emily Carr. She painted trees.

CHARLIE: Oh yes. (*with great gravity*) Emily Carr painted trees. (*pause*) I don't think I intended to say that.

MOO: EEEEEEEK! Wally! My God, you're disgusting.

WALLY: Have another shot, Mooley. (*pours her more wine*)

CHARLIE: And Moo painted trees, too. Yes and some people say hers were better than Emily's. Hem, hem.

DITTY: You've got that story all wrong, Charlie.

CHARLIE: Mmmmph.

DITTY: I painted trees. Moo couldn't paint to save her life.

MOO: Ditty, you dodo brain. I painted that tree and you know it.

DITTY: You did not.

MOO: Did too!

DITTY: Did not!

MOO: Did too!

SARAH: Would you two please shut up! It's your birthday, Mooley. Remember that and behave yourself.

CHARLIE: Yes—well—where was I? Aside from being a painter, Moo is a remarkable cook.

DITTY: Remarkable is right.

MOO: (*to DITTY*) What did you say?

CHARLIE: We have been treated to the world's cuisines …

DITTY: Dogfish.

CHARLIE: At the capable hands of Moo.

DITTY: No one else would try and make a meal out of dogfish.

SARAH: Ditty!

CHARLIE: And today, hem, hem—

WALLY tries to pull MOO's dress off her shoulder.

SUSAN: Mummy, what is that old man trying to do!

JANE: He's making a speech. Sssssh.

SUSAN: Not Grandpa. Him! (*points to WALLY*)

JANE: He's trying to pull her dress off. Now shut up!

SUSAN: But why, Mummy?

MOO: I'm an old fucking woman as of today.

WALLY continues to maul MOO.

CHARLIE: She's an old fucking …

SARAH: Charlie!

CHARLIE: Oh sorry. Right—hem, hem—

SARAH: A toast, dear.

CHARLIE: Right. So, let's propose a toast to Moo. Sixty years old today. Will you all please rise.

Everyone, except for MOO and WALLY, rises.

CHARLIE: (*with glass raised*) To Moo!

CROWD: To Moo!

CHARLIE turns round to face MOO, who is under the table with WALLY.

MOO: (*giggling*) Oh Wally!

WALLY snorts.

SUSAN: What a creepy old man.

MOO: I'm an old fucking woman as of today.

WALLY: You'll never be too old for me, Mooley.

MOO: A corpse wouldn't be too old for you, SnortSnort.

CHARLIE: Yes. Well. To Moo.

CROWD: To Moo.

MOO: I'll drink to that. (*giggles*)

They politely try to ignore the commotion under the table. JANE walks over to SARAH and drags her off to one side.

JANE: This is disgraceful. I asked you not to invite him.

SARAH: Moo likes him.

JANE: That is apparent.

SARAH: It's her birthday.

JANE: Must she celebrate here and now.

SARAH: I don't think she's doing anything wrong.

MOO giggles.

JANE: Have you looked, Mother?

SARAH: No. Have you?

JANE: Certainly not!

DITTY: I'll look.

SARAH: Ditty!

SUSAN: (*walks up to JANE*) Why is she called Moo, Mummy?

JANE: Not now, dear.

SUSAN: Why have I never seen her before?

DITTY: You're not seeing much of her now, either.

SUSAN wanders over to the main table.

JANE: SUSAN! (*SUSAN wanders back.*) She does a lot of travelling.

SUSAN: Gee, that must be exciting. I'd like to travel.

MOO: (*rises from beneath table*) That's enough, Wally. (*giggles*) Jane, little Janie, did you arrive late? I didn't see you. Wally's been very distracting. How the hell are ya?

JANE: Mmmmph.

MOO: Oh Jane—sorry—oh sorry, Jane, gotta watch the language in front of the kid.

JANE: My daughter, Susan.

MOO: So, you two finally had a kid. (*to SUSAN*) Hi, kiddo, I'm your aunt Moo-Cow.

SUSAN: You have a funny name.

MOO: Don't we all, kiddo. Don't we all. Sarah, this is a great party. Just great. Almost makes me forget I'm an old trout now. Never too old to play with Wally. Isn't he disgusting? I think he's the most repulsive man I've ever come across. And that's saying something.

JANE: He certainly is vile.

MOO: Hey Wally, SnortSnort, what are you doing with that piano?

WALLY: Tuning.

MOO: Let's see. (*goes over to join WALLY*)

JANE: She gets more garrulous every year.

SUSAN: What's garrulous, Mummy?

SARAH: She's had a very unhappy life.

JANE: That's no excuse.

There is a knock at the door. SUSAN goes to answer it

SUSAN: (*returns*) Mummy, there's a telegram for Aunt Moo.

JANE: You give it to her, dear.

SUSAN: (*walks over to MOO and WALLY*) Oh Aunt Moo—here's a telegram for you.

MOO: (*takes it*) Thanks kiddo. (*opens it, reads and screams*) AAAAAAAAaaaaahhh! (*rails around the room, knocks tables over, hurls furniture about*) THE BASTARD THE FUCKING BASTARD!!! (*runs out of the room*)

SARAH: Moo?

WALLY: Moo?

SARAH: What's got into her?

DITTY: She's had too much to drink.

JANE: The telegram.

WALLY: (*walks over to telegram, opens it and reads*)
"On the white sands of Micronesia,
People live and die,
Just to please ya."

(*looks up, confused*) Who's Harry?

Scene Four

Moo, aged 65, and SUSAN, aged 13. MOO is wearing a muumuu and beads about her neck. She is sitting cross-legged on the floor and drinking gin.

MOO: Never give the suckers a break, kiddo. Know what I mean?

SUSAN: I wish you were my mother, Aunt Moo.

MOO: Pardon?

SUSAN: I do. I hate my mother. She never lets me do anything I want. And she's so straight.

MOO: Straight. (*pours more gin*)

SUSAN: You know, everything follows in a straight line for her. Cause and effect. Cause and effect. It's so boring. I hate it.

MOO: Your mother's a special case, kiddo. Sarah spent a lot of time raising her to be nice and proper. Ruined her for good.

SUSAN: Why couldn't you be my mother. You'd be a perfect mother for me.

MOO: No, I wouldn't.

SUSAN: Why, Aunt Moo?

MOO: We've got more important things to discuss, kiddo. Now, what was I saying?

SUSAN: Never give the suckers a break.

MOO: Right. And the only thing men understand is sex. Know what I mean?

SUSAN: I think so.

MOO: And you don't give it to them. Here's a little song you should know. (*sings*)

"I'm just gonna keep sitting on it,
'fore I'm gonna give it away."

Whenever you get thoughtful, just sing that song. It'll smarten you up.

SUSAN: I'm only thirteen, Aunt Moo.

MOO: They start them young in Micronesia. Now, I've been taking these anthropology courses.

SUSAN: Anthropology?

MOO: Study of man. It's essential these days. Particularly if you're a woman. Now, some of these books claim that man is essentially a wanderer. The men are out there hunting and stuff while the woman sits at home and watches the camp. But other books say that there are societies where it's totally reversed. The women are the ones who are out screwing around while the men have to do all the boring stuff.

SUSAN: Micronesia?

MOO: Samoa. So, the key thing to remember is don't get married and don't let any man run your life. Right?

SUSAN: Right.

MOO: I'll drink to that. (*sips gin*)

SUSAN: So, what should we do?

MOO: Do?

SUSAN: Yeah. What should we do? How should we start?

MOO: Hell, I don't know. Do we have to start right away? Can't we sit and talk about it for a while?

SUSAN: I think we should start.

MOO: Well, you go right ahead, kiddo. You go right ahead.

Scene Five

SUSAN: I want to be just like Aunt Moo when I grow up.

JANE: No, you don't.

SUSAN: Yes, I do, Mum. Boy, remember the way she threw that furniture around. That was fun!

JANE: That wasn't funny, Susan. Your Aunt Moo is a very sick woman.

SUSAN: I want to be just like her. I'll never get married. I'll have boyfriends instead. Well, not like Wally. He was really repulsive. I'll get some nice boyfriends and I can do whatever I like with them.

JANE: Don't you want to get married, dear?

SUSAN: Like you, Mum?

JANE: Well—yes.

SUSAN: No way. What a bore. What a fucking bore.

JANE: WHAT DID YOU SAY!

SUSAN: Sorry.

JANE: I don't like the way you visit her all the time. It's affecting you. What do you talk about, anyway?

SUSAN: Everything. Women's rights, labour unions, female oppression—

JANE: She looks absolutely ridiculous. In that stupid muumuu and wearing those silly beads around her neck. Who does she think she is anyway?

SUSAN: She's liberated, Ma.

JANE: The hell she is. She's obsessed.

Scene Six

DITTY is at MOO's apartment. They are hanging curtains while standing precariously on a book-case.

DITTY: We worry about you, Mooley.

MOO: Who worries about me?

DITTY: Sarah and I.

MOO: I'm happy by myself.

DITTY: You live like a hermit, dear. What if something happened to you? Who'd ever find out about it?

MOO: No one, I suppose.

DITTY: And what would happen to you?

MOO: I'd die, I guess.

DITTY: That's not good enough, Moo.

MOO: Can you pass me some of those curtain hooks?

DITTY: (*reaches down to a ledge on the bookcase, picks up some hooks*) You drink too much.

MOO: It's none of your business, Dit.

DITTY: We're your family.

MOO: I don't want you. Doesn't that ever dawn on you. What good are you anyway. You're always trying to have me put away somewhere.

DITTY: Harry did that, Moo.

MOO: Well, what about this old folks home you want to stick me into.

DITTY: It's not an old folks home. It's a hotel for retired people.

MOO: Why me? Why not you? You're older than me.

DITTY: But you don't have anyone, Moo. It's bad for someone to be by themselves as much as you are.

MOO: You know, I've never stopped looking for him, Dit. I've travelled all over the world looking for him.

DITTY: That was silly of you, Moo.

MOO: Obsessive. I can't help it.

DITTY: He's living in Seattle.

MOO: WHAT!

DITTY: He married Maude Gormley and he's living in Seattle.

MOO: MAUDE!

DITTY: I thought you knew that, Moo.

MOO: Maude Gormley.

DITTY: Everyone knew, Moo. Didn't anyone tell you?

MOO: AAAAAAGH! (*falls off the bookcase*)

DITTY: OH MOO! OH MOOLEY!! (*teeters on top of bookcase*) Oh dear, Moocow. (*jumps, lands on MOO*)

MOO: OOOOOOOOWWW!

DITTY: Of course, I think they got divorced and I think he's married someone else. He threw her down the stairs. Maude, that is. Not his new wife. (*MOO groans.*) Oh Moo, I'm sorry to upset you. I thought you knew. We all thought you knew.

MOO: Get off.

DITTY: She was very angry. Enough was enough, she said. My God, that was years ago. It all seems like yesterday.

MOO: GET OFF.

DITTY: Pardon, Moo.

MOO: My hip.

DITTY: Oh Moo. We do worry about you. (*gets off*) Are you all right?

MOO: Hospital.

DITTY: Pardon, Moo?

MOO: Hospital. I can't move.

DITTY: Oh dear. Oh no. Oh now, Mooley. Oh dear. Oh no.

MOO: Call the hospital.

DITTY: Oh dear. I always panic. Oh dear, where's the phone?

MOO: JESUS F. CHRIST.

DITTY: Don't get upset, Moo. Lie still. Keep calm. Remember, I'm here for you.

MOO: JESUS F. CHRIST. SINGAPORE, HONG KONG, MONTSERRAT, MICRONESIA. ALL THIS TIME IT'S BEEN GODDAMN SEATTLE. JESUS F. CHRIST.

Scene Seven

Nursing home. MOO is in bed.

NURSE: We have a surprise for you, Miss Parker.

MOO: Mrs. Parker. Goddammit!

NURSE: My, my, let's not be cranky.

MOO: I can be as cranky as I like. I'm paying you to let me be cranky.

NURSE: Now, Miss Parker, your relatives are paying for your stay here.

MOO: Big deal. Goddamned hell hole. Why am I with all these old people, anyway? Why aren't I with the broken hip people? I hate hospitals.

NURSE: This isn't a hospital.

MOO: What!

NURSE: This is a nursing home.

MOO: WHAT! (*starts to get up*)

NURSE: Now please, Miss Parker. Don't move or you'll aggravate that hip.

MOO: Get out of my way. (*tries to get up*) OW! (*falls back in bed*)

NURSE: Now, see what I said. (*to doorway*) Oh, she's really in a bad state. I don't think she should see you.

DITTY: Nonsense! Moo! Moo, it's me.

MOO: Get away from me, you old cow!

DITTY: Oh Mooley, what have they done to you?

MOO: They? You, you mean!

DITTY: Oh Moo, so angry.

MOO: Get your long false teeth away from me.

DITTY: Oh Mooley, what's happened to you? And your hip? Is your hip all right?

MOO: Who put you up to it? Did Sarah put you up to it?

DITTY: I don't know what you're talking about. (*to NURSE*) Is she all right?

NURSE: About the same.

MOO: (*mimics*) Is your hip all right? You jumped on it. You should know.

DITTY: No Mooley, I didn't jump on your hip. I fell.

MOO: Fell! Ha!

SARAH: (*enters*) Sorry, I'm late. Moo darling, how are you?

MOO: It was your idea, wasn't it? Lock me up for good this time.

SARAH: (*to DITTY*) What's she talking about?

MOO: (*to DITTY*) Don't try to deny it. I saw you looking at me. Goddammit, you paused, counted to three and then you jumped.

DITTY: I did not jump on your hip.

MOO: I watched you from the ground. I saw your lips move.

DITTY: Well, whose fault was it that I was on top of your rickety old bookcase.

MOO: I asked you to help me hang the curtains. I didn't ask you to jump on my hip.

DITTY: Well, what was I to do. I had to get down somehow.

MOO: You could have jumped on your own hip. You didn't need to jump on mine.

SARAH: Moo? Are you going senile?

MOO: So help me, you may think you've got me right where you want me. But I'm getting out of here if it's the last thing I do.

SARAH: Yes, dear. Whatever you say, dear.

MOO: Don't humour me. I mean it.

DITTY: She's going senile, isn't she, Sarah?

SARAH: Yes, dear. I'm afraid she is.

MOO: SENILE!!

SARAH: Too much gin.

MOO: THAT'S IT. OUT, OUT! EVERYBODY OUT!!!

Scene Eight

HARRY sits in a large black easy chair. There is a large globe on a stand beside the chair. He spins it occasionally.

HARRY: Sometimes, I send her postcards. Spite, I suppose. It's a thing with me. Express the universe on a four-by-six card. Of course, I make them totally banal. I know that will irritate her. I like to go to small far-off places of the globe (*laughs*) and send her postcards. (*laughs*) And I never write: "Having a wonderful time. Wish you were here." (*laughs*) I never say: "Wish you were here." (*laughs*)

Scene Nine

Moo and her son, DOUGALL. He is wearing a hat and playing with a capgun.

DOUGALL: Mummy, when's Daddy coming home?

MOO: I've told you, kiddo. He's not coming home.

DOUGALL: Are you going to Bora Bora again? Can I stay with Aunt Sarah and Jane while you're away?

MOO: I'm not going to Bora Bora.

DOUGALL: Why not, Mummy?

MOO: You only go to those places once, kiddo.

DOUGALL: When are you going to go away?

MOO: I'm not going away.

DOUGALL: Why not, Mummy?

MOO: I'm tired of it. I've had enough.

DOUGALL: Oh. (*pause*) I could try and find him. When I grow up, I'll find Daddy for you.

MOO: I don't want him.

DOUGALL: Why not? What's wrong with him?

MOO: He's not here, is he. That's enough for a start.

DOUGALL: Jane says Daddy ran away. Did Daddy run away?

MOO: Look kiddo, I don't want to talk about it. It's all over and done with.

Pause.

DOUGALL: You got another postcard, Mummy.

MOO: What!

DOUGALL: It came in the mail today. I put it on the mantelpiece. Where's Banyu Wangi? (*MOO gets up.*) Mummy, mummy. Where're you going, Mummy?

MOO: (*rushes out*) See you later, kiddo.

Scene Ten

Hotel shack in Banyu Wangi. MOO arrives, soaking wet, with suitcase. The DESK CLERK is asleep. She rings the bell.

CLERK: (*starts up*) Oh! Oh! Many pardons. We no get visitors in Banyu Wangi in rainy season and now, two in one month.

MOO: Yes. Where is he?

CLERK: He?

MOO: Other visitor. Him man, no?

CLERK: Yes.

MOO: Where is he? What room?

CLERK: Him gone. Him no like rain.

MOO: When did he leave?

CLERK: Gone. Long ago.

MOO: When?

CLERK: You want room?

MOO: I'm not sure yet. When did he go?

CLERK: Rooms cost twelve renigos.

MOO: When did the man go?

CLERK: What man!

MOO: Man. Named Harry Parker. His name Harry Parker. No? (*CLERK stares at MOO.*) Oh. I see. (*takes out money*)

CLERK: (*takes money*) Tuan Parker left three weeks ago.

MOO: Where'd he go?

CLERK pauses. MOO pulls out more money.

CLERK: Me not know. Me think other islands.

MOO: That's all there is here. Nothing but bloody islands!

CLERK: Him go further east. Easter Island. Ha ha. Small joke. (*MOO takes back a bill.*) Sorry. Me think he go to Atapupu. Him might have gone to Pugobengo but me think he go to Atapupu. Him mention Kotomobagu. Him go to visit Tejakula then to Klungklung then he stay in Pugobengo. That when he mention Kotomabagu. (*MOO moans, collapses in nearby chair.*) But me try Atapupu. Atapupu nice. No rainy season now. Oh! Tuana lady no feel good. Here, you go to bed. Nice rooms here. You rest. (*draws her up*) Room three good. No roaches. You like. No jiggers. Some earwig, though. Stop up ears before sleeping. Otherwise earwig make home and nasty nasty. You get good rest.

CLERK leads MOO out.

Scene Eleven

Moo is unpacking. DOUGALL watches her.

MOO: (*brings out a small stuffed alligator*) There you are, kiddo. A nice stuffed alligator.

DOUGALL: Where's Daddy?

MOO: Your guess is as good as mine, kiddo.

DOUGALL: I want Daddy.

MOO: You can't have Daddy. How 'bout a nice stuffed alligator instead?

DOUGALL: I don't want a stuffed alligator. I want to see Daddy. You get to see Daddy. Why can't I see Daddy?

MOO: Who told you I saw your father?

DOUGALL: Jane.

MOO: She's telling you stories.

DOUGALL: I wish I had a father.

MOO: Oh Dougall. Stop it.

DOUGALL: But I'd like a father.

MOO: I brought you a shrunken head.

DOUGALL: You did! Oh Mummy!! Where is it, Mummy! Where is it!!! (*MOO pulls out a shrunken head.*) Oh. (*draws away*)

MOO: What's the matter, kiddo?

DOUGALL: (*whispers*) Is that Daddy?

MOO: Of course not.

DOUGALL: Who is it then?

MOO: I don't know. It's not anyone. It's a shrunken head.

DOUGALL stares at the head. MOO continues unpacking.

DOUGALL: Daddy, is that you? Was Mummy mean to you in Borneo?

MOO: (*hearing DOUGALL say "Daddy," stops unpacking and watches him*) WHAT THE HELL DO YOU THINK YOU'RE DOING!

DOUGALL: Oh! I'm just playing with him, Mummy.

MOO: You just called that shrunken head "Daddy." That is not your Daddy, Dougall. Do you hear me?

DOUGALL: Yes, Mummy.

MOO: It's a horrible thing anyway. I should never have brought it back. (*takes it from DOUGALL*)

DOUGALL: No, Mummy, no! Please let me have it. Please, please, please!

MOO: No. This one's going in a drawer. You're too young. It'll just give you bad dreams. (*puts it in a drawer*)

DOUGALL: Please, Mummy, please!

MOO: NO! (*closes drawer*) And that's final. Maybe when you're older. Now stop blubbering and play with your alligator.

DOUGALL: Yes, Mummy. (*MOO starts to leave.*) Where're you going, Mummy?

MOO: Mummy's going downstairs to pour herself a good stiff drink.

DOUGALL: Oh.

DOUGALL waits till MOO is gone. He goes over to the drawer, opens it and stares at the shrunken head.

Scene Twelve

SARAH, DITTY and MOO, who is gardening.

SARAH: You know, you really ought to think about getting married again, Moo. All this brooding isn't good for you.

MOO: I'm quite content, Sarah. I have Dougall.

SARAH: That's another thing, Moo. Ditty and I have been noticing and well, we really don't know quite how to put this, but you aren't exactly pleasant to your son.

MOO: What do you mean "pleasant"?

SARAH: Well. Nice, then.

DITTY: You aren't very nice to Dougall.

MOO: Dougall's never told me.

SARAH: No. I don't think he would. Children are like that.

DITTY: I don't even think he knows you're being mean to him.

MOO: Maybe, ladies, the possibility exists and please don't think I'm pressing a point but perhaps I'm not being mean to my son at all. Which is why he hasn't noticed. Which is why I haven't noticed. Which is just something you two meddling farts would imagine.

SARAH: Did you or did you not tell Dougall he was ugly?

MOO: (*to SARAH*) You told Dougall he didn't look like his father. (*to DITTY*) And you told Dougall his father was handsome. So Dougall put two and two together and came to the conclusion that he must be ugly. Which is not far off. He certainly is not an attractive boy.

SARAH: There! Now how can you say that about your own son.

MOO: Because it's true. The boy's homely. Maybe he'll outgrow it. Chances are he won't. But there's always hope.

SARAH: Jane says you told Dougall he was stupid.

MOO: Jane! What does your daughter have to do with it. Anyway, he's not that bright.

SARAH: You can't tell him that.

MOO: Well—do you think Dougall is highly intelligent?

SARAH: He's a dear, sweet boy.

MOO: Yes. But is he highly intelligent?

SARAH: Well—no—he isn't. But I just think that being his mother, you, of all people, should at least think he's intelligent.

MOO: Lie to him then.

SARAH: Try to be nicer. That's all. Now, Charlie's brother Arthur—

MOO: NO.

SARAH: But Moo, I haven't—

MOO: No. I don't want to meet him. He'll be just like his brother. Boring!

SARAH: Charles and I have been very happy together and I've never found him boring.

MOO: Do you know why that is?

SARAH: Compatibility, I expect.

MOO: No, osmosis. Now, you're both boring.

SARAH: WELL, I'VE …

DITTY: Montserrat.

MOO: What!

DITTY: He's just come back from Montserrat.

SARAH: We thought you'd have a lot to talk about. Just meet him. It can't hurt.

MOO: All right.

SARAH: Good. And Moo!

MOO: Yes, Sarah.

SARAH: Try to be nice.

MOO: Yes, Sarah.

Scene Thirteen

DOUGALL: Why'd you have to get rid of Daddy?

MOO: That man was not your Daddy, Dougall.

DOUGALL: Well, why'd you get rid of him? I liked Uncle Arthur.

MOO: You hardly knew him.

DOUGALL: He played ball with me.

MOO: I could play ball with you.

DOUGALL: You're never here.

MOO: You could play ball with Jane then.

DOUGALL: Jane can't catch. And she can't throw either. What's wrong with Uncle Arthur? He and Uncle Charlie are really funny. They tell good jokes. This man met this girl and his friend said: "What's she like?" and the guy said "Well, she's sort of pretty and she's sort of ugly, so guess I'd say she was both. PRETTY UGLY!" Ha! Ha! Isn't that funny, Mummy.

MOO: A laugh riot.

DOUGALL: (throws himself on the ground in a huge fit of temper) WELL, I THOUGHT IT WAS FUNNY! I had a good time with Uncle Arthur and now I don't have a daddy anymore. All the kids at school are going to ask me where my new daddy went to. They're going to think I made him up. They already think I made you up. And if you go away again, they'll know I made you up! (bursts into tears)

MOO: Stop snivelling. I am not going away.

DOUGALL: Jane says my old Daddy sends you postcards and you go off to meet him. Why can't I meet him, too?

MOO: Jane is a spiteful little brat and she's dead wrong. I used to get postcards from your father but I told him not to send them anymore. I travel because I enjoy travelling.

DOUGALL: Then why can't I come with you?

MOO: You have school.

DOUGALL: You just don't want me to come. (pulls out postcard) Here! Take it!

MOO: (grabs postcard) Oh, Dougall.

DOUGALL: It came in the mail today.

MOO: (reads) Novo Rodondo. (looks at DOUGALL) I could try and bring him back.

DOUGALL: I know why you go.

MOO: Dougall?

DOUGALL: Go on! Go! You two play your stupid little game! See if I care. (storms out)

Scene Fourteen

MOO and DOUGALL. He, aged sixteen, enters in army uniform.

DOUGALL: How do I look?

MOO: Dreadful. I hate uniforms.

DOUGALL: I think I look pretty good.

MOO: You're too young. You're only sixteen.

DOUGALL: I'm in and there's nothing you can do about it. This time, I'll get to see the world.

MOO: It's a pretty stupid way to go about it. It's not a pleasure cruise, Dougall. It's a war. You could get killed.

DOUGALL: Would that disturb you?

MOO: God, how melodramatic you are. It's really very tiresome.

DOUGALL: That's me. Ever present and tiresome.

MOO: Please don't try to be cynical, Dougall. It's unbecoming.

DOUGALL: You never take me seriously, do you. I simply don't exist for you. Well, I'm remedying the situation. I, too, am vanishing out of your life. (laughs) I'll send you a postcard.

MOO: What!

DOUGALL: I'll find him for you, Mother. Don't worry. We'll both write. Two postcards. A matching set! (*leaves*)

MOO: Dougall? DOUGALL!

Scene Fifteen

Moo in the nursing home.

MOO: The facts of life. I'm old and Harry Parker never loved me. I have done selfish things in my time, but I did them all out of a certain conviction that everything would come together. My youth and my love—foolish, frail self-deceits. I wallow in them. And my son. No point even thinking about him. No point even thinking about anything. I'm an old dog left out in the rain. No one likes my smell and it's time to die.

Scene Sixteen

Nursing home. MOO's room. SUSAN enters tentatively. She is carrying some presents.

SUSAN: Hello, Aunt Moo.

MOO: Who are you?

SUSAN: Susan.

MOO: Susan.

SUSAN: Susan. Your niece. You and I were going to move to Samoa.

MOO: I'm sorry. I don't remember you.

SUSAN: I brought you Christmas presents.

MOO: Oh. Is it Christmas already?

SUSAN: It will be. Next week. You haven't really forgotten me, have you, Aunt Moo? I know you got mad at me for not going to Samoa but I couldn't just then. I had to finish Grade Eleven. I know you haven't forgotten. You're just pretending. All the relatives say you're senile but I know you're not. Don't worry. I'll get you out of here. You've been shut up too long. That's all. Your hip's all better so I don't know why they're keeping you here. Do you want to escape?

MOO: Who are you?

SUSAN: I'll help you escape. What do you need? Ropes? A file?

MOO: Gin.

SUSAN: You shouldn't drink, Aunt Moo.

MOO: Gin. I want gin.

SUSAN: Here's your presents. (*hands them to her*)

MOO: Is there gin?

SUSAN: I don't think so.

MOO: (*takes present and sings*) Happy Birthday to me …

SUSAN: It's Christmas, Aunt Moo.

MOO: (*continues*) Happy Birthday to me, Happy Birthday to Moragh, Happy Birthday to me. (*opens present*) My Sin. My favourite perfume, you know. It suits me. One should always have a perfume that suits one. An essence to leave behind. Men hate perfume. But I wear it anyway. It tells them where I am. I used to wear this perfume as a joke. Of course, I liked the fragrance, but it was a joke. A sly joke. It backfired. I should have worn Joy. It would have been smarter to have worn Joy.

Pause.

SUSAN: I'm studying anthropology, Aunt Moo.

MOO: What?

SUSAN: You remember. We talked about it before. I have to ask you something.

MOO: Do you know those Chinese watercolour paintings? You know, the pretty pale ones with the little bird sitting on the jasmine branch—

SUSAN: This is important, Aunt Moo. I can't tell my mother. She'd have an absolute fit.

MOO: Whenever I see one of those paintings, with that tiny little bird sitting on the branch, do you know what I want to do? I want to take out my gun and shoot it! Blast its little brains out! (*bursts out laughing*) Isn't that awful?

SUSAN: Are you all right, Aunt Moo?

MOO: Of course, I'm just fine.

SUSAN: I have to tell you because you'd understand—

MOO: What perfume do you wear?

SUSAN: I don't wear perfume. You see—

MOO: How old are you?

SUSAN: Twenty.

MOO: Only twenty. You have your whole life ahead of you. (*laughs*)

Scene Seventeen

SUSAN: (*alone on stage*) Of course, he doesn't love his wife. She means nothing to him. Well, he hasn't exactly told me that. Not in so many words. But I can tell. I know he doesn't love her. I suppose it's in little things he does. The way he refers to her. As though she were an appendage. "Smith and I went down to the beach the other day. Of course, Smith likes all that stuff." He calls her "Smith," her maiden name. They went to school together and they used to call each other by their last names. He probably calls her "honey" when they're alone. Or "dear" so I'm not ruining a wonderful marriage. It's not as though they have something great going together. It's the pits. They have a perfectly lousy relationship. He's just used to her. That's all. She's like the weather. It's only a matter of time before he leaves her. It's just a matter of time.

Scene Eighteen

SUSAN: I'm not going.

JANE: (*holds out presents*) It'll only take a minute, dear.

SUSAN: I'm not going. Why do I always have to give her the presents? I go every year and she doesn't even remember me.

JANE: She doesn't remember anyone, dear.

SUSAN: She'd remember you, Mother.

JANE: Would you please just do this for me?

SUSAN: She hates the perfume, Mother.

JANE: Oh. It used to be her favourite.

SUSAN: Well, she hates it now.

JANE: Should I give her something else?

SUSAN: No. I think she's gotten used to hating it.

JANE: Please do this for me. She's had a very unhappy life.

SUSAN: You always say that, Mother. Do you really think that just because a man leaves you it should ruin your life.

JANE: Her son left her, too. And I think both of them disappear—

SUSAN: Her son.

JANE: Yes. Dougall.

SUSAN: She had a son?

JANE: Yes. He disappeared during the war.

SUSAN: She never told me she had a son. Why didn't she talk about him?

JANE: (*matter-of-fact*) She never liked him much. But I'm sure she missed him. Once he was gone. I don't think he ran away. She was cruel to him but he never seemed to mind. I don't think he even noticed it. She was his mother after all.

SUSAN: Mother, are you all right?

JANE: Yes. Yes, I'm all right.

SUSAN: Were you in love with him?

JANE: I loved him. Yes.

SUSAN: Did you have a love affair?

JANE: No. I just loved him. That's all.

SUSAN: Don't worry, Mother. I'll take the present to her.

JANE: Thank you, dear.

SUSAN: I'll take it every year from now on.

JANE: Thank you, dear.

Scene Nineteen

Nursing home. MOO's room.

SUSAN: (*enters with presents*) Merry Christmas, Aunt Moo.

MOO: Who are you?

SUSAN: Susan.

MOO: Do I know you?

SUSAN: You used to.

MOO: Sorry. I don't remember.

SUSAN: How about your son. Do you remember him?

MOO: (*muses*) My son.

SUSAN: We used to have long talks together. You and I. But you never mentioned your son. That was supposedly when you weren't senile. You had no excuse then.

MOO: I'm old and I'm tired. I'm sorry. I don't understand what you're saying.

SUSAN: Why didn't you ever tell me about your son?

MOO: (*points to presents*) Those are presents, aren't they? Are they for me?

SUSAN: I'd like to talk about your son. I don't want to talk about your presents, women's rights, female oppression, your fucking "topics." I want to know what you did to your son.

MOO: See this. (*rolls up sleeve*) The nurses did this to me.

SUSAN: (*grabs her and shakes her*) What about your son!

MOO: See, there's a bruise. Look at my bruise.

SUSAN: You're pathetic. You know that. You're absolutely pathetic. I'm not going to wind up like you. Rambling. Senile. All those years and you didn't even mention his name.

MOO: All I wanted was some cigs and they wouldn't let me have them.

SUSAN: We're different, you know. I'm not like you.

MOO: Do you have any cigs? (*starts to paw SUSAN for cigs*)

SUSAN: You're fucking feeble-minded and it's all because of some man.

MOO: They tried to take my lighter away from me but I wouldn't let them have it.

SUSAN: I know what I want and I'm going after it.

MOO: The nurses grabbed me and they pinched me (*grabs SUSAN's arm*) so I'd let go of the lighter. But I didn't let go.

SUSAN: (*grabs MOO and shakes her*) And I'm not letting go.

MOO: They pinched my arm but I didn't let go.

SUSAN: (*still shaking her*) I'm not letting go of you. You selfish old cow!

MOO: OW! OOOOOOOWW!! NURSE! NURSE! HELP ME NURSE!!!

ORDERLY: (*enters*) Miss Parker—

MOO: (*shakily, pointing to SUSAN*) This woman—

SUSAN: I'm sorry. I gave her the presents and she attacked me.

ORDERLY: Yes. She's been doing that a lot lately. You know how it is. The mind goes and they're just like children again.

SUSAN: Yes. I understand.

MOO: (*holds out arm to ORDERLY*) My bruise.

Scene Twenty

Nursing home. HARRY and PATSY enter. MOO is sitting in a chair nearby. HARRY sees MOO, stares at her.

PATSY: I couldn't keep an eye on her all the time. And I mean she couldn't live with us.

HARRY: Mmmmmm.

PATSY: Are you all right?

HARRY: Yeah.

PATSY: It's sweet you're getting so depressed about my mother.

HARRY: Yeah.

PATSY: Honey, do you mind waiting here. I just want to go back and make sure she's okay. It might be a bit of a shock for her. You don't mind, do you?

HARRY: Hurry.

PATSY: You're a doll. (*leaves*)

MOO: (*looks up, sees HARRY*) Do you have a cig?

HARRY: No.

MOO: Oh. (*pause; rolls up sleeve*) See this. The nurses did this to me. I wanted some cigs but the nurses wouldn't let me have them. I found some though but they tried to take them away from me. But I wouldn't let go.

HARRY: I'm sure they didn't mean to.

MOO: Yes. They did. They grabbed me and tried to pinch me till I let go. Like this. (*grabs HARRY's arm and pinches him*)

HARRY: OW!

MOO: They kept pinching and pinching but I wouldn't let go.

HARRY: Let go of me!

MOO: I held on and I wouldn't let go.

HARRY: Get the hell off me. (*throws her off his arm*)

MOO: They got my lighter, though. But they didn't get my cigs.

HARRY: Christ. What's happened to you. You're an old woman.

MOO: (*looks at him*) You're an old man.

HARRY: I guess I am. You don't remember, do you?

MOO: I could really use a cig.

HARRY: Here. (*hands her one*)

MOO: Thanks. Don't let the nurses know.

HARRY: No. I won't.

MOO: Do you have a light?

HARRY lights it for her.

PATSY: (*enters*) Sorry to take so long, dear. She's a bit upset. They gave her some sedatives so she should be all right.

HARRY: Let's go. (*starts to leave*)

MOO: Harry, HARRY!!

PATSY: That woman is pointing at you, dear. Do you know her?

HARRY: I lit her cigarette.

MOO: HARRY!!

PATSY: She knows your name.

HARRY: Coincidence. Come on, let's get out of here.

HARRY pushes PATSY out.

MOO: Harry. Are you going to send me a postcard? Do you have a postcard for me, Harry? Do you have a postcard?

Scene Twenty-one

Nursing home. MOO's room. Darkness. MOO is in bed, asleep.

HARRY: (*opens door*) Moo? (*goes to MOO, takes her hand*) What beautiful hands you have. You always had beautiful hands.

MOO: (*wakes up*) Harry!

HARRY: (*pulls out a small handgun, places MOO's hand on the gun*) Yes, Moo. It's me.

HARRY raises the gun to MOO's heart. MOO does not resist. She and HARRY pull the trigger. The gun goes off quietly. He leaves by the window.

Scene Twenty-two

HARRY and PATSY in front of the television set.

PATSY: Are you happy with me, Harry?

HARRY: Of course, Patsy.

PATSY: Really happy?

HARRY: Yes.

PATSY: You wouldn't rather be somewhere else.

HARRY: No. Not right now.

PATSY: I thought you always wanted to live on a desert island.

HARRY: I did.

PATSY: Do you still want to?

HARRY: Patsy, life with you is a desert island.

PATSY: Harry.

END

MICHEL MARC BOUCHARD (b. 1958)

Of the generation of Québécois playwrights following Michel Tremblay, two have most successfully bridged the gap dividing the solitudes of French- and English-Canadian theatre. Robert Lepage's markedly internationalist and spectacularly trans-linguistic approach has made his plays popular not just across Canada but world-wide. Michel Marc Bouchard has also garnered a national and international reputation, with many productions in English as well as Spanish, Italian, German, Dutch, Japanese, Polish, Scots and European French translations. Most of Bouchard's plays are rooted firmly within Quebec, specifically in Lac-Saint-Jean, the rural region north of Quebec City where he grew up. But their geographical and historical settings are often secondary to the imaginary worlds his characters evoke in order to make their lives more tolerable and more beautiful. Typically, they are isolated by sexual preference or artistic sensibility, wounded by physical or sexual abuse, devastated by family entanglements. Unable or unwilling to endure a "reality" too painful or too mundane, they resort to fantasy and myth, role-playing and story-telling. In *The Orphan Muses* four siblings try to come to terms with their mother's desertion twenty years earlier in a fascinating tale of cross-dressing, reconciliation and resurrection.

Born in the Lac-Saint-Jean village of Saint Coeur-de-Marie, Bouchard studied tourism at CEGEP, then theatre at the University of Ottawa, graduating with honours in 1980 and going to work as an actor with various Franco-Ontarian companies. Sudbury's Théâtre du Nouvel-Ontario produced his first play, *Les Porteurs d'eau* (1981), a musical about the economic exploitation of Lac-Saint-Jean at the turn of the century. It would prove atypical of his future work. His trademark style and themes were established by *Le Contre-nature de Chrysippe Tanguay, écologiste* (1983), produced by Montreal's Théâtre d'Aujourd'hui. In it, two gay men wanting to adopt a child immerse themselves in Greek mythology and role-playing fantasies about the women in their lives. The title character has the same last name as the family in *The Orphan Muses*, and Bouchard has referred to the two plays as part of the same series. Another in that series is *La Poupée de Pélopia* (1984), produced in English as *Pelopia's Doll*. This psychological drama about a master puppet-maker's incestuous relationship with his daughters garnered a Governor General's Award nomination.

Bouchard's breakthrough occurred with *Les Feluettes ou la Répétition d'un drame romantique* (1987), first produced by Montreal's Théâtre Petit à Petit and directed by Michel Tremblay's collaborator, André Brassard. A play within a play within a play set in 1952 with male actors playing the female roles, *Les Feluettes* tells a story of gay love, creative and delusional fantasy, abuse and betrayal at a Lac-Saint-Jean Catholic school in 1912. The English translation, *Lilies or The Revival of a Romantic Drama*, premiered at Theatre Passe Muraille in 1991, and the play has since been widely produced in Europe, Asia and South America. It won best play awards in Montreal, Ottawa, Toronto and Vancouver, and the 1996 film version, *Lilies*, directed by John Greyson, won Canada's Genie Award for best picture.

The Orphan Muses has a similar history. Directed by André Brassard for Théâtre d'Aujourd'hui as *Les Muses orphelines* (1988), it was a major success, revived (and revised) in Montreal in 1994 and again in 1995, followed by a tour of Quebec, winning the Grand prix littéraire du Journal de Montréal and the Prix du critiques de théâtre de l'Outaouis. The English version premiered at New York City's Ubu Repertory Theatre in 1993, followed by productions across Canada. It won multiple awards in Vancouver and Toronto including the 1999 Chalmers. The play was also translated for productions in France, Belgium, Germany, Italy, Mexico and Uruguay, and made into a film (*La Résurrection* [1999]—*The Orphan Muses* in subtitled English), directed by Guy Favreau.

Bouchard's other most produced and honoured play is *L'Histoire de l'oie* (1991), translated as *The Tale of Teeka* (1992). Staged in English and French by Théâtre des Deux Mondes, the story of a battered child who shares his fantasies with a goose has toured widely around the world, winning numerous awards as have its TV versions in both French and English. *Le Voyage du couronnement* (1995) had the honour of being the first Quebec play in fifteen years to premiere at Montreal's prestigious Théâtre du Nouveau Monde. Set aboard an ocean liner carrying various Quebeckers to the coronation of Queen Elizabeth in 1953, it focuses on a father's sexual sacrifice of his son in exchange for political favours. In translation as *The Coronation Voyage* (2000), it has had productions in Calgary, Victoria and Vancouver. Montreal's Compagnie Jean-Duceppe premiered *Le Chemin des passes-dangereuses* (1998), a dream-like tale of love and hate involving three brothers reuniting on the fifteenth anniversary of their father's death. It was first performed in English by Vancouver's Ruby Slippers Theatre as *Down Dangerous Passes Road* (2000), the road in the title the same one where *The Orphan Muses'* Isabelle works, counting logging trucks.

In addition to his serious dramas, Bouchard has had great success writing romantic comedies for both French and English summer theatres in Quebec. Among his most popular are *Les Grandes Chaleurs* (*Heat Wave*—1995), *Le Désir* (*Desire*—1996) and *Pierre et Marie ... et le démon* (*Pierre and Marie ... and the Devil with the Deep Blue Eyes*—1998). He has also served as artistic director of Ottawa's Théâtre du Trillium (1988–90) and taught at the University of Ottawa, l'Université du Québec and the National Theatre School.

The Orphan Muses is set in 1965, the same year as Tremblay's *Les Belles-Soeurs*. In the midst of Quebec's Quiet Revolution Isabelle Tanguay has decided to stage her own. Whether considered as individuals or as social microcosms of Quebec, her family has somewhat more success than the extended family of *Les Belles-Soeurs* in liberating itself from the lies, fears and repression that tie it to the past. In reconstructing the events of two decades earlier, the play evokes that past: the dark days of the war and the Duplessis regime when rural Quebec was at its most insular and intolerant. Nonconformity—much less eccentricity—was anathema. To have brought a foreigner into her home was bad enough: from the pulpit the priest thunders that even "to learn a foreigner's language is to sell our soul to the devil." But when Madame Tanguay dares to flaunt her relationship with the foreigner, to betray her marriage and sing Spanish songs in public, the good folk of Saint-Ludger de Milot riot. Having driven her husband away and lost her lover, she herself finally leaves on Easter Sunday, 1945. In Luc's romantic literary version their mother departs on a heroic note: "I'll go sing my liberation at the Easter Vigil." But in reality she orphans her four children, leaving them burdened with a legacy of confusion, loss and regret.

Twenty years later the village is hardly more tolerant. Luc gets himself beaten up for trying to enter the church dressed in his mother's Spanish skirt. But the orphans are adults now, and the twentieth anniversary reunion provides them an opportunity to test the adequacy of the fictions they have constructed, the coping mechanisms each has honed to a fine point. (The echoes of Chekhov's *Three Sisters* are surely intentional.) Despite Isabelle's sarcastic characterization—"A sicky, a mongoloid and a slut!"—the siblings have actually cast themselves in complex roles, all of them artists of their own self-creation, all each other's muses. Catherine, bitter and censorious, plays the substitute mother, sacrificing Isabelle to her own sterile need. Martine, the lesbian soldier in exile from the family, emulates the father and considers herself happy. Both discover another dimension to themselves in the face of their mother's impending return. Obsessed with his mother and possessed by her, Luc wears her clothes and takes on her voice in what seems like a desperate attempt to exorcise her from his imagination. With his book, he claims, "I have turned her life into my liberating work of art." But ultimately it is up to Isabelle, the family "retard," to orchestrate the scenario that might allow them genuine liberation.

The symbolism of the Easter setting seems blatant, but the resurrection that occurs is as ambiguous as the wreaths of flowers, delivered for the funeral of Luc who is not dead, and transformed into bouquets of welcome for the mother, who may or may not be. The revelation, when it comes, certainly does not effect radical change in every character. The final tableau suggests that Catherine and Luc may have found mutual comfort and reconciliation, but they may also just be reiterating old roles and patterns. In contrast to *Les Belles-Soeurs*, however, which ends with young Lise deciding to abort her pregnancy in despair, *The Orphan Muses* ends with a decision not to abort but to embrace the future. The homecoming proves to be a resurrection after all.

Les Muses orphelines premiered on September 7, 1988, at Théâtre d'Aujourd'hui in Montreal, with the following cast:

CATHERINE	Anne Caron
ISABELLE	Dominique Quesnel
LUC	Roy Dupuis
MARTINE	Louise Saint-Pierre

Directed by André Brassard
Set and Costume Design by Meredith Caron
Props Design by Louise Campeau
Lighting Design by Paul Mathieson
Musical Supervision by Pierre Moreau
Soundtrack by Patrice Saint-Pierre

The English translation of *Les Muses orphelines* was first produced by Ubu Repertory Theater in New York in December 1993. The first English-language production in Canada of *The Orphan Muses*, directed by David Ross, opened at the Western Canada Theatre Company in Kamloops, B.C., on January 20, 1995.

Translator's Note: The text presented here includes revisions made to the script by the playwright prior to the second production at Théâtre d'Aujord'hui in 1994.

THE ORPHAN MUSES
Translated by Linda Gaboriau

AUTHOR'S NOTE

My Picture Book: Ten years ago, I was writing *Dans les bras de Morphée Tanguay*, a satire about child-rearing: a dark, psychedelic look at the family and the education system. This play proved to be the genesis of *La Contre-nature de Chrysippe Tanguay, écologiste*; *La Poupée de Pélopia* (*Pelopia's Doll*); and *Les Muses orphelines* (*The Orphan Muses*).

In the Tanguay series, I compare myself to a painter who over the years pursues a study of the same images, the same colours, the same pre-occupations. I'm pleased to invite you to the vernissage of the fourth painting in this egotistically personal series. A fourth painting coloured by the past, by desertion and by family secrets. A questioning without censorship, without a real answer, of the fateful core of our existence: our family, our genesis.

CHARACTERS

CATHERINE Tanguay, *the eldest sister, 35 years old, elementary school teacher in Saint-Ludger de Milot*

ISABELLE Tanguay, *the youngest sister, 27 years old, employee at the gate to Dangerous Passes Road*

LUC Tanguay, *their only brother, 30 years old, pseudo-writer*

MARTINE Tanguay, *the middle sister, 33 years old, Captain in the Canadian Armed Forces, stationed in Baden-Solingen, Germany*

SCENE

Saint-Ludger de Milot, in the Lac-Saint-Jean region of Québec. April 1965. The set evokes the sitting room-dining room in a two-story country house. The front door opens into this room. A dining room table. Some chairs. An electric organ.

ACT ONE

Holy Saturday. Late afternoon. CATHERINE, puffing on her cigarette, takes inventory of the contents in a woman's suitcase.

CATHERINE: Three scarves, three red scarves, two blouses with polka dot prints.

ISABELLE: (*enters from outside, carrying a bag*) I lost track of the time.

CATHERINE: (*stubbing out her cigarette, furtively*) Close the door! Damn sand! We're gonna end up buried alive … (*closes the door*)

ISABELLE: It takes half an hour to walk into the village.

CATHERINE: It's not a broom you need to keep this place clean, it's a shovel.

ISABELLE: I got your ham. (*beat*) I lost track of the time. It happens.

CATHERINE: Twenty-seven years old and you don't know how to close a door. You waiting for the whole hillside to move into the house before you close the door? Some inheritance! Honest to God! Ten acres of sand with a house on top of a hill Ma called Calvary. Ten cold, windy acres of sand, and a twenty-seven year old girl who still doesn't know how to close a door.

ISABELLE: I got your ham.

CATHERINE: There must've been some change.

ISABELLE: The ham was four twenty-three. You gave me five bucks. Here's your seventy-seven cents. (*CATHERINE takes the change.*) You're not running off to hide it? You should buy me a gun. Walking back from town with a fortune like that, it's pretty risky.

CATHERINE: You owe me your pay cheque. You're late on your board. One … three … six pairs of socks: the red ones, the blue ones …

ISABELLE: (*opening the door*) Nobody came while I was out?

CATHERINE: Use your head! A car out here is the event of the year.

ISABELLE: Get off my back, Catherine. I lost track of the time!

CATHERINE: Don't tell me you went out like that, in the middle of spring thaw! (*beat*) "An ounce of prevention is worth a pound of cure."

ISABELLE: "Best cure, stay pure." "Practice prevention, avoid detention." God, I bet the kids at school make fun of you.

CATHERINE: If Ma could hear you.

ISABELLE: She can hear me, don't worry. She can hear me.

CATHERINE: Close the door! (*ISABELLE closes the door, but continues to look outside.*) Two fans … I've counted everything three times now, and I'm still missing a Spanish skirt.

ISABELLE: He's wearing it.

CATHERINE: Don't tell me he went into the village dressed like that again! I didn't see him leave.

ISABELLE: How come you're going through Ma's clothes?

CATHERINE: Did you see him in the village?

ISABELLE: I hate it when you answer me with another question! No, I saw him down at the foot of the hill. He was writing. How come you wanted me back before supper?

CATHERINE: You have to go back to the village.

ISABELLE: What am I, your workhorse? Take your car!

CATHERINE: I have to cook the ham.

ISABELLE: I'm expecting company.

CATHERINE: Who?

ISABELLE: Company!

CATHERINE: You're going to take this suitcase to the thrift shop. I couldn't give it to you before, with him hanging around.

ISABELLE: Oh, sure! We'll do it behind his back, and he'll hate my guts when you tell him I'm the one who got rid of Ma's clothes!

CATHERINE: Just take the suitcase. Before he comes back. If he knows it was you, he won't make a scene. I don't know how many times I've warned him that I'd get rid of these rags if he left

the house in them. He can dress up all he wants … here at home.

ISABELLE: We haven't seen hide nor hair of him for three years …

CATHERINE: He'll take off again, and he'll forget all about this place …

ISABELLE: You could make an effort and get off his back.

CATHERINE: … but what about us? We're stuck living here with these people who have memories like history books.

ISABELLE: He says we inspire him. He says we're his "muses." Muses are women who help people and ideas. That's what he says. And he says we're going to help him finish his book, *Letters from a Spanish Queen to Her Son.*

CATHERINE: When? He's been working on it for ten years now! Longer … He was eleven years old when I told him he'd do better to write what was going on in his head, instead of dressing up like Ma. God, I shouldn't have been so understanding. A good slap in the face, that's what, then dump the suitcase at the thrift shop! Get going, before he comes back. Go on!

ISABELLE: Burn it. Throw it out!

CATHERINE: What if Ma heard you?

ISABELLE: She can hear me.

CATHERINE: Ma never missed a chance to play the organ, every Sunday, every holy day, year in and year out. We can't burn her clothes during Lent! (*Silence.*) Why did you ask him to come back? If you're hoping to get some money out of him, forget it. He doesn't have a cent.

ISABELLE: God, you're a pain about money. I missed him.

CATHERINE: I'd rather miss him than have to deal with him here. I spent years telling the whole village that he'd changed.

ISABELLE: What a liar!

CATHERINE: I even told them his book was about to come out. I'd finally convinced them he might not be as crazy as they thought. And then you had to get him to come back. Things weren't extravagant enough for you.

ISABELLE: Wait a minute. (*exits*)

CATHERINE: Isabelle, get going before it's dark out. He'll be back any minute now.

ISABELLE: (*returns with a pencil and a little notebook*) "Extravagant?" What does that mean?

CATHERINE: Put something on, you'll freeze!

ISABELLE: What does "extravagant" mean? "When you know what words mean and how to use them, you're freer, and you're closer to the truth." That's what he says.

CATHERINE: "Extravagant" means something excessive, unreasonable, fantastic. Like extravagant spending. Extravagant behaviour.

ISABELLE: Well, that's true. When he's around, things stop being reasonable. "Extravagant" with an "x"?

CATHERINE: That's right, an "x."

ISABELLE: E. X. T.?

CATHERINE: E. X. T. He doesn't belong here! B. E. L. O. N. G.

ISABELLE: I'm warning you, if you tell him to leave, I'm leaving with him.

CATHERINE: Look at the way he behaves, you know as well as I do, he's not the right company for a young lady.

ISABELLE: Suddenly I'm a young lady. Guess it's better than being a ree-tard.

CATHERINE: He's sick, Isabelle.

ISABELLE: The mood you're in, guess it's been a while since you showed your bum to your boyfriend, eh!

CATHERINE: Isabelle! You shouldn't talk to your sister like that on Holy Saturday!

ISABELLE: Who you going out with now? Oh yeah, Dr. Lemieux. I guess he spends his life looking at bums. You dropped Sergeant Claveau for a doctor. You're moving up in life. You've gone through just about every profession in Saint-Ludger! What a family! A sicky, a mongoloid and a slut!

CATHERINE: Isabelle, come over here! Sit down. (*dangerously gentle*) What's the matter, Isabelle? You're usually so considerate, so sweet …

ISABELLE: So dumb, so retarded …

CATHERINE: Isabelle … Catherine's going to tell you something, but I don't want to have to repeat it … Isabelle …

ISABELLE: Here we go, the big words, the tears in your eyes … If you can't do your own dirty work, don't ask other people to do it for you. I'm not gonna get rid of the suitcase, you hear me?

CATHERINE: A little respect! Today's Holy Saturday, Isabelle.

ISABELLE: God, you're a pain. So it's Lent. Big deal. Tomorrow we'll have indigestion from too much ham and too much chocolate. Does that make it such a special day of the year, I should suddenly show you some respect?

CATHERINE: Do I have to remind you of everything I've done for you since Ma's death? Ungrateful brat!

ISABELLE: Ungrateful! Ungrateful! I knew we'd get to that word sooner or later. Don't bother telling me what it means. I have a whole page full of what that damn word means.

CATHERINE: I didn't mean it.

ISABELLE: I wasn't close enough for a slap in the face!

CATHERINE: It just came out, before I could stop it.

ISABELLE: Lots of things have come out of you, before you could stop them. Whenever something makes you mad, you hit me with your famous last words, using Ma's remains. You've used Ma's dead body once too often, Catherine. Tomorrow's Easter. A good day for resurrections.

CATHERINE: What's that supposed to mean?

ISABELLE: So nobody came while I was out?

CATHERINE: So you refuse to go to the thrift shop?

ISABELLE: Stop answering me with more questions!

CATHERINE: No, Isabelle, nobody came while you were out. Use your head. You refuse to go? (*picks up the suitcase*)

ISABELLE: Stay here. We can play poker. We're expecting company.

CATHERINE: I've got better things to do than entertain your ghosts, Isabelle.

ISABELLE: Go ahead, don't get sidetracked. Go take the sicky's clothes to the poor so they can look crazy too.

LUC: (*voice off*) Thanks a lot! (*enters dressed in the missing Spanish skirt*) They're real gentlemen, those policemen.

CATHERINE: Policemen!

LUC: They come around and open the car door for you, they help you out …

CATHERINE: Now what have you done? Close the door!

LUC: (*to CATHERINE*) You leaving on a trip, Catherine? Put that suitcase down.

CATHERINE: You know what people around here call a guy who dresses up in his mother's old rags … Never mind, we'll try to forget their word for it.

LUC: I told you to put that suitcase down. You can take it back to my room. If you try to get rid of it again, I'm warning you, what I just did in the village will seem tame compared to what I'll do next time.

CATHERINE: (*to ISABELLE*) You said you saw him at the foot of the hill! Liar!

LUC: I went to visit Madame Tessier at the post office.

CATHERINE: I don't believe you. She was closed today!

LUC: I went in through her kitchen. The minute she saw me, she tensed up, got stiff as a board. "Madame Tessier, my mother forgot something here a long time ago. Do you remember? I was with her. I was ten years old."

ISABELLE: What did she say?

LUC: She said that Ma came on a Maundy Thursday when the post office was open, but today's Holy Saturday and the post office is closed.

CATHERINE: She's right, you had no business going there today.

LUC: Then it was my turn to tense up, and I told her she just might have to make an exception today.

CATHERINE: Don't tell me you threatened her?

LUC: I told her I'd never gotten rough with a woman before, but I just might have to make an exception myself. She turned white as an envelope and she followed me into the backroom of the post office.

CATHERINE: You did threaten her!

LUC: I leaned on the counter, graciously—

ISABELLE: Graciously?

LUC: "Graciously" means the way Mama knew how to behave, "with elegance," not like the lady lumberjacks from around here. "Madame Tessier, twenty years ago my mother came to pick up a package she'd received from Québec City."

ISABELLE: What was in the package?

LUC: A Spanish dictionary.

CATHERINE: Isabelle doesn't need to know all that!

LUC: When Ma asked for her package, Madame Tessier had already opened it.

ISABELLE: How come?

LUC: There was a war going on and we had a foreigner living in our house. She figured that gave her the right to open our mail. She told Ma she read too much, that too much reading was bad for you, and that Spanish looked like a real pretty language, even though the only word she knew was *corrida*, but she didn't know what it meant. So Ma decided to explain to her what the word *corrida* meant.

ISABELLE: Ma explained that to Madame Tessier?

LUC: Yeah, and since she's the kind who gets lost in a blueberry patch, Ma practically had to draw her a picture.

CATHERINE: Show some respect for your elders.

ISABELLE: Go cook your ham, Catherine!

LUC: Mama explained that a *corrida* was like having some farmer invite everyone in Saint-Ludger to the hockey rink to watch him kill his bull. She explained that in the middle of the rink there was the toreador—the toreador was like the local farmer dressed up in fancy upholstery material. Ma's patience was put to a test. She had to explain everything, step by step. How the toreador waved a big red curtain called a *muleta* and that drove the bull crazy. How the bull would charge the *muleta*, and keep missing it, and everyone from Saint-Ludger would shout "Olé!" When the bull had charged and missed dozens of times and was getting out of breath, and people were fed up with shouting "Olé," the toreador would stab the animal with big knitting needles!

ISABELLE: Madame Tessier must've laughed?

CATHERINE: Not at all.

LUC: She got all choked up with her ugly thoughts and spit them out in Mama's face, saying that it took a loose woman who slept with foreigners to shout "Olé" when a farmer killed his bull.

ISABELLE: She said that to Ma?

CATHERINE: Filthy rumours!

LUC: Mama came home in tears. I was running behind her, saying "Your package, Ma! You forgot your package."

ISABELLE: And how did things end today?

LUC: After refreshing her memory about the little *corrida* scene, I told Madame Tessier that I refused to leave her post office empty-handed. It was the Spanish dictionary or her chignon.

CATHERINE: More threats?

LUC: So twenty years later, she took a little book covered with dust out from under her counter. (*takes the little Spanish dictionary out from under his skirt and hands it to ISABELLE*) "Don't be late for the Easter Vigil tonight, Madame Tessier, I wouldn't want you to miss the sequel."

ISABELLE: So how did she react?

LUC: She was pretty shaken, but she had enough strength left to call Sergeant Claveau. He's the one who "escorted" me home.

ISABELLE: (*thumbing through the Spanish dictionary*) It sounds so beautiful when you talk, Luc.

CATHERINE: What do you intend to do at Easter Vigil?

LUC: I just told you. The sequel.

CATHERINE: You're still not satisfied? Madame Tessier today, your tantrum at the grocery store yesterday, crying your eyes out because they didn't have the makings of a paella. It's useless reminding them of all that, Luc. Nobody cares about it any more. It was twenty years ago. Forget it!

LUC: Forget it. Forget that bunch of filthy minds who dragged our mother through the mud?

CATHERINE: When Ma … died, they decided to let bygones be bygones. You should do the same with them. Forget it.

LUC: I don't want to forget! I can't forget! I need to bug those pious souls who love to remind you that when you were a poor orphan, they used to bring you a box of groceries at Christmas and a bag of rags every spring … and you were their ticket to a good conscience. I want to remind them of their responsibility in our little family drama. They're here, stuck in my brain like a clot, blocking my imagination.

CATHERINE: Write about what you'd like to do to them. It's not so dangerous.

LUC: My writing is too precious for me to waste it on a bunch of illiterates. Writing means going beyond … until I've settled Mama's unfinished business with them, I'll never be able to pay her the homage I owe her.

CATHERINE: There are so many other beautiful subjects that could inspire you.

LUC: I don't feel like rewriting Maria Chapdelaine's romance in the wild, just to make you happy. Jesus Christ!

CATHERINE: Swearing during Lent is a sacrilege!

ISABELLE: God, you're a pain with your neat little sentences. Jesus Christ! Stop interrupting him! That's what I missed. It's so beautiful when he loses his temper. (*looking at the Spanish dictionary*) It's always so *extravagante*.

CATHERINE: You should take a rest, Luc. Your nerves are shot. (*takes back the suitcase and heads towards the door*) You'll end up with a nervous breakdown.

ISABELLE: Where you going with the suitcase?

CATHERINE: Do you remember how to cook the ham?

ISABELLE: I hate it when you answer me with another question!

CATHERINE: I've always saved us, Isabelle.

LUC: The suitcase!

CATHERINE: (*leaving the suitcase*) I'm going to apologize to Madame Tessier, poor old lady!

LUC: Sure, go apologize for being my sister.

CATHERINE exits. We hear the car start up. LUC takes out a manuscript and starts writing.

ISABELLE: Did your tantrum "inspire" you? (*beat*) When are you gonna let me read your book?

LUC: Soon.

ISABELLE: Right now, okay?

LUC: Not right now. Soon.

ISABELLE: You want to see the notebook with all my words? And correct my mistakes? (*hands him her notebook*)

LUC: (*reading*) You still writing by ear? "Extravagant" has an "a" not a "u." "Deliverance" —to take groceries to people's homes?

ISABELLE: Lionel Fraser's the one who said that when I bought the ham. He said: "You want me to deliver that to your house? We got free deliverance."

LUC: It's "delivery" for groceries, Isabelle, not "deliverance." Gotta be more selective about who you ask what words mean.

ISABELLE: (*yanks her notebook away from him*) You think I'm a mongoloid too, don't you?

LUC: Don't say that! (*gently*) "Deliverance" is a word. It means helping someone out of an unpleasant place or situation.

ISABELLE: Monday we can leave for Montreal together.

LUC: Give me back your notebook. I haven't finished correcting your words.

ISABELLE: Monday you're gonna take me with you.

LUC: Give me your notebook!

ISABELLE: If you say yes to Monday.

LUC: Monday's two days away. Lots of things can happen between then and now.

ISABELLE: When you send me those long love letters from Montreal, they're imaginary letters, right? Don't bother, you're wasting your paper on me.

LUC: Don't say that!

ISABELLE: I wrote to you because I missed you and I wanted you to come back. But you came back just to make the whole village sweat it out … not to see me, not to "deliver" me!

LUC: Don't say that, Belle. Luc loves you, big love, like the dam on the Peribonka! That's pretty big, eh?

ISABELLE: Leave me alone! I'm not seven years old any more. You're gonna take me with you, right? Just for a week?

LUC: (*playing his mother*) Tonight Mama's going to the Easter Vigil. She's going to climb the stairs to the organ loft. She's going to push fat Madame Claveau off the bench and play … (*sits down at the electric organ and plays and sings*) "*Una canción me recuerda a aquel ayer*"

ISABELLE: You're gonna take me to Montreal with you!

LUC:
"*Cuando se marchó en silencio un atardecer,
Se fue con su canto triste a otro lugar,
Dejó como campañera mi soledad,
Una paloma blanca me canta al alma …*"

ISABELLE: (*at the window*) It's Monsieur Savard's taxi. Luc, go hide.

LUC: How come?

ISABELLE: We'll surprise Martine!

LUC: (*stops playing*) Martine?

ISABELLE: I called her in Germany yesterday and asked her to come home.

LUC: How come?

ISABELLE: Go hide, you'll find out later.

LUC hides. ISABELLE sits down at the organ and sings, to the tune of "La Paloma."

"If at your window you see a gentle dove
Treat it with care, and welcome it there with love
It may be I, so do not deny its plea
Crown it with flowers, grant love its hours for me."

MARTINE enters dressed in civilian clothes and carrying her suitcases. She's exhausted.

MARTINE: Sounds like Ma singing.

ISABELLE: Leave the door open.

MARTINE: (*shaking ISABELLE's hand*) Isabelle!

ISABELLE: Martine!

MARTINE: Too bad we have to see each other again on such a sad occasion. (*takes ISABELLE into her arms*)

ISABELLE: It's all right, Martine. You can let go of me. Catherine doesn't want you to hold me too much. She says it's not normal for two women to smooch together.

MARTINE: In the taxi, Monsieur Savard didn't even know.

ISABELLE: You told Monsieur Savard?

MARTINE: Yes.

ISABELLE: You weren't supposed to. He didn't want anyone to know. He wrote it … in his will.

MARTINE: How did he die?

ISABELLE: Dr. Lemieux doesn't know yet. Dr. Lemieux's Catherine's new boyfriend.

MARTINE: Sickness? An accident? … Suicide?

ISABELLE: Catherine doesn't want us to say words like that in this house.

MARTINE: How come Dr. Lemieux was taking care of him? I thought he was in Montreal? Was he visiting here?

ISABELLE: Yeah.

MARTINE: I got on the plane in Stuttgart yesterday afternoon. I couldn't sleep. You know what time it is in Germany right now?

ISABELLE: I can't even keep track of the time here.

MARTINE: Where's he being laid out, at the sacristy or the school?

ISABELLE: He didn't want to be laid out.

MARTINE: Where's Catherine?

ISABELLE: If you'd arrived on time, you would've seen her. You said five o'clock!

MARTINE: I'm a half hour late on a twenty-hour trip! Besides, the bus from Alma to Saint-Ludger isn't the most reliable, and taxis are pretty rare around here.

ISABELLE: Still, it's a drag for the people who are organizing things!

MARTINE: How come Catherine didn't come to meet me at the bus?

ISABELLE: She's taking care of the funeral arrangements for tomorrow.

MARTINE: I'm going to take a bath.

ISABELLE: Martine, did you love Luc?

MARTINE: I know you had a lot of admiration for him. Personally, I always found him a bit strange.

ISABELLE: You could wait till he's six feet under before you shit on him.

MARTINE: Look, you must be old enough to understand that I didn't have to love him, just because he was my brother.

ISABELLE: I'm too dumb to understand things like that.

MARTINE: Let's just say I never considered him essential to my happiness.

ISABELLE: "Essential." What does that mean?

MARTINE: Something necessary, something important …

ISABELLE: "Essential." (*writing the word in her notebook*) This is my notebook for words. I feel like I don't have enough words. I try to use every new word once a day. (*beat*) So how's the war going over there?

MARTINE: (*faint smile*) There's no war where I am.

ISABELLE: They usually send soldiers where there's a war.

MARTINE: Baden-Solingen is a strategic base …

ISABELLE: What does "strategic" mean?

MARTINE: Isabelle, I don't have the strength to explain every word I use.

ISABELLE: You could make an effort. I haven't seen you for four years.

MARTINE: I'm tired. (*beat*) How have you been? Must be lots of guys hanging around you these days?

ISABELLE: Only when I go square dancing. I got other things to take care of before I start thinking about guys.

MARTINE: I don't really like being here. It feels macabre.

ISABELLE: "Macabre?"

MARTINE: It means "pertaining to death," "something sad or grim." Aren't you going to write it in your book?

ISABELLE: It's not a pretty word. I only like joyful words, words that are "grandiose," "splendid," "en-rap-turing."

CATHERINE: (*as she enters*) The door's wide open! Who cares? Catherine'll pay for the heat! Madame Tessier refused to come to the door. I passed Monsieur Savard's taxi on my way back … (*turns around and finds herself facing MARTINE; unenthusiastically*) Martine? What a nice surprise! (*MARTINE goes to hug her.*) Sorry, I've never been much for hugs and kisses.

MARTINE: That's a shame.

CATHERINE: So you decided to spend Easter with us. You could've warned me.

MARTINE: You getting cynical in your old age? If you're not capable of showing some emotion at tragic moments like this, you're colder than I thought.

CATHERINE: What's so tragic?

MARTINE: Death doesn't affect you any more?

CATHERINE: Don't tell me you've become more Catholic than the Pope! He died at three o'clock yesterday and he'll rise from the dead tomorrow, like every Easter Sunday.

MARTINE: Who are you talking about?

LUC enters.

LUC: So you crossed the Atlantic to come cry over my grave?

MARTINE: Is this some joke?

LUC: That's you all right—the dead meat specialist.

MARTINE: A joke! (*beat*) You got me to cross the Atlantic for a joke?

CATHERINE: Can someone tell me what's going on?

MARTINE: Isabelle called me in Germany yesterday so I could come to Luc's funeral.

CATHERINE: No!

ISABELLE: I missed her!

MARTINE: I spent the last twenty-four hours in a black hole and now I find out it's a joke. Twenty-four hours of remorse about everything we've been through together … "Remorse," write it down, Isabelle. It's not a pretty word but it's apt to be useful in any language. It means deep and painful regret, it means feeling goddamn guilty …

ISABELLE: "Remorse," with a "c" or an "s."

MARTINE: Somebody buy her a dictionary, for chrissakes!

LUC: How's the war going? When are you going to come back to Saint-Ludger with a Russian's head strapped on the top of your tank like antlers?

MARTINE: I swore I'd never come back here!

CATHERINE: Nobody's normal in this family. We have to live with it.

ISABELLE: Catherine says I have a behaviour problem.

LUC: You should've worn your soldier's uniform, we could've played Ma and Pa.

MARTINE: I'm never going to play that game again, Luc! (*beat*) Aren't you ever going to grow up, the lot of you?

Silence.

CATHERINE: It's been a long time since the four of us were together. Could I offer anyone a drink?

MARTINE: Why not! Drag out the photo albums. Let's try laughing at how we looked back then. Family get-togethers stopped being my idea of a good time years ago! When you leave home, you start looking ahead and family becomes a thing of the past. The only intense moments we'll share now are when we're closing the lid on someone's coffin. I just missed one of those memorable moments today.

LUC: Aren't you glad to know I'm still alive?

MARTINE: I closed your coffin on the plane on the way over here, and it was a relief.

CATHERINE: That's an awful way to talk.

MARTINE: I thought I could stop worrying about Catherine who's spent her life putting up with your moods, your crises and your financial problems.

CATHERINE: Mind your own business, Martine.

MARTINE: She sold the land, the barn ... the cottage to finance the inspiration of the male in the family. She mortgaged herself to the hilt so that Monsieur could experience Europe. So he could make his dream come true. He wanted to write! Write a book nobody's ever read a line of.

LUC: A real little soldier! You like to see your enemies dead.

ISABELLE: (sincere and delighted) I never knew anyone who could insult people as good as Martine!

MARTINE: Isabelle, if Catherine never taught you any manners, I will. There are other ways of letting your sister know that you love her and you miss her.

LUC: You got money problems, Catherine?

CATHERINE: Martine's the one who said that.

LUC: But it's true!

CATHERINE: It's personal. And my personal affairs are nobody else's business. Isabelle, come over here. You better find some way to make Martine forgive you.

ISABELLE: How come?

CATHERINE: (slaps her) Ungrateful brat!

ISABELLE: Ungrateful! You've all hidden behind Ma's corpse too much. You've used it so much there's nothing left for the worms. So much she's decided to rise from her grave and come back to straighten things out around here. Tomorrow's Easter, resurrection day. (exits)

CATHERINE: The door, Isabelle. Poor child!

MARTINE: You want to pity her or hit her? Make up your mind!

CATHERINE: I only do it because I love her.

MARTINE: Good thing you don't hate her!

LUC: She's never known how to handle her.

MARTINE: She can't exactly call you a success either.

LUC: Watch it, you goddamn butch soldier, if you don't shut up—

CATHERINE: Luc, why don't you take your Spanish skirt off first!

LUC: Federico gave it to Mama.

CATHERINE: Stop talking about Ma!

LUC: He sent her a whole suitcase full of them.

CATHERINE: (to MARTINE) Ever since he came back ... I'm not responsible for my actions.

LUC: She looked so beautiful in this skirt.

CATHERINE: Ever since he's been back, I can't control Isabelle. Sometimes, I feel like hitting her, hitting her so hard we'd forget everything ... everything we did to her. (to LUC) Yes, it's true. I'm up to my ears in debt because of you. This year I'm teaching first grade and second grade just to make ends meet. And if I have any spare time, I substitute teach in grade five. Don't think I gave you that money so you could write ... I gave it to you so you'd stay away from Isabelle. So you'd stop putting ideas into her head. I'd teach gym if I thought I could get rid of you once and for all. And don't get any ideas, you're not gonna take her with you to Montreal. (beat) She's acting so strange these days. You heard what she said: Ma's gonna rise from her grave, that she's gonna come back, she's gonna rise from the dead on Easter Sunday. So when I don't know what else to invent to defend us, I hit her.

MARTINE: Stop feeling guilty about it. It's all right what we told her. We were just kids ...

CATHERINE: Remember how pitiful she was, huddled in the corner of her room in the dark? And she kept repeating: "When's she gonna come back? When? Her trip to Spain is taking too long. Too long."

MARTINE: She hadn't eaten for two days. The three of us were ready to burst into tears. And she kept repeating ... "When's she gonna come back? When?" Then the letter arrived.

LUC: "Dear Children, I asked a travelling companion who was on her way home to mail this letter from Québec City so it would reach you sooner. I will not be coming back. I have gone to join Federico. Don't look for me … "

MARTINE: "Don't try to find me … "

CATHERINE: "Perhaps some day you'll understand. Adios … "

LUC: "Adios!"

MARTINE: "Adios!" (*beat*) It's touching to see us like this. The only time we show any emotion is when we act out that goddamn story. Like vultures feeding off carrion!

CATHERINE: It is touching. (*silence*) How are things in Germany?

MARTINE: Great! (*silence*) Have you finished your book yet?

LUC: Almost! (*to MARTINE, who's laughing*) What's so funny?

MARTINE: Sorry! I can't stop picturing you in your grave.

They all laugh.

CATHERINE: I'm going out with Dr. Lemieux these days.

MARTINE: You want to know who I'm going out with?

Silence.

LUC: I was happy to see you, Martine. I had to meet you head-on, I had to attack, but I was happy …

CATHERINE: I'm happy to see you too. (*opens her arms*)

MARTINE: (*doesn't respond*) So, how do you like being rejected?

CATHERINE: Emotions don't last long with you!

MARTINE: I thought you would've told her. It was your responsibility, as her guardian.

LUC: She didn't want her to know. It was easier for her to play mother, if the kid didn't think that her real mother might come back to get her some day.

CATHERINE: If you're going to shit on people, there's a mop in the kitchen.

MARTINE: I was hoping she was no longer the kid everyone pitied, the village retard. I even figured she would've met some guy.

CATHERINE: As if a guy could solve a woman's problems. It takes a lesbian to say something like that.

MARTINE: You must have swallowed too much sand. You talk like a dried-up old maid.

LUC: Looks like we're going to need the mop. Welcome to Saint-Ludger! Charming little hamlet of seven hundred souls, more commonly known as "the ass end of the dead end."

CATHERINE: How can you tell the truth to a twenty-seven year old woman who acts like an eleven year old who has tantrums no one can control? Am I supposed to apologize for spending the last twenty years of my life making her believe her mother died in Spain? Was I supposed to admit that she's still alive and that she simply abandoned us? "Don't try to find me. Never try to find me. Perhaps some day you'll understand." Well, the day I understand how a mother can abandon her children, I'll explain it to her.

MARTINE: Guess I didn't come back for nothing. You need a soldier to send to the front lines? Here I am. I've been trained to clean up other people's shit without asking any questions. Twenty years ago, I inherited the job of telling her the big lie we'd invented … It'll be my pleasure to tell her the truth today. Then never ask me to come back here again. I'm gonna make sure I forget all about you, even your names … (*calls*) Isabelle!

CATHERINE: What you don't know can't hurt you.

ISABELLE enters soaking wet, and holding a bouquet of thistles.

CATHERINE: The door, Isabelle!

CATHERINE goes to close the door. ISABELLE walks over to MARTINE and hands her the thistles.

MARTINE: Thank you, Isabelle. I forgive you.

ISABELLE: I never said I was sorry. Put the "burrs" in water, they're not for you.

MARTINE: (*preparing her speech*) Isabelle …

ISABELLE: What does "strategic" mean?

MARTINE: It means something that's part of a strategy, a plan.

ISABELLE: Like you. (*beat*) So you find it hard to take, Martine, someone who's supposed to be dead but isn't? A long time ago, you were the one who came into my room to tell me Ma had died in Spain. The three of you were standing there with these tragic looks on your face … Well, a month ago a lady phoned here. A lady who spoke really well, with lots of beautiful words. I didn't understand them all. She wanted to know how we were.

I told her that Catherine was a school teacher and that she was going out with a doctor, that Martine was a captain in the army in Germany, that Luc was going to publish a book … and that I was nothing, just the dumb girl who works at the gate where they count the logging trucks that enter Dangerous Passes Road.

LUC: Mama phoned here?

ISABELLE: And I realized I was nothing because I never got to hope that some day I could report to a lady like that. I never thought the dead could return to earth.

MARTINE: Is she making this up again?

CATHERINE: No, I can tell when she's making things up.

ISABELLE: How do you think you react when you find yourself talking on the phone with your mother who died twenty years ago and you can't even understand all the words? Eh? I bet no dictionary in the world has a word for how you feel! She was disappointed in me. You hear me? She was disappointed because I didn't have anything to tell her. Because I hadn't "emancipated," that's what she said. "Emancipated." And Catherine told me "to emancipate" meant to "grow up." She asked me to get you all together here. The "burrs" are for Ma. She'll be here tomorrow … and I haven't had time to learn enough beautiful words.

MARTINE: Ma's gonna be here tomorrow?

CATHERINE: Did she tell you why she was coming back?

ISABELLE: No. And I'm still trying to understand why she left. Guess I better catch up.

MARTINE: Ma's gonna be here tomorrow?

LUC: She'll be here tomorrow!

The phone rings four times. CATHERINE goes to answer it.

CATHERINE: (*into the phone*) Hello. Yes, just a minute. It's Madame Talbot. She wants to know when Luc's funeral is. Who wants to answer?

LUC: (*taking the phone*) Madame Talbot? It's Jacqueline Tanguay here! I'll be arriving tomorrow!

ACT TWO

Holy Saturday. Evening. ISABELLE enters from outside, carrying funeral wreaths. She arranges a few in the living room and exits to take one to a bedroom. She comes back.

CATHERINE enters. She's carrying a package. She notices the wreaths.

ISABELLE: They're for Luc. They didn't know where to make the "delivery." They left them on the porch. They're still afraid to come into the house. Guess they didn't know where to send them. It's "macabre," eh? That one's from the ladies at the library. That one's from the Saint-Ludger Recreation Committee … We put one of them in your room, the one from your buddies at school. Luc says we should make them into bouquets for Ma. Leave the door open! … Please.

CATHERINE: (*leaves the door open*) I hate the sound of the wind whining in the cypress trees.

ISABELLE: When the snow started to melt and the weather got warmer, Federico always asked us to leave the door open. He'd sit on the porch and sing his songs with his guitar. He used to say that back home, in his country, the doors are always open. That way the air can circulate and chase away bad thoughts. That's one thing I remember about him.

CATHERINE: (*closing the door*) What I remember is how he used to make us freeze. Where is everybody?

ISABELLE: In their rooms. Martine said she was having trouble with her "jet log." They must be thinking about what they're gonna say to Ma. (*CATHERINE lights up a cigarette.*) When did you start smoking?

CATHERINE: Ages ago. I didn't want to set a bad example for you.

ISABELLE: Can I have one! (*CATHERINE offers her a cigarette.*) At the gate, the guys all smoke Export A's. (*lights up.*) I like menthols. Have you thought about what you're gonna say to her?

CATHERINE: Poor Madame Tessier had palpitations after listening to Luc's little scene about the *corrida*.

ISABELLE: So did you go show your bum to the doctor?

CATHERINE: (*surprisingly candid*) Yes. I needed a bit of consolation.

ISABELLE: "Consolation." Oh, forget it. I'm tired of asking what words mean. I got so many to learn, one more or less won't make no difference, she'll still see that I'm just a dummy.

CATHERINE: Don't say that, sweetie.

ISABELLE: "Sweetie?" I'd like to know what that word means when you use it.

CATHERINE: It means what it means. A sign of affection. You want me to bring you a beer?

ISABELLE: Two signs of affection in the same sentence, something's fishy. You're not supposed to drink during Lent.

CATHERINE: Well, sometimes you can negotiate with God! Isabelle, I'm going to tell you something, but don't make me repeat it.

ISABELLE: Here we go. One of your emotional sentences.

CATHERINE: I just want to tell you that I love you, Isabelle. You're my little girl. There, I said it. Here's an Easter present for you.

ISABELLE: (*opens it*) A dictionary!

CATHERINE: I stopped by the school. I've got the keys. I stole it ... It's even got illustrations.

ISABELLE: There are so many words, where do I start?

CATHERINE: "Reconciliation," maybe you can start with the word "reconciliation."

ISABELLE: You've never been any good at poker. You always show your hand too soon. It's gonna take longer than one night for me to forgive you.

CATHERINE: I love you!

ISABELLE: You had years to prove it. But instead, you called me every name in the book, you never let me do what I wanted, you never gave me a cent and once I had some money, you started charging me board. You never helped your "little girl" act like a woman, and when she tried, you made fun of her. Do I have to remind you of what you did a couple of months ago? The night you sent your old boyfriend, Sergeant Claveau, after me?

CATHERINE: A trucker. You didn't realize how dangerous it was.

ISABELLE: A trucker or a doctor, what's so dangerous if he makes you feel good ... I had fun with my trucker—and maybe your policeman got there too late.

CATHERINE: It's my duty to protect you.

ISABELLE: Tomorrow you're gonna have to explain yourself to Ma.

CATHERINE: What's this address in Montreal that Dr. Lemieux wants to give you?

ISABELLE: He had no business talking to you about that!

CATHERINE: What's this all about? (*beat*) Isabelle, I love you!

ISABELLE: I think you got worse vocabulary problems than me.

LUC: (*enters, dressed in another Spanish skirt and a few accessories*) Give me the car keys.

CATHERINE: Where do you think you're going decked out like that?

LUC: To church.

CATHERINE: Over my dead body. I'm not letting you out of here dressed like that. (*rushes over to block the door*)

LUC: The car keys!

CATHERINE: Never!

ISABELLE: (*referring to the Spanish dress*) You chose the prettiest one!

CATHERINE: I don't mind here in the house. But not at Easter Vigil!

LUC: Isabelle, where does Catherine hide the car keys?

CATHERINE: Ma will be here tomorrow!

LUC: Precisely. I want everyone to have paid for what they did to her by tomorrow.

CATHERINE: You've taken enough revenge already!

LUC: Where are the keys, Isabelle?!

CATHERINE: Isabelle, I swear, there's gonna be hell to pay if you tell him where the keys are!

LUC: All right, I'll walk.

CATHERINE: (calling) Martine! Martine, come help me!

ISABELLE: Luc, what are you gonna say to Ma tomorrow?

MARTINE enters dressed in her uniform.

CATHERINE: Martine, he wants to go into the village dressed like that!

MARTINE: I'm not the family bouncer.

CATHERINE: Stop him!

MARTINE: Let him go, I don't give a damn.

ISABELLE: What are you gonna say to her, Luc?

CATHERINE: They'll kill you!

ISABELLE: Luc, what are you gonna say to her tomorrow?

CATHERINE: (hands him the keys) All right, go ahead! Get yourself killed!

ISABELLE: Answer me, Luc!

CATHERINE: Go ahead!

ISABELLE: Luc!

CATHERINE: We've already got the flowers for your grave.

ISABELLE: What are you gonna say to Ma, Luc?

LUC: (to ISABELLE) Will you give me a break with your retarded questions!

MARTINE: Luc!

Silence.

LUC: (realizing he has hurt ISABELLE; beat) Sorry! Look at me, Belle. I didn't mean to say that.

ISABELLE: But you said it. You said what everybody thinks. Retarded.

LUC: I feel ridiculous. (takes off a few Spanish accessories, including the mantilla) If you love me, look at me. (She looks at him.) I'm sorry. Do you forgive me?

Beat.

ISABELLE: What are you gonna say to Ma tomorrow?

LUC: I'm going to give her my book.

ISABELLE: Really?

CATHERINE: Have you finished it?

LUC: Yes.

ISABELLE: Can you read us some of it tonight?

LUC: I have to go to church.

CATHERINE: Just read a bit of it. Here ... in the house. We'd really like that, wouldn't we, Martine?

MARTINE: Sure.

LUC: (heading for the door) I've got the Easter Vigil.

ISABELLE: It goes on for four hours. You can go later.

MARTINE: You mean that book actually exists? (LUC opens the door. We hear the wind.) The wind! His book's gone with the wind!

LUC: (closes the door and goes to get his book) Stay right there!

CATHERINE: (whispers) Thanks, sweetie!

ISABELLE: How come?

CATHERINE: Now he's going to stay home.

ISABELLE: (loudly) I didn't get insulted just to make you happy.

CATHERINE starts arranging the chairs.

MARTINE: Luc's book, Ma coming back! I guess I didn't come this far for nothing.

The three sisters are obviously excited.

CATHERINE: Everybody have a seat!

ISABELLE: Martine, you sit here.

CATHERINE: Anyone want popcorn?

ISABELLE: Me!

MARTINE: Go easy on the butter.

ISABELLE: Don't listen to her.

MARTINE: And don't let it burn!

LUC: (re-enters; calmly) Forget the popcorn!

MARTINE: Is there any beer?

CATHERINE: Cold or room temperature?

MARTINE: Room temperature.

ISABELLE: Cold.

LUC: Could everybody just settle down! This isn't the Saturday night movies. This is my life's work.

MARTINE: Oh, excuse us!

ISABELLE: That's beautiful, what he just said. (sits down with her dictionary and her notebook on her lap)

CATHERINE: (whispering) Go ahead, Luc. We're listening.

LUC: Letters from a Queen of Spain to Her Beloved Son.

ISABELLE: Your title's longer than it was yesterday.

LUC: (reading) "Dear Reader, This book contains all the letters which betray my mother's silence. The silence where she buried her unfulfilled desires, her aborted dreams. I had the mission of putting this silence into words. Her life was my inspiration. I have dissected her memory, spied on her destiny. I have transformed her, I have worshipped her and magnified her. I have turned her life into my liberating work of art." Prologue.

ISABELLE: What's a "prologue?"

CATHERINE: Write it down and look it up afterwards.

ISABELLE: I need to learn them in "context."

CATHERINE: (exasperated) Isabelle! (beat) Go ahead, Luc, we're listening.

LUC: (reading) "First letter from Canada. 20 January 1944. Dear Son. Tonight, on the hillside, the wind has crystallized waves of snow, like a sea where the ebb of the tide suddenly stood still. Two dark knights on horseback emerge from this sea beyond time. I recognize my husband, my duty. And there's the other one, beside him, mystery and the unknown. As he turns his gaze on me, this stranger says: "Buenas tardes, Señorita." He could have said "I love you" and I wouldn't have felt more embarrassed. I lowered my eyes. It was as if he'd mysteriously made the statue of the toreador a cousin once brought back from a trip come to life. That plaster matador with his perfect body made me doubt my devotion to Christ, so thin and emaciated. I fear I am a woman who prefers the muleta to the cross. Federico Rosas will board in our house during the construction of the dam on the Peribonka River. Lots of love, Mama."

"11 May 1944. Dear Son, Spring is back … and so is the sand. Federico has been part of the family for more than three months now. Isabelle loves to play with him. Yet she still cries whenever he smiles at her. Catherine is becoming more and more flirtatious with Federico and Martine more distant with me. And you ask too many embarrassing questions at the supper table."

MARTINE: Ma, how come you only go fishing with Federico? How come you close the doors to the sitting room at night? How come Pa's been sleeping in the attic?

LUC: (reading) "He's learning to speak French better all the time. I bought him a little notebook so he could keep a record of his new words."

ISABELLE: Like me.

LUC: "Yesterday I played the organ at all three masses. The priest gave the same sermon all three times. He says that to learn a foreigner's language is to sell our soul to the devil."

MARTINE: Move ahead in time! We know all that!

ISABELLE: It sounds nicer when it's written.

LUC: "Yesterday Catherine went for a walk with Federico. Since that walk, she's stopped being flirtatious with him, and she's stopped speaking to me."

ISABELLE: What did you talk about on your walk, you and Federico?

CATHERINE: (defensively) It's been so long. I don't remember.

ISABELLE: Did you talk to him about your bum?

CATHERINE: May I remind you that you haven't had your quota of slaps today.

LUC: "At night, the smell of his skin, the taste of his lips … I'm struggling with my desire, with his desire."

CATHERINE: We can do without those details, Luc.

ISABELLE: Have a beer, Catherine.

LUC: (reading) "Madame Claveau has been replacing me more and more often at church. The priest saves the weddings and baptisms for me. He rattles on about the innocence of children and our duties as parents. Catherine has been taking care of Isabelle more often, as if she was trying to keep her away from me. Martine has joined the Cadets. She's away every weekend. And you are spying on me. Studying my every move. Your loving mother."

"3 July 1944. Dear Son. Last night we went to the organ party."

ISABELLE: The organ party!

CATHERINE: The church wardens had organized a party in the Knights of Columbus hall to finance a new organ …

LUC: (reading) "They want me to play something. I don't have anything to wear!"

ISABELLE: You could wear one of the dresses Federico gave you!

LUC: (playing his mother) I'll wear the white one. The white one with the mantilla.

MARTINE: She had absolutely no sense of decency!

LUC: (playing his mother) Your father can't come to hear me play. He says he can't take the time off.

ISABELLE: But Federico's coming, isn't he?

LUC: (playing his mother) Of course, sweetie!

MARTINE: No decency.

CATHERINE: When we arrived at the Knights of Columbus Hall, the party had already started. We could hear everyone singing along with Florence Giroux. She was doing La Bolduc's songs.

LUC: (playing his mother) Federico pushed open the front doors of the hall and proudly offered me his arm. We walked in together.

CATHERINE: Everyone stopped singing. Even Madame Giroux stopped and since she wasn't used to the mike, everyone in the hall heard her gasp: "She's outta her mind."

LUC: (playing his mother) The whole village stood there, watching us walk in together. Nothing's as silent as two hundred people being silent. The women lowered their eyes at the sight of the matador. The men lowered their eyes at the sight of the señorita.

ISABELLE: I was holding Luc's hand.

CATHERINE: Martine and I completed the procession.

MARTINE: The head warden tried to relax the atmosphere. He pushed old lady Giroux away from the mike and said: "Welcome to Madame Tanguay and her little brood."

CATHERINE: He missed a great opportunity to keep his mouth shut. We heard a few people laugh.

LUC: (playing his mother) "Her little brood," just to remind me that I didn't have fourteen kids like all the other women. Four kids wasn't enough to keep a woman busy … It left her with too much time to get into trouble.

CATHERINE: The head warden tried again. "Welcome to our talented organ player, Mrs Lucien Tanguay."

MARTINE: And he started to clap like a seal.

CATHERINE: Nobody joined in.

LUC: (playing his mother) Suddenly I felt very peaceful.

MARTINE: The lull before the storm.

LUC: (playing his mother) Federico helped me up onto the stage. I looked at him as if I was looking at him for the first time. To encourage me, Federico began to hum. After a moment of giddiness, I began to play …

ALL: (singing)

"Una canción me recuerda a aquel ayer
Cuando se marchó en silencio un atardecer
Se fue con su canto triste a otro lugar

Dejó como campañera mi soledad.
Una paloma blanca me canta al alma
Viejas melancólicas cosas del alma
Llegando del silencio de la mañana
Y cuando salgo a verla vuela a su casa
Donde va que mi voz
Ya no quiere escucharla
Donde va que mi vida se apaga
Si junta a mi no está
Si quisiera volver
Yo la íria a esperar
Cada día cada madrugada
Para quererla mas."

CATHERINE: Two men grabbed Federico. Two minutes later there were ten of them on top of him. People were throwing anything they could get their hands on at Ma: ashtrays, glasses, candles ...

MARTINE: And in the middle of all that, there were two kids dancing like Federico had taught them.

CATHERINE: Pa arrived in the middle of the riot. Ma stopped playing.

MARTINE: There was another long silence.

LUC: (*playing his mother*) Your father walked to the middle of the hall. Everyone backed off and stood against the walls. There was your father, dressed in a soldier's uniform, as dignified as a toreador, standing over Federico, lying on the floor in a pool of blood, like a bull in the middle of the arena, waiting for the final blow. (*to MARTINE*) Lucien, what are you doing dressed up like a soldier?

MARTINE: No, Luc. Never!

ISABELLE: Play, Martine! Just this once. For the last time. Just for tonight!

MARTINE: No.

LUC: (*playing his mother*) Why are you dressed up like a soldier?

MARTINE: (*stands up*) I'm leaving.

LUC: (*playing his mother*) You think that's the solution?

MARTINE: I'd rather leave than go on pretending that it doesn't bother me.

LUC: (*playing his mother*) That's so cowardly of you! (*beat*) Children! We're going home now!

MARTINE: (*playing her father*) No. Stay here. We're gonna settle this right now. You want to show the whole village how happy you are? Well, let's show them the rest.

LUC: (*playing his mother*) You knew very well that bringing Federico home ...

MARTINE: (*playing her father*) I never was able to invent the world you wanted, Jacqueline. I can't teach you anything about my country, it's the same as yours, and you don't even like it. Every morning, we open our eyes and we see the same trees, the same hillside, the same faces. Maybe I can't talk about love to you ... I learned to say it, but I don't know how to babble about it ... Maybe I'm not ... a great ...

LUC: (*playing his mother*) The word is "lover!"

MARTINE: (*playing her father*) Maybe I'm nothing but ...

LUC: (*playing his mother*) You're just an ordinary guy from Saint-Ludger, like dozens of others. You're just the guy I couldn't choose, because there was no choice. You're just what my children are turning into: ordinary people living ordinary lives.

MARTINE: (*playing her father*) Any other guy, another one of your dozens of guys like me, would have killed you by now. I prefer to go kill where it'll count.

CATHERINE: Then he turned on his heels and walked towards the main door of the hall. And just before disappearing forever, he turned and looked at Ma one last time.

MARTINE: (*playing her father*) My family warned me. They told me to watch out for beautiful women. It's the devil who gave them their beauty. At birth, he gave them a poisoned present called desire. Jacqueline, you'll always feel desire and it will be your downfall. You better pick up what remains of the Spaniard, his mistress is probably already desiring somebody else. (*turns away from the others*)

CATHERINE: Thank you, Martine.

ISABELLE: You were really good, Martine.

MARTINE: She better not show up tomorrow saying she's repented!

ISABELLE: What does "repented" mean?

MARTINE: It means someone who comes back on all fours, licking the floor, looking for forgiveness! She's not going to put us through the epitome of pardon! "Epitome" means the cherry on the sundae! Use your dictionary, for chrissakes!

LUC: (*returning to his book*) "21 September 1944. My Beloved Son. The autumn winds are sweeping over the hill and there's no escaping the sand. Federico has recovered from his wounds. I received an official letter from the Canadian Armed Forces. Your father is dead. He died in the Normandy landing. His soldier friends had nicknamed him "the suicide case." When I announced the news, Martine smashed the matador statue."

"The next day, when she got back from training, Martine aimed your father's old .22 at Federico and froze, as if paralyzed. For her Christmas present, she wants Federico to leave … otherwise, next time, she'll pull the trigger."

CATHERINE: I always wondered, would you have shot him?

MARTINE: No … I would've shot her. Just wait, tomorrow when we see her walk in the door, we're going to feel vulnerable, like scared little kids, 'cause time's stood still for us since she left. If I see one of you make the slightest friendly gesture, I'll get out the old .22 and this time, believe me, I'll pull the trigger.

LUC: (*goes on reading*) "Last letter from Canada. April 1945. Five months have gone by since Federico left. The day he left … *Adiós, adiós!* … The wind has once again crystallized the snow into immobile waves. This morning I went to the post office to pick up the Spanish dictionary Federico sent me. Madame Tessier was as mean as usual, like the grocer, the priest, the two old maids at the library … You and Isabelle help me pack my suitcase. I've decided to leave you my Spanish dresses. There'll be other prettier ones where I'm going. Before leaving Saint-Ludger, I'll go sing my liberation at the Easter Vigil. I'll leave the house without kissing you goodbye … The slightest sign of emotion could undermine my decision. My destiny is elsewhere. Signed: Your mother, who will always love you. Goodbye."

ISABELLE: Goodbye.

LUC: (*suddenly pushing his manuscript aside*) They must've reached the blessing of the candles at church. (*stands up and heads for the door.*)

CATHERINE: (*grabs his manuscript*) What's in the rest of the pages?

LUC: Her life in Spain.

MARTINE: Do you mean you actually believe that she wrote to you after she left? You've been imagining that for the last twenty years?

LUC: Haven't you ever tried to imagine what's become of her?

MARTINE: I tried to forget her.

LUC: How about you, Catherine?

CATHERINE: I didn't have any time to waste on that!

LUC: Are you telling me that you never thought about what your own mother might be doing for the past twenty years? How do you manage to look in the mirror without seeing her in your own features?

ISABELLE: I never had a chance to imagine her. Catherine told me she was in purgatory and since she couldn't explain what purgatory was, well, I couldn't imagine it. The priest tried to explain. He said it was like a long line at the confessional. So I saw her standing in line, waiting, and sometimes I brought her a chair so she could rest.

LUC: I imagined her so clearly that when I finally found her in Spain, five years ago, she was exactly like she was in my dreams.

MARTINE: Found who?

LUC: Mama.

MARTINE: You found Ma in Spain?

ISABELLE: You found her and you never told me?

MARTINE: Is this literature or truth?

CATHERINE: Literature. (*exits*)

LUC: When I arrived in Barcelona, I had no trouble finding them. I met Federico on horseback in the middle of their fields. They had a huge estate. Mama was the queen of a huge estate.

CATHERINE: (*returns with a box full of letters*) Since Ma's gonna be here tomorrow, there's no sense in trying to hide it from you any more. (*passes out letters to MARTINE and ISABELLE*)

LUC: Federico told me Mama was playing the organ at the Iglesia de la Sagrada Familia. I went back into town. When I arrived at the entrance of the Iglesia, I heard the organ.

MARTINE: (*reading a letter*) "Hello Catou, I'd like you to send me your father's death certificate ... "

LUC: It was so majestic.

MARTINE: (*reading a letter*) "I might need it in view of a possible marriage. Love, Mama."

LUC: I hadn't seen her for fifteen years.

ISABELLE: (*reading a letter*) "Dear Catou, I'm sending a hundred dollars to buy the children some clothes in view of the upcoming winter. Love, Jacqueline Rosas."

LUC: I walked down the centre aisle of the huge empty church so I could see her in the organ loft ...

ISABELLE: (*reading*) "Catou, I am enclosing two hundred dollars to help you with Isabelle's education. Ma."

LUC: My heart was beating so fast.

CATHERINE: Read the address in the corner of the envelope.

MARTINE: 102 Saint-Marc Avenue, Québec City.

LUC: She stopped playing.

CATHERINE: She never went to Spain. She made all that up so we wouldn't try to find her.

ISABELLE: My stomach aches!

CATHERINE: Yes, Luc. I thought about her often. Every day. I imagined her sweating in Québec City, in those factories in Lower Town. Having to struggle all day with a sewing machine, making corsets for the ladies in Upper Town ... to pay for her desire.

MARTINE: She's in Québec City! Now I can stop wracking my brains. I felt like half my brain had turned into a map of the world, I spent so much time looking for a possible address for her. She's in Québec City.

LUC: Isabelle, go pack your suitcase. We're going to Montreal tomorrow.

CATHERINE: Luc, I've got a thousand dollars in the co-op ... Leave her alone ...

LUC: Leave her alone? You sent me half way round the world, you let me believe that Mama was in Spain, just so I'd leave her alone. "Leave her alone!" We left her with you and look what you've done to her! A twenty-seven year old woman with the maturity of a child of twelve and the vocabulary of a telephone book!

ISABELLE: Mind your own business, Luc!

CATHERINE: Tomorrow I don't want to hear any comments about how I've raised her. I gave her everything I could. And she's not going to take her away from me.

LUC: (*playing his mother*) I've come back for her, Catou, because I can't stand leaving her here, just waiting for you to have a kid of your own ... Because you know very well you'll never have one. You've gone through every stud in the village but your problem, your little tragedy, is that you're not just sterile in your head. Isabelle, go pack your suitcase.

ISABELLE goes to get her suitcase.

CATHERINE: (*crying*) I would like to have had twelve kids! Twelve just to get to her, dammit! Twelve just to show her how beautiful a family can be, a real family.

MARTINE: Can you imagine if you had twelve kids? Twelve devastating departures. Imagine asking yourself twelve times why you bothered to sacrifice your life to them ... Turning into a cloying bloodsucker twelve times, so they won't leave ... Twelve thousand sleepless nights because they're gone ... Worrying about their love problems, money problems, career problems. Wondering twelve times over whether you were a good mother, wondering twelve times about the woman you were before they arrived ... Realizing twelve times over that you are nothing but a lousy link in the masterpiece called humanity. Glorious humanity that takes such pleasure in suffering and killing ... I thought our mother was courageous because she dared take off before we did. Imagine ... She didn't even have to feel guilty about me being a lesbian. You can explain that word to Isabelle, Catherine. You can go throw up first, and then explain it to her. I think she's a coward to come back. I don't understand how she can be so masochistic. Or why she needs to know that we really suffered, to know that when we're not hurting each other, we go on hurting inside …

ISABELLE: (*re-enters with her suitcase and picks up her dictionary*) "Masochistic?"

MARTINE: Don't bother to look it up. Just look at your brother. The worst kind of "masochist." A real nutcase who's been trying to imitate our mother since the day she left. He's put on the same damn show, every time we've seen him … for the last twenty years. (*to LUC*) Stop imagining that you're her! Your heroine: "the Queen of Spain." A beautiful book built on thin air! Tomorrow, when you see her and she tells you about the Chateau Frontenac Hotel … and her corset factory, there'll be nothing left to say, nothing to write, nothing to play, because she won't tell the exotic tale you've been waiting for.

ISABELLE: Let's go, Luc!

LUC: No!

ISABELLE: How come? Five minutes ago you wanted to leave.

LUC: No. That's how come.

CATHERINE: Thank you, Luc.

ISABELLE: How come?

LUC: 'Cause you're just a dummy. And I don't see myself stuck in Montreal with a mongoloid.

ISABELLE: Luc, you must know the worst word in the world you can say to someone? Well, I'm shouting it at you right now!

LUC runs out of the house, grabbing the car keys. We hear the car start up.

CATHERINE: What's the taxi number? Isabelle, get me Monsieur Savard's number!

MARTINE: He must be at Easter Vigil too.

CATHERINE: Monsieur Tessier told Dr. Lemieux that if he ever saw Luc again he'd have his twins beat him to a pulp.

MARTINE: I don't see what you can do about it. (*beat*) Can you believe what we just said to each other and we were stone sober! Any beer left?

CATHERINE: (*after dialling a number*) Dr. Lemieux must be at church.

MARTINE: I guess God's never been on your side!

CATHERINE: (*throwing on her coat*) Go ahead, joke about it. What am I gonna look like walking down the road at one in the morning?

MARTINE: If he kills himself, or if they kill him, or if he dies, don't forget that's what I came home for. It will look better on my leave papers than a resurrection.

CATHERINE exits. ISABELLE comes back with a beer. She hands it to MARTINE.

ISABELLE: You want to play poker?

MARTINE: Goddamn crazy family!

ISABELLE: You never would've come if I told you Ma was coming back!

MARTINE: I never wanted to come back here. There's no soul left. I've made a life for myself somewhere else.

ISABELLE: Is it true you never tried to imagine her?

MARTINE: Sometimes. (*beat*) I went to Spain too. I didn't look for her, but I felt that she was there.

ISABELLE: Are you afraid to see her again? "Martine made Federico leave. Martine told Isabelle that Ma was dead."

MARTINE: I wish she'd been here tonight to see the damage. You think that's awful? You must think I'm heartless? Isabelle, I've stopped asking myself questions. I've learned to stop wondering why I'm a soldier like my father, why I'm a lesbian, why I get pleasure out of life.

ISABELLE: Martine, do you think that people should have kids?

MARTINE: How can you ask me that?

ISABELLE: Whenever I ask Catherine something, she uses it against me, and Luc has so much imagination, you never know what he'll do with what you say to him. Do you think that it's possible to have a kid and to really love it? Do you think it's possible for a kid to love its mother too? Do you think we're gonna do to our kids what was done to us?

Do you think people should have kids?

Do you think it's better to take it out on them, or on the people who hurt us?

MARTINE: (*touched by the question*) Not on them … Not on them …

ISABELLE: I'm gonna cook the ham.

MARTINE: Isabelle, I do feel love for you. You know that?

ISABELLE: I guess that's the only word I know by heart, but I sure would like to have it explained to me again. Most of the time, it seems to mean, I want something.

MARTINE: Not me. I don't want anything from you. Good night. (*exits*)

ISABELLE: (*putting on makeup*) Ma always used to wear red lipstick … real red … scarlet. She was always … radiant. Ma's clothes were … splendid. Tomorrow, Ma's gonna think I'm splendid … radiant. I guess everything's ready for Ma's return.

ACT THREE

The following morning. Around eight o'clock. Easter Sunday. MARTINE and ISABELLE are busy decorating the table tastefully. MARTINE is in uniform.

ISABELLE: Stems aren't very long on funeral flowers, eh? I'll tear out some more.

MARTINE: That's enough. We don't want her to think we're congratulating her!

ISABELLE: (*removing some of the flowers already arranged*) You're right. Don't want to overdo it. We've already made enough of a fuss.

MARTINE: Pretty, eh?

ISABELLE: (*places a pitcher of water in the middle of the table*) I went to get some spring water when the sun came up. It's Easter water. They say this water stays pure all year. Never goes bad. In a family that's gone bad like ours, a little glass of this water can't hurt. (*silence*) Luc and Catherine better show up on time!

MARTINE: Stop worrying.

ISABELLE: They were out all night and they didn't even call.

MARTINE: Don't worry. Nobody called to ask where they were going to be laid out so don't panic.

ISABELLE: I feel real nervous. I've already cried twice since I got up this morning.

MARTINE: You must have good mascara, it doesn't show. You look pretty made up like that.

ISABELLE: I want to show her I've "emancipated." (*suddenly*) The ham!

MARTINE: It's all right! You've checked it three times in the last ten minutes. It's gonna start screaming if you stab it any more.

ISABELLE: Where should we have Ma sit? Catherine always took her place.

MARTINE: We can have her sit in the guest's place.

ISABELLE: Ma always spoke so beautifully, eh?

MARTINE: Ma spoke the way people speak in books. Books were her only friends. She'd probably already met Federico in a book before he even arrived in Saint-Ludger. She should've started reading before she met Pa.

ISABELLE: You don't seem so mad at her any more.

MARTINE: Last night I read all the letters she sent Catherine. Cold, practical letters, as if she'd broken all ties with everything here. I still don't understand why she's coming back … I don't understand.

ISABELLE: Every word I learn opens another door for me … the pretty ones and the not so pretty ones. The not so pretty ones open more doors than the pretty ones. You just have to get used to hearing them too. I know why she's coming back. She's coming to open the doors that are still waiting to be opened.

MARTINE: You're getting pretty poetic.

ISABELLE: Me? Poetic already? I have to make sure I speak well when she's here. I have to speak as well as her.

MARTINE: You can speak any way you want.

ISABELLE: No. As well as her. (*silence*) Do they think women look pretty in that suit?

MARTINE: I'm not a model, I'm a soldier.

ISABELLE: It must be a "strategy" to scare the enemy, eh? You sleep with women?

MARTINE: Yes. With one in particular.

ISABELLE: Two and a half months ago, I met a guy at the gate. He made me feel good … I guess you must feel as good with her as I feel with him?

MARTINE: I hope so, for your sake. (*They both laugh.*)

ISABELLE: I really like telling dirty stories. It makes me feel better. I guess that's what they mean by "grown-up talk," eh?

MARTINE: Depends upon the grown-ups.

ISABELLE: You're not supposed to talk about that with Catherine. I'd like to talk about it for hours … It'd be a change from all the stories about our past.

MARTINE: What do you want to start with?

ISABELLE: (*looking out the window*) Catherine and Luc are here.

MARTINE: Guess today's not the day we get to talk about sex in this house.

ISABELLE: Luc looks like he's in rough shape.

MARTINE: Thank God! He finally got the beating he deserved!

LUC enters dressed in men's clothes. His head is bandaged, his arm in a sling. He has trouble walking. CATHERINE is helping him.

CATHERINE: Stop staring like you're watching some sideshow. Come help me.

They help LUC sit down.

MARTINE: So how was Easter Vigil? Did you bring us a candle?

CATHERINE: Looks like the two of you stayed up all night telling jokes.

MARTINE: (*sarcastic*) Looks like the Queen of Spain got one helluva beating!

LUC: (*barely audible*) Bitch!

CATHERINE: Shut up, Luc, you'll tear your stitches.

MARTINE: It's been a long time since we've seen you wearing pants.

CATHERINE: Dr. Lemieux lent him some clothes.

MARTINE: He makes a pretty little boy!

LUC: (*barely audible*) Isabelle, I want to apologize for yesterday.

ISABELLE: (*almost shouting as if LUC were deaf*) What did you say?

LUC: I want to apologize for what I said yesterday.

ISABELLE: I can't understand a thing you say, you're talking like a mongoloid.

CATHERINE: I got there too late. He was sitting in a pool of blood on the church steps. Tessier's twins jumped on him the minute they saw him walk into the church. Luc didn't even have time to go up to the organ loft. In no time at all, there were four or five of them on top of him. Then they threw him out on the steps. Barbarians …

LUC: Tell them what you did!

CATHERINE: I had to go into the church to get Dr. Lemieux. When I found him, I realized I was right in the middle of the centre aisle. I don't know why but I stared at them all and began humming. (*hums "La Paloma"*) The harder Dr. Lemieux tugged on my coat to get me to leave, the louder I sang. I walked out of the church singing at the top of my lungs, and the organist started to play along with me.

MARTINE: You actually did that?

CATHERINE: I felt so good. I felt so good and so free. I had nothing left to hide. I was taking revenge. (*picks up the suitcase*) Now there's something else I've wanted to do for ages. (*walks out the door, only to come back in*) There's a strange car headed this way.

MARTINE: (*goes to the door*) Anyone else on the road waiting for their mother? The car went right by.

Long wait. ISABELLE is scribbling in her notebook. The clock strikes nine, ten, eleven o'clock, noon. Throughout this time, ISABELLE can be seen getting ready. At noon, ISABELLE exits, then re-enters dressed in a 1940s style suit. She enters with the ham, playing her mother.

ISABELLE: Happy Easter, children! (*puts the ham on the table*) I've been waiting for this moment for so long. I've been dreaming of it for months. Hello, Martine! Hello, Luc! Hello, Catou! The house hasn't changed much … You worked hard to keep everything the same.

CATHERINE: What is this supposed to mean, Isabelle?

ISABELLE: (*playing her mother*) Yes, tell me about Isabelle. (*silence*) She isn't here with you? She's in a faraway country? Her work made it impossible for her to come? What has become of her, Catherine? What has she become?

CATHERINE: Not much of anything.

ISABELLE: (*playing her mother*) I'd like to thank you for everything you did for her.

CATHERINE: Fuck off!

LUC: (*making an effort to be understood*) Does this mean Mama isn't coming?

ISABELLE: (*playing her mother*) Here I am, dear.

LUC: The phone call ... the phone call ...

ISABELLE: The phone call? It was Isabelle's turn to make up a lie.

CATHERINE: (*sarcastically*) So, "Ma," where are you arriving from?

ISABELLE: (*playing her mother*) I was supposed to come back from Spain but at the very last minute I decided to come back from Québec City. (*starts to pour water into the glasses*) Let's drink some Easter water. I won't give you any, Luc, you'll spill it. It's Easter water to purify us. To your health!

MARTINE: I'd love to chat a bit longer, but I've got to catch a plane in Bagotville this afternoon. I'm afraid I don't have time to play. So would you mind telling us why?

ISABELLE sits down on the chair reserved for her mother.

ISABELLE: (*playing her mother*) Two and a half months ago, Isabelle met a man who told her that the whole village knew that her mother wasn't dead, that she had simply abandoned them. That man was the truth for Isabelle, and today Isabelle is expecting the child of truth.

MARTINE: You're pregnant?

ISABELLE: (*playing her mother*) Yes, Isabelle's two and a half months pregnant.

CATHERINE: You wanted to go to Montreal to get rid of the baby, is that it?

ISABELLE: (*playing her mother*) Isabelle's baby is a muse. It was the baby who inspired her to do all this. Isabelle preferred to take revenge on you, not on her muse ... not on her muse.

CATHERINE: You can't have the baby! I'm going to take you to Montreal!

ISABELLE: (*playing her mother*) She's going to have twelve kids, just to show you that children are beautiful. Twelve who will leave home ... The most beautiful thing about a family is knowing how to leave it!

CATHERINE: You can't do this to me!

We hear a trailer truck pull up outside and honk.

ISABELLE: (*playing her mother*) You told her how courageous I had to be to abandon you ... Isabelle is abandoning you today.

CATHERINE: Isabelle, I'll sell the house, I've got a thousand dollars in the co-op, we could ...

ISABELLE: You can buy whatever you want, Catherine. Don't forget to eat the ham. It's a family tradition. (*exits*)

MARTINE: That's how I imagined our mother ... free. (*exits with her suitcase*)

LUC: I really wish ... she had come ... for real ... I wanted her to take me in her arms and tell me ...

CATHERINE: (*taking LUC in her arms*) Don't worry, Luc, Catherine will take care of you.

(*singing softly*)
"If at your window, you see a gentle dove
Treat it with care and welcome it there with love
It may be I, so do not deny its plea
Crown it with flowers, grant love its hours for me."

END

MORRIS PANYCH   (b. 1952)

With its roots firmly fixed in the cultural nationalism of the 1965–75 era, and with an implicit mandate to hold up the theatrical mirror to reflect Canadians as they are and have been, Canadian drama has generally tended to favour the social problem play, the family play, the history play: theatre grounded in the particularities of Canadian experience. Just as George F. Walker bucked that trend in the 1970s, Morris Panych's work has been a rare exception in the past two decades. Perhaps because he came of age, theatrically speaking, at the tail end of the nationalist period; perhaps because he cut his teeth on introspective west coast experimentalism rather than the naturalistic, socially committed alternate theatre more common in the era; certainly for personal reasons of temperament and philosophy, Panych has gone his own way. As a triple-threat writer, director and actor, he has built a body of work that draws on an array of cosmopolitan influences from literature, music, philosophy and the stage, but rests primarily on the mid-twentieth-century paradigms of existentialism and the absurd. In *7 Stories* he has written an existential parable and absurdist fantasy that Pat Donnelly, reviewing a Montreal production, called "a revelation of intelligent theatricality … guaranteed to change one's perception of Canadian playwriting forever."

Born in Calgary and raised in Edmonton, Panych got a diploma in radio and television from the Northern Alberta Institute of Technology. He worked briefly at CBC radio before enrolling at the University of British Columbia to study creative writing and theatre (BFA, 1977). After two years at E. 15 acting school in London, he returned to Vancouver where he quickly established himself as the city's most dynamic and versatile actor, beginning with his own sensational playwriting debut.

Last Call, subtitled *A Post-Nuclear Cabaret*, was first produced by Tamahnous Theatre in 1982, then toured Canada and was filmed for CBC-TV. A two-man musical structurally similar to *Billy Bishop Goes to War*, which Tamahnous had also premiered, and with distinct echoes of Beckett's *Endgame*, *Last Call* is set amid the rubble of a nuked Vancouver. The only survivors are a couple of vaudevillians who sing and dance their way through the apocalypse. The play introduced Panych's characteristic dramatic theme and strategy: the meaning of life in the face of death explored through witty meta-theatricality. Panych's partner Ken MacDonald, who also wrote and played the music, was the other actor in the show. His creative collaboration—especially his imaginative set designs—has been a key element in virtually all Panych's subsequent successes.

As artistic director of Tamahnous from 1984–86, Panych co-wrote two more musicals with MacDonald, *Contagious* (1985) and *Cheap Sentiment* (1985), and both performed in Panych's *Simple Folk, Songs of a Generation* (1987), a lovely play about coming of age during the folk music era, which toured Russia after its Tamahnous debut. *7 Stories* opened at Vancouver's Arts Club in 1989, directed by Panych with a startlingly effective set by MacDonald. It swept the city's Jessie awards, then had a successful run at Toronto's Tarragon. The Arts Club-Tarragon connection has proven productive for Panych, the two theatres having subsequently premiered nearly all his major plays. *7 Stories* has since had 100 productions across Canada and the United States as well as in Hungary, Australia and the UK.

7 Stories kicked off over a decade of existential comedies written and directed by Panych, variations on the theme of "this little nothing of a man" (who, he told critic Barbara Crook, "is me") struggling to make sense of it all. *The Necessary Steps* (1990) and *The Ends of the Earth* (1992), the latter a Governor General's Award winner, tell relatively epic versions of this story, with casts of four and five taking on multiple roles. In *The Story of a Sinking Man* (1993) Panych himself played the Beckettian solo character literally sinking into the muck. A misanthropic man sits at the bedside of a dying old woman named Grace in *Vigil* (1995), among his very best plays. (The *Washington Post* called it "delectably weird" and "a morbid masterpiece.") Another darkly comic two-hander is *Lawrence & Holloman* (1998). *Earshot* (2001) Panych describes as a one-character play about "a man who hears too much." Perhaps the most acclaimed of his forays into the fate of the little man has been *The Overcoat* (1997), co-created and co-directed with Wendy Gorling for the Vancouver Playhouse, featuring rubber-limbed actor Peter Anderson. (Both Gorling and Anderson were in the original cast of *7 Stories*.) Adapted from Gogol's classic tale, *The Overcoat* is theatre wholly without words, every movement of the 22-member cast carefully choreographed to the music of Shostakovich.

Panych has had success in a wide range of theatrical endeavours. His plays for young audiences—*Cost of Living* (1990), *2B WUT UR* (1992) and *Life Science* (1993)—have toured nationally and internationally, produced by Vancouver's Green Thumb Theatre and published under the title *Other Schools of Thought*. In addition to three Sydney Risk awards for best new play in the Vancouver theatre, he has received 13 Jessies and a number of Dora award nominations for his acting and directing. Besides his own plays, directorial highlights include *Sweeney Todd*, *The Imaginary Invalid*, *The Comedy of Errors*, *Hamlet* and Judith Thompson's *White Biting Dog*. He has directed operas for the Banff Centre and Vancouver Opera, and music videos for the band Spirit of the West. Among his film and TV credits is a recurring role on *The X-Files*.

"There is but one truly serious philosophical problem, and that is suicide," Albert Camus wrote in *The Myth of Sisyphus*. "Judging whether life is or is not worth living amounts to answering the fundamental question of philosophy." The (every)Man on the ledge in *7 Stories* is clearly in crisis. Costumed in the original production like a silent-movie Buster Keaton, he seems to be undergoing an existential nervous breakdown. As he explains to Lillian, the routine terms of existence that allowed him to cruise thoughtlessly through his daily life have mysteriously dissolved. His "faith in the days of the week has been seriously undermined"; his hands look strange; his shoes and hat and car seem to contain him like prisons. He has confronted the fact of mortality that makes life in a godless universe absurd: "I saw in the mirror a condemned man, serving a life sentence inside his body." So he climbed out on the ledge "to get a better perspective on my exact situation." Perhaps in the hope of a last-minute reprieve, an answer to the ultimate question, he asks Lillian, "There really is no reason to live, is there?" When she answers "Not really," he is left in the fundamental existential quandary: without help from outside himself, confronting "the dizziness of freedom" (in Kierkegaard's phrase), having to choose whether to be or not to be.

The Man is not alone in this predicament. Standing precariously on the seventh-story ledge, he serves as a lens through which we see the other people in the building trying frantically to make sense of their lives in a world where Luigi Pirandello meets Woody Allen. Totally immersed in their own personal fictions, the "stories" they tell themselves to give their existence some semblance of meaning, no one even notices until near the end of the play that the Man might be thinking of jumping. Charlotte the poet and Rodney the lawyer find a superficial antidote to their boredom in the sado-masochistic game of trying to kill each other. Leonard the psychiatrist derives meaning from his own paranoia. For Marshall, acting is so perfect a metaphor for life that he literally transforms himself into his character "for a long run." Rachel plays God, while Michael and Joan decide that "style is absolute," and embrace the lifetime challenge of continuous interior decoration. Percy, Jennifer and Al find ultimate value in the social whirl. As Nurse Wilson observes, no one is interested in other people's problems because everyone is too busy "finding reasons not to jump themselves."

Only Lillian seems to have really figured things out. With the benefit of a century's wisdom she calmly acknowledges that nothing has any intrinsic meaning, that each experience she recounts is "just a story," that "when you're a hundred years old you'll understand. And then you'll die." But through exploring her own rich internal life, she has realized the immense possibilities of transcendence in the free play of the creative imagination. In what Camus calls "a blind act of human confidence" ("nothing logically prepares this reasoning"), she gives the Man the courage to take the existential leap of faith that leads to the play's exhilarating conclusion.

7 Stories was first produced at the Arts Club Theatre in Vancouver in May, 1989 with the following cast:

MAN	Peter Anderson
CHARLOTTE, JOAN, NURSE WILSON	Sherry Bie
RODNEY, MARSHALL, PERCY	David King
JENNIFER, LILLIAN, RACHEL	Wendy Gorling
LEONARD, AL, MICHAEL	Norman Browning

Directed by Morris Panych
Set Design by Ken MacDonald
Lighting Design by Marsha Sibthorpe
Costume Design by Nancy Tait
Original Music by Jeff Corness

7 STORIES

CHARACTERS

MAN
CHARLOTTE
RODNEY
JENNIFER
LEONARD
MARSHALL
JOAN
MICHAEL
RACHEL
PERCY
AL
NURSE WILSON
LILLIAN
POLICE *(megaphone voice)*
FOUR NEIGHBOURS

SCENE

The action of the play takes place outside an apartment building—on the ledge, outside various windows of the seventh storey. As the play progresses, the lights emphasize the time elapsed between early evening and late night.

As the play opens, we hear a party in progress from one of the windows. MAN stands on the ledge, in a state of perplexity, contemplating the depths below. He seems disturbed, confused. Then he comes to what seems to be a resolution. He prepares to jump. As he is about to leap, the window next to him flies open. CHARLOTTE appears. She has a man's wallet, which she attempts to throw out the window. RODNEY, charging up from behind, grabs her hand. A window-ledge struggle ensues.

CHARLOTTE: Let GO of me!!! Let GO!!

RODNEY: *(threatening)* So-help-me-GOD-Charlotte ... !!

CHARLOTTE: *(daring him)* What?? WHAT??!!

RODNEY: Give me back my wallet!

She tries to throw it again. They struggle.

RODNEY: What's WRONG with you? Are you CRAZY?!

CHARLOTTE: YES! YES I AM!!!

RODNEY: MY GOLD CARD is in there!!

CHARLOTTE: Oh? Is it? Is your GOLD CARD in here ... *(She searches through his wallet as he tries to retrieve it.)* Oh my goodness! So it is!! And your RACQUET CLUB membership!! Oooo! And a LOVELY picture of your LOVELY wife! We mustn't drop THAT, must we? We wouldn't want someone picking HER up off the street!!

RODNEY: Give it here!

CHARLOTTE: Leave me alone, or I'll call the police!

RODNEY: You wouldn't dare.

CHARLOTTE: HELP! POLICE!

RODNEY: SHUT UP!!

CHARLOTTE: You STRUCK me!!

RODNEY: I did not!

CHARLOTTE: Yes you did! He STRUCK me! HELP!

RODNEY: I did not!! SHUT UP!

CHARLOTTE: Yes you did! You bastard!

CHARLOTTE goes to strike him. They struggle violently out the window, as MAN watches on, in terror. RODNEY manages to grab CHARLOTTE by the throat and starts to strangle her.

CHARLOTTE: HELP! Helgpjhhgghp!

RODNEY: *(strangling her)* You're quite unattractive when you're dying. Did you know that, Charlotte?

CHARLOTTE: Gddldjkiqk!!!

RODNEY: *(calmly)* You lose all your CHARM! You lose all your SPARKLE! Charlotte! I believe you're turning blue! It's most unbecoming!

CHARLOTTE: Gahhghh!

RODNEY: Is that all you've got to say, Charlotte? Ordinarily you're so outspoken. One might even say LOUD and CONSPICUOUS! What's that you say, Charlotte?

CHARLOTTE: Grrghaah!

RODNEY: Yes, the view from here is BREATH-TAKING, isn't it!

MAN: Excuse me.

RODNEY and CHARLOTTE are stopped cold.

MAN: Would you mind letting go of her. You're hurting her.

RODNEY: (*with feigned surprise*) Hurting her!? (*looks at CHARLOTTE*) Am I hurting you, Charlotte?

CHARLOTTE: Yeghhgg!

RODNEY: (*letting go*) What's that Charlotte?

CHARLOTTE: (*hoarsely*) Yes!

RODNEY: I *am* sorry! (*to MAN*) You were right. I was hurting her. And thank you for pointing that out. Why don't we go inside, Charlotte? We seem to be attracting a crowd.

CHARLOTTE: I am not going anywhere with you! You tried to KILL me!

RODNEY: Kill you! Really Charlotte! Now why would I do that? (*to MAN*) She has an overactive imagination, you know. Dabbles in the creative arts.

MAN: Oh.

CHARLOTTE: Dabbles!

RODNEY: You're misinterpreting the facts once again, Charlotte. (*to MAN*) Apparently she misunderstood my intentions. Come inside, Charlotte.

CHARLOTTE: Misunderstood, nothing! You tried to kill me Rodney. He saw the whole thing. Didn't you?

MAN: I—

CHARLOTTE: He's a key witness. And we know all about key witnesses, don't we? (*to MAN*) Rodney's a lawyer.

MAN: Oh.

RODNEY: Charlotte! I'm warning you—

CHARLOTTE: And of course we know all about lawyers, don't we?

MAN: Actually, he's the only one I've ever met.

CHARLOTTE: Really?!

RODNEY: Oh, for heaven's sake!

CHARLOTTE: Well, in that case, let me fill you in. Lawyers are the people who BORE you to death with the facts. (*to RODNEY*) By the way, Rodney. Why would you go to all the trouble of strangling me, when you simply could have BORED me to death?

RODNEY: You're making a public spectacle!

CHARLOTTE: My goodness that would have been the perfect crime. I would have died, slowly, over the course of one of our romantic evenings together. Hanging, as it were, on his every word—

RODNEY: I need a drink.

CHARLOTTE: Would you like a drink? (*to RODNEY*) Fix us a drink, would you Rodney?

RODNEY goes.

MAN: I—

CHARLOTTE: Yes … I suppose you're wondering why I don't just leave him.

MAN: Well, I—

CHARLOTTE: That's a very good question. (*to RODNEY*) Rodney! What the gentleman wants to know is why I don't just leave you.

RODNEY: Does he?

MAN: I don't really—

CHARLOTTE: Shall I tell him? (*no answer*) He's not answering. He's standing there, giving me that LOOK again. (*to RODNEY*) Don't just stand there giving me that stupid LOOK. I'm not threatened by you in the least. (*to MAN*) He thinks I'm threatened. (*to RODNEY*) In case you forgot, I have a key witness here who fully intends to testify at your attempted murder trial.

MAN: I don't think I'll be around, I—

CHARLOTTE: You won't? Why not?

RODNEY: (*now at the window*) What a pity, Charlotte. Your KEY WITNESS won't be here. (*to MAN*) I can quite understand your reservations. Considering her history. (*to CHARLOTTE*) Get in here!!

CHARLOTTE: Don't listen to him. He'll say anything. He spins a web of lies, like a spider.

RODNEY: Really Charlotte. I'm surprised at your use of such a tired metaphor. And you call yourself a poet.

CHARLOTTE: You see! He tries to make you lose your train of thought.

RODNEY: I shouldn't think you'd need any help with that.

CHARLOTTE: Where's my drink?

RODNEY: Haven't you had enough. (*to MAN*) She loses count after ten cocktails. (*to CHARLOTTE*) Anyway, I'm leaving.

CHARLOTTE: (*to MAN*) Ha!

RODNEY: Where are my Italian brogues?

CHARLOTTE: (*to MAN*) Most people wear shoes. (*to RODNEY*) I have no idea. Perhaps I threw them out the window.

They all look down.

RODNEY: Did you?

CHARLOTTE: I honestly can't remember.

RODNEY: You've hidden them. Where are they? (*to MAN*) What's she done with my shoes?

MAN: I—

CHARLOTTE: I TOLD you—I can't remember. Besides—you happen to be interrupting our conversation.

RODNEY: Oh really? I'm sorry. (*He goes.*)

MAN: It's quite all right!

CHARLOTTE: Don't pay any attention to him. As I was saying … the reason I don't leave here is because Rodney and I are inseparable. The question of leaving, although it arises constantly, is—dare I say—moot. (*to RODNEY*) MOOT? Is that right, Rodney?

RODNEY: WHAT!!?

CHARLOTTE: Can I say "the question of my leaving is MOOT"?

RODNEY: You can say whatever you like.

CHARLOTTE: He's not usually so generous with my word usage. He finds himself correcting just about everything I say.

RODNEY: (*correcting her*) Irrelevant!

CHARLOTTE: What?

RODNEY: The question of your leaving is irrelevant.

CHARLOTTE: Thank you. (*to MAN*) You see.

MAN: Yes, I see.

CHARLOTTE: But I suppose you don't think the question is irrelevant? Since he just tried to kill me.

MAN: Well—

CHARLOTTE: Rodney!

RODNEY: WHAT, for heaven's sake?!

CHARLOTTE: He doesn't think the question of my leaving is irrelevant.

RODNEY: Who doesn't?

CHARLOTTE: He doesn't.

RODNEY: Well, he doesn't know the facts.

CHARLOTTE: Oh. Apparently you don't know the facts. Only Rodney, of course, knows the facts. "The World According to Rodney." My God. Where would we be without all those specific details? Life would be so—vague. Perhaps even meaningless.

MAN: Yes.

CHARLOTTE: When you come to think of it, the Rodneys of this world are man's salvation in a way. They build us the ramparts, stone by stone, each one another absolute little certainty. Another "fact." All piled high against the onslaught of the absurd truth!

RODNEY: (*appearing with two drinks*) Really, Charlotte. You sound like a cheap novelist.

CHARLOTTE: IT'S POETRY!! (*taking drinks*) Thank you. (*giving MAN one of the drinks*) Naturally he despises poetry. He despises all art. Because art is the act of climbing to the top of that ridiculous wall of his—and standing on the ledge—to look out into a cruel and pointless world—devoid of meaning—where fact is merely fiction. And anybody with any courage would simply leap off the edge and be done with it.

RODNEY: I could give you a little push if you'd like.

CHARLOTTE: Go ahead and push me!

RODNEY goes.

MAN: I wouldn't provoke him.

CHARLOTTE: Oh good heavens. That would be much too quick for him. He'd rather kill me little by little than all at once.

RODNEY approaches from behind and points what seems to be a gun at the back of CHARLOTTE's head.

RODNEY: One more word and I'll blow your head off.

CHARLOTTE: I do hope that's a gun, Rodney, and not just your finger.

RODNEY: That's our little secret. Now come inside. I don't want any witnesses this time.

CHARLOTTE: Will you excuse us?

CHARLOTTE slowly closes the window. After a brief moment, a shot rings out. As MAN stands, martini glass in hand, JENNIFER appears from the party window.

JENNIFER: Was that gunfire?

MAN: Uh—I don't …

JENNIFER: (*looking down*) Was somebody gunned down, or what?

MAN: I'm not sure.

JENNIFER: I just LOVE your neighbourhood. It's so … third world!

LEONARD appears from his window, dressed in pajamas.

LEONARD: SHUT UP!! SHUT UP for GOD'S SAKE!! SHUT UP!! I'm TRYING to get some SLEEP!!

JENNIFER: Oh, I know! I tried that once. Scary isn't it?

LEONARD: What's she talking about?

JENNIFER: I was just lying there … and I could hear myself breathing? You know? I thought Oh, God! I can hear myself breathing!! I'll never try THAT again! (*LEONARD quietly closes his window.*) Wow! Your friend is so intense!

MAN: He's not—

JENNIFER: (*looking down*) Do you ever feel like throwing yourself out of a building?

MAN: (*pause*)

JENNIFER: Whenever I get too close to the edge, I just feel like jumping. Isn't that wild?!

MAN: (*pause*)

JENNIFER: It's probably symbolic.

MAN: (*pause*)

JENNIFER: Will you excuse me. It's not that I don't like you or anything—'cause I really do— it's just that there's too many pauses in this conversation.

She disappears, closing the window. After a moment, LEONARD opens his window.

LEONARD: Listen lady … where did she go? She wasn't even there. Oh, my God! (*to MAN*) She wasn't even there! (*He closes his window again. After a brief moment, he opens it again.*) What do you want?

MAN: Uh …

LEONARD: A likely story! What?

MAN: I think there might have been a murder committed.

LEONARD: A murder! So THAT'S where she went.

MAN: No. Your neighbours.

LEONARD: My neighbours murdered her!?

MAN: No.

LEONARD: She murdered my neighbours?

MAN: It's got nothing to do with her. I think there's been a murder committed. I think you should call the police.

LEONARD: Let me get this straight. You murdered the neighbours?

MAN: I didn't say that!

LEONARD: Yes, you did. Are you trying to tell me I'm hearing things? Is that what you're saying. I distinctly heard you say you murdered my neighbours. That it had nothing to do with her!

MAN: All I said was: I think there's been a murder committed. There was an argument. Didn't you hear the gunshot?

LEONARD: Gunshot! I didn't hear any gunshot! Are you sure it was a gunshot?

MAN: Positive.

LEONARD: Oh dear. This is a new twist. Usually I'm hearing things. Now, I'm *not* hearing things. Oh dear. I've gone deaf.

MAN: Hadn't we better call the police?

LEONARD: Did you say something just now?

MAN: Yes.

LEONARD: Are you sure?

MAN: Of course I am. I said, we'd better call the police.

LEONARD: Oh good. Well, I heard that quite distinctly. Every word of it.

MAN: Look—this could be serious.

LEONARD: Do you think so? I'm only a little tense. That's all. If I had some sleep I'd be just fine. Maybe it's just a little wax build-up.

MAN: What are you talking about?

LEONARD: What are *you* talking about? Aren't we both talking about the same thing?

MAN: I was talking about your neighbours. About the gunshot.

LEONARD: The gunshot! Yes! About whether I heard it or not.

MAN: Look—that doesn't matter.

LEONARD: It matters to me!

MAN: There was a gunshot. That's all that matters. Just call the police!

LEONARD: Now how can you expect me to do that? I didn't even hear a gunshot. What am I supposed to tell them—when and if they answer? Am I supposed to *admit* that I didn't even hear a gunshot from twenty feet away? Or am I supposed to pretend that I'm hearing things. They'll think I'm insane!

MAN: What difference does it make?

LEONARD: They ask for your name. Am I supposed to lie about that as well? They'll just find out anyway. Because they'll trace the call back to me. Why did I have to get dragged into this?

MAN: Why are you taking it so personally? It's got nothing to do with you.

LEONARD: Oh, that's right! Accuse me of being one of those!

MAN: One of what?

LEONARD: Those people who shut themselves off from the rest of the world.

MAN: Good God! I wasn't accusing you of anything.

LEONARD: Yes you were!

MAN: No I wasn't!

LEONARD: Are you positive about that?

MAN: Of course I am. I don't even know you.

LEONARD: There was a tone of accusation in your voice. You have to admit it.

MAN: I think you're just being paranoid.

LEONARD: Why would you say that? (*pause*) You don't know anything about paranoia. What experience do you have in that field—if any?

MAN: None.

LEONARD: A likely story! (*pause*) What did you say?

MAN: I said I don't have any experience in the field.

LEONARD: What's that supposed to mean?

MAN: I mean I don't know anything about paranoia.

LEONARD: Implying that I'm paranoid.

MAN: Not at all.

LEONARD: By inference. Saying that you don't know anything about it. Inferring that I know a great deal.

MAN: You said so yourself.

LEONARD: I did not.

MAN: You indicated as much.

LEONARD: This is a trap! You're trying to trap me into something. Aren't you? You think I'm insane! That I've completely lost my grip on reality. And that's where you're wrong. I happen to be painfully cognizant of the world around me. I might be going deaf, but I'm not blind. I'm a qualified professional, and I'm trained to keep my eyes wide open.

LEONARD instantly falls asleep. MAN studies LEONARD for a moment, then looks at his martini glass, goes back over to CHARLOTTE's window. He raps on the pane. RODNEY opens the window.

RODNEY: What do YOU want?

MAN: Is everything all right?

RODNEY: Couldn't be better.

MAN: I heard a gunshot. I thought maybe there'd been an accident.

RODNEY: Charlotte!?

CHARLOTTE: (*inside*) What?!

RODNEY: The gentleman heard a gunshot. He thought there'd been an accident. Isn't that amusing?

CHARLOTTE: Ha! Ha!

RODNEY: As a matter of fact there was a bit of an accident. I aimed for her head and accidentally hit the wall. But thank you for your concern.

RODNEY slams the window shut, waking LEONARD.

LEONARD: Ah! What happened?

MAN: I don't know. You fell asleep.

LEONARD: No I didn't. What?

MAN: You—fell—asleep.

LEONARD: I did? Well, of course I did! What did you expect?

MAN: I don't know.

LEONARD: That's right, you don't. I haven't slept more than two hours in the past month. I never sleep. I work nights.

MAN: So why don't you sleep during the day?

LEONARD: Why do you want me to go to sleep?

MAN: I don't. It makes no difference to me.

LEONARD: Just what are you planning?

MAN: Me? I'm not planning anything. I was only thinking … for your well-being …

LEONARD: My well-being? You think I'm not well.

MAN: I never said that.

LEONARD: Somebody told you something, didn't they?

MAN: No. Nobody told me anything.

LEONARD: Why didn't they? Why would they want to keep YOU in the dark?

MAN: Who?

LEONARD: I don't know!! Has it occurred to you yet that you could be an innocent pawn in all this? A dupe?

MAN: No.

LEONARD: Well, you see! You're naive. You're the perfect candidate for them to carry out their insane plan.

MAN: What insane plan?

LEONARD: Well, they didn't tell you of course. They wouldn't want YOU to know!!

MAN: Know what? Who's they?

LEONARD: You said you heard a gunshot. Right?

MAN: Yes. I did. But …

LEONARD: Coming from where?

MAN: Your neighbours, but …

LEONARD: Well, they're in on it too. Don't you see?

MAN: No. It's all been a mix-up. I mean, I heard a gunshot, but it turns out it was nothing.

LEONARD: Nothing? You don't know what's going on in the world, do you?

MAN: I used to think I did. I don't know. No … I don't.

LEONARD: I suppose you think all these things happen by chance? Just one GREAT BIG HAPPY coincidence. Gunshots are fired. Then they're not fired. A woman appears who was never there. That light in that apartment over there. I guess you didn't notice that either. Because you don't think these things are important.

MAN: Light?

LEONARD: Over there. It just went on. Don't look.

A slight pause as MAN considers this.

MAN: And?

LEONARD: And!? And WHAT?!

MAN: I don't get it.

LEONARD: Of course you don't get it. You don't know the code. Fortunately—I do. I have deciphered the code. I know EXACTLY what's going on. Ah. There goes that other light. Don't look.

MAN: There's lights going on and off all over the place. You don't think everybody's in on it.

LEONARD: In on WHAT? There IS something, isn't there?

MAN: I'm not really sure anymore.

LEONARD: And you think I'm confused!

MAN: I never said you were.

LEONARD: Well, who said I was, then?

MAN: Nobody.

LEONARD: Well, where did you get the information?

MAN: I have no information. I don't know anything.

LEONARD: Oh. (*pause*) Well, I don't know anything either. In fact, I don't even know what we were talking about.

MAN: That makes two of us.

LEONARD: Two of us?

MAN: I don't know what you're talking about either.

LEONARD: Oh. (*pause*) You don't?

MAN: No.

LEONARD: Was I being incoherent?

MAN: I don't know what to say.

LEONARD: What does that mean?

MAN: You're bound to take it the wrong way.

LEONARD: What?

MAN: Whatever I say.

LEONARD: What are you going to say?

MAN: Nothing.

LEONARD: You can tell me. What is it? Is there something I should know about myself?

MAN: Look—it's none of my business.

LEONARD: What? What's none of your business?

MAN: You asked if you were being incoherent. I don't know what to say. If I tell you you were, you'll fly into a panic. If I tell you you weren't, you'll think I'm trying to hide something from you. You take everything I say the wrong way.

LEONARD: You think I'm insane.

MAN: Now there's a case in point. I don't think you're insane. I don't think anything. The word *insane* didn't even enter into it.

LEONARD: Yes it did.

MAN: Well, you said it. I didn't say it. I'm in no position to judge the state of your mind. I'm not a psychiatrist.

LEONARD: A psychiatrist? Why did you mention a psychiatrist? I never said anything about a psychiatrist.

MAN: I was only making a point.

LEONARD: Well, you can make a point without mentioning a psychiatrist, can't you? You could have mentioned a proctologist.

MAN: Why would I do that?

LEONARD: Precisely!

MAN: Very well, then. Have it your way. Let me correct myself. What I meant to say is: I'm in no position to judge the state of your mind. I'm not a proctologist. Is that better?

LEONARD: Why are you making fun of me?

MAN: I'm sorry.

LEONARD: Do you find psychiatry amusing? Well, let me tell you—it's no joke.

MAN: I didn't say it was.

LEONARD: Oh, I realize, it's an easy target for satire. One might even say an obvious one. But it's serious work, involving a lot of time and dedication. And we don't get paid nearly as much as you'd like to think.

MAN: You're a psychiatrist?

LEONARD: Why do you say it like that? What are you implying?

MAN: I'm not implying anything. I'm a little surprised. That's all.

LEONARD: Why should you be? Do you think there's something strange about it? Why are you looking at me like that?

MAN: I'm not even looking at you.

LEONARD: Why aren't you looking at me? Are you afraid of me? Are you afraid I'll find something out about you? Some dark, terrible secret? You can tell me—I'm a psychiatrist. Here—why don't you take my card. You can set up an appointment with my secretary. I work nights at the loony bin. But I have a private practice in the mornings. I've got to run now. It's time to get up and go to work. I haven't slept in three years but what difference does that make to them? They're all on drugs. They sleep all the time. I hate insane people. They drive me crazy. I don't mean literally crazy. You didn't take that literally, did you?

MAN: No.

LEONARD: Are you patronizing me?

MAN: No.

LEONARD: In the future, don't patronize me. I'm the doctor, and I'll do all the patronizing. You'll find, once we've begun to develop a professional relationship, that you'll come to rely on me for emotional support. I'll be carrying the weight of all your problems, so that you can feel free to let go. You won't have to hang on to your sanity. I'll be the one who's hanging on. That's my job.

LEONARD closes the window. The MAN studies the card. As he is pocketing the card, MARSHALL, wearing a tuxedo, opens another window and climbs out onto the ledge. Without noticing the MAN, he takes out a cigarette and lights it. For a moment he luxuriates in this obviously great pleasure. As he exhales he notices the MAN looking at him. MARSHALL speaks with a very "theatrical" accent.

MARSHALL: Oh, pardon me. I hope you don't mind my smoking. It's my last cigarette.

MAN: That's all right.

MARSHALL: Would you like one?

MAN: I don't know. I've never tried one before.

MARSHALL: Here. Be my guest. You can take them all.

MAN: (*making his way a little along the ledge*) I guess it can't do any harm now.

MARSHALL: And *I* certainly won't be smoking them. (*hands the MAN his cigarettes*)

Suddenly, LEONARD's window opens once again, behind him.

LEONARD: I have a question I forgot to ask you. (*not noticing that he has moved*) My God! He wasn't even there!

MAN: I'm over here. I'm having a cigarette.

LEONARD: Who's that?

MAN: A gentleman. I don't know his name. We only just met.

MARSHALL: It's Marshall. Actually, it's Mike.

LEONARD: Well, who is he?

MAN: I don't know. We only just met. (*Now he climbs along the ledge, a little way back to LEONARD's window.*) What was your question?

LEONARD: What question?

MAN: You have a question you forgot to ask me.

LEONARD: What sort of question?

MAN: I don't know.

LEONARD: Well, what? Was it a personal question?

MAN: *You* were the one who wanted to ask it.

LEONARD: Then it *was* personal.

MAN: I really don't know.

LEONARD: Could I have a word with you for a moment.

MAN: What is it?

LEONARD: (*sotto voce*) What does he want?

MAN: I don't think he wants anything. I think he's just having a cigarette.

LEONARD: Does he know about our conversation?

MAN: No, I don't think so.

LEONARD: Well, don't say a word to him. Keep it private.

MAN: All right.

LEONARD: We must pretend that we never spoke.

MAN: We're speaking now.

LEONARD: Act like you don't know me.

MAN: I don't.

LEONARD: Otherwise, he might get the wrong idea. He'll think that just because you're seeing a psychiatrist that you're insane. And that kind of information can get into the wrong hands.

Without saying another word, LEONARD slowly closes the window, putting his finger to his lips in a secret gesture.

MARSHALL: (*who has been watching*) Friend of yours?

MAN: No. I don't know him.

MARSHALL: Best to keep it that way. People know far too much about each other these days. I much prefer to form my own false impressions. Don't you?

MAN: I really don't like to speculate.

MARSHALL: What difference does it make? The truth is irrelevant. One's own opinion on the other hand is far more appealing. One should always form a strong opinion, one way or the other. Regardless of the facts.

MAN: That seems to be a popular theme around here.

MARSHALL: After all, it's about the only thing people are entitled to. Except for me. I've completely relinquished my personality. I've even relinquished my hair colour. Can you believe it?

MAN: That's not your real hair colour?

MARSHALL: Oh, there's no need to pretend you didn't know.

MAN: I didn't.

MARSHALL: I won't be offended if you don't like it. I'm not that sort of person. But you can decide what sort of person I am for yourself. And anyway—it's got nothing to do with me. It's my wife's decision really. Well, it's not really a decision. But then, she's not really my wife, is she? Not yet. But almost.

MAN: You're getting married.

MARSHALL: Yes. In a little over a half an hour, my life, as you and I know it, will be over. Finished. Butted out. Extinguished.

MAN: I suppose congratulations are in order.

MARSHALL: Don't be absurd. Congratulations aren't in order at all. On the other hand, I don't expect any sympathy. You wouldn't feel the least bit sorry for me if you knew the whole story. (*suddenly switching to another, more natural voice*) Is my moustache on straight?

MAN: It looks fine.

MARSHALL: (*returning to accent*) Of course it doesn't look fine. Don't be ridiculous. I'm only asking if it's straight. This damn glue doesn't stick properly.

MAN: You mean it's false?

MARSHALL: (*normal voice*) Couldn't you tell?

MAN: No.

MARSHALL: (*accent*) Oh good. Of course, I suppose it'll fall off in the middle of the ceremony, and that'll be the end of it. I really ought to have grown one. But I can't stand moustaches. The itching drives me mad. Oh God. I've only got half a cigarette left! It seems to be burning awfully fast. Isn't that always the way? You're not smoking yours.

MAN: I'm sorry. I don't find it very pleasant.

MARSHALL: (*normal voice*) Well, don't waste it, for God's sake. Here. I'll finish it. (*He now has two cigarettes, which he smokes alternately. As he continues to speak he gradually loses his accent.*) If I had the time, I'd smoke the whole pack. But the Best Man is waiting for me. He thinks I'm in the bathroom. Thank God for bathrooms. Where would we be without them, eh? Those little private oases in the desert of eternal wedlock. Wedlock! There's a good name for it.

Sounds like padlock, doesn't it? What a perfect description for marriage. Wed—*Lock*. The penitentiary of betrothal! I imagine I'll be spending the rest of my life locked in a bathroom somewhere. Oh, there's no need to be concerned about it. The house has seven different bathrooms. Excluding the *en suites*.

MAN: No. It's not that.

MARSHALL: What is it, then? You look troubled.

MAN: I'm sorry. It's no business of mine, but why are you wearing a false moustache?

MARSHALL: Well, it's part of my character, isn't it?

MAN: It is?

MARSHALL: He wears a moustache. His hair is auburn. And he doesn't smoke, among other things. And his name is Marshall. And I keep losing my accent.

MAN: You mean to say that's not your real accent?

MARSHALL: (*accent*) Well, it is now. Now that I've fully adopted this character.

MAN: You had *me* fooled.

MARSHALL: That's the idea.

MAN: It's so realistic.

MARSHALL: (*changes to normal voice*) Well, there's a lot at stake, isn't there?

MAN: There is?

MARSHALL: About a hundred and fifty million, I'd say. Give or take a million. But who's counting?

MAN: Dollars?

MARSHALL: Dollars. Debentures. Stocks. Bonds. Futures. Securities. You name it.

MAN: Yours?

MARSHALL: If I play my part well enough. If the moustache doesn't fall off at the altar.

MAN: And what if it does?

MARSHALL: Then they'll wonder, won't they? Wouldn't you?

MAN: Well, yes. I'm wondering now.

CHARLOTTE bursts forth.

CHARLOTTE: Help!

MARSHALL: (*assuming accent again*) Are you in some sort of trouble, madam?

CHARLOTTE: Help me.

MARSHALL: Should I call the police this time?

CHARLOTTE: He tried to kill me!

MARSHALL: Oh, dear. Again?

MAN: Again?

Offstage, we hear a little girl's voice.

EFFIE: Marshall!!! Marshall!!!

MARSHALL: (*own voice, to MAN*) It's that horrible little flower girl. Will you excuse me. (*He goes.*)

MAN: Again?

CHARLOTTE: What?

MAN: You mean to say he's tried to kill you before.

CHARLOTTE: On several occasions. Not the least of which was my BIRTHDAY!!

RODNEY: (*from off*) Oh, for heaven's sake … get in here!!

CHARLOTTE: Don't you think that's insensitive?

MAN: Well, yes, I …

CHARLOTTE: Rodney!

RODNEY: What!?

CHARLOTTE: This gentlemen thinks it's incredibly insensitive that you tried to kill me on my birthday.

RODNEY: Oh, does he?

MAN: I—

RODNEY: He doesn't know the whole story.

CHARLOTTE: Oh. You don't know the whole story.

RODNEY: And what's more, it wasn't your birthday.

CHARLOTTE: It was MY BIRTHDAY!! He has a tremendous sense of occasion.

RODNEY: You're distorting the facts once again.

MAN: Why do you treat each other this way?

CHARLOTTE: It's all words and gestures. Pomp. There's absolutely no substance to it.

MAN: He was choking you to death.

CHARLOTTE: Oh, that. It gives him a tremendous sense of power to hear me gasping helplessly for air.

MAN: And the gun?

CHARLOTTE: Blanks.

MAN: You were both just pretending?

CHARLOTTE: Oh, I don't know. There's such a fine line between truth and fiction, isn't there. It's the subject of a number of foreign films. (to RODNEY) Oh, for God's sake, Rodney. What are you doing now?

RODNEY: I'm killing all your goldfish.

CHARLOTTE: Did you hear that? He's killing all my goldfish.

MAN: Yes. I heard.

CHARLOTTE: The neighbours can hear you, Rodney.

RODNEY: What? Killing a fish?

CHARLOTTE: He's not really doing anything. He's standing there *looking* at my goldfish. Giving them that LOOK. That DEADLY LOOK. Yes. I was only acting.

MAN: Pardon?

CHARLOTTE: I was pretending to die. He finds it amusing.

MAN: Oh. Well, I don't.

CHARLOTTE: Then why were you watching us?

MAN: I happened to be here. That's all.

CHARLOTTE: I see.

RODNEY: (inside) Come inside, Charlotte. I've got a knife and I want to cut your head off.

CHARLOTTE: (to RODNEY) That knife isn't even sharp. You'd have to poke my head off with that!

RODNEY: Now there's an idea!

CHARLOTTE: He's threatening to cut my head off with a butter knife. Can you imagine?!

MAN: No, not really.

CHARLOTTE: Well, at least it's something. I suppose there's a certain affection in it. It keeps the relationship alive anyway. It used to be one of those dreary, mindless little affairs that start with a bang and end with a whimper. We weren't even lovers anymore. Just zombies. You can't imagine. He started reading the paper at dinner. I started having another affair. You can't believe how complicated that is. Cheating on the man you're cheating with. Anyway—it had all the trappings of a marriage. Which is precisely what both of us were trying to escape. We began to dread seeing one another. Finally, I suppose out of sheer exasperation, dear Rodney, the boring lawyer, tried to run me down with his car. It's hard to explain, but as I lay on the curb, half-conscious, I felt—revitalized. We both did. And we've been trying to kill each other ever since.

RODNEY: Charlotte … ?

CHARLOTTE: (to MAN) It's not entirely an act. We really do hate each other. But there's something to be said for that, isn't there. There's a certain zeal to it. (She leaves.)

MARSHALL returns, now speaking in his normal voice.

MARSHALL: They're quite an item, those two.

MAN: You know them?

MARSHALL: I've seen them around. She tried to stab him to death in the hallway last week. It's really an incredible love story.

MAN: Love?

MARSHALL: What would you call it?

MAN: I—

MARSHALL: Oh. I forgot. You don't like to speculate on these things.

MAN: No.

MARSHALL: I do. I think they're deeply and passionately in love, and I think that one day soon, quite by accident, there will be casualties. It's not my kind of love, mind you. I'm much more inclined toward the romantic. The sentimental. The sort of love that brings a tear to the eye. Like a good television commercial. Counterfeit emotion is really my style. Counterfeit everything.

MAN: Like your moustache?

MARSHALL: It is perfect when you think about it.

MAN: What is?

MARSHALL: This masquerade.

MAN: Wouldn't it be easier just to be who you are?

MARSHALL: I wonder what that would be? Anyway—it wouldn't be what she wants. This is what she wants so this is what she gets. After all, I'm being well compensated for it. So what do I care? It's no worse than what I was doing. Just a little more involved.

MAN: What were you doing?

MARSHALL: Acting. I was acting for a living.

MAN: Oh. You're an actor.

MARSHALL: Well, not anymore. I've forfeited that as well. Along with my name. It used to be Mike. Michael Merchant. I take it you've never heard of me.

MAN: I, uh …

MARSHALL: But then, why would you have? I was never really very good. Quite second-rate, in fact. I've played all the great roles, but I've played them all very badly. Acting is such a desperately futile profession anyway. Playing out the lives of other men. Knowing of their failures and successes long before they ever do. Living, suffering, murdering, dying … all in the space of three hours. Sometimes only two. And in such a confined little area. And over and over again every night. Can you imagine anything more perfectly stupid? Squeezing a whole existence into a measly evening's entertainment on the stage? And not only that—in the middle of it all—pausing for an intermission. It makes one's own life seem unbearably preposterous, doesn't it?

MAN: Yes. I suppose it does.

MARSHALL: So I'm more than happy to give it up.

MAN: But you're acting now.

MARSHALL: Well, yes, but this is different, isn't it?

MAN: Is it?

MARSHALL: Most certainly and definitely. This is one play where the curtain never goes down. I will play this character until I die. Or until she does. But that's another story.

JOAN and MICHAEL burst forth from another window, struggling with an antique vase.

JOAN: No. No, Michael. Please!

MICHAEL: Pull yourself together, Joan. Be a little more objective.

JOAN: Michael … Michael …

MICHAEL: Joan!

In their struggle, the vase breaks.

JOAN: Oh, no. It was family!

MICHAEL: Yes, but it was completely out of fashion.

JOAN: It meant a great deal to me, Michael.

MICHAEL: My mother meant a great deal to me, Joan, but she didn't go with anything either.

They go.

MAN: I don't get it. I just can't understand why your fiancée would want you to be someone else.

MARSHALL: She doesn't want me to be someone else. As far as she's concerned, I *am* someone else. I'm Marshall. She doesn't know anything about Michael Merchant, and she never will. In about five minutes from now, Michael Merchant will disappear from the face of the earth. He'll be nothing but a fleeting memory.

MAN: Where will he go?

MARSHALL: That's probably a very interesting philosophical question. But I'm not a philosopher. I'm Marshall.

MAN: So you said.

MARSHALL: Yes. Well, it doesn't hurt to remind myself. (*normal voice*) She first met me, that is, she first met *him* one night about a year ago. I was playing Horatio, and as usual, playing it very badly. Not only that—but on this particular evening, I was also playing it very fast. The flights of angels had never so quickly sung poor Hamlet to his rest. I had a date with destiny, you see. Actually, I had a date with a sailor.

MAN: A sailor? A *male* sailor?

MARSHALL: Yes. It's funny, now that I think about it. Well, it's all an act anyway. Isn't it? The whole stupid dumb show. Life, I mean. His name was Marshall. And it was him I was thinking about, as I dashed from the theatre, still in make-up, and in this ridiculous hair colour, and moustache, when this sleek, red Mercedes came roaring around the corner …

MAN: So she hit you.

MARSHALL: Almost hit me. But she'll never know. I must say—it was a much better performance than the one I'd just given. And I thought—well, a Mercedes … there's got to be a little money here somewhere. And as it turns out, there was. Quite a little.

MAN: A hundred and fifty million.

MARSHALL: It does come trippingly off the tongue, doesn't it? Like the name Marshall. It seemed to suit the scenario. More like the name of the sort of person who might be worth her while. Anyway, it worked. She loved the name, she loved the hair colour, and she adored the moustache. And the rest of the character just slowly fell into place, until it was exactly what she wanted. She couldn't have done better if she'd ordered me from a catalogue, which is just the sort of thing she usually does. Who'd believe it, eh?

MAN: I would think she's bound to find out the truth.

MARSHALL: Well, as I say. Who'd believe it?

MAN: But what about family and friends?

MARSHALL: They go with the forfeit. Vanish into thin air.

MAN: They'll see you in the street.

MARSHALL: We'll hardly be travelling in the same circles. And if they ever do see me, I'll simply remind them of someone they used to know.

MAN: But what about records of birth. That sort of thing. Don't you have to prove who you are? Even to get a marriage license?

MARSHALL: I have a friend in props. He's very good.

MAN: Well, you can't just appear out of nowhere. What about parents?

MARSHALL: Yes. Those were difficult parts to cast.

MAN: You mean, there are others in on this?

MARSHALL: Oh, just a couple of old actors, in need of a steady job. I have to admit *she's* a bit of a ham. Calls me "son" too much. But I've passed it off as eccentricity. The in-laws find them terribly charming. And there's an uncle. He's an old friend of mine. I owe him a few favours, so he's part of the family now. It's quite a collection. Between them, they've come up with more than a few fond memories of my childhood.

MAN: This is total fraud!

MARSHALL: Well, we're looking at it more like a long run.

MAN: What's more, it's immoral!

MARSHALL: Don't be ridiculous. It's nothing of the kind. It's simply patronage of the arts. It all depends on your point of view. And anyway, no one's doing anyone any harm.

MAN: But you've given up your family. Your friends. You're making a complete mockery out of your existence. A joke. Doesn't your life mean anything?

MARSHALL: Well, I've lived so many, haven't I? Lives are just short little episodes. You're on and then you're off. Just like that. Which reminds me. I'm off.

Just as MARSHALL is leaving, RACHEL opens her window.

RACHEL: Oh, excuse me.

LEONARD reappears as RACHEL closes her window.

LEONARD: Oh good. You're still here. (*producing pills*) Here, take a couple of these.

MAN: What are they?

LEONARD: Oh, you know. The usual.

MAN: There's nothing wrong with me. Nothing—psychiatric. I don't really have any of the necessary symptoms.

LEONARD: (*another bottle*) Then you'll want to take a couple of these first before you take a couple of those. Otherwise, there's no reason to take any of those. These ones pick you up and those ones bring you down. So it's really better if you take them both at the same time. That'll keep you more or less balanced until I get back from the booby hatch.

He goes. MAN studies the pills. RACHEL opens her window.

RACHEL: How long are you going to be out there? Roughly speaking?

MAN: Huh?

RACHEL: Are you going to be out there for long?

MAN: I have no idea.

RACHEL: Oh. Well, don't rush. I can wait. (*pause*) Will it be more than ten minutes?

MAN: What?

RACHEL: Will it be more than ten minutes, or less than ten minutes?

MAN: I don't really know.

RACHEL: Oh. (*Pause. She watches, as he contemplates the depths.*) So you really don't know how long you'll be.

MAN: Does it make any difference?

RACHEL: No. I suppose not. Not if you're preoccupied.

MAN: Preoccupied?

RACHEL: With your thoughts.

MAN: Oh. Yes. I am.

RACHEL: You have your thoughts and you need somewhere to think them. Someplace private. I understand.

MAN: You do?

RACHEL: Well, of course. I value my privacy, too. A person needs to be alone with God.

MAN: God.

RACHEL: So go ahead. I'm not going to bother you anymore.

As he contemplates, she lowers money on a string.

MAN: (*muttering to himself*) Monday, Tuesday, Thursday, Friday ... (*noticing the money*) What are you doing?

RACHEL: (*retrieving money*) Oh. It's nothing. Really.

MAN: What *is* that?

RACHEL: What?

MAN: In your hand?

RACHEL: Are you asking me what I've got in my hand? Is that what you want to know?

MAN: Yes. Well, no. Well, I know what you've got. You've got some money.

RACHEL: Well, then you don't need to ask.

MAN: On a string?

RACHEL: I thought you had some thinking to do?

MAN: I do. But I just couldn't help noticing. That's all.

RACHEL: I'm sorry if I was distracting you.

MAN: Well, it's not my place, really. I mean—I don't belong here. It's your business what you do with your money. If you want to lower it on a string that's your business.

RACHEL: It does seem odd from this perspective, I'll admit; when you see it from above. You're getting the seventh-storey perspective. If you were on the sixth storey, this would look quite different.

MAN: Yes. I'm sure it would.

RACHEL: But please don't let me interrupt. You were in the middle of prayer.

MAN: No, I wasn't. In fact I'm not even sure I believe in God.

RACHEL: Sometimes in a person's life, they're not really sure. They lose their faith. They become pragmatic about things. They need hard evidence of God's existence. But the evidence of God is everywhere.

MAN: Where?

RACHEL: Well, since you asked about the money, I'll tell you. There's a man here. Just below us. On the sixth floor? Last night, he turned to God for help. He's in a great deal of trouble. He drinks quite heavily, you see. His wife left him three years ago. Then he lost his job. He was a carpet wholesaler, or a carp-fish processor. I'm not really sure. He slurs his words quite a bit. Last year his son was killed on a motorbike. Or murdered with a knife. And six months ago, a close friend of his was killed in what sounds like a freak accident, involving either a stray piece of glass, or the spraying of some gas, or a suspension bridge collapse. And now, they're evicting him. He's asked for money. And God is answering. Could the evidence be clearer?

MAN: It's not clear to me.

RACHEL: Unfortunately, you're on the wrong floor. I can't help people up here on the seventh storey. But the people on the sixth and fifth are well looked-after.

MAN: You're answering all their prayers?

RACHEL: Not all. I try to spread things around a little. A toaster here, an electric heater there. Besides, they can't have everything they ask for. I've only got so much. And I wouldn't want them taking it for granted. Miracles don't just happen, you know. They require a great deal of prayer. Even little miracles.

MAN: But you can't expect people to believe that this is God's work. They might as well believe in Santa Claus! And what's the procedure if they don't believe? Do you lower down overdue electric bills and eviction notices? (*pause*) You didn't!

RACHEL: What difference does it make?

MAN: You sent him that eviction notice?

RACHEL: I'm giving him the rent money. Everything will be fine now. He was lost and now he's found.

MAN: Lost! The poor man lost his wife, his job, his son, his best friend. Isn't that punishment enough? You weren't involved with any of that, were you?

RACHEL: That's so typical.

MAN: What is?

RACHEL: It's just so easy to be cynical, isn't it?

MAN: Under the circumstances.

RACHEL: These people's lives have changed! You've never heard so many prayers as the ones that rise up from directly below this window.

MAN: No. I don't doubt it.

RACHEL: And that is the power of faith!

MAN: What is? Hoping for a toaster? How do you know it isn't the power of greed?

RACHEL: I don't know who you are, and I don't know who sent you, but I have a pretty good idea. And you're not going to alter my relationship with God.

MAN: I have no interest in your relationship with God.

RACHEL: You want to make me say something, but I won't.

MAN: I don't want to make you say anything. Don't be ridiculous. What on earth would I want you to say?

RACHEL: Oh, you know perfectly well.

MAN: No I don't.

RACHEL: Yes you do.

PERCY appears from the party window.

PERCY: Say—where did you get that drink? I've been looking everywhere. Nobody's drinking anything. Is this a new trend or what? First nobody was smoking, so I had to give up smoking. I never really liked smoking, you know, but everybody was smoking, so I started smoking, and then I got hooked. Then everybody was quitting so I had to quit. And now it looks like nobody's drinking. Everybody's walking. Everybody used to run. I'm glad that's over. Now everybody is walking. Nobody's running anymore. Well, I guess it's because everybody's getting older. Well—nobody's getting younger, that's for sure! Yeah—everybody's in the same boat, and nobody's rocking it anymore. Everybody used to rock the boat. Everybody used to be different from everybody else, so nobody would be the same. But that didn't work, because everybody was the same, because everybody was different. Now everybody is just plain "the same." Except for you. You're drinking. I wish I was.

RACHEL: You've got your priorities all wrong, mister. You don't need a drink. You need God.

PERCY: God? Nobody's doing God! Okay—*some* people were doing God, but not everybody. And that was before everybody was doing sex and hardly anybody's doing sex anymore.

Everybody's doing children. Children—and walking—and gas ranges. Not God! (*He goes.*)

RACHEL: He's the devil.

MAN: No he's not.

RACHEL: Well, he's not actually the devil. The devil doesn't make personal appearances. He acts through people.

MAN: What? You don't think that people are capable of acting on their own? You think the devil sent me?

RACHEL: Can you think of any other explanation?

MAN: Yes. I can.

RACHEL: Well, of course you can. You could probably come up with at least a dozen reasons why you're standing on the ledge outside my window. He's very good at making even the most perverse things seem perfectly reasonable.

MAN: Well, if you must know the truth …

RACHEL: The truth! How clever! Go ahead. Try and seduce me.

MAN: Seduce you. I haven't got the slightest interest in you.

RACHEL: You know what I mean.

MAN: No. I don't.

RACHEL: Try and convince me that God doesn't exist.

MAN: Why would I do that? No. Really. Why would I try and convince you that God doesn't exist? In the first place, I don't care whether you believe in him or not. In the second place, I'm not really sure myself.

RACHEL: This is amazing! You are so devious. Pretending that you don't care. Even pretending that you sort of believe in God yourself.

MAN: But I'm not pretending.

RACHEL: And even pretending that you're *not* pretending.

MAN: This is hopeless.

RACHEL: Yes. It's hopeless. You won't make me say it.

MAN: Say *what*?

RACHEL: Well, I'm not going to say it, am I?

MAN: How do I know if I don't even know what you're going to say?

RACHEL: I have to admit that you're very shrewd. You think that if you act stupid enough, that somehow I'll confess to my doubts. But you'll never make me.

MAN: If I'm not mistaken, you already have.

RACHEL: I have not.

MAN: You said that you'll confess to your doubts.

RACHEL: You've turned this whole thing inside out.

MAN: Well, I won't argue the point. I really don't care. I was merely concerned about the effects of your faith on other people. Especially poor, desperate people.

RACHEL: What do you know about desperate people? When have you ever been desperate? Ask *me* about desperation. I'll tell you all about it. God has tested my faith in many horrible ways! He has sent me almost every disease imaginable. He has crippled me, and bruised me, and pushed me around. And, as if that isn't enough, he shoved my mother down a flight of stairs, and turned her into a human vegetable. I had to care for her. I had to change her dirty clothes and feed her like a baby. She was my daily torment for sixteen years, until finally, out of sheer divine mercy, he gave her an overdose of two thousand milligrams of diazepam!

RACHEL cries. The MAN is in shock at what RACHEL has just told him. Another window opens. JOAN, holding two bolts of cloth, leans out the window.

JOAN: It's even worse in the street light, darling. There's *red* in it!

MICHAEL: (*from inside*) Oh, please! Are you blind?

JOAN: It's not beige at all. It's pink! Look!

MICHAEL: (*appearing*) Why do I even argue with you? It's pointless!

JOAN: But can't you see the red?

MICHAEL: It's the reflection of the neon, dear. There's too much bounce out here from the lights. Where's your sense of colour?

JOAN: Well, what's wrong with this other shade?

MICHAEL: It's not a *shade!* It's a tint for heaven's sake! Please!

JOAN: What's wrong with it?

RACHEL cries.

MAN: (*to RACHEL*) Stop crying for heaven's sake!

MICHAEL and JOAN stop and notice the MAN, who smiles back.

JOAN: Are we interrupting something?

MAN: No. Nothing. Sorry. Carry on.

RACHEL: No one will ever destroy my faith! Not you—not even God!

JOAN: At least let her have her faith, for heaven's sake.

MAN: She can have it. I'm not stopping her.

JOAN: What sort of faith are we talking about anyway?

RACHEL: My faith in God.

JOAN: Oh. How interesting. Well, I know what it's like.

MICHAEL: Yes. She has absolutely no faith in me!

JOAN: Don't be ridiculous, Michael. Of course I do!

MICHAEL: Then why don't you believe me when I tell you this has absolutely no pink tones?!

JOAN: Because it does! (*to RACHEL and the MAN*) Would you mind giving us your opinion?

MICHAEL: Really Joan! You're not serious. You can't be!

JOAN: I'm only asking.

MICHAEL: This is an outrage! (*He leaves the window.*)

JOAN: Oh dear. I've upset him. Excuse me. (*She leaves.*) Michael!

MAN: That's murder, you know.

RACHEL: What is?!

MAN: Giving your mother an overdose of diazepam. That's cold-blooded murder.

RACHEL: I didn't give her an overdose. *She* took the pills.

MAN: Oh!

RACHEL: She wanted to die, so God gave her the strength to do it.

MAN: Suicide is not an act of God.

RACHEL: How do you know?

MAN: Because it's a human act. It's the one act that defies all pre-destiny. And it's got nothing to do with anybody else. It stands alone. Complete and of itself. What are you doing?

RACHEL: I'm praying.

MAN: Well, please don't. You're wasting your time. Unless there's somebody just like you up on the eighth floor. Look. Please. Don't bother.

RACHEL: Do you want to go to Hell someday?

MICHAEL returns, leaning out of the window, sulking.

JOAN: (*from behind*) Michael. Please. I'm sorry.

RACHEL: Well, I can't help you if you want to go to Hell.

JOAN: I'm sorry darling.

MICHAEL: Go ahead and make a fool out of me. See if I care.

JOAN: Nobody's trying to make a fool out of you.

MICHAEL: (*referring to the MAN*) What does *he* know about hue? About value, or intensity? About pair interpretation, for that matter? It's all subjective with him. Low and common. Is that what you want? The lowest common denominator? Consensus? A thousand people all shouting "beige! beige!"? And who asks the all-important question: "which beige?" Someone's got to ask that question, Joan. Or the world becomes nothing. Just an ugly great wash!

RACHEL: (*to MAN*) If you change your mind and decide to go to Heaven, let me know. (*closes her window*)

MICHAEL: Heaven? My goodness—she has a very high opinion of herself.

MAN: She was speaking theologically.

JOAN: (to MICHAEL) Am I forgiven, then?

MICHAEL: You must stop questioning my stylistic perceptions.

JOAN: I don't.

MICHAEL: You can't just go out and buy an ashtray—or a vase.

JOAN: I can't help it.

MICHAEL: You've got to learn to disassociate yourself with your emotions a little and finally come to terms with style.

JOAN: I'm trying, Michael. I'm really trying.

MICHAEL: And you can't just go asking any idiot off the street what he thinks.

JOAN: Well, he looked like he might be objective.

MICHAEL: But what does he know about the physiological capacities? What does he know about black, about white? About anything at all, for that matter? He's nothing but an animal, in an animal world. (They both study the MAN.) Look at the way he's dressed. Can you seriously take his word for anything?

MAN: What's wrong with the way I'm dressed?

JOAN: Nothing darling. You look perfectly charming.

MICHAEL: There's no thought. There's no justification. It's all mood. Stream of consciousness.

MAN: I beg your pardon …

MICHAEL: He's a walking fatality. A casualty of function!

MAN: Excuse me …

JOAN: Yes?

MAN: Well, I couldn't help overhearing you.

MICHAEL: I'm sorry. I was just being emphatic.

JOAN: Michael is very emphatic.

MAN: If I'm not mistaken, you called me an idiot.

JOAN: Try not to take it personally, darling.

MICHAEL: I wasn't referring to you. You're no more idiotic than the next person.

MAN: I don't mind being called an idiot. It's not that. It's just that you don't know me.

MICHAEL: Well, no. I don't. Why on earth would I?

MAN: Well, if you don't know me, how do you know I'm an idiot? What if I said you were an idiot?

MICHAEL: You'd be an idiot for saying it. (back to JOAN) Now, let's discuss this green thing for a moment. I'm not entirely adverse, but you must remember that unlike nature, where it's so pervasively vital, green can take on a role of defensiveness and obstinacy. It has its devious side.

JOAN: But don't you think it reflects my character?

MICHAEL: The character of a colour depends entirely on the colours around it. You can't take a colour out of context.

MAN: Just how is it that you can call me an idiot, but if I call you an idiot, then I'm an idiot for saying it?

MICHAEL: (to MAN) Do you mind? (to JOAN) Who is this man?

JOAN: I suppose he's a neighbour. Are you a neighbour?

MAN: No. And there's nothing wrong with the way I'm dressed, either.

MICHAEL: Nobody said there was. I don't make value judgements. I'm not a fascist.

JOAN: Michael never makes value judgements.

MAN: I didn't say you were a fascist.

JOAN: He's just being sensitive, aren't you Michael?

MICHAEL: I'm not being sensitive. I am sensitive.

JOAN: Of course you are.

MAN: I merely took exception to your sweeping generalizations. About me—and about the world at large. After all—you said I was nothing but an animal, in an animal world.

MICHAEL: I can't deal with this, Joan.

JOAN: Of course you can't. You go inside for a moment, darling, while I send the gentleman away.

MICHAEL: (*goes*) I just can't deal with it.

MAN: What's he so upset about? I'm the one who's been insulted.

JOAN: Of course you have. Can I write you a cheque or do you want cash?

MAN: Why would I want cash?

JOAN: Good. I'll write you a cheque, then.

MAN: I don't want a cheque either.

JOAN: No? Well, what do you want?

MAN: Nothing.

JOAN: Oh. How interesting.

MAN: I certainly don't want money.

JOAN: I'm sorry if my offer offended you. It's just that … so often, in situations involving Michael, it's much more expedient to simply buy one's way out.

MAN: Does he always go around insulting people?

JOAN: Michael is an artist. People don't understand him. He's intensely visual. The sight of red with yellow gives him heart palpitations. Certain shades of magenta make him physically nauseous. He can feel the space around him so much so that he becomes the space. The presence of Dacron gives him the flu. So you can imagine how difficult he is. Very hard to keep up with. He's cost me a fortune but it's worth it. Left on my own, I couldn't decorate a closet. I have absolutely no imagination. But I admire a perfect work of art. Although it's something we've yet to achieve. Since I've known him, Michael and I have redecorated my apartment eighteen times. Including this one. Eighteen times. Top to bottom. We're only half way through this one and already I know we'll have to start again. So I hope you can understand the frustration. And if Michael insulted you, I—we apologize.

MAN: Well, thank you for explaining the situation. Although, as situations go, I have to admit, I don't really get it. Why would you go to all the trouble?

JOAN: It is a lot of trouble, of course, yes. There are times when I've felt like giving up. Michael gives me the inspiration to keep searching for that perfect constellation of form, texture, and colour. We look on it as a lifetime challenge.

MAN: A lifetime is a lot of time.

JOAN: There are a lot of choices. Probably too many.

MAN: It sounds to me like you'll never be satisfied.

JOAN: Yes. It does, doesn't it? But one day we'll find what we're looking for.

MAN: And then what?

JOAN: Oh. What an interesting question. Perhaps it's a little too interesting. (*calling*) Michael!

MICHAEL: I won't be compromised!

JOAN: Nobody's compromising anybody. (*to MAN*) He thinks you're putting in your two-cents worth about the apartment. People usually do. They think they know how to decorate because they think they know what they like. I used to be the same. But I'm trying not to have any opinions now. Sometimes it's difficult to be objective though, isn't it? But one has to be. Especially if you live in it. After all, on a purely subjective level, my apartment looks ridiculous. And I don't even have a decent, comfortable bed to sleep in. So you can understand why it's necessary for us to disassociate ourselves from our personal feelings. Personal feelings are so difficult anyway. Whereas style is absolute. Whether it's absolutely this, or absolutely that.

Another window opens, and PERCY leans out. He emits an audible sigh. Inside, behind him, a party is in full-swing.

PERCY: Dreary, isn't it?

MAN: Sorry?

PERCY: My God I feel like jumping. Right here and now. I'd rather splatter my guts all over the pavement than go back in there.

JOAN: Oh, don't do that darling. You leave too much up to chance. If you want to convey the right message, you may want to slash your wrists over a simple, pale cotton print, for instance. It has a stronger impact. More clarity.

MAN: You don't really want to jump, do you?

JOAN: Of course he doesn't. People don't jump from buildings anymore.

MAN: Why not?

JOAN: The trend is much lighter. More whimsical.

MAN: He's talking about suicide.

PERCY: No I'm not. I'm talking about dying of boredom.

JOAN: Well, if you'll excuse me ... (*She starts to go.*)

PERCY: I wonder if you could do me a favour.

JOAN: Yes?

PERCY: I wonder if you could call next door here in about five minutes, asking for me and sounding quite urgent. Say your name is Rhonda. I'll give you the number.

JOAN: I'd love to oblige you, darling, but I no longer have a telephone. It didn't fit in with the decor.

JOAN leaves and closes her window. The MAN and PERCY are left alone.

PERCY: Everybody has a telephone. Nobody doesn't have a telephone. How on earth does she survive?

MAN: It wouldn't be so bad.

PERCY: I'd be lost. I wouldn't have a single friend. As it is now, I have nine hundred and forty.

MAN: Friends?

PERCY: Yes.

MAN: You have that many friends?

PERCY: Yes. Isn't it fabulous? People are always saying "I can't *count* the number of friends I have!" When what they actually mean is that they only have a handful. Maybe two, three hundred. But I can, and I've got nine hundred and forty.

MAN: I didn't think it was possible to be intimate with that many people.

PERCY: Who said anything about being intimate? I couldn't care less about most of them.

MAN: Well, then they're not really your friends, are they?

PERCY: Why not?

MAN: The whole idea of friendship is that you like someone.

PERCY: Why would I like them? They're awful. What an odd notion!

MAN: You don't like any of them.

PERCY: *Like* is a big word. If we're counting friends that I *like*, I've actually got more sweaters. I've got two hundred and sixty-eight sweaters, but actually sort of *like* three of them. Of the friends I have—uh ... let's see ... (*He thinks.*) No. I don't really like her, but I *love* her work. Uh ... can I count you?

MAN: What? As a friend?

PERCY: No. As a friend I *like*. I already count you as a friend.

MAN: But I'm not.

PERCY: I beg your pardon.

MAN: I'm not your friend.

PERCY: Oh. Well, I guess I'll have to put you in the "don't like" column, then.

MAN: Don't put me in *any* column.

PERCY: What?

MAN: I don't want to be in one of your columns.

PERCY: Well, where would you suggest I put you.

MAN: Don't put me anywhere. You don't own me. I'm not a sweater.

PERCY: What are you taking about? Of course you're not a sweater. You're not even *wearing* a sweater.

JENNIFER pokes her head through the same window.

PERCY: Jennifer. I want you to meet a friend of mine.

MAN: I'm not his friend.

JENNIFER: Well, any friend of Jack's is a friend of mine.

MAN: I'm—not—his—friend!

PERCY: That's all right. I'm not Jack.

JENNIFER: You're not? Why aren't you?

PERCY: Because I'm Percy.

JENNIFER: Yes—well … It's the details that start to ruin a perfectly good relationship. I like to know as little about a person as possible. Preferably nothing at all.

Now AL leans out the same window.

AL: I hope you guys don't think this is the way out.

PERCY: Not unless you want to jump.

All laugh.

MAN: What's so funny about that?

AL: (*to MAN*) Hi! Don't I know you?

MAN: No.

AL: Are you sure?

MAN: Of course I'm sure.

JENNIFER: I don't know a soul.

PERCY: Well, I can introduce you. They're all my friends.

AL: Are they? Well, they're certainly not mine.

JENNIFER: I don't even know which one is the host.

AL: I am.

JENNIFER: Oh! Well, it's a fabulous party. I wasn't invited. That's the only reason I'm here.

PERCY: It's the best party I've been to in a long time. I've been to one hundred and eleven parties this year, and this is one of the best. Oh! Look! I think I see a friend of mine. Excuse me, will you? (*He leaves.*)

AL: Who's *he?*

JENNIFER: (*referring to MAN*) A friend of *his.*

AL: Oh!

MAN: No. He's not.

AL: Well, whoever he is, I hope he leaves and takes everybody else with him. Except for you two, of course.

JENNIFER: I'm afraid I can't stay. As much as I'm enjoying this one, I'm due at another party any minute now.

AL: Oh? Whose party?

JENNIFER: I'm sure you know her.

AL: Probably.

JENNIFER: But I can't remember her name. I'm not sure I even know her address. It's … somewhere.

AL: I'd love to come.

JENNIFER: Why don't you? Why don't you both come?

MAN: I wasn't invited. I don't even know what you're talking about.

JENNIFER: (*to AL, referring to MAN*) I just love your friend. He's so specific. (*as she goes*)

AL: Isn't he! (*She's gone.*) Who's *she?*

MAN: I haven't got any idea.

AL: You meet the worst people at your own party.

MAN: Then why give a party?

AL: Well, I don't want to be antisocial. Don't get me wrong. I love parties. If only it wasn't for the people at them. But this is really the worst part, isn't it?

MAN: What is?

AL: The actual event. It's always such a crushing disappointment. From the minute the first guests arrive, I just want to evaporate into thin air. At my last party, I had to start a fire in the kitchen to get rid of them.

MAN: You started a fire!?

AL: Just a small one. But there was a lot of smoke. It cleared the place out quite nicely. It wasn't fifteen minutes before I was finally alone again.

MAN: Someone could have been seriously hurt.

AL: Oh, the fire department was there instantaneously. I called them ahead of time. But I'll never try that one again. There was a hell of a mess. This time I'm taking a more subtle approach. There's no food, no drinks, and the music is far too loud. Lots of people have already left.

Another window opens. NURSE WILSON pokes her head out.

NURSE WILSON: Turn that God-awful music down!

AL: I was actually planning on turning it up!

NURSE WILSON: Oh, were you? Well, we'll just see about that!

AL: Why don't you call the police, if you don't like it.

NURSE WILSON: That's exactly what I intend to do!

AL: If you do call, though—please don't tell them about all the drugs.

NURSE WILSON: Drugs! (*She goes inside.*)

AL: Well, thank God for the neighbours. This thing might have gone on forever, and we've got that other party to go to. You don't happen to remember the address, do you?

MAN: No.

AL: Well, someone else is bound to know. That's where all these people will be going after they've been herded out of here.

MAN: Why would you bother getting rid of them, just to follow them to another party?

AL: I'm always hearing about parties I didn't go to. How great they were. What a fabulous time everybody had. The ones I miss are always the good ones. So I never miss one now. Are you coming?

MAN: I don't like parties.

AL: Why did you come to this one, then?

MAN: I didn't.

AL: Well, what are you doing here?

MAN: Actually—

AL: You're not thinking about jumping, are you? It's seven storeys.

MAN: Yes. I know.

AL: A guy could kill himself.

MAN: Well ... yes ... he could, but ...

The next window opens.

NURSE WILSON: I called the police!

AL: This guy's gonna jump, lady.

NURSE WILSON: Really!

AL: You sure you wouldn't rather go to this party?

NURSE WILSON: If he wants to jump, why don't you let him?

MAN: Look—I didn't say I wanted to. I don't know what I'm doing. I really—

NURSE WILSON: Would you like us to convince you?

LILLIAN: (*a voice from inside*) Is that Albert?

NURSE WILSON: (*to LILLIAN*) No. It isn't Albert. It's a man. He's thinking about jumping off the side of the building.

LILLIAN: (*inside*) Why doesn't he then?

NURSE WILSON: (*to LILLIAN*) That's what I asked him.

MAN: Look—this has nothing to do with either of *you*. Why don't you both go inside and just carry on with your lives?

AL: You don't mind if I go to this party then?

MAN: No. Of course I don't mind.

AL: It's not that I don't care about your plight or anything. It's just such a downer—that's all. Anyway, this lady looks pretty serious. Maybe she can talk you out of it.

NURSE WILSON: I am serious and I'm not talking him out of anything.

AL: Look—the police'll be here any minute. Just hang on until they get here. I gotta go. I don't even know where I'm going so who knows how long it'll take to get there. (*He goes, closing his window.*)

NURSE WILSON: Some friend.

MAN: He's not a friend.

LILLIAN: (*inside*) Albert?

NURSE WILSON: (*to LILLIAN*) It's not Albert, Mrs. Wright. Albert's gone! He FLEW AWAY!!

LILLIAN: Why?

NURSE WILSON: You *know* why. Because he's a *bird*. (*to MAN*) God, I hate old people.

LILLIAN: (*inside*) Who's a bird?

NURSE WILSON: Albert! Albert's a bird. We let him go, remember? We let him go because he was unhappy.

LILLIAN: (*inside*) Oh!

NURSE WILSON: She remembers the whole thing.

LILLIAN: (*inside*) No I don't!

NURSE WILSON: She's supposed to be deaf but she can hear the grass growing. So what's stopping you?

MAN: Huh?

NURSE WILSON: What's stopping you from jumping? Wait—let me guess. You're afraid of heights. Now that's a pity. Letting a little thing like that stand in the way of your suicide, when really it's such a perfectly logical thing to do.

MAN: Logical?

NURSE WILSON: I started out my career thinking I wanted to save people's lives. Imagine!

MAN: I think that's very noble.

NURSE WILSON: A lot you know. Where's the nobility in watching people hang on to the last shred of a meagre existence? Hooked up to every imaginable medical apparatus. Jumping is the only way to go these days, otherwise you run the serious risk of a protracted survival. My! Doesn't the sidewalk look inviting from here!

MAN: I'd rather not look down if you don't mind.

NURSE WILSON: Aren't you even the least bit curious?

MAN: I can imagine what it's like.

NURSE WILSON: I suppose you expect me to ask you what your reasons are for jumping.

MAN: You're probably not interested.

NURSE WILSON: You're probably right.

MAN: Nobody seems terribly interested.

NURSE WILSON: Why should they be? Death isn't terribly interesting. I work in a hospital when I'm not here cleaning up after this thing and I can tell you first hand, death isn't the least bit interesting. In fact—it's very routine. Besides, people are too busy to be interested in other people's problems. These days you have to pay someone to be interested.

MAN: Busy doing what?

NURSE WILSON: Finding reasons not to jump themselves.

MAN: So what's your reason?

NURSE WILSON: Me? I'm a humanitarian.

MAN: You don't seem the type.

NURSE WILSON: Oh? What type is that?

MAN: You don't seem very—well—very friendly.

NURSE WILSON: Why should I be friendly. I despise almost everyone I meet.

MAN: I thought humanitarians were supposed to *like* people.

NURSE WILSON: I like people on the whole. It's individuals I can't stand.

LILLIAN: (*from inside*) Has he jumped yet?

NURSE WILSON: No. He's vacillating.

LILLIAN: (*inside*) What?

NURSE WILSON: He hasn't made up his mind, yet—one way or the other.

LILLIAN: He shouldn't be so tentative.

MAN: I *have* made up my mind.

NURSE WILSON: Oh. (*to LILLIAN*) He has made up his mind. The police will be here soon. You'd better go now or they'll definitely talk you out of it. They're experts. They listen to all your problems. They sympathize with every one of them. Eventually, they convince you that life has some meaning. That there's some little thread to hang onto. So you hang on, as they slowly reel you in. But you never let go again, not for the rest of your life. The next thing you know, you're old, and by that time you've been hanging on so long and so tightly to that little thread that it practically has to be pried loose.

MAN: You know something—you're astonishingly morbid.

LILLIAN: (*close to the window*) What seems to be the problem?

NURSE WILSON: I already told you, Mrs. Wright. I'm not going to tell you again.

LILLIAN: (*appearing now in window*) Well, get out of my way then.

NURSE WILSON: You're not supposed to be up and around.

LILLIAN: Where is this man?

NURSE WILSON: Die of heart failure. See if I care.

LILLIAN: She doesn't really want me to die because then she'd have to fill out a form.

NURSE WILSON: I've already filled it out!

LILLIAN: I'm a hundred years old. Does that impress you?

MAN: That's very old.

LILLIAN: Yes. They send people like her to look after me.

MAN: She's not very nice.

LILLIAN: She doesn't have a very nice job. Looking after sick people. Waiting for them to die. So she thinks that she has to pretend she has no feelings.

NURSE WILSON: I haven't!

LILLIAN: But she's afraid. (*NURSE WILSON goes.*) Don't pay any attention to her.

Pause.

LILLIAN: Oh my, what a lovely evening.

MAN: I never noticed.

LILLIAN: I haven't looked out this window in years. I used to go out on evenings like this. I walked down to the end of that street and took the streetcar as far as it went. Up where there weren't any houses. That's where we stopped. That's where the streetcar turned around. As though the world was flat, and that was the end of it, where you fell off. That was about seventy years ago, so I imagine the houses go quite a bit further now. But not far enough, of course. I imagine the streetcar eventually stops somewhere and turns around.

MAN: There isn't any streetcar.

LILLIAN: There isn't?

MAN: There hasn't been one for about thirty years.

LILLIAN: Well, that just goes to show you what I know. I haven't gone out since ... well, in about fifty years.

MAN: Fifty years?

LILLIAN: Well, as I said—you can really only go out so far, and then you've got to turn around and come back. I find that somewhat limiting. I prefer to go nowhere at all. As it turns out my apartment is much larger than I thought. In fact, it's enormous.

MAN: It can't be more than a few hundred square feet at the most.

LILLIAN: Yes. It's almost too much to grasp, isn't it? Of course, it looks a lot smaller now. Since she came to look after me. She cleaned it all up. Put everything in order. Kicked Albert out. She has a very sanitary point of view. Doesn't like pigeons. I imagine he'll come back though. When he's had enough of flying.

NURSE WILSON: (*inside*) He's not coming back in here.

LILLIAN: I used to have all kinds of things piled up against this window. Until *they* came and took everything away. And once Albert saw the window, there was just no keeping him. After all those years, his little head was suddenly filled with big ideas.

MAN: All what years?

LILLIAN: Those years.

MAN: Pigeons don't live that long.

LILLIAN: How long?

MAN: How many years are we talking about exactly?

LILLIAN: Oh, I don't know. About fifty.

MAN: That doesn't make any sense.

LILLIAN: No. It doesn't. (*pause*) Must be a riddle.

Pause.

MAN: I don't get it.

LILLIAN: Neither do I. Well—it's just a story. It's not important. People attach too much importance to these things. That reminds me of another story.

MAN waits as she loses her train of thought. Finally, he coughs, which arouses her.

LILLIAN: Oh, my! What a lovely evening.

MAN: You were going to tell me something?

LILLIAN: What about?

MAN: I don't know. Something reminded you of a story.

LILLIAN: A story?—Let's see …

A long pause.

MAN: I guess you don't remember. It's not important. Really. I thought—I thought it might be—well—important, somehow.

LILLIAN: You're looking for something important.

MAN: No. Well, I—I need—I'm looking for something, yes.

LILLIAN: I don't have anything. Just an empty room. It'll be coming up for rent soon, if you're interested.

MAN: No. I'm not looking for a room.

LILLIAN: It's a place to hang your hat. To sort out all your shoes.

MAN: I don't need to sort out my shoes. All my shoes are the same. Every pair identical. All seven pairs. I have seven hats also. All like this one. I have one for every day of the week. Only I can't remember what day it is.

LILLIAN: Oh.

MAN: I've lost track, you see. I went to sleep and I had a dream. I—I think it was a dream. I dreamt that I got up, and made my way to work, and when work was over I came home and went to bed. And then I woke up. I think I woke up.

LILLIAN: It's Wednesday.

MAN: It is?

LILLIAN: I don't know, but I thought it would make you feel better.

MAN: (*Now he speaks slowly and deliberately, in an attempt to understand his own words.*) Not really. You see—my faith in the days of the week has been seriously undermined. When I woke up this morning, I wasn't exactly sure what day it was. And for that brief moment—it was only a

matter of seconds—I think it was seconds—I stood—or I should say I "lay" on very shaky ground. After all—how could I act with assuredness. How could I rise up and plunge headlong into Friday's world, if it was actually Saturday? And so I lay completely still for a moment, pondering this question. That's when I noticed my hands. I'd never noticed them before. How they moved with amazing dexterity. But this flexibility, this movement of hands, can never extend beyond the boundaries of its own flesh—can only reach as far as the fingertips and no further, much as the movement of time is restricted by the days of the week. So I got up and tried to erase these things from my mind. I tried to get dressed. But then I began to understand other things—for example the meaning of shoes. They were little prisons for my feet. Absolute definitions of space. I could run a million miles, in any direction, and still not escape them. And my hat—forming a firm idea around my head, as if to say, "Well, that's about the size of it." My mind could expand into infinite space, and still never change the shape of my head. I saw in the mirror a condemned man, serving a life sentence inside his body. Even the car—I drove—to work. My car. This thing. This instrument of liberation. It wasn't freedom. It was merely the idea of freedom, bound in metal. A kind of hope, but with a speed limit attached to it. Now I was travelling an unknown route along a familiar road. It led in exactly the direction I was going, but not by coincidence. The asphalt was not laying itself a path in front of me. I was merely following a prearranged course and then something happened, something that had never happened before. When I finally arrived in town at my usual space it was taken. I was late for work you see and there was another car in my space. Someone had taken my space you see. I sat in my car for a moment, not knowing where to go. Just staring straight ahead. And then, I put my car into gear and drove into it. Drove right into this other car. There didn't seem to be any other choice. No place else to go, you see.

So I put my car in reverse, backed up, and rammed into this car again. And then again, and again and again, until finally this other car, this intruder of my space was smashed up against the side of the building, like an accordion. So now I had my space back, and I parked. I got out of the car, and turned to head for my office. That's when

I realized. It wasn't my space at all. Somehow I got completely turned around. This wasn't anywhere near where I work. I didn't know where I was. I hadn't any idea. I had always depended on the road which led there. The way I've always believed that one thing leads to another. Then I saw this building. I thought I'd come up here to get a better perspective on my exact situation. And from here the view is quite clear. There are no spaces left, you see. I have no place to park my car.

LILLIAN: Have you tried The Bay?

MAN: Don't you understand?

LILLIAN: Of course I understand. You didn't need to make such a long speech. When you're a hundred years old you'll understand everything. And then you'll die.

MAN: Why wait?

LILLIAN: Something interesting might happen. But then again, it might not. I think you should jump now.

MAN: You do?

LILLIAN: If that's what you want to do, I think you should do it.

MAN: There really is no reason to live, is there?

LILLIAN: Not really.

MAN: (*as he prepares to jump*) It's sort of disappointing. I wonder where they'll tow my car.

LILLIAN: Oh. Now I remember!

MAN: (*stopping*) What?

LILLIAN: That story. Some years ago, I went to Paris to see the *Mona Lisa*. It's in the Louvre, the largest building in the world, probably. But the *Mona Lisa*, as it turns out, is very small. So naturally I couldn't find it. I kept looking for something—big. Then I saw a huge crowd of people all standing around—looking disappointed. And there she was—smiling as if she knew.

MAN: That's it? That's the whole story?

LILLIAN: You do like a long story, don't you. Let's see. There was a young Frenchman standing next to me, in a terrible state of despair. He began talking to me as if he'd known me all his life. I didn't understand a word he was saying, but he didn't seem to take any notice. I thought I'd lose him in the crowd, but he followed me right out of the museum. He told me a very long and involved story, often punctuating the words with his fists. Occasionally he would sink into a sadness the like of which I'd never seen. And then he would start raving again. The further we walked, the more distressed he became—the more enraged. By the time we reached the Pont Neuf he was sobbing uncontrollably. It seemed very clear that he wanted me to say something. We hadn't walked halfway across, when he started to climb over the side of the bridge. I didn't know what to say. So I blurted out the only thing in French that I'd ever learned. "*La pamplemousse est sur la table.*" I don't even know what it means. But he responded very positively. He thought about it for a moment, and then smiled. After that his mood changed considerably. In fact, he was delighted. Whatever it was I said, it seemed to be something for him to hang his hat on. And he walked away a new man. Determined, it seemed, to live by this philosophy the rest of his life.

MAN: It doesn't mean anything.

LILLIAN: It must mean something. I learned it in school.

MAN: "The grapefruit is on the table"?

LILLIAN: Oh. Is that what it means? (*pause*) Well, that's not a bad philosophy to live by. As philosophies go. It has a certain—preciseness.

MAN: How have you managed to stay alive so long?

LILLIAN: I forget.

MAN: Shut up in your room like that? Never going out?

LILLIAN: There are other places to go besides *out*. There's *in*. There's *around*. There's *under*. *Over*. *Between*.

MAN: Down.

LILLIAN: Well, you might go down. But you might go up. If you're going to go to all the trouble of jumping, you might as well try going up and see what happens. Albert went up. Straight up.

MAN: Albert was a pigeon.

LILLIAN: He didn't know that. Not for sure. He'd never flown a day in his whole life, not until the day we let him go. You could be the first of a kind. Imagine what a story that would make! You'd be interviewed by just about every newspaper in the world. You'd travel around giving lectures. You'd be an inspiration to others. There'd be people flying all over the place. That sort of thing has to start somewhere. It might as well start with you. If you're going to give your life up anyway, you may as well give it up to something. The principle is very simple. You just have to let go and let the wind currents do the rest. You know about airflow, don't you?

MAN: I really don't think …

LILLIAN: No. Don't think. The important thing is to just let it happen. Let it take you where it wants. Don't try to go any place special this first time. Just do a circle once around the building, and come back. Once you get a better feel for it, you can go a little further.

Suddenly, a huge spotlight on MAN.

POLICE MEGAPHONE: Stop! This is the police!

LILLIAN: Go!

MAN: I don't know what to do—I can't—fly—

POLICE MEGAPHONE: Just stay calm. Don't move.

LILLIAN: Don't listen to them. They're all trying to put the world in order. They don't want people flying around all over the place. They'd have to make up a whole bunch of new regulations. That's just bullshit. Just go.

MAN: Are you sure?

LILLIAN: Just up and away.

POLICE MEGAPHONE: Stop!

MAN: Just like that?

POLICE MEGAPHONE: Stay right where you are!

MAN: I'm supposed to stay right where I am.

LILLIAN: Go!

MAN: All right—I'm going.

LILLIAN: Then go!

MAN: Goodbye!

A blackout.

MAN: Ahhhhhhhhhhhhhhhhhhhhhhhhhh!

As the lights come up the MAN flies with the aid of his umbrella. He then lands on the ledge of another building. Four people open their windows.

ONE: We saw that.

MAN: What?

TWO: We saw you fly over here from that building across the street.

MAN: You did?

THREE: We've been watching the whole thing.

MAN: You have?

FOUR: Yes. We have.

TWO: We saw you talk to that old lady.

FOUR: To all those people.

TWO: We saw the whole thing from beginning to end.

THREE: And then we saw you fly over here and land!

FOUR: There's just one thing …

TWO: We don't get it.

ONE: What's the flying supposed to represent? Is it an existential statement or what?

TWO: It's a Jungian thing, isn't it?

THREE: I don't agree. I think it's political.

ONE: Is it about enlightenment?

THREE: There's a suggestion of mass revolt.

TWO: There's an archetypal quality about it.

ONE: I detect strong religious overtones.

THREE: It's a struggle against tyranny, isn't it?

FOUR: I think it's just weird.

MAN: Will you excuse me?

Suddenly the MAN is airborne and he flies through the stars. He then returns to the original window ledge. LILLIAN is gone. Below, an ambulance light flashes. The MAN knocks at the window.

MAN: Hello! HELLO—O!!

NURSE WILSON appears.

NURSE WILSON: Yes?

MAN: The old lady. I'd like to speak to her. I have to tell—her about—something—something quite incredible!!

NURSE WILSON: Yeah … well, she's gone.

MAN: Gone? (*They look down.*) So sudden? She was here just a few minutes ago.

NURSE WILSON: Yeah, well … that's the way it always happens. So—what's this "something incredible"? As if I really want to know.

MAN: It was … it was nothing.

NURSE WILSON: I thought you were going to jump off the ledge.

MAN: I did.

NURSE WILSON: Oh. You did, did you?

MAN: Yes, I did. I flew across the street to that building and back.

NURSE WILSON: I suppose you want to come inside now.

MAN: I'm just fine where I am.

NURSE WILSON: You can't stay perched out there forever.

MAN: Why not?

NURSE WILSON: Because it's abnormal behaviour.

MAN: Not for a pigeon.

NURSE WILSON: You're not a PIGEON!!

MAN: Yes … I know that now. (*She goes.*) But for a moment … for a brief … moment … I didn't know. And the wind carried me up and took me along for a ride. And I forgot. I forgot my own story … and I flew … flew on the wings of someone else's.

POLICE MEGAPHONE: This is the police.

MAN: I have to forget … try … to forget everything. Forget everything that has ever happened to me … everything that ever *will* happen … everything … and wait … just wait for the wind again … and do nothing … nothing … and … wait … just …

The sound of the wind increases and the music, as the lights fade. In the blackout we hear the police megaphone.

POLICE MEGAPHONE: All right, ladies and gentlemen—break it up. Just break it up now and go home. Come on, move along—move along now ladies and gentlemen. Everything will be fine. Everything's under control, so let's just disperse with this little gathering and go home. The show's over.

END

TOMSON HIGHWAY (b. 1951)

In 1967 George Ryga's *The Ecstasy of Rita Joe* awoke theatre audiences to a new awareness of Native people and their situation in Canada. Rita, Jaimie and David Joe were shown to be capable of joy, ambition, disappointment, rage: the whole gamut of thoughts and feelings that whites had always been deemed to have, but which Natives, when they appeared on stage at all, were generally denied. But Ryga's Native characters are ultimately imprisoned by despair. Oppressed by a white society that refuses to see them as fully, autonomously human, Rita and Jaimie are doomed. The play reflects the vision of a white writer of conscience berating his own culture and bemoaning its victims. Rita herself, in the first production, was played by a white actress.

Two decades later Tomson Highway appeared in the vanguard of a group of Native theatre artists ready to write and perform their own stories. They tell of oppression but also of hope, of tragedies but also of the ordinary daily pleasures and absurdities of life experienced from inside the skin of Native women and men. For the first time the Canadian theatre heard Native voices telling Native stories. The voices are distinctly post-colonial, appropriating forms and styles from the dominant culture while incorporating traditional formal and spiritual elements of Native art and life. In Highway's *The Rez Sisters* and *Dry Lips Oughta Move to Kapuskasing*, the result is a brilliant theatrical synthesis bursting with vitality and speaking to Native and non-Native alike. "You feel as if you've been somewhere after one of these plays," writes critic Lucy Bashford, "as if you're still alive under the armor of twentieth-century life."

Highway's life spans two radically different worlds. Born on a trap-line on the remote Brochet reserve in northern Manitoba, the eleventh of twelve children, he spoke only Cree until the age of six when he was sent off to residential school in The Pas. Later he lived in white foster homes while attending a Winnipeg high school where he was the only Native student. Developing an interest in classical piano, he enrolled at the University of Manitoba and studied with music professor William Aide, who invited Highway to join his family for a sabbatical year in England. Highway spent 1972–73 touring England and the continent, immersing himself in European culture and civilization. Returning to Canada, he transferred to the University of Western Ontario in London, earning an honours degree in music and a B.A. in English (1975–76). Fast-tracked for a career as a concert pianist, Highway was brought up short by the poverty and alcoholism he saw other Native people suffering in the cities where he was playing Bartók and Chopin. Unable to reconcile the two worlds, he gave up music and worked for seven years with Native social service agencies in London and Toronto. While still in London he also became involved in James Reaney's play development workshops on *Wacousta* and *The Canadian Brothers*. He saw *The Donnellys*, too, and was struck by Reaney's use of myth, folklore, music and poetry, and his evocation of a community—elements Highway would later incorporate into his own work.

In the early 1980s, now living in Toronto, Highway started writing theatre pieces for himself and his brother Rene, a professional dancer, in an attempt to combine Native life and spirituality with what he called his "high art" training. In 1983 he joined Native Earth Performing Arts, an aboriginal theatre company founded the year before. He wrote and directed music as well as acting in a series of collective shows for Native Earth, and studied mask and clown techniques for dramatizing the traditional figure of the Trickster. From 1986–90 Highway served as the company's artistic director, nurturing an important group of Native plays through development into production. But meanwhile he had also begun workshopping a new play of his own with another Ontario Native company, De-ba-jeh-mu-jig Theatre on Manitoulin Island. In November 1986, Act IV Theatre Company and Native Earth Performing Arts presented *The Rez Sisters*, directed by Larry Lewis at the Native Canadian Centre in Toronto, marking a new era in Canadian theatre.

The Rez Sisters follows seven women on the fictional Wasaychigan Hill reserve on Manitoulin Island, better known as "Wasy" or "the rez," as they work, dream, compare notes on life, and make their way to Toronto to play THE BIGGEST BINGO IN THE WORLD. Pelajia Patchnose fantasizes about paving the dusty rez roads with her winnings. Philomena Moosetail would buy a new toilet, and Veronique St. Pierre a stove to cook for her mentally disabled daughter Zhaboonigan, who was raped by two white guys with a screwdriver. Marie-Adele Starblanket wants a little island with a picket fence for her fourteen kids. Manic Annie Cook and bisexual biker Emily Dictionary round out the group who are shadowed by a seagull—actually Nanabush, the Ojibway Trickster—played by a male dancer (Rene Highway in the original production). Only Zhaboonigan and Marie-Adele, who is dying of cancer, can see Nanabush and talk to him in Cree. Inspired in part by Michel Tremblay's *Les Belles-Soeurs* but lacking its bitterness, *The Rez Sisters* offers an earthy comic vision of a world in which suffering is a daily reality, but by no means the primary one, and in which sisterhood is very powerful. It won the Dora Mavor Moore award for best new play and a Governor General's Award nomination, had a triumphant cross-Canada tour and went to the Edinburgh Festival in 1988. The play and its exciting production established Tomson Highway as a major theatrical talent, and Native theatre as a potent new force on the Canadian scene.

Highway continued working with Native Earth, consolidating his theatrical ideas and techniques. Further exploring the condition of Native women, he wrote and played piano on *Aria* (1987), a solo show for Greenland Inuit actress Makka Kleist. In 1988 he collaborated with brother Rene on *New Song … New Dance*, performing on piano as Weesageechik, the Cree Trickster, in this multimedia treatment of the traumas suffered by Natives displaced from their families and culture. *The Sage, the Dancer, and the Fool* (1989), co-created by Tomson, Rene and Billy Merasty, with words and music by Tomson, looked at a day in the life of a Native man in the city. Once again the Trickster appears, this time adapting to contemporary urban realities in a show Highway described as a combination of Cirque du Soleil, dance theatre and pow wow.

Dry Lips Oughta Move to Kapuskasing also appeared in 1989, co-produced by Native Earth and Theatre Passe Muraille, and directed by Larry Lewis. It won the Chalmers, as well as Dora awards for outstanding new play, best production, male lead (Graham Greene) and featured female (Doris Linklater). Following its first showing, Highway was given the Wang Festival Prize for contributions to the literary community. *Dry Lips* next played Winnipeg, then was remounted in 1991 by mega-producer David Mirvish at the National Arts Centre and in a major commercial production at Toronto's lavish Royal Alex. This was the most extravagant production of a Native play to date on any Canadian stage, and confirmation of Highway's mainstream success—although some people felt that bigger did not necessarily make it better.

The second in what Highway has announced as an intended cycle of seven "rez" plays, *Dry Lips Oughta Move to Kapuskasing* (originally titled *The Rez Brothers*) focuses on the male side of the society dramatized in *The Rez Sisters*. Here we get to meet Big Joey, the rez-ident stud so prominent in the women's conversations, along with Veronique St. Pierre's boozy husband Pierre, and Simon Starblanket, one of Marie-Adele's sons. Rez sisters Veronique, Annie Cook and "that terrible Dictionary woman" become out-characters in *Dry Lips*, names on the Wasy Wailerettes hockey team roster. The notorious Gazelle Nataways and Black Lady Halked, first mentioned in *The Rez Sisters*, appear here as incarnations of Nanabush the Trickster.

The eagerly awaited third installment in the "rez" cycle did not appear until 2000, and then only in a student production at the University of Toronto. *Rose* is a large-cast musical set on the Wasaychigan Hill reserve in 1992, featuring many of the same characters as the first two plays. Emily Dictionary takes centre stage again along with some of her female biker pals, and Big Joey returns with plans to open a casino. Bob Rae, premier of Ontario at the time, makes an appearance in a land claims negotiation with band chief Rose, and violence against women is a featured theme once more. Partly out of frustration with the difficulty of getting *Rose* professionally produced, Highway turned to writing fiction and had great success with his first novel, *Kiss of the Fur Queen*

(1998). This semi-autobiographical, tragicomic tale follows two brothers from their birth on a trap-line through the agonies of residential school to adult life as artists in the city, accompanied all the while by the Trickster.

Dry Lips is a harsher, more complex and ambitious play than either *The Rez Sisters* or *Rose*, examining the possibility of spiritual renewal for contemporary Native culture in a radical mélange of styles that combines broad comedy with brute tragedy. The rivalry between Big Joey and Zachary Jeremiah Keechigeesik for band funds to support their entrepreneurial projects—Joey's radio station and Zachary's bakery—suggests an economic approach to the reserve's malaise, and finds a comic echo in their sexual rivalry. The conflict between Simon Starblanket and Spooky Lacroix has higher stakes. Simon seeks nothing less than the return of traditional Native spirituality: the resurrection of old dance and drum rituals, and the recuperation of Nanabush. He reaches back to tradition through his engagement to Patsy Pegahmagahbow, stepdaughter of the last medicine woman on the reserve. Simon also wants to reach back through Dickie Bird Halked, whose grandfather was a great medicine man until the priest turned the people against him. But Dickie's uncle Spooky has embraced the religion of the priest, as has his mother, Black Lady Halked. Highway wouldn't seem to have much sympathy for the white man's religion in this battle for the Native soul, except that Spooky Lacroix himself was saved from the hell of alcoholism by Christianity. In the context of the play's central iconic event, that provides a potent argument. *Dry Lips* actually features two such events. The first, in flashback, is the nightmarish birth of Dickie Bird in the bar with Kitty Wells wailing on the jukebox, his mother "drunk almost senseless" and his father, Big Joey, running away. Highway seems here to be directly confronting Native people with their own responsibility for their condition. The result of the mother's drunkenness and the father's evasion is Dickie's fetal alcohol syndrome, made worse by Big Joey's continued denial of his paternity. Seventeen years later we see Dickie driven over the edge by his spiritual crisis arising from Spooky's evangelism. The *tableau vivant* that ends the first act illustrates these relationships in a vivid theatrical moment that captures the stylistic audacity of the play. All this leads directly to the second iconic event, Dickie's horrible rape of Patsy begotten by and enacted with the symbolically loaded crucifix, the phallic weapon with which this patriarchal religion has ravaged Native culture. And once again Big Joey stands by and does nothing.

In the program for the original production, Highway included an epigraph from Native elder Lyle Longclaws: " … before the healing can take place, the poison must first be exposed … " The ellipses suggest an ongoing, incomplete process, and in *Dry Lips* the process of exposure is painful and ugly. Finally forced to account for his inactions, Big Joey blames Native women for taking "the fuckin' power away from us faster than the FBI [at Wounded Knee] ever did." His fear of women's power is reflected in the other men's frantic responses to the women's hockey team, especially the comic chorus characters Pierre St. Pierre and Creature Nataways, and perhaps too in the grotesque male-fantasy forms Nanabush assumes in becoming the three women with their huge breasts, belly and bum. The rape, the blame, the fear, the exaggerated sexuality all add up to misogyny. Robert Cushman, reviewing the Royal Alex production for the *Globe and Mail*, called *Dry Lips* "the most powerful play I have seen about misogyny." Other commentators, including a number of Native women, felt that the play itself was misogynist. Highway is appalled at that suggestion. "To me *Dry Lips* is about the return of God as a woman," he told *Toronto Life*. "I wrote it as a hymn—of pain, yes—but a hymn to the beauty of women and the feminine energy that needs to come back into its own if this world is going to survive."

The figure of Nanabush is perhaps the most difficult element of the play to comprehend for a non-Native audience or reader. As Highway explains in his prefatory note, the Trickster, like the languages of Cree and Ojibway, is not bound by gender, so s/he tends to assume exaggerated or contradictory gendered characteristics. S/he is neither solemn nor distant like the central figures in Judeo-Christian theology, but rather clownish, earthy and immediate. Native playwright and poet Daniel David Moses says, "The trickster is the embodiment of our sense of humour about the way we live our lives. It's a very central part of our attitude that things are funny even though horrible things happen." So Nanabush makes the poster of Marilyn Monroe fart when Dickie Bird tries to kill himself, and Nanabush as Jehovah in drag sits on a mock-heavenly toilet "nonchalantly filing his/her fingernails" as Zachary keens over the terrible wastefulness of Simon's death.

At the end of the play everything is resolved and nothing is. If the dream-frame suggests that nothing that happened is real, then what has been learned? What progress has been made? In another program note Highway wrote that "dreams—and the dream-life—have traditionally been considered by native society to be the greatest tool of instruction … " Zachary awakens to a lesson in his native language from his wife with the goddess' name and the "magical, silvery Nanabush laugh," to his beautiful laughing baby girl—and to *The Smurfs* on television. Creating a living harmony out of such contradictions is the challenge of Highway's provocative and exhilarating theatre.

Dry Lips Oughta Move to Kapuskasing premiered at Theatre Passe Muraille in Toronto on April 21, 1989, produced by Theatre Passe Muraille and Native Earth Performing Arts Inc., with the following cast:

NANABUSH (as the spirit of GAZELLE NATAWAYS, PATSY PEGAHMAGAHBOW and BLACK LADY HALKED)	Doris Linklater
ZACHARY JEREMIAH KEECHIGEESIK	Gary Farmer
BIG JOEY	Ben Cardinal
CREATURE NATAWAYS	Errol Kinistino
DICKIE BIRD HALKED	Kenneth Charlette
PIERRE ST. PIERRE	Graham Greene
SPOOKY LACROIX	Ron Cook
SIMON STARBLANKET	Billy Merasty
HERA KEECHIGEESIK	Doris Linklater

Directed by Larry Lewis
Set and Costume Design by Brian Perchaluk
Lighting Design by Stephan Droege
Music written and performed by Carlos Del Junco
Choreography by Rene Highway

DRY LIPS OUGHTA MOVE TO KAPUSKASING

CHARACTERS

NANABUSH (*as the spirit of GAZELLE NATAWAYS, PATSY PEGAHMAGAHBOW and BLACK LADY HALKED*)
ZACHARY JEREMIAH KEECHIGEESIK*, 41 years old
BIG JOEY, 39
CREATURE NATAWAYS, 39
DICKIE BIRD HALKED, 17
PIERRE ST. PIERRE, 53
SPOOKY LACROIX, 39
SIMON STARBLANKET, 20
HERA KEECHIGEESIK, 39

SPOOKY LACROIX's baby, towards the end of Act Two, can and should be played by a doll wrapped in a blanket. But for greatest effect, ZACHARY's baby at the very end of the play should be played by a real baby, preferably about five months of age.

SCENE

*The Wasaychigan** Hill Indian Reserve, Manitoulin Island, Ontario. Between Saturday, February 3, 1990, 11:00 p.m., and Saturday, February 10, 1990, 11:00 a.m.*

SET

The set for the original production of Dry Lips Oughta Move to Kapuskasing *contained certain elements which I think are essential to the play.*

First of all, it was designed on two levels, the lower of which was the domain of the "real" Wasaychigan Hill. This lower level contained, on stage-left, BIG JOEY's living room/kitchen, with its kitchen counter at the back and, facing downstage, an old brown couch with a television set a few feet in front of it. This television set could be made to double as a smaller rock for the forest scenes. Stage right had SPOOKY LACROIX's kitchen, with its kitchen counter (for

which BIG JOEY's kitchen counter could double) and its table and chairs.

In front of all this was an open area, the floor of which was covered with teflon, a material which looks like ice and on which one can actually skate, using real ice skates; this was the rink for the hockey arena scenes. With lighting effects, this area could also be turned into "the forest" surrounding the village of Wasaychigan Hill, with its leafless winter trees. The only other essential element here was a large jutting rock beside which, for instance, ZACHARY JEREMIAH KEECHIGEESIK and SIMON STARBLANKET meet, a rock which could be made to glow at certain key points. PIERRE's "little bootleg joint" in Act Two, with its "window," was also created with lighting effects.

The upper level of the set was almost exclusively the realm of NANABUSH. The principal element here was her perch, located in the very middle of this area. The perch was actually an old jukebox of a late 60s/early 70s make, but it was semi-hidden throughout most of the play, so that it was fully revealed as this fabulous jukebox only at those few times when it was needed; the effect sought after here is of this magical, mystical juke-box hanging in the night air, like a haunting and persistent memory, high up over the village of Wasaychigan Hill. Over and behind this perch was suspended a huge full moon whose glow came on, for the most part, only during the out-door scenes, which all take place at nighttime. All other effects in this area were accomplished with lighting. The very front of this level, all along its edge, was also utilized as the "bleachers" area for the hockey arena scenes.

Easy access was provided between the lower and the upper levels of this set.

SOUND

The soundscape of Dry Lips Oughta Move to Kapuskasing *was mostly provided by a musician playing, live, on harmonica, off to the side. It is as though the dreamscape of the play were laced all the way through with ZACHARY JEREMIAH*

---

* "Keechigeesik" means "heaven" or "great sky" in Cree.
** "Wasaychigan" means "window" in Ojibway.

KEECHIGEESIK's "idealized" form of harmonica playing, permeated with a definite blues flavour. Although ZACHARY ideally should play his harmonica, and not too well, in those few scenes where it is called for, the sound of this harmonica is most effectively used to underline and highlight the many magical appearances of NANABUSH in her various guises.

LANGUAGE

Both Cree and Ojibway are used freely in this text for the reasons that these two languages, belonging to the same linguistic family, are very similar and that the fictional reserve of Wasaychigan Hill has a mixture of both Cree and Ojibway residents.

Note: Words and passages in Cree and Ojibway are translated in parentheses, except as noted.

A NOTE ON NANABUSH

The dream world of North American Indian mythology is inhabited by the most fantastic creatures, beings and events. Foremost among these beings is the "Trickster," as pivotal and important a figure in our world as Christ is in the realm of Christian mythology. "Weesageechak" in Cree, "Nanabush" in Ojibway, "Raven" in others, "Coyote" in still others, this Trickster goes by many names and many guises. In fact, he can assume any guise he chooses. Essentially a comic, clownish sort of character, his role is to teach us about the nature and the meaning of existence on the planet Earth; he straddles the consciousness of man and that of God, the Great Spirit.

The most explicit distinguishing feature between the North American Indian languages and the European languages is that in Indian (e.g., Cree, Ojibway), there is no gender. In Cree, Ojibway, etc., unlike English, French, German, etc., the male-female-neuter hierarchy is entirely absent. So that by this system of thought, the central hero figure from our mythology—theology, if you will—is theoretically neither exclusively male nor exclusively female, or is both simultaneously. Therefore, where in The Rez Sisters Nanabush was male, in this play—"flip-side" to The Rez Sisters—Nanabush is female.

Some say that Nanabush left this continent when the white man came. We believe she/he is still here among us—albeit a little the worse for wear and tear—having assumed other guises. Without the continued presence of this extraordinary figure, the core of Indian culture would be gone forever.

ACT ONE

The set for this first scene is the rather shabby and very messy living room/kitchen of the reserve house BIG JOEY and GAZELLE NATAWAYS currently share. Prominently displayed on one wall is a life-size pin-up poster of Marilyn Monroe. The remains of a party are obvious. On the worn-out old brown couch, with its back towards the entrance, lies ZACHARY JEREMIAH KEECHIGEESIK, a very handsome Indian man. He is naked, passed out. The first thing we see when the light comes up—a very small "spot," precisely focused—is ZACHARY's bare, naked bum. Then, from behind the couch, we see a woman's leg, sliding languorously into a nylon stocking and right over ZACHARY's bum. It is NANABUSH, as the spirit of GAZELLE NATAWAYS, dressing to leave. She eases herself luxuriously over the couch and over ZACHARY's bum and then reaches under ZACHARY's sleeping head, from where she gently pulls a gigantic pair of false, rubberized breasts. Then NANABUSH/GAZELLE NATAWAYS sashays over to the side of the couch, picks a giant hockey sweater up off the floor and shimmies into it. The sweater has a huge, plunging neck-line, with the capital letter "W" and the number "1" prominently sewn on. Then she sashays back to the couch and behind it. Pleasurably and mischievously, she leans over and plants a kiss on ZACHARY's bum, leaving behind a gorgeous, luminescent lipstick mark. The last thing she does before she leaves is to turn the television on. This television sits facing the couch that ZACHARY lies on. NANABUSH/GAZELLE does not use her hand for this, though; instead, she turns the appliance on with one last bump of her voluptuous hips. Hockey Night in Canada comes on. The sound of this hockey game is on only slightly, so that we hear it as background "music" all the way through the coming scene. Then NANABUSH/GAZELLE exits, to sit on her perch *on the upper level of the set. The only light left on stage is that coming from the television screen, giving off its eerie glow.*

Beat.

The kitchen door bangs open, the "kitchen light" flashes on and BIG JOEY and CREATURE NATAWAYS enter, CREATURE carrying a case of beer on his head. At first, they are oblivious to ZACHARY's presence. Also at about this time, the face of DICKIE BIRD HALKED emerges from the shadows at the "kitchen window." Silently, he watches the rest of the proceedings, taking a particular interest—even fascination—in the movements and behaviour of BIG JOEY.

BIG JOEY: (*calling out for GAZELLE who, of course, is not home*) Hey, bitch!

CREATURE: (*At regular intervals he bangs the beer case down on the kitchen counter, rips it open, pops bottles open, throws one to BIG JOEY, all noises that serve to punctuate the rat-a-tat rhythm of his frenetic speech.*) Batman oughta move to Kapuskasing, nah, Kap's too good for Batman, right, Big Joey? I tole you once I tole you twice he shouldna done it he shouldna done what he went and did goddawful Batman Manitowabi the way he went and crossed that blue line with the puck, man, he's got the flippin' puck right in the palm of his flippin' hand and only a minute-and-a-half to go he just about gave me the shits the way Batman Manitowabi went and crossed that blue line right in front of that brick shithouse of a whiteman why the hell did that brick shithouse of a whiteman have to be there ...

ZACHARY: (*talking in his sleep*) No!

CREATURE: Hey!

BIG JOEY raises a finger signalling CREATURE to shut up.

ZACHARY: I said no!

CREATURE: (*in a hoarse whisper*) That's not a TV kind of sound.

BIG JOEY: Shhh!

ZACHARY: ... goodness sakes, Hera, you just had a baby ...

CREATURE: That's a real life kind of sound, right, Big Joey?

BIG JOEY and CREATURE slowly come over to the couch.

ZACHARY: ... women playing hockey ... damn silliest thing I heard in my life ...

BIG JOEY: Well, well ...

CREATURE: Ho-leee! (*whispering*) Hey, what's that on his arse look like lip marks.

ZACHARY: ... Simon Starblanket, that's who's gonna help me with my bakery ...

CREATURE: He's stitchless, he's nude, he's gonna pneumonia ...

BIG JOEY: Shut up.

CREATURE: Get the camera. Chris'sakes, take a picture. (*CREATURE scrambles for the Polaroid, which he finds under one end of the couch.*)

ZACHARY: ... Simon! (*jumps up*) What the?!

CREATURE: Surprise! (*camera flashes*)

ZACHARY: Put that damn thing away. What are you doing here! Where's my wife? Hera! (*He realizes he's naked, grabs a cast iron frying pan and slaps it over his crotch, almost castrating himself in the process.*) Ooof!

BIG JOEY: (*smiling*) Over easy or sunny side up, Zachary Jeremiah Keechigeesik?

ZACHARY: Get outa my house.

CREATURE: This ain't your house. This is Big Joey's house, right, Big Joey?

BIG JOEY: Shut up.

ZACHARY: Creature Nataways. Get outa here. Gimme that camera.

CREATURE: Come and geeeet it! (*grabs ZACHARY's pants from the floor*)

ZACHARY: Cut it out. Gimme them goddamn pants.

CREATURE: (*singing*) Lipstick on your arsehole, tole da tale on you-hoo.

ZACHARY: What! (*straining to see his bum*) Oh lordy, lordy, lordy gimme them pants. (*He tries to wipe the stain off.*)

CREATURE: Here doggy, doggy. Here poochie, poochie woof woof! (*ZACHARY grabs the pants.*

They rip almost completely in half. CREATURE yelps.) Yip!

Momentary light up on NANABUSH/GAZELLE, up on her perch, as she gives a throaty laugh. BIG JOEY echoes this, CREATURE tittering away in the background.

ZACHARY: Hey, this is not my doing, Big Joey. (*As he clumsily puts on what's left of his pants, CREATURE manages to get in one more shot with the camera.*) We were just having a nice quiet drink over at Andy Manigitogan's when Gazelle Nataways shows up. She brought me over here to give me the recipe for her bannock apple pie cuz, goodness sakes, Simon Starblanket was saying it's the best, that pie was selling like hot cakes at the bingo and he knows I'm tryna establish this reserve's first pie-making business gimme that camera.

BIG JOEY suddenly makes a lunge at ZACHARY but ZACHARY evades him.

CREATURE: (*in the background, like a little dog*) Yah, yah.

BIG JOEY: (*slowly stalking ZACHARY around the room*) You know, Zach, there's a whole lotta guys on this rez been slippin' my old lady the goods but there ain't but a handful been stupid enough to get caught by me.

He snaps his fingers and, as always, CREATURE obediently scurries over. He hands BIG JOEY the picture of ZACHARY naked on the couch. BIG JOEY shows the picture to ZACHARY, right up to his face.

BIG JOEY: Kinda em-bare-ass-in' for a hoity-toity educated community pillar like you, eh Zach?

ZACHARY grabs for the picture but BIG JOEY snaps it away.

ZACHARY: What do you want?

BIG JOEY: What's this I hear about you tellin' the Chief I can wait for my radio station?

ZACHARY: (*As he proceeds around the room to collect and put on what he can find of his clothes, BIG JOEY and CREATURE follow him, obviously enjoying his predicament.*) I don't know where the hell you heard that from.

BIG JOEY: Yeah, right. Well, Lorraine Manigitogan had a word or two with Gazelle Nataways the other night. When you presented your initial proposal at the band office, you said: "Joe can wait. He's only got another three months left in the hockey season."

ZACHARY: I never said no such thing.

BIG JOEY: Bullshit.

ZACHARY: W-w-w-what I said was that employment at this bakery of mine would do nothing but add to those in such places as those down at the arena. I never mentioned your name once. And I said it only in passing reference to the fact ...

BIG JOEY: ... that this radio idea of mine doesn't have as much long-term significance to the future of this community as this fancy bakery idea of yours, Mr. Pillsbury dough-boy, right?

ZACHARY: If that's what you heard, then you didn't hear it from Lorraine Manigitogan. You got it from Gazelle Nataways and you know yourself she's got a bone to pick with ...

BIG JOEY: You know, Zach, you and me, we work for the same cause, don't we?

ZACHARY: Never said otherwise.

BIG JOEY: We work for the betterment and the advancement of this community, don't we? And seeing as we're about the only two guys in this whole hell-hole who's got the get-up-and-go to do something ...

ZACHARY: That's not exactly true, Joe. Take a look at Simon Starblanket ...

BIG JOEY: ... we should be working together, not against. What do you say you simply postpone that proposal to the Band Council ...

ZACHARY: I'm sorry. Can't do that.

BIG JOEY: (*cornering ZACHARY*) Listen here, bud. You turned your back on me when everybody said I was responsible for that business in Espanola seventeen years ago and you said nothin'. I overlooked that. Never said nothin'.

ZACHARY remembers his undershorts and proceeds, with even greater desperation, to look for them, zeroing in on the couch and under it. BIG JOEY catches the drift and snaps his fingers, signalling CREATURE to look for the shorts under the couch. CREATURE jumps for the couch. Without missing a beat, BIG JOEY continues.

BIG JOEY: You turned your back on me when you said you didn't want nothin' to do with me from that day on. I overlooked that. Never said nothin'. You gave me one hell of a slap in the face when your wife gave my Gazelle that kick in the belly. I overlooked that. Never said nothin'. (*CREATURE, having found the shorts among the junk under the couch just split seconds before ZACHARY does, throws them to BIG JOEY who holds them up to ZACHARY, smiling with satisfaction.*) That, however, was the last time …

ZACHARY: That wasn't my fault, Joe. It's that witch woman of yours Gazelle Nataways provoked that fight between her and Hera and you know yourself Hera tried to come and sew up her belly again …

BIG JOEY: Zach. I got ambition …

ZACHARY: Yeah, right.

BIG JOEY: I aim to get that radio station off the ground, starting with them games down at my arena.

ZACHARY: Phhhh!

BIG JOEY: I aim to get a chain of them community radio stations, not only on this here island but beyond as well …

ZACHARY: Dream on, Big Joey, dream on.

BIG JOEY: … and I aim to prove this broadcasting of games among the folks is one sure way to get some pride …

ZACHARY: Bullshit! You're in it for yourself.

BIG JOEY: … some pride and dignity back so you just get your ass on out of my house and you go tell that Chief your Band Council Resolution can wait until next fiscal year or else …

ZACHARY: I ain't doing no such thing, Joe, no way. Not when I'm this close.

BIG JOEY: (*eases himself down onto the couch, twirling the shorts with his forefinger*) … or else I get my Gazelle Nataways to wash these skivvies of yours, put them in a box all nice and gussied up, your picture on top, show up at your doorstop and hand them over to your wife.

Silence.

ZACHARY: (*quietly, to BIG JOEY*) Gimme them shorts. (*no answer; then to CREATURE*) Gimme them snapshots. (*still no response*)

BIG JOEY: (*dead calm*) Get out.

ZACHARY: (*seeing he can't win for the moment*) You may have won this time, Joe, but …

BIG JOEY: (*like a steel trap*) Get out.

Silence. Finally ZACHARY exits, looking very humble. Seconds before ZACHARY's exit, DICKIE BIRD HALKED, to avoid being seen by ZACHARY, disappears from the "window." The moment ZACHARY is gone, CREATURE scurries to the kitchen door, shaking his fist in the direction of the already-departed ZACHARY.

CREATURE: Damn rights! (*strutting like a cock, he turns to BIG JOEY*) Zachary Jeremiah Keechigeesik never shoulda come in your house, Big Joey. Thank god, Gazelle Nataways ain't my wife no more … (*BIG JOEY merely has to throw a glance in CREATURE's direction to intimidate him. At once, CREATURE reverts to his usual nervous self.*) … not really, she's yours now, right, Big Joey? It's you she's livin' with these days, not me.

BIG JOEY: (*sits on the couch with his beer, mostly ignoring CREATURE and watching the hockey game on television*) Don't make her my wife.

CREATURE: (*trying to clean up the mess around the couch, mostly shoving everything back under it*) I don't mind, Big Joey, I really don't. I tole you once I tole you twice she's yours now. It's like I loaned her to you, I don't mind. I can take it. We made a deal, remember? The night she threw the toaster at me and just about broke my skull, she told me: "I had enough, Creature Nataways, I had enough from you. I had your kids and I had your disease and that's all I ever want from you, I'm leavin'." And then she grabbed her suitcase and she grabbed the kids, no, she didn't even grab the kids, she grabbed the TV and she just sashayed herself over here. She left me. It's been four years now, Big Joey, I know, I know. Oh, it was hell, it was hell at first but you and me we're buddies since we're babies, right? So I thought it over for about a year … then one day I swallowed my pride and I got up off that chesterfield and I walked over here, I opened your door and I shook your hand and I said: "It's okay, Big Joey, it's okay." And then we went and played darts in Espanola except we kinda got side-tracked, remember, Big Joey, we ended up on that three-day bender?

BIG JOEY: Creature Nataways?

CREATURE: What?

BIG JOEY: You talk too much.

CREATURE: I tole you once I tole you twice I don't mind …

PIERRE ST. PIERRE comes bursting in, in a state of great excitement.

PIERRE: (*addressing the case of beer directly*) Hallelujah! Have you heard the news?

CREATURE: Pierre St. Pierre. Chris'sakes, knock. You're walkin' into a civilized house.

PIERRE: The news. Have you heard the news?

CREATURE: I'll tell you a piece of news. Anyways, we come in the door and guess who …

BIG JOEY: (*to CREATURE*) Sit down.

PIERRE: Gimme a beer.

CREATURE: (*to PIERRE*) Sit down.

PIERRE: Gimme a beer.

BIG JOEY: Give him a fuckin' beer.

But PIERRE has already grabbed, opened and is drinking a beer.

CREATURE: Have a beer.

PIERRE: (*talking out of the side of his mouth, as he continues drinking*) Tank you.

BIG JOEY: Talk.

PIERRE: (*putting his emptied bottle down triumphantly and grabbing another beer*) Toast me.

BIG JOEY: Spit it out.

CREATURE: Chris'sakes.

PIERRE: Toast me.

CREATURE: Toast you? The hell for?

PIERRE: Shut up. Just toast me.

CREATURE/BIG JOEY: Toast.

PIERRE: Tank you. You just toasted "The Ref."

CREATURE: (*to PIERRE*) The ref? (*to BIG JOEY*) The what?

PIERRE: "The Ref!"

CREATURE: The ref of the what?

PIERRE: The ref. I'm gonna be the referee down at the arena. Big Joey's arena. The Wasaychigan Hill Hippodrome.

CREATURE: We already got a referee.

PIERRE: Yeah, but this here's different, this here's special.

BIG JOEY: I'd never hire a toothless old boot-legger like you.

PIERRE: They play their first game in just a coupla days. Against the Canoe Lake Bravettes. And I got six teeth left so you just keep your trap shut about my teeth.

CREATURE: The Canoe Lake Bravettes!

BIG JOEY: Who's "they"?

PIERRE: Haven't you heard?

BIG JOEY: Who's "they"?

PIERRE: I don't believe this.

BIG JOEY: Who's "they"?

PIERRE: I don't believe this. (*BIG JOEY bangs PIERRE on the head.*) Oww, you big bully! The Wasaychigan Hill Wailerettes, of course. I'm talkin' about the Wasy Wailerettes, who else geez.

CREATURE: The Wasy Wailerettes? Chris'sakes …

PIERRE: Dominique Ladouche, Black Lady Halked, that terrible Dictionary woman, Fluffy Sainte-Marie, Dry Lips Manigitogan, Leonarda Lee Starblanket, Annie Cook, June Bug McLeod, Big Bum Pegahmagahbow, all twenty-seven of 'em. Them women from right here on this reserve, a whole batch of 'em, they upped and they said: "Bullshit! Ain't nobody on the face of this earth's gonna tell us us women's got no business playin' hockey. That's bullshit!" That's what they said: "Bullshit!" So. They took matters into their own hands. And, holy shit la marde, I almost forgot to tell you my wife Veronique St. Pierre, she went and made up her mind she's joinin' the Wasy Wailerettes, only the other women wouldn't let her at first on account she never had no babies—cuz, you see, you gotta be pregnant or have piles and piles of babies to be a Wasy Wailerette—but my wife, she put her foot down and she says: "Zhaboonigan Peterson may be just my adopted daughter and she may be retarded as a doormat but she's still my baby." That's what she says to 'em. And she's on and they're playin' hockey and the Wasy Wailerettes, they're just a-rarin to go, who woulda thunk it, huh?

CREATURE: Ho-leee!

PIERRE: God's truth …

BIG JOEY: They never booked the ice.

PIERRE: Ha! Booked it through Gazelle Nataways. Sure as I'm alive and walkin' these treacherous icy roads.

BIG JOEY: Hang on.

PIERRE: … god's truth in all its naked splendour. (*He pops open yet another beer.*) I kid you not, gentlemen, not for one slippery goddamn minute. Toast!

BIG JOEY: (*grabbing the bottle right out of PIERRE's mouth*) Where'd you sniff out all this crap?

PIERRE: From my wife, who else? My wife, Veronique St. Pierre, she told me. She says to me: "Pierre St. Pierre, you'll eat your shorts but I'm playin' hockey and I don't care what you say. Or think." And she left. No. First, she cleaned out my wallet, (*grabs his beer back from BIG JOEY's hand*) grabbed her big brown rosaries from off the wall. Then she left. Just slammed the door and left. Period. I just about ate my shorts. Toast!

CREATURE: Shouldn't we … shouldn't we stop them?

PIERRE: Phhht! … (*CREATURE just misses being spat on.*)

CREATURE: Ayoah!

PIERRE: … Haven't seen hide nor hair of 'em since. Gone to Sudbury. Every single last one of 'em. Piled theirselves into seven cars and just took off. Them back wheels was squealin' and rattlin' like them little jinger bells. Just past tea-time. Shoppin'. Hockey equipment. Phhht! (*Again, CREATURE just misses getting spat on.*)

CREATURE: Ayoah! It's enough to give you the shits every time he opens his mouth.

PIERRE: And they picked me. Referee.

BIG JOEY: And why you, may I ask?

PIERRE: (*faking humility*) Oh, I don't know. Something' about the referee here's too damn perschnickety. That drum-bangin' young whip-perschnapper, Simon Starblanket, (*grabbing yet another beer*) he's got the rules all mixed up or somethin' like that, is what they says. They kinda wanna play it their own way. So they picked me. Toast me.

CREATURE: Toast.

PIERRE: To the ref.

CREATURE: To the ref.

PIERRE: Tank you. (*They both drink.*) Ahhh. (*pause; to BIG JOEY*) So. I want my skates.

CREATURE: Your skates?

PIERRE: My skates. I want 'em back.

CREATURE: The hell's he talkin' about now?

PIERRE: They're here. I know they're here. I loaned 'em to you, remember?

BIG JOEY: Run that by me again?

PIERRE: I loaned 'em to you. That Saturday night Gazelle Nataways came in that door with her TV and her suitcase and you and me were sittin' right there on that old chesterfield with Lalala Lacroix sittin' between us and I loaned you my skates in return for that forty-ouncer of rye and Gazelle Nataways plunked her TV down, marched right up to Lalala Lacroix, slapped her in the face and chased her out the door. But we still had time to make the deal whereby if I wanted my skates back you'd give 'em back to me if I gave you back your forty-ouncer, right? Right. (*produces the bottle from under his coat*) Ta-da! Gimme my skates.

BIG JOEY: You sold them skates. They're mine.

PIERRE: Never you mind, Big Joey, never you mind, I want my skates. Take this. Go on. Take it.

BIG JOEY fishes one skate out from under the couch.

CREATURE: (*to himself; as he sits on the couch*) Women playin' hockey. Ho-leee!

BIG JOEY and PIERRE exchange bottle and skate.

PIERRE: Tank you. (*He makes a triumphant exit. BIG JOEY merely sits there and waits knowingly. Silence. Then PIERRE suddenly re-enters.*) There's only one. (*silence*) Well, where the hell's the other one? (*Silence. PIERRE nearly explodes with indignation.*) Gimme back my bottle! Where's the other one?

BIG JOEY: You got your skate. I got my bottle.

PIERRE: Don't talk backwards at me. I'm your elder.

CREATURE: It's gone.

PIERRE: Huh?

CREATURE: Gone. The other skate's gone, right, Big Joey?

PIERRE: Gone? Where?

CREATURE: My wife Gazelle Nataways.

PIERRE: … your ex-wife …

CREATURE: … she threw it out the door two years ago the night Spooky Lacroix went crazy in the head and tried to come and rip Gazelle Nataways' door off for cheatin' at the bingo. Just about killed Spooky Lacroix too, right, Big Joey?

PIERRE: So where's my other skate?

CREATURE: At Spooky Lacroix's, I guess.

PIERRE: Aw, shit la marde, youse guys don't play fair.

BIG JOEY: You go over to Spooky Lacroix's and you tell him I told you you could have your skate back.

PIERRE: No way, José. Spooky Lacroix's gonna preach at me.

BIG JOEY: Preach back.

PIERRE: You come with me. You used to be friends with Spooky Lacroix. You talk to Spooky Lacroix. Spooky Lacroix likes you.

BIG JOEY: He likes you too.

PIERRE: Yeah, but he likes you better. Oh, shit la marde! (*takes another beer out of the case*) And I almost forgot to tell you they decided to make Gazelle Nataways captain of the Wasy Wailerettes. I mean, she kind of … decided on her own, if you know what I mean.

BIG JOEY: Spooky Lacroix's waitin' for you.

PIERRE: How do you know?

BIG JOEY: God told me.

Pause. PIERRE actually wonders to himself. Then:

PIERRE: Aw, bullshit. (*exits*)

Silence. Then BIG JOEY and CREATURE look at each other, break down and laugh themselves into prolonged hysterical fits. After a while, they calm down and come to a dead stop. They sit and think. They look at the hockey game on the television. Then, dead serious, they turn to each other.

CREATURE: Women … Gazelle Nataways … hockey? Ho-leee …

BIG JOEY: (*still holding PIERRE's bottle of whisky*) Chris'sakes …

Fade out.

From this darkness emerges the sound of SPOOKY LACROIX's voice, singing with great emotion. As he sings, the lights fade in on his kitchen, where DICKIE BIRD HALKED is sitting across the table from SPOOKY LACROIX. DICKIE BIRD is scribbling on a piece of paper with a pencil. SPOOKY is knitting (pale blue baby booties). A bible sits on the table to the left of SPOOKY, a knitting pattern to his right. The place is covered with knitted doodads: knitted doilies, a tea cozy, a tacky picture of The Last Supper *with knitted frame and, on the wall, as subtly conspicuous as possible, a crucifix with pale blue knitted baby booties covering each of its four extremities. Throughout this scene, SPOOKY periodically consults the knitting pattern, wearing tiny little reading glasses, perched "just so" on the end of his nose. He knits with great difficulty and, therefore, with great concentration, sometimes, in moments of excitement, getting the bible and the knitting pattern mixed up with each other. He has tremendous difficulty getting the "disturbed" DICKIE BIRD to sit still and pay attention.*

SPOOKY: (*singing*) Everybody oughta know. Everybody oughta know. Who Jesus is. (*speaking*) This is it. This is the end. Igwani eeweepoonas-keewuk. ("The end of the world is at hand.") Says right here in the book. Very, very, very important to read the book. If you want the Lord to come into your life, Dickie Bird Halked, you've got to read the book. Not much time left. Yessiree. 1990. The last year. This will be the last year of our lives. Clear as a picture. The end of the world is here. At last. About time too, with the world going crazy, people shooting, killing each other left, right and centre. Jet planes full of people crashing into the bushes, lakes turning black, fish choking to death. Terrible. Terrible.

DICKIE BIRD shoves a note he's been scribbling over to SPOOKY.

SPOOKY: What's this? (*reads with some difficulty*) "How ... do ... you ... make ... babies!" (*shocked*) Dickie Bird Halked! At your age? Surely. Anyway. That young Starblanket boy who went and shot himself. Right here. Right in the einsteins. Bleeding from the belly, all this white mushy stuff come oozing out. Yuch! Brrr! I guess there's just nothing better to do for the young people on this reserve these days than go around shooting their einsteins out from inside their bellies. But the Lord has had enough. He's sick of it. No more, he says, no more. This is it.

DICKIE BIRD shoves another note over. SPOOKY pauses to read.

SPOOKY: Why, me and Lalala, we're married. And we're gonna have a baby. Period. Now. When the world comes to an end? The sky will open up. The clouds will part. And the Lord will come down in a holy vapour. And only those who are born-again Christian will go with him when he goes back up. And the rest? You know what's gonna happen to the rest? They will die. Big Joey, for instance. They will go to hell and they will burn for their wicked, whorish ways. But we will be taken up into the clouds to spend eternity surrounded by the wondrous and the mystical glory of God. Clear as a picture, Dickie Bird Halked, clear as a picture. So I'm telling you right now, you've got to read the book. Very, very, very important.

DICKIE BIRD shoves a third note over to SPOOKY. SPOOKY reads and finishes.

SPOOKY: Why, Wellington Halked's your father, Dickie Bird Halked. Don't you be asking questions like that. My sister, Black Lady Halked, that's your mother. Right? And because Wellington Halked is married to Black Lady Halked, he is your father. And don't you ever let no one tell you different.

Blackout.

From the darkness of the theatre emerges the magical flickering of a luminescent powwow dancing bustle. As it moves gradually towards the downstage area, a second—and larger—bustle appears on the upper level of the set, also flickering magically and moving about. The two bustles "play" with each other, almost affectionately, looking like two giant fireflies. The smaller bustle finally reaches the downstage area and from behind it emerges the face of SIMON STARBLANKET. He is dancing and chanting in a forest made of light and shadows. The larger bustle remains on the upper level; behind it is the entire person of NANABUSH as the spirit of PATSY PEGAHMAGAHBOW, a vivacious young girl of eighteen with a very big bum (i.e., an over-sized prosthetic bum). From this level, NANABUSH /PATSY watches and "plays" with the proceedings on the lower level. The giant full moon is in full bloom behind her. From the very beginning of all this, and in counterpoint to SIMON's chanting, also emerges the sound of someone playing a harmonica, a sad, mournful tune. It is ZACHARY JEREMIAH KEECHIGEESIK, stuck in the bush in his embarrassing state, play-ing his heart out. Then the harmonica stops and, from the darkness, we hear ZACHARY's voice.

ZACHARY: Hey.

SIMON hears this, looks behind, but sees nothing and continues his chanting and dancing. SIMON chants and dances as though he were desperately trying to find the right chant and dance.

ZACHARY: Pssst!

SIMON: Awinuk awa! ("Who's this?")

ZACHARY: (*in a hoarse whisper*) Simon Starblanket.

SIMON: Neee*, Zachary Jeremiah Keechigeesik. Awus! ("Go away!") Katha peeweestatooweemin. ("Don't come bothering me [with your words].")

Finally, ZACHARY emerges from the shadows and from behind a large rock, carrying his harmonica in one hand and holding his torn pants together as best he can with the other.

---

* "Neee" is probably the most common Cree expression, meaning something like "Oh, you" or "My goodness."

SIMON ignores him and continues with his chanting and dancing.

ZACHARY: W-w-w-what's it cost to get one of them dough-making machines?

SIMON: (*not quite believing his ears*) What?

ZACHARY: Them dough-making machines. What's it cost to buy one of them?

SIMON: A Hobart?

ZACHARY: A what?

SIMON: Hobart. H-O-B-A-R-T. Hobart.

ZACHARY: (*to himself*) Hobart. Hmmm.

SIMON: (*amused at the rather funny-looking ZACHARY*) Neee, machi ma-a, ("Oh you, but naturally,") Westinghouse for refrigerators, Kellogg's for corn flakes igwa ("and") Hobart for dough-making machines. Kinsitootawin na? ("Get it?") Brand name. Except we used to call it "the pig" because it had this ... piggish kind of motion to it. But never mind. Awus. Don't bother me.

ZACHARY: What's it cost to get this ... pig?

SIMON: (*laughing*) Neee, Zachary Jeremiah here you are, one of Wasy's most respected citizens, standing in the middle of the bush on a Saturday night in February freezing your buns off and you want to know how much a pig costs?

ZACHARY: (*vehemently*) I promised Hera I'd have all this information by tonight we were supposed to sit down and discuss the budget for this damn bakery tonight and here I went and messed it all up thank god I ran into you because now you're the only person left on this whole reserve who might have the figures I need what's this damn dough-making machine cost come on now tell me!

SIMON: (*a little cowed*) Neee, about four thousand bucks. Maybe five.

ZACHARY: You don't know for sure? But you worked there.

SIMON: I was only the dishwasher, Zachary Jeremiah, I didn't own the place. Mama Louisa was a poor woman. She had really old equipment, most of which she dragged over herself all the way from Italy after the Second World War. It wouldn't cost the same today.

ZACHARY: Five thousand dollars for a Mobart, hmmm ...

SIMON: Hobart.

ZACHARY: I wish I had a piece of paper to write all this down, sheesh. You got a piece of paper on you?

SIMON: No. Just ... this. (*holding the dancing bustle up*) Why are you holding yourself like that?

ZACHARY: I was ... standing on the road down by Andy Manigitogan's place when this car came by and wooof! My pants ripped. Ripped right down the middle. And my shorts, well, they just ... took off. How do you like that, eh?

SIMON: Nope. I don't like it. Neee, awus. Kigithaskin. ("You're lying to me.")

ZACHARY: W-w-w-why would I pull your leg for? I don't really mind it except it is damn cold out here.

At this point, NANABUSH/PATSY, on the upper level, scurries closer to get a better look, her giant powwow dancing bustle flickering magically in the half-light. SIMON's attention is momentarily pulled away by this fleeting vision.

SIMON: Hey! Did you see that?

But ZACHARY, too caught up with his own dilemma, does not notice.

ZACHARY: I'm very, very upset right now ...

SIMON: ... I thought I just saw Patsy Pegahmagahbow ... with this ...

ZACHARY: (*looks, perplexed, in the direction SIMON indicates*) ... do you think ... my two ordinary convection ovens ...

SIMON: (*calling out*) Patsy? ... (*Pause. Slowly, he turns back to ZACHARY.*) ... like ... she made this for me, eh? (*referring to the bustle*) She and her step-mother, Rosie Kakapetum, back in September, after my mother's funeral. Well, I was out here thinking, if this ... like, if this ... dance didn't come to me real natural, like from deep inside of me, then I was gonna burn it. (*referring to the bustle*) Right here on this spot. Cuz then ... it doesn't mean anything real to me, does it? Like, it's false ... it's driving me crazy, this dream where Indian people are just dropping off like flies ...

NANABUSH/PATSY begins to "play" with the two men, almost as if, with the help of the winter night's magic and the power of the full moon, she were weaving a spell around SIMON and ZACHARY.

ZACHARY: (*singing softly to himself*) Hot cross buns. Hot cross buns. One a penny, two a penny, hot cross buns …

SIMON: … something has to be done …

ZACHARY: (*speaking*) … strawberry pies …

SIMON: … in this dream …

ZACHARY: … so fresh and flaky they fairly bubble over with the cream from the very breast of Mother Nature herself …

SIMON: … the drum has to come back, mistig-wuskeek ("the drum") …

ZACHARY: … bran muffins, cherry tarts …

SIMON: … the medicine, the power, this … (*holding the bustle up in the air*)

ZACHARY: … butter tarts …

SIMON: … has to come back. We've got to learn to dance again.

ZACHARY: … tarts tarts tarts upside-down cakes cakes cakes and not to forget, no, never, ever to forget that Black Forest cake …

SIMON: … Patsy Pegahmagahbow …

ZACHARY: … cherries jubilee …

SIMON: … her step-mother, Rosie Kakapetum, the medicine woman …

ZACHARY: … lemon meringue pie …

SIMON: … the power …

ZACHARY: … baked Alaska …

SIMON: … Nanabush! …

ZACHARY: (*then suddenly, with bitterness*) Gazelle Nataways, K'skanagoos! ("The female dog!")

All of a sudden, from the darkness of the winter night, emerges a strange, eerie sound; whether it is wolves howling or women wailing, we are not sure at first. And whether this sound comes from somewhere deep in the forest, from the full moon or where, we are not certain. But there is

definitely a "spirit" in the air. The sound of this wailing is undercut by the sound of rocks hitting boards, or the sides of houses, echoing, as in a vast empty chamber. Gradually, as SIMON speaks, ZACHARY—filled with confusing emotion as he is—takes out his harmonica, sits down on the large rock and begins to play a sad, mournful melody, tinged, as always, with a touch of the blues.

SIMON: … I have my arms around this rock, this large black rock sticking out of the ground, right here on this spot. And then I hear this baby crying, from inside this rock. The baby is crying out my name. As if I am somehow responsible for it being caught inside that rock. I can't move. My arms, my whole body, stuck to this rock. Then this … eagle … lands beside me, right over there. But this bird has three faces, three women. And the eagle says to me: "the baby is crying, my grandchild is crying to hear the drum again." (*NANABUSH/PATSY, her face surrounded by the brilliant feathers of her bustle, so that she looks like some fantastic, mysterious bird, begins to wail, her voice weaving in and out of the other wailing voices.*) Then the eagle is gone and the rock cracks and this mass of flesh, covered with veins and blood, comes oozing out and a woman's voice somewhere is singing something about angels and god and angels and god …

The wailing has now faded into complete silence. ZACHARY finally rises from his seat on the rock.

ZACHARY: … I dreamt I woke up at Gazelle Nataways' place with no shorts on. And I got this nagging suspicion them shorts are still over there. If you could just go on over there now … I couldn't have been over there. I mean, there's my wife Hera. And there's my bakery. And this bakery could do a lot for the Indian people. Economic development. Jobs. Bread. Apple pie. So you see, there's an awful lot that's hanging on them shorts. This is a good chance for you to do something for your people, Simon, if you know what I mean …

SIMON: I'm the one who has to bring the drum back. And it's Patsy's medicine power, that stuff she's learning from her step-mother Rosie Kakapetum that … helps me …

ZACHARY: I go walking into my house with no underwear, pants ripped right down the middle, not a shred of budget in sight and wooof! …

PIERRE ST. PIERRE comes bursting in on the two men with his one skate in hand, taking them completely by surprise. NANABUSH/PATSY disappears.

ZACHARY: Pierre St. Pierre! Just the man …

PIERRE: No time. No time. Lalala Lacroix's having a baby any minute now so I gotta get over to Spook's before she pops.

SIMON: I can go get Rosie Kakapetum.

PIERRE: Too old. Too old. She can't be on the team.

SIMON: Neee, what team? Rosie Kakapetum's the last midwife left in Wasy, Pierre St. Pierre, of course she can't be on a team.

ZACHARY: (*to PIERRE*) You know that greasy shit-brown chesterfield over at Gazelle Nataways'?

SIMON: (*to ZACHARY*) Mind you, if there was a team of midwives, chee-i? ("eh!") Wha!

PIERRE: Gazelle Nataways? Hallelujah, haven't you heard the news?

ZACHARY: What? … you mean … it's out already?

PIERRE: All up and down Wasaychigan Hill …

ZACHARY: (*thoughtfully, to himself, as it dawns on him*) The whole place knows.

PIERRE: … clean across Manitoulin Island and right to the outskirts of Sudbury …

ZACHARY: Lordy, lordy, lordy …

PIERRE: Gazelle Nataways, Dominique Ladouche, Black Lady Halked, that terrible Dictionary woman, Fluffy Sainte-Marie, Dry Lips Manigitogan, Leonarda Lee Starblanket, Annie Cook, June Bug McLeod, Big Bum Pegahmagahbow …

SIMON: Patsy Pegahmagahbow. Get it straight.

PIERRE: Quiet! I'm not finished … all twenty-seven of 'em …

SIMON: Neee, Zachary Jeremiah, your goose is cooked.

PIERRE: Phhht! Cooked and burnt right down to a nice crispy pitch black cinder because your wife Hera Keechigeesik is in on it too.

ZACHARY, reeling from the horror of it all, finally sits back down on the rock.

SIMON: Patsy Pegahmagahbow is pregnant, Pierre St. Pierre. She can't go running around all over Manitoulin Island with a belly that's getting bigger by the …

PIERRE: Aw, they're all pregnant, them women, or have piles and piles of babies and I'll be right smack dab in the middle of it all just a-blowin' my whistle and a-throwin' that dirty little black thingie around …

ZACHARY: (*rising from the rock*) Now you listen here, Pierre St. Pierre. I may have lost my shorts under Gazelle Nataways' greasy shit-brown chesterfield not one hour ago and may have lost my entire life, not to mention my bakery, as a result of that one very foolish mistake but I'll have you know that my shorts, they are clean as a whistle, I change them every day, my favourite colour is light blue, and black and crusted with shit my shorts most certainly are not!

SIMON: (*surprised and thrilled at ZACHARY's renewed "fighting" spirit*) Wha!

PIERRE: Whoa! Easy, Zachary Jeremiah, easy there. Not one stitch of your shorts has anything whatsoever to do with the revolution.

SIMON: Pierre St. Pierre, what revolution are you wheezing and snorting on about!

PIERRE: The puck. I'm talkin' about the puck.

ZACHARY: The puck?

SIMON: The puck?

PIERRE: Yes, the puck. The puck, the puck, the puck and nothin' but the goddamn puck they're playin' hockey, them women from right here on this reserve, they're playin' hockey and nothin', includin' Zachary Jeremiah Keechigeesik's bright crispy undershorts, is gonna stop 'em.

SIMON: Women playing hockey. Neee, watstagatch! ("Good grief!")

PIERRE: "Nee, watstagatch" is right because they're in Sudbury, as I speak, shoppin' for hockey equipment, and I'm the referee! Outa my way! Or the Lacroixs will pop before I get there. (*He begins to exit.*)

ZACHARY: Pierre St. Pierre, get me my shorts or I'll report your bootleg joint to the police.

PIERRE: No time. No time. (exits)

ZACHARY: (calling out) Did Hera go to Sudbury, too? (But PIERRE is gone.)

SIMON: (thoughtfully to himself, as he catches another glimpse of NANABUSH/PATSY and her bustle) … rocks hitting boards …

ZACHARY: (to himself) What in God's name is happening to Wasaychigan Hill …

SIMON: … women wailing …

ZACHARY: (with even greater urgency) Do you think those two ordinary convection ovens are gonna do the job or should I get one of them great big pizza ovens right away?

SIMON: … pucks …

ZACHARY: Simon, I'm desperate!

SIMON: (finally snapping out of his speculation and looking straight into ZACHARY's face) Neee, Zachary Jeremiah. Okay. Goes like this. (very quickly) It depends on what you're gonna bake, eh? Like if you're gonna bake bread and, like, lots of it, you're gonna need one of them great big ovens but if you're gonna bake just muffins …

ZACHARY: … muffins, nah, not just muffins …

SIMON: … then all you need is one of them ordinary little ovens but like I say, I was only the dishwasher …

ZACHARY: How many employees were there in your bakery?

SIMON: … it depends on how big a community you're gonna serve, Zachary Jeremiah …

ZACHARY: … nah, Wasy, just Wasy, to start with …

SIMON: … like, we had five, one to make the dough—like, mix the flour and the water and the yeast and all that—like, this guy had to be at work by six a.m., that's gonna be hard here in Wasy, Zachary Jeremiah, I'm telling you that right now …

ZACHARY: … nah, I can do that myself, no problem …

SIMON: … then we had three others to roll the dough and knead and twist and punch and pound it on this great big wooden table …

ZACHARY: … I'm gonna need a great big wooden table?

SIMON: … hard wood, Zachary Jeremiah, not soft wood. And then one to actually bake the loaves, like, we had these long wooden paddles, eh? …

ZACHARY: … paddles …

SIMON: … yeah, paddles, Zachary Jeremiah, real long ones. It was kinda neat, actually …

ZACHARY: … go on, go on …

SIMON: Listen here, Zachary Jeremiah, I'm going to Sudbury next Saturday, okay? And if you wanna come along, I can take you straight to Mama Louisa's Pasticerria myself. I'll introduce you to the crusty old girl and you can take a good long look at her rubbery old Hobart, how's that? You can even touch it if you want, neee …

ZACHARY: … really? …

SIMON: Me? I'm asking Patsy Pegahmagahbow to marry me …

ZACHARY: … Simon, Simon …

SIMON: … and we're gonna hang two thousand of these things (referring to his dancing bustle) all over Manitoulin Island, me and Patsy and our baby. And me and Patsy and our baby and this Nanabush character, we're gonna be dancing up and down Wasaychigan Hill like nobody's business cuz I'm gonna go out there and I'm gonna bring that drum back if it kills me.

ZACHARY: (pause; then quietly) Get me a safety pin.

SIMON: (pause) Neee, okay. And you, Zachary Jeremiah Keechigeesik, you're gonna see a Hobart such as you have never seen ever before in your entire life!

SIMON/ZACHARY: (smiling, almost laughing at each other) Neee …

Blackout.

Lights come up on the upper level, where we see this bizarre vision of NANABUSH, now in the guise of BLACK LADY HALKED, nine months pregnant (i.e., wearing a huge, out-sized prosthetic belly). Over this, she wears a maternity gown and, pacing the floor slowly, holds a huge string of rosary beads. She recites the rosary *quietly to herself. She is also drinking a beer and, obviously, is a little unsteady on her feet because of this.*

Fade-in on the lower level into SPOOKY LACROIX's kitchen. DICKIE BIRD HALKED is on his knees, praying fervently to this surrealistic, miraculous vision of the Madonna (i.e., his own mother), which he actually sees inside his own mind. Oblivious to all this, SPOOKY LACROIX sits at his table, still knitting his baby booties and preaching away.

SPOOKY: Dickie Bird Halked? I want you to come to heaven with me. I insist. But before you do that, you take one of them courses in sign language, help me prepare this reserve for the Lord. Can't you just see yourself, standing on that podium in the Wasaychigan Hill Hippodrome, talking sign language to the people? Talking about the Lord and how close we are to the end? I could take a break. And these poor people with their meaningless, useless ...

PIERRE ST. PIERRE comes bursting in and marches right up to SPOOKY. The vision of NANABUSH/BLACK LADY HALKED disappears.

PIERRE: Alright. Hand it over.

SPOOKY: (*startled out of his wits*) Pierre St. Pierre! You went and mixed up my booty!

PIERRE: I know it's here somewhere.

SPOOKY: Whatever it is you're looking for, you're not getting it until you bring the Lord into your life.

PIERRE: My skate. Gimme my skate.

SPOOKY: I don't have no skate. Now listen to me.

PIERRE: My skate. The skate Gazelle Nataways threw at you and just about killed you.

SPOOKY: What the hell are you gonna do with a skate at this hour of the night?

PIERRE: Haven't you heard the news?

SPOOKY: (*pauses to think*) No. I haven't heard any news.

DICKIE BIRD gets up and starts to wander around the kitchen. He looks around at random, first out the window, as if to see who has been chanting, then, eventually, he zeroes in on the crucifix on

the wall and stands there looking at it. Finally, he takes it off the wall and plays with its cute little booties.

PIERRE: The women. I'm gonna be right smack dab in the middle of it all. The revolution. Right here in Wasaychigan Hill.

SPOOKY: The Chief or the priest. Which one are they gonna revolution?

PIERRE: No, no, no. Dominique Ladouche, Black Lady Halked, that terrible Dictionary woman, that witch Gazelle Nataways, Fluffy Sainte-Marie, Dry Lips Manigitogan, Leonarda Lee Starblanket, Annie Cook, June Bug McLeod, Big Bum Pegahmagahbow, all twenty-seven of 'em. Even my wife, Veronique St. Pierre, she'll be right smack dab in the middle of it all. Defence.

SPOOKY: Defence? The Americans. We're being attacked. Is the situation that serious?

PIERRE: No, no, no, for Chris'sakes. They're playin' hockey. Them women are playin' hockey. Dead serious they are too.

SPOOKY: No.

PIERRE: Yes.

SPOOKY: Thank the Lord this is the last year!

PIERRE: Don't you care to ask?

SPOOKY: Thank the Lord the end of the world is coming this year! (*Gasping, he marches up to DICKIE BIRD.*)

PIERRE: I'm the referee, dammit.

SPOOKY: Watch your language. (*grabbing the crucifix from DICKIE BIRD*)

PIERRE: That's what I mean when I say I'm gonna be right smack dab in the middle of it all. You don't listen to me.

SPOOKY: (*puts the little booties back on the crucifix*) But you're not a woman.

PIERRE: You don't have to be. To be a referee these days, you can be anything, man or woman, don't matter which away. So gimme my skate.

SPOOKY: What skate?

PIERRE: The skate Gazelle Nataways just about killed you with after the bingo that time.

SPOOKY: Oh, that. I hid it in the basement. (*PIERRE opens a door, falls in and comes struggling out with a mousetrap stuck to a finger.*)

SPOOKY: Pierre St. Pierre, what the hell are you doing in Lalala's closet?

PIERRE: Well, where the hell's the basement? (*He frees his finger.*)

SPOOKY: Pierre St. Pierre, you drink too much. You gotta have the Lord in your life.

PIERRE: I don't need the Lord in my life, for god's sake, I need my skate. I gotta practice my figure eights.

SPOOKY: (*begins to put the crucifix back up on the wall*) You gotta promise me before I give you your skate.

PIERRE: I promise.

SPOOKY: (*unaware, he threatens PIERRE with the crucifix, holding it up against his neck*) You gotta have the Lord come into your life.

PIERRE: Alright, alright.

SPOOKY: For how long?

PIERRE: My whole life. I promise I'm gonna bring the Lord into my life and keep him there right up until the day I die just gimme my goddamn skate.

SPOOKY: Cross my heart.

PIERRE: Alright. Cross your heart.

Neither man makes a move until SPOOKY, finally catching on, throws PIERRE a look. PIERRE crosses himself.

SPOOKY: Good. (*exits to the basement*)

PIERRE: (*Now alone with DICKIE BIRD, half-whispering to him. As PIERRE speaks, DICKIE BIRD again takes the crucifix off the wall and returns with it to his seat, taking the booties off in haphazard fashion.*) Has he been feedin' you this crappola, too? Don't you be startin' that foolishness. That Spooky Lacroix's so fulla shit he wouldn't know a two thousand year-old Egyptian Sphinxter if he came face to face with one. He's just preachifyin' at you because you're the one person on this reserve who can't argue back. You listen to me. I was there in the same room as your mother when she gave birth to you. So I know well who you are and where you come from. I remember the whole picture. Even though we

were all in a bit of a fizzy ... I remember. Do you know, Dickie Bird Halked, that you were named after that bar? Anyone ever tell you that? (*DICKIE BIRD starts to shake. PIERRE takes fright.*) Spooky Lacroix, move that holy ass of yours, for fuck's sakes! (*DICKIE BIRD laughs. PIERRE makes a weak attempt to laugh along.*) And I'll never forgive your father, Big Joey oops ... (*DICKIE BIRD reacts.*) ... I mean, Wellington Halked, for letting your mother do that to you. "It's not good for the people of this world," I says to him, "it's not good for 'em to have the first thing they see when they come into the world is a goddamn jukebox." That's what I says to him. Thank god, you survived, Dickie Bird Halked, thank god, seventeen years later you're sittin' here smack-dab in front of me, hale and hearty as cake. Except for your tongue. Talk, Dickie Bird Halked, talk. Say somethin'. Come on. Try this: "Daddy, daddy, daddy." (*DICKIE BIRD shakes his head.*) Come on. Just this once. Maybe it will work. (*He takes DICKIE BIRD by the cheeks with one hand.*) "Daddy, daddy, daddy, daddy." (*DICKIE BIRD jumps up and attacks PIERRE, looking as though he were about to shove the crucifix down PIERRE's throat. PIERRE is genuinely terrified. Just then, SPOOKY re-enters with the skate.*) Whoa, whoa. Easy. Easy now, Dickie Bird. Easy.

SPOOKY: (*Gasping again at the sight of DICKIE BIRD man-handling the crucifix, he makes a bee-line for the boy.*) Dickie Bird Halked? Give me that thing. (*He grabs the crucifix with a flourish. Then he turns to PIERRE and holds the skate out with his other hand.*) Promise.

PIERRE: Cross my heart. (*crosses himself*)

SPOOKY: (*replacing the crucifix on the wall and pointing at PIERRE*) The Lord.

PIERRE: The Lord.

SPOOKY hands the skate over to PIERRE. Just then, CREATURE NATAWAYS stumbles in, now visibly drunk.

CREATURE: The Lord!

Picking on the hapless DICKIE BIRD, CREATURE roughly shoves the boy into a chair.

PIERRE: (*holding up both his skates*) I got 'em both. See! I got 'em.

CREATURE: Hallelujah! Now all you gotta do is learn how to skate.

SPOOKY: Creature Nataways, I don't want you in my house in that condition. Lalala is liable to pop any minute now and I don't want my son to see the first thing he sees when he comes into the world is a drunk.

PIERRE: Damn rights!

SPOOKY: … you too, Pierre St. Pierre.

CREATURE: Aw! William Lacroix, don't give me that holier-than-me, poker-up-the-bum spiritual bull crap …

SPOOKY: … say wha? …

CREATURE: Are you preachin' to this boy, William Lacroix? Are you usin' him again to practice your preachy-preachy? Don't do that, William, the boy is helpless. If you wanna practice, go practice on your old buddy, go preach on Big Joey. He's the one who needs it.

SPOOKY: You're hurting again, aren't you, Creature Nataways.

CREATURE: Don't listen to Spooky Lacroix, Dickie Bird. You follow Spooky Lacroix and you go right down to the dogs, I'm tellin' you that right now. Hair spray, lysol, vanilla extract, shoe polish, Xerox machine juice, he's done it all, this man. If you'd given William Lacroix the chance, he'd have sliced up the Xerox machine and ate it …

PIERRE: (mockingly) No!

CREATURE: … He once drank a Kitty Wells record. He lied to his own mother and he stole her record and he boiled it and swallowed it right up …

PIERRE: Good heavens!

BIG JOEY enters and stands at the door unseen.

CREATURE: … Made the Globe and Mail, too. He's robbed, he's cheated his best friend …

SPOOKY: Alphonse Nataways! Why are you doing this, may I ask?

CREATURE: Oh, he was bad, Dickie Bird Halked, he was bad. Fifteen years. Fifteen years of his life pukin' his guts out on sidewalks from here to Sicamous, B.C., this man …

SPOOKY: Shush!

CREATURE: … and this is the same man …

BIG JOEY: (Speaking suddenly and laughing, he takes everyone by surprise. They gasp. And practically freeze in their tracks.) … who's yellin' and preachin' about "the Lord!" They oughta retire the beaver and put this guy on the Canadian nickel, he's become a national goddamn symbol, that what you're sayin', Creature Nataways? This the kind of man you wanna become, that what you're sayin' to the boy, Creature Nataways? (close up to DICKIE BIRD) A man who couldn't get a hard-on in front of a woman if you paid him a two dollar bill?

SPOOKY: (stung to the quick) And is this the kind of man you wanna become, Dickie Bird Halked, this MAN who can't take the sight of blood least of all woman's blood, this MAN who, when he sees a woman's blood, chokes up, pukes and faints, how do you like that?

PIERRE, sensing potential violence, begins to sneak out.

BIG JOEY: (pulls a bottle out of his coat) Spooky Lacroix, igwani eeweepoonaskeewuk. ("The end of the world is at hand.")

PIERRE, seeing the bottle, retraces his steps and sits down again, grabbing a tea cup en route, ready for a drink.

SPOOKY: (shocked) Get that thing out of my house!

BIG JOEY: Tonight, we're gonna celebrate my wife, Spooky Lacroix, we're gonna celebrate because my wife, the fabulous, the incredible Gazelle Delphina Nataways, has been crowned Captain of the Wasy Wailerettes. The Rez is makin' history, Spooky Lacroix. The world will never be the same. Come on, it's on me, it's on your old buddy, the old, old buddy you said you'd never, ever forget.

SPOOKY: I told you a long time ago, Big Joey, after what you went and done to my sister, this here boy's own mother, you're no buddy of mine. Get out of my house. Get!

BIG JOEY: (handing the bottle of whisky to CREATURE) Creature Nataways, celebrate your wife.

CREATURE: (raising the bottle in a toast) To my wife!

PIERRE: (*holding his cup out to the bottle*) Your ex-wife.

BIG JOEY: (*suddenly quiet and intimate*) William. William. You and me. You and me, we used to be buddies, kigiskisin? ("Remember?") Wounded Knee. South Dakota. Spring of '73. We parked my van over by that little lake, we swam across, you almost didn't make it and nothin' could get you to swim back. Kigiskisin? So here we're walkin' back through the bush, all the way around this small lake, nothin' on but bare feet and wet undershorts and this black bear come up behind you, kigiskisin? And you freaked out. (*laughs*)

PIERRE *tries, as best he can, to create a party atmosphere, to little avail. CREATURE nervously watches BIG JOEY and SPOOKY. DICKIE BIRD merely sits there, head down, rocking back and forth.*

SPOOKY: (*obviously extremely uncomfortable*) You freaked out too, ha-ha, ha-ha.

BIG JOEY: That bear gave you a real spook, huh? (*Pause. Suddenly, he jumps at the other men.*) Boo! (*The other men, including SPOOKY, jump, splashing whisky all over the place. BIG JOEY laughs. The others pretend to laugh.*) That's how you got your name, you old Spook …

SPOOKY: You were scared too, ha-ha, ha-ha.

BIG JOEY: … we get back to the camp and there's Creature and Eugene and Zach and Roscoe, bacon and eggs all ready for us. Christ, I never laughed so hard in my life. But here you were, not laughin' and we'd say: "What's the matter, Spook, you don't like our jokes?" And you'd say: "That's good, yeah, that's good." I guess you were laughin' from a different part of yourself, huh? You were beautiful …

SPOOKY: That's good, yeah, that's good.

BIG JOEY: (*getting the bottle back from CREATURE and PIERRE*) So tonight, Bear-who-went-and-gave-you-a-real-Spooky Lacroix, we're gonna celebrate another new page in our lives. Wounded Knee Three! Women's version!

PIERRE: Damn rights.

BIG JOEY: (*raising the bottle up in a toast*) To my wife!

SPOOKY: Ha! Get that thing away from me.

PIERRE: Spooky Lacroix, cooperate. Cooperate for once. The women, the women are playing hockey.

CREATURE: To my wife!

PIERRE: Your ex-wife.

CREATURE: Shut up you toothless old bugger.

SPOOKY: Big Joey, you're not my friend no more.

BIG JOEY: (*Grabs SPOOKY roughly by the throat. CREATURE jumps to help hold SPOOKY still.*) You never let a friend for life go, William Hector Lacroix, not even if you turn your back on your own father Nicotine Lacroix's spiritual teachings and pretend like hell to be this born-again Christian.

SPOOKY: Let go. Creature Nataways, let go of me! (*to BIG JOEY*) For what you did to this boy at that bar seventeen years ago, Joseph Jeremiah McLeod, you are going to hell. To hell!

BIG JOEY *baptizes SPOOKY with the remainder of the bottle's contents. Breaking free, SPOOKY grabs DICKIE BIRD and shoves him toward BIG JOEY.*

SPOOKY: Look at him. He can't even talk. He hasn't talked in seventeen years!

DICKIE BIRD *cries out, breaks free, grabs the crucifix from the wall and runs out the door, crying. SPOOKY breaks down, falls to the floor and weeps. BIG JOEY attempts to pick him up gently, but SPOOKY kicks him away.*

SPOOKY: Let go of me! Let go!

CREATURE: (*lifting the empty bottle, laughing and crying at the same time*) To my wife, to my wife, to my wife, to my wife, to my wife …

BIG JOEY *suddenly lifts SPOOKY off the floor by the collar and lifts a fist to punch his face.*

Blackout.

Out of this blackout emerges the eerie, distant sound of women wailing and pucks hitting boards, echoing and echoing as in a vast empty chamber. The lights come up on DICKIE BIRD HALKED and SIMON STARBLANKET, standing beside each other in the "bleachers" of the hockey arena, watching the "ice" area (i.e., looking out over the audience). The bleachers area is actually on the upper level of the set, in a straight line directly in front of NANABUSH's perch. DICKIE BIRD is still holding SPOOKY's crucifix and SIMON is still holding his dancing bustle.

SIMON: Your grandpa, Nicotine Lacroix, was a medicine man. Hell of a name, but he was a medicine man. Old priest here, Father Boucher, years ago—oh, he was a terrible man—he went and convinced the people old Nicotine Lacroix talked to the devil. That's not true. Nicotine Lacroix was a good man. That's why I want you for my best man. Me and Patsy are getting married a couple of months from now. It's decided. We're gonna have a baby. Then we're going down to South Dakota and we're gonna dance with the Rosebud Sioux this summer. (*sings as he stomps his foot in the rhythm of a powwow drum*) " ... and me I don't wanna go to the moon, I'm gonna leave that moon alone. I just wanna dance with the Rosebud Sioux this summer, yeah, yeah, yeah ... " (*breaks into a chant*)

DICKIE BIRD watches, fascinated, particularly by the bustle SIMON holds up in the air.

At this point, ZACHARY JEREMIAH KEECHIGEESIK approaches timidly from behind a beam, his pants held flimsily together with a huge safety pin. The sound of women wailing and pucks hitting boards now shifts into the sound of an actual hockey arena, just before a big game.

ZACHARY: (*to SIMON*) Hey! (*But SIMON doesn't hear and continues chanting.*) Pssst!

SIMON: Zachary Jeremiah. Neee, watstagatch!

ZACHARY: Is Hera out there?

SIMON: (*indicating the "ice"*) Yup. There she is.

ZACHARY: Lordy, lordy, lordy ...

SIMON: Just kidding. She's not out there ...

ZACHARY: Don't do that to me!

SIMON: ... yet.

ZACHARY: (*coming up to join the young men at the "bleachers"*) You know that Nanabush character you were telling me about a couple of nights ago? What do you say I give his name over to them little gingerbread cookie men I'm gonna be making? For starters. Think that would help any?

SIMON: Neee ...

Just then, BIG JOEY enters to get a microphone stand ready for broadcasting the game. ZACHARY goes to stand as far away from him as possible.

ZACHARY: (*looking out over the "ice"*) It's almost noon. They're late getting started.

BIG JOEY: (*yawning luxuriously*) That's right. Me and Gazelle Nataways ... slept in.

CREATURE NATAWAYS comes scurrying in.

CREATURE: (*still talking to himself*) ... I tole you once I tole you twice ... (*then to the other men*) Chris'sakes! Are they really gonna do it? Chris'sakes!

SPOOKY LACROIX enters wearing a woollen scarf he obviously knitted himself. He is still knitting, this time a pale blue baby sweater. He also now sports a black eye and band-aid on his face. All the men, except PIERRE ST. PIERRE, are now in the "bleachers," standing in a straight line facing the audience, with DICKIE BIRD in the centre, SIMON and SPOOKY to his immediate right and left, respectively.

SPOOKY: It's bad luck to start late. I know. I read the interview with Gay Lafleur in last week's Expositor. They won't get far.

He sees Gazelle Nataways entering the "rink," unseen by the audience. All the hockey players on the "ice" are unseen by the audience; it is only the men who can actually "see" them.

SPOOKY: Look! Gazelle Nataways went and got her sweater trimmed in the chest area!

Wild catcalls from the men.

CREATURE: Trimmed it! She's got it plunging down to her ootsee ("belly button").

ZACHARY: Ahem. Smokes too much. Lung problems.

BIG JOEY: Nah. More like it's got somethin' to do with the undershorts she's wearin' today.

ZACHARY: (*fast on the up-take*) Fuck you!

BIG JOEY: (*blowing ZACHARY a kiss*) Poosees. ("Pussy cat." [Zachary's childhood nickname])

SPOOKY: Terrible. Terrible. Tsk, tsk, tsk.

PIERRE ST. PIERRE enters on the lower level, teetering dangerously on his skates towards the "ice" area downstage. He wears a referee's top and a whistle around his neck.

PIERRE: (*checking the names off as he reads from a clipboard*) Dominique Ladouche, Black Lady Halked, Annie Cook, June Bug McLeod, Big Bum Pegahmagahbow ...

SIMON: (*calling out*) Patsy Pegahmagahbow, turkey.

PIERRE: Shut up. I'm workin' here ... Leonarda Lee Starblanket, that terrible Dictionary woman, Fluffy Sainte-Marie, Chicken Lips Pegahmagahbow, Dry Lips Manigitogan, Little Hand Manigitogan, Little Girl Manitowabi, Victoria Manitowabi, Belinda Nickikoosimeenicaning, Martha Two-Axe Early-in-the-Morning, her royal highness Gazelle Delphina Nataways, Delia Opekokew, Barbra Nahwegahbow, Gloria May Eshkibok, Hera Keechigeesik, Tall Mary Ann Patchnose, Short Mary Ann Patchnose, Queen Elizabeth Patchnose, the triplets Marjorie Moose, Maggie May Moose, Mighty Moose and, of course, my wife, Veronique St. Pierre. Yup. They're all there, I hope, and the world is about to explode!

SPOOKY: That's what I've been trying to tell you!

PIERRE ST. PIERRE, barely able to stand on his skates, hobbles about, obviously getting almost trampled by the hockey players at various times.

BIG JOEY: (*Now speaking on the microphone. The other men watch the women on the "ice"; some are cheering and whistling, some calling down the game.*) Welcome, ladies igwa gentle-men, welcome one and all to the Wasaychigan Hill Hip-hip-hippodrome. This is your host for the big game, Big Joey—and they don't call me Big Joey for nothin'—Chairman, CEO and Proprietor of the Wasaychigan Hill Hippodrome, bringin' you a game such as has never been seen ever before on the ice of any hockey arena any-where on the island of Manitoulin, anywhere on the face of this country, anywhere on the face of this planet. And there ...

CREATURE: ... there's Gazelle Nataways, number one ...

BIG JOEY: ... they are, ladies ...

SPOOKY: ... terrible, terrible ...

BIG JOEY: ... igwa gentlemen ...

CREATURE: ... Chris'sakes, that's my wife, Chris'sakes ...

BIG JOEY: ... there they are, the most beautiful ...

SIMON: ... give 'em hell, Patsy Pegahmagahbow, give'em hell ...

BIG JOEY: ... daring, death- ...

SIMON: (*to ZACHARY*) ... there's Hera Keechigeesik, number nine ...

BIG JOEY: ... defying Indian women ...

SPOOKY: ... terrible, terrible ...

BIG JOEY: ... in the world ...

ZACHARY: ... that's my wife ...

BIG JOEY: ... the Wasy Wailerettes ... (*clears his throat and tests the microphone by tapping it gently*)

ZACHARY: ... lordy, lordy, lordy ...

CREATURE: Hey, Gazelle Nataways and Hera Keechigeesik are lookin' at each other awful funny. Something bad's gonna happen, I tole you once I tole you twice, something bad's gonna happen ...

SPOOKY: This is a sign from the Lord. This is THE sign ...

BIG JOEY: Number One Gazelle Nataways, Captain of the Wasy Wailerettes, facing off with Number Nine, Flora McDonald, Captain of the Canoe Lake Bravettes. And referee Pierre St. Pierre drops the puck and takes off like a herd of wild turtles ...

SIMON: Aw, Spooky Lacroix, eat my shitty shorts, neee ...

BIG JOEY: Hey, aspin ("there goes") Number Six Dry Lips Manigitogan, right-winger for the Wasy Wailerettes ...

ZACHARY: ... look pretty damn stupid, if you ask me. Fifteen thousand dollars for all that new equipment ...

BIG JOEY: ... eemaskamat ("and steals the puck from") Number Thirteen of the Canoe Lake Bravettes anee-i-puck ...

CREATURE: ... Cancel the game! Cancel the game! Cancel the game!

BIG JOEY: ... igwa aspin sipweesinskwataygew. Hey, k'seegoochin! ("and skates off. Hey, is she ever flying!") (off microphone) Creature Nataways. Shut up. (to the other men) Get that asshole out of here ...

SIMON: Yay, Patsy Pegahmagahbow! Pat-see! Pat-see! Pat-see!

BIG JOEY: (back on microphone) How, Number Six Dry Lips Manigitogan, right-winger for the Wasy Wailerettes, soogi pugamawew igwa anee-i puck igwa aspin centre-line ispathoo ana puck ... ("shoots the puck and the puck goes flying over towards the centre-line ... ")

CREATURE: (to SIMON) Shut up. Don't encourage them ...

BIG JOEY: ... ita ("where") Number Nine Hera Keechigeesik, left-winger for ...

SIMON: (to CREATURE) Aw, lay off! Pat-see! Pat-see! Pat-see!

BIG JOEY: ... the Wasy Wailerettes, kagatchitnat ("catches it"). How, Number Nine Hera Keechigeesik ... (He continues uninterrupted.)

CREATURE: ... Stop the game! Stop the game! Stop the game! ...

ZACHARY: Goodness sakes, there's gonna be a fight out there!

CREATURE continues his "stop the game," ZACHARY repeats "goodness sakes, there's gonna be a fight out there," SIMON'S "Pat-see!" has now built up into a full chant, his foot pounding on the floor so that it sounds like a powwow drum, his dancing bustle held aloft like a shield. SPOOKY finally grabs the crucifix away from DICKIE BIRD, holds it aloft and begins to pray, loudly, as in a ceremony. DICKIE BIRD, caught between SIMON's chanting and SPOOKY's praying, blocks his ears with his hands and looks with growing consternation at "the game." PIERRE blows his whistle and skates around like a puppet gone mad.

SPOOKY: The Lord is my shepherd; I shall not want. He maketh me to lie down in green pastures; he leadeth me beside the still waters. He restoreth my soul; he leadeth me in the paths of righteousness for his name's sake. Yea, though I walk through the valley of the shadow of death, I will fear no evil; for thou art with me. Yea,

though I walk through the valley of the shadow of death, I will fear no evil; for thou art with me ... (He repeats the last phrase over and over again.)

Finally, DICKIE BIRD freaks out, screams and runs down to the "ice" area.

BIG JOEY: (continuing uninterrupted above all the other men's voices) ... igwa ati-ooteetum blue line ita Number One Gazelle Nataways, Captain of the Wasy Wailerettes, kagag-weemaskamat anee-i-puck, ma-a Number Nine Hera Keechigeesik mawch weemeethew anee-i puck. Wha! "Hooking," itwew referee Pierre St. Pierre, Gazelle Nataways isa keehookiwatew her own team-mate Hera Keechigeesikwa, wha! How, Number One Gazelle Nataways, Captain of the Wasy Wailerettes, face-off igwa meena itootum asichi Number Nine Flora McDonald, Captain of the Canoe Lake Bravettes igwa Flora McDonald soogi pugamawew anee-i puck, ma-a (" ... approaching the blue line where Number One Gazelle Nataways, Captain of the Wasy Wailerettes, tries to get the puck off her, but Number Nine Hera Keechigeesik won't give it to her. Wha! "Hooking," says referee Pierre St. Pierre, Gazelle Nataways has apparently hooked her own team-mate Hera Keechigeesik, wha! How, Number One Gazelle Nataways, Captain of the Wasy Wailerettes, facing off once again with Number Nine Flora McDonald, Captain of the Canoe Lake Bravettes and Flora McDonald shoots the puck, but") Number Thirty-seven Big Bum Pegahmagahbow, defence-woman for the Wasy Wailerettes, stops the puck and passes it to Number Eleven Black Lady Halked, also defence-woman for the Wasy Wailerettes, but Gazelle Nataways, Captain of the Wasy Wailerettes, soogi body check meethew ("gives a mean body check to") her own team-mate Black Lady Halked woops! She falls, ladies igwa gentlemen, Black Lady Halked hits the boards and Black Lady Halked is singin' the blues, ladies igwa gentlemen, Black Lady Halked sings the blues. (off microphone, to the other men) What the hell is goin' on down there? Dickie Bird, get off the ice! (back on microphone) Wha! Number Eleven Black Lady Halked is up in a flash igwa seemak n'taymaskamew Gazelle Nataways anee-i puck, holy shit! The ailing but very, very furious Black Lady Halked skates back, turns and takes aim, it's gonna be a slap shot, ladies igwa gentlemen, slap shot keenatch taytootum Black Lady Halked igwa

Black Lady Halked shootiwoo anee-i puck, wha! ("Wha! Number Eleven Black Lady Halked is up in a flash and grabs the puck from Gazelle Nataways, holy shit! The ailing but very, very furious Black Lady Halked skates back, turns and takes aim, it's gonna be a slap shot, ladies and gentlemen, Black Lady Halked is gonna take a slap shot for sure and Black Lady Halked shoots the puck, wha!") She shoots straight at her very own captain, Gazelle Nataways and holy shit, holy shit, holy fuckin' shit!

All hell breaks loose; it is as though some bizarre dream has entered the arena. We hear the sound of women wailing and pucks hitting boards, echoing and echoing as in a vast empty chamber. The men are all screaming at the same time from the "bleachers," recalling Black Lady Halked's legendary fall of seventeen years ago.

BIG JOEY: (*dropping his microphone in horror*) Holy Christ! If there is a devil in this world, then he has just walked into this room. Holy Christ! (*He says this over and over again.*)

ZACHARY: Do something about her, goodness sakes, I told you guys to do something about her seventeen years ago, but you wouldn't do fuck-all. So go out there now and help her … (*repeated*)

CREATURE: Never mind, Chris'sakes, don't bother her. Let me out of here. Chris'sakes, let me out of here! … (*repeated*)

SPOOKY: … Yea, though I walk through the valley of the shadow of death, I fear no evil; for thou art with me … (*repeated*)

SIMON continues chanting and stomping.

PIERRE: (*from the "ice" area*) Never you mind, Zachary Jeremiah, never you mind. She'll be okay. No she won't. Zachary Jeremiah, go out there and help her. No. She'll be okay. No she won't. Yes. No. Yes. No. Help! Where's the puck? Can't do nothin' without the goddamn puck. Where's the puck?! Where's the puck?! Where's the puck?! (*He repeats this last phrase over and over again.*)

Centre and downstage, on the "ice" area, DICKIE BIRD is going into a complete "freak-out," break-ing into a grotesque, fractured version of a Cree chant. Gradually, BIG JOEY, ZACHARY and CREATURE join PIERRE's refrain of "where's the

puck?!" with which they all, including the chanting SIMON and the praying SPOOKY, scatter and come running down to the "ice" area. As they reach the lower level and begin to approach the audience, their movements break down into slow motion, as though they were trying to run through the sticky, gummy substance of some horrible, surrealistic nightmare.

PIERRE/BIG JOEY/ZACHARY/CREATURE: (*slower and slower as on a record that is slowing down gradually to a stop*) Where's the puck?! Where's the puck?! Where's the puck?! …

SIMON continues chanting and stomping. SPOOKY continues intoning the last phrase of his prayer and DICKIE BIRD continues his fractured chant. Out of this fading sound collage emerges the sound of a jukebox playing the introduction to Kitty Wells' "It Wasn't God Who Made Honky Tonk Angels," as though filtered through memory. At this point, on the upper level, a giant luminescent hockey stick comes seemingly out of nowhere and, in very slow motion, shoots a giant luminescent puck. On the puck, looking like a radiant but damaged Madonna-with-Child, sits NANABUSH, as the spirit of BLACK LADY HALKED, naked, nine months pregnant, drunk almost senseless and barely able to hold a bottle of beer up to her mouth. All the men freeze in their standing positions facing the audience, except for DICKIE BIRD who continues his fractured chanting and whimpering, holding his arms up towards NANABUSH/BLACK LADY HALKED. The giant luminescent puck stops at the edge of the upper level. NANABUSH/BLACK LADY HALKED struggles to stand and begins staggering toward her perch. She reaches it and falls with one arm on top of it. The magical, glittering lights flare on and, for the first time, the jukebox is revealed. NANABUSH/BLACK LADY HALKED staggers laboriously up to the top of the jukebox and stands there in profile, one arm lifted to raise her beer as she pours it over her belly. Behind her, the full moon begins to glow, blood red. And from the jukebox, Kitty Wells sings:

As I sit here tonight, the jukebox playing,
That tune about the wild side of life;
As I listen to the words you are saying,
It brings memories when I was a trusting wife.

It wasn't God who made honky tonk angels.
As you said in the words of your song;
Too many times married men think they're still single,
That has caused many a good girl to go wrong.

During the instrumental break of the song, DICKIE BIRD finally explodes and shrieks out towards the vision of NANABUSH/BLACK LADY HALKED.

DICKIE BIRD: Mama! Mama! Katha paksini. Katha paksini. Kanawapata wastew. Kanawapataw wastew. Michimina. Michimina. Katha pagitina. Kaweechee-ik nipapa. Kaweechee-ik nipapa. Nipapa. Papa. Papa. Papa. Papa. Papa. Papa! ("Mommy! Mommy! Don't fall. Don't fall. Look at the light. Look at the light. Hold on to it. Hold on to it. Don't let it go. My daddy will help you. My daddy will help you. My daddy. Daddy. Daddy.") (He crumples to the floor and freezes.)

Kitty Wells sings:

It's a shame that all the blame is on us women,
It's not true that only you men feel the same;
From the start most every heart that's ever broken
Was because there always was a man to blame.

It wasn't God who made honky tonk angels;
As you said in the words of your song;
Too many times married men think they're still single,
That has caused many a good girl to go wrong.

As the song fades, the final tableau has DICKIE BIRD collapsed on the floor between SIMON, who is holding aloft his bustle, and SPOOKY, who is holding aloft his crucifix, directly in front of and at the feet of BIG JOEY and, above BIG JOEY, the pregnant NANABUSH/BLACK LADY HALKED, who is standing on top of the flashing jukebox, in silhouette against the full moon, bottle held up above her mouth. ZACHARY, CREATURE and PIERRE are likewise frozen, standing off to the side of this central grouping.

Slow fade-out.

ACT TWO

When the lights come up, DICKIE BIRD HALKED is standing on a rock in the forest, his clothes and hair all askew. He holds Spooky's crucifix up to the night sky; he is trying, as best he can, to chant after SIMON STARBLANKET's fashion. As he

does, NANABUSH appears in the shadows a distance behind him (as the spirit of GAZELLE NATAWAYS, minus the gigantic breasts, but dressed this time as a stripper). She lingers and watches with interest. Slowly, DICKIE BIRD climbs off the rock and walks offstage, his quavering voice fading into the distance. The full moon glows. Fade-out.

Fade-in on SPOOKY LACROIX's kitchen, where SPOOKY is busy pinning four little pale blue baby booties on the wall where the crucifix used to be, the booties that, in Act One, covered the four extremities of the crucifix. At the table are PIERRE and ZACHARY. PIERRE is stringing pale blue yarn around ZACHARY's raised, parted hands. Then SPOOKY joins them at the table and begins knitting again, this time a baby bonnet, also pale blue. ZACHARY sits removed through most of this scene, preoccupied with the problem of his still missing shorts, his bakery and his wife. The atmosphere is one of fear and foreboding, almost as though the men were constantly resisting the impulse to look over their shoulders. On the upper level, in a soft, dim light, NANABUSH/GAZELLE can be seen sitting up on her perch, waiting impatiently for "the boys" to finish their talk.

PIERRE: (*in a quavering voice*) The Wasy Wailerettes are dead. Gentlemen, my job is disappeared from underneath my feet.

SPOOKY: And we have only the Lord to thank for that.

PIERRE: Gazelle Nataways, she just sashayed herself off that ice, behind swayin' like a walrus pudding. That game, gentlemen, was what I call a real apostrophe ...

ZACHARY: Catastrophe.

PIERRE: That's what I said, dammit ...

SPOOKY: ... tsk ...

PIERRE: ... didn't even get to referee more than ten minutes. But you have to admit, gentlemen, that slap shot ...

SPOOKY: ... that's my sister, Black Lady Halked, that's my sister ...

PIERRE: ... did you see her slap shot? Fantastic! Like a bullet, like a killer shark. Unbelievable!

ZACHARY: (*uncomfortable*) Yeah, right.

PIERRE: When Black Lady Halked hit Gazelle Nataways with that puck. Them Nataways eyes. Big as plates!

SPOOKY: Bigger than a ditch!

PIERRE: Them mascara stretch marks alone was a perfectly frightful thing to behold. Holy shit la marde! But you know, they couldn't find that puck.

SPOOKY: (losing his cool and laughing, falsely and nervously) Did you see it! It fell ... it fell ... that puck went splat on her chest ... and it went ... it went ... plummety plop ...

PIERRE: ... plummety plop to be sure ...

SPOOKY: ... down her ... down her ...

PIERRE: Down the crack. Right down that horrendous, scarifyin' Nataways bosom crack.

The kitchen lights go out momentarily and, to the men, inexplicably. Then they come back on. The men look about them, perplexed.

SPOOKY: Serves ... her ... right for trimming her hockey sweater in the chest area, is what I say.

PIERRE: They say that puck slid somewhere deep, deep into the folds of her fleshy, womanly juices ...

ZACHARY: ... there's a lot of things they're saying about that puck ...

PIERRE: ... and it's lost. Disappeared. Gone. Phhht! Nobody can find that puck.

At this point SPOOKY gets up to check the light switch. The lights go out.

ZACHARY: (in the darkness) Won't let no one come near her, is what they say. Not six inches.

PIERRE: I gotta go look for that puck. (Lights come back on. PIERRE inexplicably appears sitting in another chair.) Gentlemen, I gotta go jiggle that woman.

Lights go out again.

ZACHARY: (from the darkness) What's the matter, Spook!

SPOOKY: (obviously quite worried) Oh, nothing, nothing ... (Lights come back on. PIERRE appears sitting back in his original chair. The men are even more mystified, but try to brighten up anyway.) ... just ... checking the lights ... Queen of

the Indians, that's what she tried to look like, walking off that ice.

PIERRE: Queen of the Indians, to be sure. That's when them women went and put their foot down and made up their mind, on principle, no holds barred ...

A magical flash of lavender light floods the room very briefly, establishing a connection between SPOOKY's kitchen and NANABUSH's perch, where NANABUSH/GAZELLE is still sitting, tapping her fingers impatiently, looking over her shoulder periodically, as if to say: "Come on, boys, get with it." PIERRE's speech momentarily goes into slow motion.

PIERRE: ... no ... way ... they're ... takin' up ... them hockey sticks again until that particular puck is found. "The particular puck," that's what they call it. Gentlemen, the Wasy Wailerettes are dead. My job is disappeared. Gone. Kaput kaput. Phhht!

SPOOKY: Amen.

Pause. Thoughtful silence for a beat or two.

ZACHARY: W-w-w-where's that nephew of yours, Spook?

SPOOKY: Dickie Bird Halked?

PIERRE: My wife, Veronique St. Pierre, she informs me that Dickie Bird Halked, last he was seen, was pacin' the bushes in the general direction of the Pegahmagahbow acreage near Buzwah, lookin' for all the world like he had lost his mind, poor boy.

ZACHARY: Lordy, lordy, lordy, I'm telling you right now, Spooky Lacroix, if you don't do something about that nephew of yours, he's liable to go out there and kill someone next time.

SPOOKY: I'd be out there myself pacing the bushes with him except my wife Lalala's liable to pop any minute now and I gotta be ready to zip her up to Sudbury General.

PIERRE: Bah. Them folks of his, they don't care. If it's not hockey, it's bingo she's out playin' every night of the week, that Black Lady of a mother of his.

ZACHARY: Went and won the jackpot again last night, Black Lady Halked did. All fifty pounds of it ...

PIERRE: Beat Gazelle Nataways by one number!

ZACHARY: ... if it wasn't for her, I'd have mastered that apple pie recipe by now. I was counting on all that lard. Fifty pounds, goodness sakes.

SPOOKY: This little old kitchen? It's yours, Zachary Jeremiah, anytime, anytime. Lalala's got tons of lard.

PIERRE: Ha! She better have. Zachary Jeremiah hasn't dared go nowhere near his own kitchen in almost a week.

ZACHARY: Four nights! It's only Wednesday night, Pierre St. Pierre. Don't go stretching the truth just cuz you were too damn chicken to go get me my shorts.

PIERRE: Bah!

SPOOKY: (to ZACHARY) Your shorts?

ZACHARY: (evading the issue) I just hope that Black Lady Halked's out there looking after her boy cuz if she isn't, we're all in a heap of trouble, I have a funny feeling. (Suddenly, he throws the yarn down and rises.) Achh! I've got to cook! (He goes behind the kitchen counter, puts an apron on and begins the preparations for making pie pastry.)

SPOOKY: (to PIERRE, half-whispering) His shorts?

PIERRE merely shrugs, indicating ZACHARY's pants, which are still held together with a large safety pin. SPOOKY and PIERRE laugh nervously. SPOOKY looks concernedly at the four little booties on the wall where the crucifix used to be. Beat.

Suddenly, PIERRE slaps the table with one hand and leans over to SPOOKY, all set for an argument, an argument they've obviously had many times before. Through all this, ZACHARY is making pie pastry at the counter and SPOOKY continues knitting. The atmosphere of faked jocular camaraderie grows, particularly as the music gets louder later on. NANABUSH/GAZELLE is now getting ready for her strip in earnest, standing on her perch, spraying perfume on, stretching her legs, etc. The little tivoli lights in the jukebox begin to twinkle little by little.

PIERRE: Queen of Hearts.

SPOOKY: Belvedere.

PIERRE: Queen of Hearts.

SPOOKY: The Belvedere.

PIERRE: I told you many times, Spooky Lacroix, it was the Queen of Hearts. I was there. You were there. Zachary Jeremiah, Big Joey, Creature Nataways, we were all there.

From here on, the red/blue/purple glow of the jukebox (i.e, NANABUSH's perch) becomes more and more apparent.

SPOOKY: And I'm telling you it was the Belvedere Hotel, before it was even called the Belvedere Hotel, when it was still called ...

PIERRE: Spooky Lacroix, don't contribute your elder. Big Joey, may he rot in hell, he was the bouncer there that night, he was right there the night it happened.

ZACHARY: Hey, Spook. Where do you keep your rolling pin?

SPOOKY: Use my salami.

PIERRE: (to SPOOKY) He was there.

ZACHARY: Big Joey was never the bouncer, he was the janitor.

SPOOKY: At the Belvedere Hotel.

PIERRE: Never you mind, Spooky Lacroix, never you mind. Black Lady Halked was sittin' there in her corner of the bar for three weeks ...

SPOOKY: Three weeks? It was more like three nights. Aw, you went and mixed up my baby's cap. (getting all tangled up with his knitting)

ZACHARY: Got any cinnamon?

SPOOKY: I got chili powder. Same colour as cinnamon.

Faintly, the strip music from the jukebox begins to play.

PIERRE: ... the place was so jam-packed with people drinkin' beer and singin' and smokin' cigarettes and watchin' the dancin' girl ...

SPOOKY: Gazelle Nataways, she was the dancing girl ...

The music is now on full volume and NANABUSH/GAZELLE's strip is in full swing. She dances on top of the jukebox, which is now a riot of sound and flashing lights. SPOOKY's kitchen is *bathed in a gorgeous lavender light. BIG JOEY and CREATURE NATAWAYS appear at SPOOKY's table, each drinking a bottle of beer. The strip of seventeen years ago is fully re-created, the memory becoming so heated that NANABUSH/GAZELLE magically appears dancing right on top of SPOOKY's kitchen table. The men are going wild, applauding, laughing, drinking, all in slow motion and mime. In the heat of the moment, as NANABUSH/GAZELLE strips down to silk tassels and G-string, they begin tearing their clothes off.*

Suddenly, SIMON STARBLANKET appears at SPOOKY's door. NANABUSH/GAZELLE disappears, as do BIG JOEY and CREATURE. SPOOKY, PIERRE and ZACHARY are caught with their pants down. The jukebox music fades.

SIMON: Spooky Lacroix.

The lavender light snaps off, we are back to "reality" and SPOOKY, PIERRE and ZACHARY stand there, embarrassed. In a panic, they begin putting their clothes back on and reclaim the positions they had before the strip. SPOOKY motions SIMON to take a seat at the table. SIMON does so.

SIMON: Spooky Lacroix. Rosie Kakapetum expresses interest in coming here to birth Lalala's baby when the time comes.

SPOOKY: Rosie Kakapetum? No way some witch is gonna come and put her witchy little fingers on my baby boy.

SIMON: Rosie Kakapetum's no witch, Spooky Lacroix. She's Patsy Pegahmagahbow's step-mother and she's Wasy's only surviving medicine woman and midwife ...

SPOOKY: Hogwash!

PIERRE: Ahem. Rosie Kakapetum says it's a cryin' shame the Wasy Wailerettes is the only team that's not in the Ontario Hockey League.

ZACHARY: Ontario Hockey League?

PIERRE: Absolutely. The OHL. Indian women's OHL. All the Indian women in Ontario's playin' hockey now. It's like a fever out there.

ZACHARY: Shoot. *(referring to his pastry)* I hope this new recipe works for me.

PIERRE: Well, it's not exactly new without the cinnamon.

SPOOKY: *(to SIMON)* My son will be born at Sudbury General Hospital ...

SIMON: You know what they do to them babies in them city hospitals?

SPOOKY: ... Sudbury General, Simon Starblanket, like any good Christian boy ...

PIERRE: *(attempting to defuse the argument)* Ahem. We got to get them Wasy Wailerettes back on that ice again.

SIMON: *(refusing to let go of SPOOKY)* They pull them away right from their own mother's breast the minute they come into this world and they put them behind these glass cages together with another two hundred babies like they were some kind of scientific specimens ...

PIERRE: ... like two hundred of them little monsters ...

ZACHARY: Hamsters!

PIERRE: ... that's what I said dammit ...

SPOOKY: ... tsk ...

PIERRE: ... you can't even tell which hamster belongs to which mother. You take Lalala to Sudbury General, Spooky Lacroix, and your hamster's liable to end up stuck to some French lady's tit.

SIMON: ... and they'll hang Lalala up in metal stirrups and your baby's gonna be born going up instead of dropping down which is the natural way. You were born going up instead of dropping down like you should have ...

PIERRE: Yup. You were born at Sudbury General, Spooky Lacroix, that's why you get weirder and weirder as the days get longer, that's why them white peoples is so weird they were all born going up ...

SIMON: ... instead of dropping down ...

ZACHARY: *(sprinkling flour in SPOOKY's face, with both hands, and laughing)* ... to the earth, Spooky Lacroix, to the earth ...

SPOOKY: Pooh!

PIERRE: ... but we got to find that puck, Simon Starblanket, them Wasy Wailerettes have got to join the OHL ...

SPOOKY: (to SIMON) If Rosie Kakapetum is a medicine woman, Simon Starblanket, then how come she can't drive the madness from my nephew's brain, how come she can't make him talk, huh?

SIMON: Because the medical establishment and the church establishment and people like you, Spooky Lacroix, have effectively put an end to her usefulness and the usefulness of people like her everywhere, that's why Spooky Lacroix.

SPOOKY: Phooey!

SIMON: Do you or your sister even know that your nephew hasn't been home in two days, since that incident at the hockey game, Spooky Lacroix? Do you even care? Why can't you and that thing (pointing at the bible that sits beside SPOOKY) and all it stands for cure your nephew's madness, as you call it, Spooky Lacroix? What has this thing (the bible again) done to cure the madness of this community and communities like it clean across the country, Spooky Lacroix? Why didn't "the Lord," as you call him, come to your sister's rescue at that bar seventeen years ago, huh, Spooky Lacroix? (pause; tense silence) Rosie Kakapetum is gonna be my mother-in-law in two months, Spooky Lacroix, and if Patsy and I are gonna do this thing right, if we're gonna work together to make my best man, Dickie Bird Halked, well again, then Rosie Kakapetum has got to birth that baby. (He begins to exit.)

SPOOKY: (in hard, measured cadence) Rosie Kakapetum works for the devil.

SIMON freezes in his tracks. Silence. Then he turns, grabs a chair violently, bangs it down and sits determinedly.

SIMON: Fine. I'll sit here and I'll wait.

SPOOKY: Fine. You sit there and you wait.

Silence. SIMON sits silent and motionless, his back to the other men.

PIERRE: Ahem. Never mind, Spooky Lacroix, never you mind. Now as I was sayin', Black Lady Halked was nine months pregnant when she was sittin' in that corner of the Queen of Hearts.

SPOOKY: The Belvedere!

PIERRE: Three weeks, Black Lady Halked was sittin' there drinkin' beer. They say she got the money by winnin' the jackpot at the Espanola bingo just three blocks down the street. Three weeks, sure as I'm alive and walkin' these treacherous icy roads, three weeks she sat there in that dark corner by herself. They say the only light you could see her by was the light from the jukebox playin' "Rim of Fire" by Johnny Cash ...

ZACHARY: "Rim of Fire." Yeah, right, Pierre St. Pierre.

SPOOKY: Kitty Wells! Kitty Wells!

The sound of the jukebox playing "It Wasn't God Who Made Honky Tonk Angels" can be heard faintly in the background.

PIERRE: ... the place was so jam-packed with people drinkin' and singin' and smokin' cigarettes and watchin' the dancin' girl ...

SPOOKY: ... Gazelle Nataways, she was the dancing girl, Lord save her soul ...

PIERRE: ... until Black Lady Halked collapsed.

SPOOKY, PIERRE and ZACHARY freeze in their positions, looking in horror at the memory of seventeen years ago.

On the upper level NANABUSH, back in her guise as the spirit of BLACK LADY HALKED, sits on the jukebox, facing the audience, legs out directly in front. Nine months pregnant and naked, she holds a bottle of beer up in the air and is drunk almost senseless. The song "It Wasn't God Who Made Honky Tonk Angels" rises to full volume, the lights from the jukebox flashing riotously. The full moon glows blood red. Immediately below NANABUSH/BLACK LADY HALKED, DICKIE BIRD HALKED appears, kneeling, naked, arms raised toward his mother. NANABUSH/BLACK LADY HALKED begins to writhe and scream, laughing and crying hysterically at the same time and, as she does, her water breaks. DICKIE BIRD, drenched, rises slowly from the floor, arms still raised, and screams.

DICKIE BIRD: Mama! Mama!

From here on, the lights and sound on this scene begin to fade slowly, as the scene on the lower level resumes.

PIERRE: ... she kind of oozed down right then and there, right down to the floor of the Queen of Hearts Tavern. And Big Joey, may he rot in hell, he was the bouncer there that night, when he saw the blood, he ran away and puked over on the other side of the bar, the sight of all that woman's blood just scared the shit right out of him. And that's when Dickie Bird Halked, as we know him, came ragin' out from his mother's womb, Spooky Lacroix, in between beers, right there on the floor, under a table, by the light of the jukebox, on a Saturday night, at the Queen of Hearts ...

SPOOKY: They went and named him after the bar, you crusted old fossil! That bar, which is now called the Belvedere Hotel, used to be called the Dickie Bird Tavern ...

SIMON: (*suddenly jumping out of his chair and practically lunging at SPOOKY*) It doesn't matter what the fuck the name of that fucking bar was! (*The lights and sound on NANABUSH and the jukebox have now faded completely.*) The fact of the matter is, it never should have happened, that kind of thing should never be allowed to happen, not to us Indians, not to anyone living and breathing on the face of God's green earth. (*Pause. Silence. Then dead calm.*) You guys have given up, haven't you? You and your generation. You gave up a long time ago. You'd rather turn your back on the whole thing and pretend to laugh, wouldn't you? (*silence*) Well, not me. Not us. (*silence*) This is not the kind of Earth we want to inherit. (*He begins to leave, but turns once more.*) I'll be back. With Patsy. And Rosie. (*He exits. Another embarrassed silence.*)

SPOOKY: (*Unwilling to face up to the full horror of it, he chooses, instead, to do exactly what SIMON said: turn his back and pretend to laugh.*) That bar, which is now called the Belvedere Hotel, used to be called the Dickie Bird Tavern. That's how Dickie Bird Halked got his name. And that's why he goes haywire every now and again and that's why he doesn't talk. Fetal Alcohol something something, Pierre St. Pierre ...

ZACHARY: (*from behind the counter, where he is still busy making pie crust*) Fetal Alcohol Syndrome.

SPOOKY: ... that's the devil that stole the baby's tongue because Dickie Bird Halked was born drunk and very, very mad. At the Dickie Bird Tavern in downtown Espanola seventeen years ago and that's a fact.

PIERRE: Aw, shit la marde. Fuck you, Spooky Lacroix, I'm gonna go get me my rest. (*Throws the yarn in SPOOKY's face, jumps up and exits.*)

SPOOKY sits there with a pile of yarn stuck to his face, caught on his glasses.

ZACHARY: (*proudly holding up the pie crust in its plate*) It worked!

Blackout.

On the upper level, in a dim light away from her perch, NANABUSH/BLACK LADY HALKED is getting ready to go out for the evening, combing her hair in front of a mirror, putting on her clothes, etc. DICKIE BIRD is with her, naked, getting ready to go to bed. SPOOKY's crucifix sits on a night-table to the side. In DICKIE BIRD's mind, he is at home with his mother.

DICKIE BIRD: Mama. Mama. N'tagoosin. ("I'm sick.")

NANABUSH/BLACK LADY: Say your prayers.

DICKIE BIRD: Achimoostawin nimoosoom. ("Tell me about my grandpa.")

NANABUSH/BLACK LADY: Go to bed. I'm going out soon.

DICKIE BIRD: Mawch. Achimoostawin nimoosoom. ("No. Tell me about my grandpa.")

NANABUSH/BLACK LADY: You shouldn't talk about him.

DICKIE BIRD: Tapweechee eegeemachipoowamit nimoosoom? ("Is it true my grandpa had bad medicine?")

NANABUSH/BLACK LADY: They say he met the devil once. Your grandpa talked to the devil. Don't talk about him.

DICKIE BIRD: Eegeemithoopoowamit nimoosoom, eetweet Simon Starblanket. ("Simon Starblanket says he had good medicine.")

NANABUSH/BLACK LADY: Ashhh! Simon Starblanket.

DICKIE BIRD: Mawch eemithoosit awa aymeewatik keetnanow kichi, eetweet Simon Starblanket. ("Simon Starblanket says that this cross is not right for us.") (*He grabs the crucifix from the night-table and spits on it.*)

NANABUSH/BLACK LADY: (*Grabbing the crucifix from DICKIE BIRD, she attempts to spank him but DICKIE BIRD evades her.*) Dickie Bird! Kipasta-ood! ("You're committing a mortal sin!") Say ten Hail Marys and two Our Fathers.

DICKIE BIRD: Mootha apoochiga taskootch nimama keetha. Mootha apoochiga m'tanaw-gatch kisagee-in. ("You're not even like my mother. You don't even love me at all.")

NANABUSH/BLACK LADY: Dickie Bird. Shut up. I'll say them with you. "Hail Mary, full of grace, the Lord is with thee … " Hurry up. I have to go out. (*She prepares to leave.*) "Hail Mary, full of grace, the Lord is with thee … " (*She gives up.*) Ashhh! Your father should be home soon. (*exits*)

DICKIE BIRD: (*speaking to the now absent NANABUSH/BLACK LADY*) Mootha nipapa ana. ("He's not my father.") (*He grabs his clothes and the crucifix and runs out, down to the lower level and into the forest made of light and shadows.*) Tapwee anima ka-itweechik, chee-i? Neetha ooma kimineechagan, chee-i? ("It's true what they say, isn't it? I'm a bastard, aren't I?") (*He is now sitting on the rock where SIMON and ZACHARY first met in Act One.*) Nipapa ana … Big Joey … (*to himself, quietly*) … nipapa ana … Big Joey … ("My father is … Big Joey.") (*silence*)

A few moments later, NANABUSH comes bouncing into the forest, as the spirit of the vivacious young PATSY PEGAHMAGAHBOW, complete with very large, oversized bum. The full moon glows.

NANABUSH/PATSY: (*to herself, as she peers into the shadows*) Oooh, my poor bum. I fell on the ice four days ago, eh! And it still hurts, oooh. (*She finally sees DICKIE BIRD huddling on the rock, barely dressed.*) There you are. I came out to look for you. What happened to your clothes? It's freezing out here. Put them on. Here. (*She starts to help dress him.*) What happened at the arena? You were on the ice, eh! You feel like talking? In Indian? How, weetamawin. ("Come on, tell me.")

BIG JOEY and CREATURE NATAWAYS enter a distance away. They are smoking a joint and BIG JOEY carries a gun. They stop and watch from the shadows.

CREATURE: Check her out.

NANABUSH/PATSY: Why do you always carry that crucifix? I don't believe that stuff. I traded mine in for sweetgrass. Hey. You wanna come to Rosie's and eat fry bread with me? Simon will be there, too. Simon and me, we're getting married, eh? We're gonna have a baby …

CREATURE: What's she trying to do?

NANABUSH/PATSY: … Rosie's got deer meat, too, come on, you like my Mom's cooking, eh? (*She attempts to take the crucifix away from DICKIE BIRD.*) But you'll have to leave that here because Rosie can't stand the Pope …

DICKIE BIRD grabs the crucifix back.

CREATURE: What's he trying to do?

NANABUSH/PATSY: … give it to me … Dickie … come on …

CREATURE: He's weird, Big Joey, he's weird.

NANABUSH/PATSY: … leave it here … it will be safe here … we'll bury it in the snow … (*Playfully, she tries to get the crucifix away from DICKIE BIRD.*)

CREATURE: Hey, don't do that, don't do that, man, he's ticklish.

NANABUSH/PATSY: (*As DICKIE BIRD begins poking her playfully with the crucifix and laughing, NANABUSH/PATSY gradually starts to get frightened.*) … don't look at me that way … Dickie Bird, what's wrong? … ya, Dickie Bird, awus …

DICKIE BIRD starts to grab at NANABUSH/PATSY.

CREATURE: Hey, don't you think, don't you think … he's getting kind of carried away?

NANABUSH/PATSY: … awus …

CREATURE: We gotta do something, Big Joey, we gotta do something. (*BIG JOEY stops CREATURE.*) Let go! Let go!

NANABUSH/PATSY: (*now in a panic*) Awus! Awus! Awus! …

DICKIE BIRD grabs NANABUSH/PATSY and throws her violently to the ground. He lifts her skirt and shoves the crucifix up against her.

BIG JOEY: (*to CREATURE*) Shut up.

NANABUSH/PATSY: (*screams and goes into hysteria*) ... Simon! ...

DICKIE BIRD raped NANABUSH/PATSY with the crucifix. A heart-breaking, very slow, sensuous tango breaks out on off-stage harmonica.

CREATURE: (*to BIG JOEY*) No! Let me go. Big Joey, let me go, please!

BIG JOEY: (*suddenly grabs CREATURE violently by the collar*) Get out. Get the fuck out of here. You're nothin' but a fuckin' fruit. Fuck off. (*CREATURE collapses.*) I said fuck off.

CREATURE flees. BIG JOEY just stands there, paralyzed, and watches.

NANABUSH/PATSY, who has gradually been moving back and back, is now standing up on her perch again (i.e., the "mound"/jukebox which no longer looks like a jukebox). She stands there, facing the audience, and slowly gathers her skirt, in agony, until she is holding it up above her waist. A blood stain slowly spreads across her panties and flows down her leg. At the same time, DICKIE BIRD stands downstage beside the rock, holding the crucifix and making violent jabbing motions with it, downward. All this happens in slow motion. The crucifix starts to bleed. When DICKIE BIRD lifts the crucifix up, his arms and chest are covered with blood. Finally, NANABUSH/PATSY collapses to the floor of her platform and slowly crawls away. Lights fade on her. On the lower level, BIG JOEY, in a state of shock, staggers, almost faints, and vomits violently. Then he reels over to DICKIE BIRD and, not knowing what else to do, begins collecting his clothes and calming him down.

BIG JOEY: How, Dickie Bird. How, astum. Igwa. Mootha nantow. Mootha nantow. Shhh. Shhh. ("Come on, Dickie Bird. Come. Let's go. It's okay. It's okay. Shhh. Shhh ... ") (*Barely able to bring himself to touch it, he takes the crucifix from DICKIE BIRD and drops it quickly on the rock. Then he begins wiping the blood off DICKIE BIRD.*) How, mootha nantow. Mootha nantow. How, astum, keeyapitch uplsees ootee. Igwani. Igwani. Poonimatoo. Mootha nantow. Mootha nantow. ("Come on, it's okay. It's okay. Come on, a little more over here. That's all. That's all. Stop crying. It's okay. It's okay ... ") (*DICKIE BIRD, shaking with emotion, looks questioningly into BIG JOEY's face.*) Eehee. Nigoosis keetha.

Mootha Wellington Halked kipapa. Neetha ... kipapa. ("Yes. You are my son. Wellington Halked is not your father. I'm ... your father.")

Silence. They look at each other. DICKIE BIRD grabs BIG JOEY and clings to him, BIG JOEY reacting tentatively at first, and then passionately, with DICKIE BIRD finally bursting out into uncontrollable sobs. Fade-out.

Out of this darkness gunshots explode. And we hear a man's voice wailing, in complete and utter agony. Then comes violent pounding at a door. Finally, still in the darkness, we hear SIMON STARBLANKET's speaking voice.

SIMON: Open up! Pierre St. Pierre, open up! I know you're in there!

PIERRE: (*still in the darkness*) Whoa! Easy now. Easy on that goddamn door. Must you create such a carpostrophe smack dab in the middle of my rest period?

When the lights come up, we are outside the "window" to PIERRE ST. PIERRE's little bootleg joint. PIERRE pokes his head out, wearing his night clothes, complete with pointy cap.

PIERRE: Go home. Go to bed. Don't be disturbin' my rest period. My wife, Veronique St. Pierre, she tells me there's now not only a OHL but a NHL, too. Indian women's National Hockey League. All the Indian women on every reserve in Canada, all the Indian women in Canada is playin' hockey now. It's like a fever out there. That's why I gotta get my rest. First thing tomorrow mornin', I go jiggle that puck out of Gazelle Nataways. Listen to me. I'm your elder.

SIMON shoots the gun into the house, just missing PIERRE's head.

SIMON: (*dead calm*) One, you give me a bottle. Two, I report your joint to the Manitowaning police. Three, I shoot your fucking head off.

PIERRE: Alright. Alright. (*He pops in for a bottle of whisky and hands it out to SIMON.*) Now you go on home with this. Go have yourself a nice quiet drink. (*SIMON begins to exit. PIERRE calls out.*) What the hell are you gonna do with that gun?

SIMON: (*calling back*) I'm gonna go get that mute. Little bastard raped Patsy Pegahmagahbow. (*exits*)

Pause.

PIERRE: Holy shit la marde! (*pause*) I gotta warn him. No. I need my rest. No. I gotta warn that boy. No. I gotta find that puck. No. Dickie Bird's life. No. The puck. No. Dickie Bird. No. Hockey. No. His life. No. Hockey. No. Life. Hockey. Life. Hockey. Life. Hockey. Life. Hockey. Life. Hockey. Life …

Fade-out.

Lights up on SPOOKY LACROIX's kitchen. CREATURE NATAWAYS is sitting at the table, silent, head propped up in his hands. SPOOKY is knitting, with obvious haste, a white christening gown, of which a large crucifix is the centre-piece. SPOOKY's bible still sits on the table beside him.

SPOOKY: Why didn't you do something? (*silence*) Creature. (*Silence. SPOOKY stops knitting and looks up.*) Alphonse Nataways, why didn't you stop him? (*silence*) You're scared of him, aren't you? You're scared to death of Big Joey. Admit it. (*silence*)

CREATURE: (*quietly and calmly*) I love him, Spooky.

SPOOKY: Say wha?!

CREATURE: I love him.

SPOOKY: You love him? What do you mean? How? How do you love him?

CREATURE: I love him.

SPOOKY: Lord have mercy on Wasaychigan Hill!

CREATURE: (*rising suddenly*) I love the way he stands. I love the way he walks. The way he laughs. The way he wears his cowboy boots …

SPOOKY: You're kidding me.

CREATURE: … the way his tight blue jeans fall over his ass. The way he talks so smart and tough. The way women fall at his feet. I wanna be like him. I always wanted to be like him, William. I always wanted to have a dick as big as his.

SPOOKY: Creature Alphonse Nataways! You know not what you say.

CREATURE: I don't care.

SPOOKY: I care.

CREATURE: I don't care. I can't stand it anymore.

SPOOKY: Shut up. You're making me nervous. Real nervous.

CREATURE: Come with me.

SPOOKY: Come with you where?

CREATURE: To his house.

SPOOKY: Whose house?

CREATURE: Big Joey.

SPOOKY: Are you crazy?

CREATURE: Come with me.

SPOOKY: No.

CREATURE: Yes.

SPOOKY: No.

CREATURE: (*suddenly and viciously grabbing SPOOKY by the throat*) Cut the goddamn bull crap, Spooky Lacroix! (*SPOOKY tries desperately to save the christening gown.*) I seen you crawl in the mud and shit so drunk you were snortin' like a pig.

SPOOKY: I changed my ways, thank you.

CREATURE: Twenty-one years. Twenty-one years ago. You, me, Big Joey, Eugene Starblanket, that goddamn Zachary Jeremiah Keechigeesik. We were eighteen. We cut our wrists. Your own father's huntin' knife. We mixed blood. Swore we'd be friends for life. Frontenac Hotel. Twenty-one years ago. You got jumped by seven white guys. Broken beer bottle come straight at your face. If it wasn't for me, you wouldn't be here today, wavin' that stinkin' bible in my face like it was a slab of meat. I'm not a dog. I'm your buddy. Your friend.

SPOOKY: I know that.

CREATURE tightens his hold on SPOOKY's throat. The two men are staring straight into each other's eyes, inches apart. Silence.

CREATURE: William. Think of your father. Remember the words of Nicotine Lacroix.

Finally SPOOKY screams, throwing the christening gown, knitting needles and all, over the bible on the table.

SPOOKY: You goddamn fucking son-of-a-bitch!

Blackout. Gunshots in the distance.

Lights up on BIG JOEY's living room/kitchen. BIG JOEY is sitting, silent and motionless, on the couch, staring straight ahead, as though he were in a trance. His hunting rifle rests on his lap. DICKIE BIRD HALKED stands directly facing the life-size pin-up poster of Marilyn Monroe, also as though he were in a trance. Then his head drops down in remorse. BIG JOEY lifts the gun, loads it and aims it out directly in front. When DICKIE BIRD hears the snap of the gun being loaded, he turns to look. Then he slowly walks over to BIG JOEY, kneels down directly in front of the barrel of the gun, puts it in his mouth and then slowly reaches over and gently, almost lovingly, moves BIG JOEY's hand away from the trigger, caressing the older man's hand as he does. BIG JOEY slowly looks up at DICKIE BIRD's face, stunned. DICKIE BIRD puts his own thumb on the trigger and pulls. Click. Nothing. In the complete silence, the two men are looking directly into each other's eyes. Complete stillness. Fade-out. Split seconds before complete blackout, Marilyn Monroe farts, courtesy of Ms. NANABUSH: a little flag reading "poot" pops up out of Ms. Monroe's derriere, as on a play gun. We hear a cute little "poot" sound.

Out of this blackout emerges the sound of a harmonica; it is ZACHARY JEREMIAH KEECHIGEESIK playing his heart out. Fade-in on PIERRE ST. PIERRE, still in his night-clothes but also wearing his winter coat and hat over them, rushing all over the "forest," ostensibly rushing to BIG JOEY's house to warn DICKIE BIRD HALKED about the gun-toting SIMON STARBLANKET. He mutters to himself as he goes.

PIERRE: … Hockey. Life. Hockey. Life. Hockey.

ZACHARY appears in the shadows and sees PIERRE.

ZACHARY: Hey!

PIERRE: (*not hearing ZACHARY*) … Hockey. Life. Hockey. Life …

ZACHARY: Pssst!

PIERRE: (*still not hearing ZACHARY*) Hockey. Life. Hockey. Life. (*pause*) Hockey life!

ZACHARY: (*finally yelling*) Pierre St. Pierre!

PIERRE: (*jumps*) Hallelujah! Have you heard the news?

ZACHARY: The Band Council went and okayed Big Joey's radio station.

PIERRE: All the Indian women in the world is playin' hockey now! World Hockey League, they call themselves. Aboriginal Women's WHL. My wife, Veronique St. Pierre, she just got the news. Eegeeweetamagoot fax machine. ("Fax machine told her.") It's like a burnin', ragin', blindin' fever out there. Them Cree women in Saskatchewan, them Blood women in Alberta, them Yakima, them Heidis out in the middle of your Specific Ocean, them Kickapoo, Chickasaw, Cherokee, Chepewyan, Choctaw, Chippewa, Wichita, Kiowa down in Oklahoma, them Seminole, Navajo, Onondaga, Tuscarora, Winnebago, Micmac-paddy-wack-why-it's-enough-to-give-your-dog-a-bone! … (*Getting completely carried away, he grabs his crotch.*)

ZACHARY: Pierre. Pierre.

PIERRE: … they're turnin' the whole world topsy-turkey right before our very eyes and the Prime Minister's a-shittin' grape juice … (*A gunshot explodes in the near distance. PIERRE suddenly lays low and changes tone completely.*) Holy shit la marde! He's after Dickie Bird. There's a red-eyed, crazed devil out there and he's after Dickie Bird Halked and he's gonna kill us all if we don't stop him right this minute.

ZACHARY: Who? Who's gonna kill us?

PIERRE: Simon Starblanket. Drunk. Power mad. Half-crazed on whisky and he's got a gun.

ZACHARY: Simon!

PIERRE: He's drunk and he's mean and he's out to kill. (*another gunshot*) Hear that!

ZACHARY: (*to himself*) That's Simon? I thought …

PIERRE: When he heard about the Pegahmagahbow rape …

ZACHARY: Pegahmagahbow what?

PIERRE: Why, haven't you heard? Dickie Bird Halked raped Patsy Pegahmagahbow in most brutal fashion and Simon Starblanket is out to kill Dickie Bird Halked so I'm on my way to Big Joey's right this minute and I'm takin' that huntin' rifle of his and I'm sittin' next to that Halked boy right up until the cows come home. (*exits*)

ZACHARY: (*to himself*) Simon Starblanket. Patsy …

Blackout.

Out of this blackout come the gunshots, much louder this time, and SIMON's wailing voice.

SIMON: Aieeeeee-yip-yip! Nanabush! …

Fade-in on SIMON, in the forest close by the large rock, still carrying his hunting rifle. SIMON is half-crazed by this time, drunk out of his skull. The full moon glows.

SIMON: … Weesageechak! Come back! Rosie! Rosie Kakapetum, tell him to come back, not to run away, cuz we need him …

NANABUSH/PATSY PEGAHMAGAHBOW's voice comes filtering out of the darkness on the upper level. It is as though SIMON were hearing a voice from inside his head.

NANABUSH/PATSY: … her …

SIMON: … him …

NANABUSH/PATSY: … her …

Slow fade-in on NANABUSH/PATSY, standing on the upper level, looking down at SIMON. She still wears her very large bum.

SIMON: … weetha ("him/her"—i.e., no gender) … Christ! What is it? Him? Her? Stupid fucking language, fuck you, da Englesa. Me no speakum no more da goodie Englesa, in Cree we say "weetha," not "him" or "her," Nanabush, come back! (*Speaks directly to NANABUSH, as though he/she were there, directly in front of him; he doesn't see NANABUSH/PATSY standing on the upper level.*) Aw, boozhoo how are ya! Me good. Me berry, berry good. I seen you! just seen you jumping jack-ass thisa away …

NANABUSH/PATSY: (*as though she/he were playing games behind SIMON's back*) … and thataway …

SIMON: … and thisaway and …

NANABUSH/PATSY: … thataway …

SIMON: … and thisaway and …

NANABUSH/PATSY: … thataway …

SIMON: … and thisaway and …

NANABUSH/PATSY: … thataway …

SIMON: … etcetra, etcetra, etcetra …

NANABUSH/PATSY: etcetERA. (*pause*) She's here! She's here!

SIMON: … Nanabush! Weesageechak! (*NANABUSH/PATSY peals out with a silvery, magical laugh that echoes and echoes.*) Dey shove dis … whach-you-ma-call-it … da crucifix up your holy cunt ouch, eh? Ouch, eh? (*SIMON sees the bloody crucifix sitting on the rock and slowly approaches it. He kneels directly before it.*) Nah … (*laughs a long mad, hysterical laugh that ends with hysterical weeping*) … yesssss … noooo … oh, noooo! Crucifix! (*spits violently on the crucifix*) Fucking goddamn crucifix, yesssss … God! You're a man. You're a woman. You're a man? You're a woman? You see, nineethoowan poogoo neetha ("I speak only Cree") …

NANABUSH/PATSY: … ohhh …

SIMON: … keetha ma-a? ("How about you?") Nah. Da Englesa him …

NANABUSH/PATSY: … her …

SIMON: … him …

NANABUSH/PATSY: … her …

SIMON: … him! …

NANABUSH/PATSY: … her! …

SIMON: … all da time …

NANABUSH/PATSY: … all da time …

SIMON: … tsk, tsk, tsk …

NANABUSH/PATSY: … tsk, tsk, tsk.

SIMON: If, God, you are a woman/man in Cree but only a man in da Englesa, then how come you still got a cun …

NANABUSH/PATSY: … a womb.

With this, SIMON finally sees NANABUSH/PATSY. He calls out to her.

SIMON: Patsy! Big Bum Pegahmagahbow, you flying across da ice on world's biggest puck. Patsy, look what dey done to your puss … (*NANABUSH/PATSY lifts her skirt and displays the blood stain on her panties. She then finally takes off the prosthetic that is her huge bum and* holds it in one arm.) Hey! (*NANABUSH/PATSY holds an eagle feather up in the air, ready to dance. SIMON stomps on the ground, rhythmically, and sings.*) " … and me I don't wanna go to the moon, I'm gonna leave that moon alone. I just wanna dance with the Rosebud Sioux this summer, yeah, yeah, yeah … " (*SIMON chants and he and NANABUSH/PATSY dance, he on the lower level with his hunting rifle in the air, she on the upper level with her eagle feather.*) How, astum, Patsy, kiam. N'tayneemeetootan. ("Come on, Patsy, never mind. Let's go dance.")

We hear ZACHARY JEREMIAH KEECHIGEESIK's voice calling from the darkness a distance away.

ZACHARY: Hey!

But SIMON and NANABUSH/PATSY pay no heed.

NANABUSH/PATSY: … n'tayneemeetootan South Dakota? …

SIMON: … how, astum, Patsy. N'tayneemeetootan South Dakota. Hey, Patsy Pegahmagahbow … (*He finally approaches her and holds his hand out.*)

NANABUSH/PATSY: (*holds her hand out toward his*) … Simon Starblanket …

SIMON/NANABUSH/PATSY: … eenpaysageeitan ("I love you to death") …

ZACHARY finally emerges tentatively from the shadows. He is holding a beautiful, fresh pie. NANABUSH/PATSY disappears.

ZACHARY: (*calling out over the distance*) Hey! You want some pie?

SIMON: (*silence; calling back*) What?! (*Not seeing ZACHARY, he looks around cautiously.*)

ZACHARY: I said. You want some pie?

SIMON: (*calling back, after some confused thought*) What?

ZACHARY: (*approaches SIMON slowly*) Do you want some pie?

SIMON: (*Silence. Finally, he sees ZACHARY and points the gun at him.*) What kind?

ZACHARY: Apple. I just made some. It's still hot.

SIMON: (*long pause*) Okay.

Slowly, NANABUSH/PATSY enters the scene and comes up behind SIMON, holding SIMON's dancing bustle in front of her, as in a ceremony.

ZACHARY: Okay. But you gotta give me the gun first. (*The gun goes off accidentally, just missing ZACHARY's head.*) I said, you gotta give me the gun first.

Gradually, the dancing bustle begins to shimmer and dance in NANABUSH/PATSY's hands.

SIMON: Patsy. I gotta go see Patsy.

ZACHARY: You and me and Patsy and Hera. We're gonna go have some pie. Fresh, hot apple pie. Then, we go to Sudbury and have a look at that Mobart, what do you say?

The shimmering movements of the bustle balloon out into magical, dance-like arches, as NANABUSH/PATSY manoeuvres it directly in front of SIMON, hiding him momentarily. Behind this, SIMON drops the base of the rifle to the ground, causing it to go off accidentally. The bullet hits SIMON in the stomach. He falls to the ground. ZACHARY lets go of his pie and runs over to him. The shimmering of the bustle dies off into the darkness of the forest and disappears, NANABUSH/PATSY manoeuvring it.

ZACHARY: Simon! Simon! Oh, lordy, lordy, lordy … Are you alright? Are you okay? Simon. Simon. Talk to me. Goodness sakes, talk to me Simon. Ayumi-in! ("Talk to me!")

SIMON: (*barely able to speak, as he sinks slowly to the ground beside the large rock*) Kamoowanow … apple … pie … patima … neetha … igwa Patsy … n'gapeetootanan … patima … apple … pie … neee. ("We'll eat … apple … pie … later … me … and Patsy … we'll come over … later … apple … pie … neee.") (*He dies.*)

ZACHARY: (*kneels over SIMON's body, the full moon glowing even redder*) Oh, lordy, lordy … Holy shit! Holy shit! What's happening? What's become of this place? What's happening to this place? What's happening to these people? My people. He didn't have to die. He didn't have to die. That's the goddamn most stupid … no reason … this kind of living has got to stop. It's got to stop! (*talking and then just shrieking at the sky*) Aieeeeeee-Lord! God! God of the Indian! God of the Whiteman! God-Al-fucking-mighty!

Whatever the fuck your name is. Why are you doing this to us? Why are you doing this to us? Are you up there at all? Or are you some stupid, drunken shit, out-of-your-mind-passed-out under some great beer table up there in your stupid fucking clouds? Come down! Astum oota! ("Come down here!") Why don't you come down? I dare you to come down from your high-falutin' fuckin' shit-throne up there, come down and show us you got the guts to stop this stupid, stupid, stupid way of living. It's got to stop. It's got to stop. It's got to stop. It's got to stop. It's got to stop …

He collapses over SIMON's body and weeps. Fade-out.

Towards the end of this speech a light comes up on NANABUSH. Her perch (i.e., the jukebox) has swivelled around and she is sitting on a toilet having a good shit. He/she is dressed in an old man's white beard and wig, but also wearing sexy, elegant women's high-heeled pumps. Surrounded by white, puffy clouds, she/he sits with her legs crossed, nonchalantly filing his/her fingernails. Fade-out.

Fade-in on BIG JOEY's living room/kitchen. BIG JOEY, DICKIE BIRD HALKED, CREATURE NATAWAYS, SPOOKY LACROIX and PIERRE ST. PIERRE are sitting and standing in various positions, in complete silence. A hush pervades the room for about twenty beats. DICKIE BIRD is holding BIG JOEY's hunting rifle. Suddenly, ZACHARY JEREMIAH KEECHIGEESIK enters, in a semi-crazed state. DICKIE BIRD starts and points the rifle straight at ZACHARY's head.

CREATURE: Zachary Jeremiah! What are you doing here?

BIG JOEY: Lookin' for your shorts, Zach?

From his position on the couch, he motions DICKIE BIRD to put the gun down. DICKIE BIRD does so.

ZACHARY: (*to BIG JOEY*) You're unbelievable. You're fucking unbelievable. You let this young man, you let your own son get away with this inconceivable act …

CREATURE: Don't say that to him, Zachary Jeremiah, don't say that …

ZACHARY: (*ignoring CREATURE*) You know he did it and you're hiding him what in God's name is wrong with you?

SPOOKY: Zachary Jeremiah, you're not yourself …

PIERRE: Nope. Not himself. Talkin' wild. (*Sensing potential violence, he sneaks out the door.*)

BIG JOEY: (*to ZACHARY*) He don't even know he done anything.

ZACHARY: Bullshit! They're not even sure the air ambulance will get Patsy Pegahmagahbow to Sudbury in time. Simon Starblanket just shot himself and this boy is responsible …

SIMON rises slowly from the ground and "sleep walks" right through this scene and up to the upper level, towards the full moon. The men are only vaguely aware of his passing.

BIG JOEY: He ain't responsible for nothin'.

ZACHARY: Simon Starblanket was on his way to South Dakota where he could have learned a few things and made something of himself, same place you went and made a total asshole of yourself seventeen years ago …

CREATURE: Shush, Zachary Jeremiah, that's the past …

SPOOKY: … the past …

CREATURE: … Chris'sakes …

ZACHARY: What happened to all those dreams you were so full of for your people, the same dreams this young man just died for?

SPOOKY: (*to BIG JOEY, though not looking at him*) And my sister, Black Lady Halked, seventeen years ago at that bar, Big Joey, you could have stopped her drinking, you could have sent her home and this thing never would have happened. That was your son inside her belly.

CREATURE: He didn't do nothing. He wouldn't let me do nothing. He just stood there and watched the whole thing …

SPOOKY: Creature Nataways!

CREATURE: I don't care. I'm gonna tell. He watched this little bastard do that to Patsy Pegahmagahbow …

BIG JOEY: (*suddenly turning on CREATURE*) You little cocksucker!

DICKIE BIRD hits CREATURE on the back with the butt of the rifle, knocking him unconscious.

SPOOKY: Why, Big Joey, why did you do that?

Silence.

ZACHARY: Yes, Joe. Why?

Long silence. All the men look at BIG JOEY.

BIG JOEY: (*raising his arms, as for a battle cry*) "This is the end of the suffering of a great nation!" That was me. Wounded Knee, South Dakota, Spring of '73. The FBI. They beat us to the ground. Again and again and again. Ever since that spring, I've had these dreams where blood is spillin' out from my groin, nothin' there but blood and emptiness. It's like … I lost myself. So when I saw this baby comin' out of Caroline, Black Lady … Gazelle dancin' … all this blood … and I knew it was gonna come … I … I tried to stop it … I freaked out. I don't know what I did … and I knew it was mine …

ZACHARY: Why? Why did you let him do it? Why? Why did you let him do it? Why? Why did you let him do it? Why? Why did you let him do it? (*finally grabbing BIG JOEY by the collar*) Why?! Why did you let him do it?!

BIG JOEY: (*breaking free from ZACHARY's hold*) Because I hate them! I hate them fuckin' bitches. Because they—our own women—took the fuckin' power away from us faster than the FBI ever did.

SPOOKY: (*softly, in the background*) They always had it.

Silence.

BIG JOEY: There. I said it. I'm tired. Tired. (*He slumps down on the couch and cries.*)

ZACHARY: (*softly*) Joe. Joe.

Fade-out.

Out of this darkness emerges the sound of SIMON STARBLANKET's chanting voice. Away up over NANABUSH's perch, the moon begins to glow, fully and magnificently. Against it, in silhouette, we see SIMON, wearing his powwow bustle. SIMON STARBLANKET is dancing in the moon. Fade-out.

Fade-in on the "ice" at the hockey arena, where PIERRE ST. PIERRE, in full referee regalia, is gossiping with CREATURE NATAWAYS and SPOOKY LACROIX. CREATURE is knitting, with great difficulty, pink baby booties. SPOOKY is holding his new baby, wrapped in a pale blue knit blanket. We hear the sound of a hockey arena just before a big game.

PIERRE: … she says to me: "Did you know, Pierre St. Pierre, that Gazelle Nataways found Zachary Jeremiah Keechigeesik's undershorts under her chesterfield and washed them and put them in a box real nice, all folded up, and even sprinkled her perfume all over them and sashayed herself over to Hera Keechigeesik's house and handed the box over to her? I just about had a heart attack," she says to me. "And what's more," she says to me, "when Hera Keechigeesik opened that box, there was a picture sittin' on top of them shorts, a colour picture of none other than our very own Zachary Jeremiah Keechigeesik … (*Unseen by PIERRE, ZACHARY approaches the group, wearing a baker's hat and carrying a rolling pin.*) … wearin' nothin' but the suit God gave him. That's when Hera Keechigeesik went wild, like a banshee tigger, and she tore the hair out of Gazelle Nataways which, as it turns out, was a wig … " Imagine. After all these years. " … and she beat Gazelle Nataways to a cinder, right there into the treacherous icy door-step. And that's when 'the particular puck' finally came squishin' out of them considerable Nataways bosoms." And gentlemen? The Wasy Wailerettes are on again!

CREATURE: Ho-leee!

SPOOKY: Holy fuck!

PIERRE: And I say shit la ma … (*finally seeing ZACHARY, who is standing there listening to all this*) … oh my … (*turns quickly to SPOOKY's baby*) … hello there, koochie-koochie-koo, welcome to the world!

SPOOKY: It's not koochie-koochie-koo, Pierre St. Pierre. Her name's "Kichigeechacha." Rhymes with Lalala. Ain't she purdy!

Up in the "bleachers," BIG JOEY enters and prepares his microphone stand. DICKIE BIRD enters with a big sign saying "WASY-FM" and hangs it proudly up above the microphone stand.

PIERRE: Aw, she'll be readin' that ole holy bible before you can go: "Phhht! Phhht!"

PIERRE accidentally spits in the baby's face. SPOOKY shoos him away.

SPOOKY: "Phhht! Phhht!" to you too, Pierre St. Pierre.

CREATURE: Spooky Lacroix. Lalala. They never made it to Sudbury General.

SPOOKY: I was busy helping Eugene Starblanket out with Simon …

SPOOKY/PIERRE: … may he rest in peace …

ZACHARY: Good old Rosie Kakapetum. "Stand and deliver," they said to her. And stand and deliver she did. How's the knitting going there, Creature Nataways?

CREATURE: Kichigeechacha, my god-daughter, she's wearin' all the wrong colours. I gotta work like a dog.

PIERRE: (*calling up to DICKIE BIRD HALKED*) Don't you worry a wart about that court appearance, Dickie Bird Halked. I'll be right there beside you tellin' that ole judge a thing or two about that goddamn jukebox.

SPOOKY: (*to CREATURE*) Come on. Let's go watch Lalala play her first game.

He and CREATURE go up to the "bleachers" on the upper level, directly in front of NANABUSH's perch, to watch the big game.

PIERRE: (*reading from his clipboard and checking off the list*) Now then, Dominique Ladouche, Black Lady Halked, Annie Cook, June Bug McLeod … (*He stops abruptly for BIG JOEY's announcement, as do the other men.*)

BIG JOEY: (*on the microphone*) Patsy Pegahmagahbow, who is recuperating at Sudbury General Hospital, sends her love and requests that the first goal scored by the Wasy Wailerettes be dedicated to the memory of Simon Starblanket …

CREATURE and SPOOKY, with knitting and baby, respectively, are now up in the "bleachers" with DICKIE BIRD and BIG JOEY, who are standing beside each other at the microphone stand. PIERRE ST. PIERRE is again skating around on the "ice" in his own inimitable fashion, warming up. ZACHARY, meanwhile, now has his apple pie as

well as his rolling pin in hand, still wearing his baker's hat. At this point the hockey arena sounds shift abruptly to the sound of women wailing and pucks hitting boards, echoing and echoing as in a vast empty chamber. As this hockey game sequence progresses, the spectacle of the men watching, cheering, etc., becomes more and more dreamlike, all the men's movements imperceptibly breaking down into slow motion until they fade, later, into the darkness. ZACHARY "sleepwalks" through the whole lower level of the set, almost as though he were re-tracing his steps back through the whole play. Slowly, he takes off his clothes item by item until, by the end, he is back lying naked on the couch where he began the play, except that this time it will be his own couch he is lying on.

BIG JOEY: … And there they are, ladies igwa gentlemen, there they are, the most beautiful, daring, death-defying Indian women in the world, the Wasy Wailerettes! How, Number Nine Hera Keechigeesik, CAPTAIN of the Wasy Wailerettes, face-off igwa itootum asichi Number Nine Flora McDonald, Captain of the Canoe Lake Bravettes. Hey, soogi pagicheeipinew "particular puck" referee Pierre St. Pierre … ("and referee Pierre St. Pierre drops the 'particular puck' … ")

CREATURE: Go Hera go! Go Hera go! Go Hera go! … (*repeated all the way through—and under—BIG JOEY's commentary*)

BIG JOEY: … igwa seemakwathay g'waskootoo ("and takes off") like a herd of wild turtles …

SPOOKY: Wasy once. Wasy twice. Holy jumpin' Christ! Rim ram. God damn. Fuck, son-of-a-bitch, shit! (*repeated in time to CREATURE's cheer, all the way through—and under—BIG JOEY's commentary*)

BIG JOEY: … Hey, aspin Number Six Dry Lips Manigitogan, right-winger for the Wasy Wailerettes, eemaskamat Number Thirteen of the Canoe Lake Bravettes anee-i "particular puck" … (" … Hey, and there goes Dry Lips Manigitogan, right-winger for the Wasy Wailerettes, and steals the 'particular puck' from Number Thirteen of the Canoe Lake Bravettes … ")

DICKIE BIRD begins chanting and stomping his foot in time to CREATURE's and SPOOKY's cheers. Bits and pieces of NANABUSH/GAZELLE NATAWAYS' strip music and Kitty Wells' "It

Wasn't God Who Made Honky Tonk Angels"
begin to weave in and out of this sound collage,
a collage which now has a definite pounding
rhythm to it. Over it all soars the sound of
ZACHARY's harmonica, swooping and diving
brilliantly, recalling many of NANABUSH's
appearances throughout the play. BIG JOEY
continues uninterrupted.

BIG JOEY: … igwa aspin sipweesinskwataygew.
Hey, k'seegoochin! How, Number Six Dry Lips
Manigitogan igwa soogi pugamawew anee-i
"particular puck" ita Number Twenty-six Little
Girl Manitowabi, left-winger for the Wasy
Wailerettes, katee-ooteetuk blue line ita Number
Eleven Black Lady Halked, wha! defence-woman
for the Wasy Wailerettes, kagatchitnat anee-i
particular puck" igwa seemak kapassiwatat
Captain Hera Keechigeesikwa igwa Hera
Keechigeesik mitooni eepimithat, hey, kewayus
graceful Hera Keechigeesik, mitooni Russian
ballerina eesinagoosit. Captain Hera
Keechigeesik bee-line igwa itootum straight for
the Canoe Lake Bravettes' net igwa shootiwatew
anee-i "particular puck" igwa she shoots, she
scores … almost! Wha! Close one, ladies igwa
gentlemen, kwayus close one. But Number Six
Dry Lips Manigitogan, right-winger for the Wasy
Wailerettes, accidentally tripped and blocked the
shot … (" … and skates off. Hey, is she ever flying. Now, Number Six Dry Lips Manigitogan
shoots the 'particular puck' towards where
Number Twenty-six Little Girl Manitowabi, left-
winger for the Wasy Wailerettes, is heading
straight for the blue line where Number Eleven
Black Lady Halked, wha! defence-woman for the
Wasy Wailerettes, catches the 'particular puck'
and straightway passes it to Captain Hera
Keechigeesik and Hera Keechigeesik is just a-
flyin', hey, is she graceful or what, that Hera
Keechigeesik, she looks just like a Russian
ballerina. Captain Hera Keechigeesik now makes
a bee-line straight for the Canoe Lake Bravettes'
net and shoots the 'particular puck' and she
shoots, she scores … almost! Wha! Close one,
ladies and gentlemen, real close one. But
Number Six Dry Lips Manigitogan, right-winger
for the Wasy Wailerettes, accidentally tripped
and blocked the shot … ")

BIG JOEY's voice begins to trail off as CREATURE
NATAWAYS marches over and angrily grabs the
microphone away from him.

BIG JOEY: … How, Number Nine Flora
McDonald, Captain of the Canoe Lake Bravettes,
igwa ooteetinew anee-i "particular puck" igwa
skate-oo-oo behind the net igwa soogi heading
along the right side of the rink ita Number
Twenty-one Annie Cook … (" … How, Number
Nine Flora McDonald, Captain of the Canoe Lake
Bravettes, grabs the 'particular puck' and skates
behind the net and now heading along the right
side of the rink where Number Twenty-one Annie
Cook … ")

CREATURE: (*off microphone, as he marches over
to it*) Aw shit! Aw shit! … (*He grabs the microphone and, as he talks into it, the sound of all the
other men's voices, including the entire sound
collage, begins to fade.*) … That Dry Lips
Manigitogan, she's no damn good. Spooky
Lacroix, I tole you once I tole you twice she
shouldna done it she shouldna done what she
went and did godawful Dry Lips Manigitogan
they shouldna let her play, she's too fat, she's
gotten positively blubbery lately, I tole you once
I tole you twice that Dry Lips Manigitogan oughta
move to Kapuskasing, she really oughta, Spooky
Lacroix. I tole you once I tole you twice she
oughta move to Kapuskasing, Dry Lips oughta
move to Kapuskasing! Dry Lips oughta move to
Kapuskasing! Dry Lips oughta move to
Kapuskasing! Dry Lips oughta move to
Kapuskasing Dry Lips oughta move to
Kapuskasing Dry Lips oughta move to
Kapuskasing Dry Lips oughta move to
Kapuskasing Dry Lips oughta move to
Kapuskasing …

*And this, too, fades into first a whisper, magnified
on tape to other-worldly proportions, then into a
slow kind of heavy breathing. On top of this we
hear SPOOKY's baby crying. Complete fade-out
on all this (lights and sound), except for the
baby's crying and the heavy breathing, which
continue in the darkness. When the lights come
up again, we are in ZACHARY's own living room
(i.e., what was all along BIG JOEY's living
room/kitchen, only much cleaner). The couch
ZACHARY lies on is now covered with a "starblanket" and over the pin-up poster of Marilyn
Monroe now hangs what was, earlier,
NANABUSH's large powwow dancing bustle.
The theme from* The Smurfs *television show
bleeds in. ZACHARY is lying on the couch face*

down, naked, sleeping and snoring. The television in front of the couch comes on and The Smurfs are playing merrily away. ZACHARY's wife, the "real" HERA KEECHIGEESIK, enters carrying their baby, who is covered completely with a blanket. HERA is soothing the crying baby.

ZACHARY: (*talking in his sleep*) ... Dry Lips ... oughta move to ... Kapus ...

HERA: Poosees.

ZACHARY: ... kasing ... damn silliest thing I heard in my life ...

HERA: Honey. (*bends over the couch and kisses ZACHARY on the bum*)

ZACHARY: ... goodness sakes, Hera, you just had a baby ... (*Suddenly, he jumps up and falls off the couch.*) Simon!

HERA: Yoah! Keegatch igwa kipageecheep-'skawinan. ("Yoah! You almost knocked us down.")

ZACHARY: Hera! Where's my shorts?!

HERA: Neee, kigipoochimeek awus-chayess. ("Neee, just a couple of inches past the rim of your ass-hole.")

ZACHARY: Neee, chimagideedoosh. ("Neee, you unfragrant kozy": Ojibway.) (*He struggles to a sitting position on the couch.*)

HERA: (*correcting him and laughing*) "ChimagideeDEESH." ("You unfragrant KOOZIE.")

ZACHARY: Alright. "ChimagideeDEESH."

HERA: And what were you dreaming abou ...

ZACHARY: (*finally seeing the television*) Hey, it's the Smurfs! And they're not playing hockey da Englesa.

HERA: Neee, machi ma-a tatoo-Saturday morning Smurfs. Mootha meena weegatch hockey meetaweewuk weethawow Smurfs. ("Well, of course, the Smurfs are on every

Saturday morning. But they never play hockey, those Smurfs.") Here, you take her. (*She hands the baby over to ZACHARY and goes to sit beside him.*) Boy, that full moon last night. Ever look particularly like a giant puck, eh? Neee ...

Silence. ZACHARY plays with the baby.

ZACHARY: (*to HERA*) Hey, cup-cake. You ever think of playing hockey?

HERA: Yeah, right. That's all I need is a flying puck right in the left tit, neee ... (*But she stops to speculate.*) ... hockey, hmmm ...

ZACHARY: (*to himself*) Lordy, lordy, lordy ... (*HERA fishes ZACHARY's undershorts, which are pale blue in colour, from under a cushion and hands them to him. ZACHARY gladly grabs them.*) Neee, magawa nipeetawitoos ("Neee, here's my sharts ... ")

HERA: (*correcting him and laughing*) "NipeetawiTAS." ("My SHORTS")

ZACHARY: Alright. "NipeetawiTAS." (*Dangles the shorts up to the baby's face and laughs. Sing-songy, bouncing the baby on his lap.*) Magawa nipeetawitas. Nipeetawitas. Nipeetawitas. Nipeetawitas ...

The baby finally gets dislodged from the blanket and emerges, naked. And the last thing we see is this beautiful naked Indian man lifting this naked baby Indian girl up in the air, his wife sitting beside them watching and laughing. Slow fade-out. Split seconds before complete blackout, HERA peals out with this magical, silvery NANABUSH laugh, which is echoed and echoed by one last magical arpeggio on the harmonica from offstage. Finally, in the darkness, the last sound we hear is the baby's laughing voice, magnified on tape to fill the entire theatre. And this, too, fades into complete silence.

END

JOAN MacLEOD (b.1954)

Canadian drama in the 1990s offered vivid reflections of the nation's changing demographics and its evolving relationships within the late twentieth century global village. Whereas *Bordertown Café* reflects a long Canadian tradition of negotiation across a single, relatively stable national border, subsequent plays explore more multi-dimensional geopolitics. Issues of race, gender and ethnicity as well as postmodern notions of state and citizenship make nationalistic self-definition especially complicated in plays such as *Fronteras Americanas* and *Harlem Duet*. In Joan MacLeod's *Amigo's Blue Guitar*, the delicate balance of a family with tangled Canadian and American roots is upset by the arrival of a Salvadoran refugee. Elias' presence challenges the family members' personal myths, and tests the limits and integrity of their liberal empathy. For all our vaunted Canadian compassion, MacLeod asks, can we really understand, much less embrace, those whose experiences lie beyond even our vocabulary?

MacLeod was born and grew up in Vancouver, earning degrees in creative writing from the University of Victoria (BA, 1978) and UBC (MFA, 1981). While attending a poetry workshop at the Banff Centre in 1984, she met playwright Alan Williams who encouraged her to try her hand at drama. The result was the monologue *Jewel*, which she sent to Tarragon Theatre in Toronto. Tarragon invited her to join its Playwrights Unit in 1985, and subsequently premiered her first four plays. MacLeod remained playwright-in-residence there for six years. Her first produced work, however, was the libretto for a chamber opera, *The Secret Garden*, presented by Toronto's Comus Music Theatre in 1985. Based on the classic children's novel, it won MacLeod a Dora Mavor Moore Award for best new musical.

Jewel premiered at the Tarragon in 1987. Set in 1985, it takes the form of a widow's Valentine to her husband who drowned in the sinking of the oil rig *Ocean Ranger* three years earlier. The woman addresses the dead man in a poignant effort to kick-start her own life again. Emotional and moving, as is all MacLeod's work, *Jewel* received Dora and Chalmers award nominations for best new play. It also marked her first (and last) experience as a stage actor when, the day before opening and with no previous experience, MacLeod replaced the actress who had been rehearsing the part. She later reprised the role for radio. Retitled *Hand of God*, the radio adaptation of *Jewel* garnered honourable mention in the prestigious Prix Italia competition, and has been produced in French, German, Danish and Swedish.

Toronto, Mississippi, also premiered by Tarragon in 1987 and widely produced since then, had its genesis in MacLeod's experience as a child care worker and life skills instructor for mentally handicapped people in the late 1970s and early '80s. A funny and moving play about a single mother, her mildly autistic teenage daughter, the poet who boards with them, and the girl's estranged father, a professional Elvis impersonator, *Toronto, Mississippi* sensitively explores the mother-daughter relationship while deconstructing and reconstructing the concepts of nuclear family and mental disability. MacLeod next wrote *Amigo's Blue Guitar* for Tarragon. After its 1990 premiere (with Guillermo Verdecchia in the role of Elias), the play was produced across western Canada as well as in Ottawa, Chicago, London, England and Juneau, Alaska. The published text of *Amigo's Blue Guitar* won the Governor General's Award for drama in 1991.

The Hope Slide premiered in 1992, a one-woman play about an actress who assumes the characters of three dead Doukhobors in an attempt to comprehend the deaths of her friends from AIDS, and to rally her own crumbling hope. The Tarragon production won a Chalmers best play award, and the show has since been done in Vancouver, Victoria, Edmonton, Ottawa and elsewhere. *Little Sister* (1994), a play for young audiences about body image and eating disorders, was co-produced by Vancouver's Green Thumb and Toronto's Theatre Direct. MacLeod's millennial comic drama *2000* (1996) was first produced in Ottawa by the Great Canadian Theatre Company and subsequently in Toronto and Vancouver. Set on the border between city and wilderness in North Vancouver, the play combines west coast mysticism (evoking the ghost of Chief Dan George) with the concerns of an upper-middle-class couple wrestling with mid-life crisis. *The Shape of a Girl*, a one-woman play about a teenager affected by Victoria's notorious Reena Virk murder, was co-produced by Calgary's Alberta Theatre Projects and Vancouver's Green Thumb Theatre in 2001.

MacLeod has lived in and around Vancouver since 1992 and teaches at Kwantlen College. She has also taught at UBC and been writer-in-residence at the University of Northumbria in England. She has published poetry and fiction in more than a dozen literary journals, written radio plays and episodes of the TV series *Edgemont*, and adapted *Jewel* and *Amigo's Blue Guitar* for television.

In an interview with Rita Much, MacLeod explains that the immediate motivation for *Amigo's Blue Guitar* came from her involvement with refugee sponsorship groups in Toronto, but that the centre of the play is the brother-sister relationship between Sander and Callie: "my work always feels political, and it always feels personal." While exploring the internal politics of family as she had done in *Toronto, Mississippi* and would do again in *2000*—the dynamic entanglements of love, power and need within and across generations—MacLeod also looks at this particular family's interventions in the larger political realm represented by Elias' nightmarish experience. Like Wendy Lill's *Heather Rose*, Sander and Callie bring to bear a naïve and clumsy do-gooder mentality inflected by unconscious self-interest and a tendency to romanticize. In this they are very much their father's heirs, and their grandmother's, too.

MacLeod's plays have always involved radical acts of imaginative identification that transcend time, place and ethnic difference—the Alberta wife reaching across to her husband dead in the ocean off Newfoundland, the young girl conflating Toronto and Mississippi, the actress imagining herself a Doukhobor. In most of the plays the impulse appears positive, with the potential to effect powerful and creative transformations. The primary beneficiary, however, usually turns out to be the very one doing the imagining.

In *Amigo's Blue Guitar* Sander's attachment to Elias is, initially at least, therapeutic and revivifying—for Sander, that is—and proof to himself of both his altruism and his manhood. But even if his motives may not have been pure, he does get Elias out of El Salvador. And when he tells Elias that "it was the best thing I ever did," the line rings with absolute sincerity. Similarly, Callie uses Elias to fulfill both his needs and her own. Just as she tries to imagine the sub-strata below the geography of the Spanish-named Gulf Islands where they live, she wants to know what lies beneath Elias' external scars. Is this just liberal slumming and sexual adventurism? Does she really love Elias or only, as he tells her, "these terrible things that I remember"? In her frustrated desire for romantic authenticity she can't get anyone to believe that she was born in a row-boat; but with Elias she can feel, "it's like this chance to change the whole world."

Owen's insistence on romanticizing his Viet Nam-era "great escape" across the Canadian border seems trivial and somewhat insensitive in the face of Elias' experience, despite the real suffering he underwent. And even grandma Martha, who bonds with Elias from the start, is almost solipsistically self-referential in her conversations with him. Her liberal impulse is evident: she collects eyeglasses for her church to send to Africa. And her empathetic credentials are strong. She has, after all, seen in her own husband the awful reality of post-traumatic stress syndrome. But can she do any more than scratch at the surface of Elias' darkness? The Kitty Wells song she sings to him, which gives the play its title, superficially reflects Elias' lonely exile but also smacks of country & western kitsch and faux-Hispanic nostalgia.

The personal anguish each of these characters feels is real enough to themselves; a person ultimately lives within his or her own life. Owen genuinely suffered from his father's estrangement. Callie insists without irony, "I was born!" But Elias is finally a test that none of them can ever pass. He doesn't want his dreams to come out because they are too terrible, and because the others could never fully understand them. The name Marina, the image of the silver airplane, the word *desaparecido*, "disappeared"—a noun—these accrue their meanings through accumulated experiences that render them virtually incommunicable to even the most liberal consciousness forged in the sheltered experience of bourgeois North American life. In the play's final stage direction, as Anne Nothof points out, Callie and Martha can only console each other.

Amigo's Blue Guitar was first presented by the Tarragon Theatre, Toronto, on January 2, 1990, with the following cast:

ELIAS	Guillermo Verdecchia
MARTHA	Patricia Hamilton
OWEN	David Fox
CALLIE	Brooke Johnson
SANDER	Christopher Shore

Directed by Dennis Foon
Set Design by Adam and Irena Kolodziej
Costume Design by Melanie Huston
Lighting Design by Kevin Fraser
Sound Design by Keith Thomas

AMIGO'S BLUE GUITAR

CHARACTERS

ELIAS, *twenty-four, Salvadoran refugee*
MARTHA, *sixty-five, Owen's mother*
OWEN, *forty-two, Sander and Callie's father*
CALLIE, *twenty*
SANDER, *nineteen, Callie's brother*

SCENE

An island that is a short ferry ride from Vancouver. The time is the present [1990.]

SET

The set should have playing areas for the dock and shoreline, ELIAS' room and a living room/ dining area of the house. The interior of the house should be simple. What dominates the set is the exterior. It contains earth, water and sky and conveys a feeling of being on the edge of an ocean.

ACTION

Although blackouts can be used, the action of the play is more or less continuous, with the end of one scene often overlapping the start of another. Running time is 1 hour and 45 minutes.

PROLOGUE

Spot up on ELIAS. He speaks directly to the audience. Initially, his manner is very welcoming until he makes a fist.

ELIAS: What I sleep is my own. I am in my bed, in my room and there are no countries. There is no language to sleep. This is a true thing to all peoples. Now you are asking for the nightmare, for the dreams of me. I am not going to tell you. They are mine.

Do you see the girl in my bed? It is too dark. You must touch to see. You must see her by what you remember. I will tell you her arms, her eyes, her skin. She too would like to see the dream come out of me. This is one stupid girl.

You let the dream come out and there is no place left for me. In this house, this country. No place left inside a girl in my bed. (*makes a fist*)

This is it. This is how the dream comes out. This is the dream I will bring you.

ACT ONE

Scene One

Interior, late afternoon, November. MARTHA and OWEN enter. They have just driven up from Oregon.

MARTHA: John Wayne looked tired. That was my first impression—give the man a rest. It should've been the happiest day of my life. How many other women look up from the breakfast dishes and see John Wayne out their window, John Wayne tying up to their dock.

OWEN: He fished up here every year. It was no big deal.

MARTHA: Speak for yourself mister. I'm running to beat the band—trying to find Sander's autograph book, braiding Callie's hair. By the time we got down there the water was calm again but he stayed on so we could all say hello. He was polite as could be. I was so mad at you, Owen. Sitting up here on your duff like it was a daily occurrence. The man was a legend.

OWEN: The man was a fascist.

MARTHA: A polite legend. You were nasty just like that today.

OWEN: To who?

MARTHA: The border man. He asked if we had anything to declare and you almost took his head off.

OWEN: You know what they are, Mom? Failed cops.

MARTHA: Don't you start with me. Carter forgave you. The whole bunch of you. Stevie Newton moved back home as soon as they granted amnesty. And Kitty's boy up in Portland?

He was a draft dodger too. I never liked that expression. Draft dodger. It made you sound sneaky.

OWEN: We were. That was the point. And while we're on the subject, I'm still waiting. I didn't want a pardon. I want a goddamn apology.

CALLIE: (enters) You two at it already? (embraces MARTHA and OWEN)

OWEN: Hi sweetheart.

MARTHA: Callie. God love us you're like your mother.

CALLIE: Hi Grandma. Dad.

OWEN: You and your brother get along okay this week?

CALLIE: No. How was the drive up?

MARTHA: We stopped at Denny's near Snohomish. I had clam strips. They were tough. Are you on one of your diets, Callie? You're thin.

CALLIE: No.

OWEN: Where is Sander?

CALLIE: Town.

MARTHA: What was that diet you were on the last time you were in Oregon? What was it you were eating?

CALLIE: Tab and ju-jubes.

MARTHA: Tab and ju-jubes! I thought we'd have to haul you out on a stretcher. You still seeing that guy with all the hair? Riley? Are you dating Riley?

CALLIE: No.

MARTHA: I didn't like all that hair. Did you?

CALLIE: It ruined our relationship. I'm going out with this guy that works on the ferries.

OWEN: Who?

CALLIE: Roddy Glass.

MARTHA: Is he the one who steers? We met him this afternoon.

CALLIE: Roddy parks cars. He bought his own place. You know that A-frame on Harbour Road?

OWEN: Gone five days and you found a boyfriend.

CALLIE: He's not my boyfriend. Did you see Mum?

OWEN: I talked to her on the phone. I didn't do much visiting. Just went down to pick up your grandma really.

MARTHA: The Peace Arch was dirty. Did you notice that, Owen? That poor old monument used to gleam in the sun.

OWEN: It looked about the same as ever to me.

MARTHA: "Children of a common mother." That's what's written up top and today you could barely see it. I always thought common meant cheap.

OWEN: I like that: a regular floozy …

MARTHA: Don't you start with me …

OWEN: I'm glad you're here.

MARTHA: Your dad wants me to stay right through the winter. He thinks I'm old.

CALLIE: We all want you to stay …

MARTHA: Meatloaf and canned corn for supper. I brought two turkeys up for Thanksgiving. Your father here wouldn't declare them.

CALLIE: We already had Thanksgiving last month.

MARTHA: Well, you're having it again. This coming Thursday. Does everyone still like canned corn?

CALLIE: That's fine.

MARTHA: I don't know how to gauge the time on that old stove. Is it in the metric too?

CALLIE: Grandma, it's a woodstove.

MARTHA: Well I know that. I grew up with one of those and believe you me we didn't think it was anything special. I suppose your father here will be getting rid of electricity soon so we can all ruin our eyes with a coal oil lamp. That's why your mother left. Owen wouldn't be modern. (exits)

CALLIE: No it wasn't.

OWEN: You tell her, Cal. How were your midterms?

CALLIE: Easy. You know, Dad, Roddy Glass is a perfectly fine person. He's just not very good with words …

OWEN: You don't meet anyone in your classes?

CALLIE: Roddy's going to night school.

OWEN: What's he taking?

CALLIE: Air brakes. If you're so down on island guys, how come you made us grow up here?

OWEN: I could rent a place in town for you and Sander. You're spending half your day on a bus or a ferry …

CALLIE: Sander doesn't need to live near campus. He only shows up there twice a week, tops. And all he does is sit in the cafeteria. Or else he's down at immigration driving them all crazy. That's the only reason they're letting that guy come. It's so they'll have Sander off their case …

OWEN: What guy?

CALLIE: The refugee.

OWEN: I thought he died.

CALLIE: Apparently not. Immigration phoned right after you left. Sander's been unbearable, Dad. He's walking around like the new Gandhi or something. Better yet he won't tell me anything. He says it's all top security.

OWEN: Where's the guy from?

CALLIE: El Salvador. Guess how much Sander knows about El Salvador?

OWEN: Give him a chance. How much do you know, Cal?

CALLIE: The tallest peak is Santa Ana …

OWEN: Armed only with her major in geography Callie takes on the third world …

CALLIE: But the most famous is the volcano Izalco …

Spot up on ELIAS.

ELIAS: El faro del Pacifico …

CALLIE: The lighthouse of the Pacific. All of El Salvador is covered by layer upon layer of ash.

Scene Two

Spot up on ELIAS.

ELIAS: Estoy muy contento que usted me puede ver ahora. Tengo mis papeles listos si usted los quiere. (I'm glad that you can see me now. I have my papers ready if you need them.)

I am happy to work in Canada is good.

I like to work. My English is great.

Speak again please and slowly.

Que quiere? No entiendo lo que usted quiere y he dicho que quiero trabajar. Me gusta trabajar. (I don't understand what you want. I want to work. I like to work.)

No. I come to Canada to … porque … not to work solamente. I come to Canada porque … estoy inquieto. I am afraid.

I am afraid of my house. Please let me come.

Scene Three

Exterior, the next day.

SANDER: Right now I could take the 10:15 to Vancouver, Highway 99 to the States, then the I-5 all the way to Mexico then bang! We're there—El Salvador, Guatemala. I think about that. I think about taking Dad's truck and his Esso card and driving right inside those places. There are these soldiers everywhere and these Indian women making tortillas or pounding silver or something. I talk to them in Spanish and they understand exactly what it is I'm saying.

CALLIE: Did you talk to Dad yet?

SANDER: No. Okay, Cal. This is what you say when he arrives. Buenas dias Elias (*pronounces it as E-lie-as*). Yo soy Callie. Try it.

CALLIE: You better talk to him pretty soon.

SANDER: I will. He was already out on the boat when I got up.

CALLIE: I told him the guy might come but I never said he was going to live here.

SANDER: What's your problem? Dad will love it. C'mon. Buenas dias Elias … Yo soy …

CALLIE: Yo soy pissed off, Sander! Yo soy wants to know exactly when this guy's coming, what he looks like and how long he's going to stay. Yo soy also wants to know how come we don't hear anything about this for a whole year then it's guess what?

SANDER: For your information, Callie, I stood in line at immigration yesterday for five hours. It was incredible: all these different languages flying around, all these very desperate people …

CALLIE: You missed your midterms.

SANDER: These very brave people. It certainly wouldn't hurt you any to spend some time down there.

CALLIE: What about your midterms?

SANDER: I didn't have any.

CALLIE: What about English?

SANDER: I dropped out.

CALLIE: Ah Christ …

SANDER: I didn't flunk out. I withdrew. Sociology too.

CALLIE: Dad is going to go insane.

SANDER: It doesn't go on my transcript; it just says withdrawn or gone or …

CALLIE: So that's great, Sander. That means you're only taking two courses. You know normal people have full-time jobs and families and a variety of hobbies and they can still do two courses.

SANDER: Well, normal people are not concerned with saving other people's lives.

CALLIE: Give me a break.

SANDER: I'm on the waiting list to take industrial first aid.

CALLIE: What?

SANDER: So if I get my first aid ticket, I can work in a logging camp or even a mill. And I'll have lots of time for Elias.

CALLIE: You don't know the first thing about first aid.

SANDER: I can learn. Besides, you know what a first aid attendant does all day? Nothing.

CALLIE: What if somebody really got hurt?

SANDER: The most important thing is to not do anything. I mean I could put on Band-Aids and stuff but anything big and it's completely illegal to even touch them. And I know how to do the hug-of-life.

CALLIE: What the hell is the hug-of-life?

SANDER: The Heimlich manoeuvre.

CALLIE: Well, God help the guy who falls on top of his chain-saw.

SANDER: Get off my case, Cal. I haven't even signed up yet. I couldn't find it in the phone book.

CALLIE: And now because of some bullshit school project you've got some orphan-guy being hauled out of the jungle and forced to live with you.

SANDER: Okay, okay, okay! You know it all. I am terrible at everything. But there's one thing I do know about, Callie, and that's Elias. I know how I feel about him and I know I helped save someone's life—and if you think midterms or Roddy Glass or first aid mean more than that then you're absolutely stupid.

CALLIE: (pause) I can help. I can help you with the first aid. School too.

SANDER: I don't give a shit about school. This refugee stuff is way more important. It should be important to all of us.

CALLIE: What'd Elias do? Why'd he have to run away?

SANDER: You don't have to do anything to get nailed down there. He was a student …

CALLIE: He could stay at Roddy's place. He's got lots of room.

SANDER: Roddy Glass is practically an alcoholic.

CALLIE: No he isn't.

SANDER: When I think of Roddy, I just remember him leaning over the wharf and throwing up on some guy's speedboat. Not a terrific example for new Canadians. Stand up.

CALLIE: Why?

SANDER: Just do it.

SANDER places his arms around CALLIE from behind and hugs her

CALLIE: Sander! Jesus, ow! What are you doing?

SANDER: Saving you. I rescued Grandma once. Remember when she was practically dying over that muffin that had gone down the wrong way? I made it fly.

OWEN: *(enters)* Made this crap sail right out of her like a little wet bird thumping against the window.

SANDER: Hi Dad. How was the trip? *(releases CALLIE, embraces OWEN)*

OWEN: Good.

CALLIE: You've probably punctured my god-damned lung. *(exits)*

OWEN: School alright?

SANDER: Yeah.

OWEN: Cal said you did an essay on Mussolini.

SANDER: Right.

OWEN: That you copied it word for word from the *Junior Worldbook*.

SANDER: I changed some stuff.

OWEN: That's bullshit, Sander.

SANDER: So's school. I've been busy.

OWEN: You do some work on the boat?

SANDER: Sort of.

OWEN: Sort of.

SANDER: I ran out of paint. Lives have been at stake, Dad.

OWEN: Pardon me?

SANDER: You know that group I formed last year to sponsor a refugee?

OWEN: I know you left everything until the last minute and …

SANDER: Well, he's coming. Elias.

OWEN: You told me he died.

SANDER: No way.

OWEN: Sander, you said he died.

SANDER: He could've been killed a million times. I said he was in danger. Grave danger.

OWEN: There is a slight difference between being dead and being in danger.

SANDER: Elias filled out the wrong forms. He said he wanted to work here and they gave him the stuff for a work visa and he got turned down. Immigration does it on purpose to slow things up because so many want in. But he reapplied and now he's coming.

OWEN: Where?

SANDER: Well, here.

OWEN: To Canada.

SANDER: Right. He's just waiting in Guatemala City while they do these security checks …

OWEN: Where's he going to live, Sander?

SANDER: With us. Isn't that great?

OWEN: You know what I think? That you're as organized as a two year old and you do stuff behind my back even when you don't have to.

SANDER: You're the one who's always going on about how hard it was being booted out of your own country …

OWEN: I didn't say it was a bad idea. But you've got to get organized.

SANDER: I already signed him up for English. The waiting lists are huge. Muy grande. My Spanish is really coming back.

OWEN: Where'd it go, Sander? Aren't you doing Spanish this term?

SANDER: By tutorial. How's Mum?

OWEN: Actually she's going in the hospital …

SANDER: What's wrong?

OWEN: She's fine. She's getting her tubes tied. She should've done it years ago …

SANDER: Thanks a lot.

OWEN: Now this guy's gonna need some warm clothes.

SANDER: I know.

OWEN: How long will he be staying here?

SANDER: We're responsible for the first year but most refugees are on their own after three months …

OWEN: It would've been nice to have a little warning, Sander.

SANDER: That's not how it works.

OWEN: If you had followed up on this properly and not forgot about …

SANDER: I never forgot him! I've written letters, stood in lines … Just because I don't announce everything I do to you and Callie doesn't mean I don't do anything. He's important to me, Dad.

OWEN: Okay.

SANDER: I've thought about him every single day this year. Elias.

Scene Four

Interior, one week later.

ELIAS: Hello.

MARTHA: Why, you're not a boy at all. You're a full-grown man.

ELIAS: Hon … honoured to meet you.

MARTHA: You're Elias. (*mispronounces his name E-lie-as*) Sander's on his way. He was so disappointed not to be able to go to the airport.

ELIAS: Elias, yes. Hello …

MARTHA: E-lee-as? You're sure?

ELIAS: Elias.

MARTHA: Alright, Elias it is. I'm Martha. Have you had your lunch?

ELIAS: Como … I am honoured to meet you.

MARTHA: You can call me Grandma.

ELIAS: Me Grandma.

MARTHA: CALL ME GRANDMA!

ELIAS: GRANDMA! HELLO!

MARTHA: HELLO!

ELIAS: Hello.

MARTHA: Do you like Cheez Whiz?

ELIAS: Cheez Whiz?

MARTHA: And there's enough turkey left over to feed an army.

ELIAS: (*removing carton of cigarettes from a duty-free bag*) For you.

MARTHA: Oh, no. I'm not a smoker. This house is smoke-free except for that damn stove.

ELIAS: Sugars? (*offers little packets of sugar*)

MARTHA: Isn't that nice of you. Thank you. We'll have it in our tea. How was your trip?

ELIAS: Que? Lo puede repetir por favor? (Can you repeat that please?)

MARTHA: The airplane?

ELIAS: Yes!

MARTHA: You're a long way from home. This isn't really my home either but I guess I'm the welcome wagon. Welcome! I've been to Mexico.

ELIAS: Mexico. Yes. I am El Salvador.

MARTHA: Just Tijuana but that was enough. We were in San Diego; we went down for the afternoon. Reg brought the car. Can you imagine?

ELIAS: Disculpame. Puede hablar un poco mas despacito por favor? (Can you speak a little slower please?)

MARTHA: (*pause*) We were afraid to leave the car by itself. Mexico is one hot country. You'll be from a hot place too. Canada is cold but not here. It's just like home. I'm an Oregonian.

ELIAS: I … am … speaking … slowly … please.

MARTHA: You certainly are!

ELIAS: Yes.

MARTHA: Or … e … gon. I am from Oregon.

ELIAS: Como? No entiendo … (I don't understand …)

MARTHA: Just north of California …

ELIAS: California! Yes!

MARTHA: Actually we're closer to the Washington end, up by Portland. Are you married?

ELIAS: Disculpame Señora pero no entiendo muy bien el ingles. (Excuse me but my English is not very good.)

MARTHA: Married! A wife?

ELIAS: Wife. No. No wife for me. Please.

MARTHA: But you have a family. Sisters? Brothers?

ELIAS: Two brother. Four sister.

MARTHA: You must be a Catholic.

ELIAS: Yes. Catholic. Now—no. No Catholic.

MARTHA: We're Baptist. Owen doesn't go. Sander and Callie are agnostics. Are your parents in El Salvador?

ELIAS: Parents?

MARTHA: Mother, father …

ELIAS: Mother dead. Father dead.

MARTHA: My husband's gone. He was sick a long time. Owen came down but he couldn't go to the funeral. The FBI were there, right in the chapel. That's sad isn't it? Having to stay away from your own father's funeral. Him and his father didn't see eye to eye. Reg was ashamed of him over this draft business.

ELIAS: Do you have a birthday?

MARTHA: July the fifth. My mother went into labour during the fireworks. You've run away too now. Like Owen.

ELIAS: Yes?

MARTHA: I'm glad he didn't go. Mabel Roderick's boy was killed over there. Mabel hates me. She hates me because I can hop on the Greyhound and go see my son. Viet Nam was a dreadful business.

ELIAS: Viet Nam, yes. I am El Salvador.

MARTHA: Then everyone blamed Catherine. She was the one that made him leave. And I kept my mouth shut but I would've told him the same: run oh run, head for the hills everyone, head for the hills.

ELIAS: Very bad Viet Nam.

MARTHA: Wasn't it terrible? And it split our town right down the middle. Some people wouldn't talk to me because of Owen. I never stopped saying hello to anyone. Cheerful too. Water off a duck's back. The FBI used to visit me.

ELIAS: FBI …

MARTHA: Listen to me, Elias! (*mispronouncing his name again*)

ELIAS: Elias.

MARTHA: Sorry, Elias. Nattering away at you and you're probably starving to death.

ELIAS: I am fine. How are you?

MARTHA: Fine! Reg bought a plaster donkey in Tijuana. It was blue. I thought he'd put it out in the garden but he kept it at the foot of our bed. Can you imagine that?

ELIAS: Como?

MARTHA: I thought it was creepy … I do! I do speak Spanish. "Amigo's Guitar." Do you know Kitty Wells?

ELIAS: How are you?

MARTHA: She's a country and western singer. The best country and western singer ever.

ELIAS: Country and western.

MARTHA: You like it?

ELIAS: No me gusta. Sorry. (I don't like it.)

MARTHA: I told you a fib. It did hurt me. All those people who wouldn't give me the time of day because of Owen. Berty Barnes said there was no difference between a draft dodger and a child molester or any other common criminal. It broke Reg's heart. Berty used to be one of our best friends.

ELIAS: Amigos.

MARTHA: "Amigo's Guitar" is a song by Kitty Wells and it's Spanish. Or some of it anyway. Mexican. I believe it's from south of the border.

ELIAS: Me va cantar una cancion de Mexicana? (You're going to sing me a song from Mexico?)

MARTHA: It'll break your heart in two if you're at all sensitive. I can tell already that you're sensitive.

ELIAS: Sing please.

MARTHA: You want me to sing? Aren't you brave.

ELIAS: Honoured …

MARTHA: Pretend my hair's black.

ELIAS: Yes.

MARTHA: Pretend I'm beautiful.

ELIAS: Usted es muy hermosa. (You are very beautiful.)

MARTHA: (*sings*)
Tonight they're singing in the village,
Tomorrow you'll be gone so far,
Hold me close and say you love me,
While Amigo plays his blue guitar.
Aye yi, aye yi the moon is so lonely,
Tomorrow you'll be gone so far …

SANDER: (*enters*) Grandma don't …

MARTHA: Ssssshhhh! (*sings*) Mañana morning …

ELIAS: Mañana …

MARTHA: (*sings*) I'll be blue as Amigo's guitar.

SANDER: Hi. Yo soy Alexander.

ELIAS: I am hon … hon …

SANDER: Grandma! You made him upset. (*in dreadful Spanish*) Estoy feliz que tu estas aqui. (I am very glad you're here.)

MARTHA: We were only singing …

ELIAS: I am very honoured to meet you. Grandma.

Scene Five

Interior, later the same day.

OWEN: (*to ELIAS*) It's Labour Day. Catherine and I met this guy in a parking lot at Penny's. He was head of the Bellingham cell. You've gotta remember what year it was.

CALLIE and SANDER: 1968.

OWEN: And I'm not kidding here, his name was Orbit Galaxy. Orbit had the distinction of being the first hippy in all of the Northwest.

CALLIE: How can you prove who was the first?

OWEN: Undisputed. Orbit was the original freak. But he had everything in order: Canadian passports, this old Valiant with B.C. plates. Great car. We wrecked the engine a week later but whatever … Sander?

SANDER: What?

OWEN: You're supposed to be translating.

SANDER: Mi padre tiene un amigo qui llama Orbit Galaxy. El tiene un auto como una Valiant …

OWEN: Valiant.

SANDER: El tiene Viet Nam. La guerra.

ELIAS: Si, Viet Nam.

OWEN: Because of the holiday the border is packed, which was also all part of the master plan. There's campers everywhere, families on picnics at the Peace Arch. We're in line forever and Catherine's gone dead quiet. My heart is crawling up my throat but this old guy in the booth, he just asked where we were born and I said "Chilly Whack!" and he waved us through. It was a big deal. We wanted it to be a big deal. We'd just gone over the wall, under the wire, crawled out on our bellies and arrived at a safe place. We're heroes, man. The great escape. Then Catherine threw up all over her shoes not one mile into Canada and it dawns on us for the first time that she might be pregnant. She was in a hell of a mood but then she was usually in a hell of a mood no matter what … Sander!

SANDER: El paso la frontiera, no problema. Mi madre es infermo porque ella tiene mi hermana Callie.

CALLIE: What about me?

SANDER: I said you made Mum sick.

OWEN: (*pause*) That's it? That's a pretty short translation.

SANDER: C'mon, Dad. You drove up and they waved you through. You're always making it sound like the Berlin Wall or something. Quieres dormir ahora?

ELIAS: No.

CALLIE: What'd you say?

SANDER: I asked if he wanted to go to sleep. He's had a big day.

ELIAS: Callie.

CALLIE: What?

ELIAS: Your name—Callie. Es un nombre familiar? Un apodo? De adonde viene Callie?

SANDER: Caligula.

CALLIE: What?

SANDER: He wants to know what Callie stands for …

ELIAS: Cal … ig … u … la …

CALLIE: No, no … Calico.

ELIAS: Calico. Very pretty.

CALLIE: It's ridiculous. It's a terrible name. My parents were insane. Tell him to never call me that.

SANDER: Callie. No Calico.

CALLIE: Great translating, Sander.

ELIAS: Okay. Okay, Callie. Hello.

CALLIE: Hi.

OWEN: Bienvenido to soo nueva casa.

SANDER: Oh brother.

ELIAS: Thank you. Thank you very much.

OWEN: I hope you can feel at home here. I know how lonely it's going to feel at first. I hope I can help you a little with that …

SANDER: Dad …

OWEN: What's your problem, Sander?

SANDER: It isn't the same. You've been pardoned. You can go back anytime.

OWEN: Well, I didn't want a pardon …

OWEN and SANDER: I want a goddamn apology.

ELIAS: Yo tengo una novia Marina. Ella se parece a Callie.

CALLIE: What's he talking about?

SANDER: I don't know.

ELIAS: Mi novia, Marina. Se parece a Callie.

CALLIE: I could learn as much Spanish as Sander knows in half an hour.

SANDER: He thinks you look like his girlfriend. Marina.

CALLIE: Marina?

ELIAS: Si.

CALLIE: Where is she now? Ask him, Sander.

SANDER: Adonde esta Marina?

ELIAS: El Salvador. Hace un año que no la veo. (I have not seen her for a year.)

SANDER: He doesn't see her anymore.

OWEN: Man, it's great. A new language. It makes the whole house feel different.

CALLIE: Ask him what he's run away from.

SANDER: No.

CALLIE: Why not?

SANDER: It's none of our business.

OWEN: And that we're sorry he had to run, that his country's in such a mess.

SANDER: He's had a long day.

OWEN: I'm very glad you're here. I'm going to bed now. Buenas noches.

ELIAS: Good night. Me too. I go.

SANDER: Tienes todos? Requerdas a donde es tu camo y el quarto de baño? (Do you have everything? Do you remember where the bed and bathroom are?)

ELIAS: I no understand you.

SANDER: Buenas noches.

ELIAS: Thank you. Thank you Sander. Good night Callie.

CALLIE: Elias? Are you happy to be here?

ELIAS: Happy, yes. Thank you.

OWEN and ELIAS exit.

CALLIE: No he isn't.

SANDER: How do you know? He's just tired.

CALLIE: And sad. I thought he'd be, you know, more excited.

SANDER: He is excited. He's a warrior.

CALLIE: What?

SANDER: He's a warrior.

Scene Six

Interior, six weeks later, New Year's Eve day. CALLIE is wrapping ELIAS in bandages. ELIAS is studying his English books.

ELIAS: "Where is the monkey?"

CALLIE: Hold still …

ELIAS: "The monkey is in the tree." Yeah!

CALLIE: Hold still. Make your fingers curl under. See?

ELIAS: Si. "The monkey eats the banana."

CALLIE: You're supposed to be an amputee. Your hand has been chopped off below the wrist. Comprende?

ELIAS: No I am not understanding you.

CALLIE: I'm going to wrap it. I'm going to wrap the stump.

SANDER: Gross.

CALLIE: What's this called, Sander?

SANDER: What's what called?

CALLIE: This type of injury … C'mon.

SANDER: I haven't got that far in the book.

CALLIE: Saw mill accident number six.

ELIAS: You are helping me.

CALLIE: You better believe it.

SANDER: It's illegal to touch the patient.

CALLIE: What people do behind closed doors is their own business.

ELIAS: Close the door! We are closed.

SANDER: You going to give him the hug-of-life too? I'll bet Elias would like that …

ELIAS: Take off your clothes.

SANDER: Unwrap Elias. Him and me are going to a party.

ELIAS: (verb) Party!

CALLIE: Elias?

ELIAS: Yes Callie.

CALLIE: Have you ever killed someone?

ELIAS: Pardon me?

SANDER: Shut up, Callie.

CALLIE: It's just a question.

ELIAS: No I have not. I have not killed someone. And you?

CALLIE: You know something, Sander? You still have a great deal of trouble with emotional honesty. Sander and I ran into these scientologists on the Granville Mall once. They hooked us up to this machine thing called the E-Meter.

SANDER: Scientology is pure crap.

CALLIE: The E-meter measures your emotional and spiritual honesty

ELIAS: The E-meter.

CALLIE: I, as usual, passed. Sander flunked completely. He ripped the wires right off … So. Where's the party?

SANDER: You don't want to know where the party is …

ELIAS: My friend Roddy Glass.

CALLIE: You're going to a party at his place? Thanks a lot.

SANDER: He's working. He won't even be there.

CALLIE: Does he know there's a party at his house?

SANDER: He doesn't mind. He likes it.

CALLIE: He also has trouble with emotional honesty. When Roddy and I split up he couldn't even cry.

ELIAS: Where is the Christmas tree?

SANDER: Grandma took it down this morning.

CALLIE: If it's not down by New Year's it's bad luck.

ELIAS: I was loving the Christmas tree.

SANDER: We light it on fire.

ELIAS: Why?

CALLIE: It's tradition. A Canadian tradition.

SANDER: If you want to come tonight you can. Roddy won't be there.

CALLIE: No thank you very much.

SANDER: It's New Year's Eve.

CALLIE: No kidding.

SANDER: What'll you do?

CALLIE: I want to be alone.

SANDER: Grandma will be here.

CALLIE: I love the elderly! I don't need to get drunk and picked up and puke all night. Who'll be there?

SANDER: Everyone.

MARTHA enters.

ELIAS: Hello Grandma.

MARTHA: Hello Elias.

ELIAS: Happy New Year Grandma.

MARTHA: And to you as well.

SANDER: Where's Dad?

MARTHA: Walking on the beach. Owen's mad at me.

SANDER: Why?

MARTHA: He's mad I didn't breast feed him. Who likes ham?

ELIAS: I like ham.

MARTHA: Sander?

SANDER: Yes. Cal too. We all love ham.

MARTHA: Reg loved a ham supper. I'm moving to China. The old are honoured there. They wear crowns of gold and are asked advice.

CALLIE: I think that's Japan.

MARTHA: Owen just told me I should have walked into the woods to give birth. He could've fallen out on the dirt while I howled at the moon. Isn't that a terrible thing to say?

ELIAS: Yes Grandma.

CALLIE: I was born in a row-boat.

SANDER: You were not.

CALLIE: I was practically born in a row-boat. When Mum went into labour Dad was out fishing. She tried to row to the mainland all by herself.

SANDER: You were born in Lions Gate Hospital.

CALLIE: I was nearly born in a row-boat.

ELIAS: I like to eat ham and eggs.

SANDER: Nearly being born somewhere is slightly different than …

CALLIE: I was! I was born!

Scene Seven

Exterior, New Year's Eve night. CALLIE, ELIAS and SANDER have been drinking beer for several hours.

CALLIE: I ruined our night.

SANDER: No you didn't.

CALLIE: You know that song? "December 31st is the very worst day of the year … "

SANDER: It was a lousy party. This is way better.

ELIAS: Happy New Year! Trienta y una!

CALLIE: Don't tell me when it's midnight. We'll just let it slip by, okay?

ELIAS: Okay Callie.

CALLIE: Do you think Roddy saw me crying?

SANDER and ELIAS: (*together*) Yeah/Si.

ELIAS: Before on this night, I am with my friends and with Marina. We go to one house and the other house to drink and all the time we are more friends. Then we go to the square and there are singers—Tepehuany—very good. We drink and sing and then we light the sky on fire.

SANDER: Fireworks. We should have bought some. We could light off some flares on the boat.

CALLIE: Do you miss Marina?

ELIAS: I have said good-bye and this is a long time before.

CALLIE: He changed his mind. He's going to buy a place in the Caribbean.

SANDER: Who?

CALLIE: David Bowie. He doesn't want to live here.

SANDER: No one does.

CALLIE: That's not true …

SANDER: You're always going on about all the rock stars who come here to relax, who come because it's so pretty. So we've all lived here forever and how many have we met?

CALLIE: Boz Scaggs.

SANDER: We saw him from the back. It could have been anyone …

CALLIE: It was Boz Scaggs. He owns a whole island north of here. It's common knowledge.

ELIAS: I do not know him. I do not know Boz Scaggs.

SANDER: Now Springsteen.

ELIAS: The Boss.

SANDER: I wouldn't mind having him for a neighbour …

CALLIE: Do you know why Bruce's marriage ended? She wouldn't have his child. I'd have his child in a second.

SANDER: Well, maybe he'll buy a place here and you can have his baby …

CALLIE: Bruce Springsteen only lives in industrialized areas. It's common knowledge. … Okay! Everybody lie back and shut their eyes …

SANDER: Christ, Cal. It's freezing.

CALLIE: It's August. The sun's so hot you fall asleep in a second. The dock begins to drift. You sleep for hours and hours and when you wake up, you're in another country. A foreign country.

SANDER: I remember this. We used to play this all the time.

ELIAS: When you are children?

SANDER: Yeah.

ELIAS: We play these things too. We play the sand is made of snow and is so cold it will hurt you.

CALLIE: In this country, the men all wear dresses …

SANDER: And the ladies don't wear any clothes …

ELIAS: Take off your clothes!

CALLIE: I have to disguise myself as a boy and look after Sander the rest of my life. Sander'd say—tell me a better story. Tell me something funny that doesn't have any people.

SANDER: You always loved scaring the shit out of me …

CALLIE: We loved it, being scared.

ELIAS: (*toasting the others*) Happy New Year! Trienta y una!

SANDER: You tell 'em, partner.

CALLIE: Is midnight past?

SANDER: This year is officially twelve minutes old. (*to ELIAS*) So you had fun last year eh? That's great.

ELIAS: This was not last year. Last year I have lost this day.

CALLIE: How can you lose a day?

ELIAS: I am in a little room. There is no night and no day. I am in a prison.

SANDER: Right.

CALLIE: How'd you get out?

SANDER: You don't have to talk about it …

ELIAS: About the prison?

SANDER: Unless you want to. I mean you can if you want …

CALLIE: That's just so sad …

ELIAS: No. We are here, now. Trienta y una. Thirty One and I would like to drink with you. Sander. I would like to drink to you. I wish to thank you for bringing me here and to your house.

CALLIE: You don't have to thank him.

SANDER: You're welcome.

ELIAS: I think you must care very much for my country.

SANDER: Yeah, I do.

ELIAS: You worry with me for the trouble there.

SANDER: I think it's very important that we help. I mean there are twelve million refugees …

ELIAS: I hope one day to help you.

SANDER: I heard how five people can sponsor one. I had to do something. And even though it did cut into school and that, I think those sacrifices are essential.

ELIAS: Thank you very much, Sander.

CALLIE: I can't stand this.

SANDER: This Jesuit came to my sociology class and he gave a lecture. He was incredible.

ELIAS: Lecture?

SANDER: A talk.

ELIAS: What does he talk of?

SANDER: Well … torture. He gave a talk about the effects of torture …

CALLIE: And?

SANDER: And mercy. "Mercy occurs when those in power act with kindness and compassion." He meant us …

CALLIE: What else, Sander?

SANDER: I loved that. I loved what he said about mercy and what we could do. So I did something. I mean I really did something …

CALLIE: It's March and Sander's done nothing in this course all year. He makes a deal …

SANDER: Lay off, Cal …

CALLIE: Instead of writing a term paper, Sander forms a sponsoring group.

SANDER: Look Callie, I'm really sorry that Roddy Glass dumped you for the stupidest woman on the entire west coast …

CALLIE: This also means he gets to cut out of Spanish and English class and hang out at Immigration. Everyone thinks he's some kind of hero plus he gets credit in three courses without doing any work.

SANDER: It was not that simple. You know it, Cal …

ELIAS: (to SANDER) I am your homework?

SANDER: No!

ELIAS: I am the work the teacher gives you?

CALLIE: A direct quote from Sander: "It'll never happen. The guy won't ever really get here, most groups wait for years. It's all red tape and paper-work."

SANDER: Fuck you. You and Dad both. You can't stand it when I do anything right.

CALLIE: And all of a sudden you're a real person and you're in real danger. You have a name and a face and you're coming here. You're coming to our house. Sander isn't your saviour, Elias. He was just trying to get out of writing an essay.

SANDER: Well, you've written the book on saving people, Callie. You've "saved" half the guys on this island.

CALLIE: It's bullshit, Sander. You walking around trying to make Elias feel grateful …

SANDER: I'm not!

CALLIE: When we both know exactly why this whole thing got started.

SANDER: Who cares how it started. The point is that Elias is here and he's okay.

CALLIE: The point is you've been going around for a year thinking you're Jesus.

ELIAS: Is this true?

SANDER: I'm glad Elias has come and he's glad too.

ELIAS: I do not come because I want to. I come because I have no place to go. I am a thing for your studies? This is a funny thing. This is something I have not been before. Where is the monkey? The monkey is in the tree.

SANDER: It wasn't like that.

ELIAS: Trienta y una! Hello Canada! Do you need more help?

SANDER: You don't owe us anything …

ELIAS: No. I very much want to help you. (pushes SANDER down) You are in this chair.

SANDER: What chair?

ELIAS: You are sitting in a chair. The chair is wood and pretty. (He lifts his hand suddenly as if he's about to strike SANDER but refrains.) I hit you across the face.

SANDER: What did I do?

ELIAS: I hit you again so you will tell me.

SANDER: Right. I get it. Okay.

SANDER tries to stand. ELIAS pushes him down more roughly this time.

ELIAS: What did you do?

SANDER: I haven't done anything.

ELIAS: Bullshit! No shit! Canada is alright!

SANDER: Right … We should go in now eh?

ELIAS: What did you do?

SANDER: Nothing.

ELIAS: I hit you again.

CALLIE: I don't like this ...

ELIAS: You are not here! I hit you again. What do you do to me?

SANDER: Noth ... I, I hit you back.

ELIAS: I am much bigger than you.

SANDER: I beat the crap out of you. Now let me get up.

ELIAS will not let SANDER move.

ELIAS: Your hands are tied behind you back. Your legs too ...

CALLIE: Quit it.

ELIAS: I am now hurting every part of you. Your back, your legs, your family. Your mouth is full of blood.

SANDER: Callie!

CALLIE: Don't touch him! Don't you go near my brother!

ELIAS: You think we are stopped? I am only starting ...

SANDER: *(terrified)* Oh Jesus. Don't. Please. Leave me alone! *(frees himself from ELIAS)*

ELIAS: This is pretending.

CALLIE: Bullshit.

ELIAS: No shit! Canada is alright!

CALLIE: You're nuts ...

ELIAS: I am helping Sander with his studies.

SANDER is stunned. Still sitting, he is afraid to look at ELIAS. CALLIE kneels in front of him.

CALLIE: Are you okay?

SANDER: Don't touch me, nobody touch me.

CALLIE: Look, I'm sorry ...

SANDER: Just keep away.

CALLIE: Let's go home.

ELIAS: I would like this. I would like to go home.

CALLIE: He wanted to help you. It wasn't just homework ...

ELIAS: I did not ask for the help of Sander.

SANDER: That isn't true.

CALLIE: *(to ELIAS)* Did that stuff happen? Did that stuff really happen to you?

ELIAS: Si quieres entender mi historia, aprende mi lengua. (If you want to know my story, then you can learn my language.)

CALLIE: What?

ELIAS: Si quieres entender mi historia, aprende mi lengua.

CALLIE: Sander? What's he talking about?

ELIAS: Quiero que pongas tu pecho en mi boca. (I want you to put your breast in my mouth.)

CALLIE: *(to ELIAS)* What are you saying to me? *(to SANDER)* What's he talking about?

SANDER: I don't understand him. I don't understand either of you.

ELIAS: Si quieres entender mi historia, aprende mi lengua!

SANDER: If you want to know his story, then you can learn his language.

SANDER exits. CALLIE is very upset but she can't leave ELIAS. She yells at SANDER who is already offstage.

CALLIE: I'm sorry.

ELIAS: Quiero que me des tu mano ... (Place your hand in mine.)

CALLIE: You know damn well I don't know what you're talking about.

ELIAS: Si quieres entender lo que digo vas ...

CALLIE: That isn't fair. You know how to talk to me.

ELIAS: Hablas español?

CALLIE: Yo soy ... Yo soy. C'mon give me a break here. I want to talk to you. We shouldn't have done that. Sander takes everything too personally.

ELIAS: No entiendo. (I don't understand.)

CALLIE: I am. Yo soy. Yo soy sorry.

ELIAS: No entiendo.

CALLIE: Yo ... yo tengo?

ELIAS: Si?

CALLIE: I am sad. (*She touches ELIAS' face, running her fingers down his cheek as though she is tracing tears.*) Sad.

ELIAS: Triste.

ELIAS kisses CALLIE.

CALLIE: Yo soy triste.

ELIAS: I understand. Estoy triste. I am sad now too.

ACT TWO

Scene One

Interior, New Year's Day, early morning. ELIAS and CALLIE are in bed.

CALLIE: Did you sleep?

ELIAS: I sleep a little.

CALLIE: I wanted to watch you sleeping.

ELIAS: Why?

CALLIE: But you were always at the window or smoking …

ELIAS: Watch me sleeping. I think I sleep like any man.

CALLIE: Can you see anything?

ELIAS: The sea.

CALLIE: Is it calm?

ELIAS: Calm?

CALLIE: Quiet.

ELIAS: Everything is quiet.

CALLIE: Does it look at all the same as down there?

ELIAS: El Salvador is very beautiful.

CALLIE: You don't think it's pretty here?

ELIAS: Oh yes but everything is very different.

CALLIE: I know what it looks like a little. I know the geology, the geography there.

ELIAS: Geografia.

CALLIE: The science of the earth's form.

ELIAS: This is the thing you study …

CALLIE: Your whole country is covered by ash. The volcano Izalco …

ELIAS: El faro del Pacifico …

CALLIE: The lighthouse of the Pacific. We could hear the bang when Mount St. Helens blew. Dad and Sander were out on the boat. I was afraid something had gone wrong. I love trying to imagine, you know, what's underneath these islands. When I was a kid I used to think the American border was this big red rope like in a bank line-up and when the draft dodgers were pardoned it had been let down forever. I want to learn everything. I want to know everything about you.

ELIAS: Do you have many boyfriends?

CALLIE: I went out with this guy Riley but that ended nearly a year ago now. And Roddy Glass. You know the story there. What about Marina? Does she write you or …

ELIAS: No.

CALLIE: When was the last time you saw her?

ELIAS: No te preocupas de Marina. (Don't worry about Marina.)

CALLIE: Did you see her after you got out of jail?

ELIAS: These are many questions.

CALLIE: How did you get out?

ELIAS: (*beat*) Avion plateado. The silver airplane is how you make your escape.

CALLIE: Is that what you did? You and your brother took a plane to …

ELIAS: To the mountains. Si.

CALLIE: Which mountains? I know how it looks …

ELIAS: Geografia … And here. (*touches CALLIE'S face*) This is my geography.

CALLIE: My face.

ELIAS positions CALLIE so that she is upright and kneeling. He then uses her body as a map; he runs his hands down CALLIE'S arms.

CALLIE: My arms.

ELIAS: North America. The head, the thinking. The strong part. This part of you is telling the other part what to do. It is telling your legs to work …

CALLIE: Yes …

ELIAS: Here. (*kisses CALLIE'S feet and legs*) South America. Underneath and working. Working for the top of you.

CALLIE: What are you talking about?

ELIAS: Your body. Geography. No?

CALLIE: Yes.

ELIAS: And here. (*puts his arms around CALLIE'S hips*) Central America. This is the asshole.

CALLIE: I don't think so …

ELIAS: Everybody very happy to screw Central America.

CALLIE: No.

ELIAS: Soy un idiota. Estaba loco a noche. (I am an idiot. I was crazy last night.)

CALLIE: What? What is it?

ELIAS: The anger. Last night the anger comes out of me.

CALLIE: But good stuff too …

ELIAS: This will never happen again. I will make apology to your brother.

CALLIE: It's not your problem. He'll just blame everything on me … (*examines ELIAS' back*) The scars on your back. All the things that have happened to you …

ELIAS: Scars? No, no. They are … enfermedad, viruela … pox.

CALLIE: Chicken pox? Oh. What were you like when you were little?

ELIAS: I don't know, Callie. Bad and lazy and loving to play. Just a boy.

CALLIE: Say something. Say something to me in Spanish.

ELIAS: Pienso que deberias volver a tu cuarto …

CALLIE: What? What does it mean?

ELIAS: I think you should go back to your room.

CALLIE: Why?

ELIAS: This must be kept away from your father. Your brother and grand …

CALLIE: It doesn't matter. Riley used to spend the weekends here.

ELIAS: Riley does not look like me. Riley does not live in this house.

CALLIE: You didn't want this. You didn't want this to happen.

ELIAS: I want and wanted. I wanted you. Pienso que deberias volver a tu cuarto. Good bye, Callie.

CALLIE: What happened last night with you and Sander, that isn't something you should feel bad about. You can't keep everything hidden inside …

ELIAS: Go back to your room.

CALLIE: What happened between you and me isn't a bad thing either.

ELIAS: You and me. Volve a tu cuarto …

CALLIE: I don't want to.

ELIAS: Please go.

Scene Two

Interior, later the same morning.

MARTHA: Do you remember the wave after the Alaskan earthquake?

SANDER: I wasn't born. Have you seen Callie or Elias?

MARTHA: No I haven't. It put our row-boat in the rose garden and it completely demolished the town pier.

SANDER: This isn't a tidal wave, Grandma. It's just a bunch of brown crud that washed up on the beach last night. Did you hear them come in?

MARTHA: Weren't you with them?

SANDER: They stayed out later.

MARTHA: Reg wouldn't move that boat back. For ten years, everyone that came to our house heard about the earthquake, something that happened thousands of miles away that made our row-boat land in the garden …

SANDER: There's a sailboat from Seattle at the government wharf. They probably dumped something.

MARTHA: It just made me sad. Every time I'd see that silly old thing rotting out there in the bushes I'd think of all those Alaskans being swallowed up by the earth …

SANDER: Or maybe it's from a tanker …

MARTHA: I can't see anything.

SANDER: Well it's there on the shore. It looks like brown soap. An American tanker …

MARTHA: When Reg died I chopped that old boat up and put it in the trash. The past is past.

SANDER: Where's Dad?

MARTHA: He went into Horseshoe Bay first thing.

SANDER: Why?

MARTHA: I don't know. Maybe he's got a girl there. Do you think?

SANDER: No.

MARTHA: I wish Owen would date more. He was seeing that Evelyn, the pot thrower, but that's nearly two years ago now.

SANDER: Evelyn was alright. I hate this. I hate never knowing where anyone is. Communication in this house is at an all time low.

MARTHA: Well. Someone woke up with a chip on their shoulder.

SANDER: I woke up clear, Grandma. I'm a new man.

MARTHA: That Evelyn made me a tea pot. It had two spouts and you couldn't make a cup of tea in it for love or money. So I put it on the mantel. It's a wonder the whole mantel didn't come down.

SANDER: You should learn Spanish.

MARTHA: Why?

SANDER: So you can know what's going on. Everyone in this house should.

MARTHA: We don't have many Spaniards in Oregon.

SANDER: They're not called Spaniards, all the Spanish speaking people in this world are not Spaniards.

MARTHA: Five years ago I was in the dog house because I couldn't speak French.

CALLIE: (enters) Hi.

MARTHA: (to CALLIE) You and your little friend would come down to visit and pretend you were from Quebec City.

CALLIE: (to SANDER) Hi. (pause)

SANDER: You see the shit all over the beach?

CALLIE: Where?

SANDER: C'mon, Cal, it's everywhere. Open your eyes.

CALLIE: Everything looks the same as ever to me.

SANDER: Well, it isn't.

CALLIE: You okay?

SANDER: Oh yeah. I'm a freak of nature; I'm happy all the time.

MARTHA: Sander's decided to start this year off contrary …

CALLIE: I know it wasn't …

SANDER: What?

CALLIE: I know it wasn't all selfish, you bringing Elias here …

SANDER: She's the one who should feel bad.

CALLIE: Grandma? What's she got to do with this?

MARTHA: I stayed in last night and watched television. I didn't whoop and holler out on the dock half the night …

SANDER: You should go right down to his room and say you're sorry.

MARTHA: Whose room?

SANDER: Elias.

CALLIE: What's with you?

MARTHA: I consider Elias to be a friend. I have certainly never had a falling out with him, never heard him get lippy …

SANDER: It's your government, Grandma! Yours. They're behind everything down there. It's the Americans who are responsible for his going to jail, his being tortured, his having to run away …

CALLIE: He hasn't … been …

MARTHA: Elias is my friend. And in his country, young man, grandmothers are a respected commodity.

SANDER: He should hate your guts …

MARTHA: I would no sooner cause him harm than myself or you or your sister.

SANDER: Why do you keep voting for them?

MARTHA: Who's them? Huey Angus the mayor? And we've got a Democrat in …

SANDER: I hate them. I hate Americans. They're just such liars. They're all overweight big-mouth right-wing fanatical religious nuts except they're too stupid to even know it …

CALLIE: He's mad at me. This is nothing to do with …

MARTHA: Just who do you think your mother and father are? Where do you think you come from?

CALLIE: This has nothing to do with you, Grandma …

MARTHA: Where do you think you come from?

SANDER: Here! I was born here!

CALLIE: I'm sorry, Sander. Okay?

SANDER: I am not, repeat, not an American!

MARTHA: You should be ashamed of yourself.

ELIAS enters.

SANDER: I was born here.

ELIAS: Do not yell at the grandma.

SANDER: Don't you ever tell me what to do.

MARTHA: You owe me an apology. You should bow your head in shame. (*exits*)

CALLIE: Grandma … Jesus Christ, Sander. What do you think you're doing?

ELIAS: (*to SANDER*) Buenos dias.

SANDER: It's more her fault than ours.

CALLIE: What? Is someone trying to blame someone here?

SANDER: He is. It's not my fault for saving his life.

ELIAS: Quiero hablar de lo que paso anoche. Sander? (I wish to talk to you of last night.)

SANDER: I don't understand you.

ELIAS: Dije que quiero hablar con …

SANDER: What?

ELIAS: Quiero … I wish to talk of last night. (*pause*) Do you wish me to go from your house?

CALLIE: No! We all just had too much beer …

ELIAS: Sander?

SANDER: Where are you going to go? This is it for you. The last stop. Like it or not, this is home.

ELIAS: Thank you very much.

CALLIE: (*to ELIAS*) Stop thanking people all the time. It's unnatural … (*to SANDER*) You made Grandma cry.

ELIAS: I go to her. I go to Grandma. (*exits*)

CALLIE: God, Sander. What's with you?

SANDER: Listen.

CALLIE: You're acting like a little dictator.

SANDER: Cal, listen to me. I saw him last night.

CALLIE: Who?

SANDER: Elias. I saw him up close.

CALLIE: So did I.

SANDER: He put something in me. Something so sour from inside him.

CALLIE: No he didn't …

SANDER: He's full of poison.

CALLIE: Look, people who've been through stuff like he has …

SANDER: I know. Trying to help them is ridiculous. He's doomed. He was doomed way before he ever got here. And I've read about this stuff …

CALLIE: You got it all backwards, Sander.

SANDER: We shouldn't have done this. I shouldn't have brought him here. People who've been tortured—it's all business as usual then all of a sudden—snap.

CALLIE: Last night he opened up, just a crack. And now you're making him pay through the teeth for it …

SANDER: I mean, we hardly know anything about him or what he's been through, what he could do. How come he got out of prison? What did he do to get out?

CALLIE: The scars on his back … He says it's chicken pox.

SANDER: Right. So last night he was showing me what it was like to have chicken pox. You turned on me, Callie. You made that all happen. You should keep away from him.

CALLIE: It was just fooling around …

SANDER: He scared me.

CALLIE: We can help him.

SANDER: You're crazy.

CALLIE: When I look at him it's like this chance to change the whole world.

SANDER: When I look at him I wish we'd never brought him here.

CALLIE: A chance to set things right.

SANDER: Exactly. That's what he wants, that's why he's in our house. He wants to get even.

Scene Three

Six weeks later, exterior.

ELIAS: El Salvador is not maybe going to war. It is not maybe going to war in another country. It is not the same …

OWEN: I didn't say it was the same.

ELIAS: El Salvador is at war. At war inside herself.

OWEN: Itself.

ELIAS: Hitting herself. Itself.

OWEN: I don't think you followed what I was saying …

ELIAS: I follow good.

OWEN: Get things straightened out at your English course and you'll understand a whole lot better.

ELIAS: Do not change the words for me. Continue please.

OWEN: There was just this time, this time between getting my draft notice and coming to Canada. Everything was very sharp, defined. Instant overview. Made the food taste better and women … man. You put all that on top of really getting to know women for the first time and it was incredible. You know when the sea goes crazy? Comes right up over the breakwater? There's something so great about that. We're all longing to be threatened. We're all longing to be threatened again by the natural world. Cal knows that. She's very in tune with old mother earth.

ELIAS: Yes she is …

OWEN: Sander of course used to wet the bed worrying about earthquakes. Are you hearing anything from your people down there? In El Salvador?

ELIAS: Some of them yes.

OWEN: And they're fine?

ELIAS: Some of them yes. Fine thank you.

OWEN: How do they feel about your having to come here? To Canada?

ELIAS: Fine thank you.

OWEN: Did you understand my question?

ELIAS: Fine … They are sad. Grandma, she is sad too when you leave her house.

OWEN: My mother? That's what she told you?

ELIAS: She tells you run but her heart is sad when you go …

OWEN: Well, that's a long time ago now …

ELIAS: She is very good, your mother.

OWEN: I burnt my draft notice. There was this group of us, we went to Portland for the afternoon. This very big deal demonstration. It made the news. When I get home that night all my stuff has been packed up, stacked neatly by the front door. My room is bare, pictures off the wall, little league trophies cleared away. Even the bed is stripped.

ELIAS: They are helping you to leave?

OWEN: I don't exist anymore. Even the air reeks of disinfectant, they're getting rid of the stink. Not one trace. Her and the old man are eating dinner. They won't even look up from their plates. I'm asking what the hell is going on and all they give me is silence. Both of them. Now I know damn well this is all his idea but she's not saying a word. That means she's nodding approval. It's A-okay. Turn up the juice.

ELIAS: A-okay. But your mother is a friend to you now ...

OWEN: She helped out with the kids when Catherine left. It was a pretty rough time.

ELIAS: For you she goes against her husband ...

OWEN: He was dead. ... So. Your English teacher says you're not there half the time and when you are you're asleep.

ELIAS: My English is okay.

OWEN: I couldn't give a damn whether you go or not. But if you don't go to your English class, C.E.I.C. doesn't pay. Period.

ELIAS: Canada Employment si. Que se joda la C.E.I.C. Los puercos in Manpower ... I look for a job.

OWEN: You don't have to yet ... That's the point of this program: Skills Development.

ELIAS: I have found a job for next week. I do not go back for the English.

OWEN: Where?

ELIAS: Pizza 222-2222.

OWEN: Oh Christ ...

ELIAS: I clean their house in the morning.

OWEN: Whose house?

ELIAS: Pizza 222 ...

OWEN: You're making a hundred dollars a week to study English. What's the rush?

ELIAS: I am an assistant-manager trainee.

OWEN: Well you can tell your manager to go screw his job and ...

ELIAS: He is a good man, the manager. He is a chemist from Somalia. I pay them back.

OWEN: Who?

ELIAS: (producing letter from his coat) The government, Immigration. ... I am in debt to them.

OWEN: (reading) Your plane ticket ...

ELIAS: I am pay them back for the airplane. Guatemala City to Vancouver. It is a lot of money.

OWEN: They're asking when you can start paying. You can pay them as little as ten dollars a month if that's all you can afford ...

ELIAS: They are your friends at the C.E.I.C.?

OWEN: No, they're not my friends ...

ELIAS: The man at there talks to you on his machine?

OWEN: What machine?

ELIAS: I talk to him. I have the interview and he turns on the little tape machine.

OWEN: A dictaphone ...

ELIAS: Who does he talk to?

OWEN: I don't know. He's probably just, you know, making a memo to your file. Maybe telling his secretary to write a letter.

ELIAS: To who?

OWEN: It's just paper work. I wouldn't worry about it ...

ELIAS: I have read the paper. They are very angry here with the refugees. Go home Tamil! Go home Iran! I have read these things. How do we go?

OWEN: Slow down. Nobody is going to make you go anywhere. Legally, whatever, they're not allowed to.

ELIAS: I have no other place to go. Eleven countries I am apply to before Canada ...

SANDER enters.

OWEN: I will see to it personally. You are not going to be made to leave ...

ELIAS: Ecuador, Columbia, Panama ...

OWEN: And you don't have to work until you finish English. You don't have to pay back the plane ticket until you have a job. You don't have to move from here until you're ready. You got all that?

ELIAS: Si …

OWEN: And I've got a big contract with fisheries this spring tagging fish. You can work on the boat if you want, with us. Right, Sander? I count and mark the fish. We put this silver tag on their fins.

ELIAS: Why?

OWEN: So we can see where they're going. It'll be good to have another hand. Eh Sander?

SANDER: It's pretty crowded already.

OWEN: Then maybe Elias can do the first contract. You'll still have classes then. Or exams. You should be into exams by then.

SANDER: I'm finished.

ELIAS: You follow the fish.

OWEN: Sort of. And I pay a lot better than Pizza-Pizza.

ELIAS: You should kill the fish.

OWEN: They come down from Alaska to spawn and we keep track of how many stay here, and how many make it down to Juan de Fuca, to the States.

ELIAS: You wish to know the nationality of a fish.

OWEN: Right. We don't start until April so you can finish English.

SANDER: I said I'm finished school.

OWEN: What?

SANDER: I withdrew.

ELIAS: You should kill the fish.

OWEN: You've flunked out.

SANDER: I withdrew …

ELIAS: You would make more monies if you kill the fish.

OWEN: I usually kill the fish!

ELIAS exits.

SANDER: It's just a "W" on my transcript. It doesn't mean anything.

OWEN: Oh. I'm glad it doesn't mean anything. For a while there I thought we were in serious trouble. When did this happen?

SANDER: I don't know. Two weeks ago. This first aid stuff is taking up a lot of my time.

OWEN: Right.

SANDER: I'm doing okay at it. It's easier than I thought.

OWEN: Glad to hear it, Sander. I wouldn't want you straining any muscles or exercising your brain …

SANDER: College. I mean it was all crap, Dad. All the other students, I didn't know how to talk to anyone. They're all just pre-law, pre-business, pre-historic morons …

OWEN: Some poor son-of-a-bitch like Elias—he must be appalled by the privileges you have, the choices.

SANDER: Then let him fish the whole season.

OWEN: You bring Elias all the way up here and now you ignore him too. Withdrawn.

SANDER: I'll have my first aid ticket. You can pull your Captain Ahab routine with him.

OWEN: Fine.

SANDER: And the forest industry pays a lot better than you.

OWEN: Alright. You've got no worries then.

SANDER: That's right.

OWEN: Nothing keeping you awake at night.

SANDER: Nothing.

OWEN: What is it you care about, Sander? What's important?

SANDER: Nothing.

OWEN: Whole goddamned planet's dying! What are you going to do about it, Sander?

SANDER: Nothing.

OWEN exits. Light remains on SANDER.

Scene Four

Interior, six weeks later. CALLIE and ELIAS in bed.

CALLIE: Do you ever dream you can't speak? Maybe I'm with Dad on the boat and something really terrible will happen if I can't warn him. But my throat is full of concrete. Only little noises come out, like a bird.

SANDER'S light goes out. He exits.

ELIAS: I do not dream.

CALLIE: That's because you never sleep …

ELIAS: And that, Callie, is because you will not let me. Always you are coming to my room.

CALLIE: Tell me not to.

ELIAS: This is a hard thing.

CALLIE: Exactly. It's snowing again. Snow in April.

ELIAS: I like the snow.

CALLIE: Coming in from the north. Maybe it will travel all the way to El Salvador. Big clouds of snow.

ELIAS: I don't think so.

CALLIE: It'll cover up the cities, the mountains …

ELIAS: We do never have snow in Salvador.

CALLIE: The layers of ash … What scares you more than anything?

ELIAS: Many things have scared me.

CALLIE: The most scared you've been, ever.

ELIAS: When I hear the knock on the door, softly …

CALLIE: Yes?

ELIAS: And there you are, back in my room.

CALLIE: I'm serious.

ELIAS: And I wish to talk of the snow.

CALLIE: Will you miss me?

ELIAS: Yes of course.

CALLIE: I miss you already. Only three more days. I wish you weren't going.

ELIAS: This is a good thing, working on your father's boat.

CALLIE: Yeah well, just wait until you've been cooped up out there for a month with Dad and a bunch of dead fish.

ELIAS: We do not kill the fish.

CALLIE: Dead or alive they all stink and Dad's a pain in the ass.

ELIAS: And what scares you the most?

CALLIE: More than anything?

ELIAS: Yes.

CALLIE: Drunk people. People so pissed their eyes roll back in their head and you can't, you know, reason with them.

ELIAS: You have drunk people in your family?

CALLIE: No, no … just guys I've gone out with, that sort of thing.

ELIAS: Yes you do have many boyfriends.

CALLIE: No I don't.

ELIAS: Pretend the drunk man you are afraid of is under the bed or behind the door, is there in your room, always.

CALLIE: That's terrible.

ELIAS: And when you close your eyes he is there also. He never goes away, ever.

CALLIE: The people that put you in prison, they …

ELIAS: No. I am talking about a different thing. I am talking about a big fear in my country that you would not know of.

CALLIE: But I want to know. How can I understand the things that have happened to you if you won't tell me?

ELIAS: They are good things to leave behind.

CALLIE: Look at your scars. They're whiter at night, nearly silver …

ELIAS: Plateado, enfermedad, pox.

CALLIE: Bullshit.

ELIAS: No shit, Canada is alright … avion plateado.

CALLIE: The silver airplane.

ELIAS: In my prison there is an old kitchen. On the ceiling a silver wheel with a rope … una maquina … (a machine)

CALLIE: A winch.

ELIAS: We are take to this room to wait for the avion plateado. When the guard comes my brother's hands are put behind his back and legs and like this he is hung from the winch. Avion plateado. It is my brother that is the silver airplane …

CALLIE: But you said …

ELIAS: And the guard asks him do you wish to fly with or without a piloto …

CALLIE: A pilot.

ELIAS: Without he says. He swings my brother so hard his head is hit and hit and hit and hit into the wall and he tells him an airplane that flies without a pilot always will … choquar (*makes crash sound*) …

CALLIE: Crash …

ELIAS: By the time it is dark he has finished breathing. Then it is my turn. I cry that I wish to fly with a pilot. The guard laughs: "Yo soy el piloto—I am the pilot." The guard climbs onto my back. My arms break. My skins open. My eyes close.

CALLIE: (*pause*) I'm sorry.

ELIAS: This is my story. What is it you wish to do with it now?

CALLIE: To … I don't know.

ELIAS: What? This is the thing you have been wanting. No?

CALLIE: Let me hold you.

ELIAS: This is not what I wish.

CALLIE: Your other brother. Is he in danger too?

ELIAS: Everyone is in danger.

CALLIE: Let me help them or …

ELIAS: Eso es imposible.

CALLIE: Then let me help you forget.

ELIAS: This is not a true thing you are wanting.

CALLIE: I love you.

ELIAS: No Callie.

CALLIE: Yes I do.

ELIAS: You love these terrible things that I remember.

Scene Five

Interior, a couple of days later.

MARTHA: Now every spring I'd go around door to door collecting everyone's old eyeglasses. The church would send them to Africa. They used to send them to the Eskimos but the Eskimos are modern now. Remember that, Sander.

SANDER: The Eskimos are modern …

MARTHA: Remember to always do something extra. You should be proud of your sister. She's learned from your example.

SANDER: What'd she do?

MARTHA: She's formed a group, just like you did for Elias.

SANDER: She has?

MARTHA: Only this time it's for his brother. And she's left papers for me to sign somewhere. I'm joining her group to bring him here …

SANDER: Did you sign, Dad?

OWEN: Of course I signed.

MARTHA: (*to OWEN*) Do you think your signature on something will help or hurt Callie's efforts?

OWEN: What's that supposed to mean?

MARTHA: Those terrible letters, all those terrible letters that you used to write to the draft board.

OWEN: I was expressing my world view.

MARTHA: Threatening to blow up Fort Lewis. What was the use? Writing nasty letters with no return address. Your father, Sander, in his day, was quite the character.

SANDER: I know.

MARTHA: The FBI used to visit us. Your grandfather would have a holy fit. Getting me to make tea. Reg would even offer them salmon to take home from the freezer. Now if your father stayed in college he wouldn't have been drafted, wouldn't have had to run off to Canada.

OWEN: And you'd have nothing to complain about.

MARTHA: Oh blow me up, Owen! Blow up me and the Pentagon and the whole country. I am guilty on all counts. I didn't breast feed, I'm an American citizen, a senior ...

OWEN: Nobody wants to blow you up, Mom.

SANDER: And I'm not going to be drafted for withdrawing ...

OWEN: Quitting.

SANDER: Withdrawing from college. You told stuff about Dad to the FBI?

MARTHA: No sir, I did not.

SANDER: Good for you, Grandma.

OWEN: Not the old man though. He'd have put on his old uniform and signed up if that's what they wanted.

MARTHA: That's not true, Owen. Reg never said a word about your whereabouts or ...

OWEN: That's because he didn't know where we'd gone. I couldn't trust him. Couldn't trust my own father.

MARTHA: Poor Sander here was eight months old before we even knew he existed. The underground—Lord. I used to worry Sander'd been born in a gopher hole. I'd think of you, Owen, six years old trying to dig a hole to China in the front yard. "Check there," I'd tell Agent Beatty. This did not go over well with Reg or the FBI.

CALLIE: (enters) Elias back yet?

OWEN: He's still in town. He'd better not miss the last ferry. We leave the dock tomorrow at five a.m. sharp. You sure you don't want to change your mind, Sander?

SANDER: I have an interview.

OWEN: For what?

SANDER: A job, you know, industrial first aid.

OWEN: Where?

SANDER: In this logging camp near Gold River. Just until June.

OWEN: You finished this first aid thing?

SANDER: Sort of ...

OWEN: Here we go ...

SANDER: I still have to do the exam.

OWEN: You didn't quit or ...

SANDER: I'm doing okay.

MARTHA: Good for you, Sander. Maybe you'll be a doctor one day. Or a nurse.

OWEN: So I guess you'll be going away from home then?

SANDER: It's just an interview, Dad. I don't have the job or anything.

MARTHA: I could see Sander as a nurse.

CALLIE: Me too.

OWEN: I can't wait to get back to work. All this sitting around in the winter makes me crazy.

CALLIE: Dad? In two weeks, when you're around Campbell River, I might come up for the weekend.

OWEN: Why?

CALLIE: I thought the boat was family property, we're all in this together.

OWEN: You've just always hated it ...

SANDER: Where're you gonna sleep?

CALLIE: With Elias. Is there any supper left?

OWEN: Pardon me?

MARTHA: You can't do that ...

CALLIE: I love him.

MARTHA: I love him too, honey but ...

CALLIE: No, Grandma, I love him. I sleep with him, you know, we make love.

SANDER: I don't believe this ...

OWEN: How long has this been going on, Cal?

CALLIE: I don't know. A couple of months maybe ...

SANDER: Since New Year's Eve.

CALLIE: Yeah, New Year's Eve to be more specific.

SANDER: I knew it ...

MARTHA: Do you know about birth control?

SANDER: Grandma ...

MARTHA: It's a good question! And safety. Safety sex.

OWEN: Yeah she knows all about it.

CALLIE: What's your problem, Dad?

OWEN: Did I say I have a problem?

CALLIE: How come it was no sweat when Riley stayed here. Or Evelyn or Sofie …

MARTHA: Who's Sofie?

OWEN: One thing at a time here …

CALLIE: He loves me.

OWEN: You should take it slow, Cal. He comes from a whole different place, a whole other set of rules.

CALLIE: I know that.

SANDER: Maybe he'll want to fight a duel with Roddy Glass. It's very macho, Central America.

CALLIE: Shut up, Sander.

SANDER: Or marry you.

CALLIE: He's been living right in the middle of a war. He hasn't exactly had a great life. You could show a little compassion, Sander. All of you could.

MARTHA: I like Elias.

SANDER: I didn't know being in a war made somebody a great guy.

OWEN: Sander, you're way out of line.

SANDER: I brought him here.

CALLIE: Do you want him to say thank you every day of the week?

SANDER: I want you to admit, admit it, Callie, that he was a shit to me.

OWEN: What did he do?

SANDER: And you too. You set the whole thing up, you let that happen. And now you're in love. That's great. The two of you deserve each other …

OWEN: Sander …

SANDER: You don't know anything about it, Dad.

OWEN: I have some sort of idea of how he might be feeling.

MARTHA: When your grandfather came home from the war …

OWEN: Oh Jesus. Here we go …

MARTHA: You listen to me, Owen. Your father (pause) … he had seen, he had participated in some things that I believe were unspeakable. Terrible things.

OWEN: Why would someone who'd been through such awful things be so anxious for their kid to go through the same thing?

MARTHA: Maybe it was a way of letting you in …

OWEN: I would walk through hell for Sander. If I thought someone was going to harm him or hurt him in any way. That is slightly different than getting Sander to walk through hell for me.

CALLIE: (pause) Did Grandpa talk to you about the war? About all that stuff?

MARTHA: No. But you'd know he was thinking about it, even years later when he was home safe and sound.

CALLIE: How?

MARTHA: Well, he'd do odd things.

SANDER: Elias does odd things.

MARTHA: He'd finally get around to filling in the potholes on the driveway but it would be four in the morning and raining. There he'd be. Out there in his pajamas and overcoat, digging and grading in the black of night.

CALLIE: You wouldn't ask him about it?

MARTHA: You can't get inside someone's skin, Callie. I think I tried to do that when we were first married. But those things were, well, they were his. People don't always work things out. Young people don't know that. Isn't that strange? Young people don't know that at all … I want to sign the form to help Elias' brother. I want to help.

CALLIE: It's here.

SANDER: Grandma can't sign. You've got to be a Canadian citizen or landed.

MARTHA: Landed! I'm landed. What on earth is that supposed to mean?

OWEN: You're still in orbit, Mom. Same old track, round and round.

MARTHA: Well, I can give some money.

OWEN: (to SANDER) Are you going to sign?

SANDER: No.

OWEN: No?

CALLIE: What an asshole, Sander …

SANDER: You're all so phoney about him.

CALLIE: I love him.

SANDER: He's taking money from Grandma, he took my job on the boat and now he's screwing Callie and that's all just fine. It's all so phoney.

CALLIE: It is not screwing …

SANDER: You invent stuff. He's just another foreign guy in a ski jacket. He wants a big car and …

OWEN: (handing him the envelope) Read this. Try remembering all the reasons you brought Elias here in the first place.

SANDER: I know all about sponsorship. I know how good you feel when you're filling out the goddamn forms. I also know it was the most dumbfuck thing I ever did in my life.

MARTHA: Sander!

OWEN: Read Callie's reasons for bringing his brother here. They're good.

SANDER: I tried to be a friend to him. He hasn't been fair to me.

OWEN: This isn't about making friends. It's about saving lives.

SANDER: It's sealed.

CALLIE: It can't be. Elias hasn't filled out his part yet.

SANDER: (opens envelope and reads) Yes he has.

MARTHA: Elias is kind. I would consider it a privilege to help his family.

CALLIE: Thanks, Grandma.

SANDER: How come Elias' brother has a different last name than him?

CALLIE: He doesn't.

SANDER: And his first name's Marina.

OWEN: Marina?

MARTHA: Who's that?

SANDER: He wants to bring her here. He wants to bring his real girlfriend here behind everyone's back.

CALLIE: Marina …

Scene Six

Interior, a couple of hours later. SANDER has been waiting up for ELIAS in Elias' room.

ELIAS: Hola Sander.

SANDER: Hola fuckhead.

ELIAS: Fuckhead? Okay fuckhead hello. I am at Park Royal. I have bought rubber boots for the fishing.

SANDER: Gumboots.

ELIAS: Gumboots?

SANDER: Any word from Marina?

ELIAS: Marina …

SANDER: Marina Martinez?

ELIAS: Tienes noticias de Marina? (There is word of Marina?)

SANDER: How stupid do you think we are? Did you think she'd just walk off the plane one day and Grandma would set an extra place for supper?

ELIAS: Please tell me if you have heard from Marina.

SANDER: I mean lying like that.

ELIAS: I don't understand …

SANDER: You're a liar! (pushes ELIAS)

ELIAS: When I leave Salvador my leaving puts Marina in an even bigger danger. Please …

SANDER: And Callie's got feelings too, you know. You hurt her.

ELIAS: I am sorry. I do not mean to make a hurt to Callie.

SANDER: When Mum left, Cal kept weapons in her bed. A rock, a stick, this old umbrella. No one was ever going to hurt her.

ELIAS: But if you have heard of news of Marina I am asking you to tell me please!

SANDER: Cal hasn't even filed the sponsorship yet. It'll take years.

ELIAS: Years …

SANDER: You know that. I knew who you were way over a year ago. I knew your name. There's this office in a church in Vancouver. A cardboard box full of files. All these names, all the people in danger. I chose you. I chose your name.

ELIAS: Why my name Elias?

SANDER: Your name (beat) talked to me. I invented the place you were from: this little village in the mountains. I'd try to imagine your day and …

ELIAS: San Salvador is big like Vancouver.

SANDER: I wished something good for you every morning. First thing. I'd wish for your safety and then I'd wish something so you wouldn't give up hoping. Maybe something that tasted good. Maybe a good dream. Something that would keep you going. It was the best thing I ever did. You turned on me. You tried to put your hate inside me. You lied to me, you lied to my family. That name in the box turned on me.

ELIAS: Venenos. Venenos adentro de mi.

SANDER: English.

ELIAS: Poison, bad stories live inside me. I try. I am try very hard to not let the bad dream go outside me.

SANDER: This whole thing just got so messed up …

ELIAS: The name in the box in the church. The name is now Marina. Make the name talk to you. The name goes into you and you will wish her one good thing everyday. Do you like her name? If you do not like her name there are also the names of others. Miguel, Alberto, Theresa, Juan … You do not have to pretend the place they live. I can tell you these things. Sander? Marina is small. She comes from the north. Let me tell you her house. Marina. Let her name talk to you. Let me tell you her voice, her hair, her eyes, her skin …

SANDER comforts ELIAS.

Scene Seven

Exterior, six weeks later.

MARTHA: (*sings*)
They've hushed the singing in the village,
All is quiet beneath the stars,
Amigo sings Hasta Luega …

CALLIE: (*comes up under MARTHA*) Gabriola, Cortes, Galiano, Valdez …

MARTHA: Upon his lonely blue guitar.

CALLIE: I always thought the names were fancier than the islands themselves. Very lady-like.

MARTHA: What names?

CALLIE: Saturna, Texada … the names of these islands. Like a piece of lace dropped over the same old rocks and trees.

MARTHA: (*referring to envelope at CALLIE'S feet*) What's this, Cal? Is there news?

CALLIE: I don't know.

MARTHA: You haven't even opened it.

CALLIE: Sander and I used to think all the islands went all the way to the south pole … None of the Spanish explorers stuck around here. Why do you suppose that was?

MARTHA: You owe it to Elias. He'll be anxious for any word …

CALLIE: I don't owe him anything.

MARTHA: And they're still out fishing for another week …

CALLIE: I tried, Grandma. I wanted to listen.

MARTHA: I know, sweetheart.

CALLIE: He wouldn't trust me. He can't trust anyone. And it's only been a month since I filed the sponsorship. It takes Immigration a month to answer the phone. Central America is made up of a series of shifting plates. Did you know that?

MARTHA: Well I don't think Immigration would write to you just for the fun of it.

CALLIE: No wonder it's so screwed up. They're all walking on eggshells. You open it … (*MARTHA opens the letter and reads.*) Sander thought that once we were big enough we could walk and row and sail and follow the islands all the way to South America. He wanted to visit the people that lived underneath the world …

MARTHA: "The proposed sponsorship of Marina Martinez has been declined."

CALLIE: She can't come? Why?

MARTHA: They can't find her. Well, maybe no news is good news.

CALLIE: I don't think so …

MARTHA: You try again then, Callie, or phone them. Maybe you filled out her name wrong or …

CALLIE: I never meant her any harm. We better get in touch with the boat, with Elias.

MARTHA: People don't just disappear.

CALLIE: Yes, Grandma, they do.

Light remains on CALLIE and MARTHA. Another light comes up on ELIAS. He is kneeling before his empty bed.

Epilogue

ELIAS: What I sleep is my own.
I am in my bed, in my room and there are no countries.
There is no language to sleep.
This is a true thing to all peoples.
Do you see the girl in my bed?
It is too dark. You must touch to see her.
Her arms break, her eyes close.
She is gone. Desaparecido, disappeared.
Do you want it?
Do you have a place to put her story?

MARTHA: (*comforts CALLIE*) Oh mercy. Oh mercy me.

END

JUDITH THOMPSON (b. 1954)

Nothing else in the Canadian theatre really prepares us for the strange and savage intensity of Judith Thompson's world. Her characters wear their psyches and their emotions on their sleeves. They talk about and sometimes act out—"really" or in their minds, although often we can't be sure of the distinction—their deepest insecurities, fantasies and fears. They live on the edge of madness, and sometimes over the edge. All Thompson's plays explore what she calls "the huge chasm" between the rational, everyday self we like to think comprises our life and the dangerous, primeval places where so much of our real life goes on. At the same time her characters are often in desperate search of something like spiritual grace or salvation. A lapsed Catholic and daughter of a psychology professor, Thompson infuses her characters with an obsessive need to reconcile the innate violence of their unconscious life—the animal, the dark side, or whatever other metaphors she uses for the Freudian id—with their equally profound pull toward some unnameable, transcendent pole of experience. All this is forged in a language remarkable for its vivid colloquial qualities and haunting imagery. Considered by many the most exciting playwright in the English-Canadian theatre, she has written in *Lion in the Streets* perhaps her most powerful and disturbing play.

Born in Montreal, Thompson grew up in Kingston, Ontario. She attended Catholic schools and by age eleven was acting in plays directed by her mother, an English teacher. After a B.A. at Queen's University (1976), where her father was head of the psychology department, she went on to the acting program at Montreal's National Theatre School. There, during a summer job as a social worker with adult protective services, Thompson met a mentally handicapped woman on whom she modelled a character she began to perform in her mask class. Writing monologues to develop the character, Theresa, Thompson eventually built a play around her. After graduating theatre school in 1979 and acting for a year, she premiered *The Crackwalker* at Theatre Passe Muraille in 1980.

This remarkable first play scrapes the lower depths of Kingston where two couples struggle to construct normal lives for themselves in the face of severe disabilities: mental limitations, abuse, environmental degradation, and their own irrational terrors. Superficially naturalistic, *The Crackwalker*, like all Thompson's plays, continually fractures its own realist surface with a kind of psycho-surrealism. Often in monologues, the characters' deepest fears break through into their language, a vulgar, supercharged colloquial language that is one of the great strengths of Thompson's dramaturgy. The play also embodies Thompson's spiritual impulse. Theresa, "sucking off queers down the Lido for five bucks," is perceived by her boyfriend as the Madonna, and that perception transforms her. Though degraded in nearly every way, she appears late in the play described by a stage direction as "reminiscent of Cassandra in *The Trojan Women*." *The Crackwalker* had only moderate success in its Toronto debut, but in 1982 a highly praised production by Montreal's Centaur Theatre, subsequently remounted in Toronto, garnered rave reviews. The play has since been produced across the country and abroad.

White Biting Dog (1983), first performed at Tarragon Theatre, which has since premiered each of Thompson's new plays, won the Governor General's Award for Drama. The play concerns young Cape Race who is saved from suicide by a dog who gives him a mission: he must save his dying father's life by reconciling his father and his adulterous mother. Cape's attempt to regenerate himself and the family with the help of a strange, psychic young woman named Pony ends with mixed results. The play's themes of the quest for grace and the problematic nature of love and home recur throughout Thompson's work.

Thompson wrote and developed *I Am Yours* while playwright-in-residence at the Tarragon, winning the Chalmers New Play Award for 1987. It explores with an almost hallucinatory intensity the ramifications of human attachment suggested by its title: the deep desire to be loved and possessed, the psychic damage that can be caused by that desire's remaining unrealized, and the costs of possession itself. Battles rage between sisters, husbands and wives, children and their living and dead parents, as well as an unborn/newborn child and those who claim it as their own. The play's subsequent productions included a Québécois translation in Montreal titled *Je suis à toi*. Also in 1987 her CBC radio play *Tornado* won the ACTRA Award for Best Radio Drama. The powerful story of an epileptic woman on welfare who is conned by a middle-class social worker into giving up her newborn, *Tornado* was collected along with *The Crackwalker* and *I Am Yours* in a volume titled *The Other Side of the Dark* (1989), which garnered Thompson her second Governor General's Award. Another radio drama, *White Sand* (1991), a study of racist demagoguery, won the B'nai B'rith Media Human Rights Award.

Thompson herself directed the premiere of *Lion in the Streets* in 1990, winning another Chalmers. A French version, *Lion dans les rues*, played Montreal in 1991. She has never stopped rewriting the play: the version printed here, for example, contains a newly revised Sherry-Edward scene and, following it, a new alternate scene involving Ben and his mother. Thompson adapted and directed *Hedda Gabler* at the Shaw Festival in 1991, then returned to the Tarragon with *Sled* (1997), a play about innocence and loss set in the Canadian North, featuring a kidnapping, three murders, ghosts, pornography, the Northern Lights, and the usual Thompsonian possibility of redemption. In *Perfect Pie* (2000) two childhood friends from rural Ontario re-unite in middle age, their lives having taken very different turns. As the women recall their younger selves, the play flashes back and forth, weaving social ostracism and brutality, epilepsy, a train crash and pie-baking.

Thompson's forays into screenwriting include co-authoring a study of domestic violence, *Life with Billy* (1994), for CBC-TV, and adapting Susan Swan's novel about a girls' boarding school, *The Wives of Bath*, for the feature film *Lost and Delirious* (2000), directed by Léa Pool. A mother of five children, Thompson has taught in the faculty of drama at the University of Guelph since 1993.

In interviews Thompson frequently employs vivid physical metaphors of invasion and possession to describe her creative processes and the plays that emerge from them. An idea enters her unconscious "the same way a disease begins … and starts to reproduce itself in the nucleus of your cells." Developing characters involves her "stepping into the[ir] blood." She imagines her own mild epilepsy as "a screen door swinging between the unconscious and the conscious mind," putting her "in contact with the dark." ("It's like they forgot to nail in the storm windows in my head.") The shock of her plays, she says, derives less from their language, sex and violence than from our buried fears: "It's this animal we all have tucked away in the corner of our unconscious, and it is very frightening to see the cage unlocked."

The text of *Lion in the Streets* opens with a stage direction explaining that the character we would be seeing on the stage if we were in the theatre, a nine-year-old girl played by an adult actress, is actually a ghost. It says she was killed by a man seventeen years earlier and she does not yet know she is dead. This information would not be available to us if we were watching the play. Only gradually would we, as does Isobel herself, come to understand that she has been murdered, and that the "home" to which she is trying to return is both the scene of the crime, where she will finally confront her killer, and the "heaven" to which, at the end, she will ascend "in her mind."

Thompson's strategy is to disorient us, to jolt us out of our normal expectations of the world to make us see the frightening reality that lies beneath the benign appearance of things. Surface appearance is the "pickshur" of which, Isobel assures us, we shouldn't be scared because we know it as we know her. She is our neighbour; she plays with our kids in our parks. But this is also *not* our familiar neighbourhood, but some strange and terrifying place, a kind of limbo where souls live in torment. On her journey through this purgatory Isobel will observe a variety of lives. Like her, unobserved, we will see the darkness beneath the bright surface of the "pickshur," and learn about our need to create such comforting pictures of what we assure ourselves is our reality (the need for lyin' in the streets). We will catch glimpses of the lions of anger and fear, repression and denial that lie in wait not just in the streets but in the abysses of the human heart.

In the opening sequence Isobel, too, is dominated by the lion of rage and violence, growling threats to kill the children who torment her. Rescued by Sue who tells of having been saved herself from a similar childhood experience, Isobel will spend much of the rest of the play alternately seeking such a saviour or offering herself as one. "I am your HARMY! I am your SAINT!" she will declare, a soldier of virtue like Saint George, going out to slay the dragon with her "great crooked stick." But at the end she will forego the way of violence and revenge in an extraordinary leap of faith generated, at least in part, by the bestial behaviour she observes on her journey.

Isobel first watches Sue, whose humiliating experience at the dinner party is a nightmare brought to life, one of the many scenes in the play that exist on the border between expressionism and naturalism, at once hallucinatory and all too real. As the polite surface of the party fractures, fearful images break through: phone sex, the striptease, colon cancer. Laura, the hostess, who mocks Sue, turns out to be no more secure herself. Her overwrought reaction in the "Sugar Meeting" suggests that middle class privilege offers no respite from personal demons. Socio-economic status does matter, as we see in Rhonda's violent response to Laura's condescending accusations. Yet in the next scene class issues seem relatively superficial next to the fear of death, Joanne desiring to dress up the horrible reality of her illness by emulating the pre-Raphaelite picture of Ophelia, who "dies good." Formal religion masks similar fears. The scene between David and Father Hayes is a revelation of guilt, regret and unfulfilled desire. Act Two extends the ideas of the first act in the intense confrontations between Christine and Scarlett, Michael and Rodney, and Sherry and Edward.

Edward's terrifying evocation of misogynist violence leads inevitably to Isobel's showdown with Ben and the play's stunning conclusion. Does the play sanction the idea that women who are victims of violence should turn the other cheek and forgive their aggressor? Thompson says the decision is Isobel's, not hers. Just as Isobel ascends "in her mind" to heaven, *she* resolves the battle between "the forces of vengeance and forgiveness warring inside her." She has come to realize that "to have your life" you have to take control of it yourself; no one can do it for you. She has learned how to take back her life by watching those whose lives lie beyond their control, in the claws and maws of their terrible beasts.

Lion in the Streets was first produced by Tarragon Theatre at the du Maurier Theatre Centre in Toronto as part of the du Maurier World Stage Theatre Festival in June 1990, with the following cast:

ISOBEL	Tracy Wright
NELLIE, LAURA, ELAINE, CHRISTINE, SHERRY	Jane Spidell
RACHEL, LILY, RHONDA, ELLEN, SCARLETT	Ann Holloway
SCALATO, TIMMY, GEORGE, DAVID, RODNEY, BEN	Stephen Ouimette
MARTIN, ISOBEL'S FATHER, RON, FATHER HAYES, MICHAEL	Andrew Gillies
SUE, JILL, JOANNE, BECCA, JOAN	Maggie Huculak

Directed by Judith Thompson
Set and Costume Design by Sue LePage
Lighting Design by Steven Hawkins
Sound Effects by Evan Turner

LION IN THE STREETS

CHARACTERS

ISOBEL, *9 years old, a ghost*
NELLIE
SCALATO
MARTIN } *children*
RACHEL
TIMMY
SUE, *Timmy's mother*
ISOBEL'S FATHER
LAURA
BILL, *Timmy's father, Sue's husband*
LILY
GEORGE
MARIA, *Isobel's mother*
RON
JILL
RHONDA
JOANNE
DAVID
FATHER HAYES
CHRISTINE
ELLEN
SCARLETT
RODNEY
MICHAEL
EDWARD
SHERRY
BEN
JOAN, *Ben's adoptive mother*

ACT ONE

The ghost of ISOBEL, a deranged and very ragged looking nine-year-old Portuguese girl, runs around and around in a large circle, to music, terrified of a remembered pursuer: in fact, the man who killed her in this playground seventeen years before the action of the play. There are autumn leaves all over the playground, and the kids who approach her all have large handfuls of leaves, which they throw at her. At this point ISOBEL does not know she is a ghost, but she knows that something is terribly wrong. She is terrified.

ISOBEL: Doan be scare. Doan be scare. *(turns to audience)* Doan be scare of this pickshur! This pickshur is niiiice, nice! I looove this pickshur, this pickshur is mine! *(gesturing behind her)* Is my house, is my street, is my park, is my people! You know me, you know me very hard! I live next house to you, with my brother and sisters, Maria, Luig, Carla and Romeo we play, we play with your girl, your boy, you know me, you know me very hard. But ... when did tha be? Tha not be now! Tha not be today! I think tha be very long years ago I think I be old. I think I be very old. Is my house but is not my house is my street but is not my street my people is gone I am lost. I am lost. I AM LOOOOOOOOOOST!!

Four children—two girls and two boys—laugh and approach ISOBEL.

NELLIE: Take a bird why doncha?

RACHEL: Go back with the nutties to the nutty-house!

SCALATO: She looks like a crazy dog!

MARTIN: *(barks)* Hey!

All bark.

ISOBEL: Peoples! Peoples, little boy little girl peoples! Hey!

ISOBEL walks towards them.

MARTIN: What's she doin?

NELLIE: She's coming over here!

RACHEL: She's gonna get us!

ISOBEL: You, girl, you help to me. I am lost you see! You help!

NELLIE: She smells.

RACHEL: You should dial 911 so the police could help you.

SCALATO: Where do you live?

MARTIN: With all the other pork and cheese west of Christie Street?

RACHEL: Martin that's not nice.

ISOBEL: *(overlapping)* Portuguese, Portuguese, yes ... I catch a bus! Is there a bus, bus maybe? To take me to my home? You know a bus?

SCALATO: No buses here.

ISOBEL: Yah, bus right here, bus right here, number ten, eleven, I take with my mother to cleaning job, where this bus?

SCALATO: I said there's no buses here you ugly little SNOT.

ISOBEL: (*points*) You! YOU bad boy you bad boy say Isobel, BAD.

SCALATO: Why don't you get your ugly little face outa here, snot?

MARTIN: Snotface!

ISOBEL: Shut up boy, shut up, I kill you I kill you boy.

SCALATO: Hey she's gonna kill me!

RACHEL: She's a witch.

ISOBEL tosses rocks at them.

MARTIN: She's throwin rocks! Hey she's throwin rocks!

NELLIE: STOP IT.

RACHEL: Stop throwin rocks or we'll tell the police!

ISOBEL: You BAD boy you BAD I will kill you!

SCALATO: (*jumping off and attacking her*) You just try it you goddamned faggot!! Faggot! Faggot!! (*hitting her*)

ISOBEL: (*growling like a dog*) G-r-r-r-r. G-r-r-r-r.

They circle one another.

MARTIN: What's she doing?

NELLIE: I don't like her.

ISOBEL and SCALATO scrap and the others join in. SUE, a thirty-eight-year-old woman in a grey sweatsuit, walking home from a meeting, spies the fight and rushes up.

SUE: Hey! Hey hey hey stop that right now! (*pries them apart*) HEY! Listen! What is going on??

ISOBEL: I KILL YOU BOY!

SCALATO: She started it!

MARTIN: She was throwing rocks at us!

RACHEL: She's crazy.

ISOBEL leaps towards SCALATO. SUE catches her. She falls to the ground.

SUE: Little girl? Little girl!

ISOBEL: (*overlapping*) I kill that stupid boy.

SCALATO: She started it, lady.

MARTIN: I'm getting out of here.

SCALATO: Me too.

NELLIE & RACHEL: Wait for me!!

SCALATO: You chicken, Martin! You suck!

ISOBEL: I kill that stupid boy! (*beat*) I no like those boys.

SUE: I'm sorry if they hurt you.

ISOBEL: They no want play with me. Why they no want play with me? Why all the kids no want play with Isobel? Ha?

SUE: Ohhh … sometimes kids are just … mean, that way, Isobel, when I was little kids were mean like that to me once.

ISOBEL: Kids? Mean no play to you?

SUE: That's right. We had just moved to a new town, Cornwall actually, near Montreal? Well my sisters and I went for a walk around the neighbourhood and these big boys on bikes started firing arrows at us.

ISOBEL: Boys on bikes?

SUE: That's right, just like those nasty boys!

ISOBEL: Nasty boys, to you, too! Mean to you!!

SUE: That's right. And those arrows, they hurt! They really hurt!! And I was the oldest so I told my sisters, "Just cry, just start to cry and then maybe they'll feel sorry for us," so we all started to cry.

ISOBEL: Cry.

SUE: But you know what? It didn't work! They kept shooting those arrows anyways. They were just mean.

ISOBEL: Mean boys shoot arrows. Haaah!

SUE: AND suddenly, a bigger boy, about sixteen, came along and made them stop, and you know, he was like an angel, to us, an angel who came down from the sky on his big blue bicycle. I've never forgotten that.

ISOBEL: Never forgetting.

SUE: Nope. I guess I'm your helper today.

ISOBEL: Helper.

ISOBEL'S FATHER: (on porch) Hey! Is-o-bel.

SUE: Isobel is that your father?

ISOBEL: Father. My father. Eu pensava que té tinha perdedo!

ISOBEL'S FATHER: (ordering ISOBEL to go around to the back door) Vai pela porta das traseiras.

SUE: Hello. (ISOBEL'S FATHER grunts.) My name is Sue Winters and I don't know if you're aware of it, but some of the boys in the neighbourhood have been well I'd say doing some not very nice teasing of your daughter. I just … thought … you might … (ISOBEL'S FATHER goes in, slamming the door.) Poor man probably works all day in construction and then all night as a janitor in some Bay Street office building. What a life. (exits)

ISOBEL: My father? My father is not there. My father is dead. Yes, was killed by a subway many many years; it it breathed very hard push push over my father; push over to God. Hi my father.

Music. Lights come up just a bit. SUE is in her son TIMMY'S room, in the dark. TIMMY is in bed. ISOBEL watches.

SUE: And so the giant starfish saved the drowning boy.

TIMMY: What was the starfish's name?

SUE: The starfish's name? Uh … Joey. It was Joey.

TIMMY: Mummy? Why isn't magic true? I want magic to be true.

SUE: Well. It is true, in a way, it …

TIMMY: Not it's not. It's not true. And ya know what else?

SUE: What, darling?

TIMMY: I think tonight's the night.

SUE: That what, Tim?

TIMMY: That we're all gonna die. Tonight's the night we're gonna die.

Music. A dinner party, around a table. ISOBEL is there, invisible. The conversation is simultaneous.

LAURA: There was nothing to do! Nothing to bloody do but sing in the church choir!! And go to baked-bean suppers!! The snow at one point was actually up to the second-floor window.

BILL: No, she had the gall to ask my male students to "Please leave the room," for her senior seminar. She did "not wish to be dominated by men." Where did that leave me, I asked her?

LILY: No, no no, you have to pat the dough, pat it for ohh a good five minutes then put it in the microwave for one, then take it out, then pat it again.

GEORGE: St. Paul said, "We are as vapour," what is it? Like "vapour vanisheth" or—something. "We are no more." So I got up this notion of Martians—being these—wisps of vapour … no, you see your problem is you want the aliens to be like you, you are anthropomorphizing, you …

LAURA: That's so boring. That's so knee-jerk boring.

BILL: And she launched into the most savage tirade—

SUE rushes in, dressed in her sweatsuit and sneakers. Everyone turns and freezes, except BILL, who continues to talk until SUE's third "Bill."

SUE: Bill … Bill … Bill!! We have to talk!

BILL: Sue! Hi! Who's with the boys?

SUE: Mum came over, Bill I need to talk, NOW.

LAURA: Would you like a drink, Sue? We have …

GEORGE: Yeah, come in and sit down …

SUE: No, no thank you, I just … want to talk to my husband.

ISOBEL: My helper, Suuuuusan!

BILL: Oh—okay, Sue, I'll just finish this conversation. Anyway—

SUE: He thinks he's going to die.

BILL: Who?

SUE: Timmy! Your son! He—

BILL: What, did he say that tonight? Oh, that's just kids, he's—

SUE: BILL, come home, your son is very depressed his father is never there, why are you never never …

BILL: Sue PLEASE, we'll talk about it later, okay? So as I was saying, Laura …

SUE: Come with me.

BILL: I'll come in a while. I'll just finish this conversation, and then I'll come, okay?

SUE: YOU COME WITH ME NOW!

BILL: Sue.

SUE: Bill, I need you, please, why won't you come?

BILL: Why won't I come? Why won't I come? Because … (*walks over to the others*) I'm … not … I am not coming home tonight.

SUE: Bill! Stop it, this is private—

BILL: It is not private, Sue, nothing we do is private for Christ's sake, you tell your friends everything, they all—know everything—about us, don't they? How many times we had sex in the last month.

LAURA: I don't think that's true, Bill.

GEORGE: I haven't heard anything.

SUE: Bill, I think you're being very unreasonable.

There is an awkward pause in which BILL and SUE lock eyes.

LAURA: (*to LILY and GEORGE*) Well, it's a lovely night out there. Why don't the three of us go for a walk?

BILL: No.

SUE: You stay and finish up that wonderful looking chocolate paté, Laura, I'm sure you spent a lot of time on it. I'll just get Bill's coat and we'll go on home.

BILL: There is … somebody else, Sue. And I will be going home with her.

GEORGE: I think we've all had a little too much to drink, why don't we just …

SUE: Don't worry guys this isn't real. He's just drunk he's just trying to scare me because we had this argument about the new sofa—Come on honey, let's go home. Who is it. Who is it, Bill? She's not here, is she? You didn't, you didn't bring her to my neighbours', OUR friends' dinner party, to which I was invited. Laura! Laura for God's sake.

LILY: It's me. (*SUE laughs.*) Why do you think I'm joking?

SUE looks at LILY, then looks at BILL.

SUE: Bill??

BILL: This is—Lily.

LILY: How do you do, Susan?

SUE: Don't you call me by my name you FAT!! Please, I don't think you know what you're doing. This is not just me, this is a family, a family, we have two children.

LILY: I'm sorry.

SUE: Bill you are not leaving your children.

BILL: Sue, please.

SUE: YOU TOOK A VOW! In a CHURCH in front of a priest and my mother and your mother and your father and you swore to LOVE and honour and cherish till DEATH US DO PART till DEATH US DO PART BILL, it's your WORD your WORD.

BILL: I am breaking my word.

SUE: No!

BILL: YOU turned your back on me!! You you—look at you in that … sweatsuit thing you're not—I mean look at her, really, you're you're you're a kind of … cartoon now, a … cartoon mum a … with your day care meetings and neighbourhood fairs, you know what I mean Laura! Your face is a drawing your body, lines. The only time, the only time you are alive, electric again is … when you talk on the phone, to the other mums, there's a flush in your face, excitement, something rushing through your body, you laugh, loudly, you make all those wonderful female noises, you cry, your voice, like … music, or in the park, with Timmy and John, while they cavort with the other children at the drinking fountain, spraying the water and you talking and talking with all the mothers, storming,

storming together your words like crazy swallows, swooping and pivots and ... landing ... softly on a branch, a husband, one of us husbands walk in and it's like walking into ... a large group of ...

LILY: You see, I love ... his body, Sue. I mean, I really love it. I love to suck it. I love to kiss it his body is my God, okay? His body—

SUE slaps LILY twice.

SUE: YOU ... DON'T LIVE ON THIS STREET. You don't belong in this neighbourhood. (*LILY contains herself from slapping SUE back.*) Where did you meet this ... woman? On the street? (*BILL starts to try to answer.*) In a house of prostitution? I demand to know—

LILY: I fucked him on the telephone, Susan, many many times.

SUE: That is a disgusting ... lie.

LILY: Come on Suzy, don't you remember? You caught him a couple of times, on the downstairs phone with his pyjamas around his ankles, he told me!

SUE: (*the wind totally out of her*) I thought he was making ... obscene phone calls.

BILL: Hello.

LILY: Hi there.

BILL: You got back to me quickly.

LILY: Fucking right.

BILL: Fucking right.

LILY: Your voice makes me crazy.

BILL: My voice.

LILY: I'm wet, Bill, wet just from hearing your voice.

BILL: What are you wearing?

LILY: Black silk underwear, red spiked heels, black lace bra.

BILL: Yeah? And what do you want? What do you want?

LILY: I want to suck your big cock, Bill, would you like me to do that? Would you like me to suck your big cock?

BILL: Oh baby, baby.

LILY: And then I want you to fuck me from behind all night long, can you do that? Can you do that for me, Bill?

BILL: Yes, yes, oh yes! Yes! Yes!

LILY: Oh, Bill!

SUE: BILLLLLLLLLLLLLLLLLLLLLL!!!!!!! (*She physically attacks LILY.*) Aghhhh! Listen, you, if you take my husband away from me and my children I will ... kill you, I will I will ... come when you are sleeping and I will pull your filthy tongue out of your filthy mouth. And then I will ... feed it to our cat.

BILL: Susan.

SUE: (*forced laugh*) I didn't mean that, I really didn't. I'm sorry everybody, this is all just so ridiculous and embarrassing and I'm sure we'll all laugh about it someday I KNOW we will, but um ... Bill? Won't you just ... give me a chance? To show you? That I can? Be sexy? 'Cause I can, you know, much much more so than THAT creepy shit ... Don't you remember? Don't you remember before we were married how you loved to watch me dance? Come on, you did! Remember remember that wedding, Kevin and Leslie's? I wore that peach silk that you loved so much that dress drove you crazy! And after after the wedding we were in that room in the Ramada Inn over the water and I danced? You lay on the bed and you just ... watched me you loved it I ... whooshed whooshed in that dress, back and forth to this thing on the radio back and oooh and back and you were laughing and and (*laughs*) and whoosh. (*Music beats louder, filling the room, and SUE begins a slow striptease.*) And whoosh ... and ... close to you, you're hard ... and far away and ... turn ... and whooosh ... and ... let ... my ... hair ... down ... you—love my hair whoosh and ... zipppper ... whoooo down so slowwwww turn and turn ... you watching lying on the bed and ease ... off my shoulders you love my shoulders, elegant ohhh Billy, and down. Over my body the soft silky down and whooooooooooooooooo whooOOOOOOOO Billy. Take me home, Billy, take me home and let's make mad passionate love! Please.

BILL and LILY leave. GEORGE and LAURA pick up SUE's clothing and bring it to her. LAURA dresses her.

LAURA: Honey, I'm sorry.

SUE: Aghh don't feel sorry for me it's fine, everything will be fine because … his colon cancer's gonna come back, don't you think? Dr. Neville said he had a sixty-forty chance, it will. And she'll drop him, for sure, don't you think? And he will let me nurse him I will … feed him broth, with a spoon, like I did my mum, and I will hold, I will hold his sweet head in my chest till till his lips are black and his eyes … like bright dead stars and he is dead and I will stay I will stay with his body, in the hospital room because I did love that body … oh I did *love—that—body* once.

ISOBEL: Susan, Susan, Susan. The boy with the arrow ha *killed* you, ha? Where's your helper now? Oh Susan, you can't help me now you can't take me home. (*to the audience*) Hey! Who gonna take me home? You? You gotta car? What kinda car you got? Trans-Am? What about bus tickets? You gotta bus tickets? C'mon. Come on. COME ON. SOMEBODY. What I'm sposed to do, ha? Who gonna take me home? Who gonna take me home?

ISOBEL finds a watching place. A few hours later, at LAURA and GEORGE's, LAURA clears the table.

LAURA: Poor Suzy. Poor poor Suzy.

GEORGE: (*half asleep*) Yeahh. Chee.

LAURA: God, that is the worst thing I have ever seen happen to anybody.

GEORGE and LAURA laugh hysterically and imitate SUE in the previous scene.

GEORGE: Whoosh! That peach silk, oh baby take me home.

LAURA: Take me home, Bill. Let's make mad passionate love. (*stops imitating SUE*) I don't know, I mean I know she needs a friend badly, I am her friend I mean I love her. George, how can you laugh? This is important. If she calls me tomorrow, what should I say? I'm just going to say, I'm going to say, "SUZY? I feel really badly for you and I think you're a wonderful person but you will have to look somewhere else for—"

GEORGE: Nice.

LAURA: GEORGE, you KNOW—

GEORGE: You always say she's your best friend, Laura, "my BEST—"

LAURA: She is! But George, are you forgetting Maria? I had a nervous breakdown because of that woman and her problem how could you FORGET?

GEORGE: I was on the book tour, Loo.

LAURA: I told you about it a hundred times, how could you forget?

GEORGE: I was on the book tour—Loo.

LAURA: George, you are so insensitive, I can't believe this. I told you about it one hundred times. How can you forget?

GEORGE grabs a tablecloth and wraps it around his head, like a shawl, speaking in a Portuguese accent.

GEORGE: How could I forget, how could I forget?

LAURA: George.

GEORGE: Looka this. Me? I donta forget nothing.

LAURA: George I'm going to bed, Molly gets up in two hours and it's always me that gets up with her of course.

She walks around the circle.

GEORGE/MARIA: LAURA.

Now he speaks as MARIA, ISOBEL'S mother. ISOBEL recognizes her.

LAURA: George! Come to bed.

GEORGE/MARIA: LAURA.

LAURA: Maria.

MARIA: I am … so sorry to be coming to your house, maybe you busy, I don't know—

LAURA: No, no, please come in Maria, I'm just—reading the paper the kids are at school and—

MARIA starts shaking violently and keening. She looks like she is in shock.

LAURA: Maria? … uh … Maria? Are you alright? You look—why don't you sit down. Here. Sit down. Can I get you a drink of water?

MARIA starts to keen with grief, quite quietly.

MARIA: Eeeeeeee

LAURA: Maria? Maria … are you alright? Maria, Maria please tell me … what's …

MARIA: … think … I think … Antonio—

LAURA: Your husband? Something happened to your husband? (*MARIA continues to keen.*) It's okay, Maria, you don't have to tell me if you don't—

MARIA: Five o'clock in the morning I cook: smelt and three scramble eggs, nice bread, coffee. For Antony must work long day, construction on highway, long day in the sun, he come from his shower to kitchen, but he don't want. He gotta rat in his stomach that day he say, make a joke, don't want my cooking eat a little bitta bread and just small glass of milk and he go, catch his subway. I fold. I fold clothes one pile for Antony, one pile for me, one for Maria, Romeo, Isobel and Luig, my hands fold the clothes but my … (*gesture indicating self or soul*)

LAURA: Sure, you go on automatic—I—

MARIA: Like I fold myself too, and I go in his body, maybe, you know, his … hand to, wipe off his face when he hot and too sweat I am there. (*She walks operatically downstage to deliver the rest of the speech, which should be like an aria.*) I am foldin a light sheet of blue then and sudden, I can see through his eye, am at subway, in him, he stands on the platform, is empty, empty and I am his head, circles and circles like red birds flying around and around I am his throat, tight, cannot breathe enough air in my body the floor the floor move, and sink in, rise up rise like a wall like a killin wave turn turn me in circles with teeth in circles and under and over I fall!

ISOBEL falls on an imaginary track in front of her mother.

I fall on the silver track nobody move I hearing the sound. The sound of the rats in the tunnel their breath like a basement these dark rats running running towards me I am stone I am earth cannot scream cannot move the rats tramp … trample my body flat-ten and every bone splinter like …

We hear the sound of a strong wind as the "Sugar Meeting" is being set up on the stage. By the end of the wind, LAURA is at her table, addressing the meeting.

LAURA: Good evening everybody.

GEORGE: Good evening.

RON: Hi Laura.

LAURA: I uh might as well get straight down to business. As head and sole member of the menu research committee, I have spent some three weeks doing … a great deal … of … research, and even a little detective work …

RON and GEORGE are talking to one another.

… and I would like to make my presentation tonight without too much interruption, thank you.

GEORGE: Go for it.

RON: No problem.

LAURA: POINT ONE. Sugar: I strongly recommend that we make a concerted effort to eradicate all sugar from the children's diet. Sugar is an overstimulant, sugar is empty calories, sugar rots …

RON: Uh, I have to say, that, while I agree, sure, too much sugar is not a good thing, that once in a while …

LAURA: Would you let your four-year-old smoke "once in a while"?

A murmur from the crowd.

RON: (*with a little laugh*) I don't really think you can equate …

ISOBEL rises and walks into the meeting.

LAURA: Sugar is a known carcinogen, Ron, I have a study right here …

JILL: Lettuce is a known carcinogen, for God's sake!

ISOBEL: Hey! Boys! Girls! Looka this! I think tha they can't see me! They no see Isobel! Wha happen? Wha happen?

JILL: Okay as chairperson, I say—let's cut the comments and raise our hands for questions. Laura? You want to go ahead?

LAURA: Yes, thank you, Jill. Uh. (*clears her throat*) It has come to my attention … (*GEORGE groans.*) Excuse me, I have to ask you why you groaned like that, George, did I say something wrong?

JILL: George, penalty for groaning out of turn, just kidding.

GEORGE: No, no, I'm sorry, I just, I don't know, I just ... have a kind of a hard time with "meeting ... talk" ... "it has come to my attention."

LAURA: Well, I'm very sorry, George, if you have a better way of—

JILL: That was uncalled for George, really.

RON: George, your mother's calling you.

General laughter.

JILL: Let's let Laura continue please, so we can get out of here ...

ISOBEL: I think I invisible!

LAURA: Thank you Jill. I have NOTICED, if you don't like "it has come to my attention," I have noticed that in this nursery school they are ... subtly, and I'm sure unwittingly, encouraging an addiction to sugar in our children.

RHONDA: Hey, that's not true.

LAURA: Rhonda, I'm SAYING it's not intentional ...

RHONDA: The kids are not ...

LAURA: PLEASE LET ME TALK.

JILL: Go ahead, Laura, please.

LAURA: I have noticed that sugar is used as a reward. If you're good we'll make cookies tomorrow. If you tidy up you get chocolate cake as a reward. You are creating ... unwittingly, I concede, you are creating TOMORROW'S COKE ADDICTS ... TO—

RHONDA: EXCUSE ME I HAVE TO SAY THAT, AS THE CAREGIVER, I RESENT THIS.

LAURA: Rhonda, I'm not accusing just you, I think you are fabulous with the kids, it's our whole society ...

RHONDA: I am not creating drug addicts.

JILL: Rhonda, Laura does not mean any of this personally, I think that's ...

LAURA: I'm saying it's a small step from sugar addiction to—

RON: Excuse me, I have to say, all food is sugar ...

LAURA: REFINED SUGAR IS FAST-ACTING, RON, IT BURDENS THE PANCREAS.

GEORGE: I think you are taking this a little too seriously, Laura, we're just talking about a few cookies now and then for heaven's sake.

LAURA: WE ARE TALKING ABOUT A LIFETIME ADDICTION AND I DON'T THINK IT SHOULD BE TAKEN LIGHTLY.

JILL: Laura, are you willing to listen to a response from Rhonda?

LAURA: Sure.

RHONDA: I would just ... like to say that I, also have done ... a great deal of studying diet and menu and that, and I fully agree with Laura that sugar is ... something to be avoided, IF YOU CAN. Listen, if I'm giving the kids yoghurt, they won't eat it without honey they won't, so I figure, a bit of honey is worth getting the yoghurt down em ...

LAURA: BULLSHIT THAT IS ABSOLUTE UNADULTERATED BULLSHIT.

RHONDA: I beg your pardon, Laura?

LAURA: You don't know what you're saying, Rhonda.

RHONDA: If you don't trust me, Laura ...

LAURA: Rhonda ...

RHONDA: I do not encourage sugar, I do not hold it up as a reward, ever, I have never done that.

LAURA: You're lying, Rhonda.

RON: WAIT A MINUTE HOLD ON JUST A ...

LAURA: SHUT UP RON. LISTEN. LISTEN TO ME RHONDA. I FOUND OUT THAT JUST LAST FRIDAY, LAST FRIDAY, AS A REWARD, YOU TOOK SIX KIDS, INCLUDING MY TWINS, TO A DOUGHNUT SHOP. YOU TOOK THEM TO A DOUGHNUT SHOP AND BOUGHT THEM EACH A JELLY DOUGHNUT. I think I screamed for five minutes when the twins told me that I just couldn't believe it they started harassing me every five minutes, "Mum, if we're good, can we have a jelly doughnut?" I don't think they'd ever HEARD OF JELLY DOUGHNUTS BEFORE THAT!! I find it unconscionable, UNCON-

SCIONABLE that a jelly doughnut would be the sole purpose of an excursion.

RHONDA: Um, I can explain that. It was a Friday, right, and I happen to get severe cramps with my period, right? And I was very sick that day and the kids had bad bad cabin fever, well …

LAURA: (overlapping) And the Friday before that it was popsicles, Rhonda, I'm not blaming you I'm saying you need to be re-educated, we all do, smelling the flowers is a reason to go for a walk, not getting a poisonous body-destroying drug …

RHONDA: LET MEEEEE TALLLLLK. LET ME TALK LET ME TALLLLLLLLLLLLLK!! I feel … nailed to the wall by you lady, nailed right to the fucking wall. I have to say and something else I have to say is that I think you are … are very … inconsiderate … of feelings! I brought up two kids on what I feed your kids, and they turned out just fine, are you telling me what I feed my kids isn't good enough for your kids? You know the funny thing is, Laura, you may be a bitch on wheels, but lookin at all the rest of you, Laura? at least you're honest you are. Youse others, what you're thinkin is … it really doesn't matter what they get at the day care the real learning is at home, that's where youse teach your kids to become—huh. Here I am saying "youse" I haven't said that since I was a kid! that's how flustered I am—at home you teach your kids … to be … higher kind of people, higher kind of people don't eat Kraft slices and *tuna casserole*, I've seen that kinda laugh in your voices, all of you, when you say, "Oh, they had tuna casserole," I seen, I have seen the roll in your eyes at the grace before meals, or the tidy-up song, or the stars we give out for citizen of the week, you think, oh well the kid is happy, well cared for, we can undo all that and we can make the kids high people like ourselves better people, more better people than the poor little teacher who reads ROMANCE, yes, yes, JILL MATHINS, I saw you showin my book, my novel to RON there and Cathy and havin a big giggle, you think I didn't see that? You think the books you read are deeper more … higher, well it's the same story, don't you see that? What's makin me cry in my book is, when ya come right down to it, is exactly the same thing that's makin you cry in your book, oh yes, oh yes and I'll tell you something, I'll tell all of you I GREW UP ON THAT. I grew up on jelly doughnuts and butter tarts, and chocolate ice-cream, and I happen to think they're a wonderful thing. I happen to agree with the mice and the cockroaches and the horses and birds that treats are a wonderful thing, you need treats, you need treats in this life, each bit of a treat can wipe out a nasty word, every bite of a jelly doughnut cleans out your soul it is a gift from GOD, a wonderful gift from GOD and I for one … I for one … I … for … your eyes, eh? Your eyes are all the same colour and shape like a picture, a … freaky art picture all the same in a row like dark soldiers raisin your …

ISOBEL shoots everybody there except RHONDA with her finger. There are real shot sounds although ISOBEL is imagining this.

ISOBEL: (big laugh, then struts) Rho-HONDA! Bebbe! Beautiful belle! I have killed those dirty bastards, babe, I have killed them dirty dead. I am your harmy, Rhohonda! And you! You gonna take me home!

ISOBEL falls and wraps herself around RHONDA's feet. Music. A restaurant. DAVID takes his place behind the bar. Another person is sitting alone at a table. RHONDA and her friend JOANNE meet for drinks. They are laughing. ISOBEL watches.

RHONDA: Oh man is this Singapore Sling fantastic.

JOANNE: My Fuzzy Navel is warm. Hot!

RHONDA: SEND it back! We're paying through the teeth for these drinks. Waiter, take this thing back!

JOANNE: No, I like it this way, honest, Rhonda, I do.

DAVID: Is there a problem with your cocktail?

JOANNE: No no no no please …

DAVID: I could take it back—

JOANNE: No.

RHONDA: Are you sure?

JOANNE: I'm sure.

DAVID: Okaaay.

RHONDA: Ohhh Christ, I'd like to just sit and drink all afternoon to tell you the truth.

JOANNE: I thought you quit heavy drinkin.

RHONDA: I did. I'm just … down in the dumps.

JOANNE: Why, ya on your time?

ISOBEL: Is this my home? This is not my home!

RHONDA: No no no, I get happy then, no, it's just … work.

JOANNE: Yeah, Jeez I'm glad I'm not workin it made me crazy, what's goin on? the kids at the day care gettin to ya?

RHONDA: No no it's not the kids, the kids are great, it's the parents.

JOANNE: Uh oh. That same B-I-T-C-H?

RHONDA: No, she was quite good this time, strangely enough, it's another one.

JOANNE: They all look like bitches to me in their leather pants. Stuck up, puttin their kids in forty-five-dollar shoes, I looked at the price of them REEboks for kids—the other day when I picked you up I saw three of those kids had those shoes on I couldn't believe my eyes.

RHONDA: Yeah, well, they're pretty well-off, but I don't hold that against them, I mean, who wouldn't be if they had the chance, right?

JOANNE: Well that's a good point SO …

RHONDA: We had this meeting, okay?

JOANNE: RHONDA. Excuse me!

RHONDA: What?

JOANNE: (intake of breath) … I don't know.

RHONDA: What do you mean?

JOANNE: I mean … no, I don't know.

RHONDA: Joanne.

JOANNE: I mean … oh God, I wasn't going to tell nobody—

RHONDA: You're pregnant again?

JOANNE: No no no no, if only, I …

RHONDA: JOANNE, I'M YOUR BEST FRIEND.

JOANNE: YOU'RE MY BEST FRIEND?

RHONDA: Yes, you know that!

JOANNE: THEN SWEAR ON YOUR MOTHER'S LIFE.

RHONDA: What?

JOANNE: That you will do what I'm gonna ask you.

RHONDA: Joanne, what is this?

JOANNE: Just … swear.

RHONDA: I'm not swearing on my mother's life without knowing what it is, she's got enough problems …

JOANNE: Okay, your husband's life.

RHONDA: Okay, I swear on the asshole's life. There. Now what?

JOANNE: You remember … I had this pain in my back?

RHONDA: Yeah, for the last few months, every time ya bend down.

JOANNE: SEARING pain, every time I moved …

RHONDA: … Okay …

JOANNE: Well remember I told you I went to that specialist and he said he was gonna do some tests?

RHONDA: Right, uh-huh.

JOANNE: Well—

RHONDA: You gotta go in and have an operation and you want me to take your kids, no problem of COURSE I'll take them Jo, for God's—

JOANNE: (overlapping) No. No, I mean, you might have to take the kids but that's only … part of it.

RHONDA: Joanne, I really don't like guessing games.

JOANNE: Shadows … that's what they call them, and … it is … the very worst thing it could be, and the … kind, the kind is of the bone.

RHONDA: Oh boy.

JOANNE: Yeah.

RHONDA: (whispers) Jo …

JOANNE: Don't … don't touch me. I'll go hysterical please.

RHONDA: YOU … want a cigarette?

JOANNE: Yeah. (RHONDA lights one and gives it to her.) Ya know, I have to go to the bathroom, like, real bad but I'm not gonna go, ya know why? 'Cause every time … I sit down to pee I feel my whole life drainin out of me, just draining out with the pee, goin … outa me, into the water down in the pipes, and under the … friggin … GROUND. That's where I'll be, Rho, that's where I'm gonna … (*fights to regain her composure*) I'll come home with the groceries? Like after dark? and I'll see Frank and the kids through the window, in the livin-room, right? Watchin TV, or drawing on paper, cuttin out stuff, whatever, and I'll stand on the porch and watch em, just … playing … on the floor, and I think … that's life, that's life goin on without me, it'll be just like that, only I won't be here with the groceries, I'll be under the ground under the ground with my flesh fallin off a my face and I just can't take it. You know in that picture? That picture I had in my bedroom growing up?

RHONDA: UHH—

JOANNE: My aunt and uncle sent me that from England, the poster it's OPHELIA, from this play by Shakespeare, right? And she she—got all these flowers, tropical flowers, wild flowers, white roses, violets and buttercups, everything she loved and she kinda weaved them all together. Then she got the heaviest dress she could find … you know how dresses in the olden days were so long and heavy, with petticoats and that? And she got this heavy heavy blue dress, real … blue and then she wrapped all these pretty pretty flowers round and round her body, round her head, and her hair, she had this golden, wavy hair, long, and then she steps down the bank, and she lies, on her back, in the stream. She lies there, but the stream runs so fast she's on her back and she goes. It pulls her along so fast and she's lookin at the sky and the clouds, and she's singing little songs—"I'm lookin over a four-leaf clover"—and being pulled so fast by a clear cold water pulled along and she's not scared, she's not scared at all, she's calm, so happy! And just ever so slowly her dress, gets heavier, right? Then, then, she gets caught on a stick, like a branch, of a willow tree, and her dress pulls her down, soft, she's still singin down deep deep deep to the bottom of the stream and with all these "fantastic garlands," these beautiful flowers all around her—"one's for the roses that blew down the lane"—she dies, Rhon, she dies … good. She dies good.

RHONDA: That's … something.

JOANNE: I want to die like that. But … I don't … want to do it all alone, I mean, I want you to help me, with the flowers, and with the dress, and my hair, I want you to make sure the willow branch is there, and the stream is right, and maybe … maybe that … Frank … sees I … wouldn't mind him seein … me in that stream, with the flowers, and the heavy blue dress … I wouldn't mind if you took maybe some pictures of me like that and then you could have them printed and given out at the funeral, something like that … just, you know, two by four, colour, whatever, it's the one thing that would make it alright—it's the one thing …

RHONDA: I just … I don't know, Jo, you know I'd do anything to make it alright …

JOANNE: Well this is what I want, Rhonda, it's really really really what I want. Are you going to help me?

RHONDA: I uh—think you need to see a counsellor, Jo, you know they have counsellors that … specialize in these … situations I'm surprised your doctor didn't …

JOANNE: You think I'm crazy.

RHONDA: No no, Joanne, I just think that … your situation is so hard that you are not quite yourself, I mean this is not … you, the Joanne I know is practical she … you should believe in the treatments, Jo, they do work sometimes, they really do, and the Joanne I know—would never ask a friend to help … her … is one of the most thoughtful people that I know, of other people and how the hell, how the hell do you think that I could live with that after, eh?? I mean it's all very lovely and that, your picture, in your room but that's a picture, that's a picture, you dimwit! The real of it would be awful, the stalks of the flowers would be chokin you, and the smells of them would make you sick, all those smells comin at you when you're feelin so sick to begin with, and the stream, well if you're talking about the Humber River or any stream in this country you're talkin filth, in the Humber River you're even talkin sewage, Jo, you're talkin cigarette packages and used condoms and old tampons floating by you're talking freezin, you'd start shakin from head to toe you're talkin rocks gashin your head you're talkin a bunch of longhairs and goofs on the banks yellin at you callin you whorebag sayin what they'd like to do to you,

you're talkin … and where would you get a dress like that, eh? You'd never find the one in the picture, Jo, it'd be too tight at the neck and the waist, it'd be a kind of material that itches your skin, even worse wet, drives you nut-crazy, the blue would be off, wouldn't look right your shoes wouldn't match you could never find the same colour, Joanne. You can't become a picture, do you know what I mean? I mean you can't … BE … a picture, okay?

They freeze. ISOBEL runs from her watching place, around the circle, screaming. She has realized, listening to JOANNE, that she is not lost but dead, murdered seventeen years before.

ISOBEL: AAHHHHHHHHHHHH!! I am dead! I have been bones for seventeen years, missing, missing, my face in the TV and newspapers, posters, everybody lookin for, nobody find, I am gone, I am dead, I AM DEADLY DEAD! Down! It was night, was a lion, roar!! with red eyes: he come closer (*silent scream*) come closer (*silent scream*) ROAR tear my throat out ROAR tear my eyes out … ROAR I am kill! I am kill! I am no more! (*Music; to JOANNE*) We are both pictures now. WHO WILL TAKE US? WHO WILL TAKE US TO HEAVEN, HA?

Lights down. Cathedral bells ring. DAVID is outside, walking down the street.

DAVID: God, that customer dying of bone cancer. I didn't even want to touch her glass. I don't know she had that look, that dead look. I mean I almost felt hostile.

ISOBEL: (*inside the cathedral*) I WANT TO GO TO HEAVEN NOW! (*She sees a life-size statue of the Virgin Mary and approaches it.*) Holy Mary Mother of God. Will you take Isobel to heaven now, please? (*She lies at the base of the statue, her hand touching its foot.*)

DAVID: God that cathedral is beautiful, funny, I've passed it every day on my way out from work and I've never really looked at it. Look at the stonework, those *spires*—(*He opens the church doors and enters. The doors slam behind him.*) Oh I love this it's so … the air is so … holy it IS, look at those bird-bath things full of holy water, I love it it's so primitive. (*splashes some on his face*) In the name of the Father … the Son, and the Holy—

FATHER HAYES: Good evening. (*DAVID shrieks, startled. His shriek echoes.*) It's alright, it's alright. Have you come for …

DAVID: Confession. I've come for confession, 8:30, yes? I'm not too late, am I, see, I just finished work, and …

FATHER HAYES: Not too late, of course not. (*goes into his part of the confessional*)

DAVID: (*to himself*) I guess just—God I don't remember a THING about what to do!!

We hear the wooden barrier being opened, and the priest begins the Latin prayer.

FATHER HAYES: In the name of the Father, and the Son, and the Holy Spirit.

DAVID: (*overlapping*) Oh God he's saying something—

FATHER HAYES: May the Lord be in your heart and help you to confess your sins with true sorrow. Let us listen to the Lord as he speaks to us: I will give them a new heart and put a new spirit within them; I will remove the strong heart from their bodies and replace it with a natural heart, so that they will live according to my statutes, and observe and carry out my ordinances; thus they shall be my people and I will be their God.

DAVID: (*overlapping*) I think it's Latin, isn't that against Papal Law? I should report him to the Vatican and have him defrocked here goes nothing—(*FATHER HAYES finishes the prayer.*) AHH—FORGIVE ME FATHER FOR I have sinned. It has been … four weeks since my last confession. These are my sins? … OKAY, told Barb I'd be there last night for dinner with her and the niece and nephew—didn't show up didn't phone nothing, was in a mad PASH with my hockey player. I was very cruel to Daniel Thursday, saw him at Billy's—the club? And I don't know, the way he was looking at me drove me CRAZY CRAZY he was mooning! Well I walked up to him and told him to "quit mooning I'd rather see your hairy ass than that pathetic face, face it!" I said, "Face it you old fag, you have been dumped, DUMPED!" That was really mean, that's gotta be more than a venial sin, AND THEN, then, yesterday, I walked through a park? And I saw a large group of poor children playing, and I just thought they were trouble; I wondered why God had put them in the world, really, isn't that unkind? THEN today I saw a fat lady eating an ice-cream cone and I said, I think quite audibly I said "disgusting" oh AND I did not stand up in the subway the incredibly packed subway, for a hugely pregnant lady and her kid, I just didn't feel like it. Quite the catalogue, eh? Oh and another thing, I've lied to you already. I haven't been to confession in fifteen years, haven't stepped in a church in fifteen years, just … did it on a whim, don't ask me why I was passing by on my way …

FATHER HAYES: AND you felt the hand of GOD?

DAVID: Well … it was just a whim—really …

FATHER HAYES: David.

DAVID: How do you know my name?

FATHER HAYES: David I know your name better than I know my own.

DAVID: Wait a minute, wait a minute, I think maybe this is some odd coincidence because although my name is DAVID, I don't actually know you at all, so …

FATHER HAYES: There's nothing odd about it, David, you were an altar boy for me, two years, for two years you served, in 1957 and 1958 at St. Bernard's in Moncton, New Brunswick. Remember?

DAVID: Moncton? We were around there for a couple of years—

FATHER HAYES: You were a believer, David, the other boys were just forced into it by their parents, you believed in every statue every—

DAVID: Father Hayes? You—are Father Hayes?

FATHER HAYES: I am.

DAVID: You're still alive?

FATHER HAYES: I think.

DAVID: But you were so old even way back then!

FATHER HAYES: Not really.

DAVID: I remember you now. I remember you did look old, because you stooped, and you had white hair already didn't you?

FATHER HAYES: Indeed, I was prematurely white …

DAVID: White hair and … and … red eyes.

FATHER HAYES: I … suffered from allergies, hay fever. I'm sorry if it frightened you.

DAVID: I guess maybe it did frighten me a bit, Father, but you know how young boys are—

FATHER HAYES: I am sorry, but, but …

DAVID: No no, I … look, I uh—

FATHER HAYES: David, I want …

DAVID: … don't mean to be impolite but I'd like you to be honest with me, sort of man to man I … I always got the impression that you were looking at me much more than you looked at the other boys am I right?

FATHER HAYES: Well …

DAVID: I felt … I felt as though your eyes were devouring me.

FATHER HAYES: No, no, no …

DAVID: No?? I'm gay, Father, you can be honest with me. I'll forgive you, I mean you never actually did anything, you never even touched me, you just … looked. You kept looking at me—tell me, tell me the truth.

FATHER HAYES: It was not what you think, no, no please—

DAVID: Confess to me Father, come on, come on …

FATHER HAYES: I make my confessions on a regular …

DAVID: Have you confessed this sin?

FATHER HAYES: No, no I haven't, but—

DAVID: God loves sinners who confess, Father, you taught me that, as long as you speak up and you're sorry as hell, you're okay, you still got your ticket to heaven, but you won't you won't Father, if you don't tell me, you'll wither in LIMBO! I suffered, I need you to tell me! CONFESS …

FATHER HAYES: I'm due to a christening. I have to shave first, there's a big party, I—

DAVID: You would christen a baby with this sin, bobbing on the surface, bobbing? Confess, you son of a bitch. Con—

FATHER HAYES: Forgive me Father for I have sinned.

DAVID: Alright.

FATHER HAYES: I looked at you, David, because … I … because … I wanted … to … remember … you.

DAVID: Remember me?

FATHER HAYES: Because … of what was to happen, in the water: oh OH when the day arrived, when the picnic came round, in July, that Canada Day picnic? I had a bad feeling, I had … a very bad feeling indeed. We all piled out of the cars: families, priests, nuns, altar boys, piled out and lugged all those picnic baskets to tables under trees. The grownups all fussed with food and drink while the kids, all of you children, ran ran in your white bare feet to the water, throwing stones and balls, and a warning sound a terrible, the sound of deep nausea filled my ears and I looked up and saw you, dancing on the water, and I saw a red circle, a red, almost electric circle, dazzling round and round like waves, spinning round your head and body. I thought watch, watch that boy, on this day he will surely drown, he *will*. David, *I knew that you would die*. And all because of the chicken. The twenty-nine-pound chicken brought there by Mrs. Henry grown on her brother's farm, everyone had talked and talked about that chicken, who would carve that chicken, Mrs. Henry took it out you skipped along the shore, she laid it on the table, "FATHER HAYES, YOU GO AHEAD AND CARVE, AND DON'T MAKE A MESS OF IT OR YOU WON'T SEE ME AT MASS NEXT SUNDAY." Everyone laughed laughed the men, the men drinking beer, watching me, sure they're thinking, "Watch him carve like a woman," most men hate priests, you know this is a fact, I could see them thinking cruel thoughts under hooded eyes and practised grins; my sin was the sin of pride! The sin of pride David, I started to carve, didn't want to look up, lest I wreck the bird. You see at that moment that chicken was worth more, indeed worth more … than your LIFE, David I SHUT OUT the warning voice and I—carved. I carved and carved and ran into trouble, real trouble I remember thinking, "Damn how does any person do it, it's a terrible job," people behave as if it's nothing, but it's terrible, I kept at it, I wouldn't give up, I wouldn't look up till I'd finished, and I finished carving, and I had made a massacre. The men turned away the women … murmured comfort, and before I looked up I had a hope, a hard hope, that you were still skipping on the rocks and shouting insults to your pals all hands reached for chicken and bread, potato salad, chocolate cake I looked I looked up and your hand from the sea, your hand, far away, was reaching, reaching for me far away … oh no! I ran, and tripped, fell on my face ran again, I could not speak ran to the water and shouted as loud as I could but my voice was so tiny; I saw your hand, ran to the fisherman close, he wasn't home his fat daughter and I, in the skiff, not enough wind no wind, paddling paddling, you a small spot nothing then nothing the sun burns our faces our red red faces.

DAVID: And I … was … never found?

FATHER HAYES: And now … you have come!! You have finally come!!

DAVID: And what have I come for? (*FATHER HAYES is sleeping.*) Uh … Father? Uh—listen … I'm sorry. I'm sorry but I never died. You got the wrong guy I knew you … some other time—I mean, shit, I wish I had died, I only wish, it would have made my life so much more interesting … I grew up, I grew up. Listen if I had drowned in the sea, in Moncton, New Brunswick a beautiful perfect young boy, if I was … pulled by the sea if I reached and was lost, and all those people felt this loss, a loss all their lives, mother father brothers and sister friends a dark ache, somewhere in their chest for what could have been, they could all imagine, you see, what could have been Father Father? I forgive you, I forgive you Father, it was nice on the water, you know? It was neat, so calm, as I slipped underneath I wasn't scared, I'll tell ya. I wasn't scared a bit. The water was so … nice!!

Music. ISOBEL dances, joined by the cast one by one until they are all dancing fully. Cast dance off one by one leaving ISOBEL, who freezes. Blackout.

ACT TWO

Sounds of kids playing in a park. A group of mothers chat. ISOBEL watches.

CHRISTINE: How's your pregnancy going, dear?

Lion roar.

ISOBEL: I hear the LION, I hear the Lion ROAR!!

ELLEN: Wonderful! I finally feel … good for something. LEO, SHARE IT. Share it please.

CHRISTINE: Not me NOT me when I was pregnant I felt as useful as a cow. A large, stupid …

ELLEN: Christine!!

CHRISTINE: EMMA! Five more minutes honey! Mummy's got to go to work! Well, considering I despised the man whose child I was carrying—

ELLEN: I suppose that would … alter things— GOOD CATCH, Leo!

SUE: Hi guys. Timmy, just five minutes. Remember, your father's coming to get you at five.

CHRISTINE: Sue, I love that blouse! Really suits you!

ELLEN: Gorgeous!

SUE: Thank you, I'm organizing a bake sale, if you can believe it, for the community centre over on Ash Street. PLEASE say you'll bake, or sell tickets, even a promise to buy—

ISOBEL: I must tell these peoples, I must tell them now!

ELLEN: Forget me, I'm a diabetic! I can't even look at the stuff.

SUE: Tim! Why don't you try the swing? You love swings.

CHRISTINE: Okay, put me down for fudge brownies, *if* my kids don't eat them first. (*GEORGE enters with a kid's bicycle.*) George! How's the book going?

GEORGE: Well, well, very well indeed!! And how's the busiest freelancer in town? Bradley, don't push so hard!

CHRISTINE: Overworked and underpaid.

GEORGE: What else is new? (*RON enters.*) Ron! Why aren't you at your office?

ELLEN: We're telling!

GEORGE: Good. Bradley!

SUE: Tim? Why don't you try the swing?

CHRISTINE: RON did you get my note? EMMA PUT IT BACK!

RON: Yes, I did, I—I—I—

ISOBEL: (*hitting them*) Shut up Boy! Shut up Girl! I say I say it's time!! He's in the streets get them out he's in the streets save your children take their hand take their leg.

SUE: Isobel! I saw this girl before, she—

ISOBEL: I say shut up! I say LISTEN TO ME NOW! Can you no hear? Listen! Can you nooo—

All freeze except SUE, who crosses slowly towards the children.

SUE: Timmy?

ISOBEL: (*goes to her*) The lion is here, in your streets. He is trying to kill you, to kill all of your children. He really really is. (*She picks up a great crooked stick which she will carry until she says "I love you" to BEN in the final scene.*) Watch me! (*laughs*) I am your HARMY! (*laughs*) I am your SAINT! I am your HARMY! Watch me, watch me, (*a war cry*) I WILL KILL THE LION NOW!!*

Thunderstorm as SUE shouts "TIMMMYY!!" and the others ad lib to their children, e.g., "Quick, you don't want to get wet!" All exit. A kid's bike is left onstage. Blackout.

Lights up on CHRISTINE walking towards SCARLETT'S basement apartment, "tracked" by ISOBEL.

ISOBEL: This girl, Christine, Christine, this girl, SHE will take me to the lion, yes, for she … she is very hard. Harrrrd. HARRRRRRRD!!

CHRISTINE: 116 Carlisle. Lord what a stench. What could that be? (*knocks*)

SCARLETT: Come in!

CHRISTINE: Scarlett Deer?

SCARLETT: That's my name, don't wear it out, has to last a lifetime!!

CHRISTINE: I'm Christine Pierce from the *Telegraph.* We talked on the phone.

SCARLETT: Have a seat.

CHRISTINE: Thank you. Nice place.

SCARLETT: What, this hole? Sorry if it stinks, I cooked chicken today an ever since I ate it I been fartin up a storm. Dead chicken farts, that's what my brother always said.

CHRISTINE: Scarlett, I don't have a lot of time, so is it all right if I ask you some questions?

SCARLETT: Sure, How does it feel to be an ugly geek? Fine thank you, fuck you very much.

CHRISTINE: Scarlett, advanced cerebral palsy is a serious handicap. Don't you feel that living on your own is dangerous?

SCARLETT: Would you like to live in a freak-house?

CHRISTINE: Well, Scarlett, I—

SCARLETT: Freedom, freedom girl, I'd rather fuckin rot on the floor of my own home than be well-fed and cared for in a freakhouse.

CHRISTINE: What you're saying, then, is that above all things, you cherish freedom. That you would rather risk—

SCARLETT: Once when my volunteers were sick? All of em were sick, right? And I just wanted to see what the hell I would do? I lay in my own shit and piss for three days.

CHRISTINE: Good Lord, what—

SCARLETT: I coulda phoned somebody, my parents live down the street, but I just wanted to see ... I wanted to see how long I'd survive, I wanted to see if I could do it.

CHRISTINE: Well, who did you eventually—

SCARLETT: My mother, my poor mother. And it makes me sick, sick, because what will I do when they die? They're old you know, they're gonna die soon.

CHRISTINE: What will you do?

SCARLETT: I'll die on the floor in my shit and piss.

CHRISTINE: Scarlett, do you have any hobbies; that is, what do you do between volunteers, do you have favourite soap operas or game shows, or—

SCARLETT: I screw my brains out.

CHRISTINE: (a weak laugh) No, seriously, Scarlett.

SCARLETT: You think I'm kiddin? You think I sit around and watch game shows and uh stare out the window waitin for the next volunteer? No way, girlie, I git it ONNN.

CHRISTINE: You're ... sexually active, then?

SCARLETT: Shocked, aren't you, pretty pea?

CHRISTINE: No.

SCARLETT: YOU ARE TOO YOU LYING BITCH!!

CHRISTINE: Alright, I will admit, I am ... surprised. I suppose the public perception of handicapped people is somewhat—skewered.

SCARLETT: You think you're bettern me, dontcha?

CHRISTINE: Oh Scarlett, really I ...

SCARLETT: Well I'll tell you somethin, Christine, my boyfriend wouldn't rub your tittie. And you think he's handicapped? No way, babe, I'm not fucking a freak.

CHRISTINE: Well, I'm very happy for you, really Scarlett.

SCARLETT: Bullshit, you think it's sick.

CHRISTINE: No, honestly Scarlett, I don't! I think everybody deserves to have a happy sex life.

SCARLETT: Yeah? Wanna hear more?

CHRISTINE: Sure!

SCARLETT: But don't print this part in your article, right, just the crap about how noble I am copin on my own and that shit, and how good the United Church is helpin me out, all that shit right?

CHRISTINE: Scarlett, I won't print anything that you don't want me to. I despise journalists that do that kind of thing. I want you to think of me as a friend. Maybe we could even go out sometime, catch a movie, or go to dinner ...

SCARLETT: Sure, if you like.

CHRISTINE: So! How did it all start with your boyfriend?

SCARLETT: It all started one night, I'd just been watching TV for sixteen hours straight, from eight in the morning, right? And that's hard on the eyes, I was bone tired. So I go to bed, I look out the window and there's no moon, right? And I lie there for hours, can't sleep, itchy, bored, just wishin I was dead, as usual, when I hear, my door open.

CHRISTINE: Were you frightened?

SCARLETT: I couldnta cared. I thought it was, you know, a guy with a knife, come to carve me up. I thought good, great, what a way to go. I laughed thinkin a Monica, she's my morning volunteer, thinkin a her comin in findin me dead—so I wait to be cut, but I don't hear nothin, nothin, I figure he's in his socks, not a sound then … he sits on the edge of my bed, and and and, and then he start … he start … he start … touchin my foot just touchin my foot so soft, and nice, and I … laugh. I laugh and laugh, and Christine, I don't think I ever laughed so long and so long in my life.

CHRISTINE: Who was it?

SCARLETT: That's the question, isn't it Chris? Who the hell is it?

CHRISTINE: Did he … ever come again?

SCARLETT: He come every time there isn't no moon, in like a big cat sit on the bed, and me, like a big piece of fruit, (*Dance music starts. She gets up.*) explodin in the heat, exploding up and out the whole night, I can MOVE when my boy comes, (*she twirls*) I am movin, I know I am, I am turnin and swishin and holdin …

A MAN enters. He and SCARLETT dance romantically around the set. He leaves her back in her chair, immobile, and exits.

… like eels, you ever seen eels? Lamprey eels, brilliant light moving fast fast they swim from the Saint John River down to Montego Bay to spurt their young, I swim like that coloured-up, bright and fast when my boy comes, swirlin and movin in the dark no moon …

CHRISTINE: Hey, is he handsome?

SCARLETT: I tole you there's no moon.

CHRISTINE: You mean you haven't—

SCARLETT: He's my midnight man, you dick! My midnight man he is my midnight man, get it? You can't SEE night, you can't SEE when there's no moon why? Why do you think it's so big to see your boyfriend two eyes, nose, a mouth, what the diff, what the hell is the—

CHRISTINE: I must go, I … have an appointment.

SCARLETT: You're not gonna print that.

CHRISTINE: I have a job, Scarlett, I have a child to support …

SCARLETT: I'll slit your throat if ya print that.

CHRISTINE: Goodbye.

SCARLETT: (*grabs CHRISTINE's clothing*) PLEASE!! PLEASE!! Please, Christine, my old lady and old man, they're old, my mum's had a stroke, my dad's got MS, this'd kill em, please!!

CHRISTINE: That is not my business, Scarlett, Scarlett, let go of me, LET GO!

SCARLETT: Reverend Pete and everybody down the church, they'd think I was a slut, they'd send me to the freakhouse.

They struggle.

CHRISTINE: Let me go!!

SCARLETT: (*falls on top of CHRISTINE*) You're gonna kill me, you're gonna kill me.

CHRISTINE: (*rolls her off and onto the floor*) You are trying to obstruct the freedom of the press, lady.

SCARLETT: You can't do this you can't do this!

CHRISTINE: (*frees herself and gets away*) I'm sorry. I'm doing it.

SCARLETT: I'll see you in hell!!

This stops CHRISTINE.

CHRISTINE: What?

SCARLETT: I said you'll go right to hell for this!!

CHRISTINE: I don't believe in hell.

SCARLETT: Joke's on you, girl, 'cause I'm in it, right now, live from hell, and if you do this, you're gonna be burning here with me, maybe not today, maybe not tomorrow but soon, soon, you'll be whizzing down the highway with a large group of handsome friends to some ski resort or other, and your male driver will decide to pass on the right, you will turn over and over, knocking into each other's skulls breaking each other's necks like eggs in a bag, falling through windshields it's gonna rain blood and I will open my big jaws and swallow youuuu! YOU will spend the rest of eternity inside me. Inside my … body and ooooh time goes slowwwwwe …

CHRISTINE: You're crazy.

SCARLETT: I am waiting for you Chrissy, I'm waiting for you Chrissy, I am waiting for you Chrissy, I am …

CHRISTINE: STOP THAT. Stop that craziness NOW there is no such thing, there is no such thing as any of that ANY of it. You live and you die in your own body and you go up to heaven or just nowhere.

SCARLETT: Into the middle of Scarlett …

CHRISTINE: You don't know ANYTHING.

SCARLETT: Inside my big wet behind …

CHRISTINE: Stop it. Stop saying those things.

SCARLETT: In the bummy of a big dead fish …

CHRISTINE: Stop it, I said stop it now.

SCARLETT: Your left arm and your head too, Chrissy, gonna be severed you'll be all over the highway and your mean little soul will …

CHRISTINE: (beats SCARLETT to the ground, screaming) STOP IT! STOP IT! (kicking her) STOP IT! STOP IT!

CHRISTINE collapses. SCARLETT breathes with difficulty.

Oh no. Oh no. Scarlett, are you okay? You're okay. You're okay. Your mother will be by soon or a volunteer and, and I'll call, I, I, I'll call an ambulance. You shouldn't have made me do that, Scarlett. You shouldn't have made me kick you like that. The way you, you, you talked to me like that. Like, like, like you belong. In the world. As if you belong. Where did you get that feeling? I want it. I need it. (pause, about to exit) I need it.

SCARLETT: OOOOOOH! Come down and kiss me, put your tongue in my mouth!! Come on, NOW, RIGHT now, there's no one around, right now, on the ground, do me, kiss me, come down and kiss me, like a lion, so hot right here right now, swirl, swirl me twirl, twirl me, make me light, light exploding into … (laughs)

CHRISTINE returns, swooping down like a condor, and gives SCARLETT the kiss of death. SCARLETT, thinking it is her lover, responds passionately and then, without air, dies.

ISOBEL: (to CHRISTINE, touching her) SLAVE! You are a slave of the lion! You lie with him you laugh you let him bite your neck, you spread your legs. You will take me to him now.

Music, blackout. Lights up on CHRISTINE's office. She is moving things in an angry way.

ISOBEL: Shhh. I wait for the lion!!

RODNEY, an early-middle-aged man with a stoop, CHRISTINE's research assistant, comes in and waits until she addresses him. He has an armload of papers.

CHRISTINE: Yes, Rodney, what is it?

RODNEY: I've … uh … brought the research material you asked for.

CHRISTINE: Good. Great. Thank you … how was your weekend?

RODNEY: Quiet.

CHRISTINE: Rodney. Rodney—Rodney I told you I wanted stats on CP, cerebral palsy, not just "handicapped people." I wanted information on cerebral palsy!

RODNEY: You did NOT specify cerebral palsy, Christine.

CHRISTINE: Oh yes I most certainly did, I said—

RODNEY: I have it on tape, Christine!

CHRISTINE: Rodney! Are you or are you not a professional researcher?

RODNEY: Yes.

CHRISTINE: Well then start doing professional work! NOW! Or you are out. Is that understood? IS THAT UNDERSTOOD?

RODNEY: … of … course …

CHRISTINE exits. RODNEY is at his desk.

RODNEY: You will NOT EVER SPEAK TO ME THAT WAY AGAIN CHRISTINE YOU WILL NOT TREAT ME AS AN OBJECT do you understand? Is that understood? IS THAT UNDERSTOOD?? (knock on the door) Yes? Hello. May I help you?

MICHAEL: Yes, I'm looking for a Rodney LeHavre—I was directed to this office.

RODNEY: I … am … Mr. LeHavre.

MICHAEL: Rodney?

RODNEY: Do I know you?

MICHAEL: Michael … Lind … from St. George's, '60 to '64. How are you? You remember me, don't you?

RODNEY: Michael … Lind? No. No, I'm afraid I don't, I'm sorry. Were you in my class?

MICHAEL: Yeah, yeah, we were good friends for a while even; don't you remember? Come on. We played chess. You were a great player. You taught me … how to play. You must remember.

RODNEY: Chess.

MICHAEL: I guess you don't remember. I'm sorry. I was sure that you'd remember. I … I … (backing out)

RODNEY: Would you like to come in and sit down? I can take ten minutes I think. Would you like to sit down?

MICHAEL: Oh, oh, okay, if you don't mind …

RODNEY: No. A cup of coffee … I could—get the secretary—Sherry—to—

MICHAEL: (laughs) You've got to remember the fly collection. It was really hot. July, I think. We caught it must have been fifty house flies, and, and we stuck them with Elmer's glue, to a piece of Bristol board. To a big piece of Bristol board. And labelled them in Latin. Don't you remember? You must remember.

RODNEY: Wait a minute … wait a minute … yeah, yeah, and we even named them, didn't we? Didn't we name each one?

MICHAEL: Yeah, yeah … I'll never forget. You even named one Clarence. I thought it was brilliant.

RODNEY: Right! And yours were all names like Fred, Joe, Cindy, weren't they? Right!

MICHAEL: And yours were all royalty— Elizabeth, Margaret, Clarence. God!

RODNEY: God. A fly collection. So what did we do with it?

MICHAEL: I think … we had it arranged … to show someone. A colleague of my father's. Someone in insect …

RODNEY: Entomology.

MICHAEL: Yeah, that's it. And it was raining or something …

RODNEY: Pouring, yes, pouring, and all the flies—

RODNEY & MICHAEL: —FELL OFF THE BRISTOL BOARD!

RODNEY: God. Michael Lind. Michael LIND! I'm sorry.

CHRISTINE: (off) Rodney I need that material as SOON as possible, please!

MICHAEL: Well I see that you have to get back to work, I'd better go … ahhh … just before I go, there's one thing. I uh … this is going to sound strange, but … I've been having … sort of … dreams … about … back then, I … have them a lot—

RODNEY: Oh?

MICHAEL: Yes, only … I always wake up at the same spot, fairly distressed, actually, and … I just … wondered … if you could … help me … remember … what actually happened. Back then … when we were … kids. Do you think you could—

RODNEY: Sure, I could try …

MICHAEL: Okay, let's start at the beginning. It was something to do with chess.

RODNEY: Chess.

MICHAEL: You loved to play chess you … brought me to your house after school, it was a Tuesday, I think, cold, we went through a short cut it said "Pedestrians Only" I thought it said "Protestants Only" and I was terrified. (RODNEY laughs.) And we went to your room, with all the paper airplanes hanging from the ceiling all over the room! And we lay on the floor. Do you remember? You remember lying on the floor? Rodney, your carpet. Your carpet was brown and orange, sort of circles or something. There was the sound of a snowblower outside. My queen. You took my queen. And then, and then, Rodney, didn't we laugh, or or or or … some touch some touch Rodney and you made a strange sound. What was that sound. Please help me! I need to go back there. I need to go back there, you see? You were the only—friend that I—we saw the world the same way. Remember? We saw the world the same way. I want to go back there. (caresses his shoulder) I want to go back there …

RODNEY: I want to go back there, too. I want to go back there, too.

MICHAEL and RODNEY embrace. RODNEY makes the sound. MICHAEL pulls him back and throws him to the ground.

MICHAEL: QUEER!! Queer queer queer queer queer queer QUEER! FAIRY SISSY LITTLE CREEP!! DON'T YOU EVER ever remember again. YOU have WRECKED my life, your slimy memory, using me over and over and over again like an old porno magazine you will RELIN-QUISH that memory you will wipe it OUT, YOU understand?

RODNEY: You're crazy, you need psychiatric ...

MICHAEL: You will NOT remember me again because if you do, if you do, I will feel it, oh yes, and I will come and I will kill you. I could feel you remembering, almost daily, I would be in the middle, the middle of a crucial business meeting all the way in Vancouver and suddenly I would feel you ... holding my memory, turning it over and over, folding it, caressing it, reliving it, SPEWING, spewing your filth all over me. How how I always wondered how could you do it in the middle of the day? Did you do it here, at work, at this desk is this where you—

RODNEY: Anywhere I can, Michael. You see, my life has been terribly disappointing.

MICHAEL: You will ... free me—

RODNEY: Of course. I'll try, but memory ... does seem to have a will of its own, I can't really help what—

MICHAEL hits him. They fight, rolling and punch-ing, and end up on the floor. Very, very slowly MICHAEL raises his head and extends his tongue. RODNEY does the same. They come together and their tongues touch. It is an ecstatic moment for both of them. MICHAEL pulls out a knife. RODNEY takes it from him and cuts his throat. MICHAEL dies. Music. The actor playing MICHAEL gets up and exits. ISOBEL goes to RODNEY and touches him, then RODNEY gets up and straightens himself.

RODNEY: "Hello, welcome to St. George's. My name is Rodney LeHavre, grade seven, and you're ... ? Michael Lind! Welcome! You just came from Vancouver? I have a cousin there! Do you play chess?" Chess, every day ... chess,

Monday, Tuesday, Wednesday, Thursday, chess, with ... Michael ... at school, at my house at his house in his room, lying on our stomachs staring at the chess board, he sticks his tongue out at me because he had just captured my queen and then I stuck my tongue out back at him and he moved forward just a bit till his tongue was touching mine, and my whole life jumped into my tongue we didn't move just lay there touching tongues, "Would you boys like some tuna sandwiches?" his mother the best mother in the world with her red bangles and bourbon sour at six, "Okay Mrs. Lind, thanks!" And we had a secret, an atomic secret nobody else in the whole entire world knew that we had touched tongues oh OH wrote his name, MICHAEL, over and over one thousand times one thousand times; on the fifth day, the fifth day after, I'm at the blackboard doing math, very good at math, superb mind for mathematics the other boys jealous, always been jealous of my superior brain throwing spitballs, used to that, yelling "Froggy, froggy frog" because of my francophone name, used to that, I turn, I catch his face white darkened so quickly like a sky, he caught, he knew, suddenly he knew, Michael, that he had been playing chess with the loser "FROGGY, HEY FROGGY" they scream "HEY FROG." He stands up! They look expectantly, is the new kid going to defend his friend? What's he going to say, I to myself, "Oh thank you, Michael, thank you thank you the first to ever defend me oh what what are you going to say to defend me?" He takes a breath, I'm holding mine, he smiles he speaks he says: "Is he a frog ... OR A TOAD!!" They laugh and laugh and laugh screaming their laughter slapping their desks shaking their fists triumphing a new member of the PACK!! Is he a frog, or a toad—Am I a frog or am I a toad?

SHERRY enters.

SHERRY: RODDEE! RODDEEE!! Baby Bunny.

ISOBEL: She!

SHERRY: You'll never guess what I have! Milk chocolate bar with lots of gushy cream in it. Two squares for you, and two squares for me.

ISOBEL: She!

SHERRY: One hundred and forty calories a square who gives a shit. I heard Christine chewin ya out, what a fuckin cow.

ISOBEL: She ... I see, I smell the spray, the Lion's spray ...

SHERRY: *(notices that RODNEY is very upset)* What happened?

SHERRY runs from RODNEY's office back home to the apartment she shares with her boyfriend of two years, EDWARD, an out-of-work actor. When she comes in, he is practising a tap routine for an audition. Newspapers are all over the floor.

SHERRY: JeSUS I'm peed off—I'm standing on the escalator, right? Goin down to the subway? My back hurts, I don't feel like takin the stairs? So I'm standin there when this woman shoves by me right into the wall and goes, "Can't *you* move? Some people are in a hurry!" And I just STAND there like a fucking WETWIPE with my mouth open FUCK if I see that bitch again—

EDWARD: That's very interesting, Sherry.

SHERRY: Whatcha workin on that dance try-out thing?

EDWARD: Uh, no. I'm fixing the faulty wiring with my feet, it's magic, Sherry, really! Right through the—

SHERRY: Ah Jeez, you're not mad at me again are ya? Whad I do now?

EDWARD: I don't know, Sherry, what did you do now?

SHERRY: I get off work at five-thirty, Ed, it's ten to six what the hell am I supposed to do? Fly home?

EDWARD: I phoned work at four o'clock, Sherry, and Arlene said that you had left for the day.

SHERRY: Oh well THAT—I was havin a coffee and a piece of cake with Rodney, he—

EDWARD: Don't lie, please.

SHERRY: I was, Eddie, ask Rodney, ask—

EDWARD: You've rehearsed them all.

SHERRY: Listen to me! Rodney had some kind of fit today, Christine just about called the cops he was yelling and screaming at nobody all afternoon—he's right nuts.

EDWARD: It is a skillful liar it is.

SHERRY: *Don't call me "it."*

EDWARD: I beg your pardon?

SHERRY: Have you been drinking? Or doin coke or some shit? You have, haven't you? You—

EDWARD: We're out of toilet paper.

SHERRY: No, there's more right under the—

EDWARD: No there's NOT!

SHERRY: Alright, I'll go and get some now—

EDWARD: YOU'LL stay right where you are, Sherry. Please. PLEASE I'm asking you. Don't leave me alone—here—I don't want to be alone.

SHERRY: Aww Eddie, you know I love you, don't you.

EDWARD: If—if you're not happy with my performance in bed ... I wish you'd just ... tell me and—and—

SHERRY: Honey, I love your performance in bed.

EDWARD: You don't really, do you?

SHERRY: Listen I was just tellin Arlene today you got the best hands of I bet any guy there is on the whole fuckin planet!

EDWARD: You were?

SHERRY: The way you touch me, Eddie, Christ, I feel like a whole bouquet, you know? A bouquet of red flowers just ... poppin open, poppop pop pop pop just like on one of them nature specials. I love makin love with you, I think about it all day, half the time my pants are wet thinkin about you.

EDWARD: They're not, really?

SHERRY: They are. Feel ... feel that. *(puts his hand under her dress)* Oh honey I want you to make love to me. Please?

EDWARD: *(kissing her)* Oh! Oh! I've been thinking about you too, all day, every day.

SHERRY: Oh Eddie, I want you.

EDWARD: You want me ... ?

SHERRY: Did you not get that part in the TV series? About the runaway kid or whatever? Is that why you're—Eddie what's wrong? Did I say something wrong?

EDWARD: YOU ARE A FLAMING ASSHOLE!

SHERRY: Eddie!

EDWARD: Who are you dreaming about every night?

SHERRY: What?

EDWARD: Every night you're moaning like an animal in heat, who?

SHERRY: What?

EDWARD: Who are you dreaming about, Sherry?

SHERRY: Nobody! I'm not dreaming about—nobody.

EDWARD: WHO ARE YOU DREAMING ABOUT?

SHERRY: Just forget it, I'm going over to Arlene's, I'll see you later.

EDWARD: You tell me who you are dreaming about or I will cancel the wedding.

SHERRY: Eddie.

EDWARD: I will ... TODAY, if you don't stop lying to me treating me like a fucking maggot—

SHERRY: I'm not lying to you Ed, please, just—

EDWARD: I'll cancel the wedding! I'll phone up Father Hayes and I'll cancel the whole fucking thing.

SHERRY: I paid nine hundred dollars for that dress, Eddie.

EDWARD: I don't give a flying fuck what you paid for it.

SHERRY: EDDIE my mum's got her ticket from Florida, my sisters—

EDWARD: I don't give a hot damn miss—

SHERRY: OKAY OKAY OKAY OKAY you're right, you're right. There is someone I'm dreaming about ... it's ... uh ... it's ...

EDWARD: Now we are cookin' with GAS, Sherry. This is what I always knew in my heart never DARED with all this feminist shit going down. Come on, come on tell me if I'm going to be your husband I want to know it all.

SHERRY: Tell you. Tell ... you ... ?

EDWARD: You were walking home from the subway, yes?

SHERRY: Yes.

EDWARD: About one thirty in the morning, yes?

SHERRY: Yes. Well. I had been at my great aunt's doin'—

EDWARD: I don't give a fuck where you were Sherry you were walking home, one thirty in the morning, right?

SHERRY: Right.

EDWARD: And you hear steps behind you.

SHERRY: Steps.

EDWARD: Clack clack clack like cowboy boots.

SHERRY: Clack. Clack.

EDWARD: And a voice ...

SHERRY: Like a housefly.

EDWARD: A VOICE.

SHERRY: Asks me if I had been seein' that ... porno show down the street.

EDWARD: And you said ...

SHERRY: I didn't say, Ed, I walked faster.

EDWARD: But your heels, were so high, so provocative, that you turned on your ankle.

SHERRY: I sprained my ankle.

EDWARD: And he grabbed you.

SHERRY: By the arm!

EDWARD: He was all man.

SHERRY: Oh no! No!

EDWARD: And then what happened, Sherry? What happened then?

SHERRY: You know what happened Ed.

EDWARD: I forget, Sherry. Tell me again. Tell me again, come on, come ON or I ... cancel ...

SHERRY: You know what happened.

EDWARD: ORICANCEL ...

SHERRY: He threw me between two houses, Ed.

EDWARD: And you are breathing fast. And hot.

SHERRY: And he smashed my head against the fire wall, Ed.

EDWARD: You dream about that, don't you Sherry?

SHERRY: And he told me he was going to kill me.

EDWARD: His voice. MASTERFUL …

SHERRY: And he held my throat and he …

EDWARD: And he …

SHERRY: Please, Eddie. Please please, I am asking you … I can't do this again, I can not go through it for you, Eddie. I'm tired, I'm …

EDWARD: And? And?

SHERRY: And I fought like a cat, Ed, you know that! I scratched him and bit him and twisted and screamed but he—

EDWARD: But he … ?

SHERRY: He—

EDWARD: He—

SHERRY: Eddie please …

EDWARD: Say it!!!

SHERRY: NO!

EDWARD: Say it now Sherry.

SHERRY: Eddie!

EDWARD: You *are* the snake.

SHERRY: No.

EDWARD: Because the snake tempts others to sin, uh huh? SATAN tempts others to sin. Say it Sherry. Come on, "I am the snake," come on, "I am the snake," "I am the snake" come on COME ON.

SHERRY: I … am … the snake.

EDWARD: With the diamond back, glittering.

SHERRY: Yeah. I am. The snake. With the back.

EDWARD: Oh yes!! You ARE the snake, baby, come on, "I am the snake!"

SHERRY: I am. The snake! I am the snake! I am the snake! I AM THE SNAKE I AM THE SNAKE I AM THE SNAKE I AM THE SNAAAAAAAAAKE!

SHERRY breaks down in tears. She collapses on the floor. EDWARD cleans up and then sits down.

Eddie? Will you come with me tomorrow then to Ashley's to pick out a pattern? Like I've made the appointment and everything Ed, and after all, you are going to have to live with the dishes. I mean, I know guys hate goin' in there, all guys do, but everyone that gets married goes to Ashley's, everyone that gets married—

EDWARD: Alright. But nothing with flowers on it. I just want something clean, maybe—white, with a black stripe.

SHERRY thinks, changes her mind, then turns away. ISOBEL enters the room and offers her hand to SHERRY, who takes it gratefully. Arm in arm, they walk away from SHERRY and EDWARD's apartment to a graveyard. At first ISOBEL is helping SHERRY, but by the time they reach the graveyard, it is SHERRY who helps ISOBEL find her grave, and gently lays her down, and disappears.

PLAYWRIGHT'S NOTE: The next section has two scene options.

Scene Option 1:

In the graveyard, sitting on another tombstone, is BEN, the man who killed ISOBEL seventeen years before.

BEN: There's one thing, you know. There's one thing that I always … wanted to tell somebody and that is that … I done her a favour. I was— kindly—yeah, see, I pull her outa the car and throw her on the cement in front of the ware-house there's a streetlight and … and she says to me she says, "Please," she says, "Please no strangle, I so … scared of strangle," in this voice of breath just … purely of breath so I stopped, eh? I did. I stepped out of the twister 'cause that's what it's like, when you're doin something like that, you're inside a twister and to step out, is like … liftin a dishwasher, eh, but I did. So I go back of the warehouse and I picked up a brick and I hit her—'cause she touched me okay? She touched me, right?

ISOBEL approaches with her weapon.

(Scene Option 1 continues after Scene Option 2.)

Scene Option 2:

In the graveyard a group of mourners exits, leaving BEN and his mother, JOAN, alone.

JOAN: Dear, you're looking quite uncomfortable, shall we go?

BEN: Yeah, yeah, let's go. No. No. Let's stay here. Here, sit on a tombstone why dontcha? (*reading*) "Harvey J. Walker, 1920–1973." What's that make him?

JOAN: Dear, it's getting quite chilly, don't you think?

BEN: It's summer, Joanie!

JOAN: Yes dear, but there is a wind! I'm afraid my silly old hair will just—

BEN: JOAN! I wanna siddown and pay my respects. SIDDOWN! SIT DOWN!

JOAN: (*sitting down awkwardly*) All right. Somebody hasn't watered these impatiens in a very long time. Poor old Father Hayes, I will miss him.

BEN: He was an old fruit.

JOAN: Benny he was not, how can you say that about Father Hayes?

BEN: Because he talked like a fruit; he walked like one too.

JOAN: Now now, you don't mean that.

BEN: I sure as hell do.

JOAN: BEN PLEASE your language!!

BEN: So, whatdya been up to, Joan, lots a charity work, what?

JOAN: Yes, I'm still working in the shop, at the hospital.

BEN: What about bridge, you still play bridge?

JOAN: Oh yes, every week, heavens, I guess it's been every week for the last … fifteen years. Ben I wish you would call me Mum.

BEN: I can't. I told you that before.

JOAN: You are my son. We've had you since you were three weeks old for heaven's sake.

BEN: I don't give a shit. You're Joan, I like you, you're just not my mother.

JOAN: You break my heart, Christine still calls me Mum.

BEN: Christine's different.

JOAN: How? How is Christine different?

BEN: 'Cause … she's … like you, see; she's the same. Her mother was some kinda student or something, her father a professor or some shit, me, I wasn't from nothin, I'm different, I'm different from you, see?

JOAN: I love you Ben, I hope you …

BEN: Don't say that word.

JOAN: I'm sorry, but it's true, I love every hair on your sweet head …

BEN: Joan.

JOAN: And I will till the day I die.

BEN: DO YOU LOVE ME?

JOAN: Well yes, I just—

BEN: Do you love me?

JOAN: Terribly.

BEN: Well then gimme some money.

JOAN: I beg your pardon?

BEN: I need a loan. About sixty thousand bucks. And I need it tonight.

JOAN: Oh so that's why you agreed to come with me to Father Hayes' funeral, stupid me, I actually thought …

BEN: Shutup, I came because I knew it meant something for you, I hadn't seen you in a while—

JOAN: Eight months.

BEN: Yeah well I was busy.

JOAN: You're only seeing me because you want money.

BEN: Shutup, don't give me that shit …

JOAN: It's obviously true, Ben.

BEN: Okay, it's true. Can you get the money?

JOAN: What do you need it for?

BEN: I said can you get it?

JOAN: I don't know, Ben, I don't know until you tell me what you need it for.

BEN: Okay I'm leaving.

JOAN: Ben WAIT, WAIT. (*crying*) I'm sorry.

BEN: WELL don't cry, I hate it when an old woman cries, it's friggin gross youse are ugly enough to begin with but when you start with the water …

JOAN: Ben that's enough.

BEN: I'm just being straight, Joan, come on, the old "visage" is NOT what it used to be, HEY, you can take a little tease can't ya?

JOAN: Well I know I've aged, dear, but I didn't think—

BEN: You're old and ugly. But you're okay. Wanta smoke?

JOAN: No thank you Ben, you know I don't.

BEN: The cancer thing, right, right, well I don't give a shit myself, so I'm gonna smoke myself sick.

JOAN: Ben, why do you say you don't care?

BEN: 'Cause I'm a sittin duck. Unless you give me that cash money now, I'll be dead news anyways, so what do I care.

JOAN: I don't follow you, Ben.

BEN: I'm saying that there's people after me, Joanie, bad bad dudes, these jokers don't think nothin, nothin of blowin a guy's head off and stickin him in a trunk.

JOAN: Oh Benny how did you get involved with these …

BEN: Don't ask questions, Joanie, for crying out loud, I did time in a federal penitentiary, I did twenty years in friggin Collins Bay the place is crawlin with creeps they follow you out …

JOAN: Why are they … after you?

BEN: Why are they after me? Why are they after me? You are askin me why they are after me? Why do you think?

JOAN: Well goodness anybody who knows anything knows you did not kill that little girl, all the magazines wrote about the suppressed evidence, and impossibility of the time factor, everybody knows it was a miscarriage of justice—

BEN: I know that you know that, butcha think the turkeys know that? Hey, they just gotta feel upper than somebody, right? They're the lowest on the social ladder they gotta have somebody lower, that's me, scum of the earth.

JOAN: Oh Benny.

BEN: You never thought I done it.

JOAN: Not for a second.

BEN: May I ask why?

JOAN: Because—because—you would fall asleep only in my arms till you were six years old.

BEN: ONLY IN YOUR ARMS.

JOAN: And you brushed my hair, your favourite pastime in the world was for us to lie on the bed and you would brush and brush my hair, my hair was long then black …

BEN: I still like brushin chicks' hair.

JOAN: I always knew, I always knew it wasn't you.

BEN: I know. I know you always knew that.

JOAN: I am your mother …

BEN: NO!

JOAN: I AM.

BEN: You are not! You are … my guardian, LIKE a mother to me not my mother. My mother is probably some whore living outa Dominion bags now.

JOAN: Oh Benny.

BEN: Are you gonna give me the cash?

JOAN: Just … please, please tell me what it's for? Please darling?

BEN: Surgery. Changin my face so those jokers won't know me, then I'm gonna start in on the pasta, the milkshakes, gain fifty pounds, then dye the hair red.

JOAN: But surely that won't cost—

BEN: LET ME FINISH, Christ, did ya ever let anybody finish anything?

JOAN: I'm sorry.

BEN: You better be. Now where was I …

JOAN: About why you need so much—

BEN: Okay, after the looks change, I go into business. I got a idea for a business gonna make me a millionaire. Alls I gotta do is have some cash up front.

JOAN: Ben, dear, I don't mean to be discouraging, but I've watched so many of these schemes of yours—

BEN: What?

JOAN: Fail!!

BEN: They didn't fail! They didn't fail they just didn't work 'cause of people rippin me off 'cause my heart was too big!! Well this time I learned my lesson I know I know to be ruthless, okay?

JOAN: Well I don't think you have to be "ruthless," I mean Walter was a brilliant business man, but he was never never—

BEN: (spits) HE WAS A SON OF A BITCH.

JOAN: Walter loved you, Benny.

BEN: Don't you mention that man's name the man was a pig.

JOAN: Ben you are talking about your father, my husband.

BEN: NOT MY FATHER NOT MY FATHER YOU only saw one face, Joanie one WALTER face, the other face was secret, between him and me, only I saw the …

JOAN: Oh Ben how can you—

BEN: He he he he he used to force me …

JOAN: He forced you to do what?

BEN: Well … forget it.

JOAN: Ben, please, I don't understand what you—

BEN: WHY DO YOU THINK THIS BOY IS HELL, I was hell for you from the time I was seven, killin the cats, wrecking the car, sellin your stereo WHY? 'Cause my mother was a fifteen-year-old kid from Gerrard and Parliament with stringy hair … who couldn't say her alphabet? You think it's that? Why do you think it is, Joanie, why do you think I am hell?

JOAN: I think that when we told you that you were adopted, you were crushed and we were never able to help you.

BEN: No. So whaddya think it is, Joan?

JOAN: … Something … Walter … ?

BEN: Yeah. Yeah. Yeah … something Walter said.

JOAN: You are saying that he … did something to you—he struck you?

BEN: Joanie bein hit, I wouldn'ta minded, hell it was a relief when it was that. It's … the other …

JOAN: It's not true.

BEN: You never noticed anything, NOTHIN strange? Whyd'ja think, whyd'ja think he left the bed every night?

JOAN: To have a snack, he … always said that he had had a … snack.

BEN: (laughs) Yeah right.

JOAN: I'm … really in a state of shock.

BEN: Believe me, Joan.

JOAN: I thought I knew Walter so well …

BEN: Yeah.

JOAN: OH GOD. My little boy, my poor little …

BEN: Poor Joanie, no one told her. No one ever told her that 95% of the human population is maggots. You got fooled into thinkin life was nice tea parties and hot cocoa after skatin and tuckin your kids in and singing a pretty song about the fuckin moon … 'Member that rabbit I used to have?

JOAN: Honey.

BEN: Yeah Honey, well, Honey always made me think of you, you know, with those big wide apart eyes, believe everything thinkin everything is nice, so trusting, she was so trustin it made me mad, you know? Like why do you trust me don't you know I could pull your eyes out? You should hop away when my hands are in your cage, hop away, you stupid pest, don't just stand there. With those eyes.

JOAN: Is that why you—

BEN: I DON'T LIKE STUPIDITY.

JOAN: Oh dear.

BEN: Look, Joan, I'm short on time here, so do we have a deal?

JOAN: Sixty ... thousand ... ?

BEN: You got it.

JOAN: Oh Ben. Oh Ben. Walter. I am shattered to know that my Walter—

BEN: Hey. Would I lie to you Joanie? Just to score some cash? Come on ...

JOAN: Now I know, Ben, I know ...

BEN: Whaddya know.

JOAN: Her picture, in the papers on all those posters, that picture, her eyes, she had unusually trusting, wide apart—

BEN: Back off, I'm tellin ya Joanie—

JOAN: YOU HATE TRUSTING EYES because— they reminded you of me and how ... I trusted Walter, how I let it go on, how dumb I was how dumb I was, you were killing me, killing—WAL- TER! It's all my fault!! That little girl's death is all my fault!

BEN: There's one thing, you know. There's one thing that I always ... wanted to tell somebody and that is that ... I done her a favour. I was— kindly—yeah, see, I pull her outa the car and throw her on the cement in front of the ware- house there, and ... I put my hands around her neck and she says to me she says "Please," she says, "please no strangle, I so ... scared of strangle" in this ... voice of breath just ... purely of breath and I stopped, eh? I stepped out of the twister 'cause that's what it's like, Joanie, when you're doin somethin like that you're inside a twister and to step out, is like ... liftin two hundred pounds but I did 'cause she touched me, okay? She touched me right—she was me, right? She was me, under Walter, asking him askin him please Daddy, please, please, Daddy so I done what I always wanted Walter to do, what I always wished what I wished every night, I got a brick a plain red brick, yeah, killed her with a brick, smashed her little face in. To this day I can't watch them Brick commercials, you know, the furniture warehouse? No money down—turn the set right off, right off for the night. Hey! Did I really used to brush your hair?

He puts his head in her lap. She extricates herself and backs off in horror. ISOBEL approaches with her weapon.

Scene Option 1 and Scene Option 2 both resume at this point in the play:

ISOBEL: BEN ... ja ... men. (*He looks.*) BEN ja men BEN ja men.

BEN: Who are you?

ISOBEL: Is ... o ... bel.

BEN: Isobel.

ISOBEL: July. Isobel in July July the one, remem- ber? Don't you remember? CANADA day day for CANADA Birthday. I selling tickets tickets on a Chrysler car, for boys' and girls' club, one dollar fifty for a ticket. I have five tickets left. Don't you remember? I see you in park. It is raining. In my park I ask you, "you want to buy ticket on a Chrysler car?" You say, "yes, yes, I buy all five all five tickets. Come into my car, come into my silver car with dark red seats, come into my car. I will give you the money for the tickets I have the money in my car" you said ...

BEN: I'm hallucinatin.

ISOBEL: I'm Isobel.

BEN: You're a picture.

ISOBEL: I'm Isobel.

BEN: What ... do you want?

ISOBEL: I have come.

BEN: What do you want?

ISOBEL: I am here.

BEN: WELL GO AWAY! You hear me? GO AWAY.

She is about to kill him with the stick, the forces of vengeance and forgiveness warring inside her. Forgiveness wins.

ISOBEL: I love you.

BEN: NO!!

ISOBEL: *You took my last breath!*

BEN: Christ I'm sick, I'm so sick.

ISOBEL: *I want back my life. Give me back my life!*

The players enter singing a religious-sounding chorale with a sense of sadness and triumph.

They place a veil on ISOBEL's head, the actor playing BEN joining them.

ISOBEL: (*an adult now*) I want to tell you now a secret. I was dead, was killed by lion in long silver car, starving lion, maul maul maul me to dead, with killing claws over and over my little young face and chest, over my chest my blood running out he take my heart with. He take my heart with, in his pocket deep, but my heart talk. Talk and talk and never be quiet never be quiet. I came back. I take my life. I want you all to take your life. I want you all to have your life.

Players sing a second, joyful chorale, walking off. ISOBEL ascends, in her mind, into heaven. The last thing we see is her veil.

END

DANIEL MacIVOR (b. 1962)

The year 1988 marked a turning point in Daniel MacIvor's playwriting career. Sandwiched between his first two successes—the hard-hitting female monologue *See Bob Run*, co-produced by his Da Da Kamera company in 1987, and the bleakly comic, wildly surreal one-man show *Wild Abandon* (1988), his first performance of his own work—came an invitation to write for Tarragon Theatre. MacIvor's project was a memory play about growing up in Cape Breton called *Somewhere I Have Never Traveled*. It proved, in his own words, "a disaster." Writing discursively in a conventional mode and letting a major producer stage his work was not to be his path to success. Creating offbeat plays that intimately connect performer and audience; maintaining firm artistic control as well as personal involvement as actor or director—that would become MacIvor's hallmark. His best work involves the simplicity of a single actor or two or three on a nearly bare stage spinning a bizarre but compelling narrative with precisely choreographed theatricality. *Never Swim Alone* is classic MacIvor: "a beautiful piece," said *Books in Canada*, "spare, evocative, funny, and sad."

Born to a working-class family in Sydney, Nova Scotia, MacIvor studied theatre for a couple of years at Dalhousie University before leaving to work as an actor with Newfoundland's Stephenville Festival. He moved to Toronto in 1984, completed the theatre program at George Brown College and founded Da Da Kamera in 1986. After some early experimental work with Sky Gilbert's Buddies in Bad Times Theatre and the debacle of *Somewhere I Have Never Traveled*, MacIvor quickly developed Da Da Kamera into one of Toronto's premier cutting-edge companies. He surrounded himself with a group of like-minded theatre artists with whom he has collaborated on nearly all his subsequent projects: actress Caroline Gillis, actor-director Ken McDougall (until his death in 1992), producer Sherrie Johnson, composer Richard Feren, and writer-director Daniel Brooks.

The 1990s proved extraordinarily productive for MacIvor whose first four plays of the decade all received Chalmers Best New Canadian Play Award nominations, as had *See Bob Run*. Co-producing with two other companies, MacIvor co-wrote, co-directed and performed in *White Trash Blue Eyes* (1990), a large-cast barroom play about neighbourhood gentrification. He also wrote and performed in *Never Swim Alone* (1991), which reunited actress Gillis and director McDougall from *See Bob Run*, and *2-2-Tango* (1991), a highly choreographed duet about gay mating rituals, directed by McDougall. *House* (1991) took the form and flavour of the earlier *Wild Abandon*. It inaugurated MacIvor's relationship with Daniel Brooks who directed him in this remarkable solo piece that has a dyspeptic character named Victor regaling and abusing the audience with details of his "fucked up" life and family, his experiences in group therapy, and other bizarre misadventures. *House* won the Chalmers Award and has probably been MacIvor's most widely produced play. In 1995 he reprised his role as Victor in the film version. *This Is a Play* (1992), directed by McDougall with MacIvor and Gillis in the cast, hilariously exposes what actors *really* think when onstage. It was published in a volume with *Never Swim Alone* in 1993. MacIvor directed McDougall and Gillis in *Jump* (1992), a wordless play about weddings, co-produced with Theatre Passe Muraille which revived it to strong reviews in 2001.

He performed in the otherwise all-female *The Lorca Play* (1992), deconstructing the Spanish playwright's *House of Bernardo Alba*. MacIvor co-wrote and co-directed the play with Brooks, the two sharing the Dora Mavor Moore Award for best director. They collaborated again on the movement piece *Excerpts from the Emo Project* (1994), and co-created *Here Lies Henry* (1995), a sound and light show in which MacIvor, directed by Brooks, assaulted the audience in the guise of a pathological character much like Victor in *House*. The play won MacIvor his second Chalmers and initiated an innovative program which has Da Da Kamera touring each new show before and after its official opening to "development partners" in different cities while the work continues to evolve. Festival Antigonish in Nova Scotia, the Vancouver East Cultural Centre, Calgary's High Performance Rodeo and Edinburgh's Traverse Theatre have been among the regular partners. In 1998 Da Da Kamera won a Chalmers Award for Innovation in Theatre.

With *The Soldier Dreams* (1997) and *Marion Bridge* (1998) MacIvor re-entered more conventional territory: the deathbed vigil play. In the former, for which he and Brooks once again shared a Dora for best director, a family gathers around a young man (MacIvor) dying of AIDS. In the latter, co-produced by Nova Scotia's Mulgrave Road Theatre, three sisters await their mother's death in Cape Breton. *Marion Bridge* earned MacIvor his first Governor General's Award nomination. *Monster* (1998) got him, with Brooks, his second. Rounding out what might be considered MacIvor's monologue tetralogy, it presents his character, here called Adam, engaging the audience in an outrageous psychodrama involving oedipal revenge fantasies. After opening in Toronto, *Monster* toured the U.S., Ireland, Australia, Norway and Israel, and became the first English-language play ever staged at Montreal's Théâtre de Quat'Sous. *In on It* (2001), a two-hander about playmaking and memory, was directed by and featured MacIvor along with the unlikely musical combination of Maria Callas and Leslie Gore. It premiered in Vancouver after stops in Antigonish, Edinburgh, Philadelphia, Washington and Calgary.

In addition to his work on and in his own plays, MacIvor has made notable appearances as an actor on stage in David Mamet's *Oleanna* and Judith Thompson's *White Biting Dog* (directed by Morris Panych), in Canadian films (among them *Justice Denied: The Donald Marshall Story*, *I Love a Man in Uniform*, and *The Five Senses*, for which he received a Genie Award nomination), and on series television (CBC's *Twitch City*). He has also written, directed and performed in his own short films. In 2000 he was writer-in-residence at the National Theatre School in Montreal.

Never Swim Alone sprang from a variety of sources. MacIvor has said that his own competitive relationship with Ken McDougall provided a thematic framework for the play, while the sophisticated, rapid-fire word games in a show he saw by Montreal's Théâtre Ubu offered a stylistic template. His Cape Breton heritage gave him both a love of story-telling and "a suspicion of language, a distance from words," he told R.M. Vaughan. "[I'm] not making poetry out of the way people speak but manipulating the way people speak into poetry. Cutting it up, rearranging it ... " Hence the lyrical, almost incantatory quality of the language in parts of the play and the self-consciously rote, mechanical quality in others.

Words are weapons for these testosterone-fueled combatants, from eloquent rhetoric to crude insult. They stand back and watch the effects of their comments on each other and on the Referee who is also the girl on the beach they want to impress, the female swimmer who claims that she can beat them to the point. "It's like a *Nature* documentary of rutting stags who can talk," *Toronto Star* critic Geoff Chapman wrote, straining metaphors to find a way to describe this curious piece. Actually, with its overt engagement of the audience whose sympathies the men attempt to enlist even before stepping onto the stage, *Never Swim Alone* seems more like a WWF wrestling match, sharing as well that spectacle's crafted artificiality and parodic (de)constructions of masculinity. Though the Referee officially scores the rounds, in performance the play's audience actively keeps its own score with laughter, cheers, boos. The only thing missing in Round Eleven is a tag team.

As an old-fashioned pissing contest, the play offers a transparently exaggerated comic portrait of white-collar machismo. The briefcase-toting men whip out penises, cell phones and cigars, and "cock their guns." They insult each other's fathers and impugn each other's wives. Bill even invokes his MASSIVE STAIRCASE—size matters to these guys. The rutting stags metaphor hits closest to home when Frank invokes the guilt-free Darwinian ethic of winning at all costs: "Compassion will lose the race ... And being first my friends is the point." Yet ironically, what makes the play so effective on stage is precisely the cooperation and harmony of the two actors working in concert, in vocal and often physical lockstep. At the level of performance, being first is specifically not the point. As another counterpoint, the play juxtaposes the bravado of adult maledom with the bittersweet memory of boys and a girl enacting one of the proto-sexual rituals of adolescence. Its disastrous outcome may be a lesson, as the title suggests. But the lessons the men think they learn seem to be something altogether different. The enigmatic final tableau leaves them and the audience suspended in the pure theatrical ether that is Daniel MacIvor's milieu.

Never Swim Alone was first produced by Platform 9 Theatre in association with Da Da Kamera at the Theatre Centre, Toronto, on February 26, 1991, with the following cast:

REFEREE   Caroline Gillis
A. FRANCIS DELORENZO   Robert Dodds
WILLIAM (BILL) WADE   Daniel MacIvor

Directed by Ken McDougall
Designed by Steve Lucas

NEVER SWIM ALONE

CHARACTERS

FRANK
BILL
REFEREE

SET

Up centre a tall referee chair. Stage left a small table and chair for BILL. Stage right a small table and chair for FRANK. A scoreboard.

As the audience enters, the woman lies onstage under a sheet. 1970s beach music plays. FRANK, a man in a blue suit, and BILL, an almost imperceptibly shorter man in a blue suit, enter through the house, greeting the audience individually. Before stepping on stage they turn and greet the audience.

FRANK & BILL: (*in unison*) Hello. Good to see you. Glad you could come.

They step onto the stage and slowly lift the sheet from the REFEREE. She rises. She wears a blue bathing suit. She looks out and steps down centre.

REFEREE:
A beach.
A bay.
The point.
Two boys on a beach. Late afternoon. They have been here all day and all day each summer. It is the last day of summer before school begins. Nearby is a girl. She as well has been here all day and all day every day all summer. She lies on her green beach towel in her blue bathing suit with her yellow transistor. The boys have been watching the girl from a distance but now that the summer is nearly over, from very close by. She reminds one boy of his sister, she reminds the other of a picture of a woman he once saw in a magazine. She turns her head a little over her shoulder and speaks to the boys: "Race you to the point?"
This is the beach.
Here is the bay.
There is the point.

The REFEREE steps to her chair and takes her place. She blows her whistle. The men exit.

REFEREE: Round one: Stature.

The REFEREE begins Round One. We hear footsteps.

FRANK & BILL:
(*offstage*) Two. Two. Two. Two. Two. Two. Two. Two. Men.
Enter a
room.

FRANK and BILL enter.

FRANK: Good to see you Bill.

BILL: Good to see you Frank.

FRANK: How long's it been?

BILL: Too long Frank.

FRANK: Too long indeed Bill.

FRANK & BILL:
How's things?
Can't complain.
How's the family?
Just great.
How's business?
Well a whole heck of a lot better than it was this time last year let me tell you.
Ha ha ha.
How's the blood pressure.
(*aside and snide*) Ha ha ha.

FRANK: Two men.

BILL: Two men.

FRANK & BILL: Two men enter a

They step downstage.

room. A taller man and—

They stop. They laugh. FRANK gestures towards BILL as he speaks the line, and vice versa. They continue.

A taller man and—
A taller man and—
A taller man and—
A taller man and—
A taller man and—

A taller man and—

REFEREE ends the round. The men stand side by side facing her. She inspects them carefully. She gives the victory to FRANK. BILL takes his seat. FRANK steps front and centre and addresses the audience.

FRANK: A. Francis DeLorenzo. My friends call me Frank. The "A" is for Alphonse and not even my enemies call me Alphonse. Alphonse Francis DeLorenzo: French, English, Italian. Behold before you a square of the Canadian Quilt. To those of you I didn't have a chance to greet as I entered I'd like to welcome you and thank you for coming. I'm sure you all have busy schedules and many other concerns in these troubled times and your presence here tonight is greatly appreciated. A hand for the audience! And if I might I would like to start off with a favourite quote of mine: "We do not place especial value on the possession of virtue until we notice its total absence in our opponent." Friedrich Nietzsche. Once again, thanks for coming. (*FRANK resumes his seat.*)

REFEREE: Round Two: Uniform.

REFEREE begins Round Two.

FRANK & BILL: Two men enter a room.

FRANK: A taller man and

BILL: an almost imperceptibly shorter man.

FRANK: They both wear

FRANK & BILL: White shirts. Blue suits. Silk ties. Black shoes. Black socks. White shirts, blue suits, silk ties, black shoes, black socks. White shirts, blue suits, silk ties, black shoes, black socks. White shirts blue suits silk ties black shoes black socks. White shirts blue suits silk ties black shoes black socks. White shirts blue suits silk ties black shoes black socks. White shirts:

BILL: A hundred and ten twenty five at Cyrus K.

FRANK & BILL: Blue suits:

FRANK: six twenty two twenty two

BILL: on sale

FRANK: at Brogue.

FRANK & BILL: Silk ties:

BILL: Came with the suit?

FRANK: Present.

BILL: From Donna?

FRANK: Ah ... no.

BILL: Oh. It's nice.

FRANK: How's Sally.

BILL: Oh good good. How's Donna?

FRANK: Oh good good.

BILL: How's the house?

FRANK: Very good.

FRANK & BILL:
How's the boy?
Just fine.
Now there's an investment eh?

FRANK: Three?

BILL: Four? Five?

FRANK: Four.

FRANK & BILL:
Right right.
Good kid?
Great kid.
Smart kid?
A little genius.
Must get it from his mother.
Ha ha ha ha ha ha ha.
Black shoes:

FRANK: two twenty five even, David's Uptown.

FRANK & BILL: Black socks:

BILL: (*excitedly noting FRANK's socks*) BLUE SOCKS!

REFEREE ends the round. She inspects the men's socks. She gives the victory to BILL. FRANK takes his seat. BILL steps forward and addresses the audience.

BILL: Hello to all the familiar faces in the audience tonight and a very extra special hello to all the friends I haven't met yet. William (Bill) Wade: Canadian, Canadian, Canadian. That's what's beautiful about this country: doesn't matter where you came from once you're here you're a Canadian, and that makes me proud. And I'd also like to add a bit of a quote myself, as my old man always used to say: "If bullshit had a brain it would quote Nietzsche." Thank you. (*BILL resumes his seat.*)

REFEREE: Round Three: Who Falls Dead The Best.

REFEREE begins Round Three.

FRANK & BILL: Two men enter a room

BILL: and each man carries

FRANK & BILL: a briefcase.

FRANK: The first man seems very much like the second man and

BILL: the first man seems very much like the second man.

FRANK & BILL: Yes.

FRANK: But

BILL: they

FRANK: are

FRANK & BILL: not.

FRANK: For two reasons.

BILL: Two.

FRANK: One:

FRANK & BILL: one man is the first man and

BILL: two:

FRANK & BILL: one man, in his briefcase has

FRANK: a gun

BILL: a gun.

FRANK & BILL: A gun.

BILL: Which man is

FRANK: the first man and

BILL: which man has

FRANK & BILL: the gun?

FRANK and BILL mime shooting one another in slow motion. They die elaborately also in slow motion. REFEREE ends the round. The men face the REFEREE. She calls a tie. FRANK and BILL step forward and address the audience.

FRANK & BILL: I've known this guy for years.

BILL: Years.

FRANK: And this is sad

FRANK & BILL: but it's true …

BILL: And when I say years

FRANK: I mean years.

FRANK & BILL: I mean

FRANK: I saw the look of another woman in his father's eyes.

BILL: I smelled the bourbon on his mother's breath.

FRANK: I kept it a secret his aunt was his sister.

BILL: I knew his brother was gay before he did.

FRANK & BILL: I mean years.

FRANK: I mean

BILL: we spent summers together.

FRANK & BILL: Real summers

BILL: when you're a kid.

FRANK: Remember real summers

FRANK & BILL: when you were a kid?

FRANK: It stayed bright 'til nine o'clock and when it did get dark it got so dark you never wanted to go home.

BILL: Smoking 'Sweet Caps' in the woods with a *Playboy* magazine and warm beer from somebody's father's basement.

FRANK & BILL: No school and Koolaid and baseball and hide and seek late at night and hot dogs and full moons and overnights outside and swimming.

FRANK: And when they said not to swim alone

BILL: this

FRANK: here

FRANK & BILL: this is the guy I swam with!

BILL: I know this guy better than he knows himself.

FRANK: And that's what makes it sad

BILL: but sad as it is it's true

FRANK & BILL: and the truth of it is:

FRANK: And this is much

BILL: much

FRANK & BILL: much more

FRANK: than something as simple as

BILL: his bum leg

FRANK: his trick knee

BILL: his weak wrist

FRANK: his slipped disc

BILL: his bad nerves

FRANK: his trouble sleeping

BILL: his dizzy spells

FRANK: his heart

FRANK & BILL: pa pa pa pa pa pa pa pa pa pa palpitations

FRANK: this is

BILL: much

FRANK: much

FRANK & BILL: much sadder than that.

FRANK: He's not happy

FRANK & BILL: he's not happy at all.

BILL: He feels cornered.

FRANK: He feels stuck.

BILL: He feels tied.

FRANK: He feels bound.

FRANK & BILL: He feels trapped.

BILL: And he's a young man

FRANK: he's still a young man.

FRANK & BILL: And that's sad.

BILL: And I'm just saying that

FRANK & BILL: That's really sad.

FRANK and BILL resume their seats.

REFEREE: Round Four: Friendly Advice Part One.

FRANK and BILL bring their chairs centre and sit. REFEREE begins Round Four.

BILL: Okay here's the story, these are the facts, this is where I stand, this is the point from which I view the situation.

FRANK: Go on.

BILL: Your situation.

FRANK: Yes.

BILL: I'm not going to pull any punches, I'm not going to cut any corners, I'm not going to give you the short shrift, I'm not going to shovel the shit.

FRANK: The only way to be.

BILL: The only way to be.

FRANK & BILL: Straight up!

BILL: Can I get personal?

FRANK: Personal?

BILL: We're friends.

FRANK: And?

BILL: Well Frank … I've got two good eyes I can't help but see, I've got two good ears I can't help but hear what's being said, and what's being said, around, is … Frank, I'm not saying I've got the goods on what makes a marriage work, God knows me and Sally, the honeymoon was over long ago but Frank … it works! And maybe that's just communication, and maybe that's just luck but Frank … All I'm trying to say here buddy is if you ever need an outside eye, if you ever need a friendly ear, then hey, I'm here.

FRANK: Are you thinner?

BILL: Wha?

FRANK: Are you thinner?

BILL: No.

FRANK: You're not thinner?

BILL: No I'm just the same.

FRANK: Really?

BILL: Same as always.

FRANK: It must just be your hair.

REFEREE ends the round. She gives the victory to FRANK. BILL takes his seat. FRANK steps forward.

FRANK: Last Saturday night I'm on the street after before dinner cocktails on my way up town. I flag a cab, I tell him where I'm going, he says, "Okay."

All right. Driving lights cars thinking so on, and he says something about the night and I say something about the moon and he says something about the weather and I say "Yeah." The radio on and I say something about the music and he says something about the singer and we both say "Yeah."

All right. Driving lights cars thinking so on.

Now; on the radio a commercial. "Butter Butter Eat Butter" or something. "Milk Milk Drink Milk" or whatever, and he says something about cows and I say something about horses and he says: "Do you like horses?" and I think about it … and I think about it and I realize … Dammit yes! Yes I do! I had never thought about it before but I am the kind of guy who likes horses. The kind of guy who likes John Wayne and Wild Turkey and carpentry and fishing on lazy August afternoons and horses. Then he says something about the moon and I say something about the night. But you see … I like horses.

Thank you. (*FRANK resumes his seat.*)

BILL: You're a real cowboy.

REFEREE calls a foul on BILL.

REFEREE: Round Five: Friendly Advice Part Two.

FRANK and BILL bring their chairs centre and sit. REFEREE begins Round Five.

FRANK: Seen Phil lately?

BILL: Oh yeah sure.

FRANK: Phil's a good guy, eh?

BILL: The best.

FRANK: The best yes. The kind of guy a guy admires. A guy who's got it all together. A guy who picks his friends carefully because he understands a friend is a mirror and a mirror is a reflection of the thing before it.

BILL: So.

FRANK: I mean … look, I'm not going to pull any punches and I don't want you to take this the wrong way but Phil mentioned it and Phil knows we're tight and I'm sure he wouldn't have mentioned it to me if he didn't think I would mention it to you. I mean he likes you. I'm almost sure he does. He thinks you're a fine guy, a good guy, he does, but he mentioned that maybe lately you … and I don't … I'm only saying this out of

concern, as I'm sure Phil was as well … but he mentioned that, maybe lately, you've been a little on the … well … a bit … how did he put it? A bit too "palpably desperate" I think was his phrase. And Bill you can't hold yourself responsible for the fact that business is bad, it's not your fault, and tomorrow is another day no matter how bad things seem right now. And Phil is worried, he wouldn't have mentioned it otherwise, and hey, I'm worried too. And I think you should be complimented … You should take it as a compliment to your character that a good guy like Phil is concerned about you.

BILL: That's funny.

FRANK: Funny?

BILL: Yeah. He didn't mention it last night.

FRANK: Last night?

BILL: We saw a movie.

REFEREE moves to end the round. FRANK stops her.

FRANK: Which movie?

BILL: *High Noon.*

FRANK: What time?

BILL: Seven-forty.

FRANK: We're going to the game on Thursday.

BILL: We're going to Montreal for the weekend.

FRANK: We're driving to Arizona for Christmas.

BILL: I'm taking his son camping.

FRANK: He asked me to lend him fifty bucks.

BILL: He wants me to help him build his house.

FRANK: His wife made a pass at me.

BILL: That dog?

REFEREE ends the round. She gives the victory to BILL. FRANK takes his seat. BILL steps forward.

BILL: Not only do I like horses I love horses, I have ridden horses, I have ridden horses bareback, I have owned a horse, I have seen my horse break its leg and I have shot my horse. And not only have I shot my horse I have made love in a stable. (*BILL resumes his seat.*)

FRANK: With who, the horse?

REFEREE calls a foul on FRANK.

REFEREE: Round Six: Members Only.

REFEREE begins the round. Slowly the men approach one another at centre. They face one another and make the sound of a telephone. They return to their briefcases, open them, pull out cellular phones.

FRANK & BILL: Yeah? Oh Hello Sir! Yes Sir.

FRANK: Thank you Sir.

BILL: I'm sorry Sir.

FRANK: Thank you Sir.

BILL: I'm sorry Sir.

FRANK: Thank you Sir.

BILL: I'm sorry Sir.

FRANK: Ha ha ha!

BILL: He he he.

FRANK: Thank you—

BILL: I'm sorry—

FRANK: Bobby.

BILL: Sir.
Good—

FRANK and BILL hang up. Slowly they approach one another at centre. They face one another and make the sound of a telephone. They return to their phones once again.

FRANK & BILL: Yeah?
Hi. I'm in the middle of something right now. Can I—Can I—Can I—
Can I call you back?
I don't know.
I told you that. Yes I'd—Yes I did this morning.
Well it's not my fault if you don't listen.
Is it!
That's right. When I get there. (*They hang up.*)

BILL: Sally says "Hi."

FRANK: Donna says "Hi."

FRANK & BILL: Hi.

FRANK and BILL slowly approach centre. They meet and turn to face the REFEREE, their backs to the audience. They take out their penises for her inspection. After some deliberation she calls a tie. Relieved, FRANK and BILL step forward.

FRANK & BILL: No One Is Perfect.

BILL: By William (Bill) Wade

FRANK: and A. Francis DeLorenzo. No one is perfect.

BILL: No one. Were our fathers perfect? Certainly not.

FRANK: Were our mothers perfect?

FRANK & BILL: Perhaps.

BILL: But I am not my mother.

FRANK & BILL: No.

FRANK: Nor is my wife my mother.

BILL: No.

FRANK: Nor will she ever be as much as I might wish she were as hard as she might try.

BILL: Frank?

FRANK: I digress.
Am I perfect?

BILL: Am I perfect?

FRANK & BILL: No.

FRANK: Yet, let us consider a moment,

BILL: a moment,

FRANK: that I am not myself

BILL: myself

FRANK: but rather

FRANK & BILL: someone else.

FRANK: Then as this person

BILL: I could

FRANK: watch me

BILL: take note

FRANK: take note

FRANK & BILL: of all the things I do

BILL: the small selfishnesses

FRANK: the minor idiosyncrasies

FRANK & BILL: the tiny spaces

BILL: between me

FRANK & BILL: and perfection.

FRANK: Perhaps then it would

FRANK & BILL: be e—be e—be easier

BILL: to see

FRANK: to look at me

BILL: and see

FRANK & BILL: be e—be e—be easier

FRANK: to change.

FRANK & BILL: But of course if I was someone else I would have my own problems to deal with.

FRANK: So what is perfect?

BILL: What?

FRANK: Besides tomorrow.

FRANK & BILL: Ah tomorrow!

BILL: Because tomorrow is an endless possibility

FRANK & BILL: and an endless possibility is the second best thing to wake up next to.

FRANK: But what?
Let us consider a moment,

BILL: a note.

FRANK & BILL: A note.

BILL:	FRANK:
Laaaaaaa	At first faltering and self-conscious
aaaaaaaa	then building up then pushed forward
aaaaaaaa	then gaining commitment then losing
aaaaaaa.	breath and trailing off near the end.

BILL: But in it there was something

FRANK & BILL: perfect.

FRANK: A happy accident?

BILL: A fluke?

FRANK: Mere chance?

FRANK & BILL: Perhaps. But back to me.

FRANK: And me

BILL: for all my weaknesses

FRANK: as a note

FRANK & BILL: let's say

BILL: a note stretched out from birth

FRANK & BILL: to death,

FRANK: I will allow

BILL: that here and there

FRANK: from time to time

BILL: there is a sound

FRANK: a thought

BILL: a word

FRANK & BILL: that touches on perfection.

BILL: But overall

FRANK: and wholly, no

FRANK & BILL: I know

FRANK: I am not perfect

FRANK & BILL: I know

BILL: I am not perfect.

FRANK & BILL: And neither is he!

FRANK and BILL resume their seats.

REFEREE: Half-time.

REFEREE comes down centre.

REFEREE: This is the beach. Here is the bay. There is the point.

FRANK and BILL come down and join her on either side.

REFEREE:
This is the beach.
Here is the bay.

	FRANK & BILL:
There is the point.	
This is the beach.	On the beach.
Here is the bay.	At the bay.
There is the point.	On the beach.
This is the beach.	At the bay.
Here is the bay.	On the beach.
There is the point.	At the bay.
This is the beach.	On the beach at the bay.
Here is the bay.	On the beach at the bay.
There is the point.	On the beach at the bay.
This is the beach.	On the beach at the bay.
Here is the bay.	On the beach at the bay.
There is the point.	On the beach at the bay.

Race you to the point?
Sun.
Boys.
Sand.
Water.
Summer.

FRANK: On the beach at the bay.

BILL: Every day that summer.

FRANK: On the beach at the bay.

BILL: All day every day.

FRANK: On the beach at the bay.

BILL: Every day that summer.

FRANK: On the beach at the bay.

BILL: All summer long.

REFEREE: It is the last day of summer before school begins. Two boys and the girl. She lies in the sun in her blue bathing suit on her green beach towel with her yellow transistor. Turning front. Turning back. And I could tell you little things about her. Turning front turning back. I could tell you that her name was Lisa. Turning front turning back. I could tell you that she had a big brother. Turning front turning back. I could tell you that she loved going to movies. Turning front. Turning back. But that doesn't matter now, all that matters is she is here on the beach with the two boys.
Turning front.
Turning back.
The boys watch the girl. She stares out past the point to where the sea makes a line on the sky. The boys are silent and shy. She can hear them blush. She reminds one boy of his sister, she reminds the other of a picture of a woman he once saw in a magazine. The boys simply watch the girl.

FRANK and BILL sing a verse of a summer song.

The sun hangs about there, just over the point. She is a little drowsy. She gets up and wanders to the edge of the water. She looks out. She feels a breeze. She turns her head a little over her shoulder and speaks to the boys:
"Race you to the point?"
This is the beach.
Here is the bay.

	FRANK & BILL:
There is the point.	
This is the beach.	On the beach.
Here is the bay.	At the bay.
There is the point.	On the beach.
This is the beach.	At the bay.
Here is the bay.	On the beach.
There is the point.	At the bay.
There is	
	On the beach at the bay.

REFEREE:	FRANK & BILL:
There is	On the beach at the bay.
There is	On the beach at the bay.
There is	On the beach at the bay.
There is	On the beach at the bay.
There is	On the beach at the bay.
There is	On the beach at the bay.
There is	On the beach at the bay.
There is	On the beach at the bay.
There is the point.	

FRANK: And we sat

BILL: on the sand

FRANK: at the edge

BILL: of the point

FRANK: and we waited

BILL: and we waited.

REFEREE: Race you to the point? Do you remember?

FRANK: One.

REFEREE: Do you remember?

BILL: Two.

REFEREE: I remember too.
I remember. Three!

REFEREE resumes her position on chair. She ends half-time. The men return to their chairs.

REFEREE: Recap: Two men enter a room. A taller man and a shorter man. They both wear white shirts, blue suits, silk ties, black shoes, black socks—

BILL: Blue socks!

REFEREE: and blue socks. And each man carries a briefcase. The first man seems very much like the second man and the second man seems very much like the first man but they are not

FRANK & BILL: No.

REFEREE: They are not for two reasons. One: one man is the first man and two: one man in his briefcase has a gun.

BILL: A gun.

FRANK: A gun.

REFEREE: Which man is the first man and which man has the gun? Round Seven: Dad.

REFEREE begins the round. FRANK and BILL approach one another at centre. FRANK does the "what's-on-your-tie" gag to BILL. BILL shoves FRANK. FRANK shoves BILL. BILL shoves FRANK, knocking him down. REFEREE calls a foul on BILL. FRANK and BILL circle one another.

FRANK: How's your Dad?

BILL: Why?

FRANK: I always liked your Dad.

BILL: Really?

FRANK: Yeah.

BILL: Well, I always liked your Dad.

FRANK: Really?

BILL: Yeah.

FRANK & BILL: Gee.

FRANK: Your Dad was a real easy going guy.

BILL: Your Dad was a real card.

FRANK: Your Dad was a real dreamer.

BILL: Your Dad was a real character.

FRANK: Your Dad was a real nice guy.

BILL: He was a real maniac.

FRANK: He was a real boozer.

BILL: Ha. He was a real wild man.

FRANK: A real cuckold.

BILL: A real wiener.

FRANK: A real dick.

BILL: A real prick.

FRANK: A lemming.

BILL: A fascist.

FRANK: An ass.

BILL: A pig!
How's your Mom?

REFEREE ends the round. She calls a tie.

FRANK:	BILL:
Please be warned that if you think I'm going to stand here and start dishing dirt and airing laundry about HIS FATHER I won't. But let's just say the desperation he displays comes from HIS FATHER. Not that I'm sure he wasn't a well-intentioned if ill	Now this is more than name calling here although that of course is the temptation but HIS FATHER drove his mother crazy I mean she did have a drinking problem but HIS FATHER didn't help at all. She
educated man but, and education isn't everything but FOR EXAMPLE:	spent the last fifteen years in and out of detox as a result of his antics. FOR EXAMPLE:
Rather than face criminal charges HIS FATHER said he could not multiply eight times nine when HIS FATHER 's company was missing some seventy-two thousand dollars at the year end audit. HIS FATHER claimed he had marked down twenty four. Twenty four? Give me a break. AND THAT'S JUST ONE EXAMPLE. Dishonest? Well he did admit to an ignorance in arithmetic and WELL I'M SURE YOU KNOW	At the Girl Guide Boy Scout banquet in grade eight HIS FATHER was supposed to make a presentation but when the time came HIS FATHER was nowhere to be found. Twenty minutes later five guys from the sixth pack found HIS FATHER in the boiler room with Suzie Walsh a sixteen-year-old Girl Guide. AND THAT'S JUST ONE EXAMPLE. Is he like that? Well they say a guy and his father are WELL I'M SURE YOU KNOW

WHAT THEY SAY ABOUT FATHERS AND SONS	WHAT THEY SAY ABOUT FATHERS AND SONS
and far be it, far be it indeed for me to say that HE IS THE PERFECT EXAMPLE. Thank you.	and I'm not saying they're right all the time, but in this case HE IS THE PERFECT EXAMPLE. Thank you.

REFEREE: Pardon me?

FRANK and BILL repeat the above at twice the speed.

REFEREE: Thank you.

FRANK & BILL: You're welcome.

REFEREE: Round Eight: All In The Palm Of His Hand.

REFEREE begins the round. FRANK and BILL come to centre. FRANK takes out two cigars. He gives one to BILL. FRANK lights them. They face one another.

FRANK: You've got auction preferreds yielding seventy percent of prime and 50/51 up either side what do you want to do? Convert with three year hard call protection, two year pay back, the hedge is a lay up? I don't think so. I say capitalize the loss by rolling it into goodwill and amortizing over forty years. Of course profits will be decreased by the switch from FIFO to LIFO. And then remember Bethlehem! Where application of FASBY 87 meant balance sheet quality went way down because of the unfunded pension liability. I mean if we were in the States I could offer at one half and give up an eighth to the market maker for three eighths net fill, but unfortunately we're not. Are you with me?

BILL puts the cigar out in the palm of his hand. REFEREE ends the round. She gives the victory to BILL. FRANK resumes his seat. BILL steps forward.

BILL: Let's go to my place everybody. Okay. Ready?
This is the back door.
We always use the back door.
Here is the rec room. There is the bar. There is the laundry room.
Hallway, stairs.
Going up stairs, going up stairs.
Out that window that's the yard.

Here's a hallway. There's the kitchen.
Microwave butcher's block breakfast nook.
Hallway.
Turn.
Dining room.
Oak table, eight chairs, hallway, French doors, living room.
It's sunken!
Big window.
Big skylight.
Grand
piano
(white).
Through the hallway into the foyer.
Front—
We never use the front door.
Window window Powder Room.
MASSIVE STAIRCASE!
One. Two. Three. Four. Five bedrooms. (Can in two).
Long hallway.
Smaller staircase.
Going up stairs. Going up stairs. Going up stairs.
Door. Locked. Key. Open the door. And this is my
secret room.

FRANK: I heard you rent.

REFEREE calls a foul on FRANK. BILL approaches FRANK.

BILL: Where'd you hear that?

FRANK: Around.

BILL: Yeah?

FRANK: Yeah.

BILL: Around where?

FRANK: Just around.

BILL: Phil?

FRANK: Might've been Phil.

BILL: Phil's full of shit.

BILL returns to centre.

BILL: As I was saying.
This is my place.
Back door rec room bar laundry out that window that's the yard
kitchen hallway turn dining room turn living room turn hallway
MASSIVE STAIRCASE

NEVER SWIM ALONE / 303

one two three four five bedrooms hallway
staircase.
Going up stairs going up stairs going up stairs
Door locked key open the door
and this is my
secret room.
And this is my secret room. And it's empty except
for a great big window right here, and when I
look out of it I see the tops of trees, and hills,
black roads with white lines, and a whole lake,
and two kinds of earth: dark wet earth and clay,
and big green fields and sky that's only ever blue.
And all of it.
Everything.
Theskythefieldsthetreesthelakethehillstheroadthe-
clay.
Everything I see, and farther where you can't see,
all of it, everything, is mine.
It's all mine. (*BILL resumes his seat.*)

REFEREE: Round Nine: Power Lunch.

*FRANK and BILL bring their chairs centre. They
sit facing one another with their briefcases on
their laps. REFEREE begins the round.*

FRANK: Been here before?

BILL: Oh yeah.

FRANK: How's the steak?

BILL: Very good.

FRANK: How's the swordfish?

BILL: Very good.

FRANK: How's the shark?

BILL: Greasy.

FRANK & BILL: Excuse me a second.

*FRANK and BILL reach into their briefcases and
take out their phones. They dial and both make a
ringing sound. As BILL speaks, FRANK continues
to ring.*

BILL: Hi doll!
Listen sorry I was short with you before.
Did you go ahead and have dinner anyway?
Ahhh … Well how bout I pick up a pizza on my
way home?
And a movie?
Something funny?
Something romantic! That sounds nice!
Okay 'Turnip.'
I do you too.

Bye bye.

FRANK and BILL hang up.

BILL: How's Donna? (*pause*) How's—

FRANK: I heard you.
She's very good.

BILL: Really?

FRANK: Yes.
How's the spaghettini?

BILL: Oily. I saw Donna at the Fullers' party.

FRANK: Oh yes.

BILL: You weren't there.

FRANK: No I wasn't.

BILL: Phil was there.

FRANK: Was he?

BILL: He was having a good time.

FRANK: Good.

BILL: So was Donna.

FRANK: Donna likes a good—

BILL: Party?

FRANK: Yes.

BILL: I've heard that.

FRANK: How's the squid?

BILL: Sneaky.

FRANK: Sneaky?

BILL: Sneaks up on you. Nice tie.

FRANK: Yes you mentioned—

BILL: Somebody has good taste.

FRANK: How's Sally?

BILL: Very good.

FRANK: Really?

BILL: She was at the Fullers'.
Strange you weren't there.

FRANK: Well I wasn't.

BILL: Working late?

FRANK: I don't believe you've ever had the steak
or the swordfish or the shark or the spaghettini or
the squid here.

BILL: No I haven't. But it was a good party.

REFEREE ends the round. She gives the victory to FRANK.

BILL: Bullshit call!

REFEREE calls a foul on BILL. BILL resumes his seat. FRANK steps forward.

FRANK: Let's not use the word "class." Class being such a nebulous word. Let's instead use the word "mountain." Mountain. And many men are born without a mountain. It is not a birthright. This is not to say that a mountain is particularly better than a valley—just as we may find from time to time that knowledge is not particularly better than ignorance. And even being second has its benefits. For example … less income tax? But some men live on mountains and some men live in valleys and if only those men standing small and insignificant in the valley would stop their futile fight to stake a claim at the crest of a hill they can never hope to own. If only they would not be so blind and for a moment consider the privilege of living in the benevolent shadow of a mountain. But to be brave enough to see that truth and face it, that takes balls, and like mountains many men are born without them. *(FRANK resumes his seat.)*

BILL: Fuck you Alphonse.

REFEREE calls a foul on BILL.

FRANK: I beg your pardon?

REFEREE calls a foul on FRANK.

REFEREE: Round Ten: Business Ties.

REFEREE begins the round. FRANK and BILL step centre. FRANK faces the audience. BILL faces FRANK and stands at an uncomfortably close distance.

FRANK: Now I don't want to harp on business Bill but I happen to be pretty tight with Bobby and Bobby runs everything and I know how things are with you and there's a chance that there might be a place opening up in accounting and from what I've heard—

BILL: Frank I really like that tie.

FRANK: And from what I've heard about business Bill—

BILL: Silk?
Of course.
How could I imagine Donna would buy a tie like that?

FRANK: I'm offering you a break here Bill I'm—

BILL: That's not Donna's taste.
Very flashy.
Yet tasteful.
Where would a person buy a tie like that?
What kind of store?

FRANK: Bill …

BILL: What kind of person would go into that kind of store and buy a tie like that?

FRANK: Don't Bill.

BILL: A very young tie!

FRANK: Shut up about the goddamn tie!

FRANK resumes his seat. REFEREE ends the round. She gives the victory to BILL. BILL steps forward.

BILL: Two stories.
The first story is a very familiar story because everybody knows it. And it's a story about a little temp, eighteen years old, who is, by the way, knocked up and who happens to have not bad taste in ties don't you think?
And the second story is a secret so just keep it to yourselves.
We're at the Fullers' party. Me and Sally. Huge spread, packed bar, beautiful house, the works. Tons of people, people everywhere. There's Donna! Where's Frank? Frank's not there. Donna's there though. She looks great! Who's that she's talking to? It's Phil. I wander over. They're talking about politics. I wander off. Have a drink, have a chat, check out the pool, come back in, poke around some more at the buffet, shoot the shit … Phil and Donna still talking! I cruise over. Now they're talking about poetry. I cruise off. Time comes to go Sally's pulling on my arm I'm talking to Mister Fuller. Look around for Donna to say goodbye … No Donna. Look around for Phil … No Phil. I gotta take a pee before we leave, walk in the can. There's Donna. In the shower. With Phil. And when she sees me she smiles and she says: "Shh! Close the door Bill." Now the first story you can repeat but the second story, that's a secret.
(BILL resumes his seat.)

REFEREE: Round Eleven: My Boy.

REFEREE begins the round. FRANK and BILL step to centre.

FRANK & BILL: Let me tell you something about my boy …

FRANK does the wrong physical choreography.

FRANK: Sorry.

FRANK & BILL: Let me tell you something about my boy.
He's a good boy, my boy.
A good boy, a smart boy.
He's the best boy my boy.
No question, he's the best—

FRANK makes another error.

BILL: (*to FRANK*) Are you with us?

FRANK & BILL: Let me tell you something about my boy …

FRANK again makes an error. FRANK steps away. REFEREE moves to end the round. BILL stops her.

BILL: What's your problem?
Hey.
Hey.
What's your problem?

BILL looks to the audience, shrugging.

FRANK: Password.

BILL does not respond.

FRANK: Password!

BILL does not respond.

FRANK: Winner rules.

BILL: That's not in the game.

FRANK: (*steps to centre*) Password.

BILL: (*joins him at centre*) Winner rules.

FRANK & BILL:
Cut!
Spit!
Mix!
Brothers brothers never part
through broken vows or covered hearts
in all our weakness, all our woes
we stick together, highs and lows.

FRANK: Pledge?

BILL: Made.

FRANK: Promise?

BILL: Kept.

FRANK: To what end?

FRANK & BILL: Never end. Transit! Transport!

FRANK and BILL join hands, arms raised over their heads, forming an arch. The REFEREE walks through this and down centre.

BILL: One.

FRANK: Two.

REFEREE: Three.

FRANK, BILL and the REFEREE begin a "swimming" action.

FRANK, BILL & REFEREE:
Cut through the water to the point. Cut through the water to the point.
Cut through the water to the point. Cut through the water to the point.
Cut through the water to the point. Cut through the water to the point.
Cut through the water to the point. Cut through the water to the point.

The three continue the "action," and the men continue the above as:

REFEREE: I'll beat you.
I'm a good swimmer.
You guys think you're so hot.
My brother taught me to swim and he's on a team.
What's your names anyway?
My name's Lisa.
My mom calls me Rosie but I hate that.
What's your names anyway?
You guys got a cottage here?
You brothers?
We've got a cottage up by the store, on the hill, you know where I mean? It used to be a farm but we don't have any animals. I wish we had a horse, I love horses. I go to the movie on Sunday. I go every Sunday even if it's one I saw already. Hey slow down it's far. Slow down.

REFEREE:	FRANK & BILL:
What's your names?	And I feel her fall back.
Hey.	And I feel her fall back.
Wait.	And I feel her fall back.

Let's not race.	And I feel her fall back.
Wait.	And I feel her fall back.
We're too far.	And I feel her fall back.
Slow down.	And I feel her fall back.
Hey.	And I feel her fall back.
Wait.	And I feel her fall back.
Hey ...	

REFEREE:	FRANK:	BILL:
His decision.	Cut through the water to the point.	And I feel her I feel her fall back.
His compassion.	Cut through the water to the point.	And I feel her I feel her fall back.
His desire.	Cut through the water to the point.	And I feel her I feel her fall back.
His jealousy.	Cut through the water to the point.	And I feel her I feel her fall back.
His guilt.	Cut through the water to the point.	And I feel her I feel her fall back.
His self-image.	Cut through the water to the point.	And I feel her I feel her fall back.
His self-knowledge.	Cut through the water to the point.	And I feel her I feel her fall back.
His self-loathing.	Cut through the water to the point.	And I feel her I feel her fall back.
His fear of death.	Cut through the water to the point.	And I feel her I feel her fall back.
His weakness.	Cut through the water to the point.	And I feel her I feel her fall back.
His pride.	Cut through the water to the point.	And I feel her I feel her fall back.
His pleasure.	Cut through the water to the point.	And I feel her I feel her fall back.
His body.	Cut through the water to the point.	And I feel her I feel her fall back.
His politics.	Cut through the water to the point.	And I feel her I feel her fall back.
His will to power.	Cut through the water to the point.	And I feel her I feel her fall back.

REFEREE:	FRANK & BILL:
His concept of God.	Cut through the water to the point.
His warrior instinct.	Cut through the water to the point.
His dreams.	Cut through the water to the point.
His memory.	Cut through the water to the point.
And first there is panic.	Cut through the water to the point.
And so much sound.	Cut through the water to the point.
Rushing.	Cut through the water to the point.
Swirling.	Cut through the water to the point.
Pulsing.	Cut through the water to the point.

FRANK slowly raises his arms in victory. BILL continues to "swim."

REFEREE: And then no sound. And then peace. And then you will float or you will sink. And if you float you will be as if flying and if you sink, when you hit bottom, you will bounce like a man on the moon.

The REFEREE returns to her chair. FRANK walks toward BILL. BILL continues to "swim."

BILL:
Cut through the water to the point. Cut through the water to the point.
Cut through the water to the point. Cut through the water to the point.
Cut through the water to the point. Cut through the water to the point.

BILL rises as he continues to speak. FRANK places his hand on BILL's shoulder.

BILL:
Cut through the water to the point. Cut through the water to the point.
Cut through the water to the point. Cut through the water to the point.

FRANK and BILL are now standing face to face. With his other hand FRANK punches BILL in the stomach. BILL goes down. REFEREE ends the round. She gives the victory to FRANK. BILL struggles to his feet and approaches FRANK. FRANK addresses the audience.

FRANK: I'd like to make a few things clear.

These are my ears, these are my eyes, this is the back of my hand.
(*FRANK strikes BILL with the back of his hand. BILL goes down.*)
And the winner has, and will always, rule.
That is the way of the world. Like battle, like business, like love. A few may fall along the way but compared to the prize what are a few. And the prize is what you want and what you want is what you hear in every mouth, every buzz, every bell, every crack, every whisper.
Don't be afraid.
The thing we must learn is how to balance compassion and desire.
For example:
Bill? You like this tie?

FRANK takes his tie off and puts it around BILL's neck.

FRANK: Have it. (*yanks on the tie*)
Say thank you.
Say thank you!

BILL: Thank you.

FRANK: No thanks necessary Bill, I've got a dozen just like it at home.
You see.
Don't be fooled.

FRANK lifts BILL and supports him.

FRANK: Beware compassion. Compassion will lose the race. Compassion is illogical. If you let it compassion will kill desire. Especially the desire to be first. And being first my friends is the point.
(*FRANK throws BILL across the room.*)
Compassion is the brother of guilt
(*FRANK lifts BILL by his tie.*)
and guilt is the mother of stomach cancer.
(*FRANK knees BILL in the stomach.*)
The first man is the man
(*FRANK knees BILL in the chest. BILL goes down.*)
who is guiltless beyond all circumstance
(*FRANK kicks BILL.*)
and sure of his right
(*FRANK kicks BILL.*)
to be first.
(*FRANK kicks BILL.*)
The first man is the man
(*FRANK kicks BILL.*)
who can recognize
the second man.

BILL lies motionless. FRANK steps forward.

FRANK: And we sat on the sand at the edge of the point and we waited and we waited and you got scared and you ran home and all night long I waited and in the morning when her body washed up on the shore I tried to comfort her but she did not respond, then to evoke some reaction I slapped her so hard my hand still hurts. And then learning my lesson I declared myself first to the point. (*FRANK resumes his seat.*)

REFEREE: Round Twelve: Rumours Of Glory.

FRANK steps to centre. BILL tries to struggle to his feet. REFEREE calls a foul on BILL. BILL continues to struggle. REFEREE calls a foul on BILL. BILL continues to struggle. REFEREE ends the round. She gives the victory to FRANK. FRANK steps forward. BILL manages to get to his feet. He approaches his briefcase.

FRANK: I have always been, will always be, the first.

FRANK resumes his seat. BILL opens his briefcase, takes out a gun, aims it at FRANK.

BILL: And I learned my lesson Frank, I won't be second again.

FRANK opens his briefcase. BILL laughs. FRANK takes out a gun and aims it at BILL.

FRANK: The game isn't over yet Bill.

REFEREE: The two men will stand here just like this for a long time to come with one thought, one thought racing through each man's mind:

FRANK & BILL:
Somebody lied.
Somebody lied.
Somebody lied.

The REFEREE steps down and to centre carrying a yellow transistor. The men continue to speak "somebody lied" through the following.

REFEREE: Two boys on a beach. The last day of summer before school begins. Nearby is a girl. She lies in the sun in her blue bathing suit on her green beach towel listening to her yellow transistor. She reminds one boy of his sister, she reminds the other of a picture of a woman he once saw in a magazine. The sun hangs about there. Just over the point. She turns her head a little over her shoulder and speaks to the boys: "Race you to the point?"

The men stop speaking.

REFEREE: And they do.
One two three.
The boys are afraid.
The boys are still afraid.
Round Thirteen:

The men cock their guns.

REFEREE: Only One Gun Is Loaded.

She begins the round. The men look at her in disbelief, still keeping aim. She places the transistor on the stage and turns it on. She exits the way the men came in. The radio plays a happy beach song. The men look at one another, still keeping aim. Lights fade.

END

GUILLERMO VERDECCHIA   (b. 1962)

"The first task of the artist is to decolonize the imagination," Guillermo Verdecchia writes in an essay called "Politics in Playwriting," in which he spells out his unapologetically political credo. As a theatre artist his work is "oppositional and critical." Against "the culture of banality" in which we live he opposes "the vigorous imagination," which recognizes the complexity of our situation and can begin the process of transforming it. But as a product of our culture with its powerful marketing and image-making machinery, even the artist's own imagination is inevitably colonized. So he tries not only to make the audience aware of its ideological blinders but to identify and expose his own complicity in the way things are. Typically then, Verdecchia's plays critique the dominant ideology through a self-conscious character—sometimes called "Verdecchia," sometimes fictionalized or distanced—who acknowledges his own failures and his indulgence in the misplaced values and social crimes he condemns. From the multiple borders on which Verdecchia lives, *Fronteras Americanas* offers a scintillating disquisition on personal and national identities in a post-national world.

Born in Buenos Aires, Argentina, Verdecchia came to Canada at the age of two. He grew up in Kitchener, Ontario, dropped out of high school, and studied theatre at Ryerson Polytechnic in Toronto where future director Peter Hinton was an early influence. He worked as an actor for a while, spent the late 1980s in France, then returned to Toronto and collaborated with Hinton and others on a play for young audiences about the police shooting of a black teenager. *i.d.* (1989) won the Chalmers New Play Award and launched Verdecchia's writing career. His next play, *Final Decisions (WAR)*, concerns a woman who discovers that her civil servant husband is involved in political torture during Argentina's "dirty war." Sharon Pollock directed its 1990 premiere at Calgary's Alberta Theatre Projects, and Verdecchia himself directed it in Vancouver.

In France Verdecchia had met Daniel Brooks—soon to enter into creative partnership with Daniel MacIvor—and back in Toronto they found themselves housemates. Discovering a common interest in political philosopher Noam Chomsky, they co-wrote and co-directed a dramatization of Chomsky's ideas about how the hidden biases of the press shape public responses to such events as the Gulf War and the Israeli-Palestinian conflict. In *The Noam Chomsky Lectures* (1990), Verdecchia and Brooks appear on stage as themselves, lecturing the audience with pointers and slides, drawing examples from the theatre world as well as the larger political sphere, smacking the Artstick or blowing the Whistle of Indignation whenever things become excessively didactic or hectoring. Funny, enlightening and tough-minded ("the real Canadian traditions are quiet complicity and hypocritical moral posturing"), the play opened at Sky Gilbert's Rhubarb! Festival and was remounted three times in the next two years, updated to keep up with current events. It won the Chalmers and earned a Governor General's Award nomination.

Fronteras Americanas was developed through workshops at Canadian Stage and Tarragon with the help of Peter Hinton. Performed by Verdecchia, it opened at Tarragon's Extra Space, played the Festival des Amériques in Montreal, then was remounted at Tarragon's larger Main Space, all in 1993, with subsequent productions in Winnipeg and Vancouver, winning both the Chalmers and Governor General's Awards. *Crucero/Crossroads*, Verdecchia's short film adaptation of the play, won awards at five international festivals in 1995.

Verdecchia moved to Vancouver in 1994 after appearing there as Elias in *Amigo's Blue Guitar,* and directed *A Line in the Sand* (1995), co-written with Marcus Youssef, for the New Play Centre. Set in the Persian Gulf, the play is based on the notorious torture and murder of a young Somali by Canadian soldiers. Its Tarragon production won Verdecchia his fourth Chalmers. He also directed for Vancouver's Rumble Theatre *The Terrible but Incomplete Journals of John D.* (1996), a solo piece for actor and cellist with echoes of Kafka and Dostoevsky's *Underground Man*. The acutely self-conscious title character examines his own personal failures in the context of his criticizing the "Wal-Mart Universe." Moving back to Toronto in the late '90s, Verdecchia hooked up with Daniel Brooks again, co-writing and co-directing *Insomnia* (1998). Its protagonist, John F. (played by Brooks), is a direct descendant of John D., trying to work through his guilt about a life badly lived while his marriage falls apart around him.

In addition to his theatre work Verdecchia has written radio documentaries and dramas for CBC, and has published a collection of short stories, *Citizen Suárez* (1998). He has been active in the Association for Canadian Theatre Research, and in 1999 was writer-in-residence at Memorial University. That same year he became artistic director of Cahoots Theatre in Toronto where he lives with actress Tamsin Kelsey and their two children.

The largely autobiographical *Fronteras Americanas* is rooted in Verdecchia's own feelings, as an immigrant, of cultural deracination and displacement. Writing in the journal *In 2 Print*, he explains: "For years—most of my life—I felt confused and divided in my tongue, my heart, my mind. I 'passed' as a Canadian, but I did not feel Canadian (whatever that might be), did not want to be Canadian, and secretly thought of myself as Argentinian (whatever that might be). However, when I was honest with myself I recognized that I was not Argentinian ... I felt like a liar, a fraud, an impostor." The play represents his journey of self-discovery as he travels "home" to Argentina, then circles back to Canada where he finally recognizes that his ultimate citizenship, his real home, is the Border. In that context the apparently straightforward opening line, "Here we are," turns out to be remarkably problematic. Where exactly is *here*? Who exactly are *we*? And what does it mean to *be* us, here, now?

"Learning to live the border" is the challenge the play presents, a challenge aimed in two directions at once. For Verdecchia it involves coming to terms with his own blurry cultural dualism and the expanded sense of personal and political responsibility (and guilt) it seems to entail. For the rest of us—North Americans, Canadians, the theatre audience—it means learning to see through the popular image of Latinos, the people with whom we share this hemisphere in intimate inter-relationship, and understanding how our conception of them has been constructed and reinforced. (Verdecchia has suggested in an interview that the play need not be quite so culturally specific: "I'd love to see—some day, I hope—a production of *Fronteras Americanas* that is transgendered and cast with an Asian actor, or something. I'd really like to see somebody take the border theme to the nth degree.") If the trick is to gain new perspective, the play's primary tool for achieving it is Wideload, Verdecchia's alter ego, the embodiment of both the privileged insider/outsider position that living the border affords, and Verdecchia's own fear of cultural inauthenticity.

With his clichéd appearance and fractured Spanglish, Wideload personifies the most blatant cultural stereotypes of the Latino at the same time as his keen critical intelligence and incisive irony undercut them. Both he and Verdecchia set about re-educating the audience à la *The Noam Chomsky Lectures*, using slides and, in the published text, scholarly footnotes. Whereas Verdecchia's lessons are mostly historical and political, Wideload's are primarily sociological. His observations about the Smiths ("my first contact with an ethnic family") and his other "friends from de Saxonian community" point out just how dependent on one's perspective the concept of ethnicity is, and how absurd generalized ethnic labeling can be. In the midst of deconstructing the Latin Lover Fantasy he provides the comic *coup de grâce* with his generous reassurance that, while Latinos like him have their rumba, mambo and tango, we "Saxons" too have our own "dance of sexual joy"—the Morris Dance.

Both Verdecchia and Wideload frequently acknowledge the theatrical nature of the proceedings. The theatre is presented as a microcosm of the nation itself, "this Noah's ark of a nation," Canada, with its rich potential for providing border-life's multiple perspectives. The metatheatrics are also a Brechtian device, reminding us that this is *theatre*, not reality; that we should not get lost in it, but *think* about what we are seeing. At the same time Wideload warns us of the danger of theatrical sugar-coating: possibly, "it doesn't really matter what I say. Because it's all been kind of funny dis evening." This is metatheatre as self-critique, recognizing that theatre itself is an apparatus of cultural construction that needs to be demystified like all the others. Finally, consider the next-to-last section of the play, titled "Consider," in which the "we" of the opening line is perhaps defined at last, and in which the binary, Wideload/Verdecchia—the divided self—comes together for the first time. Remember that the two characters are played by the same actor. This is some kind of theatrical magic. And through it "the old binary models," to quote the Gómez-Peña slide in the play, give way to the "fluctuating sense of self" which represents the true experience of living the border.

Fronteras Americanas was first produced at the Tarragon Theatre Extra Space, Toronto, in January 1993.

VERDECCHIA and
FECUNDO MORALES SECUNDO
aka WIDELOAD MCKENNAH   Guillermo Verdecchia

Directed by Jim Warren
Designed by Glenn Davidson

FRONTERAS AMERICANAS

AUTHOR'S NOTE

Fronteras Americanas began as a long letter to a close friend that I wrote during a trip to Argentina in 1989. Re-reading it—I made a copy of it for some mysterious reason—I found that hidden beneath the travelogue were some intensely personal questions that I had been struggling with for some time but which I could only now begin to articulate. In an attempt to better understand those questions I began to read, reflect and write.

Fronteras Americanas makes no claim to be the definitive explanation of the Latin experience in North America, or the immigrant experience, or anything of that nature. Our experiences on this continent are too varied, too fantastic to ever be encompassed in any single work. *Fronteras Americanas* is part of a process, part of a much larger attempt to understand and to invent. As such, it is provisional, atado con alambre. In performance, changes were made nightly depending on my mood, the public, our location, the arrangement of the planets … I hope that any-one choosing to perform this text will consider the possibilities of making (respectful) changes and leaving room for personal and more current responses.

ACT ONE

As the audience enters, James Blood Ulmer's "Show Me Your Love (America)" plays. Two slides are projected.

SLIDE: It is impossible to say to which human family we belong. We were all born of one mother, America, though our fathers had different origins, and we all have differently coloured skins. This dissimilarity is of the greatest significance.
—Simón Bolívar

SLIDE: Fronteras. Borders. Americanas. American.

Welcome

VERDECCHIA enters.

VERDECCHIA: Here we are. All together. At long last. Very exciting. I'm excited. Very excited. Here we are.

SLIDE: Here We Are

VERDECCHIA: Now because this is the theatre when I say "we" I mean all of us and when I say "here" I don't just mean at the Tarragon, I mean America.

SLIDE: Let us compare geographies

VERDECCHIA: And when I say AMERICA I don't mean the country, I mean the continent. Somos todos Americanos. We are all Americans.
Now—I have to make a small confession—I'm lost. Somewhere in my peregrinations on the continent, I lost my way.
Oh sure I can say I'm in Toronto, at 30 Bridgman Avenue, but I don't find that a very satisfactory answer—it seems to me a rather inadequate description of where I am.
Maps have been of no use because I always forget that they are metaphors and not the territory; the compass has never made any sense—it always spins in crazy circles. Even gas-station attendants haven't been able to help; I can never remember whether it was a right or a left at the lights and I always miss the exits and have to sleep by the side of the road or in crummy hotels with beds that have Magic Fingers that go off in the middle of the night.
So, I'm lost and trying to figure out where I took that wrong turn … and I suppose you must be lost too or else you wouldn't have ended up here, tonight.
I suspect we got lost while crossing the border.

SLIDE: Make a run for the border / Taco Bell's got your order

VERDECCHIA: The Border is a tricky place. Take the Latin–North American border.

SLIDE: map of the Mexico–U.S. border

Where and what exactly is the border? Is it this line in the dirt, stretching for 3,000 kilometres? Is the border more accurately described as a zone which includes the towns of El Paso and Ciudad Juárez? Or is the border—is the border the whole country, the continent? Where does the U.S. end and Canada begin? Does the U.S. end at the 49th parallel or does the U.S. only end at your living room when you switch on the CBC? After all, as Carlos Fuentes reminds us, a border is more than just the division between two countries; it is also the division between two cultures and two memories.[1]

SLIDE: Remember the Alamo?

VERDECCHIA: *The Atlantic* has something to say about the border: "The border is transient. The border is dangerous. The border is crass. The food is bad, the prices are high, and there are no good bookstores. It is not the place to visit on your next vacation."[2]

To minimize our inconvenience, I've hired a translator who will meet us on the other side.

The border can be difficult to cross. We will have to avoid the Border Patrol and the trackers who cut for sign. Some of you may wish to put carpet on the soles of your shoes, others may want to attach cow's hooves to your sneakers. I myself will walk backwards so that it looks like I'm heading north.

Before we cross please disable any beepers, cellular phones or fax machines and reset your watches to border time. It is now Zero Hour.

El Bandito

Music: "Aquí vienen los Mariachi"

SLIDE: Warning

SLIDE: Gunshots will be fired in this performance

SLIDE: Now

Gunshots. The performer appears wearing bandito outfit. He has shifted into his other persona, WIDELOAD.

WIDELOAD: Ay! Ayayayay! Aja. Bienvenidos. Yo soy el mesonero acá en La Casa de La Frontera. Soy el guía. A su servicio. Antes de pasar, por favor, los latinos se pueden identificar? Los "latinoamericanos" por favor que pongan las manos en el aire … (*He counts.*) Que lindo … mucho gusto … Muy bien. Entonces el resto son … gringos. Lo siguiente es para los gringos: Eh, jou en Méjico now. Jou hab crossed de border. Why? What you lookin' for? Taco Bell nachos wif "salsa sauce," cabrón? Forget it

gringo. Dere's no pinche Taco Bell for thousands of miles. Here jou eat what I eat and I eat raw jalopeño peppers on dirty, burnt tortillas, wif some calopinto peppers to give it some flavour! I drink sewer water and tequila. My breath keells small animals. My shit destroys lakes. Jou come dis far south looking for de authentic Méjico? Jou looking for de real mezcal wit de real worm in it? I'll show you de real worm—I'll show jou de giant Mexican trouser snake. I will show you fear in a handful of dust …

Jou wrinklin' jour nose? Someting stink? Somebody smell aroun' here? Si, I esmell. I esmell because I doan bathe. Because bad guys doan wash. Never.

Bandito maldito, independista, Sandinista, Tupamaro, mao mao powpowpow.

He removes bandito outfit.

Ees an old Hallowe'en costume. Scary huh?

Introduction to Wideload

WIDELOAD: Mi nombre es Facundo Morales Segundo. Algunos me llaman El Tigre del Barrio. También me dicen El Alacran …

Music: "La Cumbia Del Facundo," Steve Jordan

My name ees Facundo Morales Segundo. Some of you may know me as de Barrio Tiger. I am a direct descendant of Túpac Amaru, Pancho Villa, Doña Flor, Pedro Navaja, Sor Juana and Speedy Gonzalez. I am de heads of Alfredo García and Joaquín Murrieta. I am de guy who told Elton John to grow some funk of his own.

Now when I first got here people would say, "Sorry what's de name? Facoondoe?"

"No mang, Fa-cun-do, Facundo."

"Wow, dat's a new one. Mind if I call you Fac?"

"No mang, mind if I call you shithead?"

So, you know, I had to come up with a more Saxonical name. And I looked around for a long time till I found one I liked. And when I found the one I wanted I took it. I estole it actually from a TV show—*Broken Badge* or something like that.

I go by the name Wideload McKennah now and I get a lot more respect, ese.

SLIDE: Wideload

WIDELOAD: I live in de border … I live in de zone, de barrio and I gotta move 'cause dat neighbourhood is going to de dogs. 'Cause dere's a lot of yuppies moving in and dey're wrecking de neighbourhood and making all kinds of noise wif renovating and landscaping and knocking down walls and comparing stained glass.

So I gotta move.

But first I gotta make some money—I want to cash in on de Latino Boom. Ya, dere's a Latino Boom, we are a very hot commodity right now. And what I really want to do is get a big chunk of toxic wasteland up on de Trans-Canada highway and make like a third-world theme park.

You know, you drive up to like big barbed wire gates with guards carrying sub-machine-guns and you park your car and den a broken-down Mercedes Benz bus comes along and takes you in under guard, of course. And you can buy an International Monetary Fund Credit Card for fifty bucks and it gets you on all de rides.

And as soon as you're inside somebody steals your purse and a policeman shows up but he's totally incompetent and you have to bribe him in order to get any action. Den you walk through a slum on the edge of a swamp wif poor people selling tortillas. And maybe like a disappearing rain-forest section dat you can actually wander through and search for rare plants and maybe find de cure to cancer and maybe find ... Sean Connery ... and you rent little golf carts to drive through it and de golf cart is always breaking down and you have to fix it yourself. And while you're fixing de golf cart in de sweltering noon-day sun a drug lord comes along in his hydrofoil and offers to take you to his villa where you can have lunch and watch a multi-media presentation on drug processing.

I figure it would do great—you people love dat kinda *shit*. I mean if de Maharishi can get a theme park going ... And I can also undercut dose travel agencies dat are selling package tours of Brazilian slums. Dis would be way cheaper, safer and it would generate a lot of jobs. For white people too. And I would make some money and be able to move out of the barrio and into Forest Hill.

Ya, a little house in Forest Hill. Nice neighbourhood. Quiet. Good place to bring up like fifteen kids. Course dis country is full of nice neighbourhoods—Westmount in Montreal looks good, or Vancouver you know, Point Grey is lovely or Kitsilano it's kind of like de Beaches here in Toronto. Or de Annex—mang, I love de Annex: you got professionals, you got families, you got professional families. Ya I could live dere. Hey mang, we could be neighbours—would you like dat? Sure, I'm moving in next door to ... you ... and I'm going to wash my Mustang every day and overhaul de engine and get some grease on de sidewalk and some friends like about twelve are gonna come and stay with me for a few ... years. You like music? Goood!

Ya, how 'bout a Chicano for a neighbour? Liven up de neighbourhood.

SLIDE: Chicano: a person who drives a loud car that sits low to the ground?
a kind of Mexican?
generic term for a working class Latino?
a wetback?
a Mexican born in Saxon America?

WIDELOAD: Technically, I don't qualify as a Chicano. I wasn't born in East L.A. I wasn't born in de southwest U.S.A. I wasn't even born in Méjico. Does dis make me Hispanic?

SLIDE: Hispanic: someone who speaks Spanish?
a Spaniard?
a Latino?
root of the word spic?

WIDELOAD: Dese terms, *Latino, Hispanic,* are very tricky you know, but dey are de only terms we have so we have to use dem wif caution. If you will indulge me for a moment I would like to make this point painfully clear.

De term *Hispanic,* for example, comes from the Roman word *Hispania,* which refers to de Iberian peninsula or Espain. Espain is a country in Europe. Many people who today are referred to as Hispanic have nothin to do wif Hispain. Some of dem don't even speak Hispanish.

De term *Latino* is also confusing because it lumps a whole lot of different people into one category. Dere is a world of difference between de right wing Cubans living in Miami, exiled Salvadorean leftists, Mexican speakers of Nahuatl, Brazilian speakers of Portuguese, Ticos, Nuyoricans (dat's a Puerto Rican who lives in New York) and den dere's de Uruguayans—I mean dey're practically European ... As for me, let's just say ... I'm a pachuco.[3]

It Starts

VERDECCHIA: Okay, I just want to stop for a second before we get all confused.

I've known that I've been lost for quite some time now—years and years—but if I can find the moment that I first discovered I was lost, there might be a clue …

This all starts with Jorge. After I'd been in therapy for a few months, Jorge suggested I go see El Brujo. I wasn't keen on the idea, being both sceptical and afraid of things like curanderos, but Jorge was persuasive and lent me bus fare enough to get me at least as far as the border …

It actually starts before that. It starts in France, Paris, France, the Moveable Feast, the City of Light, where I lived for a couple of years. En France où mes étudiants me disaient que je parlais le français comme une vache Catalan. En France où j'étais étranger, un anglais, un Argentin–Canadien, un faux touriste. Paris, France where I lived and worked illegally, where I would produce my transit pass whenever policemen asked for my papers. In France, where I was undocumented, extralegal, marginal and where for some reason, known perhaps only by Carlos Gardel and Julio Cortázar, I felt almost at home.

Or it starts before the City of Light, in the City of Sludge: Kitchener, Ontario. There in Kitchener, where I learned to drive, where I first had sex, where there was nothing to do but eat doughnuts and dream of elsewhere. There in Kitchener, where I once wrote a letter to the editor and suggested that it was not a good idea to ban books in schools, and it was there in Kitchener that a stranger responded to my letter and suggested that I go back to my own country.

No. It starts, in fact, at the airport where my parents and my grandparents and our friends couldn't stop crying and hugged each other continually and said goodbye again and again until the stewardess finally came and took me out of my father's arms and carried me on to the plane, forcing my parents to finally board—

Maybe. Maybe not.

Maybe it starts with Columbus. Maybe it starts with the genius Arab engineer who invented the rudder. Maybe a little history is required to put this all in order.

History

SLIDE: An Idiosyncratic History of America

VERDECCHIA: Our History begins approximately 200 million years ago in the Triassic Period of the Mesozoic Era when the original supercontinent Pangaea broke up and the continents of the earth assumed the shapes we now recognize.

SLIDE: map of the world

5000 B.C.: The first settlements appear in the highlands of Mexico and in the Andes mountains. 1500 B.C.: The pyramid at Teotihuacán is built. (*SLIDE: photo of the pyramid*)

Early 1400's A.D.: Joan of Arc (*SLIDE: statue of Joan of Arc*) is born and shortly thereafter burned. At the same time, the Incas in Peru develop a highly efficient political system.

1492: Catholic Spain is very busy integrating the Moors. These Moors or Spaniards of Islamic culture who have been in Spain some 700 years suffer the same fate as the Spanish Jews: they are converted, or exiled, their heretical books and bodies burned.

SLIDE: portrait of Christopher Columbus

Yes, also in 1492: this chubby guy sails the ocean blue.

1500: Pedro Cabral stumbles across what we now call Brazil—Portugal, fearing enemy attacks, discourages and suppresses writing about the colony.

1542: The Spanish Crown passes the Laws of the Indies. These Laws state that the settlers have only temporary concessions to these lands while the real owners are the Native Americans. Curiously, the Spanish Crown does not inform the Natives that the land is legally theirs. An oversight no doubt.

1588: The invincible Spanish Armada is defeated. Spain grows poorer and poorer as gold from the New World is melted down to pay for wars and imported manufactured goods from the developed northern countries. El Greco finishes *The Burial of Count Orgaz*.

SLIDE: The Burial of Count Orgaz

Lope de Vega writes *La Dragontea*. Caldéron de La Barca and Velázquez are about to be born. 1808: Beethoven writes Symphonies 5 & 6. France invades Spain and in the power vacuum wars of independence break out all over New

Spain. Goya paints (*SLIDE: Executions of the Citizens of Madrid*) *Executions of the Citizens of Madrid*.

1812: Beethoven writes Symphonies 7 & 8 and a war breaks out in North America.

1832: Britain occupies the Malvinas Islands and gives them the new, silly name of the Falklands.

1846: The U.S. attacks Mexico.

1863: France attacks Mexico and installs an Austrian as emperor.

1867: Mexico's Austrian emperor is executed, volume one of *Das Kapital* is published and the Dominion of Canada is established.

1902: Gorki writes *The Lower Depths*, the U.S. acquires control over the Panama Canal and Beatrix Potter writes *Peter Rabbit*. (*SLIDE: illustration from* Peter Rabbit)

1961: Ernest Hemingway kills himself, (*SLIDE: photo of Ernest Hemingway*) *West Side Story* (*SLIDE: photo of the "Sharks" in mid-dance*) wins the Academy Award, a 680-pound giant sea bass is caught off the Florida coast (*SLIDE: photo of large fish*) and the U.S. attacks Cuba. (*SLIDE: photo of Fidel Castro*)

1969: Richard Nixon (*SLIDE: photo of Richard Nixon*) is inaugurated as president of the U.S., Samuel Beckett (*SLIDE: photo of Samuel Beckett*) is awarded the Nobel Prize for Literature, the Montreal Canadiens (*SLIDE: photo of the 1969 Canadiens team*) win the Stanley Cup for hockey and I attend my first day of classes at Anne Hathaway Public School.

Roll Call

Music: "God Save the Queen"

VERDECCHIA: I am seven years old. The teacher at the front of the green classroom reads names from a list.

"Jonathon Kramer?"

Jonathon puts his hand up. He is a big boy with short red hair.

"Sandy Nemeth?"

Sandy puts her hand up. She is a small girl with long hair. When she smiles we can see the gap between her front teeth.

"Michael Uffelman?"

Michael puts his hand up. He is a tall boy with straight brown hair sitting very neatly in his chair. My name is next.

Minutes, hours, a century passes as the teacher, Miss Wiseman, forces her mouth into shapes hitherto unknown to the human race as she attempts to pronounce my name.

"Gwillyou—ree—moo … Verdeek—cheea?"

I put my hand up. I am a minuscule boy with ungovernable black hair, antennae and gills where everyone else has a mouth.

"You can call me Willy," I say. The antennae and gills disappear.

It could have been here—but I don't want to talk about myself all night.

Wideload's Terms

WIDELOAD: Thank God. I mean I doan know about you but I hate it when I go to el teatro to de theatre and I am espectin' to see a play and instead I just get some guy up dere talking about himself—deir life story—who cares? por favor … And whatever happened to plays anyway—anybody remember plays? Like wif a plot and like a central character? Gone de way of modernism I guess and probaly a good thing too. I mean I doan know if I could stand to see another play about a king dat's been dead for 400 years— Anyway—

The Smiths

WIDELOAD: When I first got to América del Norte I needed a place to live and I diden have a lot of money so I stayed wif a family. The Smiths—Mr. and Mrs. and deir two kids Cindy and John. And it was nice you know. Like it was like my first contact with an ethnic family and I got a really good look at de way dey live. I mean sure at times it was a bit exotic for me, you know de food for example, but mostly I just realized they were a family like any other wif crazy aunts and fights and generation gaps and communication problems and two cars, a VCR, a microwave, a cellular phone and a dog named Buster dat ate my socks.

Dey wanted to know all about me so I told dem stories about my mafioso uncle El Gato and how he won a tank and his wife in a poker game, and stories about my aunt, the opera singer, Luisa la Sonrisa, and about my cousin, Esperanza, about her border crossings and how she almost fell in love.

I came here because I wanted some perspective—you know working for a mafioso gives you a very particular point of view about de world. You know, we all need a filter to look at de world through. Like standing in Latin America I get a clear view of Norteamérica and standing on Latin America while living in Norf America gives me a new filter, a new perspective. Anyway, it was time to change my filter so I came here to estudy. Sí, thanks to mi tío El Gato and my cousin Esperanza who always used to say, "You should learn to use your brain or somebody else will use it for you," I practically have a doctorate in Chicano estudies. Dat's right—Chicano estudies … Well not exactly a doctorate, more like an M.A. or most of an M.A., 'cause I got my credits all screwed up and I diden finish—my professors said I was ungovernable. I lacked discipline. You know instead of like doing a paper on de historical roots of the oppression of La Raza I organized an all-night Salsa Dance Party Extravaganza. I also organized de month-long "Chico and de Man" Memorial Symposium which I dedicated to my cousin, Esperanza, back home.

Going Home

VERDECCHIA: I had wanted to go home for many years but the fear of military service in Argentina kept me from buying that plane ticket. Nobody was certain but everybody was pretty sure that I had committed treason by not registering for my military service when I was sixteen, even though I lived in Canada. Everybody was also reasonably sure that I would be eligible for military service until I was thirty-five. And everybody was absolutely certain that the minute I stepped off a plane in Buenos Aires, military policemen would spring from the tarmac, arrest me and guide me to a jail cell where they would laugh at my earrings and give me a proper haircut.

I phoned the consulate one day to try to get the official perspective on my situation. I gave a false name and I explained that I wanted to go HOME for a visit, that I was now a Canadian citizen and no, I hadn't registered for my military service. The gentleman at the consulate couldn't tell me exactly what my status was but he suggested that I come down to the consulate where they would put me on a plane which would fly me directly to Buenos Aires where I would appear before a

military tribunal who could tell me in no uncertain terms what my status actually was.

"Well I'll certainly consider that," I said.

And I waited seven years. And in those seven years, the military government is replaced by a civilian one and I decide I can wait no longer; I will risk a return HOME. I set off to discover the Southern Cone.

To minimize my risk I apply for a new Canadian passport which does not list my place of birth, (SLIDE: passport photos) and I plan to fly first to Santiago, Chile and then cross the border in a bus that traverses the Andes and goes to Mendoza, Argentina.

After an absence of almost fifteen years I am going home. Going Home. I repeat the words softly to myself—my mantra: I Am Going Home—all will be resolved, dissolved, revealed, I will claim my place in the universe when I Go Home.

Music: "Vuelvo Al Sur," Roberto Goyeneche

I have spent the last fifteen years preparing for this. I bought records and studied the liner notes. I bought maté and dulce de leche. I talked to my friends, questioned my parents and practised my Spanish with strangers. I befriended former Montonero and Tupamaro guerrillas and people even more dangerous like Jorge: painter, serious smoker, maître de café. Jorge the Apocryphal, Jorge of the savage hair. Jorge who moved to Italy and left me alone with my memories. I've spent the past fifteen years reading newspapers, novels and every Amnesty International report on South America. I tracked down a Salvador Allende poster, found postcards of Che and Pablo Neruda. I drank Malbec wines and black market Pisco with a Chilean macro-economist whose cheques always bounced. I learned the words and sang along with Cafrune and Goyeneche.

I saw *Missing* three times.

Santiago

VERDECCHIA: Santiago, Chile.

Chile, your Fodor's travel guide will tell you, immediately strikes the visitor as very cosmopolitan and is known for its award-winning wines and excellent seafood. Chileans, Fodor's tells us, are a handsome, stylish people known for their openness and hospitality. My 1989 Fodor's guide also tells me that under Pinochet, Chile enjoys a more stable political climate than it did in the early seventies, but reports persist of government-sponsored assassinations, kidnappings and torture. (Tell me about it man, I saw *Missing*.)

Well, it is now 1990 and the horrific Pinochet dictatorship is a thing of the past. I ride a comfortable bus into Santiago and continue reading my Fodor's: unfortunately, South America's democracies seem to have higher street-crime rates than the police states. I guess it all depends on how you define street crime. I look out the window and read the graffiti: Ojo! La derecha no duerme. I count all the policemen, one per block it seems. What was it like under Pinochet? A policeman in every house?

Music: "Jingo," Carlos Santana

Tired from a ten-hour flight, I check into the Hotel de Don Tito, listed on page 302 of your Fodor's as a moderate, small hotel with six suites, eight twins, eight singles, bar, homey atmosphere, and it's located on one of the main streets in Santiago on Huérfanos at Huérfanos 578. (*Huérfanos*—Spanish for *orphans*.) I shower, shave and take an afternoon nap.

Three blasts from the street wake me up and pull me to the window.

There, three storeys below, directly in front of the moderate and homey Hotel de Don Tito, there on the road, directly below my window, there a man in a suit, his shirt soaked an impossible red, lies writhing as an enormous crowd gathers. I reach for my camera and begin to take photographs. I take photographs with a 135 mm. telephoto and then change lenses to get a sense of the crowd that has built up. I take photographs of the man who was shot on the first day of my return home after an absence of almost fifteen years, as more policemen arrive pulling weapons from their jean jackets. I take photographs as the man in the suit, his lower body apparently immobilized, reaches wildly for the legs that surround him, as the motorcycle police expertly push the crowd away from the Hotel de Don Tito, moderate in Fodor's, Huérfanos 578, homey, page 302. I take photographs as still more policemen arrive waving things that look like Uzis. I take photographs with a Pentax MX and a 35 mm. F2.8 lens as the dying man, one of his shoes lying beside him, his gun on the road, gives up reaching for the legs around him. I take photographs from my room in the Hotel de Don Tito, Huérfanos 578, moderate in Fodor's, as the press arrives and NO AMBULANCE EVER COMES. I take photographs, 64 ASA Kodachromes, as he dies and I take photographs as the policemen (all men) talk to each other and I wonder if anyone has seen me and I take photographs as the policemen smoke cigarettes and cover him up and I take photographs and I realize that I have willed this to happen.

Dancing

WIDELOAD: Oye, you know I do like you Saxons. Really, you guys are great. I always have a very good time whenever we get together. Like sometimes, I'll be out with some friends from de Saxonian community and we'll be out at a bar having a few cervezas, you know, vacilando, and some music will be playing and "La Bamba" will come on. And all de Saxons get all excited and start tappin' deir toes and dey get all carried away and start doing dis thing with deir heads … and dey get dis look in deir eyes like it's Christmas an dey look at me and say, "Hey Wideload, 'La Bamba.'"

"Ya mang, la puta bamba."

"Wideload man, do you know de words?"

"Do I know de words?

"Mang, do I have an enorme pinga? Of course I know de words: pala pala pala la bamba … Who doesn't know de words?"

Music: "Navidad Negra," Ramiro's Latin Orchestra

WIDELOAD: Espeaking of music I haf to say dat I love de way you guys dance. I think you Saxons are some of de most interesting dancers on de planet. I lof to go down to the Bamboo when my friend Ramiro is playing and just watch you guys dance because you are so free—like nothing gets in your way: not de beat, not de rhythm, nothing. What I especially like to watch is like a Saxon guy dancing wif a Latin woman. Like she is out dere and she's smiling and doing a little cu-bop step and she's having a good time and de Saxon guy is like trying really hard to keep up, you know he's making a big effort to move his hips independently of his legs and rib cage and he's flapping his arms like a flamenco dancer. Generally speaking dis applies just to the male Saxon—Saxon women seem to have learned a move or two …

Of course part of de problem is dat you guys wear very funny shoes for dancing—I mean like dose giant running shoes with built-in air compressors and padding and support for de ankles and nuclear laces—I mean you might as well try dancing wif snowshoes on. Your feet have got to be free, so dat your knees are free so dat your hips are free—so dat you can move your culo wif impunity.

So dere dey are dancing away: de Saxon guy and de Latin woman or de Saxon woman and de Latin guy and de Saxon, you can see de Saxon thinking: Wow, he/she can really dance, he/she can really move those hips, he/she keeps smiling, I think he/she likes me, I bet he/she would be great in bed ...

Now dis is important so I'm going to continue talking about it—even though it always gets real quiet whenever I start in on this stuff.

Now dere are two things at work here: the first is the fact that whenever a Latin and a Saxon have sex it is going to be a mind-expanding and culturally enriching experience porque nosotros sabemos hacer cosas que ni se imaginaron en la *Kama Sutra*, porque nosotros tenemos un ritmo, un calor un sabor un tumbao de timbales de conga de candomble de kilombo. Una onda, un un dos tres, un dos. Saben ... ?

Dat's de first factor at work and for dose of you who want a translation of dat come and see me after de show or ask one of de eSpanish espeakers in de audience at intermission.

De second component is the Exotica Factor. De Latin Lover Fantasy. And I'll let you in on a little secret: Latins are no sexier dan Saxons—well maybe just a little. De difference is dis: we like it. A lot. And we practise. A lot. Like we touch every chance we get.

Now I doan want you to get de impression I'm picking on you Saxons. Nothing could be further from my mind ... I have de greatest respect for your culture ... and you know, every culture has its own fertility dances, its own dance of sexual joy—you people hab de Morris Dance, (*SLIDE: photo of Morris Dancers in mid-dance*) and hey, you go to a Morris Dance Festival and it's de Latinos who look silly. You have de Morris Dance—very sexy dance—you know, a bunch of guys hopping around wif bells on and every once in a while swinging at each other. Now, I am not doing de dance justice and I am looking for a Morris Dance teacher so if you know of one

please pass deir name along. You have de Morris Dance and we have de mambo, de rumba, de cumbia, de son, son-guajiro, son-changui, de charanga, de merengue, de guaguanco, de tango, de samba, salsa ... shall I continue?

Latin Lover

WIDELOAD: Latin Lovers.

SLIDE: photo of Antonio Banderas

Dis is Antonio Banderas. He is a Spanish actor, a Spaniard from Spain. Dat's in Europe. Some of you may know him from Almódovar films like *Tie Me Up, Tie Me Down* and some of you may know him from de Madonna movie where he appears as de object of her desire and some of you may know him from *De Mambo Kings* based on de excellent book by Oscar Hijuelos. Now according to *Elle* magazine (and dey should know), (*SLIDE:* Elle *magazine cover*) Antonio Banderas is de latest incarnation of de Latin Lover. It says right here: "Antonio Banderas—A Latin Love God Is Born."

De Latin Lover is always being reincarnated. Sometimes de Latin Lover is a woman—Carmen Miranda for example. (*SLIDE: photo of Carmen Miranda*) She was Brazilian. Poor Carmen, smiling, sexy even with all dose goddamned bananas on her head—do you know she ended up unemployable, blacklisted because a certain Senator named McCarthy found her obscene?

(*SLIDE: photo of Delores Del Rio*) Dere was also Delores Del Rio,

(*SLIDE: photo of Maria Montez*) Maria Montez, some of you may remember her as Cobra Woman,

(*SLIDE: photo of Rita Moreno*) den Rita Moreno. Today we have Sonia Braga ... (*SLIDE: photo of Sonia Braga*)

(*SLIDE: photo of Rudolph Valentino*) For de men dere was Rudolph Valentino,

(*SLIDE: photo of Fernando Lamas*) Fernando Lamas,

(*SLIDE: photo of Ricardo Montalban*) Mr. Maxwell House and of course ...

SLIDE: photo of Desi Arnaz

Desi Arnaz whom we all remember as Ricky Ricardo from Ricky and Lucy those all-time-great TV lovers. Now Ricky may not exactly live up to de steamy image of unbridled sexuality we expect from our Latin Lovers but you have to admit he's a pretty powerful icon. Funny, cute, musical and more often dan not, ridiculous.

Let's see what *Elle* magazine has to say about Latin Lovers: "He's short dark and handsome, with lots of black hair from head to chest. He's wildly emotional, swinging from brooding sulks to raucous laughter and singing loudly in public. He's relentlessly romantic, with a fixation on love that looks to be total: he seems to be always about to shout, 'I must have you.'" (*SLIDE: I must have you.*) "He is the Latin Lover, an archetype of masculinity built for pleasure."

The article begins by explaining the myth of the Latin Lover and then uses the myth to explain Banderas. Banderas cannot explain himself apparently because his English is too limited.

In *Mirabella*, (*SLIDE: Mirabella cover*) another glossy magazine, there is another article on Banderas and it describes how Banderas pronounces the word LOVE. He pronounces it "Looov-aaa." Ooooh isn't dat sweet and sexy and don't you just want to wrap him up in your arms and let him whisper filthy things in your ear in Spanish and broken English? Especially when, as also described in the *Mirabella* article, he wipes his mouth on the tablecloth and asks, "What can I done?" Don't you just want to fuck him? I do. I wonder though if it would be quite so disarming or charming if it was Fidel Castro wiping his mouth on the tablecloth?

SLIDE: Gentleman's Quarterly *cover*

Dis is Armand Assante.

He plays Banderas's brother in de movie *Mambo Kings*.

He is an Italo–American.

The subtitle here says "De Return of Macho." Did macho go away for a while? I hadn't noticed. Anyway, it has returned for dose of you who missed it.

According to dis article in *GQ*, Signor Assante almost did not get de part in de movie because de estudio, Warner Brothers, wanted a name—dey wanted a big-name A-list actor—like Robin Williams to play a Cuban. But according to de article the director of the movie had the "cajones" (*SLIDE: cajones*) to buck the studio and give the part to Assante.

Cajones ... Now the word I think they want to use is cojones, (*SLIDE: cojones*) which is a colloquial term for testicles. What they've ended

up with in *GQ* magazine is a sentence that means the director had the crates or boxes to buck the studio.

SLIDE: cojones = testicles

SLIDE: cajones = crates

Could be just a typo but you never know.

Now I find it really interesting dat all of the advance publicity for dis movie was concentrated in de fashion-magazine trade. When a Hollywood trade-magazine and major newspapers tell me de movie feels authentic and when the movie is pre-sold because its stars are sexy Latino love gods and macho and 'cause dey wear great clothes, I begin to suspect dat dis movie is another attempt to trade on the look, the feel, de surface of things Latin.

It goes back to this thing of Latin Lovers being archetypes of men and women built for pleasure. Whose pleasure mang? Your movie-going pleasure? The pleasure of de Fashion–Industrial–Hollywood complex? Think about it—

In dose movies we can't solve our own problems, we can't win a revolution without help from gringos, we can't build the pyramids at Chichén Itzá without help from space aliens, we don't win the Nobel Prize, no, instead we sing, we dance, we fuck like a dream, we die early on, we sleep a lot, we speak funny, we cheat on each other, we get scared easy, we amuse you. And it's not just in de movies—it's in—

A loud buzzer goes off.

Dere goes de buzzer—indicating dat some forty-five minutes of de show have elapsed and dat less dan fifteen minutes remain till intermission. Unofficial tests indicate dat audiences grow restless at de forty-five-minute mark so we are going to take de briefest of breaks and give you de opportunity to shift around in your seats and scratch your culo and whisper to the person next to you.

And during dis break we are gonna see some clips from a mega-musical spectacular dat will be opening here soon. It's called *Miss Tijuana*. Dey are gonna be building a special theatre to house *Miss Tijuana* 'cause it's a very big show wif lots of extras. It's going to be an adobe theatre wif Adobe Sound.

Here's de break.

Video clips of cartoons and movies featuring, among other things: Latinos, Hispanics, dopey peasants, Anthony Quinn and a certain mouse. Cheesy music plays. Then the loud buzzer goes off again.

Travel Sickness

VERDECCHIA: When I travel I get sick. I've thrown up in most of the major centres of the western world: Paris, Rome, Madrid, New York, London, Venice, Seaforth, Ontario, Calgary … And it's not just too much to drink or drugs, sometimes it's as simple as the shape of the clouds in the sky or the look on someone's face in the market or the sound my shoes make on the street. These things are enough to leave me shaking and sweating in bed with a churning stomach, no strength in my legs and unsettling dreams.

Well, I'm in Buenos Aires and so far I haven't thrown up. So far, Everything's Fine.

We meet in Caballito. And Alberto and I have dinner in a bright, noisy restaurant called The Little Pigs and Everything's Fine. And now we're looking for a place to hear some music, a place in San Telmo to hear some contemporary music, not tango and not folklore. Alberto wants to go see a band called Little Balls of Ricotta and Everything's Fine, but first we have to get the flat tire on his Fiat fixed. We stop at a gomería, a word which translated literally would be a "rubbery," it's a place where they fix tires. I'm feeling like I need some air so I get out of the car and Everything's Fine, I'm looking at Alberto in the gomería there's this weird green light in the shop and I'm leaning over the car and suddenly I feel very hot and awful and just as quickly I suddenly feel better. I wake up and I'm sitting on the road and somebody's thrown up on me, then I realize the vomit is my own and I'm in Buenos Aires and I'm sick and I've thrown up and we're in a tricky part of town and the cops will be passing by any minute and I haven't done my military service—

Alberto puts me in the back of the car. From the gomería, Alberto brings me half a Coke can whose edges have been carefully trimmed and filed down—a cup of water. I lie in the back of Alberto's uncle's Fiat as we pull away. There's a knock at the window and I'm sure it's the police saying, "Excuse me but have you got a young

man who hasn't done his military service in there, a degenerate who's vomited all over the street?"—but no, it's the guy from the gomería: he wants his Coke-can cup back.

We drive back to my apartment, not mine actually, my grandmother's, but she's not there for some reason and I'm using it. I'm feeling a little better but weak, can't raise my head, I watch Buenos Aires spin and speed past and around me, through the back window, like a movie I think, ya that's it, I'm in a Costa Gavras film.

I'm on the toilet in my grandmother's apartment, I leave tomorrow, back to Canada, and I ruined this last evening by getting sick, I can't fly like this all poisoned and I have to throw up again and the bidet is right there, and for some reason I remember Alberto telling me how by the end of the month people are coming to his store on the edge of the villa, on the edge of the slum, and asking if they can buy one egg or a quarter of a package of butter or a few cigarettes, and I think yes, in a few years we will kill for an apple, and I throw up in the bidet and I just want to go home—but I'm already there—aren't I? Eventually, I crawl into my grandmother's bed and sleep.

Music: "Asleep," Astor Piazzolla and Kronos Quartet

I dream of Mount Aconcagua, of Iguaçú, of Ushuaia and condors, of the sierras yellow and green, of bay, orange, quebracho and ombu trees, of running, sweating horses, of café con crema served with little glasses of soda water, of the smell of Particulares 30, of the vineyards of Mendoza, of barrels full of ruby-red vino tinto, of gardens as beautiful as Andalusia in spring. I dream of thousands of emerald-green parrots flying alongside my airplane—parrots just like the ones that flew alongside the bus as I travelled through the interior.

The Other

VERDECCHIA: I would like to clear up any possible misimpression. I should state now that I am something of an impostor. A fake. What I mean is: I sometimes confuse my tenses in Spanish. I couldn't dance a tango to save my life. All sides of the border have claimed and rejected me. On all sides I have been asked: How long have you been … ? How old were you when … ? When did you leave? When did you arrive? As if it were somehow possible to locate on a map, on an airline schedule, on a blueprint, the precise coordinates of the spirit, of the psyche, of memory.

Music: "El Mal Dormido," Atahualpa Yupanqui

As if we could somehow count or measure these things.
These things cannot be measured—I know I tried.
I told the doctor: "I feel Different. I feel wrong, out of place. I feel not nowhere, not neither."
The doctor said, "You're depressed."
I said, "Yes I am."
The doctor said, "Well … "
I said, "I want to be tested. Sample my blood, scan my brain, search my organs. Find it."
"Find what?"
"Whatever it is."
"And when we find it?"
"Get rid of it."

SLIDES: X-rays, brain scans

They didn't find anything. Everything's absolutely normal, I was told. Everything's fine. Everything's where it should be. I wasn't fooled. I am a direct descendant of two people who once ate an armadillo—armadillo has a half-life of 2,000 years—you can't tell me that isn't in my blood-stream. Evita Perón once kissed my mother and that night she felt her cheek begin to rot. You can't tell me that hasn't altered my DNA.

El Teatro

WIDELOAD: Okay, (*the lights come up*) let's see who's here, what's everybody wearing, let's see who came to El Teatro dis evening. What a good-looking bunch of people. What are you doing here tonight? I mean don't think we doan appreciate it, we do. We're glad you've chosen to come here instead of spending an evening in front of the Global Village Idiot Box.
Are you a Group? Do you know each other? No, well, some of you know de person next to you but collectively, you are strangers. Estrangers in de night. But perhaps by the end of the evening you will no longer be strangers because you will have shared an experience. You will have gone through dis show together and it will have created a common bond among you, a common reference point.

That's the theory anyway. That the theatre is valuable because a bunch of strangers come together and share an experience. But is it true? I mean how can you be sharing an experience when you are all (thankfully) different people? You have different jobs, different sexual orientations, different lives, different histories. You are all watching dis show from a different perspective. Most of you, for example, have been awake.
Maybe the only thing you have in common is dat you are all sitting here right now listening to me speculate about what you might have in common and dat you all paid sixteen dollars to hear me do so. But not everybody paid sixteen dollars, my friends get in free. So do theatre critics. Weird, huh?
People do end up in the weirdest places. I mean some of you are from Asia, some from el Caribe, some from Africa, some of you are from de Annex, and you ended up in dis small room with me. And me, I left home to escape poverty and I ended up working in de theatre? Weird. Let's take a break, huh?
It's intermission, ladies and gentlemen. Get your hot chocolate and Wideload wine gums outside.

Music: "La Guacamaya," Los Lobos

ACT TWO

SLIDE: Every North American, before this century is over, will find that he or she has a personal frontier with Latin America.
This is a living frontier, which can be nourished by information but, above all, by knowledge, by understanding, by the pursuit of enlightened self-interest on both parts.
Or it can be starved by suspicion, ghost stories, arrogance, ignorance, scorn and violence.
—Carlos Fuentes[4]

Music: "Peligro," Mano Negra

Call to Arms

VERDECCHIA: (*voiceover*) This play is not a plea for tolerance. This is not a special offer for free mambo lessons nor an invitation to order discount Paul Simon albums. This is a citation, a manifesto. This is a summons to begin negotiations, to claim your place on the continent.

Of Ferrets and Avocado

WIDELOAD: NEVER GIVE A FERRET AVOCADO!

SLIDE: photo of a ferret

De ferret ees a northern European animal—known also as de polecat and related to de bear and de wolberine. Dey are fierce little creatures, used to kill pests like rabbits. De ferret can be domesticated. Some of you may have a ferret of your own which you have affectionately named Blinky or Squiggly or Beowulf. Ferrets, as you ferret-owners will attest, are excellent pets: intelligent, playful, affectionate, cute as all-get-out. It takes four generations to domesticate a ferret but only one generation for the ferret to revert to a feral state—dat means to go savage. Interesting, huh?

De avocado is a fruit from de southern hemisphere—known variously as avocado, aguacate and, for some reason known only to themselves, as palta to Argentinians. De avocado is a rich, nutritious fruit which can be used in all sorts of ways—as a mayonnaise, in guacamole, spread some on some pork tenderloin for a sanwich Cubano. Avocados make lousy pets. Dey are not playful and do not respond at all to commands. Never give a ferret avocado.

Because it will blow up. Deir northern constitutions cannot process de rich southern fruit.

Think about dat.

Music: "Shaloade," Wganda Kenya

Wideload Gets Attention

WIDELOAD: I want to draw some attention to myself. Some more attention. I want to talk about dat nasty "S" word: Estereotype. I would like to set the record straight on dis subject and state dat I am by no means an estereotype. At least I am no more of an estereotype dan dat other person in de show: dat neurotic Argentinian. And I know dere's a lot of confusion on dis subject so let me offer a few pointers. If I was a real estereotype, I wouldn't be aware of it. I wouldn't be talking to you about being an estereotype.

If I was a real estereotype, you would be laughing at me, not with me.

And if I was a real estereotype, you wouldn't take me seriously and you do take me seriously. Don't you?

I'm the real thing. Don't be fooled by imitations.

Border Crossings

VERDECCHIA: (*speaking to Customs Agent*) "Los Angeles. Uh, Los, Las Anngel—Lows Anjelees, uh, L.A.

"Two weeks.

"Pleasure.

"I'm a Canadian citizen.

"Pleasure." (*to audience*) Didn't I just answer that question?

(*to Customs Agent*) "I'm … an … actor actually.

"Ever seen *Street Legal?*

"Well, I'm mostly in the theatre. I don't think … Okay uh, the Tarragon uh, Canadian Stage, the—

"I'm not surprised.

"Yes, that's my book. Well, it's not *mine*. It's a novel. That I'm reading." (*to audience*) Oh, Jeeezzzuz.

(*to Customs Agent*) "A guy, you know, who has a kind of identity problem and uh—

"I told you: pleasure. Come on what is this? I'm a Canadian citizen—we're supposed to be friends. You know, Free Trade, the longest undefended border in the world … all that?" (*to audience*) I had less trouble getting into Argentina.

(*to Customs Agent*) "No, I'm not unemployed. I'm an actor. I'm between jobs, I'm on holidays.

"Thanks."

(*to audience*) Some borders are easier to cross than others. Try starting a conversation in Vancouver with the following statement: "I like Toronto."

Some things get across borders easier than others. (*SLIDE: large, angry bee*) Killer bees for example.

Music: "Muiñeira de Vilanova," Milladoiro

Music. Music crosses borders.

My grandfather was a gallego, from Galicia, Spain. This music is from Galicia and yes, those are bagpipes. Those of us with an ethnomusicological bent can only ask ourselves, "How did the bagpipes ever end up in … Scotland?"

Ponte guapa que traen el haggis!

The bandoneon, cousin to the concertina and stepbrother to the accordion, came to the Río de la Plata via Germany. Originally intended for organless churches, the bandoneon found its true calling in the whore-houses of Buenos Aires and Montevideo playing the most profane music of all: the tango.

Banned by Pope Pius X, the tango was, at first, often danced only by men because its postures were considered too crude, too sexual for women—it was after all, one of the first dances in which men and women embraced.

King Ludwig of Bavaria forbade his officers to dance it, and the Duchess of Norfolk explained that the tango was contrary to English character and manners, but the tango, graciously received in the salons of Paris, soon swept London's Hotel Savoy and the rest of Europe. Finally, even polite society in Argentina acknowledged it.

The tango, however, has not been entirely domesticated. It is impossible to shop or aerobicize to tango … porque el tango es un sentimiento que se baila.

And what is it about the tango, this national treasure that some say was born of the gaucho's crude attempts to waltz?

Music: "Verano Porteño," Astor Piazzolla[5]

It is music for exile, for the preparations, the significations of departure, for the symptoms of migration. It is the languishing music of picking through your belongings and deciding what to take. It is the two a.m. music of smelling and caressing books none of which you can carry— books you leave behind with friends who say they'll always be here when you want them when you need them—music for a bowl of apples sitting on your table, apples you have not yet eaten, apples you cannot take—you know they have apples there in that other place but not these apples, not apples like these—You eat your last native apple and stare at what your life is reduced to—all the things you can stick into a sack. It will be cold, you will need boots, you don't own boots except these rubber ones—will they do? You pack them, you pack a letter from a friend so you will not feel too alone.

Music for final goodbyes for one last drink and a quick hug as you cram your cigarettes into your pocket and run to the bus, you run, run, your chest heaves, like the bellows of the bandoneon. You try to watch intently to emblazon in your mind these streets, these corners, those houses, the people, the smells, even the lurching bus fills you with a kind of stupid happiness and regret— Music for the things you left behind in that room: a dress, magazines, some drawings, two pairs of shoes and blouses too old to be worn any more … four perfect apples.

Music for cold nights under incomprehensible stars, for cups of coffee and cigarette smoke, for a long walk by the river where you might be alone or you might meet someone. It is music for encounters in shabby stairways, the music of lovemaking in a narrow bed, the tendernesses, the caress, the pull of strong arms and legs.

Music for men and women thin as bones.

Music for your invisibility.

Music for a letter that arrives telling you that he is very sick. Music for your arms that ache from longing from wishing he might be standing at the top of the stairs waiting to take the bags and then lean over and kiss you and even his silly stubble scratching your cold face would be welcome and you only discover that you're crying when you try to find your keys—

Music for a day in the fall when you buy a new coat and think perhaps you will live here for the rest of your life, perhaps it will be possible, you have changed so much, would they recognize you? would you recognize your country? would you recognize yourself ?

WIDELOAD: Basically, tango is music for fucked-up people.

VERDECCHIA: Other things cross borders easily. Diseases and disorders. Like amnesia. Amnesia crosses borders.

Drug War Deconstruction

WIDELOAD: Hey, I want to show you a little movie. It's a home movie. It came into my home and I saved it to share with my friends. It's called *The War On Drugs*. Some of you may have seen it already so we are just gonna see some of de highlights.

An edited drug-war TV movie plays without sound. WIDELOAD explains the action.

Dis is de title: It says DE WAR ON DRUGS. In BIG BLOCK LETTERS. In English. Dis is another title: *The Cocaine Cartel*. Dey're talking about de Medellin Cartel in Colombia.

Dis is de hero. He is a Drug Enforcement Agent from de U.S. who is sent to Colombia to take on de Medellin Cartel. He is smiling. He kisses his ex-wife. (*character on-screen turns away*) Oh … he is shy.

Dis woman is a kind of judge, a Colombian judge, and she agrees to prosecute de Medellin Cartel, to build a case against de drug lords even though her life is being threatened here on de phone even as we watch. Watch.

On-screen, the judge speaks into the phone; WIDELOAD provides the dialogue.

"But … I didn't order a pizza."
Dis guy is a journalist, an editor for a big Colombian newspaper. He is outspoken in his criticism of the drug lords. He has written editorial after editorial condemning de Cartel and calling for de arrest of de drug lords. He is a family man, as we can tell by his Volvo car and by de presents which he loads into de car to take to his loved ones.
Okay, dis is a long shot so can we fast-forward through this part? (*tape speeds up*) He's going home after a hard day at de office. He is in traffic. He is being followed by two guys on a motorcycle. Dey come to an intersection. (*tape resumes normal speed*) Dey estop. De light is red. De guy gets off de motorcycle. Dum-dee-bumbe-dum. He has a gun! Oooh! And de family-man editor is killed, and as we can see he is driving one of dose Volvos wif de built-in safety feature dat when de driver is killed, de car parks itself automatically. Very good cars Volvos.
Dis is de Medellin Cartel. Dese are de drug lords. Dey are de bad guys. We know dey are bad because dey have manicured hands, expensive jewellery, even more expensive suits and … dark hair. Dere's a lot of dem, dey are at a meeting, talking business. And dis guy is de kingpin, Pablo Escobar, head of de Medellin Cartel, de baddest of de bad. We know he is bad because he has reptilian eyes.
Okay, lemme put dis on pause for a second—Dis movie shows us a lot of things. It shows us dat drugs wreck families: in dis case de family of de nice white guy who is trying to stop de drug dealers—nobody in his family uses drugs—it's just he spends so much time fighting drugs dat his family falls apart.
De movie shows us dat de drug lords are nasty people who will not hesitate to kill anybody who gets in deir way. And you all know dat de kingpin, Pablo Escobar is now dead. But did you know dat Señor Escobar was one of de richest men in de world according to *The Economist* magazine? Now Señor Escobar was not only a giant in free-market capitalism, he was also very big in public works, especially public housing. Interesting, huh? De movie doesn't show us dat. What else doesn't de movie show us?
It does not show us for example dat profits from de sale of cocaine are used to fund wars like de

U.S. war on Nicaragua which left some 20,000 Nicaraguans dead. Dis movie does not show us dat right-wing Miami-based terrorists, major U.S. drug traffickers, de Medellin Cartel, Syrian drug and arms dealers, de CIA, de State Department and Oliver North all worked together to wage war on Nicaragua. It does not show us that charges against major U.S. drug traffickers—dose are de people who bring de drugs on to dis part of de continent—charges against dose people were dropped once they became involved in the Contra war against Nicaragua.
Some of you are, naturally, sceptical, and some of you have heard all dis before because you have read de Kerry Sub-Committee report. Allow me to recommend it to those of you who haven't read it. It is incomplete at 400 pages but it does outline dese things I'm talking about. It makes excellen' bedtime or bathroom reading. I urge you to pick up a copy. And if you have any questions gimme a call.
So de next time a blatant piece of propaganda like dis one comes on, I hope we will watch it sceptically, and de next time we stick a straw up our nose I hope we will take a moment to make sure we know exactly where de money we give our dealer is going.[6]

Audition

VERDECCHIA: It's two o'clock on a wintry afternoon and I have an audition for a TV movie. (*A dialect tape plays.*) The office has sliding glass doors, hidden lighting fixtures and extravagant windows. There are four or five people seated behind a table including a guy with very expensive sunglasses.

VERDECCHIA sits down in front of a video camera. A close-up of VERDECCHIA appears on a monitor. In the following section, he sometimes speaks to the camera and sometimes off-camera to the audience.

(*on-camera*) Hi, I'm Guillermo Verdecchia. I'm with Noble Talent.
(*off-camera*) For those of you who aren't in the business this is called slating. And when I say the Business I do mean the Industry. Slating is the first thing you do when you audition for a part on a TV show or a movie—you put your face and your name and your agent's name on tape before you read the scene.

(*on-camera*) I'm 5'9". On a good day.

(*off-camera*) That's called a little joke. Always good to get the producers and director laughing.

(*on-camera*) I'm from Argentina, actually. My special skills include driving heavy machinery, tango-dancing, scuba-diving, polo-playing and badminton. I speak three languages including English and I specialize in El Salvadorean refugees, Italian bob-sledders, Arab horse-thieves and Uruguayan rugby-players who are forced to cannibalize their friends when their plane crashes in the Andes.

(*off-camera*) Actually, I've never played a horse-thief or a rugby cannibal but I have auditioned for them an awful lot.

(*on-camera*) No. I've never been on "Really—True—Things—That—Actual—Cops—Do—As—Captured—By—Totally—Average—Citizens—With—Only—A—Video—Camera" before. It's a pleasure to be here. I'm reading for the part of Sharko.

(*off-camera*) An overweight Hispanic in a dirty suit, it says here. I'm perfect for it.

(*on-camera*) Here we go.

Music: "Speedy Gonzalez Meets Two Crows From Tacos," Carl Stalling

(*reads on-camera*) A black Camaro slides into the foreground, the engine throbbing like a hard-on from hell. Cut to close-up on trunk opening to reveal a deadly assault rifle. We hear Sharko's voice. (*VERDECCHIA slips on a red bandanna.*) That's me.

(*reads Sharko's part on-camera*) There it is man. Is a thing of great beauty, no?

Sure man, I got what you ordered: silencer, bullets. I even got you a little extra 'cause I like doing business with you. A shiny new handgun.

Come on man, it's like brand-new. I got it off some old bag who used it to scare away peeping Toms.

Ah man, you take all this stuff for two grand, and I'll throw in the pistol for a couple of hundred. If you don't like it, you can sell it to some schoolkids for twice the price.

You already got one, hah? It was a present ... I see. A present from who?

From your Uncle Sam. Dat's nice. I diden know you had got an Uncle ...

(*with dawning horror*) You're a cop?

(*no longer reading; off-camera*) Well that's that. I should've done it differently. I could've been funnier.

(*on-camera*) Uh, would you like me to do the scene again? I could do it differently. I have a blue bandanna.

Okay. Thanks very much.

Nice to meet you.

SLIDE: Ay ay ay ay I am the Frito Bandito

Music: "Cielito Lindo," Placido Domingo

Santiago Two

VERDECCHIA: I went back to Santiago and looked for some sign of the man who had been shot on the first day of my return. I looked for a stain, a scrape, anything, his shoe perhaps had been left behind. Nothing.

I wondered who he might have been. I remembered the redness of his shirt, the brightness of the sun. It was five o'clock.

A las cinco de la tarde.

Eran las cinco en punto de la tarde.

Un niño trajo la blanca sábana
a las cinco de la tarde.[7]

I saw someone die, I watched him die—that's what it looks like. That's where they end up—gun men, bank robbers, criminals and those brave revolutionaries and guerrillas you dreamed of and imagined you might be, might have been—they end up bleeding in the middle of the street, begging for water.

They end up dying alone on the hot pavement in a cheap suit with only one shoe. People die like that here. Ridiculous, absurd, pathetic deaths.

I came for a sign, I came because I had to know and now I know.

SLIDE: photos of shooting

¡Que no quiero verla!
Que mi recuerdo se quema.
¡Avisad a los jazmines
con su blancura pequeña!
¡Que no quiero verla![8]

At the hotel they told me he was a bank robber. The papers said the same thing—a bank robber, died almost immediately in a shoot-out, name of Fernando Ochoa, nationality unknown, not interested. Case closed, dead gone erased.

I told them I was a Canadian writer/journalist/filmmaker. They believed me. They let me look at the files, they let me talk, very briefly, to the cops who shot him, and since no one had shown up to claim them, they let me go through his personal effects. There wasn't much. A Bic lighter, with a tiny screw in the bottom of it so it could be refilled, an empty wallet. A package of Marlboros, with two crumpled cigarettes. There was a letter to someone named Mercedes. It read: "Querida Mercedes: It is bitterly cold tonight in my little room but I can look out the window and see the stars. I imagine that you are looking at them too. I take comfort in the fact that you and Ines and I share the same sky." There was also a newspaper from August 2nd, the day I arrived, the day he was shot. The headline claimed that former President Pinochet and the former Minister of the Interior knew nothing about the bodies that had been found in the Río Mapocho. I asked about his shoe—the one I saw on the road—no one knew anything about a shoe although they knew he wore size forty-two just like me—

Decompression

VERDECCHIA: I'm sitting in the bar at Ezeiza, I'm in the bar at Heathrow, in the bar at Terminal sixty-two at LAX and I'm decompressing, preparing to surface. I'll arrive at Pearson at Mirabelle at Calgary International and I know that nothing will have changed and that every-thing will be different. I know that I've left some things behind—a sock in a hotel in Mendoza, a ring in a slum in Buenos Aires, a Zippo lighter in a lobby in Chile, a toenail in Ben's studio in Pougnadoresse, a combful of hair in the sink in the washroom at Florian in Venice.

These vestiges, these cells are slowly crawling towards each other. They are crossing oceans and mountains and six-lane expressways. They are calling to each other and arranging to meet in my sleep.

The Therapist

VERDECCHIA: So … I went to see a Therapist. He trained in Vienna but his office was in North York. I didn't tell him that I was afraid my toenails were coming after me in my sleep—I told him how I felt, what was happening. I have memories of things that never happened to me—I feel nostalgia for things I never knew—I feel connected to things I have no connection with, responsible, involved, implicated in things that happen thousands of miles away.

My Therapist asked about my family. If I'd been breast-fed. He asked about my sex life, my habits. He asked me to make a list of recurring dreams, a list of traumatic events including things like automobile accidents. I answered his questions and showed him drawings.

SLIDES: drawings

My Therapist told me I was making progress. I believed him. (Who wouldn't believe a Therapist trained in Vienna?) At about the same time that I started doing what he called "deep therapy work," or what I privately called reclaiming my inner whale, I began to lose feeling in my extremities. It started as a tingling in the tips of my fingers and then my hands went numb. Eventually, over a period of months, I lost all feeling in my left arm and I could hardly lift it.

My Therapist told me to see a Doctor.

The Doctor told me to rest and gave me pills.

Jorge made me go see El Brujo.

I said, "Jorge, what do you mean brujo? I'm not going to somebody who's gonna make me eat seaweed."

Jorge said, "No, che loco, por favor, dejate de joder, vamos che, tomate un matecito loco y vamos … "

Who could argue with that? "Where is this Brujo, Jorge?"

"En la frontera."

"Where?"

"Bloor and Madison."

El Brujo

Music: "Mojotorro," Dino Saluzzi

SLIDE: The West is no longer west. The old binary models have been replaced by a border dialectic of ongoing flux. We now inhabit a social universe in constant motion, a moving cartography with a floating culture and a fluctuating sense of self.
—Guillermo Gómez-Peña [9]

VERDECCHIA: Porque los recién llegados me sospechan,
porque I speak mejor Inglish que eSpanish,
porque mis padres no me creen,
porque no como tripa porque no como lengua,

porque hasta mis dreams are subtitled.

I went to see El Brujo at his place on Madison, and you know I'd been to see a palm reader before so I sort of knew what to expect. And he's this normal guy who looks sort of like Freddy Prinze except with longer hair. And I told him about my Therapist and about the numbness in my body and El Brujo said, "He tried to steal your soul," and I laughed this kind of honking sputtering laugh. I thought maybe he was kidding.

El Brujo asked me, "How do you feel?" and I said, "Okay. My stomach is kind of upset."

And he said, "Yes it is," and I thought oh please just let me get back to reclaiming my inner whale.

El Brujo said, "You have a very bad border wound."

"I do?"

"Yes," he said, "and here in Mexico any border wounds or afflictions are easily aggravated."

I didn't have the heart to tell him that we were at Bloor and Madison in Toronto. El Brujo brought out a bottle and thinking this would be one way to get my money's worth, I started to drink.

El Brujo said, "I remember the night Bolívar burned with fever and realized there was no way back to the capital; the night he burned his medals and cried, 'Whosoever works for the revolution ploughs the seas.'"

"You *remember* that do you?" I said. "That was what 1830 or something?" And I laughed and had another drink. And El Brujo laughed too and we had another drink and another drink and another.

El Brujo said, "I remember the Zoot Suit Riots. We were beat up for our pointy shoes and fancy clothes. I still have the scar." And he lifted up his shirt and showed me a gash. It was ugly and ragged and spotted with freshly dried blood. And that's when I first suspected that maybe we weren't at Bloor and Madison. You see, the Zoot Suit Riots were in 1943.

"What do you remember?" he asked.

"Not much."

"Try."

"I remember the Alamo?"

"No you don't."

"No, you're right I don't."

El Brujo said, "Your head aches."

"Yes it does."

"Because your left shoe is too tight. Why don't we burn it?" And maybe because I was drunk already, or maybe because I really thought that burning my shoe would help my headache, we threw it in the bathtub, doused it in lighter fluid and watched it burn this wild yellow and a weird green when the plastic caught on.

"What do you remember now?" he asked.

"I remember the French invasion of Mexico; I remember the Pastry War.

"I remember a bar of soap I had when I was little and it was shaped like a bear or a bunny and when it got wet, it grew hair, it got all fuzzy.

"I remember a little boy in a red snowsuit who ran away whenever anyone spoke to me in English. I remember la machine queso.

"I remember a gang of boys who wanted to steal my leather jacket even though we all spoke Spanish, a gang of boys who taught me I could be a long-lost son one minute and a tourist the next.

"I remember an audition where I was asked to betray and insult everything I claim to believe in and I remember that I did as I was asked.

"I remember practising t'ai chi in the park and being interrupted by a guy who wanted to start a fight and I remember thinking, 'Stupid drunken Mexican.' I remember my fear, I taste and smell my fear, my fear of young men who speak Spanish in the darkness of the park, and I know that somewhere in my traitorous heart I can't stand people I claim are my brothers. I don't know who did this to me. I remember feeling sick, I remember howling in the face of my fear …

"I remember that I had dreamt I was playing an accordion, playing something improvised, which my grandmother recognized after only three notes as a tango from her childhood, playing a tango I had never learned, playing something improvised, not knowing where my fingers were going, playing an accordion, a tango which left me shaking and sweating.

"And I remember that I dreamt that dream one night after a party with some Spaniards who kept asking me where I was from and why my Spanish was so funny and I remember that I remembered that dream the first time one afternoon in Paris while staring at an accordion in a stall at the flea market and then found 100 francs on the street."

As I passed out El Brujo said, "The Border is your … "

Music: "Nocturno A Mi Barrio," Anibal Troilo

SLIDE: Cuándo, cuándo me fui?

The Other America

VERDECCHIA: The airport is clean clean clean. And big big big. The car that takes me back into the city is big and clean. We drive through big clean empty land under a big, fairly clean sky. I'm back in Canada. It's nice. I'm back in Canada … oh well …

Why did I come back here?

This is where I work I tell myself, this is where I make the most sense, in this Noah's ark of a nation.

I reach into my pocket expecting to find my Zippo lighter and my last package of Particulares, but instead I find a Bic lighter with a tiny screw in the bottom of it so it can be refilled and a package of Marlboros with two crumpled cigarettes in it. And written on the package is a note, a quote I hadn't noticed before. It says:

No estoy en el crucero:
elegir
es equivocarse.[10]

SLIDE: I am not at the crossroads:
to choose
is to go wrong.
—Octavio Paz

And then I remember, I remember what El Brujo said, he said, "The Border is your Home."
I'm not in Canada; I'm not in Argentina.
I'm on the Border.
I am Home.
Mais zooot alors, je comprends maintenant, mais oui, merde! Je suis Argentin–Canadien! I am a post-Porteño neo-Latino Canadian! I am the Pan-American highway!

Latin Invasion

WIDELOAD: It's okay, mang. Everybody relax. I'm back. Ya, I been lying low in dis act but let me tell you I'm here to stay.

And it's quiz time. Please cast your memories way back and tell me who remembers José Imanez?

Ah-ha.

Who remembers de Frito Bandito? Who remembers Cheech and Chong?

Who remembers de U.S. invasion of Panama? Dat's okay, dat was a trick question.

Who remembers de musical *De Kiss of de Spider Woman?* I do because I paid forty-two bucks to see it: a glamorous musical celebration of the torture and repression of poor people in a far-away place called Latin America where just over the walls of the prison there are gypsies and bullfights, women with big busts and all sorts of exotic, hot-blooded delights. Dat's one of de hit songs from de show—"Big Busted Women," some of you may recall …

Who remembers de ad dat McDonald's had for deir fajitas not too long ago, featuring a guy called Pedro or Juan, and he says dat he's up here to get some McFajitas because (*reciting with supreme nasality*) "Dese are de most gueno fajitas I eber ate." What de fuck ees dat?

Can you imagine an ad dat went like: "Hey Sambo, what are you doing here?"

"Well, Mistah, I come up here to get some o' yo' pow'ful good McGrits. Mmmmm-mmm. Wif a watahmelon slice fo' deesert. Yassee."

I mean, we would be offended.

So, what is it with you people? Who do you think you are? Who do you think we are?

Yes, I am calling you you—I am generalizing, I am reducing you all to de lowest common denominator, I am painting you all with the same brush. Is it starting to bug you yet?

Of course, it is possible dat it doesn't really matter what I say. Because it's all been kind of funny dis evening.

Dat has been my mistake. I have wanted you to like me so I've been a funny guy.

Silence.

Esto, en serio ahora—

Señoras y señores, we are re-drawing the map of America because economics, I'm told, knows no borders.

SLIDE: Somehow the word "foreign" seems foreign these days. The world is smaller, so people are thinking bigger, beyond borders.
—IBM advertisement

Free Trade all de way from Méjico to Chile—dis is a big deal and I want to say dat it is a very complicated thing and it is only the beginning. And I wish to remind you, at this crucial juncture in our shared geographies, dat under dose funny voices and under dose funny images of de Frito Bandito and under all this talk of Money and Markets there are living, breathing, dreaming men, women and children.

I want to ask you please to throw out the metaphor of Latin America as North America's "backyard" because your backyard is now a border and the metaphor is now made flesh. Mira, I am in your backyard. I live next door, I live upstairs, I live across de street. It's me, your neighbour, your dance partner.

SLIDE: Towards un futuro post-Columbian

Consider

WIDELOAD & VERDECCHIA: Consider those come from the plains, del litoral, from the steppes, from the desert, from the savannah, from the Fens, from the sertão, from the rain forest, from the sierras, from the hills and high places.
Consider those come from the many corners of the globe to Fort MacMurray, to Montreal, to Saint John's to build, to teach, to navigate ships, to weave, to stay, to remember, to dream.
Consider those here first. Consider those I have not considered. Consider your parents, consider your grandparents.
Consider the country. Consider the continent. Consider the border.

Going Forward

VERDECCHIA: I am learning to live the border. I have called off the Border Patrol. I am a hyphenated person but I am not falling apart, I am putting together. I am building a house on the border.
And you? Did you change your name somewhere along the way? Does a part of you live hundreds or thousands of kilometres away? Do you have two countries, two memories? Do you have a border zone?
Will you call off the Border Patrol?
Ladies and gentlemen, please reset your watches. It is now almost ten o'clock on a Friday night—we still have time. We can go forward. Towards the centre, towards the border.

WIDELOAD: And let the dancing begin!

Music: "El Jako," Mano Negra

END

Endnotes

1. Carlos Fuentes, *Latin America: At War with the Past* (Toronto: CBC Enterprises, 1985): 8. This 1984 Massey Lecture elegantly explores, in great detail, the divisions expressed by the Mexico–North America border. Although Fuentes focuses almost exclusively on the U.S., his analysis and insights provide a useful perspective for Canadians.

2. William Langewiesche, "The Border," *The Atlantic* 269 (May 1992): 56. This excellent article deals specifically with the Mexico–U.S. border: border crossings, the Border Patrol, drug traffic, economics, etc.

3. The term *Latino* has its shortcomings but seems to me more inclusive than the term *Hispanic*. *Hispanic*—which comes from *Hispania*, the Roman word for the Iberian peninsula—is a term used in the U.S. for bureaucratic, demographic, ideological and commercial purposes. *Chicano* refers to something else again. Chicano identity, if I may be so bold, is based in the tension of the border. Neither Mexicans nor U.S. Americans, Chicanos synthesize to varying degrees Mexican culture and language—including its Indigenous roots—and Anglo-American culture and language. Originally springing from the southwest U.S., Chicanos can be found all over, in Texas, in California, in New Mexico (!), in Detroit, maybe even in Canada. Chicanos speak a variety of regional tongues including formal or standard English and Spanish, North Mexican Spanish, Tex-Mex or Spanglish and even some caló or pachuco slang. See Gloria Anzaldúa's essay, "How To Tame A Wild Tongue," in *Out There: Marginalization and Contemporary Culture* (New York and Cambridge, MA: The New Museum of Contemporary Art and M.I.T. Press, 1990): 203–11. Also of interest are the writing of Ron Arias, the poetry of Juan Felipe Herrera and the conjunto grooves of Steve Jordan.

4. Fuentes, 8.

5. Strictly speaking, Piazzolla's music is not tango with a capital T. Many purists would hotly contest my choice of music here, arguing that Piazzolla destroyed the tango. I would respond that Piazzolla re-invented and thereby rescued the tango from obsolescence. There is no forseeable end to this argument.

6. For a thorough analysis of the actual parameters of the War on Drugs, see Peter Dale Scott and Jonathan Marshall, *Cocaine Politics* (Berkeley: U of California P, 1991). See also Noam Chomsky, *Deterring Democracy* (London: Verso, 1991).

7. Federico García Lorca, "La cogida y la muerte," in *Poema del cante jondo/Llanto por Ignacio Sánchez Mejías* (Buenos Aires: Editorial Losada, 1948): 145.

8. Lorca, "La sangre derramada," in *Poema del cante jondo/Llanto por Ignacio Sánchez Mejías*, 148.

9. Guillermo Gómez-Peña, "The World According to Guillermo Gómez-Peña," *High Performance* 14 (Fall 1991): 20. A MacArthur Fellow, Gómez-Peña has been a vital contributor to the U.S. debate on "multiculturalism," urging a rigorous appraisal of terms such as assimilation, hybridization, border-culture, pluralism and coexistence. A former member of Border Arts Workshop, he continues to explore notions of identity and otherness in his writings, and in performances such as *Border Brujo* and *The Year of the White Bear*, a collaboration with Coco Fusco.

10. Octavio Paz, "A la mitad de esta frase," in *A Draft of Shadows*, ed. and trans. Eliot Weinberger (New York: New Directions, 1979): 72.

DJANET SEARS

(b. 1959)

Among the most exciting recent developments in English-Canadian theatre has been the emergence of a vibrant African Canadian theatre culture. The historical record of black involvement in Canadian theatre reaches back at least to 1849 when the Toronto Coloured Young Men's Amateur Theatrical Society performed a Restoration drama and scenes from Shakespeare. On the other side of the curtain, white resistance to black audience members' attempts to integrate theatres in Victoria in the early 1860s led to a series of near race-riots. Canada's first black professional company, the Negro Theatre Guild, established itself in Montreal in 1941, and during the headiest period of Canadian alternate theatre, from the late 1960s to the early '80s, new companies regularly came on stream: Montreal's Black Theatre Workshop, Toronto's Black Theatre Canada and Theatre Fountainhead, Vancouver's Sepia Players, Winnipeg's Caribbean Theatre Workshop, and Kwacha Playhouse in St. John, NB, among others. But until recently, African Canadian plays were still as rarely produced as indigenous Canadian plays of any kind had been in the first half of the century.

The 1990s witnessed a flourishing of African Canadian playwrights and play production reflecting the many facets of that multi-faceted culture: native-born Ottawans, Torontonians, Montrealers and Africadians from Nova Scotia; first-generation Canadians from Africa, England and the Caribbean writing in Vancouver, Regina and Toronto about life in Africa, the Caribbean, Canada and the United States. George Seremba and Archie Crail, Walter Borden, George Boyd and George Elliott Clarke, Diana Braithewaite, ahdri zhina mandiela, maxine bailey and sharon m. lewis, Lorena Gale, Andrew Moodie, and many more. In the midst of this ferment Djanet Sears has been a significant creative force as actor, director, producer, teacher, anthologist and playwright. Her own plays grapple with what George Elliott Clarke calls the "poly-consciousness" of African Canadian identity, its tangled roots and multiple cultural influences, including in Sears' case a black feminist, or womanist, perspective. *Harlem Duet*, her self-described "rhapsodic blues tragedy," tackles love and race, slavery and minstrelsy, vengeance and friendship through the lens of Shakespeare's *Othello*, refracted through the experience of Othello's black wife in contemporary Harlem and two other historical settings.

Born in England of Guyanese and Jamaican parents, Janet Sears came to Canada at the age of fifteen, spent her teens in Saskatoon and Oakville, Ontario, then moved to Toronto where she got a BFA in Theatre at York University and began working as an actor. Her first play, *Shakes*, a love story about work and relationships, was staged at York in 1980. Following a year-long trip to Africa, Sears wrote and performed *Afrika Solo*, produced by Factory Theatre and Theatre Fountainhead in 1987. A fictionalized musical autobiography, or "autobio-mythography," as she calls it, the play recounts her confusions about personal and cultural identity, the search for and discovery of her African roots, and the logic of renaming herself Djanet. It climaxes around a jungle bonfire in Zaire where she serenades her BaMbuti pygmy hosts with a soul-gospel version of "O Canada," a revelation of her polyvalent, postcolonial self as "the African heartbeat in a Canadian song," authentically African Canadian. *Afrika Solo* had a very successful series of runs on stage in Toronto and Ottawa, and won two international prizes for its CBC radio adaptation.

Double Trouble, dealing with life in public housing, was produced by Toronto Workshop Productions and toured schools in 1988. Sears collaborated with Crossroads Theatre on *The Mother Project* (1990), which examined African American female story-telling. Ground Zero Productions' *Who Killed Katie Ross?* (1996) toured Ontario, exploring the ramifications of an aboriginal woman's violent death. *Harlem Duet* was developed during Sears' 1996 tenure as playwright-in-residence at the Joseph Papp Public Theater in New York. It premiered at the Tarragon in 1997, produced by Nightwood Theatre and directed by Sears, winning four Dora Mavor Moore awards (including outstanding production, direction, and new play), the Chalmers New Play Award, and the Governor

General's Award for drama. *The Adventures of a Black Girl in Search of God*, co-directed by Sears, was workshopped at Toronto's Harbourfront in 2001 and is scheduled for a 2002 Obsidian-Nightwood Theatre co-production.

The versatile Sears has been playwright-in-residence at Nightwood, associate director of the Canadian Stage Company, writer-in-residence at the Canadian Film Centre, and visiting professor at University of Toronto. As an actor she has received both Dora and Gemini (TV) award nominations. Feature film performances include *Milk and Honey, April One* and Clement Virgo's *One Heart Broken into Song*. Among her notable directing credits are ahdri zhina mandiela's *dark diaspora ... in dub* and Monique Mojica's *Princess Pocohontas and the Blue Spots*. A founding member of Obsidian Theatre, Sears has also been artistic director of *NEGROPHILIA: An African American Retrospective, 1959–71* and the AfriCanadian Playwrights Festival. She has edited *Testifyin'*, an anthology of African Canadian drama, and *Tellin' It Like It Is*, the first collection of African Canadian monologues for actors.

Nearly a decade before *Harlem Duet*, a then unknown Ann-Marie MacDonald had revisited *Othello* in her incisive feminist comedy *Goodnight Desdemona (Good Morning Juliet)*. Also produced by Nightwood, Canada's foremost feminist theatre company, the play re-visions Shakespeare's portrait of the tragic female protagonist, imagining a Desdemona utterly unlike the passive victim of Shakespeare's play. MacDonald's Desdemona is a fearless warrior who categorically rejects the gender roles and imagery assigned her. Her battle cry is "bullshit!"

Similarly, Sears uses the template of *Othello* to explore the relatively unexamined female position in a relationship in which the male appears to have most of the power. But she focuses on gender only secondarily. Primarily, Sears foregrounds race. What is the impact on Othello's black wife, Billie, of his having left her for a white woman? What are the larger cultural and ideological ramifications of Othello's decision? The personal is very much the political in this play. Signifying on Shakespeare's *Othello*, Sears not only makes the jealous female the central figure and aggressor, but reduces Desdemona, her play's only white character, to Mona, an offstage voice invisible to the audience but for the brief appearance of her hand through a door. Moreover, Sears fractures the chronology of the play. Not content merely to re-set the story in contemporary Harlem, she utilizes fantasy or dream sequences or snatches from the African American collective unconscious—the status of these scenes is never entirely clear—to re-frame Billie and Othello as slaves in the immediate pre-Civil War South and as actors in the dressing room of a Harlem theatre in 1928. The result is a wide-ranging examination of some of the many ways in which race, as much as we might like to think otherwise, still inevitably matters.

Othello is the primary intertext cited in the play, but certainly not the only one. The 1928 scenes evoke the American theatrical tradition of minstrelsy, the cultural travesty marked by the use of grotesque blackface make-up, which some black actors themselves eventually embraced in order to secure a place in the theatrical market. The soundscapes that preface each scene introduce the voices of Martin Luther King and Malcolm X, whose names mark the Harlem streets at the crossroads of which sits Billie's apartment. Their ideological differences and divergent strategies for advancing the cause of African Americans are reflected in Othello and Billie's contrasting views on assimilation, as are the voices of Jesse Jackson and Louis Farrakhan. But the political soundtrack is not synchronized to the time-frame of the scenes. For example, we hear King's "I have a dream" speech in 1928 and Marcus Garvey's 1920s Afrocentric nationalism in the present day. Like the relevance of the *Othello* story, the struggle for racial dignity in its many forms is ongoing.

The musical prefaces also deepen and expand the tensions conveyed in the play's central plot. Billie (whose real name is Sybil but whose nickname suggests Billie Holiday) certainly has the blues. The prefatory riffs range from the deep country blues of the Mississippi delta to sophisticated urban jazz, spanning the African American experience in time and place. But the instruments (played live onstage) are cello and bass, more evocative of the European string tradition than the vernacular blues voice of African American culture, a tension again suggestive of Billie and

Othello's clash and of the latter's upwardly mobile, assimilationist aspirations. Towards the end the sound loop becomes increasingly distorted, a cacophony of strings and voices reflecting Billie's heightened emotional state as her desperate revenge plot approaches fruition. The last preface includes Langston Hughes' poem "Harlem," a commentary on what happens to "a dream deferred" too long. It speaks of Billie's final condition, refers back, through Hughes, to the Harlem Renaissance of the '20s, and contains in one of its lines the title of Lorraine Hansberry's *A Raisin in the Sun*, the play that Djanet Sears says inspired her to become a playwright.

Although the emotional arguments of *Harlem Duet* are heavily weighted against Othello, Sears gives him a good deal of counterweight (his impassioned monologue in Act One, Scene Nine, for example). She also reserves ample sympathy for Billie's father, the symbolically named Canada, who admits that he was a bad drunk and a worse parent. The father-daughter reconciliation cuts across generations, gender lines and national borders. "Canada freedom come," the slaves' cry of hope as they looked northward, expresses Billie's dream of forgiveness, healing and self-reposses-sion. The play ends with a reconfigured duet, a celebration of the rose that grows in Spanish Harlem—in this case an African-American-Canadian hybrid.

Harlem Duet premiered on April 24, 1997 as a Nightwood Theatre production at the Tarragon Extra Space, Toronto, with the following cast:

BILLIE	Alison Sealy-Smith
OTHELLO	Nigel Shawn Williams
MAGI	Barbara Barnes Hopkins
AMAH/MONA	Dawn Roach
CANADA	Jeff Jones
Double Bass	Lionel Williams
Cello	Doug Innes

Directed by Djanet Sears
Set and Costume Design by Teresa Przybylski
Lighting Design by Lesley Wilkinson
Music and Sound Design by Allen Booth
Music Composition and Arrangement by Lionel Williams

HARLEM DUET

That handkerchief
Did an Egyptian to my mother give.
She was a charmer ...
    ... There's magic in the web of it.
A sibyl ...
In her prophetic fury sewed the work.
Othello, III. iv. 55-72

CHARACTERS

OTHELLO, *a man of 40, present day*
HE, *OTHELLO, 1928*
HIM, *OTHELLO, 1860*

BILLIE, *a woman of 37, present day*
SHE, *BILLIE, 1928*
HER, *BILLIE, 1860*

CANADA, *BILLIE's father, 67*
AMAH, *BILLIE's sister-in-law, 33*
MAGI, *the landlady, 41*
MONA, *White, 30s (an off-stage voice)*

SCENE

Late summer.
Harlem: 1928, a tiny dressing room
Harlem: the present, an apartment in a renovated brownstone, at the corner of Martin Luther King and Malcolm X Boulevards (125th & Lennox)
Harlem: 1860, on the steps to a blacksmith's forge

Style note: Ellipsis marks vary; this is intentional.

ACT ONE

Prologue

Harlem, 1928: late summer—night. As the lights fade to black, the cello and the bass call and respond to a heaving melancholic blues. Martin Luther King's voice accompanies them. He seems to sing his dream in a slow polyrhythmic improvisation, as he reaches the climax of that now famous speech given at the March on Washington. Lights up on a couple in a tiny
dressing room. SHE is holding a large white silk handkerchief, spotted with ripe strawberries. She looks at HE as if searching for something. He has lathered his face and is slowly erasing the day's stubble with a straight razor. She looks down at the handkerchief.

SHE: We keep doing this don't we?

HE: I love you . . . But—

SHE: Remember . . . Remember when you gave this to me? Your mother's handkerchief. There's magic in the web of it. Little strawberries. It's so beautiful—delicate. You kissed my fingers . . . and with each kiss a new promise you made . . . swore yourself to me . . . for all eternity . . . remember?

HE: Yes. Yes . . . I remember.

Pause.

SHE: Harlem's the place to be now. Everyone who's anyone is coming here now. It's our time. In our place. It's what we've always dreamed of . . . isn't it?

HE: Yes.

SHE: You love her?

HE: I . . . I wish—

SHE: Have you sung to her at twilight?

HE: Yes.

SHE: Does your blood call out her name?

HE: Yes.

SHE: Do you finger-feed her berries dipped in dark and luscious sweets?

HE: Yes.

SHE: Have you built her a crystal palace to refract her image like a thousand mirrors in your veins?

HE: Yes.

SHE: Do you let her sip nectar kisses from a cup of jade-studded bronze from your immortal parts?

HE: Yes.

SHE: Does she make your thoughts and dreams and sighs, wishes and tears, ache sweet as you can bear?

HE: Yes.

SHE: Do you prepare her bed, deep in fragrant posies, rosemary, forget-me-nots and roses, anoint her feet with civet oil, lotus musk and perfumes, place them in gossamer slippers with coral clasps, amber beads and buckles of the purest gold, kiss her ankles and knees, caress her fragrant flower, gently unfolding each petal in search of the pearl in her velvet crown?

HE: Yes.

SHE: You love her.

HE: Yes. Yes. Yes.

He wipes his face with a towel. She stares at the handkerchief laying in her bare hand.

SHE: Is she White? (*silence*) Othello? (*silence*) She's White. (*silence*) Othello . . .

She holds the handkerchief out to him. He does not take it. She lets it fall at his feet. After a few moments, he picks it up.

Scene One

Harlem, present: late summer—morning. The strings thump out an urban melody blues/jazz riff, accompanied by the voice of Malcolm X, speaking about the nightmare of race in America and the need to build strong Black communities.

MAGI is on the fire escape, leaning on the railing, reading a magazine with a large picture of a blonde woman on the cover. As the sound fades, she closes the magazine, surveying the action on the street below.

MAGI: Sun up in Harlem. (*spots the postman*) Morning Mr. P.! Don't bring me no bill now—I warned ya before, I'm having a baby. Don't need to get myself all worked up, given my condition . . . I'm gonna have me a Virgo baby, makes me due 'bout this time next year . . . I can count. I just haven't chosen the actual father/husband candidate as yet. Gotta find me a man to play his part. I wanna conceive in the middle of December, so I've booked the Convent Avenue Baptist church for this Saturday. The wedding's at three. You sure look to be the marrying kind.

What you up to this weekend, yourself sweetness? Oh well then, wish your wife well for me. Package from where? California? Oohh. Yeh, yeh, yeh. I'll be right—Hey, hey, Amah girl . . . Up here . . . Let yourself in . . . (*throws a set of keys down to AMAH*) Mr. P., give that young lady the package . . . Yeh, she'll bring it up for me. (*beat*) Thank you, sugar. (*beat*) You have yourself a nice day now. Alright, sweetness. Mmn, mmn, mmn!

AMAH unlocks the door, enters and makes her way to the fire escape.

AMAH: Magi, look at you, out on the terrace, watching the summer blossoms on the corner of Malcolm X and Martin Luther King Boulevards.

MAGI: Nothing but weeds growing in the Soweto of America, honey. (*shouting out*) Billie!

AMAH: Where is she?

MAGI: I didn't want to wake her up 'til you got here. She didn't get to sleep 'til early morning. I could hear her wailing all the way downstairs.

AMAH: I can see a week. A couple of weeks at the most. But what is this?

MAGI: Two months—it's not like she's certifiable though. (*shouting gently to BILLIE in the bedroom*) Billie! Billie, Amah's here!

AMAH: Well, least she sleeps now.

MAGI: She's stillness itself. Buried under that ocean of self-help books, like it's a tomb. Like a pyramid over her. Over the bed. (*calling out once more*) Billie!

BILLIE's body moves slightly and an arm listlessly carves its way to the surface, shifting the tomb of books, several dropping to the floor. MAGI and AMAH make their way inside. On a large table is a vase filled with blossoming cotton branches. There is also a myriad of bottles and bags, and a Soxhlet extraction apparatus: flask, extractor and thimble, condenser, siphoning hoses, all held up by two metal stands. A Bunsen burner is placed under the flask.

MAGI: I'm just making her some coffee, can I get you a cup?

AMAH: (*inspects the table and searches for a space to put the small package*) Thanks Magi. Where d'you want this? It looks like a science lab in here.

MAGI: Some healing concoction I've been helping her make—but she's way ahead of me these days. She's got a real talent for herbs, you know. She's been sending away for ingredients—I can't even figure out what most of them are—put the package down anywhere.

AMAH: If I can find a space.

MAGI: Right there. On top of that alchemy book—right in the middle. Yeh. Thanks for doing this, Amah. For coming. It'll make her feel like a million dollars again.

AMAH: Please. Billie and me go so far back, way before Andrew. Besides, sister-in-laws are family too, you know. Jenny's been simply begging to come and see her, you know, for their once a week thing. They eat sausages, mashed potatoes, and corn. Some Canadian delicacy I guess—

MAGI: Aren't you guys vegetarians?

AMAH: Vegan.

MAGI: Vegan?

AMAH: We don't eat anything that has eyes. The sausages are tofu. You know they eat exactly the same thing every time. I was glad for the break. I guess I was kinda . . . well . . . it bugged me. Jenny's always full of Auntie Billie this, Auntie Billie that. Now I miss our one night a week without her. I mean—our time alone. And I see how it's a kind of security for her.

MAGI: Security for who?

AMAH: Oh, I can't rent your ground floor. They won't give me any insurance 'cause I don't have a licence. And I can't get a licence until I get a cosmetician's certificate. And I can't get a cosmetician's certificate until I finish this two year course on how to do White people's hair and make-up. I told them ain't no White people in Harlem. I'd learn how to do work with chemical relaxers and Jheri curls. Now, I do dreadlocks. And do they teach that? Oh no. They're just cracking down on people who do hair in private homes—something about lost tax revenues. I don't know . . . I want my own salon so bad I can taste it. 'The Lock Smiths'.

MAGI: 'The Lock Smiths'.

AMAH: Billie's supposed to be helping me with the business plan. Besides we've started trying for kid number two. I need the space.

MAGI: You're trying?

AMAH: I'm ten days late.

MAGI: No!

AMAH: It's still early. Don't tell Billie . . . you know. I'll tell her.

MAGI: Good for you, girl! Did I tell you I was having a baby?

AMAH: Oh yeh. How was he, that new candidate you were telling me about . . . Warren, no Waldo—

MAGI: Wendel? Wedded Wendel as I've discovered

AMAH: He didn't tell—

MAGI: Oh no. He believes that the nuclear family is the basis for a healthy society. That's why he's married. He keeps his own personal nuclear family at home in the event that he might someday want to spend time with it.

AMAH: Why'd you stop seeing George. I liked George.

MAGI: Well I liked him too.

AMAH: You two looked pretty serious there for a while.

MAGI: We'd been seeing each other the better part of . . . what . . . two years. I'm just not getting any younger. I mean, I kept dropping hints I was ready for him to pop the question. Seems like he don't know what question I'm referring to. So I decided to give him some encouragement. See, I've been collecting things for my trousseau, and I have this negligée . . . all white, long, beautiful lacy thing. Looks like a see-through wedding gown. So, I'm out on my balcony—you know, 'cause it's too hot inside, and I still ain't got around to putting in air conditioning. Anyway, I see him coming up the street. So I rush in and put on the wedding dress negligée, thinking, he'll see me in it, all beautiful like—want to pop the question, you know. So I open the door, me in the negligée, and he . . . He stands there. Mouth wide open. And he says, he guess he should go get a bottle of wine, seeing how this was gonna be some kind of special occasion an' all. Now I don't know whether he got lost . . . or drunk . . . But I ain't seen or heard from him since.

AMAH: Aahh nooo.

MAGI: I should have margarined his butt when I had the chance.

AMAH: Margarined his backside?

MAGI: If you want to bind a man—

AMAH: You don't mean, what I think you mean?

MAGI: If you want to keep a man then, you rub his backside with margarine.

AMAH: And it works?

MAGI: I don't know. When I'd remember, I could never figure out how to get from the bed to the refrigerator.

AMAH: Margarine, huh?

MAGI: But you've got to be careful. He might be a fool. You don't want to be dragging no damn fool behind you the rest of your days.

AMAH: You're a regular charmer, girl.

MAGI: Don't get me wrong. I don't cut the heads off chickens, or anything now.

AMAH: You know, a Jamaican lady told me about one where you rinse your underwear and use the dirty water to cook the meal.

MAGI: Nooo! Really?

AMAH: Really.

MAGI: Ooh, I like that. Boil down some greens in panty stock. Hmm!

AMAH: Once I buried his socks under the black-berry bush by the front door. Sure enough, he always finds his way back home.

MAGI: How is True Drew?

AMAH: Oh, Andrew's real good. You know him. He was up here 'til late, night before last, even, playing broad shouldered brother.

MAGI: Yep, he's a good man. They're rare. And he went all the way down to D.C. for the Million Man March. Yeh, he's one in a million. If you ever think of trading him in . . .

AMAH: Don't even think about it!

MAGI: Can't blame a girl for trying. (*calling out again*) Billie! Billie you up yet? (*gets no response; goes into the bedroom*) Billie? Billie, sorry to wake you, but Amah's here. She waiting.

BILLIE emerges. We recognize her as the woman in the prologue. She slowly makes her way to the edge of the bed.

BILLIE: If I could only stop dreaming, I might be able to get some rest.

MAGI: You should jot them down. They're messages from other realms, you know.

BILLIE: Jenny's in a large white room—the walls start pressing in all around her . . .

MAGI: You OK?

BILLIE: Mm mm. Yeh. I'm fine. I'm good.

MAGI: (*gently*) Come on sweetheart, Amah's waiting.

BILLIE: Let me just wash my face, and my mouth.

MAGI leaves BILLIE to join AMAH, who is now on the fire escape.

MAGI: She's coming . . . (*AMAH hands MAGI a cup of coffee.*) Ooh . . . Thanks.

AMAH: How is she?

MAGI: Better. Dreaming hard, though. Like she's on some archeological dig of the unconscious mind.

AMAH: His words hit her hard, huh.

MAGI: Like a baseball bat hits a mango. Like he was trying for a home run or something. The bat breaks through the skin, smashing the amber flesh, propelling her core out of the park, into the clouds. And she lays there, floating.

AMAH: Feeling sorry for herself.

MAGI: A discarded fruit sitting in a dish, surrounded by its own ripening mould.

AMAH: She feels so much.

MAGI: Yeh. Each of her emotions sprout new roots, long, tangled things, intersecting each other like strangle weed.

AMAH: She should go out though, get some fresh air once in a while.

MAGI: She does. Her trips out into the real world are brief, though. The grocer's for tubs of things you add water to, she calls food; the pharmacy for the pills, and the bookstore. All her money goes up in smokes and writings that tell her she really ain't out of her mind. They'd make her feel better, more beautiful, more well, until she'd see some nice chocolate brown-skinned man, dangling his prize in front of her. 'Cause all the rot inside her would begin to boil, threaten to shoot out. So she comes home, takes some pills and sleeps again that fitful sleep 'til she wakes.

AMAH: So she knows?

MAGI: Ooh she knows. She knows she's still up there in the clouds.

AMAH: She never used to be like that, you know, about colour.

MAGI: Guess it ain't never been personal before.

AMAH: But it seems bigger than that . . .

MAGI: Girl, you've been married what . . . six years?

AMAH: Seven this February coming . . .

MAGI: How'd you feel if Drew just upped and left you?

AMAH: I can't even imagine . . .

MAGI: They've been together nine.

AMAH: She still moving?

MAGI: So she say . . . asked me to pick up some boxes.

AMAH: (quietly) Rumour has it he's getting married.

MAGI: So soon. He hasn't told her anything. He still hasn't even moved his stuff yet.

AMAH: And she sacrificed so much. Gave up her share of the trust from her mother's life insurance to send him through school.

MAGI: No!

AMAH: So when it's her turn to go . . . All those years.

MAGI: And those babies.

AMAH: Yeh, thank god they didn't have any babies.

MAGI: No, no . . . Twice . . .

AMAH: No!

MAGI: First time, he told her he believed in a woman's right to choose, but he didn't think that the relationship was ready for—

AMAH: We didn't—

MAGI: Nobody did. Second time she miscarried.

AMAH: When? I don't—

MAGI: 'Bout the same time he left—no, it was before that. She was by herself . . . Set down in a pool of blood. She put it in a ziplock bag . . . in the freezer . . . all purple and blue . . .

AMAH: Oohh God . . . No . . . Really?

MAGI: Yeh.

AMAH: Nooo . . . For real. I'm serious . . .

MAGI: Yeh!

AMAH: Show me.

MAGI turns toward the living area and heads for the kitchen; AMAH follows closely behind. They approach the fridge and MAGI is about to open the freezer door when BILLIE enters from the bedroom. AMAH and MAGI stop abruptly, as if caught in the act.

AMAH: Billie!

MAGI: (overlapping) Hey girl! (BILLIE waves to them as she exits into the bathroom. MAGI turns to AMAH.) Or maybe I lied. Gotcha!

AMAH: You . . . You . . . little heifer—

MAGI laughs. AMAH gets infected and joins her.

Scene Two

Harlem, 1860: late summer—twilight. The instruments sing a blues from deep in the Mississippi Delta, while a mature northern American voice reads from the Declaration of Independence. HIM steeps hot metal into cool water. He places the shackles on an anvil and hammers the metal into shape. HER is making repairs to a shawl with a needle.

HER: I pray Cleotis is in heaven.

HIM: Yeh . . . I . . . um . . . I . . .

HER: You think Cleotis went to heaven?

HIM: Well, I . . . I don't . . .

HER: You think he's in hell?

HIM: No. No.

HER: Probably somewhere in between, though. Not Hades. Not God's kingdom. He's probably right there in the hardware store. Probably right there watching every time that Mr. Howard proudly hoists the mason jar. Every time they pay their penny to see through the formaldehyde. Cleotis is probably right there watching them gawk at his shriveled, pickled penis . . . You seen it?

HIM: No.

HER: You know who did the cutting, though?

HIM: No . . . Oh no . . .

HER: In France they got the vagina of a sister entombed for scientific research.

HIM: No!

HER: Venus, the Hottentot Venus. I read it in one of Miss Dessy's books. Saartjie—that's her real name, Saartjie Baartman. When Saartjie was alive they paraded her naked on a pay per view basis. Her derrière was amply endowed. People paid to see how big her butt was, and when she died, how big her pussy was.

HIM: Wooo!

HER: Human beings went and oohed and ahhed and paid money to see an endowment the creator bestowed on all of us.

HIM: That's . . . that's . . . so . . . so . . .

HER: They probably go to a special place though—Cleotis and Venus, Emmett. Purgatory. Venus and Cleotis fall in love, marry, but have no tools to consummate it. Must be a lot of us there walking around in purgatory without genitals.

Beat.

HIM: I've been meaning to . . . I want . . . (*laughing to himself*) I would like to . . .

HER: Yes . . . ?

HIM: Talk. We should talk.

HER: Talk-talk?

HIM: Talk-talk.

HER: About what . . . ? What's wrong?

HIM: Why must something be wrong—

HER: I . . . I just figured . . . figure . . .

HIM takes HER's hand and kisses it, then places a white handkerchief into her palm.

HIM: My heart . . .

HIM closes HER's fingers around the handkerchief. He kisses her fingers. Opening her hand, she examines the cloth.

HER: Little strawberries on a sheet of white. Berries in a field of snow . . . (*sighing*) Ah silk. It's beautiful.

HIM: It was my mother's. Given her by my father . . . from his mother before that. When she died she gave it me, insisting that when I found . . . chose . . . chose a wife . . . that I give it to her . . . to you heart.

HER: Oh . . . It is so beautiful.

HIM: There's magic in the web of it.

HER: So delicate . . . so old.

HIM: A token . . . an antique token of our ancient love.

HER: My ancient love . . .

HIM: My wife. My wife before I even met you. Let's do it. There's a war already brewing in the south. Canada freedom come.

HER: Yes?

HIM: Yes.

HER: We're really gonna go?

HIM: People will come to me and pay me for my work.

HER: Yes sir, Mr. Blacksmith, sir.

HIM: Can we have us a heap of children?

HER: Four boys and four girls.

HIM: And a big white house.

HER: A big house on an emerald hill.

HIM: Yeh . . . a white house, on an emerald hill, in Canada. (*pause*) I want to be with you 'til I'm too old to know. You know that.

HER: Even when my breasts fall to my toes?

HIM: I'll pick them up and carry them around for you.

HER: And when I can't remember my own name?

HIM: I'll call it out a thousand times a day.

HER: Then I'll think you're me.

HIM: I am you.

HER: And when I get old, and wrinkled, and enormously fat, you'll—

HIM: Fat? Naw. If you get fat, I'll have to leave your ass. (*kisses inside the crook of HER's arm*)

HER: Oh-oh. You're prospecting again.

HIM: I'm exploring the heightening Alleghenies of Pennsylvania. (*kisses HER*) The curvaceous slopes of California. (*kisses HER*) The red hills of Georgia, the mighty mountains of New York. (*kisses HER again*) I'm staking my claim.

HER: I don't come cheap, you know.

HIM: I know . . . I'm offering more than money can buy.

HER: How much more?

HIM: This much. (*kisses HER*)

HER: I could buy that.

HIM: Could you buy this? (*kisses HER deeply*)

HER: Beloved . . . (*kisses HIM*)

Scene Three

Harlem, the present: late summer—morning. Strains of a melodious urban blues jazz keeps time with an oral address by Marcus Garvey on the need for African Americans to return to Africa.

MAGI: No, I hate it.

AMAH: Come on. No one hates it.

MAGI: I do.

AMAH: Bah humbug?

MAGI: What?

AMAH: Scrooge?

MAGI: Oh no, no, no. You know what I hate about Christmas? Seven days to New Year's Eve. And I hate New Year's Eve. And you know what I really hate about New Year's Eve? It's not the being alone at midnight. It's not the being a wall-flower at some bash, because you fired your escort, who asked for time and a half, after 10:00

p.m. It's not even because you babysat your friend's kids the previous two. I really hate New Year's Eve because it's six weeks to Valentine's Day. And what I really really hate about Valentine's Day—well, maybe that's too strong. No. I really hate it. What I really hate about Valentine's Day is . . . it's my birthday. Don't get me wrong, now. I'm glad I was born. But I look at my life—I'm more than halfway through it, and I wonder, what do I have to show for it? Anyway . . .

AMAH: Well you come and spend Kwanzaa with us this year.

MAGI: I don't know about the seven days, girl? Look, I gotta go. I'm seeing a certain minister about a certain wedding.

AMAH: Whose wedding?

MAGI: Mine. And don't say a thing—you know, about him getting married, or anything. (*indicates the refrigerator*)

AMAH: Sealed.

MAGI: I'll drop by later.

AMAH: Alright.

MAGI: (*shouting*) Billie? I'm gonna drop by later with some boxes, OK?

BILLIE: (*offstage*) Thanks, Magi.

MAGI exits. AMAH goes to the table and examines the small chemical factory.

AMAH: Saracen's Compound . . . Woad . . . Hart's tongue . . . Prunella vulgaris . . . (*picks up a book lying among the small packages and vials*) Egyptian Alchemy: A Chemical Encyclopedia . . . (*puts the book back in its place and picks up another vial*) Nux Vomica, warning: Extremely poisonous. Can be ingested on contact with skin . . .

AMAH quickly replaces the vial, wiping her hand on her clothes. She turns her attention to the kitchen. She cautiously approaches the refrigerator, and is about to open the freezer section when BILLIE comes out of the bathroom.

BILLIE: Hey Amah.

AMAH: Oh—hi girl, how you feeling?

BILLIE: Thanks for making the house call, Amah.

AMAH: Child, you look so thin.

BILLIE: Well, I'm trying to lose a little baby fat before I die.

AMAH: Coffee?

BILLIE: Oh . . . Thanks. (*pours coffee*) You didn't have to come. I'm fine you know.

AMAH: You're very welcome. Come sit down. (*hands her the cup*)

BILLIE: I didn't mean . . . Thank you.

AMAH: You washed your hair?

BILLIE: Yesterday.

AMAH: Good. A package came for you this morning.

BILLIE: Where?

AMAH: I put it beside the chemistry set. What is all that?

BILLIE: Don't touch anything!

AMAH: Alright—alright. I—

BILLIE: No. No. I—I mean, some of this stuff can be deadly unless mixed ... or ... or diluted. Some ancient Egyptian rejuvenation tonic. If it don't kill me, it'll make me brand new—or so it says. How's my baby?

AMAH: Jenny's fine. Andrew's taking her to her first African dance class today. You should see her in the little leotard . . .

BILLIE: I should be there.

AMAH: She's dying to come over for sausages and mashed potatoes.

BILLIE: Yeh, yes, soon. Real soon.

AMAH prepares to twist BILLIE's hair. She opens a jar of hair oil and takes a generous portion, rubs it onto her hands and gently works it into BILLIE's hair.

AMAH: She was so cute, today—you know what she did? She overheard me talking to Andrew about you, and I was saying I thought your break-down was—

BILLIE: You told her I had a nervous breakdown?

AMAH: Oh—No. No. She overheard me—

BILLIE: I am not having a nervous breakdown.

AMAH: She didn't really understand. She thinks you've broken your legs and can't walk, you can't dance. She thinks you've broken your throat, and that's why she can't talk to you on the phone, that's why you don't sing to her on the phone anymore.

BILLIE: Please don't tell her I'm crazy.

AMAH: I never said you were crazy.

BILLIE: I've just been . . . tired. Exhausted. I . . . I didn't want her to see this in me. She'd feel it in me. I never want her to feel this . . .

AMAH: I know.

BILLIE: But I'm fine now. Really, I'll be fine. I registered for school, I'm only taking one course this term, but that's cool. And first thing next week, I'm redoing the business plan for the salon.

AMAH: You need to give me some of that tonic too, girl. That's the best kind of revenge, you know—living the good life.

BILLIE: I thought I was living that life.

AMAH: Maybe you were just dreaming.

AMAH takes a new lock of BILLIE's hair. Taking a large dab of oil, she applies it to the lock, rubbing the strand between her palms.

BILLIE: Remember when we moved in? The day Nelson and Winnie came to Harlem, remember? Winnie and Nelson—our welcoming committee. They'd blocked off the whole of 125th—it took us 45 minutes to convince the cops to let us through. And me and you and Othe and Drew went down to hear them speak. And Drew went off in search of some grits from a street vendor. And you asked me to hold baby Jenny while you went to the restroom, when this man came up to us and took our picture. Asked to take our picture. Jenny in my arms. Othello beside me. "The perfect Black family." That's what he called us. "The perfect Black family."

The phone rings.

AMAH: I'll get it.

BILLIE: No. Let it ring. I know who it is. I can still feel him—feel when he's thinking of me. We've spoken . . . must be three times, in the last two months. Something about $500 on my portion of his American Express card, which they'd cancel if I didn't pay the bill. Seems I did me some consumer therapy. Last time he called—mad—to announce that the card had been cancelled by AMEX, and that he hoped that I was pleased. (*beat*) And I was. Is that crazy?

AMAH: Don't sound crazy. Hold the hair oil for me.

BILLIE: I used to pray that he was calling to say he's sorry. To say how he'd discovered a deep confusion in himself. But now . . . (*phone stops ringing*) I have nothing to say to him. What could I say? Othello, how is the fairer sexed one you love to dangle from your arm the one you love for herself and preferred to the deeper sexed one is she softer does she smell of tea roses and baby powder does she sweat white musk from between her toes do her thighs touch I am not curious just want to know do her breasts fill the cup of your hand the lips of your tongue not too dark you like a little milk with your nipple don't you no I'm not curious just want to know.

AMAH: You tell Jenny colour's only skin deep.

BILLIE: The skin holds everything in. It's the largest organ in the human body. Slash the skin by my belly and my intestines fall out.

AMAH: Hold the hair oil up. (*takes a dab of oil from the jar*)

BILLIE: I thought I saw them once, you know—on the subway. I had to renew my prescription. And I spot them—him and her. My chest is pounding. My legs can't move. From the back, I see the sharp barber's line, separating his tightly coiled hair from the nape of the skin at the back of his neck. His skin is soft there . . . and I have to kick away the memory nudging its way into my brain. My lips on his neck, gently . . . holding him . . . Here, before me—his woman—all blonde hair and blonde legs. Her weight against his chest. His arm around her shoulders, his thumb resting on the gold of her hair. He's proud. You can see he's proud. He isn't just any Negro. He's special. That's why she's with him. And she . . . she . . . she flaunts. Yes, she flaunts. They are before. I am behind, stuck there on the platform. My tongue is pushing hard against the roof of my mouth . . . trying to hold up my brain, or something. 'Cause my brain threatens to fall. Fall down through the roof of my mouth, and be swallowed up. Slowly, slowly, I press forward, toward them. I'm not aiming for them though. I'm aiming with

them in mind. I'm aiming for beyond the yellow line, into the tracks. The tunnel all three of us will fall into can be no worse than the one I'm trapped in now. I walk—no, well hover really. I'm walking on air. I feel sure of myself for the first time in weeks. Only to be cut off by a tall grey man in a grey uniform, who isn't looking where he's going, or maybe I'm not—Maybe he knew my aim. He looks at me. I think he looks at me. He brushes past. Then a sound emanating from . . . from . . . from my uterus, slips out of my mouth, shatters the spell. They turn their heads—the couple. They see me. It isn't even him.

The phone rings again.

AMAH: It could be your father, you know. He's been trying to get in touch with you. Says he doesn't know if you're dead or alive. He was calling Drew even up to this morning.

BILLIE: My father . . . I wouldn't have anything to say. It's been so long. What would I say?

The phone stops ringing.

AMAH: He's been in the hospital, you know. Something about his liver.

BILLIE: He hauled us all the way back to Nova Scotia from the Bronx, to be near Granma, when Mama died.

AMAH: I love that Nova Scotia was a haven for slaves way before the underground railroad. I love that . . .

BILLIE: He's a sot. That's academia-speak for alcoholic. My Dad, the drunk of Dartmouth.

AMAH: You're still his children.

BILLIE: A detail. I'm glad he's recalled.

AMAH: Better late than never.

BILLIE: Too little, too late.

AMAH: Forgiveness is a virtue.

BILLIE: What?

AMAH: Forgiveness is a virtue.

BILLIE: Girl, patience is a virtue.

AMAH: Well . . . . . . forgiveness is up there . . .

BILLIE: Did Drew tell you about the time my father sang to me at my high school graduation dinner?

AMAH: Nooo. That's lovely. My father never sang to me at my graduation.

BILLIE: We were eating. He was standing on top of the banquet table.

AMAH: Nooo!

BILLIE: It's the truth!

Pause.

AMAH: Can I get a glass of water?

BILLIE: Yeh. Yeh, help yourself. (*AMAH goes into the kitchen.*) I've got o.j. in the fridge, if you want.

AMAH: Water will do, thanks. Do you have any . . . ice in your freezer?

BILLIE: I'll get it.

AMAH: I can get it.

BILLIE: (*gets up quickly and heads towards the kitchen*) It's OK. It's OK. I'll get it for you. (*opens the freezer and gets her the ice, closing the freezer door immediately behind her*)

AMAH: Thanks. (*beat*) What's in there?

BILLIE: Frozen shit.

The phone begins to ring again. Both women look toward it.

Scene Four

Same day: noontime. Accompanying the sound of rushing water and the polyrhythmic chorus of strings, Martin Luther King continues to assert his dream, its relationship to the American Constitution, and the Declaration of Independence.

OTHELLO: (*offstage*) Billie! (*Silence. He knocks again.*) Billie?! (*to MONA*) I don't think she's there.

OTHELLO unlocks the door. He enters. We recognize him as the man in both 1860 and 1928.

OTHELLO: Billie? Mona and I are here to pick up the rest of my things. Billie? (*He hears the shower, goes over to the bathroom door, knocks.*) Billie? . . . (*BILLIE screams. We hear something crash.*) It's just me . . . I tried to call. You should get that machine fixed.

BILLIE: (*offstage*) I'll be out in a minute.

OTHELLO returns to MONA at the entrance. We see nothing of her but brief glimpses of a bare arm and a waft of light brown hair.

OTHELLO: It's OK Mona, she's in there. Why don't you wait in the car.

MONA: (*offstage*) She'll have to get used to me sometime.

OTHELLO: I'll be down in a flash. It won't take me that long. (*She doesn't answer.*) Hey, hey, hey!

MONA: (*offstage*) Hey yourself. I do have other things to take care of, you know. (*He kisses her.*) OK . . . I still haven't found anything blue. I'll scour the stores. I'll be back in a couple of hours.

OTHELLO: Alright.

MONA: (*offstage*) Alright.

He brings in several large empty boxes. He closes the door and looks around. He sees a burning cigarette, picks it up, looks at it, then puts it out. He takes off his jacket. Then he takes several albums from a shelf and places them on the floor. He begins to form two piles. He picks up one of the albums and begins to laugh. BILLIE enters, dressed in a robe.

BILLIE: What are you doing here?

OTHELLO: I came over to pack my things. The movers are coming in the morning. I tried to call . . .

BILLIE: You took my pot.

OTHELLO: What . . .

BILLIE: My pot. The cast iron Dutch pot.

OTHELLO: Oh . . . Well, you never use it.

BILLIE: I want it back.

OTHELLO: You never use it.

BILLIE: The one with the yellow handle.

OTHELLO: We need it to make gumbo.

BILLIE: She uses it?

OTHELLO: I need it to make gumbo.

BILLIE: She needs my pot? The one with the carrying rings.

OTHELLO: It was a gift to both of us.

BILLIE: From my father.

OTHELLO: I'll bring it back tomorrow.

BILLIE: If you don't have it here for me inside of thirty minutes, I will break every jazz recording on that shelf.

OTHELLO: You want me to go all the way back for something you don't even use.

BILLIE: Let me see . . .

OTHELLO: You never used it.

BILLIE: Abbey Lincoln . . .

She takes the album from the table. Takes the record from the jacket and breaks it in two. She reaches for another album. OTHELLO picks up the broken record.

BILLIE: Aah. Max Roach. (*takes the cover off the Max Roach album*)

OTHELLO: The Abbey Lincoln was yours. (*She breaks the Max Roach record too.*) OK. OK, I'll go and get it. (*He picks up his jacket and proceeds to the door.*)

BILLIE: Fine. It's fine.

OTHELLO: Excuse me?

BILLIE: It's fine. Tomorrow's fine.

Pause. He turns toward her.

OTHELLO: OK. (*Pause. He puts his jacket down again. Pause.*) How are you? You look well.

BILLIE: I'm fine. And you?

OTHELLO: Great . . . Good.

Pause.

BILLIE: Well you know where your stuff is.

OTHELLO: Yep . . . Yes.

Pause.

BILLIE: Drink?

OTHELLO: What?

BILLIE: Would you like something to drink?

OTHELLO: Sure . . . Yes. . . . What do you—

BILLIE: Peppermint, fennel, chamomile . . . No . . . Just peppermint and fennel. Coffee, wine, cognac, water.

OTHELLO: What are you having?

BILLIE: Cognac.

OTHELLO: Oh. Well . . . That'll do. (*BILLIE goes to the kitchen.*) Where's my suitcase?

BILLIE: Where you left it.

Pause.

OTHELLO: So you're staying on then?

BILLIE: No.

OTHELLO: Where are you . . . You know . . . I mean, things are tight, money-wise, but I'll still put money in your account . . . When I can . . . I mean, I hope we can keep in touch. (*She hands him a glass of cognac.*) Thank you.

BILLIE: You're welcome.

Pause.

OTHELLO: You've lost weight. You look great. (*He takes a large gulp.*) Aaahh! Yes!

OTHELLO looks at BILLIE for a moment. He then takes one of the boxes and places it at his feet. He approaches the bookshelf. He takes down a large book.

OTHELLO: *African Mythology* . . . Is this mine or yours?

BILLIE: Mine . . . I think . . . I don't know.

OTHELLO: This is going to be interesting.

BILLIE: Take what you like. I don't care.

OTHELLO: (*takes another book*) *The Great Chain of Being?*

BILLIE: From man to mollusk. The scientific foundation for why we're not human. An African can't really be a woman, you know. My department agreed to let me take only one course this year—I'm taking a reading course.

OTHELLO: Yours . . . Yours . . . Mine . . . *Black Psychology*, you keeping this?

BILLIE: Yeh. (*takes the books from him*) You'd think there was more information on Black people and mental health. You know . . . Christ, we've been here, what, 400 years. No money in it I guess . . .

OTHELLO: What's money got to do with it?

BILLIE: You know, grants . . . scholarships . . .

OTHELLO: Race is not an obscure idea. (*He places several books into a box.*)

BILLIE: In genetics, or the study of what's wrong with people of African descent—The Heritage Foundation will give you tons of dough to prove the innate inferiority of . . . The Shakespeare's mine, but you can have it.

OTHELLO: Sure, if you don't—

BILLIE: No. The Heritage Foundation—that's where that guy Murray, et al, got most of their money for *Bell Curve*—I think . . . There's just no one out there willing to give you a scholarship to prove that we're all mad.

OTHELLO: We're all mad. This is the founding principle of your thesis?

BILLIE: Well, not mad . . . I mean . . . Well . . . Psychologically dysfunctional, then. All cultural groups are to some degree ethnocentric: We—they. But not all inter-cultural relations are of an inferior/superior type.

OTHELLO: Thus we're not all mad. (*He returns to the bookshelf.*)

BILLIE: No, no. In America, this race shit is classic behavioural disorder. Obsessions. Phobias. Delusions. Notions of persecution. Delusions of grandeur. Any one or combination of these can produce behaviours which categorize oneself as superior and another as inferior. You see, this kind of dysfunction is systemically supported by the larger society. Psychology only sees clients who can no longer function in society. We're all mad. We just appear to be functional.

OTHELLO: And your solution?

BILLIE: You'll have to buy my book. (*Pause. They continue packing.*) How's the teaching?

OTHELLO: Fine . . . Great . . .

BILLIE: Good.

Pause.

OTHELLO: I'll be heading the department's courses in Cyprus next summer.

BILLIE: I thought you told me Christopher . . . What's his name?

OTHELLO: Chris Yago?

BILLIE: Yeh, Yago.

OTHELLO: Well everyone thought he would get it. I thought he'd get it. So a whole bunch of them are challenging affirmative action.

BILLIE: Rednecks in academia.

OTHELLO: No, no . . . Well . . . . . I think it's a good thing.

BILLIE: Pul-eese.

OTHELLO: Using discrimination to cure discrimination is not—

BILLIE: We're talking put asides of 5%. 5% of everything available to Whites. They've still got 95.

OTHELLO: Billie . . . Injustice against Blacks can't be cured by injustice against Whites . . . you know that.

BILLIE: And younger people won't have the same opportunities you had.

OTHELLO: Now look who's sounding White.

BILLIE: Who said you sounded White?

OTHELLO: It's implied . . . No one at school tells me I don't know how to do my job . . . it's implied. I'll be at a faculty meeting, I'll make a suggestion and it'll be ignored. Not five minutes later, someone else will make the exact same suggestion and everyone will agree to it. Mona noticed it too. They think I'm only there because I'm Black. I've tested it.

BILLIE: So let me get this straight, you're against affirmative action in order for White people to respect you.

OTHELLO: For my peers . . . . . . my peers to respect me. You know what it's like. Every day I have to prove to them that I can do my job. I feel that any error I make only goes to prove them right.

BILLIE: Well you must be perfect. Mona respects you.

OTHELLO: Well, she really sees me. She was the only other faculty to support me on the MLK Day assembly. When we played the video—

BILLIE: The "I have a dream" speech?

OTHELLO: They understood. For a moment I got them to understand. (*He picks up several books and places them in a box.*)

BILLIE: "America has defaulted on this promissory note insofar as her . . .

OTHELLO & BILLIE: . . . citizens of colour are concerned.

OTHELLO: Instead of honoring this sacred obligation, America has given its coloured people a . . .

OTHELLO & BILLIE: bad cheque . . .

BILLIE: . . . a cheque that has come back marked . . .

OTHELLO & BILLIE: . . . 'insufficient funds.'"

BILLIE: The man was a . . . a . . .

OTHELLO: Poet . . . Visionary.

BILLIE: A prophet.

OTHELLO: After all he'd been through in his life, he could still see that at a deeper level we're all the same.

Pause.

BILLIE: I'm not the same.

OTHELLO: In the eyes of God, Billie, we're all the same.

BILLIE: One day little Black boys and little White girls—

OTHELLO: You're delusional.

BILLIE: You're the one looking for White respect.

OTHELLO: Wrong again! White respect, Black respect, it's all the same to me.

BILLIE: Right on brother man!

OTHELLO: When I was growing up . . . . . in a time of Black pride—it was something to say you were Black. Before that, I'd say . . . my family would say we're Cuban . . . It takes a long time to work through some of those things. I am a member of the human race.

BILLIE: Oh, that's a switch. What happened to all that J. A. Rogers stuff you were pushing. Blacks created the world, Blacks are the progenitors of European civilization, gloriana . . . Constantly trying to prove you're as good, no, better than White people. White people are always the line for you, aren't they? The rule . . . the margin . . . the variable of control. We are Black. Whatever we do is Black.

OTHELLO: I'm so tired of this race shit, Billie. There are alternatives—

BILLIE: Like what? Oh yes, White.

OTHELLO: Oh, don't be so—

BILLIE: Isn't that really what not acting Black, or feeling Black means.

OTHELLO: Liberation has no colour.

BILLIE: But progress is going to White schools . . . proving we're as good as Whites . . . like some holy grail . . . all that we're taught in those White schools. All that is in us. Our success is Whiteness. We religiously seek to have what they have. Access to the White man's world. The White man's job.

OTHELLO: That's economics.

BILLIE: White economics.

OTHELLO: God! Black women always—

BILLIE: No. Don't even go there . . .

OTHELLO: I . . . You . . . Forget it!

BILLIE: (*quietly at first*) Yes, you can forget it, can't you. I don't have that . . . that luxury. When I go into a store, I always know when I'm being watched. I can feel it. They want to see if I'm gonna slip some of their stuff into my pockets. When someone doesn't serve me, I think it's because I'm Black. When a clerk won't put the change into my held-out hand, I think it's because I'm Black. When I hear about a crime, any crime, I pray to God the person who they think did it isn't Black. I'm even suspicious of the word *Black*. Who called us Black anyway? It's not a country, it's not a racial category, its not even the colour of my skin. And don't give me this content of one's character B.S. I'm sorry . . . I am sorry . . . I had a dream. A dream that one day a Black man and a Black woman might find . . . Where jumping a broom was a solemn eternal vow that . . . I . . . Let's . . . Can we just get this over with?

She goes to the window. Silence. He moves toward her.

OTHELLO: I know . . . I know. I'm sorry . . .

BILLIE: Yeh . . .

OTHELLO: I care . . . you know that.

BILLIE: I know.

Silence.

OTHELLO: I never thought I'd miss Harlem.

Pause.

BILLIE: You still think it's a reservation?

OTHELLO: Homeland/reservation.

BILLIE: A sea of Black faces.

OTHELLO: Africatown, USA.

Pause.

BILLIE: When we lived in the Village, sometimes, I'd be on the subway and I'd miss my stop. And I'd just sit there, past midtown, past the upper west side, and somehow I'd end up here. And I'd just walk. I love seeing all these brown faces.

OTHELLO: Yeh . . .

BILLIE: Since they knocked down the old projects, I can see the Schomberg Museum from here. You still can't make out Harlem Hospital. I love that I can see the Apollo from our—from my balcony.

OTHELLO: Fire escape.

BILLIE: Patio.

OTHELLO: You never did find a pair of lawn chairs, and a table to fit in that space.

BILLIE: Terrace.

OTHELLO: I never saw the beauty in it.

BILLIE: Deck. My deck.

OTHELLO: I wish . . . (*He looks at her.*)

BILLIE: That old building across the street? I didn't know this, but that used to be the Hotel Theresa. That's where Castro stayed when he came to New York . . . Must have been the fifties. Ron Brown's father used to run that hotel.

OTHELLO: I . . . . . . I . . . . . . I miss you so much sometimes. Nine years . . . it's a long time.

BILLIE: I know.

OTHELLO: I'm really not trying to hurt you, Billie.

BILLIE: I know.

OTHELLO: I never meant to hurt you. (*He strokes her face.*)

BILLIE: I know.

OTHELLO: God you're so beautiful. (*He kisses her. She does not resist.*)

BILLIE: I . . . . don't . . . . I feel . . . (*He kisses her again.*) What are you doing?

OTHELLO: I . . . I'm . . . I'm exploring the heightening Alleghenies of Pennsylvania. (*kisses her again*) The curvaceous slopes of California. (*kisses her again*) The red hills of Georgia, the mighty mountains of New York. Such sad eyes. (*kisses her again*) I'm an equal opportunity employer. (*pause*) I am an equal opportunity employer. (*pause*) I say, I'm an equal opportunity employer, then you say, I don't come . . .

BILLIE: I don't come cheap, you know.

OTHELLO: I'm offering more than money can buy.

BILLIE: How much more?

OTHELLO: This much. (*He kisses her.*)

BILLIE: I could buy that.

OTHELLO: Could you buy this? (*He kisses her deeply.*)

BILLIE: Be . . . Be . . . Beloved. (*She kisses him.*)

Scene Five

Same day: early afternoon. The stringed duet croons gently as Malcolm X speaks about the need for Blacks to turn their gaze away from Whiteness so that they can see each other with new eyes. OTHELLO is lying in the bed. BILLIE is in the living room, smoking a cigarette.

OTHELLO: I've missed you.

BILLIE: That's nice.

OTHELLO: By the looks of things, I miss you even now.

BILLIE: I'm coming.

OTHELLO: I noticed.

BILLIE: Sometimes . . . Sometimes when we make love. Sometimes every moment lines up into one moment. And I'm holding you. And I can't tell where I end, or you begin. I see everything. All my ancestors lined up below me . . . . . . like a Makonde statue, or something. It's like . . . I know. I know I'm supposed to be here. Everything is here.

OTHELLO: Sounds crowded to me.

BILLIE: It's actually quite empty.

OTHELLO: Not as empty as this bed is feeling right about now.

BILLIE: I'm coming. I'm coming.

She hurriedly stubs the cigarette out, and heads toward the bedroom. The apartment buzzer rings. BILLIE goes to the intercom.

BILLIE: Hi Magi. I . . . er . . . I'm kinda busy right now.

MONA: (*through intercom*) It's Mona. Could I have a word with Othello.

OTHELLO: (*overlapping*) Shit!

BILLIE: One second please.

He rushes to the intercom, while attempting to put his clothes back on. BILLIE tries to hold back her laughter. Her laughter begins to infect OTHELLO. He puts a finger over his mouth indicating to BILLIE to be quiet.

OTHELLO: Hey Mone . . . Mone, I'm not done yet. There's more here than I imagined. Why don't I call you when I'm done. (*MONA does not respond. OTHELLO's demeanour changes.*) Mone? Mona? I'm coming, OK? I'll be right . . . Just wait there one second, OK? OK?

BILLIE is unable to hide her astonishment.

MONA: (*through intercom*) OK.

OTHELLO: OK. (*He steps away from the intercom to finish putting on his clothes. BILLIE stares at him.*) I'll be back in . . . uh . . . I just have to go straighten . . . uh . . . She wants to help . . . help pack. You'll have to get used to her sometime. I mean . . . I . . . (*BILLIE continues to stare steadily at OTHELLO as he struggles with the buttons on his shirt.*) I'm sorry . . . Well . . . . . . I'll be right . . . I'll be back.

He exits. BILLIE does not move.

Scene Six

Harlem, 1860: late summer—night. A whining delta blues slides and blurs while the deeply resonant voice of Paul Robeson talks of his fore-bears, whose blood is in the American soil. HIM is hammering a newly-forged horseshoe, HER rushes in holding a large carrying bag.

HER: Oh . . . let me catch—catch my breath . . . I thought I was seen . . . Oh my . . . I . . . I've packed a change of clothes for both of us, some loaves . . . I liberated the leftover bacon from yesterday's meal, from out the pantry, seeing how it was staring me right in the face when I was cleaning. It won't be missed. I wish I could pack old Betsy in my bag. She'd be sure an' give us some good fresh milk each mornin'. Oh—and I packed a fleece blanket. I hear the nights get good and cold further north you go. And . . . did I forget . . . no . . . Nothing forgotten. Oh yes, I borrowed the big carving knife—for the bacon, a' course. You still working on those shoes for Miss Dessy's stallion . . . Let her send it to town, or get some other slave to do that . . . She's going to be mad as hell you took off in any event . . . May as well not finish the shoes, it won't placate her none . . .

HIM picks up the horseshoe with a pair of tongs. HIM inspects it carefully. HIM puts the shoe to one side and retrieves the shackles. HIM takes a chamois and begins to polish the metal.

HER: (*pause*) O? O? Othello? The moon'll be rising. We've got to make any headway under cover of dark . . . Othello, why you trying to please her. I'm so tired of pleasing her. I'm so tired of pleasing White folks. Up in Canada, we won't have to please no White folks no how. I hear they got sailing ships leaving for Africa every day. Canada freedom come . . . O? Othello? Are you coming?

HIM: I can't.

HER: If we make it to the border there's people there'll help us wade that water—help us cross over.

HIM: I'm not going.

HER: A big white house on an emerald hill . . .

HIM: I know.

HER: You need more time, O? I can wait for you. Finish her shoes, I'll . . . I can wait—

HIM: No. No.

Pause.

HER: You love her.

HIM: Her father going to war.

HER: You love her?

HIM: I love you. It's just . . . She needs me. She respects me. Looks up to me, even. I love you. It's just . . . When I'm with her I feel like . . . a man. I want . . . I need to do for her . . .

HER: Do you love her?

HIM: Yes.

HER: Fight with me . . . . . . I would fight with you. Suffer with me, O . . . I would suffer with you . . .

Silence.

Scene Seven

Harlem, present: late summer—late afternoon. Dulcet blue tones barely swing as Louis Farrakhan waxes eloquent on African Americans being caught in the gravity of American society.

MAGI: And you know what he says, after turning on the baseball game, in the middle of my romantic dinner? Eyes glued to the screen, he says, I bet you've never made love to a man with 26-inch biceps!

BILLIE: (*smiles*) Oh . . . no . . .

MAGI: I'm telling you, girl. Macho Mack, spot him at any locale selling six-packs. Easily recognizable, everything about him is permanently flexed. His favourite pastime? Weekend NFL football, Monday night football, USFL football—even Canadian foot . . . You look like you're feeling better. Amah did a great job with your hair.

BILLIE: What's her motto? We lock heads and minds.

MAGI: Hey, can I borrow that beautiful African boubou—I got me a date with an African prince. The brother has it going on! Oh . . . you already have boxes.

BILLIE: (*begins placing some of the wrapped objects in a box*) They're his box—

MAGI: When . . . He came over?

BILLIE: I even spoke to her.

MAGI: You saw her?

BILLIE: No. Want this mask?

MAGI: You met her?

BILLIE: No. Want this mask?.

MAGI: I'll keep it for you—

BILLIE: I . . . er . . . . I don't know how long these things will have to stay in storage.

MAGI: You don't have to move, you know. It's not rented yet. I mean, I can always lower the—

BILLIE: No, no . . . I'm moving on.

MAGI: Good. Good. To where? Where are you going? You haven't given me a date or anything. I've got bills to pay too, you know. When d'you plan to leave? Where are you going?

BILLIE: I might go . . . . . . stay with Jenny. I could go home.

MAGI: I'll keep it for you—

BILLIE: I don't want anything that's—that was ours. If you don't want it, that's OK, I'll just trash it.

BILLIE throws the mask onto the floor. It breaks into several pieces.

MAGI: Something happened. What happened?

BILLIE: Nothing.

MAGI: Did he tell you about . . . What did he say to you?

BILLIE: I'm just tired. Tired of sleeping. Tired of night. It lays over me like a ton of white feathers. Swallows me up. The movers are coming in the morning to pick up his things. It's OK. I'm fine. You know . . . I've lived all my life believing in lies.

MAGI: Well, getting your Master's isn't a lie.

BILLIE: It's about proving, isn't it? Proving I'm as good as . . . I'm as intelligent as . . .

MAGI: Nothing wrong with that.

BILLIE: I don't want anything . . . believe in anything. Really. I've gotta get out of here. I don't even believe in Harlem anymore.

MAGI: Come on . . .

BILLIE: It's all an illusion. All some imagined idealistic . . . I dunno.

MAGI: When I go out my door, I see all the beauty of my Blackness reflected in the world around me.

BILLIE: Yeh, and all my wretchedness by the time I get to the end of the block.

MAGI: Billie, he's the one who wants to White wash his life.

BILLIE: Corporeal malediction.

MAGI: Corp-o-re-all mal-e . . . Oooh that's good.

BILLIE: A Black man afflicted with Negrophobia.

MAGI: Girl, you on a roll now!

BILLIE: No, no. A crumbled racial epidermal schema . . .

MAGI: Who said school ain't doing you no good.

BILLIE: . . . causing predilections to coitus denegrification.

MAGI: Booker T. Uppermiddleclass III. He can be found in predominantly White neighbourhoods. He refers to other Blacks as "them." His greatest accomplishment was being invited to the White House by George Bush to discuss the "Negro problem."

BILLIE: Now, that is frightening.

MAGI: No, what's frightening is the fact that I dated him.

BILLIE: What does it say . . . about us?

MAGI: Who?

BILLIE: You and me.

MAGI: Girl, I don't know. I can't even want to go there.

BILLIE: Ohh . . . Oh well . . . Least he's happy though. What does he say? Now he won't have to worry that a White woman will emotionally mistake him for the father that abandoned her.

MAGI: Isn't he worried the White woman might mistake him for the butler?

BILLIE: He'd be oh so happy to oblige.

MAGI: I see them do things for White women they wouldn't dream of doing for me.

BILLIE: It is a disease. We get infected as children, and . . . and the bacteria . . . the virus slowly spreads, disabling the entire system.

MAGI: Are we infected too? (*There is knocking at the apartment door.*) Speaking of White minds parading around inside of Black bodies—you want me to stay?

BILLIE: Don't you have a date?

MAGI: Hakim. But I can cancel . . .

There is knocking at the door again.

BILLIE: I'm OK. I'm OK. I'm fine . . . Truly.

BILLIE opens the door. OTHELLO enters.

OTHELLO: The pot! (*He hands the pot to BILLIE.*) Magi!

MAGI: How's Harlumbia?

OTHELLO: Columbia?

MAGI: Harlumbia—those 10 square blocks of Whitedom, owned by Columbia University, set smack dab in the middle of Harlem.

OTHELLO: Harlumbia, as you call it, is dull without you.

MAGI: You could steal honey from a bee, couldn't you. Better watch you don't get stung. Well, I'm off to doll myself up. Billie . . .

BILLIE: Yeh, I'll get that boubou . . .

BILLIE goes into the bedroom. After a few moments of silence . . .

MAGI: Why haven't you told her yet?

OTHELLO: About?—Oh yes . . . Yeh . . . I wanted to . . .

BILLIE returns with a beautiful multicoloured boubou.

BILLIE: He won't be able to resist you . . .

MAGI: Thank you, thank you. Later you two.

OTHELLO: I'll be in touch . . .

BILLIE: I'm keeping my fingers crossed for you.

MAGI: Good, I'm running out of time.

MAGI exits. OTHELLO enters. BILLIE closes the door. There is a long awkward silence. BILLIE continues placing wrapped objects into her boxes. OTHELLO steps on a piece of the broken mask. He picks it up, looks at it, then places it on the mantel. He goes over to the bookshelf and begins to pack more of his possessions into his boxes.

OTHELLO: They're coming at nine.

BILLIE: Oh . . . Er . . . I'll be out of your way.

OTHELLO: You can be here . . .

BILLIE: No. No. No. I have an appointment . . . . . . an early appointment.

OTHELLO: Either way . . . (*They continue packing.*) Ah . . . I've been meaning to tell you . . . . . . things are real . . . . . money's real tight right now, what with buying the apartment, and moving and everything . . . I won't be able to cover your tuition this semester. I'll try and put money in your account when I can. Maybe—

BILLIE: I told you, I'm only taking one course. If you cover that, I won't be taking a full load 'til next—

OTHELLO: I know, that's what I'm saying . . . . I can't . . . I just can't do it right now.

BILLIE: It's one course . . .

OTHELLO: It's $5000.

BILLIE: You promised . . .

OTHELLO: I'm mortgaged up the wazoo. I don't have it. I just don't have $5000, right now.

BILLIE: Ooh . . . . . okay.

OTHELLO: I would if I could, you know that. (*He continues to pack.*) I think I brought the bookshelf with me when we first—

BILLIE: Take it all.

OTHELLO: I don't want all of it.

BILLIE: I'm keeping the bed.

OTHELLO: What about the rest . . .

BILLIE: If you don't want it . . . I'm giving it away . . .

OTHELLO: OK, if you're throwing it out . . .

BILLIE: I'm keeping the bed.

They continue packing in silence.

OTHELLO: We're getting married. (*pause*) Me and Mona. We're engaged . . . Officially.

Very long pause.

BILLIE: Congratulations.

OTHELLO: I wanted to tell you . . . Hear it from the horse's mouth . . . Hear it from me first. You know . . .

Pause.

BILLIE: Yeh . . . Yes. Yes. Congratulations.

OTHELLO: Mona wanted me to tell you.

BILLIE: Yes. Yes. Being a feminist and every-thing—a woman's right to know—since we're all in the struggle . . . . I thought you hated feminists.

OTHELLO: Well . . . I didn't mean that. I mean . . . the White women's movement is different.

BILLIE: Just Black feminists.

OTHELLO: No, no . . . White men have main-tained a firm grasp of the pants. I mean, White men have economic and political pants that White women have been demanding to share.

BILLIE: White wisdom from the mouth of the mythical Negro.

OTHELLO: Don't you see! That's exactly my point! You . . . The Black feminist position as I experience it in this relationship leaves me feeling unrecognized as a man. The message is, Black men are poor fathers, poor partners, or both. Black women wear the pants that Black men were prevented from wearing . . . I believe in tradition. You don't support me. Black women are more concerned with their careers than their husbands. There was a time when women felt satisfied, no, honoured being a balance to their spouse, at home, supporting the family, playing her role—

BILLIE: Which women? I mean, which women are you referring to? Your mother worked all her life. My mother worked, her mother worked . . . Most Black women have been working like mules since we arrived on this continent. Like mules. When White women were burning their bras, we were hired to hold their tits up. We looked after their homes, their children . . . I don't support you? My mother's death paid your tuition, not mine . . .

OTHELLO: Can't we even pretend to be civil? Can't we? I know this isn't easy. It's not easy for me either. Do you ever consider that?

BILLIE: You like it easy, don't you.

OTHELLO: The truth is, this is too fucking difficult.

BILLIE: You wouldn't know the truth if it stood up and knocked you sideways.

OTHELLO: You don't want the truth. You want me to tell you what you want to hear. No, no, you want to know the truth? I'll tell you the truth. Yes, I prefer White women. They are easier—before and after sex. They wanted me and I wanted them. They weren't filled with hostility about the unequal treatment they were getting at their jobs. We'd make love and I'd fall asleep not having to beware being mistaken for someone's inattentive father. I'd explain that I wasn't interested in a committed relationship right now, and not be confused with every lousy lover, or husband that had ever left them lying in a gutter of unresolved emotions. It's the truth. To a Black woman, I represent every Black man she has ever been with and with whom there was still so much to work out. The White women I loved saw me— could see me. Look, I'm not a junkie. I don't need more than one lover to prove my manhood. I have no children. I did not leave you, your mother, or your aunt, with six babies and a whole lotta love. I am a very single, very intelligent, very employed Black man. And with White women it's good. It's nice. Anyhow, we're all equal in the eyes of God, aren't we? Aren't we?

BILLIE stares at OTHELLO. He continues to pack.

Scene Eight

Harlem, 1928: late summer—night. The cello and bass moan, almost dirge-like, in harmonic tension to the sound of Jesse Jackson's oratory. SHE holds a straight-edged razor in her bloodied palms. HE lies on the floor in front of her, motionless, the handkerchief in his hand.

SHE: Deadly deadly straw little strawberries it's so beautiful you kissed my fingers you pressed this cloth into my palm buried it there an antique token our ancient all these tiny red dots on a sheet of white my fingernails are white three hairs on my head are white the whites of my eyes are white too the palms of my hands and my feet are white you're all I'd ever and you my my I hate Sssshh. Shhhhh OK. OK. OK. I'm OK alright don't don't don't don't my eyes on the shadow sparrow my sense in my feet my hands my head shine the light there please scream no sing sing *(tries to sing)* and if I get a notion to jump into the ocean, ain't nobody's business if I do do do do If I go to church on Sunday then shimmy down on Monday t'ain't nobody's business if I . . .

Scene Nine

Harlem, present: late summer—early evening. The instruments sound out a deep cerulean blues, while Malcolm X almost scats the question, "What difference does colour make?" OTHELLO continues to pack. BILLIE sits on the floor by the bed watching him from the bedroom.

OTHELLO: I didn't mean—what I said. You know that. I just . . . Sometimes you make me so mad I . . . People change, Billie. That's just human nature. Our experiences, our knowledge transforms us. That's why education is so powerful, so erotic. The transmission of words from mouth to ear. Her mouth to my ear. Knowledge. A desire for that distant thing I know nothing of, but yearn to hold for my very own. My Mama used to say, you have to be three times as good as a White child to get by, to do well. A piece of that pie is mine. I don't want to change the recipe. I am not minor. I am not a minority. I used to be a minority when I was a kid. I mean my culture is not my mother's culture—the culture of my ancestors. My culture is Wordsworth, Shaw, *Leave it to Beaver*, *Dirty Harry*. I drink the same water, read the same books. You're the problem if you don't see beyond my skin. If you don't hear my educated English, if you don't understand that I am a middle class educated man. I mean, what does Africa have to do with me. We struttin' around professing some imaginary connection for a land we don't know. Never seen. Never gonna see. We lie to ourselves saying, ah yeh, mother Africa, middle passage, suffering, the Whites did it to me, it's the Whites' fault. Strut around in African cloth pretending we human now. We human now. Some of us are beyond that now. Spiritually beyond this race shit bullshit now. I am an American. The slaves were freed over 130 years ago. In 1967 it was illegal for a Black to marry a White in sixteen states. That was less than thirty years ago . . . in my lifetime. Things change, Billie. I am not my skin. My skin is not me.

Scene Ten

Harlem, same day: night. A rhapsody of sound keeps time with Christopher Darden as he asks O. J. Simpson to approach the jury and try on the bloody glove. The apartment is virtually full of boxes. BILLIE is by the chemical factory at the table. The book of Egyptian Alchemy sits open upon it. Something is boiling in the flask and steam is coming out of the condenser. With rubber-gloved hands she adds several drops of a violet liquid into the flask. She picks up a large white handkerchief with pretty red strawberries embroidered on it.

BILLIE: I have a plan, my love. My mate . . . throughout eternity. Feel what I feel. Break like I break. No more—no less. You'll judge me harsher. I know. While Susan Smith . . . She blamed some imaginary Black man for the murder of her two boys and that's why authorities didn't suspect her for nearly two weeks. Stopping every Black man with a burgundy sedan from Union, South Carolina, to the Oranges of New Jersey. And you're still wondering what made her do it. What was she going through to make her feel that this was her only way out. Yet I'll be discarded as some kind of unconscionable bitter shadow, or something. Ain't I a woman? This is my face you take for night—the biggest shadow in the world. I . . . I have nothing more to lose. Nothing. Othello? I am preparing something special for you . . . Othe . . . Othello. A gift for you, and your new bride. Once you gave me a handkerchief. An heirloom. This handkerchief, your mother's . . . . . given by your father. From his mother before that. So far back . . . And now . . . then . . . to me. It is fixed in the emotions of all your ancestors. The one who laid the foundation for the road in Herndon, Virginia, and was lashed for laziness as he stopped to wipe the

sweat from his brow with this kerchief. Or, your great great grandmother, who covered her face with it, and then covered it with her hands as she rocked and silently wailed, when told that her girl child, barely thirteen, would be sent 'cross the state for breeding purposes. Or the one who leapt for joy on hearing of the Emancipation Proclamation, fifteen years late mind you, only to watch it fall in slow motion from his hand and onto the ground when told that the only job he could now get was the same one he'd done for free all those years, and now he's forced to take it, for not enough money to buy the food to fill even one man's belly. And more . . . so much more. What I add to this already fully endowed cloth will cause you such . . . . . . such . . . wretchedness. Othe . . . Othello.

The contents of the flask have been transformed from violet to clear. BILLIE places the handkerchief onto a large tray. Then with tongs, she takes the hot flask and pours the contents over the handkerchief. She retrieves a vial from the table, opens it.

BILLIE: My sable warrior . . . Fight with me. I would fight with you . . . Suffer with me . . . I would suffer—

She starts to pour, but the vial is empty. The buzzer rings. BILLIE is surprised. The buzzer rings again. BILLIE turns off the Bunsen burner. She takes the flask into the kitchen and pours it into the sink. The buzzer rings once more. Going back to the table, she carefully takes the tray and heads toward the bathroom. There is a knock at her door.

BILLIE: *(from the bathroom)* You have a key, let yourself in . . . Make yourself right at home, why don't you—

MAGI: *(offstage)* Billie? Billie, it's me. Magi.

BILLIE: Magi?

MAGI: *(offstage)* Are you OK?

BILLIE: Yes. Yes. I'm fine. Let me call you later, OK Magi?

We hear the sound of liquid being poured. The toilet flushes. MAGI offstage mumbles something about BILLIE having a visitor.

BILLIE: What? *(MAGI mumbles something about a visitor again.)* What? Door's open!

MAGI enters and stands in the doorway. She is speaking quietly, as if not wanting someone to hear.

MAGI: Sweetie, you have a visitor. Shall I—

BILLIE: (*entering the living area*) Look I'm tired. He's been here practically all day already—

MAGI: No, no, no. He said his name is Canada. (*BILLIE turns to MAGI.*) He says he's your father. That's what he said. He said he was your father.

A man in his late sixties brushes past MAGI. He wears a hat and has a small suitcase in his hand.

CANADA: Sybil? Sybil! There's my girl. Come and give your Daddy a big hug.

ACT TWO

Scene One

Harlem, present: late summer—night. The cello and bass pluck and bow a funky rendition of Aretha Franklin's "Spanish Harlem" against the audio sound of Michael Jackson and Lisa Marie Presley's interview on ABC's Dateline. *CANADA is sitting on one of the chairs, amidst stacks of boxes.*

CANADA: The first time I came to Harlem, I was scared. Must have been '68 or '69. Yeh . . . We we're living in the Bronx, and your mother was still alive. Everything I'd ever learned told me that I wasn't safe in this part of town. The newspapers. Television. My friends. My own family. But I'm curious, see. I says, Canada you can't be in New York City and not see Harlem. So I make my way to 125th. "A" train. I'm gonna walk past the Apollo, I'm gonna see this place. I'm gonna walk the ten city blocks to Lexington and catch the "6" train back, if it's the last thing I do. So out of the subway, I put on my 'baddest mother in the city' glare. I walk—head straight. All the time trying to make my stride say, "I'm mean . . . I'm mean. Killed somebody mean." So I'm doing this for 'bout five, ten minutes, taking short furtive glances at this place I really want to see, when I begin to realize . . . No one is taking any notice of me . . . Not a soul. Then it dawns on me: I'm the same as them. I look just like them. I look like I live in Harlem. Sounds silly now. But I just had to catch myself and laugh out loud. Canada,

where did you get these ideas about Harlem from?

The kettle whistles.

BILLIE: How do you like it? (*She heads to the kitchen to make tea.*)

CANADA: Brown sugar. No milk.

BILLIE: I don't even know why I asked, I don't have any milk anyway.

CANADA: You can't take milk. Never could. When your mother stopped feeding you from her milk, that cow's milk just gave you colic. And those diapers . . . Now that's an image I'll never forget.

BILLIE: So what brings you to these parts?

CANADA: Just passing through. Since I was in the neighbourhood, thought I'd stop on in.

BILLIE: Nova Scotia's nearly a thousand miles away.

CANADA: Well, I thought I should see my grandchild. Jenny's almost six and I've only talked to her on the phone. And Andrew and his wife, and you. Nothing wrong with seeing family is there?

BILLIE: Strong or weak?

CANADA: Like a bear's bottom.

BILLIE: Polar or Grizzly?

CANADA: Grizzly. (*BILLIE returns with a tray.*) Andrew told me what happened.

BILLIE: He did, did he?

CANADA: Said you were taking it kinda hard.

BILLIE: Oh, I'll be fine. I'm a survivor. But then again, you already know that.

CANADA: Tea should be ready. Shall I be mother?

BILLIE: Go ahead. (*CANADA pours the tea.*) I hear you were in the hospital.

CANADA: My liver ain't too good. Gave out on me. I guess you reap what you sow.

BILLIE: Still drinking?

CANADA: Been sober going on five years now.

BILLIE: Good. Good for you.

CANADA: Don't mean I don't feel like it sometimes though . . .

BILLIE: Well . . . How long do you plan to be in town?

CANADA: Just a few days. See Andrew and his family. See the sights. I'm staying there—at Andrew's. Went by there earlier . . . No one home. Must have given them the wrong time. Left a note though. Told them to find me at Sybil's.

BILLIE: Billie. I've always despised that name. Sybil.

CANADA: I gave you that name. It's a good name. It was your Grandmother's name. It means prophetess. Sorceress. Seer of the future. I like it. I don't see anything wrong with that name.

BILLIE: Sounds like some old woman living in a cave.

CANADA: (reaches for his suitcase) I brought something for you. (takes out a small red box) Go on . . . open it. The box is a bit too big, but . . . (BILLIE opens the box.) It's your mother's ring. I figured she'd want you to have it.

BILLIE: I hardly remember her anymore. I get glimpses of this ghostly figure creeping in and out of my dreams.

CANADA: When Beryl first passed on, I couldn't get her off my mind, like she'd gone and left us somehow. Left me . . . with two kids, one a young girl ripening to sprout into womanhood. I was sad, but I was good and mad too. One minute I'd be trying to etch her face into my mind, 'cause I didn't want to forget. Next thing, I'd be downing another shot of rye . . . I couldn't carry the weight. I just couldn't do it by myself. That's when we moved to Dartmouth. What's that them old slaves used to say? "I can't take it no more, I moving to Nova Scotia."

BILLIE: I'm thinking of heading back there myself . . .

Pause.

CANADA: 'Cause he left you, or 'cause she's White?

Pause.

BILLIE: I remember that White woman . . . That hairdresser you used to go with . . . The one with the mini skirts . . . What was her name?

CANADA: That's going way back . . . You remember her?

BILLIE: She was boasting about knowing how to do our kind of hair. And she took that hot comb to my head . . . Sounded like she was frying chicken . . . Burnt my ears and half the hair on my head. I hated her stubby little beige legs and those false eyelashes. She taught me how to put on false eyelashes.

CANADA: Deborah.

BILLIE: Debbie . . . Yes . . . Debbie.

Pause.

CANADA: I wish . . . I wish things between . . .

The buzzer rings.

BILLIE: That must be Drew. (goes to the console by the door) Drew?

AMAH: (through intercom) It's me. Amah. Is your—

BILLIE: He's here. Come on up.

CANADA: You know, an old African once told me the story of a man who was struck by an arrow. His attacker was unknown. Instead of tending to his wound, he refused to remove the arrow until the archer was found and punished. In the meantime, the wound festered, until finally the poison infected his entire body, eventually killing him . . . Now, who is responsible for this man's death, the archer for letting go the arrow, or the man for his foolish holding on?

A knock at the door. BILLIE gets up and heads toward it.

BILLIE: The drunk?

CANADA: A drunken man can get sober but a damn fool can't ever get wise.

BILLIE opens the door. AMAH enters with some rolls of paper in her arms.

AMAH: (kissing BILLIE's cheek) Hi sweetie. And you must be Canada.

CANADA: Drew's wife . . .

AMAH: So very pleased to meet you at last.

CANADA: Delighted . . .

AMAH: We weren't expecting you until tomorrow. We ate out tonight. We would have come pick you up. Jenny's so excited.

CANADA: No, no . . . No need to fuss. I arrived safe and sound. And Sybil—Billie's been taking good care of me.

AMAH: Drew would have come himself. Jenny insisted he give her a bath tonight. You know, it's a father-daughter thing. (silence) Anyway, we should get going. (to CANADA) You're probably starving. I can rustle something up for you in no time. (CANADA reaches for his coat; to BILLIE) Look, I'm gonna have to bring that child of mine over here. She's driving me crazy asking for you—

BILLIE: No. No . . . . not yet.

AMAH: Well, if I go mad, you and Drew will have to take care of her. I want you to know that. Oh, Jenny asked me to give these to you. She made them specially for you. She wanted to give you some inspiration. You might not be able to tell, but one's of her dancing, and the other's of her singing.

BILLIE: Tell her I miss her.

AMAH: I will.

BILLIE: Tell her I'll see her real soon.

AMAH: I will.

BILLIE: (to AMAH) I still have a bone to pick with you, though. (indicating CANADA)

AMAH: No, no. You have a bone to pick with Drew.

CANADA: I'll drop in again tomorrow, if that's OK with you.

BILLIE: Tomorrow might not be so good. He's moving his stuff in the morning. We'd probably be in the way. I won't even be here until sometime in the afternoon.

CANADA: Well then . . . We'll see how things go. (kisses BILLIE on the forehead)

AMAH: Come join us over something to eat—

BILLIE: No. Thanks. I'm fine.

CANADA: Good to see you, Sybil—Billie.

BILLIE: Well it certainly was a surprise. Bye y'all.

AMAH and CANADA exit. BILLIE closes the door, then leans against it as she studies the pictures Jenny drew.

Scene Two

Harlem, the present: the next day—late morning. Lyrical strains give way to an undulating rhythm while Malcolm X recounts the tale of how George Washington sold a slave for a gallon of molasses. The apartment looks empty of furniture, save for the bed, several piles of books, and boxes strewn around the living area. OTHELLO walks into the bedroom with a large green garbage bag. After a few moments, the door is unlocked and BILLIE peers through the doorway. She hears someone in the bedroom. She quietly closes the door behind her and places a small brown paper bag in her pocket. She makes her way into the kitchen area. She waits. OTHELLO exits the bedroom, green garbage bag in tow. He walks to the centre of the living room where he stands for a few moments taking it all in.

BILLIE: Got everything?

OTHELLO: (startled) Ahh! (dropping the garbage bag, he turns around) Christ . . .

BILLIE: Got everything?

OTHELLO: God, I didn't hear you come in.

BILLIE: My meeting ended earlier than I expected. I was able to get what I needed . . . I didn't see a van. I figured you'd be done by now.

OTHELLO: They just left. I was doing a final check. See if I'd forgotten anything.

BILLIE: So the move went well.

OTHELLO: Yes . . . yeh. It's amazing how much stuff there is.

BILLIE: Yeh. It's hard to throw things away.

OTHELLO: I know what you mean. We've got a huge place though.

BILLIE: Good. Good for you.

Pause.

OTHELLO: This place looks pretty huge right now, though. Remember when we first came to look at this place?

BILLIE: Yes.

Pause.

OTHELLO: Well . . . I guess that's it.

BILLIE: I guess . . .

Pause.

OTHELLO: Anyway . . . So when do you plan on leaving?

BILLIE: Oh, I don't . . . I don't know.

OTHELLO: Ah.

BILLIE: I haven't decided.

OTHELLO: I see . . . Well . . .

BILLIE: So when's the big day?

OTHELLO: Oh . . . . . well . . . er . . . Three weeks.

BILLIE: So soon?

OTHELLO: Just a small affair.

BILLIE: Good. Good for you. Good for you both.

OTHELLO: Yeh . . .

BILLIE: I . . . I've been meaning . . . Well . . . I've been thinking.

OTHELLO: Hmn Hmn . . .

BILLIE: I . . . er . . . I . . . um . . . I want to return something you gave me . . . centuries ago.

OTHELLO: Oh?

BILLIE: The handkerchief?

OTHELLO: Oh! Really? Wow . . . No. No. It's not necessary. Really—

BILLIE: No, no, let me finish. I've . . . . been foolish. I understand that now. You can understand why. And . . . . . . I'm sorry. That's what I wanted to tell you. And the handkerchief . . . it's yours. Held by me for safekeeping really. To be passed on to our children—if we had any. Since we don't, it should be returned to you, to your line . . .

OTHELLO: Why are you doing this?

BILLIE: I just thought you might . . . I thought you would . . . After all . . . it's the only thing your mother left you . . .

OTHELLO: I don't know what to say.

BILLIE: I thought you'd be glad.

OTHELLO: Oh, I'm more than glad.

BILLIE: But I have to find it first.

OTHELLO: Are you sure about—

BILLIE: I'm sure. Give me a couple of days, to find it . . . . . . clean it up a bit.

OTHELLO: I could come by.

BILLIE: Yes. You should have it before . . . you know . . . before your . . . big day.

OTHELLO: Thank you.

BILLIE: Just trying to play my part well.

OTHELLO: Thanks.

BILLIE: Forgive me . . .

OTHELLO: I know it's been hard.

BILLIE: Yeh . . .

OTHELLO: OK. Well . . . (*He reaches to touch her face. She retreats.*)

BILLIE: I'll see you in a couple of days then.

OTHELLO: Alright.

BILLIE: Alright.

OTHELLO: Alright. And say hello to Jenny for me. (*silence*) Alright.

OTHELLO exits. BILLIE takes the small package out of her pocket. She unwraps it, revealing a small vial of fluid. She goes into the kitchen, vial in hand, turns toward the fridge, opens the freezer door and stares into it.

BILLIE: Look this way and see . . . your death . . . Othe . . . Othe . . .

She places the vial into the freezer.

Scene Three

Harlem, 1862: late summer—night. Indigo blues groan as if through a delta, while echoes of a presidential voice reads from the Emancipation Proclamation. The sound fades. HER holds HIM in her arms like Mary holds Jesus in Michelangelo's Pieta. *There is a rope around his neck. He does not move.*

HER: (*caressing him*) Once upon a time, there was a man who wanted to find a magic spell in order to become White. After much research and investigation, he came across an ancient ritual from the caverns of knowledge of a psychic. "The only way to become White," the psychic said, "was to enter the Whiteness." And when he found his ice queen, his alabaster goddess, he fucked her. Her on his dick. He one with her, for a single shivering moment became . . . her. Her and her Whiteness.

Scene Four

Harlem, present: late summer—night. A cacophony of strings grooves and collides as sound bites from the Anita Hill and Clarence Thomas hearings, the L.A. riots, the O.J. Simpson trial, Malcolm X, and Martin Luther King loop and repeat the same distorted bits of sound over and over again. BILLIE is alone in the apartment. She goes into the freezer and removes the vial. Wearing rubber gloves, she places several drops of a liquid substance onto the handkerchief. She replaces the cap of the vial. BILLIE carefully folds the handkerchief, hesitates for a moment, looks around and spots the red box on the mantle. She puts the handkerchief back down on the tray and, with her hands in the air, like a surgeon scrubbing for surgery, she gets up and goes to the red box. With one hand she takes off one of the gloves. With the ungloved hand she opens the red box and slips her mother's ring on her finger. She then takes the red box with her to the table. She very carefully replaces the one glove, picks up the handkerchief, and neatly places it in the small red box. She works slowly, and is mindful not to touch the sides of the box with the handkerchief itself.

She removes a single rubber glove once more, picks up the cover to the box, and places it on top of the other half. She is still for a few moments, staring at the box.

BILLIE gets up and crosses the room, as if looking for something, only to stop in her tracks and return to the box. She paces. Her pacing appears more methodical than hysterical. Suddenly she stops. She turns to look at the small red box.

She shakes her head and takes a seat on a large, full, cardboard box at her feet. Her breathing becomes more apparent as she begins to rock, almost imperceptibly at first. Finally she places her head in her hands.

After several moments, BILLIE's face slowly emerges from her hands.

She glares at the gloved hand incredulously, as she realizes that she has inadvertently transferred some of the potion onto her own skin. She quickly removes the second glove and proceeds to wipe her face with her own clothes.

BILLIE: (*to herself*) Oh god! Oh my god! Shit! Shit! Shit! Shit!

BILLIE gets up and rushes to the kitchen sink, turns on the tap and frantically washes her hands and face in the water.

Scene Five

The following day: early evening. In counterpoint to the cello and bass, the distorted sound loop becomes a grating repetition. MAGI and CANADA are on either side of a large box, sitting on two smaller ones. The larger box is covered by a scarf to resemble a tablecloth, on top of which is a small feast. They are eating. MAGI gets up and goes to the door of the bedroom. She peeks in. After a few moments she closes the door and returns to her seat.

MAGI: She's in distant realms. I checked in on her when I got back from church. I thought she was speaking in tongues. I couldn't understand a thing she was saying. I don't think she slept a wink all night. Those pills work like a charm, though. (*beat*) How is it?

CANADA: Mmn! Those greens . . . She looks like an angel and cooks like one too.

MAGI: Can I get you some more?

CANADA: No, no, I don't want to appear too greedy now.

MAGI: Here . . . (*serving him another helping*) There you go. And I won't tell a soul. Promise.

CANADA: I haven't tasted cooking like this in a long time.

MAGI: My Mama would say, some food is good for the mind, some is good for the body, and some food is good for the soul.

CANADA: Your Mama taught you how to cook like this?

MAGI: Once she even taught me how to cook a soufflé. She used to have a restaurant downstairs from as far back as I can recall. And I guess the boys returning home from the war in Europe kept asking for the Parisian food, and it ended up on her menu. She'd say, now this Parisian food ain't good for nothing. Soufflé ain't nothing more than baked eggs. And eggs is for breakfast. Eggs don't do no one no good past noon.

CANADA: So you've lived here all your life?

MAGI: And my mother before me, and her mother before her. My great grandmother worked for the family that lived here, most of her life. She never married, but she had two children by the man she worked for—seems his wife never knew they were his. One brown baby looks just like another to most White folks. And when the wife died, my great grandmother just stayed on. Everybody thinking she's just the maid, but she was living like the queen of the manor—him being her babies' father and everything. And his other children were all grown by then. So when he died, he left everything to his White children, 'cept this house. He left it in my great grand-mother's name, and it's been in my family ever since.

CANADA: So the White man's children ever find out? About their brown skinned relatives.

MAGI: I don't know. The Van Dykes—they were Dutch. We used to watch *The Dick Van Dyke Show*, and my Grandmother used to always say, "That there's your relative!" But we didn't pay her too much mind. More greens?

CANADA: If I eat another thing, I will truly burst. This was wonderful. Thank you. Thank you very much.

MAGI: You're more than welcome.

CANADA: When I was a boy, I used to love to sop the pot liquor.

MAGI: It's nearly the best part.

CANADA: You sure know the way to a man's heart.

MAGI: Haven't had any luck so far.

CANADA: Yet.

There is an awkward silence between them, after which they both start speaking at once.

MAGI: (*overlapping*) Well I better get started with these dishes . . .

CANADA: (*overlapping*) I should go in and check on Sybil . . . Let me give you a hand.

MAGI: No, no, it's quite alright. I can handle this.

BILLIE enters.

CANADA: Billie! Marjorie was kind enough to share her dinner with me.

MAGI: Billie, come and have something to eat.

BILLIE: I'm not hungry. I heard voices. I need to go back and lay down . . . get some reading done.

MAGI: You can't have eaten anything for the day, girl.

BILLIE: I'm fine.

CANADA: What you need is a good meal inside you.

BILLIE: I said I was fine.

MAGI: I'll just take these things downstairs. (*exits*)

CANADA: I'll make you some tea, OK.

BILLIE: I don't—don't need any tea. I don't want anything to eat. I'm fine. I'm sorry. I don't—don't—don't mean . . . to be like this . . . But I haven't seen you in God knows how long . . . And you just show up, and expect things to be all hunky dory.

Pause.

CANADA: Well, I'll be off then. (*goes for his coat*)

BILLIE: I'm sorry.

CANADA: Me too. (*heads for the door*)

BILLIE: And I am glad you came . . . Maybe this can be . . . you know . . . like a beginning of something . . . I don't know.

CANADA: I nearly came before . . . Two or three times . . . You know, when I heard. I wished your mother was here. I really wished for her . . . Her wisdom. I mean Beryl would know what to do. A girl needs her mother. And I know you didn't have her all those times . . . I mean, I couldn't tell you. What could I tell you? I kept seeing your face. It's your mother's face. You've got my nose. My mouth. But those eyes . . . The shape of your face . . . The way your head tilts to one side when you're thinking, or just listening. It's all her. You've got her moods. I used to call them her moods. Once 'bout every three months, on a Friday, when she'd have the weekend off, she'd come home from that hospital, take off her clothes and lay down in her bed and stay there 'til Sunday afternoon. She'd say she'd done turned the other cheek so many times in the past little while, she didn't have no more smiles for anybody. She'd say, better she just face God and the pillow than shower me and the children with the evil she had bottled up inside her. See, if you spend too much time among White people, you start believing what they think of you. So I'd take you and Drew and we'd go visiting. We'd take the whole weekend and visit all the folks we knew, in a fifteen mile radius . . . When we'd get home, she'd have cleaned the house, washed the clothes and even made a Sunday dinner. And after I'd pluck the guitar . . . And she'd start to sing . . . And you'd dance . . . You remember? You'd dance. You'd stomp on that floor like you were beating out some secret code to God or something . . . I know you—we don't see eye to eye. I know you haven't wanted to see very much anything of me lately. But I've known you all your life. I carried you in my arms and on my back, kissed and spanked you when you needed, and I watched you start to talk, and learn to walk, and read and I just wanted to come . . . I just wanted to come. And I know I can't make everything alright. I know. But I was there when you arrived in this world. And I didn't think there was space for a child, I loved your mother so much. But there you were and I wondered where you'd been all my life, like something I'd been missing and didn't know I'd been missing. And I don't know if you've loved anybody that long. But behind your mother's face you're wearing, I still see the girl who shrieked with laughter, and danced to the heavens sometimes . . .

CANADA slowly approaches BILLIE. She does not move. He takes her in his arms. He holds her in his arms for a long time.

Scene Six

Harlem, 1928: late summer—night. The strident movement of the strings is joined by the rising tempo of the distorted sound loop. HE and SHE are both in a tiny dressing room, as in the prologue. On a counter are a shaving brush, a straight-edged razor, greasepaint and a top hat. HE wipes his face with a towel. SHE holds the handkerchief out to him. HE does not take it. SHE lets it fall at his feet. After a few moments HE picks it up.

HE: (*referring to the handkerchief at first*) White, red, black, green, indigo . . . What difference does it make? That makes no sense . . . makes no difference. "If virtue no delighted beauty lack, Your son-in-law is far more fair than black." Far more fair than black. I want . . . I need to do this . . . For my soul. I am an actor. I—

SHE: (*kindly*) A minstrel. A Black minstrel . . .

HE: (*places the towel on the counter beside the toiletries*) It's paid my way.

SHE: (*caresses the towel*) Stay, my sable warrior . . . (*Her hand stumbles upon the razor.*)

HE: I'll not die in black-face to pay the rent. I am of Ira Aldridge stock. I am a classical man. I long to play the Scottish king. The prince of Denmark. "The slings and arrows of outrageous . . ." Or . . . Or . . . "There's a divinity that shapes our ends, Rough-hew them how we will" . . . Those words . . . I love those words. They give me life. Mona sees my gift. She's cast me as the prince of Tyre. She's breathed new life into a barren dream. She . . . She . . . She has a serene calmness about her. That smile . . . I bet they named her Mona because even at birth she had that constant half smile, like the Mona Lisa. Skin as smooth as monumental alabaster . . . As warm as snow velvet.

SHE: (*exposes the blade*) My onyx prince . . .

HE: Ooohh . . .

SHE: (*approaches him from behind*) My tourmaline king . . . (*leans her head on his back*)

HE: S'alright . . .

SHE: My raven knight . . .

She wraps her arms around him. He turns his head toward her.

HE: Oh sweet . . .

SHE: My umber squire . . .

HE: I wish . . . I wish—

Her hand rises, the razor is poised, nearly touching the skin of his neck, just below his ear, within his peripheral vision.

SHE: My Cimmerian lord . . .

He turns around, as if to see what she's holding, and in that turn his neck appears to devour the blade. The razor's shaft, at once hidden by his flesh, swiftly withdraws, leaving a rushing river of red like a scarf billowing around his neck and her hands. He yields to gravity.

Scene Seven

Harlem, the present: late summer night. The plucked strings and the distorted audio loop have become even more dissonant. BILLIE is clutching the small red box.

MAGI: . . . You know, Hakim has seven children, and he's never been married. Brother Hakim. Spot him at any street rally where the subject is prefaced by the words "Third World." He's the one with the "Lumumba Lives" button prominently displayed on his authentic kente cloth dashi—Billie? Billie, what's up? You don't look so good. *(pause)* Billie?

BILLIE: Sybil. I'm Sybil.

MAGI: That's what your Daddy calls you.

BILLIE: Yes.

MAGI: Your Daddy sure is one good-looking gentleman.

BILLIE: Trapped in history. A history trapped in me.

MAGI: I'm serious. I mean . . . I wanna know if you mind? Really. You were still a little girl when your mama died.

BILLIE: I don't remember Beryl's funeral. I see my father dressed in black, sewing a white button on to his white shirt, with an enormous needle. He attaches the button and knots the thread so many times it's like he's trying to hold onto more than just the button. Like he can't bear for anything else in his life to leave him.

MAGI: He's a nice man. Would you mind?

BILLIE: Am I nice?

MAGI: Billie, I bet you haven't eaten today.

BILLIE: Can you keep a secret?

MAGI: No, but that's never stopped you before.

BILLIE: Then sorry . . .

MAGI: OK, OK. I promise.

BILLIE: I am about to plunge into very dangerous waters. Give me your word.

MAGI: You're not going to do something stupid, now.

BILLIE: Your word?

MAGI: Yeh, OK.

BILLIE: I've drawn a line.

MAGI: A line? A line about what?

BILLIE: I'm returning the handkerchief—the one his mother give him. The one he gave to me when we first agreed to be together . . .

MAGI: I don't understand.

BILLIE: I've concocted something . . . A potion . . . A plague of sorts . . . I've soaked the hand-kerchief . . . Soaked it in certain tinctures . . . Anyone who touches it—the handkerchief, will come to harm.

MAGI: Now that is not a line, Billie, that is a trench!

BILLIE: I'm supposed to . . .

MAGI: Billie, if this kind of stuff truly worked, Africans wouldn't be in the situation we're in now. Imagine all them slaves working magic on their masters—didn't make no difference. If it truly worked, I'd be married to a nice man, with three little ones by now. But if it makes you feel better—

BILLIE: He's going to marry her . . . Officially . . .

MAGI: I know . . . I know. Remember, what goes around comes around. Karma is a strong and unforgiving force.

BILLIE: I haven't seen it affect White people too much.

MAGI: Is everything about White people with you? Is every living moment of your life eaten up with thinking about them. Do you know where you are? Do you know who you are anymore? What about right and wrong. Racism is a disease my friend, and your test just came back positive. You're so busy reacting, you don't even know yourself.

BILLIE: No, no, no . . . It's about Black. I love Black. I really do. And it's revolutionary . . . Black is beautiful . . . So beautiful. This Harlem sanctuary . . . . . here. This respite . . . like an ocean in the middle of a desert. And in my mirror, my womb, he has a fast growing infestation of roaches. White roaches.

MAGI: Billie?

BILLIE: Did you ever consider what hundreds of years of slavery did to the African American psyche?

MAGI: What? What are you . . . ?

BILLIE: Every time someone mentions traditional values or the good old days—who exactly were those days good for?

The phone rings. BILLIE goes over to it. She sits on the bare floor but does not answer.

BILLIE: Jenny . . . Is that you Jenny. My beauty. My little girl. It's Sybil . . . Auntie Sybil . . . The woman who lives in the cave. (*laughs*)

MAGI: I'll get it for you.

BILLIE: (*picks up the receiver*) Yes, yes, I'm here. Oh, Othe . . . Othello. I didn't recognize your voice. You sound . . . . . different. No. No, no, you can't pick it up. I mean—I've got it, yes. It's right here. No. No, I won't be in . . . No, no. I haven't changed my mind. But—I mean . . . I have to go . . . Roaches. Yeh, blue roaches. Green roaches. So I have to go now. I—I just have to go. (*replaces the receiver*)

MAGI: He's coming over?

BILLIE: I don't want a Mona Lisa smile . . .

MAGI: Oh Billie . . . Billie, you're all in bits and pieces.

BILLIE: I know. I know. A tumour. Suddenly apparent, but it's been there, tiny, growing slowly for a long time. What kind of therapy to take? Chop it out? Radiate it? Let it eat me alive? I see roaches all around me. In me. Blue roaches. Green roaches. Aah! Get off! Get it off. I eat roaches. I pee roaches. Help! I'm losing . . . I don't don't . . . I'm falling . . .

MAGI: Billie? Billie?

BILLIE: I have a dream today.

MAGI: You had a dream?

BILLIE: I have a dream that one day every valley shall be engulfed, every hill shall be exalted and every mountain shall be made low . . . oh . . . oh . . . the rough places will be made plains and the crooked places will be made . . .

MAGI: (*overlapping*) It's gonna be alright, Billie. (*goes to the phone and dials*)

BILLIE: (*overlapping*) . . . straight and the glory of the Lord shall be revealed and all flesh shall see it together.

MAGI: (*overlapping*) It's Magi. You all better get over here, now. No, no, no. NOW. Alright. Alright.

MAGI puts down the receiver and returns to BILLIE. She gently takes the red box from out of BILLIE's hands and places it on the mantel.

BILLIE: (*overlapping*) . . . This is our hope . . .

MAGI: (*overlapping*) It's gonna be alright. I know . . . I know . . .

BILLIE: (*overlapping*) . . . With this faith we will be able to hew out of the mountain of despair a stone of hope . . .

MAGI: (*overlapping*) It's OK. It's OK. Let's start with a little step. Come on. Come with me. (*helps BILLIE up*) Come on . . . Good. Let's get some soup into you. Warm up that frozen blood of yours. (*leads her to the door*) Warm up your insides. Come . . . Come on . . . Chase all the roaches out . . .

BILLIE breaks loose of MAGI and rushes to the window.

MAGI is no longer in the room. OTHELLO appears wearing a brightly coloured dashiki. He is inspecting a broom laying against the fridge. It is now fall, seven years earlier. Save for the broom and the fridge, the apartment is empty.

BILLIE: Look . . . Come, look . . . You can see the Apollo from the window. I love it.

OTHELLO: Where?

BILLIE: Over there. See.

OTHELLO: Oh yeh—If I crane my neck.

BILLIE: I could find some lawn chairs and table and we'd have a city terrace.

OTHELLO: On the fire escape?

BILLIE: We'd have our own little balcony.

OTHELLO: Patio.

BILLIE: Terrace . . .

OTHELLO: We could buy a house up here.

BILLIE: We can't afford to buy a house until I finish school. If I'm going to go to school full-time, this fall, like we agreed—you'd go to school, then I'd go to school—how can we afford a down payment on a house?

OTHELLO: I know. I know.

Pause.

BILLIE: I love it. Don't you love it?

OTHELLO: I love you.

BILLIE: I love you and I love it.

OTHELLO: Think Chris Yago and Mona and the other faculty will feel uncomfortable coming up here . . . for meetings and the like . . .?

BILLIE: It's on the subway line.

OTHELLO: And boy do they need to take the journey. I'll take them on a cultural field trip—blow their minds.

BILLIE: I've longed for this sanctuary.

OTHELLO: I know what you mean.

BILLIE: Black boutiques.

OTHELLO: Black bookstores.

BILLIE: Black groceries.

OTHELLO: Filled with Black doctors and dentists. Black banks.

BILLIE: Black streets teeming with loud Black people listening to loud jazz and reggae and Aretha . . . (*singing*) "There is a rose in Spanish Harlem. (*He joins her.*) A rose in Black and Spanish Harlem. Da da da, da da da . . ." Maybe later we could buy a place on 'strivers row,' that's where all the rich Black folks live.

OTHELLO: Strivers row.

BILLIE: Owned by Blacks hued from the faintest gold to the bluest bronze. That's my dream.

OTHELLO: By then you'd have your Ph.D.

BILLIE: And a small lecturer's position at a prestigious Manhattan university. We might even have enough money to get a small house in the country too.

OTHELLO: A big house in the country too?

BILLIE: A big house with a white picket fence.

OTHELLO: On a rolling emerald hill.

BILLIE: I want two-point-five kids.

OTHELLO: (*kisses her lightly*) You're mad, you know that.

BILLIE: That makes you some kinda fool for loving me, baby.

OTHELLO: Let's do it. There's an old broom right over there. Wanna jump it with me? (*retrieves the broom*)

BILLIE: Are you asking me to m—

OTHELLO: Yes . . . Yes, I am asking.

BILLIE: Yes . . . (*silence*) Then yes.

OTHELLO kisses her. He places the broom in the middle of the floor. He takes BILLIE's hand. They stand in front of it.

BILLIE: What will we use for rings?

OTHELLO: Think them old slaves had rings? Slave marriages were illegal, remember. This broom is more than rings. More than any gold. (*whispers*) My ancient love.

BILLIE: (*whispers*) My soul.

OTHELLO kisses her hand. The couple gaze at each other, preparing to jump over the broom. They jump. They hold each other. The landlady enters.

MAGI: Oh—I'm sorry.

BILLIE: No, no. We were just . . . just—

OTHELLO picks up the broom and places it to one side.

OTHELLO: I think we'll take it.

MAGI: I didn't mean to rush you. I can give you another few minutes if you need to make good and sure?

BILLIE: I think we're sure. (*to OTHELLO*) You sure? (*to MAGI*) We're sure.

MAGI looks gravely at BILLIE. They are the only ones in the room. We are back in the present. MAGI carefully approaches BILLIE. BILLIE stares at where OTHELLO stood only moments ago.

MAGI: Come on. Come with me. Come on . . . Good. Let's get some soup into you. Warm up that frozen blood of yours. (*leads her to the door*) Warm up your insides. Come . . . come on . . . Chase all the roaches out . . . One by one . . . One by one . . .

They exit.

Scene Eight

Harlem, present: late summer, afternoon. A lyrical rhapsody swings to the sound of a commentator describing the scene at the Million Man March. The apartment is virtually empty. CANADA is cleaning the kitchen, taking tubs and bags from out of the freezer. He gives them a brief once-over and then throws them into the trash. OTHELLO enters.

OTHELLO: Billie? Billie?

CANADA: Othello! Othello, good to see you son. (*They shake hands.*) Good to see you.

OTHELLO: I didn't know . . . When did you get here?

CANADA: A few days.

OTHELLO: Billie didn't say a word.

CANADA: Well, Billie's in . . . she's . . . Billie's not here right now.

OTHELLO: (*scanning the apartment*) Did she leave anything for me. An envelope . . . A package—(*sees the red box on the mantel*) Oh. Maybe . . . (*goes over to it*)

CANADA: Oh, she said no one was to touch that . . . I'm supposed to throw it out.

OTHELLO: Great! (*opens the red box and takes out the handkerchief*) It's OK, this is it. It's mine. This is what I was looking for.

CANADA: I was just about to throw it in with the trash from the fridge.

OTHELLO: Just in time, huh?

CANADA: Yeh, some of this stuff's about ready to crawl out by itself.

OTHELLO: I can imagine.

CANADA: I swear, one thing had actually grown little feet.

OTHELLO: Well, Billie wasn't one for cleaning . . . I guess neither of us was. (*an awkward silence between them*) Well . . . I should be off. (*takes some keys out of his pocket and places them where the red box lay*)

CANADA: She tells me you're getting married.

OTHELLO: I do confess the vices of my blood.

CANADA: I'm real sorry it didn't work out . . . Between you and Billie . . . I mean . . . I was hoping . . .

OTHELLO: Yes. I know.

CANADA: She's my child, so—

OTHELLO: I know, I know.

CANADA: You young'uns don't know the sweetness of molasses . . . Rather have granulated sugar 'stead of a deep clover honey, or cane sugar juice from way into the Demerara. Better watch out for that refined shit. It'll kill ya. A slow kinda killin'. 'Cause it kills your mind first. So you think you living the life, when you been dead a long time.

Silence.

OTHELLO: Well sir . . . I should be somewhere.

CANADA: (*nodding*) Well, I hope we can catch up sometime . . .

OTHELLO: (*goes to the door*) That would be great. Tell Billie I came by.

CANADA: I'll tell her that. She'll be glad to know.

OTHELLO: Good seeing you.

CANADA: You too . . . son . . . You too.

OTHELLO takes one last look at the apartment, takes out a tiny cellular phone, and exits.

CANADA is still for a few moments. From the hallway we hear OTHELLO.

OTHELLO: (*offstage*) Chris Yago, please.

CANADA returns to the fridge and continues to clean.

Scene Nine

Harlem, 1928: late summer—night. The music softly underscores the voice of Paul Robeson speaking about not being able to get decent acting roles in the U.S., and how fortunate he feels to be offered a contract to play Othello in England. HE is alone. He proceeds to cover his face in black grease paint. He begins to speak as if rehearsing at first.

HE: It is most true; true, I have married her.
It is most . . .
It is most true; true, I have married her.
For know, but that I love the gentle Desdemona,
(She) questioned me the story of my life
From year to year—the battles, sieges, fortunes,
That I have passed. These things to hear
Would Desdemona seriously incline;
But still the house affairs would draw her thence,
Which ever as she could with haste dispatch
She'd come again, and with a greedy ear
Devour up my discourse. Which I, observing,
Took once a pliant hour . . .
And often did beguile her of her tears,
When I did speak of some distressful stroke
That my youth suffered . . .

In the background we can hear a children's song. HE begins to add white greasepaint to his lips, completing the mask of the minstrel.

. . . My story being done,
She gave me for my pains a world of sighs.
She wished she had not heard it, yet she wished
That heaven had made her such a man. She thanked me,
She thanked me . . .
She thanked me . . .
She thanked me . . .

Scene Ten

Harlem, the present: late summer—night. A beryline blues improvisation of "Mama's Little Baby" cascades alongside a reading of the Langston Hughes poem "Harlem." AMAH sits beside BILLIE in the visitors' lounge of the psychiatric ward. AMAH is clearly saddened by BILLIE's state.

BILLIE: (*singing*)
. . . Step back Sal-ly, all night long.
Strut-in' down the al-ley, al-ley, al-ley,
Strut-in' down the al-ley, all night long.

AMAH & BILLIE:
I looked over there, and what did I see?
A big fat lady from Ten-nes-see.
(*BILLIE gets up and begins to dance.*)
I bet you five dollars I can beat that man,
To the front, to the back, to the side, side, side.
To the front, to the back, to the side, side, side.

The two women laugh.

BILLIE: I haven't done that in . . . in years.

AMAH: I never knew that one—I just saw Jenny do it the other day.

BILLIE: I even remember the dance. (*singing under her breath*) . . . Bet you five dollars I can beat that man . . .

AMAH: It's not so bad here.

BILLIE: You'd think the doctors at Harlem Hospital would be Black. Especially in psychiatrics. Most of the nurses are Black.

AMAH: But they're nice to you—the doctors?

BILLIE: They help. I don't—don't want any more pills. And that's OK. They don't really understand, though. I had this dream. Lucinda— she's my main doctor. Lucinda was sitting at the edge of a couch and I asked her a question. But she couldn't answer because her eyes kept flashing. Like neon lights. Flash, flash, flash. That was it. That was the dream. I knew it was important, but I didn't get it. And I told her. And she didn't get it either. But it gnawed away at me . . . for days . . . The flashing eyes. And that was it! The eyes were flashing blue. Her eyes were flashing blue. She could only see my questions through her blue eyes.

AMAH: Something in you really wants to heal.

BILLIE: Exorcism.

AMAH: Pardon?

BILLIE: Repossess.

AMAH: Self-possession?

BILLIE: I hate. I know I hate. And he loves. How he loves.

AMAH: Billie?

BILLIE: Why is that, you think?

AMAH: Some of us spend our entire lives making our own shackles.

BILLIE: Canada freedom come.

AMAH: And the experienced shackle-wearer knows the best polish for the gilt.

BILLIE: I wanna be free.

AMAH: It must be hard, though. I feel for him.

BILLIE: I'm not that evolved.

AMAH: Forgiveness.

BILLIE: Forgiveness . . .

AMAH: If I don't forgive my enemy, if I don't forgive him, he might just set up house, inside me.

BILLIE: I just . . . I—I despise—I know . . . I know . . . Moment by moment. I forgive him now. I hate—I love him so—I forgive him now. And now. (*She moves as if to speak, but stops herself.*) And I forgive him now.

AMAH: My time's up, sweetie.

BILLIE: I have a dream . . .

AMAH: Sorry?

BILLIE: I had a dream . . .

AMAH: Yes . . . I know.

BILLIE: Tell Jenny . . . Tell her for me . . . Tell her that you saw me dancing.

AMAH: I will tell her.

BILLIE: And tell her . . . Tell her that you heard me singing.

AMAH: I will.

BILLIE: And tell her . . . I'll see her real soon.

AMAH: I will tell her, Billie. I will tell her.

AMAH kisses BILLIE on the cheek and begins to exit. CANADA enters.

BILLIE: (*in the background, softly*)
Betcha five dollars I can beat that man.
To the front, to the back, to the side, side, side.
To the front, to the back, to the side, side, side.

CANADA: How's she doing?

AMAH: Mmm, so-so.

CANADA: Okay. Thanks.

AMAH: We'll really miss you when you go— back to Nova Scotia.

CANADA: Oh, I don't think I'm going anywhere just yet—least if I can help it. Way too much leaving gone on for more than one lifetime already.

BILLIE stops singing for a moment, then segues into a version of Aretha Franklin's "Spanish Harlem," more hummed than sung.

CANADA pats AMAH on the back. AMAH turns and exits. CANADA approaches BILLIE and sits down beside her.

Shortly, he joins her in the song. He rests his hand on hers.

After several moments the lights fade to black.

END

GEORGE F. WALKER   (b. 1947)

In a 1998 interview with Carole Corbeil, George F. Walker explained the impulse behind many of his plays. The only "idea that made any sense to me," he said, "was that we're all really, really pathetic, but we should try anyway! And I thought, well, that's enough." Except for the B-movie megalomaniacs in the plays of his first decade, most of Walker's protagonists have been of the pathetic variety: the down and out, the eccentric, the mad, the drunk, the fearful. On the receiving end of the social Darwinist aggression that passes for civilized behaviour in Walker's urban jungles, they survive, if at all, by improvising wildly and hoping for the best. And if that holds true for the inhabitants of the darkly comic east end neighbourhood of so many of his plays—characters with roots in the community who have something more to fight for than just their own survival—it is doubly so for the temporary tenants of *Suburban Motel*.

In the six short plays that make up this collection, the losing and the lost circulate through one dingy motel room waiting for news which, when it comes, is only ever bad. Daniel De Raey, the first director of *Problem Child*, describes the place as "a drab, camouflaged circle of hell with an ice machine." *Toronto Star* critic Vit Wagner sees it as "an uninviting way station on the road from nowhere good to somewhere worse." The characters typically depict themselves as in hell or a horrible nightmare, "very deeply in the shit" or simply "fucked." Uprooted and virtually resourceless, they recognize how pathetic they really are. And under those circumstances they face an important variation on Walker's fundamental theme. *Should* they try anyway? *Is* that enough? Or is the whole exercise pointless? Walker confronts those questions head-on in *Problem Child*, one of the bleakest, funniest and most powerful plays in his substantial canon.

Walker grew up in the working-class east end of Toronto. He was driving taxi in 1970 when he read a flyer on a lamppost soliciting scripts for Ken Gass' new Factory Theatre Lab. The play he submitted, *Prince of Naples*, was not only his first attempt at writing drama, but when he attended its opening in 1971 it was only the second play he had ever seen. Despite Walker's inexperience, Gass made him resident playwright from 1971–76, an invaluable apprenticeship and the start of an enduring association that has seen the majority of Walker's plays premiere at the Factory.

Prince of Naples and *Ambush at Tether's End* (1971) were basically absurdist exercises, more derivative of Ionesco and Beckett than original. With *Sacktown Rag* (1972) and *Bagdad Saloon* (1973) Walker began to find his own voice, planting increasingly exotic landscapes of the mind with pop icons like Gary Cooper and Gertrude Stein. This phase of his work climaxed with *Beyond Mozambique* (1974) and *Ramona and the White Slaves* (1976). The former features a B-movie jungle locale populated by a drug-addicted, pederastic priest, a disgraced Mountie, a porn-film starlet and a demonic ex-Nazi doctor whose wife thinks she is Olga in Chekhov's *Three Sisters*. *Ramona*, a murder-mystery-cum-opium-dream that marked Walker's directing debut, takes place in a Hong Kong brothel in 1919, opening with the heroine's rape by a poisonous lizard.

Walker took his next three plays to Toronto Free Theatre. *Gossip* (1977), *Zastrozzi* (1977), and *Filthy Rich* (1979) were all less obscure, more accessible and consequently more popular than his previous work. *Zastrozzi*, a stylish, anachronistic gothic romance and revenge melodrama about "the master criminal of all Europe," has been produced across the United States and Canada, in New York and London, Australia and New Zealand, and remains one of Walker's most popular plays. *Gossip* and *Filthy Rich*, heavily indebted to Humphrey Bogart and Raymond Chandler, were the first of his plays in *film noir* style. Along with *The Art of War* (1983) they comprise *The Power Plays* (1986). All feature a character named Tyrone Power as either investigative reporter or private eye, equally cynical and shabby in both incarnations, reluctantly involved in sorting out political intrigue and murder. Related in theme and mood is the Chalmers Award-winning *Theatre of the Film Noir* (1981), a bizarre murder mystery set in wartime Paris.

Exotic locales still feature prominently in *Rumours of Our Death* (1980), an anti-war parable directed by Walker as a rock musical, and *Science and Madness* (1982), a turn-of-the-century gothic melodrama. But the modern city explored by Walker in the first two Power plays became increasingly the focus of his attention. *Criminals in Love* (1984), winner of the Governor General's Award, *Better Living* (1986), a Chalmers Award winner, and *Beautiful City* (1987) were published as *The East End Plays* (1988), this time transparently the east end of Toronto itself. The nihilism of Walker's earlier work gives way in these political comedies to tenuous hope for a life of simple happiness in a city salvaged from the powerful and greedy.

Love and Anger (1989) and *Escape from Happiness* (1991), a sequel to *Better Living*, continue Walker's championing of women, the oppressed and the marginal against the patriarchal centre. These two comedies, both Chalmers Award winners, have had critical and popular success across the United States as well as Canada. But the play that really made Walker's reputation outside Canada was *Nothing Sacred* (1988), his adaptation of Turgenev's novel *Fathers and Sons*, set in pre-revolutionary Russia. Winner of the Governor General's, Chalmers, and a variety of other Canadian awards, it became so popular among American regional theatres that the *Los Angeles Times* called it "the play of the year." In 1993 Walker wrote *Tough!* for Vancouver's Green Thumb Theatre, a comedy about sex and gender relations among three young people.[1]

After taking some time off from the theatre, writing for television and moving to Vancouver, Walker returned in triumph to his first theatrical home. Toronto's Factory Theatre had suffered through difficult times and nearly folded but was now once more under the direction of Ken Gass who premiered the six new one-act plays Walker had written. *Problem Child, Adult Entertainment, Criminal Genius, Featuring Loretta, The End of Civilization* and *Risk Everything* (which brings back *Problem Child*'s R.J. and Denise, and introduces Denise's mother) run the gamut from bitter drama to wacky comedy. *Suburban Motel* (1997–98) was presented in repertory format, two plays a night. It was a huge success, winning multiple Chalmers and Dora awards and acclaimed for subsequent productions in Montreal, Vancouver and elsewhere. Walker rang in the millennium with another hit, *Heaven* (2000), an ethical revenge comedy whose characters come back from the dead, premiered by Toronto's Canadian Stage.

Walker was playwright-in-residence at the New York Shakespeare Festival's Public Theatre in 1982, and became the first resident playwright at the National Theatre School of Canada in 1991. His work for series television includes writing for *Due South* and consulting on CBC's *The Newsroom*, and he has adapted *Problem Child* for the screen. Other film versions of his plays are *Better Living* (1998), starring Olympia Dukakis, and a French production of *Beyond Mozambique* set in contemporary Montreal, titled *Rats and Rabbits* (2000).

Problem Child is a battle driven by a mother's very high stakes. In his excellent book on Walker, Chris Johnson cites Kate Taylor's *Globe and Mail* review of the play where she asks, "How far would you go to win back your child?" Johnson's own answer is "pretty damn far," and the play certainly establishes audience empathy with Denise's plight. But despite flirting with stereotypes of the stage social worker in his portrayal of the uptight, overbearing, judgmental Helen, Walker also gives her position substantial credence. We are all too familiar with those horrible incidents of severe abuse or even murder of children in which social services somehow failed to intervene aggressively enough to save them from their own parents. My students' responses to the play have been pretty evenly divided. Helen's accusation that Denise doesn't cook or go to church they dismiss as irrelevant. (When Helen asks her, "Do you clean," I can't help hearing echoes of the interview in *Billy Bishop Goes to War* where Billy, trying to become an RFC pilot, is asked by the clueless Sir Hugh, "Do you ski?") That Denise has abused drugs and turned tricks makes them wary, though most accept her self-defense. What really seems to resonate is Helen's remark, "You want me to give you the baby back so you can hang out with her, Denise? Maybe take her to the mall? Train her to give you a hug when you're feeling low … " For many, there remains enough residual suspicion about Denise's motives and the adequacy of her mothering skills to support Helen's caution. When a child's welfare is at stake, maybe it is better to be safe than sorry.

Whatever the merits of her arguments or her strategies for attempting to get her child back, Denise genuinely feels that without the child her life has no meaning or value. All she can do is go through the motions. Her deep despair at the end of the play is predicated on the conviction that things won't work out. Because "for people like us," they never do. The rest of the play and all the other plays in *Suburban Motel* pretty clearly support that assumption. Though it becomes Helen's comic refrain in *Problem Child*, "buried alive" really describes the condition of R.J. and Denise and the people like them. Their attempts to get out of the hole and fix their lives lead both to comic chaos and to the kind of failure that is not funny at all, but never to a successful outcome. So why bother?

R.J. has a variety of answers: because he loves Denise, because if you don't bother "then it all falls apart," because he believes in justice. Phillie gets practically hysterical at the mention of "justice." He finds the concept much too threatening. It means having to get involved in the world, and he has, in hilarious ways, tried to make himself immune, drinking himself unconscious and insisting that he doesn't "give a shit." He is what Denise might easily become until, stirred to action, he tentatively commits to her project. But what a feeble ally he makes. Tellingly, he is the only help she can afford, her implicit answer to R.J.'s remark that "we're trying to be the kind of people who get lawyers in circumstances like this." R.J., meanwhile, becomes ever more deeply involved with the TV talk shows where his interventions actually seem to have some effect. "Life is disgusting," he says, and "I can't do anything about life." So he pours his energies into life's absurd surrogate, content with the illusion of making a difference, while Denise sinks quietly, deeper and deeper into hell.

NOTES

1. In the late 1990s after Coach House Press went bankrupt, nearly all of Walker's plays were repackaged by his new publisher, Talonbooks. Walker took the opportunity to revise many of them, and to redefine and rearrange his East End Plays in two volumes. *The East End Plays, Part 1* comprises *Criminals in Love, Better Living* and *Escape from Happiness*. Included in *Part 2* are *Beautiful City, Love and Anger* and *Tough!*

Problem Child was first produced by Rattlestick Productions at Theatre Off Park in New York City on May 13, 1997, with the following cast:

R.J.	Christopher Burns
Denise	Tasha Lawrence
Phillie	Mark Hammer/Alan Benson
Helen	Kathleen Goldpaugh

Directed by Daniel De Raey
Set Design by Van Santvoord
Lighting Design by Chad McArver
Costume Design by Rachel Gruer
Sound Design by Laura Grace Brown

This revised version of *Problem Child* was first produced by Factory Theatre in Toronto on October 25, 1997, with the following cast:

R.J.	Shawn Doyle
Denise	Kristen Thomson
Phillie	James Kidnie
Helen	Nola Augustson

Directed by George F. Walker
Set and Costume Design by Shawn Kerwin
Lighting Design by Rebecca Picherak
Sound Design by Jonathan Rooke and Evan Turner

PROBLEM CHILD

CHARACTERS

R.J.
DENISE } *a young couple*
PHILLIE, *the motel caretaker*
HELEN, *a social worker*

SCENE

A slightly rundown motel room.

Scene One

R.J. REYNOLDS is watching TV. DENISE is in the washroom taking a shower. There are two old suitcases on the floor and a small baby crib up against the wall beside the bed.

R.J.: Ah man, will you look at that. That guy is too ugly for that woman. When they bring that woman out she's gonna pass out. You can't do stuff like that. Bring in some good looking woman and tell her she's got a secret admirer then bring her out in front of millions of people to see some ugly guy with pimples on his ears just smiling at her. She's gonna freak out when she sees him. She's gonna be embarrassed. The studio audience is gonna be embarrassed. It's a weak concept for a show so it's gotta be handled just right. Oprah never does this shit.

DENISE comes out of the bathroom drying her hair, wearing a large man's shirt.

DENISE: Can't you do anything besides watch those things.

R.J.: This is life, Denise. Don't be a snob. Just because it's on TV doesn't mean it's not real.

DENISE: Gimme a break … Mothers who confront their cross-dressing sons. That's your idea of real, eh.

R.J.: What? You think that doesn't happen. When was that anyway.

DENISE: Yesterday.

R.J.: Which one. Jerry Springer? Montel?

DENISE: (*putting on a pair of jeans*) How the hell should I know … There was that guy in a black garter belt and fish-net stockings and his mother wailing, "I don't mind that he dresses like a woman, but does he have to dress like a slut!"

R.J.: Garter belt, yeah. Sitting next to his mother in a garter belt. Sad. Kind of touching. But too extreme for daytime. What a cool thing for her to say though.

DENISE: (*shaking her head*) Yeah, cool, sure. Man, you are losing your perspective. Turn that thing off. Take a shower. Let's get out of here. Get a meal.

R.J.: Can't leave. She might call.

DENISE: It's been a week, R.J. I'm beginning to lose—

R.J.: A week isn't long. She could still call.

DENISE: We could get the guy in the office to take a message. Whatsisname.

R.J.: Philips. Phillie Philips. Yeah right. I really want to put our future in the hands of a brain-damaged drunk.

DENISE: But I'm going a bit nuts. Maybe I'll go out for a—

R.J.: You gotta stay. She told us to stay put. She was specific. We're on … you know … probation or something. We gotta obey. We'll order in. Something different … We'll order Siamese.

DENISE: Siamese? What's that.

R.J.: Not Siamese. The other one.

DENISE: What? Szechuan?

R.J.: No … Indian.

DENISE: Indian? How do you get Indian confused with Siamese?

R.J.: (*pointing at the TV*) Shush. They're bringing her out. This is gonna be awful. The audience knows. Look at their faces … It's gonna be really embarrassing … I hate it when it's this embarrassing … No I can't watch … (*pulls his sweater over his head*)

DENISE: (*in front of a wall mirror, brushing her hair*) What is Siamese food anyway ... I mean is there such a thing ... I guess there must be ... They gotta eat, don't they ... the Siamese, I mean.

R.J.: (*pulls down his sweater*) Oh man. She's laughing. She's pointing. She's laughing. She's putting her fingers in her mouth. She's making the puking sound. Oh ... oh that's just cruel. Look at the guy. He's devastated. He's ruined for life. Fuck you. Fuck you, Ricki Lake. Enough is enough. (*turns the TV off*) I'm disgusted. Did you see that.

DENISE: No.

R.J.: I think I'll write a letter. Yeah. Right now. We got any paper?

DENISE: We don't have anything, R.J. ... A change of clothes. That's it.

R.J.: Yeah but ... I have to write that letter!

DENISE: Why are you getting so worked up.

R.J.: Because I'm disgusted ... Life is disgusting.

DENISE: That wasn't life, R.J. It was a TV talk show.

R.J.: Hey that's no more disgusting than life, that show. Life is disgusting like that. Life is the place where dopes like that guy get to be humiliated ... Life is the place that fucks people like you and me up. Life is just like that show.

DENISE: No it's not.

R.J.: Yes it is ... Okay no it's not. It's worse. But I can't do anything about life. I can write that show a letter ... Paper!

DENISE: Look. Calm down.

R.J.: Forget the letter. I'll call.

DENISE: Who you gonna call? You gonna call Ricki Lake?

R.J.: The network ... Hey I've done this before. (*walks over to the phone*)

DENISE: You have?

R.J.: Once. I called Geraldo. When they had that KKK guy on with his grandchild. The old prick had the little kid—eight months old—in a Klan costume. That really disgusted me.

DENISE: I remember that one. That was bad. You called, eh. Why didn't you tell me.

R.J.: Well I didn't get through ... So there was nothing to tell ... But maybe this time I'll—shit! (*He has the phone to his ear.*)

DENISE: What's wrong.

R.J.: It's not working. It's dead.

DENISE: No way. Jesus. (*She scrambles over the bed, grabs the phone, listens.*) Ah no. No ... When was the last time you used the phone.

R.J.: I can't ... remember. (*pacing*) What is this. Is this fate. Is this a kick in the face from fate. What is it. What.

DENISE: Calm down. We'll get it fixed. We can't do anything except get it fixed. Maybe Phillie will fix it.

R.J.: If he can. If he's even around.

DENISE: (*heads for the windows*) I can see if he's in the office from here.

She throws back the drapes. And screams because PHILLIE PHILIPS' unshaven face is pressed against the window. DENISE is backing up in horror.

DENISE: Jesus. Holy shit. Look at him. Look at him. What's he doin'.

PHILLIE: (*yelling*) Your phone is broken! Your phone is broken!

R.J. runs to the door. Opens it.

R.J.: Why are you on the window, man! What are you doin'!

R.J. goes to PHILLIE. We can see through the window as he pushes PHILLIE.

R.J.: I asked you what the hell you're—(*PHILLIE falls over.*) Shit!

R.J. bends over. DENISE is straining to see. But trying not to get too close. When R.J. straightens he has PHILLIE under his arms and is dragging him towards the door.

DENISE: R.J.? R.J. What are you doing.

R.J.: He's unconscious.

DENISE: Why are you bringing him in here.

R.J.: So he can fix the phone.

DENISE: Like that?

R.J.: Well first we have to revive him.

R.J. manages to get PHILLIE in a chair.

DENISE: God. Look at him. He's so … he's so … Whatya think is wrong with him.

PHILLIE: (*eyes closed*) Drunk! He's drunk.

DENISE and R.J. look at each other.

PHILLIE: (*opens his eyes*) Yeah he's drunk. He's so drunk he just passed out against our window. Smells too. (*stands unsteadily*) Smells bad. Well why shouldn't he? Do you think he bathes. Not often. Look at him he's so … he's so. Well what I think is fuck it, wastin' all our time tryin' to figure out what brought him to this sorry state. Let's just shoot him. Bring him out back under the billboard, near the trash in the place where rats live. Fuck it … (*focuses on DENISE*) Oh yeah, a lady called … Your phone's busted. Couldn't put her through. Bitch got all … unpleasant … What did she want. Oh yeah. Something about … something …

DENISE: A baby?

PHILLIE: A what?

DENISE: A baby!?

PHILLIE: What about a baby!? Oh yeah, baby … She was callin' about a baby!! (*grabs his head*) Shit. All this excitement has made me nauseous.

He rushes into the washroom. Retching sounds. R.J. goes to DENISE. Puts his arms around her.

DENISE: This is not good. You told me everything would be all right … This is not all right.

DENISE moves away from R.J. Another loud retching sound. R.J. goes toward her.

DENISE: No. Just stay away from me. Suppose she doesn't call back … I said stay the fuck away from me.

R.J.: I was gonna … comfort you. You know?

DENISE: You wanna comfort me? Get the phone fixed.

A retching sound. R.J. gestures toward the bathroom.

R.J.: It'll probably be a minute or two more … I dunno.

DENISE continues to pace. PHILLIE continues to retch. R.J. continues to look helpless.

Blackout.

Scene Two

HELEN MACKIE stands just inside the open door. Wearing a business suit. Carrying a briefcase. DENISE and R.J. are standing. Staring at her.

HELEN: Can I … sit down.

DENISE: Where's the baby …

HELEN: I'm sorry?

DENISE: You didn't bring the baby.

HELEN: We're a long way from that yet … Can I sit down.

R.J.: Sure. There. (*points to a chair*)

HELEN: Actually over at the table would be better. I've got some paper work.

HELEN sits at the small table in the corner. DENISE has started to pace.

DENISE: What's she mean we're a long way from that … Ask her what she means.

HELEN: Did you think this would be easy, Denise.

DENISE: Look I … I just want to know what she meant.

HELEN: (*to R.J.*) What's wrong with her.

R.J.: Nothing. She's just—

HELEN: She looks pretty … edgy. (*to DENISE*) Are you on any … medication, Denise.

R.J.: No she's—Well we thought you'd be bringing—Look we've been cooped up in here for a week.

HELEN: (*opening her briefcase, putting papers on the table, a pad*) Why.

DENISE: Why? Waiting for you.

R.J.: Yeah. And we didn't go anywhere. We never left.

HELEN: Never left? I don't get it.

R.J.: You told us to stay put. We stayed put.

HELEN: I never meant you couldn't go out. I just said I'd need a week to get things moving. So you should just—

DENISE: Where's the baby!

HELEN: Denise ... Denise come over here. Sit down.

DENISE: No.

R.J.: Denise.

DENISE: No. I'm not sitting. I'm not doing anything until she tells me where the baby is.

HELEN: (*stands, goes to DENISE*) She's in the same place she's been in for the last six months. She's in a loving foster home. And we can't just take her from a place where she's secure and loved and give her back to you unless we're sure she's going to be okay ... And making sure she's going to be okay takes time. Do you understand. Time and consideration. And ... some questions.

R.J.: We'll answer questions. I've already told you that. Any questions.

HELEN: Good ... Now Denise, are you on any medication ... Lift your head. Look at me. (*DENISE obeys.*) Denise, what's that expression on your face supposed to mean. All that ... attitude. You think that's helpful? I'm just doing my job.

DENISE: I just ... I just thought you were bringing the baby ... I guess I got that wrong.

R.J.: (*to HELEN*) That's my fault. I heard you wrong. Or I misunderstood ... We both got pretty worked up ... The phone was broken ... We were cooped up ... Things ... things ...

DENISE: I'm not on anything. I haven't been on anything for a long time. We've got doctors' papers. (*to R.J.*) Show her.

R.J.: Where are they.

DENISE: In my suitcase.

R.J.: (*gets the suitcase*) Yeah we've got doctors' papers. We've got a social worker's letter. We've got a letter from our landlord.

DENISE: He's got a job.

R.J.: Yeah. I've got a job ... It's ... good ... It's—

DENISE: Okay. It's an okay job. He works for a builder. He does drywall.

R.J.: It's almost a trade ... I've got a letter from my boss. (*hands HELEN a large envelope*) They're all in there. All the letters.

HELEN: What about you, Denise.

DENISE: I've been looking. I had a part-time waitress thing. A small restaurant ...

R.J.: Well you know, it's a small town. There's not a lot of places where—She put in some applications ... but ...

HELEN: You like life in a small town?

R.J.: Yeah. It's cool.

HELEN: Denise?

DENISE: It's okay. It takes getting used to. I'll be okay. Look what are you asking. Do you wanna know if I turn tricks. Do I put stuff in my veins.

R.J.: That's not happening, Miss ... Miss ...

HELEN: Helen. Just Helen is okay ...

R.J.: Okay, Helen ... Look. Look at the letter. The letter will tell you we've got a new life in that town. It was hard at first. You know? But we did it. We went away from everyone we knew. Everything we ... did. And we started ... I mean it was hard. Denise was great. What she did was so hard. It was—

DENISE: We need our baby back. It's not gonna work if we don't get Christine back. I won't make it.

HELEN: What do you mean by that, Denise. Do you think you'll start back on drugs, Denise. Do you feel that's a possibility.

DENISE: Of course it's a possibility. Everything is a possibility. I'm not a new person. They didn't throw out the old Denise and make a new one. It's a repair job. I'm just ... repaired ... (*to R.J.*) She doesn't get it.

R.J.: (*to HELEN*) She needs the baby. Everything she's done these past few months she's done for the baby.

HELEN's cell phone rings. She answers it.

HELEN: (*into phone*) Yeah? ... Yeah. Okay ... Okay sure. About a half hour. (*puts the cell phone back in her briefcase*) Look I'm needed somewhere. Why don't I just take these letters away. Look them over. Call you. Set something up.

R.J.: Set something up like what?

HELEN: A meeting. We'll talk some more.

R.J.: We thought it was set. The court said it was okay … I mean here we are in this dump. We've come back and—

HELEN: Look the court needs our approval. If we say it's—

DENISE: We?

HELEN: Me … If things look okay to me then the court is just a rubber stamp. Listen, I'm sorry if I gave you the wrong impression but we can't rush this. We're going to have to … get to know each other a bit better. We'll have to reveal a few things. Rehash a few things probably. Do you understand what I'm saying, Denise.

DENISE shrugs. Turns away. HELEN picks up her briefcase.

R.J.: We'll … just wait then.

HELEN: I'll call you.

HELEN looks for a moment at both of them. Leaves.

R.J.: (*looks at DENISE, goes to the open door, yells after HELEN*) Goodbye … (*to DENISE*) She waved … She turned and waved.

DENISE: This is not going to happen.

R.J.: Ah don't—

DENISE: Nah, we've got a judgement against us. We've been found guilty. And no one, especially her, is going to all of a sudden find us not guilty, throw that judgement away and say here, here's your kid, start over, make a family … Ah aren't you cute—We thought you were the scum of the earth but really you're cute. We're sorry …

R.J.: (*moving toward her*) Listen, are you tired. You're probably hungry and tired so—

DENISE: Ah please stay away from me. I can't do this. I can't let you get my spirits up. I'm not up to getting positive. It's hard. Sometimes it's just like—I don't know … bullshit. Can't you just let me feel like it's all bullshit and leave it at that.

R.J.: No … I can't … Because then it all falls apart, Denise.

DENISE: I'm going out. (*grabs a jacket*) If I don't get out of here for awhile I'll go—

R.J.: It's okay. You go out. I'll stay. I'll be here if she calls. There was something in the way she waved goodbye. I think she'll call soon. Maybe she felt sorry or something but … she'll call. Don't worry … I'll be here. (*sits on the couch*)

DENISE: Yeah … I know you will … You're a rock or something. How'd that happen. I mean you used to be as messed up as me and now … now you're some kind of solid thing.

She leaves. R.J. is just staring ahead.

R.J.: Bullshit … (*lowers his head*)

Blackout.

Scene Three

PHILLIE is vacuuming the room. R.J. is watching the TV.

PHILLIE: (*shouting*) This bothering you? (*R.J. gestures that it's okay.*) 'Cause I could turn it off. Come back later. (*R.J. gestures again. PHILLIE turns off the vacuum.*) Are you sure.

R.J.: Definitely. Just do your job, man. It's okay.

PHILLIE: I appreciate that.

R.J.: Yeah … By the way, it's good to see you sober.

PHILLIE: It's Wednesday. I clean the rooms on Wednesdays. It's almost impossible to do that under the influence.

R.J.: I bet …

PHILLIE: I mean it can be done … But I gotta tell you, cleaning toilet bowls when you're smashed … is kind of … unnatural.

R.J.: Yeah.

PHILLIE turns on the machine. Vacuums awhile. Something on the TV grabs his attention. Turns off the machine.

PHILLIE: Why are those three chubby women crying.

R.J.: They're sisters … See the skinny guy with the skimpy beard next to them? He's been having sex with all of them. And today they've finally confronted him.

PHILLIE: Yeah? Confronted? So how come they're crying. And he looks …

R.J.: Kinda pleased with himself? ... Because there's no justice in the world, man. None. He thinks he's the cock of the walk. He's on national TV and he's a winner and the women are ... fools. Crying fools. There is definitely hardly any justice in the world.

PHILLIE: You think I don't know that? I know that ... The thing about me is I don't give a shit.

R.J.: I give a shit. I think justice is the only thing. Fair behaviour for fair behaviour. You know? Even breaks for everyone.

PHILLIE: No no ... Don't take me there, man. I can't get into that. Next thing I'll just get upset. I'm capable of some pretty self-destructive behaviour. I gotta concentrate on doing my job. I'm lucky to have this job. If it wasn't for my cousin Edward ... No ... No I can't get into that justice shit. The lucky and the unlucky. The haves and the have-nots. The fuckers, the fuckees—oh man. Let me just suck up some dirt. Let me just do what I can do, and suck up what little dirt I can here.

PHILLIE turns on the machine. Vacuums for awhile. PHILLIE turns off the machine.

PHILLIE: Who's the guy in the suit.

R.J.: The expert. They always have an expert.

PHILLIE: What? A social worker.

R.J.: Sometimes. Or a doctor. Or someone who's written a book.

PHILLIE: So. Yeah? Is he supposed to solve this. Is he supposed to bring justice to this situation ... I really don't think so! (*unplugging the vacuum, gathering his cleaning supplies*) Look. Here's the truth. I can't do anymore. It's that ... justice thing. Once it's in your head you can't ignore it. You just can't ... It colours everything ... It makes all work futile. (*He is leaving.*)

R.J.: Sorry ... It looks pretty clean though.

PHILLIE: There's a stain on the carpet. It's permanent. Other than that yeah it's pretty clean ... The bathroom is spotless ... not that I give a shit!

PHILLIE gets choked up and leaves, not closing the door. R.J. turns back to the TV.

R.J.: ... Oh yeah right. Take it out on her. Like it's her fault. Look at him. Look at that grin. Get

serious, man ... No no it's not about sibling rivalry you twit, it's about the guy and his dick. It's about the dick ... Go ahead ask him. Ask him about the dick! The truth is in the dick!

DENISE appears in the doorway. Doesn't come in. Just leans against the frame, watching R.J. She looks a little messed up.

R.J.: Ah man ... Enough. Look she's crying. She's really crying. Okay—Host intervention! Host intervention! Come on! Come on! Fair is fair. Come on, for chrissake. Intervene!

DENISE: Hey! (*R.J. turns to DENISE.*) Calm down! It's just a fucking TV show!

R.J.: (*looks at DENISE; at TV; at DENISE*) Yeah. (*turns off the TV; stands*) Hi.

DENISE: I mean don't we have enough problems of our own. Real ones? You have to go looking for something to get upset about on a ... a fucking TV show!?

R.J.: Where you been?

DENISE: Downtown.

R.J.: How far downtown?

DENISE: All the way.

R.J.: You see your mother?

DENISE: She wasn't there ... I went over to your place. Your mother wasn't there either. Hey, there's a show idea you can send in: "Mothers Who Aren't There When you Need Them."

R.J.: You on something?

DENISE: Ah you're gonna wanna talk about that, aren't you. I wanna talk about where our mothers are when our life is going down the toilet but you'll have to get into that "let me see your eyes" bullshit.

R.J.: I'm not gonna look in your eyes. I don't have to look in your eyes. You can't even stand up.

DENISE: Says who.

She stands. Falls back against the door frame. R.J. sits on the bed. Hangs his head between his legs.

DENISE: Ah don't go falling apart on me. Hanging your head like that. It's just booze. Six beers. Nothing. I needed to feel better than I felt. (*staggering a bit as she moves toward him*) I was feeling so bad ... I was afraid I wouldn't be able to ... you know ... make good choices ... because the way I was feeling was—fuck it ... So I thought—hey, feel better. Make better choices so ... (*sits next to him; rubs his head*) So really it's okay ... I'm not falling. I'm really not falling ... I'm still ... hopeful. Look there's still hope in me ... Look at me. Look at me. Come on. (*lifts his head*) Now is this the face of an ... optimistic person ... a basically optimistic person ... or ... isn't it. I say it is.

R.J.: Well you must know ... Why'd you go see your mother.

DENISE: Ah ... 'Cause it's hard not to go see your mother when you think ... "God I sure could use a little mother talk!" Even when you remember your mother's kind of written you off. Even when you remember it was your mother who called in "the government" and had them take away your kid ... so ... so I went to talk ... But ... well ...

R.J.: She wasn't there. Big surprise. When was she ever.

DENISE: Hey don't get uppity. Neither was yours.

R.J.: Yeah but mine has an excuse. She's dead.

DENISE: Holy shit. You're right.

R.J.: Just six beers?

DENISE: Or more ... Holy shit. That's right. She died just after I got pregnant ... I forgot. How could I forget that ... I walked over to your building. Took the elevator to the twelfth floor. Went down the hall to 1209. Knocked. Waited. Left ... I just forgot.

R.J.: It's been a rough year.

DENISE: Ah look who's trying to cheer me up. Doesn't it ever just wear you down ... Trying to make sure I'm ... okay? (*kisses his face*) Really. How could I forget your mother is dead. Do you think I've got permanent brain damage. Memory loss?

R.J.: Maybe you were just ... drunk.

DENISE: That's my man. Always got the right answer. Always looking to let me off the hook. Always looking for ... a reason ... Why?

R.J.: I don't know. I love you. I ... love you.

He kisses her. He puts his hand under her sweater. She kisses him back.

DENISE: Are we gonna have sex now?

R.J.: It's better than ...

DENISE: What.

R.J.: Thinking ... about the baby ... About mothers. I mean your mother. Of all the hypocritical bullshit in the world ... Your mother gets us busted ... your mother, the biggest screw-up in the universe gets to play Miss Citizen and—

DENISE: I did that. (*kisses him*) Shush. I did that.

R.J.: What.

DENISE: That "my mother's gotta go to hell" thing. After the six beers ...

R.J.: Or more.

DENISE: Yeah. Anyway it's been done. She's in hell. I sent her in my mind to hell. You know maybe I didn't go to see her to talk ... Maybe I went to kill her. Yeah. I think I actually went to kill her.

R.J.: Yeah. Sure.

DENISE: No really. I mean why else would I buy a gun.

R.J.: What? Get real.

DENISE: No ... No. I bought it off ... Billy Richards. Remember him? I ran into him and he says "Hey ... So? What's new" ... All that shit. And I find myself asking if he's got any weapons I can purchase ...

R.J.: Denise ... What is this—

DENISE: It's in my bag. Over there somewhere.

R.J. walks over to the door. Bends. DENISE's canvas bag is on the floor. He empties the contents onto the table. A few things. No gun.

R.J.: So?

DENISE: No gun? I guess I musta made it up.

R.J.: And why would you do something like that, Denise.

DENISE: Your worst fear, dear. What is it. Something like that? Denise gets a gun. Goes on a rampage. Takes revenge on her mother. Then ... what? Turns the gun on herself. Well whatever ...

Your worst fear ... I was just putting it out where we could both see it ... I don't know ... I don't know ...

R.J.: Maybe I should go get us some coffee.

DENISE: I guess ...

R.J.: How about food ...

DENISE: Food ... No ... Look ... I'm just going to crash ... You go out. Eat.

R.J.: No I'll—

DENISE: No I went out. You go out. It's probably good ... I mean you are talking to the TV. So ...

R.J.: Yeah ... Yeah maybe I'll just go get a—

DENISE: Take your time. I'm just going to sleep.

R.J.: She didn't call by the way. Helen. The social worker? She didn't call.

DENISE: No?

R.J.: But ... you didn't ask me if she called. Why not.

DENISE: I don't know.

R.J.: Sure you do ... You're preparing for the worst.

DENISE: Maybe.

R.J.: You are ... What's the good of that ... Denise?

She shrugs. Turns away. He leaves. She takes off her jacket. Reaches inside her pocket. Takes out a small gun. Puts it under the mattress. Lies down on the bed. Takes the bed spread. Pulls it over herself. Rolls in it until she is wrapped.

Blackout.

Scene Four

HELEN is standing over the bed. Watching DENISE sleep ... She begins to look casually around the room. Poking at a pile of newspapers. Looking in one of the dresser drawers. Eventually she goes into the bathroom. We hear glass objects being shifted. DENISE stirs. A glass crashes in the bathroom. DENISE sits up quickly.

DENISE: R.J.?

HELEN: (*coming out of the bathroom*) No ... it's just me ... I broke a glass ... Hi ... I was just ... just ...

HELEN is wrapping her hand in a towel. DENISE is up.

DENISE: Searching?

HELEN: Searching? ... No I was thirsty. So I—

DENISE: Is that a bad cut.

HELEN: I don't know.

DENISE: You're bleeding.

HELEN: A little ... Yes. There's glass all over the floor. Do you want me to ...

DENISE: I'll get it later.

HELEN: I can do it.

DENISE: I said I'll get it later! I'll do it! (*smiles*) It'll get done. Honest.

HELEN: Sure. Fine. Thanks ... So ... Can I sit down.

DENISE: Yeah, sit down ... I'll sit down too. We'll both sit down. (*sits at the table*)

HELEN: What's wrong.

DENISE: Nothing. Sit down.

HELEN: (*sitting*) You look tired—

DENISE: Do I? ... You look fine ... You look just fine. Well you've got a bad cut on your hand. And you're bleeding all over the table but other than that—

HELEN: Oh dear I better—

HELEN starts to stand. DENISE grabs her wrist.

DENISE: Where you going.

HELEN: I don't ... well to the bathroom. I'm bleeding.

DENISE: Stay put. Just for a minute.

HELEN: But I'm bleeding on the table.

DENISE: Hey it's okay. Stay put. Can you just stay put. I need to talk to you.

HELEN: Well I need to talk to you too. But—

DENISE: So good. Let's talk. It's just that I've been worried you know. Worried that you were out there doing your investigation without having all the—

HELEN: It's not really an investigation.

DENISE: Yes it is. We're suspects. And you're investigating us.

HELEN: I'm doing my job. I'm just trying to determine if you're capable of caring for your child. You're not a suspect. It's not a criminal—

DENISE: Hey, we're suspected of being inadequate. Let's not argue over the fucking word here. Look I'm sorry. But I was just worried you were out there "doing your job" without knowing something essential about me. And that is ... I need my baby. I need her.

HELEN: I know that.

DENISE: No you don't.

HELEN: Yes—

DENISE: No you don't! I didn't tell you. I should have told you how much I need her. And how much I love her. And that I never would do anything to hurt her ... And how what happened before wasn't really what they said happened. My mother ... you know, we were fighting and to get back at me she made it look like I was neglecting the baby and called you people.

HELEN: Look all that's on record.

DENISE: Some of it. Not all of it.

HELEN: The point is, it doesn't matter how we got involved. We're involved.

DENISE: Yeah but listen—

HELEN: No you listen. We were called. We got involved. We saw things we didn't like. We took action.

DENISE: Pretty drastic though ... I mean the action you took was ... pretty fucking drastic.

HELEN: Were you or were you not a drug addict.

DENISE: Hey Helen that sounded pretty ... you know "legal." Like a lawyer, that "were you or were you not" stuff.

HELEN: Were you or were you not a prostitute.

DENISE: I turned a few tricks. It happened. Hey I thought I should pay the rent.

HELEN: Please.

DENISE: Please? What's that mean. Did that sound feeble to you. I mean as an excuse.

HELEN: I didn't want to go backwards here, Denise. We have enough to deal with in the present.

DENISE: I just want to make sure you ... got it clear. I mean maybe you don't. Maybe you don't know R.J. was in jail. I was alone. Did you know that.

HELEN: Yes.

DENISE: So I was alone. I'd had this baby. My husband was in prison. I was broke.

HELEN: You were receiving welfare.

DENISE: It wasn't enough.

HELEN: Look I've told you I don't want to rehash—

DENISE: It wasn't enough. I wasn't making it.

HELEN: Others do.

DENISE: I wasn't. It wasn't enough. The rent was too high. I couldn't get them to lower it. I had expenses.

HELEN: Drugs ... Crack, speed, what else.

DENISE: No! ... No, you see, this is what makes me think you don't really know everything you should. I'd been clean since I got pregnant.

HELEN: Not according to your mother.

DENISE: My mother yeah. See? I told you. We've got to investigate my mother's part in this. I think if you were to examine her in more detail you'd see—

HELEN: Your mother isn't an issue.

DENISE: Sure she is.

HELEN: No. No you're the issue. You're a drug addict and a prostitute who wants her daughter back and that makes you the only issue ...

DENISE: (up, moving around) I was never a prostitute. I turned a few tricks and even if I was a prostitute, who says a prostitute can't raise a child.

HELEN: I do.

DENISE: You do?

HELEN: Yes I do.

DENISE: Is that an official position there Helen.

HELEN: No.

DENISE: But it's your position.

HELEN: Yes.

DENISE: Is this getting personal here, Helen. It sounds like you take this personally.

HELEN: I want to talk about your new life, Denise. I've read the letters you've given me. I've made a few calls.

DENISE: I was a drug addict though. You were right about that. I mean I kind of messed around with drugs all through my teens. I stopped when I got pregnant. But when you took my baby away I became a drug addict. That's when I became a drug addict! For the fucking record! Okay!?

HELEN: So. What strikes me about your new life in this small town is that it's really not your life. It's R.J.'s. I mean all the reference letters are about him. He seems to have become a real member of that community. But there's no reference to you at all. What do you do up there, Denise.

DENISE: I stay at home and take drugs. Sometimes I go out and fuck people for money. The guy who runs the hardware store. The mayor. The Scoutmaster. I fuck them all!

HELEN: Do you think that smart-ass mouth is going to help you out here, Denise. Do you think you're going to impress me into giving you back your baby with that smart-ass talk? Come here and sit down.

DENISE: I feel better here.

HELEN: Come here!

DENISE sits … but not on the chair HELEN has pointed to.

DENISE: Okay?

HELEN: So? … What do you do. Look for work? Watch TV?

DENISE: I look for work.

HELEN: What kind. Waitressing?

DENISE: Yeah.

HELEN: What about at home. Do you cook?

DENISE: Cook?

HELEN: Meals. Do you cook meals for R.J. Do you cook his dinner when he comes home from work.

DENISE: Ah … no.

HELEN: No? Why not.

DENISE: He doesn't like my cooking. It's not very good. He cooks better.

HELEN: So he comes home, cooks his own dinner.

DENISE: And mine. He cooks for me too, Helen. I mean he doesn't just cook for himself. That would be cruel.

HELEN: Do you clean.

DENISE: Clean. You mean vacuum? I vacuum.

HELEN: How often.

DENISE: What? What is this crap.

HELEN: I notice R.J. joined a church last month. I guess he did that to impress us.

DENISE: Probably … But with R.J. you never know. It's possible he found God. Prison changed him. He discovered the TV talk shows in prison. Maybe he discovered God there too.

HELEN: I'm assuming he did it to impress us. That's okay. It's still a good thing no matter how you come to it.

DENISE: You think so? You think church is a big deal.

HELEN: It can be. You don't think so, though. I mean you wouldn't even make the effort to impress us, I mean let alone actually sincerely looking for some true religious experience—

DENISE: I'm getting a really uneasy feeling about you Helen.

HELEN: Oh really. Why? Do you think I might be questioning your values, Denise. Do you have values Denise. Do you know what values are Denise.

DENISE: This is personal isn't it, Helen.

HELEN: You want me to give you back the baby so you can hang out with her, Denise? Maybe take her to the mall? Train her to give you a hug when you're feeling low … Is that why you want the baby, Denise. You need a "friend"?

DENISE: I want her because she's ... mine!

HELEN: Well frankly I think she's better off where she is. She's in a real family.

DENISE: I want her!

HELEN: (standing) Well I don't think you're going to get her. I really don't.

DENISE leans over the table, grabbing HELEN's injured hand. HELEN yells.

DENISE: I want her! I want her!

HELEN: Let ... go of my hand. You're hurting me.

DENISE: You shouldn't have made it personal.

HELEN: Let go! (DENISE lets go.) Ah. It's really bleeding now.

HELEN goes into the bathroom.

DENISE: What gave you the right to make it personal.

DENISE goes to the bed. Takes the gun from under the mattress.

HELEN: (from bathroom) Ah, damn. It's bleeding pretty badly.

DENISE: I mean what kind of position does that put me in? You think I should go to church and become a better cook or I'll never see my kid again. What kind of shit is that.

HELEN: (from bathroom) Look. You better help me. I'm feeling a ... little ... light-headed ...

DENISE is staring at the gun. PHILLIE comes in, carrying a pile of towels.

PHILLIE: Oh. Sorry. Should have knocked. (hits himself on the head) Moron. Learn. Why can't you learn! You wanna lose this job? Do you? (hits himself again, looks at DENISE, smiles) I brought some fresh towels.

HELEN groans loudly in the bathroom. Passes out with much noise and spilling of things. PHILLIE looks toward the bathroom. DENISE stands. Puts the gun in her waistband. Walks over to PHILLIE. Takes the towels.

DENISE: Thanks.

DENISE and PHILLIE both look into the bathroom. DENISE looks at PHILLIE intently.

DENISE: What's your name again?

Blackout.

Scene Five

R.J. is on the phone and he is very upset.

R.J.: No I won't calm down. No ... No. I've had it. It's gross, man. It's fucking pathetic and gross. Are you watching this shit. Are you watching that big prick scream at his mother. You let some big piece of garbage come on national television and humiliate a helpless pensioner. Are you nuts. Are you people insane. No! Bullshit ... No! Fuck you. It's gotta be ... stopped ... Oh really ... Oh right ... No! No! Mothers Who Never Visited Their Sons in Prison is a fucking stupid idea for a show. Ah look at that. What's he gonna do? Hit her? Do you just let him hit her? Well it looks like he's gonna hit her ... I want the producer. Get me the producer! Get me the producer. I need to tell him something ... Get him. Get him! Get him! Get him!!

PHILLIE and DENISE come in. They are both a bit messed up. R.J. sees them.

R.J.: I'll call you back. (hangs up)

DENISE: Who was that.

R.J.: No one.

DENISE: You're losing it, right? You're flipping out.

R.J.: Come here. (points to TV) Look at that. Piece of shit! Piece of shit won't stop!! It's not her fucking fault he was doing eight to ten. (to TV) I mean a fucking reality check might be in order here, son. I didn't blame MY mother when I was inside. I mean I didn't even know anyone who blamed their mother. (to DENISE) I mean where did they dig this guy up ... Look at her face. Look at that poor woman's hurt and confused face. It's a crime. I can't believe they syndicate this shit.

DENISE: Do you mind if I turn it off.

R.J.: No. Please. Turn it off. I want you to turn it off. Do you think I like watching this stuff. It's fucking infuriating.

DENISE turns off the TV.

PHILLIE: It's the injustice that gets to him.

R.J.: Yeah ... yeah ...

DENISE has taken HELEN's briefcase from under the bed.

PHILLIE: Yeah ...

R.J.: You're both covered in mud ... or something.

DENISE: I'll explain later ... I've got to give Phillie something ...

R.J.: Whose briefcase is that. Is that whatshername's.

DENISE: In a minute, okay?

DENISE has taken an address book from the briefcase. Looks through it. Tears out a page. Hands it to PHILLIE.

DENISE: It's the one on top ... Do you know where that is.

PHILLIE: Yeah. It's on top ...

DENISE: But do you know ... where it is.

PHILLIE: It's on top ...

DENISE: But do you know how to find it.

PHILLIE: Yeah.

DENISE: Do you think you can do this.

PHILLIE: Do you.

DENISE: Yeah I think you can. But you have to be sure you want to ...

PHILLIE: I want to ...

DENISE: Okay then ... Go.

PHILLIE: Yeah. Okay ... I'm going. (*He starts off. Stops.*) I feel good.

DENISE: I'm glad.

PHILLIE nods. Leaves.

R.J.: What's going on. Where you been. Where's he going ... What's going on.

DENISE: Things got a bit weird when you were out before. I'm trying to think of how to explain this to you. Trying to think if maybe there's some TV show I can compare it to for you.

R.J.: Gimme a break.

DENISE: I don't know, man. Life is just crawling all over us here and you're putting all your energy into that crap you watch on that stupid box. So I'm wondering maybe you're not really capable of understanding what I have to tell you unless ... I don't know maybe I should go on TV and sit on one of those stupid chairs. Cry. And then you'll

see me and hear my story and your heart will go out to me and you'll understand. But if I just tell you how it happened and I'm just me and you're just you ... I don't know, I don't know ...

R.J.: How bad is this.

DENISE: She's dead.

R.J.: Who's dead.

DENISE: Helen.

R.J.: Helen? Helen the social worker?

DENISE: Yeah ... She's dead ... She fell down and hit her head against the toilet.

R.J.: The toilet ... Our toilet?

DENISE: Yeah ... the bowl ... you know.

R.J.: (*walks into the bathroom; walks out*) She's not in there.

DENISE: No. She's ... gone.

R.J.: I was afraid to look. I had my eyes closed. But when I opened them she wasn't there.

DENISE: Yeah.

R.J.: A lot of blood though.

DENISE: Yeah. Some of that's from her head. Some of it from when she cut her hand.

R.J.: She cut her hand?

DENISE: On a glass. I had nothing to do with that.

R.J.: Oh. Did you have anything to do with her hitting her head.

DENISE: Not directly. I think I sped up the flow of blood from her hand when I squeezed it and that might have made her woozy. I think that's what happened ...

R.J.: Why were you squeezing her hand.

DENISE: Look we gotta skip all that and get to the important thing. I didn't shoot her. I wanted to shoot her. I didn't. She told me we weren't getting our child back. She told me to basically forget it and I thought okay, I'll forget it. I'll put a bullet in you and then one in myself and it'll be forgotten. But I didn't. Of course maybe she made the decision for me by falling and hitting her head on the toilet bowl. But I don't think so. I think I'd already decided not to use the gun. To remain hopeful. I mean I can't be sure because the timing was … tight. But I think I'd already decided. And then Phillie was standing there with the towels and my mind started to race. You know how it races sometimes when I'm upset. Like that. But different. Because this time it was clear. My mind. It had purpose. So I knew the first thing I had to do. And I did it.

R.J.: You got rid of the body.

DENISE: No. I got Phillie on my side … I mean I had to … He was right there so I had to get him on my side. It wasn't hard really. Because really he's one of us …

R.J.: What's that mean, "one of us"?

DENISE: Scum of the earth. So he knows. He knows about getting screwed … Because it's just so easy to screw us, people can do it without even trying really.

R.J.: No. Justice.

DENISE: What.

R.J.: He's just got a thing about justice. He thinks it's something that's … forbidden or something.

DENISE: No. He knew her. He knew her type, that's all. I told him what she said to me. That I won't be getting the baby 'cause I don't go to church and I don't cook.

R.J.: She said that?

DENISE: Yeah she said that.

R.J.: She said "I'm sorry Denise but you can't have your child back because we've found out you're a lousy cook"?

DENISE: Yes! She said that! Exactly!

R.J.: And so you killed her!?

DENISE: I didn't kill her.

R.J.: No you didn't kill her. You thought about killing her with the gun you told me you didn't have but you didn't really kill her. Oh you squeezed her hand a little. But that was it. Come on, Denise. There's a lot of blood in that bathroom. A lot!

DENISE: I didn't kill her. I didn't kill her, I'm telling you!

R.J.: Good thing I didn't go in there unprepared. If I'd gone in there not knowing … All that blood.

Good thing I went right for the TV. I mean you're down on me watching television but it's a damn good thing I wanted to watch television instead of taking a piss, or I might be really fucked up now! Because I would've thought that was your blood. Your blood. And I would've thought you'd hurt yourself. Really bad … And I would have freaked … Okay. But that didn't happen. Something else happened. Let's try and stay with what really happened.

DENISE: Good idea …

R.J.: She died?

DENISE: Yeah.

R.J.: Accidentally.

DENISE: Ah … Yeah …

R.J.: You got Phillie on your side and he helped you get rid of the body.

DENISE: Yeah.

R.J.: Because you had to … because you couldn't call the goddamn police or a goddamn ambulance like most people … even though it was a fucking accident you had to get rid of the body. Sure. That makes sense! Oh my God. Oh my God what have you done. We could have appealed. She wasn't the only social worker in this city. We could have appealed. (grabs DENISE) You didn't have to kill her. Killing her was not the right thing to do.

DENISE: Listen to me!

R.J.: It was a bad idea! Bad bad bad—

DENISE: Listen to me. Listen!

R.J.: Bad!

DENISE: Listen! Listen it was over before she fell. We were finished as parents. Our life. Our future. Everything we wanted to do was over. She was going to make sure it wasn't going to happen. I didn't kill her. But … it would've maybe looked like I had … so we buried her …

R.J.: Where.

DENISE: Out back.

R.J.: We could've gotten a lawyer. We're trying to be the kind of people who get lawyers in circumstances like this, Denise.

DENISE: Please. No. No lawyers. No law. No official investigation. We're not going that route. It's not our route. Listen to me. We're doing it our way. The only way we've got … really.

R.J.: Where'd you send Phillie.

DENISE: She had their names in her address book. The foster parents …

R.J.: Ah no—

DENISE: He can do it.

R.J.: Ah. No he can't.

DENISE: I gave him the gun.

R.J.: You sent him to get our baby. And you gave him a gun?

DENISE: No bullets. Just the gun. Something to … produce if he meets resistance. I think it'll be okay. They don't know him. He'll just ring the door bell. They'd recognize me probably. She's probably described me to them. Thought I might pull something … So I couldn't do it myself … Because she prepared them.

R.J.: Are you nuts.

DENISE: What.

R.J.: (grabs her) Are you fucking nuts!?

DENISE: Yes! Yes I am. I'm out of my fucking mind. I want my baby. I can't sleep, I can't eat without her. I can't live without her. And I want her now! I want her. That's all I want. Just let me have her and it will be okay. I promise. Let this happen and it will be okay. Just … please let this happen! (buries her head in his chest) Please …

R.J. is staring off. Rubbing DENISE's back.

Blackout.

Scene Six

R.J. and DENISE are waiting for the phone to ring. He paces. She sits on the bed staring at the phone.

R.J.: He said he'd call? You're sure?

DENISE: Yeah.

R.J.: And you think he … understood.

DENISE: Yeah … Understood what?

R.J.: To call.

DENISE: I said "Call when you've got her."

R.J.: There could've been a problem.

DENISE: Yes … Lots of them.

R.J.: The chances are slim he got her out of there.

DENISE: I thought he could do it. I mean they're just a nice suburban couple. They're not the mob or anything. They're not protected. He shows up. Shows the gun if he has to … Says, "give me the kid" … They should cooperate … It's human nature to cooperate.

R.J.: Yeah? Would you give her over to someone.

DENISE: I did. Remember? People came into our apartment and I gave her to them. And they didn't have a fucking gun. They just had a piece of paper.

R.J.: Well we'll see … we'll see how reckless you've been. Why doesn't he call … Why … It's been enough time.

DENISE: Shit … Oh shit. (stands and heads for the door) There's no one in the office to put the call through.

R.J.: Is that how it works.

DENISE: Yes. That's how it fucking works.

She leaves, slamming the door behind her. R.J. paces awhile. Looks at TV. Paces. Goes to TV. Turns it on. Flips the channels. Flips. Flips. A knock on the door. R.J. goes to the door. Opens it. PHILLIE is standing there.

PHILLIE: I saw Denise leave. I've been waiting. Can I come in.

R.J.: Yeah come in. (pulls PHILLIE in) Have you got her?

PHILLIE: The baby?

R.J.: Yeah, the baby!

PHILLIE: No … no. I didn't do it. I mean I thought about doing it. But I couldn't. It was a wild idea. It was like an idea from my youth. In my youth I could've done it. I had guts then. But not now. I tried though. Got in the car. Headed in the right direction. Five or six blocks. But then I stopped. Reality stopped me. I mean what am I. I'm a drunk. I'm not a kidnapper. There's a difference.

R.J.: Yeah.

PHILLIE: You understand?

R.J.: Yeah.

PHILLIE: I mean I couldn't say this to Denise … She was wild. Intense and wild. You got anything to drink?

R.J.: No.

PHILLIE: Because I need a little something.

R.J.: I'm sorry.

PHILLIE: That's okay. Don't feel bad. I was telling you about Denise … She was wild. She was intense. (*hits himself*) Well which was it. Wild or intense? She couldn't be both … She was intense. Yeah. Focused. "Why are we burying this body?" I asked her. I mean she fell. I heard her. It was an accident. (*shrugs*) You use hair tonic? I could go in the bathroom and you wouldn't have to watch me drink or anything. I'd just go in there if that's where it is. Anyway I was telling you about Denise. What Denise said about the body was "I can't take any chances." … So what about that hair tonic … Aftershave …

R.J.: There's nothing like that in there.

PHILLIE: But I need something …

R.J.: You want me to go get you a bottle?

PHILLIE: You might have to … I mean I have to face Denise. I've let her down.

R.J.: It's okay.

PHILLIE: I don't think so. I don't think it's okay.

R.J.: Denise isn't … She's not thinking clearly.

PHILLIE: Yes. She is. She's trying to survive. Look, nothing I've said should be taken as criticism of Denise. She's just trying to … what's the word I'm looking for. Survive?

R.J.: Yeah but she's … Look we've got to go dig up that body … Call the police. Get it straight.

PHILLIE: Dig up the body?

R.J.: Yeah.

PHILLIE: Tell the police?

R.J.: Yeah.

PHILLIE: Tell the police what? We buried a body. But now we think that was unwise.

R.J.: Well it was unwise. It was really really … unwise. Why didn't you call the police.

PHILLIE: Denise couldn't take a chance. That's what she said. They come in. They see the situation. They find out the social worker was going to make a bad report about her. They make Denise a suspect. She couldn't let that happen. She couldn't. Don't you know that, man. God are you her husband or not. Can't you see she's right! Denise was doing it right, man. She's gotta get that baby. And the two of you gotta take that baby and disappear. And make a great life. That's the only way for justice to be served. Okay I'm goin'. I'm going this time for sure.

R.J.: Where.

PHILLIE: To get the baby.

R.J.: No, no. No! (*grabs PHILLIE*)

PHILLIE: No listen. It's okay. I can do it. I'm worked up. I can do it.

R.J.: No I don't want you to do it.

PHILLIE: But if I do it, I'll feel better about myself. I think it's something I could take pride in.

R.J.: Someone could get hurt.

PHILLIE: It'll be all right. I'll get her. Don't you want her. She's your baby too. Don't you want her.

R.J.: Yes. Yes I want her. But not like this. I want her in a way that'll be okay …

PHILLIE: That can't happen. Nothing is ever going to be truly okay again. Everything is wrong. Everything in the world is wrong. There is no justice. Not really. There's only grab and run! … Everyone for themselves. I gotta do this.

R.J.: I can't let you.

PHILLIE: Look. I gotta. (*pulls the gun from his pocket*) I'm sorry. But I'm doing this so stay back.

R.J.: That isn't loaded.

PHILLIE: (*fires a shot into the floor*) What gave you that idea.

PHILLIE runs out of the room. R.J. is about to follow when the phone rings. He runs over. Answers it.

R.J.: (*into phone*) Yeah … yeah speaking … Yeah. Really. How'd you get my number … I did?

Oh yeah, right—Yeah … yeah well it was about that Mothers Who Didn't Visit Their Sons In Prison show. I mean don't you think you went a bit too far with that one. There was real pain on that woman's face. She didn't need … Well sure she has free will but do you think she expected to be treated like that by her own son. I mean—

DENISE bursts through the door.

DENISE: Jesus Christ! What is wrong with you!? (*She rushes over. Grabs the phone. Hangs up.*) I mean you left your number with the network? I put the call through because at first I thought … then I thought what the hell was that. Is that all you've got on your mind considering the circumstances of our life right now.

R.J.: I made the call earlier. Things were okay when I made the call.

DENISE: You made the call six months ago? 'Cause that's the last time I remember things being okay.

R.J.: No I made the call before you killed the social worker.

DENISE: Look for the last time. I didn't kill the social worker. I just buried the social worker.

R.J.: You know what though … It's gonna turn out to be the same thing. I think it's gonna have basically the same impact on our lives as if you'd killed her. So let's just say you did. Okay!?

DENISE: Why? Because it'll sound better on TV? You thinking ahead 'til when we're invited on one of those shows. Look I can't talk to you anymore. I'm waiting for Phillie's call.

R.J.: He's not calling.

DENISE: He'll call. Have faith.

R.J.: He was here.

DENISE: When.

R.J.: Just now.

DENISE: Did he have Christine.

R.J.: No he couldn't do it.

DENISE: Shit … Shit … Okay okay, we'll have to do it … We'll go get her ourselves. Come on.

R.J.: No he's doing it.

DENISE: You just said he wasn't doing it.

R.J.: He changed his mind. He went to do it. He's … doing it.

DENISE: He changed his mind?

R.J.: He convinced himself. It's something he has to do. He says it'll make him feel better.

DENISE: It will … It'll be an accomplishment.

R.J.: He's got a gun.

DENISE: I know.

R.J.: It's loaded.

DENISE: So?

R.J.: You told me it wasn't.

DENISE: I did?

R.J.: Suppose he hurts someone.

DENISE: It's a risk worth taking. Hey R.J. it's our life we're talking about here. (*R.J. goes to the phone.*) What are you doing.

R.J.: I have to call that TV guy back.

DENISE: You're kidding.

R.J.: You hung up on him. He took the time to call me and you hung up on him … He might never take the time to call anyone again. That would be a shame. Because improvements can be made in how things are done and he's in a position to make them … Probably all he needs is encouragement … and, you know … input.

DENISE: You're too much.

R.J.: So are you, Denise. So are you.

He dials the phone. Blackout.

Scene Seven

R.J. and DENISE are near the bathroom door. Looking tense. The door is closed and someone is having a shower. DENISE becomes exasperated, throws her arms in the air and begins to pace. R.J. puts his head against the bathroom door. Listens. The water stops running. R.J. gestures to DENISE. She stops pacing. They wait. Suddenly the bathroom door is opened. Steam pours into the room. They wait.

HELEN comes out of the bathroom. Wet hair. Wearing one of R.J.'s shirts.

HELEN: That feels better … A lot better. (*to R.J.*) Thanks for the shirt.

R.J. nods. HELEN looks at herself in the wall mirror. Touches her forehead.

HELEN: Nasty little bump. (*to DENISE*) Do you have a brush I could borrow.

DENISE gets a brush from the bedside table. Takes it to HELEN.

HELEN: Thanks … I said thanks.

DENISE: You're … welcome.

HELEN sits at the table. Begins to brush her hair.

HELEN: (*brushing*) It's important to be polite … Politeness is a cornerstone of civilized behaviour. I guess no one ever taught you that … That's just one of the things you weren't taught … Politeness. Moderation … Reasonable behaviour. I don't think people know these things intuitively. They have to be taught. So as I was lying in that mud under that pile of leaves and debris under that billboard out back afraid to move, not knowing if I were paralyzed, how seriously injured I was—I thought about your lack of education. Why didn't Denise call for help. Why has she taken the criminal route in this. Why hasn't she taken the reasonable moderate—yes, even polite approach and called an ambulance. And then of course I remembered all my training and everything I've been taught about people like you and I decided you just don't know any better.

R.J.: Are you going to call the police.

HELEN: (*brushing*) I don't know yet. Probably. I mean it is the reasonable thing to do. I was just buried alive.

R.J.: You see, what happened was, she panicked.

HELEN: I was buried alive! I had to claw my way up through garbage and leafy smelly muddy things because I was buried alive in a deep hole.

DENISE: (*to herself*) Not deep enough.

HELEN: I heard that.

R.J.: She didn't mean it.

HELEN: Oh she meant it.

R.J.: (*to DENISE*) Tell her you didn't mean it.

DENISE: (*to HELEN*) I didn't mean it.

HELEN: Yes you did! You meant it. What's wrong with you. Don't you have any civilized instincts left in you. Have they all been dulled or killed by your senseless self-indulgent lifestyle.

DENISE: Look I'm sorry. Don't start … with that judgement crap. I can't take it.

HELEN: Well look who's going on the offensive. I mean talk about inappropriate responses. I mean who buried who alive.

DENISE: It wasn't personal. Why are you always making it personal. I didn't do it to punish you. I thought you were dead. I was just—

R.J.: She panicked.

DENISE: I didn't panic. I thought it through. I was taking precautions. I did what I thought I had to do … so we could get on with our life.

HELEN: (*standing*) You're a bad girl, Denise. That's all you are. Someone should have just told you this a long time ago. You're a very bad girl.

DENISE: Ah shut up.

HELEN: I won't shut up! (*rubs her head*) I have a job here. I'm a representative of our government. And what government represents to me is the people's will to have a civilized society. And what that means is dealing with people like you and getting you back in line. You're out of line, Denise. Way out of line! (*rubs her head; wobbles*) Oooh. I have to sit down. (*sits*)

R.J.: Are you all right.

HELEN: No. I have a serious concussion. And I was buried alive. I'm not all right … Did you call a doctor as I asked, Denise.

DENISE: Yes.

HELEN: Did you.

DENISE: Yes!

HELEN: Did you really!?

DENISE: No! No I didn't!

HELEN: No you didn't! Couldn't you see I was maybe giving you a second chance to do the right thing. Why didn't you call a doctor, Denise. It would have been the right thing for you to do … So why didn't you do it?

DENISE: Because! … I needed to know if you were going to tell the police.

HELEN: Protecting yourself.

DENISE: Yes.

HELEN: At any cost.

DENISE: Yes.

HELEN: Bad bad girl! Bad girl! Wicked girl!

DENISE: Oh please shut up. (*to R.J.*) Make her shut up.

R.J.: How.

DENISE: Any way you can.

HELEN: Don't get him to do your dirty work. Maybe it's time you stopped dragging him down, Denise. He's trying to do better things with his life. Why don't you let him do them ... these better things.

DENISE: (*to R.J.*) She's impressed with you because you joined the church.

HELEN: Or maybe I'm impressed because he doesn't bury people alive!

R.J.: (*to HELEN*) The church thing. I just did it to make points with you people ... It's not real.

HELEN: It could be, R.J. Just open up your heart. I know you want to. I know you've got the ... right things in you.

DENISE: (*to R.J.*) I told her you could cook. She thought that was great. Well she thought it was sad you had to cook your own supper after working hard all day. She thought I was some demon bitch for making you do that. But the fact that you could cook, she thought that was cool.

R.J.: (*to HELEN*) I like to cook.

HELEN: I'm sure you do. The desire to cook. To serve. To nurture. These are good things. The things civilized people feel.

R.J.: Denise has been sick. Really sick. Sick about losing the baby.

HELEN: That's not an excuse.

R.J.: Yes it is.

HELEN: Not enough of an excuse.

R.J.: Yes it is. Losing the baby made her life ... made her feel her life was ... didn't have any value. And she hated herself ... She'd cry all night. Night after night for weeks and months.

DENISE: No, no I don't want you telling her this stuff.

R.J.: She should know. She thinks you're just some punk kid who—

DENISE: (*to R.J.*) No no listen. I don't want to ... it's not what I'm worried about, what she thinks of me. (*to HELEN*) I just want to know if you're going to tell the police.

HELEN: I ... don't know.

DENISE: When *will* you know.

HELEN: I don't know when I'll know! I mean I'm trained, you know. Trained to think things through ... Act in the best interests of people. The people in this instance are your child, R.J. here and even you, Denise. I have to weigh intent with possibility. And possibility with harsh reality.

DENISE: I don't know what you're talking about.

HELEN: Is it better if I just let this pass. Or is it better for everyone if you're put away! I have to think about these things ... And then of course there's the issue of ... compassion ... I am a Christian. I believe in Christian things.

R.J.: That's ... good ... I don't know much about it ... I mean I just started to learn and I wasn't paying a lot of attention. But I got the general feeling it was a good thing to be ... a Christian.

DENISE: Oh please ... I just want to know what she's going to do ... Maybe you can ask her. Christian to Christian. I'm tired. (*sits on the bed*)

HELEN: (*to R.J.*) Can you get my briefcase. All my muddy clothes are on the bathroom floor. Can you stuff them all in my briefcase. Can you take a twenty dollar bill out of my wallet. And put it in my hand. Can you take me and my possessions to the street and hail a cab for me. Can you get started on those things now.

R.J.: Yeah ... yeah. (*goes about his tasks*)

HELEN: Good ... because I think I need to have an x-ray. I feel that would be the best thing for me to do right now. Go to the hospital and get an x-ray.

R.J.: (*from bathroom*) I'm coming. I'm coming.

HELEN: Good ... Denise?

DENISE: What.

HELEN: Stay put ... I'll let you know what I decide.

DENISE: Sure.

HELEN: I mean the chances of you getting your child back now are slim. Very slim.

DENISE: Right.

HELEN: I mean you have really messed up ... But we'll see ... I've reclaimed worse people than you ... I have ... I'm trained ... And it's ... possible ... We'll have to meet ... and meet again.

DENISE: Here?

HELEN: Here or in prison ... Wherever. We'll see ...

R.J.: (*comes out of the bathroom*) Okay ... Ready?

PHILLIE walks by the window. Sees HELEN.

HELEN: I need some help.

R.J.: Okay.

He helps her up. They start off, HELEN holding R.J. for support. They are leaving.

HELEN: Denise?

DENISE: What.

HELEN: Remember. Hang in.

DENISE: Sure ...

HELEN: But stay put.

They are gone. DENISE goes into the bathroom. Runs water. Comes out drying her face vigorously. PHILLIE comes in.

PHILLIE: Wow. That was weird. Good thing I looked through the window before coming in. So ... she's alive. Well I guess that's better in the long run.

DENISE: I don't know. How did you get on.

PHILLIE: Did you talk to R.J. ... You know I didn't go the first time?

DENISE: Yeah ... But you went back ... So?

PHILLIE: I got up to the front porch ... I looked in the window. I saw her.

DENISE: You saw her? Really?

PHILLIE: Yeah. She looks like you. She's cute. She was playing with blocks. Blue and red and orange blocks. She looked ... happy ... I couldn't go in. I would've scared her.

DENISE: Yeah.

PHILLIE: We've got to think of a way that won't scare her.

DENISE: Yeah ...

PHILLIE: I'll be in touch ... ah ... Wednesday ... Wednesdays are my best days ... So ... we'll talk ... I mean I'm committed to this project. I think it's good ... I feel good about it.

DENISE: I'm glad.

PHILLIE: See ya.

DENISE: Yeah.

She closes the window. PHILLIE disappears. R.J. comes back in. DENISE just leans against a wall.

R.J.: I think she's bleeding internally.

DENISE: Really.

R.J.: I mean her eyes are bloodshot ... If that's a sign ... I don't know for sure.

DENISE: Me neither.

R.J.: So ... what do you think's gonna happen.

DENISE: I don't know.

R.J.: I mean should we stay here. Should we go back home. Should we go on the run. (*DENISE shrugs.*) I mean if Phillie grabs Christine we can just take off like you said ... I'm up for that if we have to ...

DENISE: I wouldn't count on that happening.

R.J.: No?

DENISE: No.

R.J.: You know something I don't?

DENISE: Yeah.

R.J.: You wanna tell me what it is?

DENISE: No. Not really ... No point ... Later maybe ...

R.J.: So ... (*shrugs*) so ...

The phone rings. R.J. looks at DENISE but she seems far away so he goes to the phone. Picks it up.

R.J.:   Hello ... Yeah hi Phillie ... Oh ... wait a sec. (*covers the receiver*) It's that guy from the television network. Can I talk to him. Will it piss you off.

DENISE looks at R.J. for a long time.

DENISE: (*shaking her head*) Go ahead.

R.J.:   Thanks ... (*into phone*) Put him through, Phillie.

R.J. smiles at DENISE. DENISE smiles sadly at R.J.

There is a lighting change. DENISE is alone in a light. Everything else is in darkness or shadow. And DENISE is talking to us.

DENISE: We stayed in that motel room for six months. We hardly left. R.J. watched his shows and took a lot of calls from network executives. They seemed to think he had some special understanding of what their shows were trying to do and they called him to ask for his advice. He'd suggest ideas and plead with them for a more human handling of their guests. He spent a lot of time explaining to these shows how it wasn't necessary to treat people like shit just to boost their ratings. And he told me he had a feeling that gradually they were coming around to his way of thinking. Phillie made a few more feeble attempts to grab Christine ... Once he made it as far as her bedroom. But she was asleep. And he didn't want to wake her up ... Anyway he was crying so hard he could barely see. Because the book she had open on her sleeping body was the same book his Aunt Jennie used to read to him when he was about Christine's age. And his Aunt Jennie was the only person other than his cousin Edward who ever treated him with justice and a fair heart ... Helen spent seven weeks in the hospital recovering from a ... subdural hematoma ... She called me from the hospital daily ... And continues to do so. Asking me questions and counselling me about moderate civilized behaviour. And I have learned to listen patiently and sigh pleasantly like I agree and like I am truly trying to change ... But I'm not agreeing with her or even thinking about what she's saying any more than I'm listening to R.J. on the phone with his TV people or even when I'm watching those shows with R.J. and listening to those sad, desperate people and all those experts telling them how to live better and everything else and blah, blah, blah ... I'm not really listening ... Because I'm not really there. I'm in hell. I'm more desperate than anybody I ever hear on those shows and I'm trapped in a sadness and an anger so deep I know I'll never get out. Because I'm just slipping deeper into the sadness. And deeper into the anger ... I have horrible thoughts about doing horrible things to people. If I were on one of those shows and I told people how I really felt and what I really wanted to do ... they wouldn't be able to give me any advice ... They wouldn't even be able to talk ... Maybe they'd just cancel the fucking show ... If I leaned over in bed and told R.J. what I felt about everything ... about life ... about our life and everyone else's life and how really useless and stupid it all is ... he'd die probably. He'd give up and die ... So I don't tell him. I tell him I'm waiting. I'm being a good girl. Seeing if things work out. I tell him maybe there's still a chance we'll get Christine ... But I know ... things don't work out ... Not for people like us. They just get worse ... until ... well you can't take it anymore ... Then you really do get bad ... Helen thinks she knows how bad I am. She probably thinks she knows how sad I am and how angry I am too. She's wrong ... She hasn't got a clue ... She might find out though ... Maybe I'll just ... come up with a way of letting her know ...

DENISE shrugs. Lights up on R.J. watching TV. Smiling. DENISE shakes her head sadly.

DENISE: You okay, R.J.?

R.J.:   Yeah. How about you. Still with me? Still hangin' in?

DENISE: Yeah.

R.J.:   Thata girl.

DENISE smiles.

Blackout.

END

A SELECTIVE BIBLIOGRAPHY OF SOURCE MATERIAL

I. Selected Websites

The CanDrama Home Page provides an index of all the most useful links and sites: www.unb.ca/web/english/candrama

John Ball and Richard Plant's *Bibliography of Theatre History in Canada: The Beginnings Through 1984*: www.lib.unb.ca/Texts/Theatre/ Bib/Search

The Canadian Theatre Encyclopedia: www.canadiantheatre.com

For recent reviews of Canadian plays in production: www.canoe.ca/TheatreReviews

II. Backgrounds, Surveys and General Studies

Anthony, Geraldine, ed. *Stage Voices: Twelve Canadian Playwrights Talk about Their Lives and Work*. Toronto: Doubleday, 1978.

Benson, Eugene, and L.W. Conolly. *English Canadian Theatre*. Toronto: Oxford Univ. Press, 1987.

———, eds. *The Oxford Companion to Canadian Theatre*. Toronto: Oxford Univ. Press, 1989.

Bessai, Diane. *Playwrights of Collective Creation*. Toronto: Simon & Pierre, 1992.

Boni, Franco, ed. *Rhubarb-o-rama! Plays and Playwrights from the Rhubarb! Festival*. Winnipeg: Blizzard, 1998.

Brask, Per, ed. *Contemporary Issues in Canadian Drama*. Winnipeg: Blizzard, 1995.

Brisset, Annie. *A Sociocritique of Translation: Theatre and Alterity in Quebec, 1968–1988*. Trans. Rosalind Gill and Roger Gannon. Toronto: Univ. of Toronto Press, 1996.

Brookes, Chris. *A Public Nuisance: A History of the Mummers Troupe*. St. John's: Institute of Social and Economic Research, Memorial Univ. of Newfoundland, 1988.

Canada on Stage: Canadian Theatre Review Yearbook. Ed. Don Rubin. Toronto: CTR Publications, 1974–88.

"Canadian Theatre Before the 60s." Special Issue. *Canadian Theatre Review* 5 (Winter 1975).

Canadian Writers Since 1960, 1st and 2nd ser. In *Dictionary of Literary Biography*. Ed. W.H. New. Vols. 53 and 60. Detroit: Gale Research, 1986–87.

Carson, Neil. *Harlequin in Hogtown: George Luscombe and Toronto Workshop Productions*. Toronto: Univ. of Toronto Press, 1995.

Conolly, L.W., ed. *Canadian Drama and the Critics*. Rev. ed. Vancouver: Talonbooks, 1995.

"Contemporary Drama." Special Issue of *Canadian Literature* 118 (Autumn 1988).

Donohoe, Joseph I., Jr. and Jonathan M. Weiss, eds. *Essays on Modern Quebec Theatre*. East Lansing: Michigan State UP, 1995.

Drainie, Bronwyn. *Living the Part: John Drainie and the Dilemma of Canadian Stardom*. Toronto: Macmillan, 1988.

Filewod, Alan. *Collective Encounters: Documentary Theatre in English Canada*. Toronto: Univ. of Toronto Press, 1987.

Fink, Howard, and John Jackson, eds. *All the Bright Company: Radio Drama Produced by Andrew Allan*. Kingston and Toronto: Quarry/CBC Enterprises, 1987.

Frick, Alice. *Image in the Mind: CBC Radio Drama, 1944–1954*. Toronto: Canadian Stage and Arts Publications, 1987.

Garebian, Keith. *A Well-Bred Muse: Selected Theatre Writings, 1978–1988*. Oakville, Ont.: Mosaic Press, 1991.

———, ed. *William Hutt: Masks and Faces*. Oakville: Mosaic, 1995.

Gilbert, Helen and Joanne Tompkins. *Post-Colonial Drama: Theory, Practice, Politics*. London: Routledge, 1996.

Glaap, Albert-Reiner with Rolf Althorp, ed. *On-Stage and Off-Stage: English Canadian Drama in Discourse*. St. John's: Breakwater, 1996.

Goldie, Terry. *Fear and Temptation: The Image of the Indigene in Canadian, Australian, and New Zealand Literatures*, Chap. 9. Kingston and Montreal: McGill-Queen's Univ. Press, 1989.

Grace, Sherrill, Eve D'Aeth and Lisa Chalykoff, eds. *Staging the North: Twelve Canadian Plays*. Toronto: Playwrights Canada Press, 1999.

Green, Lynda Mason and Tedde Moore, eds. *Standing Naked in the Wings: Anecdotes from Canadian Actors.* Toronto: Oxford Univ. Press, 1997.

Henighan, Tom. "Theatre: From Kitchen-Sink to Mega-Musical." In *Ideas of North: A Guide to Canadian Arts and Culture,* 41–74. Vancouver: Raincoast, 1997.

Hochbruck, Wolfgang and James O. Taylor, eds. *Down East: Critical Essays on Contemporary Maritime Canadian Literature.* Trier: Wissenschaftlicher Verlag Trier, 1996.

Hodkinson, Yvonne. *Female Parts: The Art and Politics of Female Playwrights.* Montreal: Black Rose, 1991.

Johnston, Denis. *Up the Mainstream: The Rise of Toronto's Alternative Theatres.* Toronto: Univ. of Toronto Press, 1991.

King, Bruce, ed. *Post-Colonial English Drama: Commonwealth Drama since 1960.* NY: St. Martin's, 1992.

Knowles, Richard Paul. *The Theatre of Form and the Production of Meaning: Contemporary Canadian Dramaturgies.* Toronto: ECW, 1999.

Lecker, Robert, ed. *Canadian Canons: Essays in Literary Value.* Toronto: Univ. of Toronto Press, 1991.

Miller, Mary Jane. *Turn Up the Contrast: CBC Television Drama Since 1952.* Vancouver: UBC Press, 1987.

Moore, Mavor. *4 Canadian Playwrights.* Toronto: Holt, Rinehart, 1973.

———. *Reinventing Myself: Memoirs.* Toronto: Stoddart, 1994.

Much, Rita, ed. *Women on the Canadian Stage: The Legacy of Hrotsvit.* Winnipeg: Blizzard, 1992.

Nardocchio, Elaine. *Theatre and Politics in Modern Quebec.* Edmonton: Univ. of Alberta Press, 1986.

New, William H., ed. *Dramatists in Canada: Selected Essays.* Vancouver: UBC Press, 1972.

Parker, Brian. "Is There a Canadian Drama?" In *The Canadian Imagination: Dimensions of a Literary Culture.* Ed. David Staines, 152–87. Cambridge, Mass.: Harvard Univ. Press, 1977.

———, and Cynthia Zimmerman. "Theatre and Drama [1972–84]." In *Literary History of Canada: Canadian Literature in English.* Ed. W.H. New. 2nd ed. Vol. 4, 186–216. Toronto: Univ. of Toronto Press, 1990.

Patterson, Tom, and Allan Gould. *First Stage: The Making of the Stratford Festival.* Toronto: McClelland and Stewart, 1987.

Perkyns, Richard, ed. *Major Plays of the Canadian Theatre, 1934–1984.* Toronto: Irwin, 1984.

———. *The Neptune Story: Twenty-Five Years in the Life of a Leading Canadian Theatre.* Hantsport, N.S.: Lancelot, 1989.

Pettigrew, John, and Jamie Portman. *Stratford: The First Thirty Years.* 2 vols. Toronto: Macmillan, 1985.

Podbrey, Maurice. *Half Man, Half Beast: Making a Life in Canadian Theatre.* Montreal: Véhicule, 1997.

Profiles in Canadian Literature, ser. 4–8. Ed. Jeffrey M. Heath. Toronto: Dundurn Press, 1982–91.

Ripley, John. "Drama and Theatre, 1960–73." In *Literary History of Canada.* Ed. Carl F. Klinck. 2nd ed. Vol. 4, 212–32. Toronto: Univ. of Toronto Press, 1976.

Rubin, Don, ed. *Canadian Theatre History: Selected Readings.* Toronto: Copp Clark, 1996.

———. "Creeping Toward a Culture: The Theatre in English Canada since 1945." *Canadian Theatre Review* 1 (Winter 1974): 6–21.

———, and Alison Cranmer-Byng, eds. *Canada's Playwrights: A Biographical Guide.* Toronto: CTR Publications, 1980.

Rudakoff, Judith, ed. *Dangerous Traditions: A Passe Muraille Anthology.* Winnipeg: Blizzard, 1992.

———, ed. *Questionable Activities: Canadian Theatre Artists Interviewed by Canadian Theatre Students.* 2 vols. Toronto: Playwrights Union of Canada, 1997.

———, and Rita Much. *Fair Play: 12 Women Speak: Conversations with Canadian Playwrights.* Toronto: Simon & Pierre, 1990.

Ryan, Toby Gordon. *Stage Left: Canadian Theatre in the Thirties.* Toronto: CTR Publications, 1981.

Saddlemyer, Ann and Richard Plant, eds. *Later Stages: Essays in Ontario Theatre from the First World War to the 1970s.* Toronto: Univ. of Toronto Press, 1997.

Stuart, E. Ross. *The History of the Prairie Theatre*. Toronto: Simon & Pierre, 1984.

Tait, Michael. "Drama and Theatre, 1920–1960." In *Literary History of Canada*. Ed. Carl F. Klinck. 2nd ed. Vol. 2, 143–67. Toronto: Univ. of Toronto Press, 1976.

Theatre Memoirs: On the Occasion of the Canadian Theatre Conference. Toronto: Playwrights Union of Canada, 1998.

Tompkins, Joanne, ed. *Theatre and the Canadian Imaginary*. Special Issue of *Australasian Drama Studies* 29 (October 1996).

Usmiani, Renate. *Second Stage: The Alternative Theatre Movement in Canada*. Vancouver: UBC Press, 1983.

Vogt, Gordon. *Critical Stages: Canadian Theatre in Crisis*. Ottawa: Oberon, 1998.

Wagner, Anton, ed. *Contemporary Canadian Theatre: New World Visions*. Toronto: Simon & Pierre, 1985.

———. "The Developing Mosaic: English-Canadian Drama to Mid-Century," In *Canada's Lost Plays*. Vol. 3, 4–39. Toronto: CTR Publications, 1980.

———, ed. *Establishing Our Boundaries: English-Canadian Theatre Criticism*. Toronto: Univ. of Toronto Press, 1999.

Wallace, Robert. *Producing Marginality: Theatre and Criticism in Canada*. Saskatoon: Fifth House, 1990.

———, ed. *Making, Out: Plays by Gay Men*. Toronto: Coach House, 1992.

———, and Cynthia Zimmerman, eds. *The Work: Conversations with English-Canadian Playwrights*. Toronto: Coach House, 1982.

Wasserman, Jerry, ed. *Twenty Years at Play: A New Play Centre Anthology*. Vancouver: Talonbooks, 1990.

Weiss, Jonathan M. *French-Canadian Theater*. Boston: Twayne, 1986.

Whittaker, Herbert. *Whittaker's Theatre: A Critic Looks at Stages in Canada and Thereabouts, 1944–1975*. Ed. Ronald Bryden with Boyd Neil. Greenbank, Ont.: The Whittaker Project, 1985.

Zimmerman, Cynthia. *Playwriting Women: Female Voices in English Canada*. Toronto: Simon & Pierre, 1994.

III. Individual Plays and Playwrights

Note: Wherever a book in this section has already appeared as an entry in Part II (Backgrounds, Surveys and General Studies), I have used the short form here. *Canadian Theatre Review* is indicated by *CTR*; *Dictionary of Literary Biography* is *DLB*; *English-Canadian Theatre* is *ECT*.

MICHEL MARC BOUCHARD

A. BIOGRAPHY AND CRITICISM

Graefe, Sara. "Reviving and Revising the Past: The Search for Present Meaning in Michel Marc Bouchard's *Lilies, or the Revival of a Romantic Drama*." *Theatre Research in Canada* 14.2 (Fall 1993): 165–77.

Mainguy, Barbara. "*Lilies*: The Adaptation of Michel Marc Bouchard's Award-Winning Play." *Point of View* 30 (Fall 1996): 35–39.

Moss, Jane. "Sexual Games: Hypertheatricality and Homosexuality in Recent Quebec Plays." *American Review of Canadian Studies* 17.3 (1987): 287–96.

Teissier, Guy. "A Theatre of 'La Répétition.'" In *Essays on Modern Quebec Theater*. Ed. Joseph I. Donohoe, Jr. and Jonathan M. Weiss. 165–82.

Wallace, Robert. "Homo Creation: Towards a Poetics of Gay Male Theatre." *Essays on Canadian Writing* 54 (Winter 1994): 212–36.

B. **THE ORPHAN MUSES**: SELECTED REVIEWS

Bonham, R.A. "*The Orphan Muses*." *CTR* 86 (Spring 1996): 63.

Chapman, Geoff. "Parental Play Needs Nurturing." *Toronto Star*, 16 January 1998, E11.

Conlogue, Ray. "A Memorable Reunion of Damaged Siblings." *Globe and Mail*, 28 November 1994, C1.

Crook, Barbara. "Vancouver Production of a Quebec Play Shows a Universal Symbol For Survival." *Vancouver Sun*, 11 March 1996, B6.

Donnelly, Pat. "Dysfunctional Family, Quebec-Style, Makes for Fine Drama." *Montreal Gazette*, 21 September 1995, C7.

———. "Give *Orphan Muses* a Chance." *Montreal Gazette*, 25 October 1997, C2.

Kennedy, Janice. "Complex *Orphan Muses* Rich, Rewarding Triumph." *Ottawa Citizen*, 22 October 1999, E1.

Morrow, Martin. "Oddball Family Drama Lacks Pathos, Depth." *Calgary Herald*, 25 October 1997, J7.

Taylor, Kate. "Director's Wisdom Coaxes the Muse from these Orphans." *Globe and Mail*, 16 January 1998, C9.

———. "Tricky Script about a Family Tragedy." *Globe and Mail*, 25 October 1996, C9.

SALLY CLARK

A. BIOGRAPHY AND CRITICISM

Clark, Sally. "Preface/Introduction to 'Ten Ways to Abuse an Old Woman.'" *Windsor Review* 30 (Spring 1997): 23–25.

Conlogue, Ray. "'I Hate Political Correctness.'" *Globe and Mail*, 21 October 1989, C1, C3.

Godard, Barbara. "(Re)Appropriation as Translation." *CTR* 64 (Fall 1990): 22–31.

Kirchhoff, H.J. "The Trials—and Plays—of Sally Clark." *Globe and Mail*, 8 August 1991, A10.

Rudakoff, Judith. "Under the Goddess's Cloak: reCalling the Wild, enGendering the Power." In *Women on the Canadian Stage*. Ed. Rita Much. 115–30.

———, and Rita Much, eds. *Fair Play*. 74–86.

Wagner, Vit. "Painter-Turned-Playwright Trying to Portray Heroines Warts and All." *Toronto Star*, 13 January 1989, E17.

B. **MOO**: SELECTED REVIEWS

Bolt, Carol. "Rotters and Cads." *Books in Canada* 19 (March 1990): 37–38.

Conlogue, Ray. "Theatrical Torchbearers." *Globe and Mail*, 23 February 1988, A20.

———. "Moo Gets Her Man and Tickles Our Funnybone." *Globe and Mail*, 16 January 1989, C9.

Crew, Robert. "*Moo* Puts Humorous Bite on Snatches of Family Life." *Toronto Star*, 15 January 1989, C2.

Doolittle, Joyce. "Olympic Arts Festival, Theatre." *NeWest Review* 13 (April 1988):12.

Gilbert, Reid. "*Moo*." *CTR* 63 (Summer 1990): 72–74.

Hunt, Nigel. "The Short Straight Jacket." *Fuse* 12 (August 1989): 46–47.

Morrow, Martin. "Miscasting Undermines Tale of Obsessive Love." *Calgary Herald*, 5 February 1988, E12.

Wasserman, Jerry. "Drama." *University of Toronto Quarterly* 60 (Fall 1990): 66.

———. "Survival Stories." *Canadian Literature* 130 (Autumn 1991): 168–69.

Wilson, Peter. "One-Act Play Didn't Need Extra Hour." *Vancouver Sun*, 4 February 1988, D6.

TOMSON HIGHWAY

A. BIOGRAPHY AND CRITICISM

Alexie, Sherman. "Spokane Voices: Tomson Highway Raps with Sherman Alexie." *Aboriginal Voices* 4 (January-March 1997): 36–41.

Baker, Marie Annharte. "Angry Enough to Spit But with Dry Lips It Hurts More Than You Know." *CTR* 68 (Fall 1991): 88–89.

Bennett, Susan. "Who Speaks? Representations of Native Women in Some Canadian Plays." *Canadian Journal of Drama and Theatre* 1.2 (1991): 13–25.

Burnham, Clint. "Lips, Marks, Lapse: Materialism and Dialogism in Tomson Highway's *Dry Lips Oughta Move to Kapuskasing*." *Open Letter* 8 (Summer 1994): 19–30.

Davison, Carol Margaret. "The Matrix Interview: Tomson Highway." *Matrix* 46 (1995): 2–7.

Enright, Robert. "Let Us Now Combine Mythologies: The Theatrical Art of Tomson Highway." *Border Crossings* 11 (1992): 22–27.

Ferguson, Ted. "Native Son." *Imperial Oil Review* 73 (Winter 1989): 18–23.

Filewod, Alan. "Averting the Colonial Gaze: Notes on Watching Native Theater." In *Aboriginal Voices: Amerindian, Inuit and Sami Theater*. Ed. Per Brask and William Morgan. Baltimore: Johns Hopkins Univ. Press, 1992. 17–28.

———. "Receiving Aboriginality: Tomson Highway and the Crisis of Cultural Authenticity." *Theatre Journal* 46 (October 1994): 363–73.

Grant, Agnes. "Canadian Native Literature: The Drama of George Ryga and Tomson Highway." *Australian-Canadian Studies* 10.2 (1992): 37–56.

Hannon, Gerald. "Tomson and the Trickster." *Toronto Life* (March 1991): 28–31, 35–44, 81–85.

Highway, Tomson. "On Native Mythology." *Theatrum* 6 (Spring 1987): 29–31.

Hodgson, Heather. "Survival Cree, or Weesakeechak Dances Down Yonge Street." *Books in Canada* 28 (Fall 1999): 2–5.

Honegger, Gitta. "Native Playwright: Tomson Highway." *Theater* 23 (Winter 1992): 88–92.

Imboden, Roberta. "On the Road with Tomson Highway's Blues Harmonica in *Dry Lips Oughta Move to Kapuskasing*." *Canadian Literature* 144 (Spring 1995): 113–24.

Innes, Christopher. "Dreams of Violence: Moving Beyond Colonialism in Canadian and Caribbean Drama." In *Theatre Matters: Performance and Culture on the World Stage*. Ed. Richard Boon and Jane Plastow. Cambridge: Cambridge Univ. Press, 1998. 76–96.

Johnston, Denis W. "Lines and Circles: The 'Rez' Plays of Tomson Highway." *Canadian Literature* 124–125 (Spring-Summer 1990): 254–64.

Knowles, Richard Paul. "Reading Material: Transfers, Remounts, and the Production of Meaning in Contemporary Toronto Drama and Theatre." *Essays on Canadian Writing* 51–52 (Winter 1993-Spring 1994): 258–95.

Loucks, Brian. "Another Glimpse: Excerpts from a Conversation with Tomson Highway." *CTR* 68 (Fall 1991): 9–11.

Maufort, Marc. "Recognizing Difference in Canadian Drama: Tomson Highway's Poetic Realism." *British Journal of Canadian Studies* 8.2 (1993): 230–40.

Methot, Suzanne. "The Universe of Tomson Highway." *Quill & Quire* 64 (November 1998): 1, 12.

Morgan, William. "The Trickster and Native Theater: An Interview with Tomson Highway." In *Aboriginal Voices: Amerindian, Inuit and Sami Theater*. Ed. Per Brask and William Morgan. Baltimore: Johns Hopkins Univ. Press, 1992. 130–38.

Moses, Daniel David. "The Trickster Theatre of Tomson Highway." *Canadian Fiction Magazine* 60 (1987): 83–88.

Nothof, Anne. "Cultural Collision and Magical Transformation: The Plays of Tomson Highway." *Studies in Canadian Literature* 20.2 (1995): 34–43.

Petrone, Penny. *Native Literature in Canada: From the Oral Tradition to the Present*. Toronto: Oxford Univ. Press, 1990. 170–75.

Preston, Jennifer. "Weesageechak Begins to Dance: Native Earth Performing Arts Inc." *TDR* 36 (Spring 1992): 135–59.

Rabillard, Sheila. "Absorption, Elimination, and the Hybrid: Some Impure Questions of Gender and Culture in the Trickster Drama of Tomson Highway." *Essays in Theatre* 12 (November 1993): 3–28.

Steed, Judy. "Tomson Highway: My Way." *Toronto Star*, 24 March 1991, D1–2.

Taylor, Drew Hayden. "Storytelling to Stage: The Growth of Native Theatre in Canada." *TDR/The Drama Review* 41 (Fall 1997): 140–52.

Tompkins, Joanne and Lisa Male. "'Twenty-One Native Women on Motorcycles': An Interview with Tomson Highway." *Australasian Drama Studies* 24 (April 1994): 13–28.

Usmiani, Renate. "The Bingocentric Worlds of Michel Tremblay and Tomson Highway: *Les Belles-Soeurs* vs. *The Rez Sisters*." *Canadian Literature* 144 (Spring 1995): 126–40.

Wasserman, Jerry. "Where the Soul Still Dances: The Blues and Canadian Drama." *Essays on Canadian Writing* 65 (Fall 1998): 56–75.

Wigston, Nancy. "Nanabush in the City." *Books in Canada* 18 (March 1989): 7–9.

Wilson, Ann. "Tomson Highway, Interview." In *Other Solitudes: Canadian Multicultural Fictions*. Ed. Linda Hutcheon and Marion Richmond. Toronto: Oxford Univ. Press, 1990. 350–55.

B. **DRY LIPS OUGHTA MOVE TO KAPUSKASING**: SELECTED REVIEWS

Bashford, Lucy. "*Dry Lips Oughta Move to Kapuskasing*." *Malahat Review* 91 (June 1990): 109–10.

Bemrose, John. "Highway of Hope." *Maclean's* 102 (8 May 1989): 62.

———. "Native Grace." *Maclean's* 104 (29 April 1991): 60–61.

Chapman, Geoff. "Royal Treatment for Dry Lips." *Toronto Star,* 14 April 1991, C1.

Conlogue, Ray. "An Emotionally Riveting Dry Lips." *Globe and Mail,* 24 April 1989, A17.

Crew, Robert. "Hope Flickers in Disturbing Probe of Native Spirit." *Toronto Star,* 23 April 1989, C1.

Crook, Barbara. "A Few Slips Twixt Audience and Lips." *Vancouver Sun,* 25 March 1995, H8.

Cushman, Robert. "From Ideal to Painfully Real." *Globe and Mail,* 15 April 1991, C3.

Donnelly, Pat. "Greene a Scene-Stealer in *Dry Lips.*" *Montreal Gazette,* 23 March 1991, E12.

Fraser, Marian Botsford. "Contempt for Women Overshadows Powerful Play." *Globe and Mail,* 17 April 1991, A13.

Godfrey, Stephen. "Trip from Comedy to Drama Is a Worthwhile, if Bumpy, Ride." *Globe and Mail,* 9 March 1991, C8.

Hunt, Nigel. "Tracking the Trickster." *Brick* 37 (Autumn 1989): 58–60.

McIlroy, Randal. "*Dry Lips* Oughta Be Reworked Despite Some Bright Moments." *Winnipeg Free Press,* 26 October 1990, 42.

Mazey, Steven. "*Dry Lips.*" *Ottawa Citizen,* 2 March 1991, G3.

Portman, Jamie. "Native Play's Impact Dulled by Buffoonery." *Calgary Herald,* 25 April 1989, D3.

Scott, Jay. "*Dry Lips'* Loss of Intimacy Transforms Visceral Images into Picturesque Tableaux." *Globe and Mail,* 21 April 1991, 9.

Smyth, Michael. "Native Play Triumphs." *Winnipeg Free Press,* 15 April 1991, 16.

Wasserman, Jerry. "Drama." *University of Toronto Quarterly* 60 (Fall 1990): 69–71.

ROBERT LEPAGE

A. BIOGRAPHY AND CRITICISM

Ackerman, Marianne. "*Alanienouidet*: Simultaneous Space and Action." *CTR* 70 (Spring 1992): 32–34.

———. "The Hectic Career of Robert Lepage." *Imperial Oil Review* 74 (Winter 1990): 14–17.

Beauchamp, Hélène. "The Repère Cycles: From Basic to Continuous Education." *CTR* 78 (Spring 1994): 26–31.

Burrows, Malcolm. "*Tectonic Plates*: Bridging the Continental Drift." *CTR* 55 (Summer 1988): 43–47.

Bunzli, James. "The Geography of Creation: Decalage as Impulse, Process, and Outcome in the Theatre of Robert Lepage." *TDR/The Drama Review* 43 (Spring 1999): 79–103.

Carson, Christie. "Celebrity by Association: *Tectonic Plates* in Glasgow." *CTR* 74 (Spring 1993): 46–50.

———. "Collaboration, Translation, Interpretation: Robert Lepage Interviewed." *New Theatre Quarterly* 33 (February 1993): 31–36.

Charest, Rémy. *Robert Lepage: Connecting Flights.* Trans. Wanda Romer Taylor. London: Methuen, 1995.

Dault, Gary Michael. "*Le Confessionnal* & *Le Polygraphe*: A Rumination." *Take One* 5 (Spring 1997): 17–21.

Feldman, Susan. "When Cultures Collide: Robert Lepage in Glasgow." *Theatrum* 24 (Summer 1991): 9–13.

Frieze, James. "Channeling Rubble: *Seven Streams of the River Ota* and *After Sorrow.*" *Journal of Dramatic Theory and Criticism* 12 (Fall 1997): 133–42.

Garner, Stanton B., Jr. "Traces: *The Dragons' Trilogy.*" In *Bodied Spaces: Phenomenology and Performance in Contemporary Drama.* Ithaca, NY: Cornell UP, 1994. 225–30.

Gibson, K. Jane. "Seeing Double: The Map-Making Process of Robert Lepage." *CTR* 97 (Winter 1998): 18–23.

Harvie, Jennifer and Erin Hurley. "States of Play: Locating Quebec in the Performances of Robert Lepage, Ex Machina, and the Cirque du Soleil." *Theatre Journal* 51 (October 1999): 299–315.

Hodgdon, Barbara. "Splish Splash and the Other: Robert Lepage's Intercultural *Dream Machine.*" *Essays in Theatre* 12 (November 1993): 29–40.

Hunt, Nigel. "The Global Voyage of Robert Lepage." *TDR/The Drama Review* 122 (Summer 1989): 104–18.

———. "The Moving Language of Robert Lepage." *Theatrum* 6 (Spring 1987): 25–28, 32.

Jacobson, Lynn. "Tectonic States." *American Theater* (November 1991): 17–22.

Knowles, Richard Paul. "From Dream to Machine: Peter Brook, Robert Lepage, and the Contemporary Shakespearean Director as (Post)Modernist." *Theatre Journal* 50 (May 1998): 189–206.

Lefebre, Martin. "Sense of Time and Place: The Chronotope in *I Confess* and *Le Confessionnal*." *Quebec Studies* 26 (Fall 1998): 88–98.

Lefebvre, Paul. "Robert Lepage: New Filters for Creation." *CTR* 52 (Fall 1987): 30–35.

McCall, Gordon. "Two Solitudes: A Bilingual *Romeo et Juliette* in Saskatoon." CTR 62 (Spring 1990): 35–41.

Manguel, Alberto. "Theatre of the Miraculous." *Saturday Night* 104 (January 1989): 32–39, 42.

Manning, Eric. "The Haunted Home: Colour Spectrums in Robert Lepage's *Le Confessionnal*." *Canadian Journal of Film Studies* 7 (Fall 1998): 49–65.

Rewa, Natalie. "Clichés of Ethnicity Subverted: Robert Lepage's *La Trilogie des dragons*." *Theatre History in Canada* 11 (Fall 1990): 148–61.

Salter, Denis. "A State of Becoming." *Books in Canada* 20 (March 1991): 26–29.

———. "Between Wor(l)ds: Lepage's Shakespeare Cycle." *Theater* 24.3 (1993): 61–70.

———. "Borderlines: An Interview with Robert Lepage and Le Théâtre Repère." *Theater* 24.3 (1993): 71–79.

Sidnell, Michael J. "*Polygraph*: Somatic Truth and an Art of Presence." *CTR* 64 (Fall 1990): 45–48.

Steen, Shannon and Margaret Werry. "Bodies, Technologies, and Subjectivities: The Production of Authority in Robert Lepage's *Elsinore*." *Essays in Theatre* 16 (May 1998): 139–51.

Ziraldo, Cristiana. "Lepage's *Polygraphe* in Italy." *CTR* 105 (Winter 2001): 16–19.

B. POLYGRAPH: SELECTED REVIEWS

Campbell, James. "The Lie of the Body." *Times Literary Supplement* (London), 3 March 1989, 222.

Crew, Robert. "Quebec Maestro in Top Form." *Toronto Star*, 21 February 1990, F4.

Donnelly, Pat. "Enigmatic Lepage Play Disappoints." *Montreal Gazette*, 18 November 1988, C4.

———. "Lepage's *Polygraph* Improves with Age." *Montreal Gazette*, 21 March 1991, D10.

Dykk, Lloyd. "Stunning Stagecraft Saves This Unlikely Tale." *Vancouver Sun*, 24 October 1992, C20.

Godfrey, Stephen. "A Riveting Exploration of Memory and Survival." *Globe and Mail*, 18 November 1988, D9.

Holden, Stephen. "Metaphysics and Crime." *New York Times*, 27 October 1990, I12.

Lacey, Liam. "*Polygraph*'s Evolving X-Ray." *Globe and Mail*, 23 February 1990, C6.

Nicholls, Liz. "Brilliant Multi-Layered Fantasia on Truth, Fiction and Memory." *Edmonton Journal*, 7 April 1991, D2.

Winston, Iris. "*Polygraph*: A Riveting, Powerful Whodunnit with a Difference." *Ottawa Citizen*, 13 March 1991, C7.

DANIEL MacIVOR

A. BIOGRAPHY and CRITICISM

Bolt, Carol. "Introduction." *Never Swim Alone & This Is a Play* by Daniel MacIvor. Toronto: Playwrights Canada, 1993. 7–9.

Brooks, Daniel. "Some Thoughts about Directing *Here Lies Henry*." *CTR* 92 (Fall 1997): 42–45.

Edemariam, Aida. "Nasty Drafts and Big Prizes." *National Post*, 28 November 1998, 5.

Halferty, Paul. Interview with Daniel MacIvor. In *Questionable Activities*. Ed. Judith Rudakoff. Vol. 2, 6–11.

Knowles, Ric. *The Theatre of Form and the Production of Meaning: Contemporary Canadian Dramaturgies*. 72–73, 198–202.

Livingstone, David. "Jump Starter." *Flare* 14 (September 1992): 76, 180.

MacIvor, Daniel. "This Is an Article." *Theatrum* 30 (September/October 1992): 15–17.

Posner, Michael. "Avant–garde Duo Creates a Monster." *Globe and Mail*, 21 April 1998, A15.

Vaughan, R.M. "A Gay Man's Everyhomo." *Books in Canada* 24 (December 1995): 10–11.

Wagner, Vit. "Playwright Daniel MacIvor: Down the Road and Back Again." *ARTSatlantic* 14 (Fall 1995): 34–36.

Wallace, Robert. "The Victor(y) of the Subject." Introduction to *House Humans* by Daniel MacIvor. Toronto: Coach House, 1992. 7–14.

Wilson, Ann. "Lying and Dying: Theatricality in *Here Lies Henry*." *CTR* 92 (Fall 1997): 39–41.

B. **NEVER SWIM ALONE**: SELECTED REVIEWS

Chapman, Geoff. "Furious Word-Duels Convey Male Idiocy." *Toronto Star*, 21 January 1994, D12.

Clark, Bob. "Bitterness Evident in Short Play." *Calgary Herald*, 10 February 2000, B13.

Donnelly, Pat. "Odd Strokes from Cult Dramatist." *Montreal Gazette*, 24 October 1997, D5.

Hall, Lynda. "*Never Swim Alone & This Is a Play*." *CTR* 82 (Spring 1995): 95–96.

Hampton, Wilborn. "13 Corporate Rounds, Mano a Mano." *New York Times*, 20 July 2000, E3.

Hood, Sarah B. "*Never Swim Alone*, A Cruel Comedy." *Theatrum* 23 (April/May 1991): 38.

Kirchhoff, H.J. "Beached Wails and Recriminations." *Globe and Mail*, 25 January 1994, C4.

Prosser, David. "Looking Past the Print." *Books in Canada* 23 (September 1994): 31.

Wagner, Vit. "MacIvor Dives Deep into Stylish Oneupmanship." *Toronto Star*, 1 March 1991, D9.

JOAN MacLEOD

A. BIOGRAPHY AND CRITICISM

Chapman, Geoff. "Unpredictable MacLeod Brings Rich Writing to Real-Life Worries." *Toronto Star*, 5 March 1992, E8.

Crew, Robert. "Play Talks to Handicapped via Elvis." *Toronto Star*, 2 October 1987, E12.

Derksen, Céleste. "BC Oddities: Interpellation and/in Joan MacLeod's *The Hope Slide*." *CTR* 101 (Winter 2000): 49–52.

Kirchhoff, H.J. "The Reincarnation of Joan MacLeod." *Globe and Mail*, 28 March 1992, C6.

MacLeod, Joan. "Interview with Joan MacLeod." *Capilano Review* 2.12 (1994): 68–90.

Nothof, Anne. "The Construction and Deconstruction of Border Zones in *Fronteras Americanas* by Guillermo Verdecchia and *Amigo's Blue Guitar* by Joan MacLeod." *Theatre Research in Canada* 20 (Spring 1999): 3–15.

Rudakoff, Judith and Rita Much, eds. *Fair Play*. 190–207.

B. **AMIGO'S BLUE GUITAR**: SELECTED REVIEWS

Bemrose, John. "Flight from Tyranny." *Maclean's* 103 (29 January 1990): 66.

Conlogue, Ray. "Guilt, Guilt, Guilt: Offstage Horrors Steal the Show." *Globe and Mail*, 4 January 1990, C5.

Crew, Robert. "Si, Amigo, a Fine Guitar." *Toronto Star*, 3 January 1990, D1.

Dykk, Lloyd. "Moral, Humorous Play Undercuts the Obvious at Every Turn." *Vancouver Sun*, 3 October 1990, C6.

Grant, Alex. "The Art of Altruism." *British Columbia Report* 2 (22 October 1990): 50.

Hood, Sarah B. "*Amigo's Blue Guitar*." *Theatrum* 24 (June-August 1991): 7.

Jones, Heather. "*Amigo's Blue Guitar*." *CTR* 79/80 (Fall 1994): 159–60.

Morrow, Martin. "Dramatic Story Only Half-Realized." *Calgary Herald*, 4 November 1990, D3.

Wasserman, Jerry. "Drama." *University of Toronto Quarterly* 61 (Fall 1991): 83.

MORRIS PANYCH

A. BIOGRAPHY and CRITICISM

Ajzenstadt, Michael. "The Unfinished Morris Panych." *Theatrum* 22 (February/March 1991): 29–30.

Crook, Barbara. "Out of the Mud Comes Panych Attack." *Vancouver Sun*, 4 March 1993, C2.

Dykk, Lloyd. "Triple-Threat Panych Fans the Stage Fires." *Vancouver Sun*, 14 June 1989, C5.

Gilbert, Reid. "Metadramatic Design in the Stage Work of Morris Panych and Ken MacDonald." *Theatre History in Canada* 11 (Fall 1990): 134–47.

_____. "The Theatrical Stories of Morris Panych." *CTR* 67 (Summer 1991): 5–11.

Panych, Morris. "Vancouver: Contradictions." *CTR* 76 (Fall 1993): 58–59.

Ryan, Denise. "The Panych Button." *Vancouver Magazine* 30 (April 1997): 20–21.

Wood, Chris. "Body—and Soul—Language." *Maclean's* 113 (7 February 2000): 60–62.

B. 7 STORIES: SELECTED REVIEWS

Conlogue, Ray. "Many Worlds on a Narrow Ledge." *Globe and Mail*, 1 March 1991, A11.

Donnelly, Pat. "Style and Substance." *Montreal Gazette*, 17 August 1992, C6.

Dykk, Lloyd. "Opening Windows on Lives in Chaos." *Vancouver Sun*, 13 May 1989, E8.

Kerslake, Barbara. "Three Keepers." *Canadian Literature* 140 (Spring 1994): 138–39.

Leiren-Young, Mark. "*7 Stories.*" *Theatrum* 15 (September/October 1989): 50.

Maclean, Colin. "7 Storeys High on Life." *Edmonton Express*, 30 January 1997.

Morrow, Martin. "Muted Metaphysical Fluff Doesn't Fly." *Calgary Herald*, 21 September 1991, F8.

Page, Malcolm. "*7 Stories.*" *CTR* 72 (Fall 1992): 81.

Thomas, Colin. "Student Actors Mostly Shine in *Stories.*" *Georgia Straight*, 23–30 January 1997, 49

Wagner, Vit. "First-Rate Cast Binds Play Together." *Toronto Star*, 27 February 1991, F3.

Wasserman, Jerry. "Drama." *University of Toronto Quarterly* 61 (Fall 1991): 87–88.

KELLY REBAR

A. BIOGRAPHY and CRITICISM

Donnelly, Pat. "Playwright a Dramatic Success." *Montreal Gazette*, 6 April 1988, B5.

Keahey, Deborah. *Making It Home: Place in Canadian Prairie Literature*. Winnipeg: Univ. of Manitoba Press, 1998. 26–34.

Morrow, Martin. "Author of Hit Café Play Insists She's Serving Pure Invention." *Calgary Herald*, 23 April 1990, D1–2.

Prokosh, Kevin. "Prairie Playwright." *Winnipeg Free Press*, 19 September 1987, 29.

Salter, Denis. "Introduction." In *New Canadian Drama 3*. Ed. Denis Salter. Ottawa: Borealis, 1984. vii–xiii.

B. BORDERTOWN CAFÉ: SELECTED REVIEWS

Doney, Diane. "*Bordertown Café.*" *City Magazine* 9 (Winter 1987/88): 42.

Donnelly, Pat. "Café Conveys Spirit of West." *Montreal Gazette*, 8 April 1988, D1.

Dykk, Lloyd. "Bordertown Marred by Tired Clichés." *Vancouver Sun*, 9 May 1990, C6.

McIlroy, Randal. "Play Lacks Strong Shape." *Winnipeg Free Press*, 2 October 1987, 19.

Morrow, Martin. "Play Delivers Sad Message about Modern Fathers." *Calgary Herald*, 25 February 1990, E1.

Skinner, C.J. "*Bordertown Café.*" *CTR* 65 (Winter 1990): 60–61.

Thiessen, Vern. "*Bordertown Café.*" *Prairie Fire* 11.3 (1990): 98–99.

Wasserman, Jerry. "Drama." *University of Toronto Quarterly* 60 (Fall 1990): 74–75.

DJANET SEARS

A. BIOGRAPHY and CRITICISM

Bennett, Susan. "Text as Performance: Reading and Viewing Djanet Sears's *Afrika Solo.*" In *Contemporary Issues in Canadian Drama*. Ed. Per Brask. 15–25.

Breon, Robin. "Blackface: Thoughts on Racial Masquerade." *CTR* 98 (Spring 1999): 60–62.

Edemariam, Aida. "Nasty Drafts and Big Prizes." *National Post*, 28 November 1998, 5.

Gilbert, Helen and Joanne Tompkins. *Post-Colonial Drama: Theory, Practice, Politics*. 249–50.

Goodman, Lizbeth. *Contemporary Feminist Theatres: To Each Her Own*. London: Routledge, 1993. 178–81.

Nurse, Donna Bailey. "*Othello* Built for the Nineties." *Globe and Mail*, 18 November 1997, C5.

Sanders, Leslie. "Othello Deconstructed: Djanet Sears' *Harlem Duet*." In *Testifyin': Contemporary African Canadian Drama, Volume One*. Ed. Djanet Sears. Toronto: Playwrights Canada, 2000. 557–59.

Sears, Djanet. "Afterword." In *Afrika Solo* by Djanet Sears. Toronto: Sister Vision, 1990. 95–101.

———. "Introduction." In *Testifyin': Contemporary African Canadian Drama, Volume One*. Ed. Djanet Sears. i–xiii.

———. "Naming Names: Black Women Playwrights in Canada." In *Women on the Canadian Stage*. Ed. Rita Much. 92–103.

———. "nOTES oF a cOLOURED gIRL: 32 sHORT rEASONS wHY i wRITE fOR tHE tHEATRE." In *Harlem Duet* by Djanet Sears. [Winnipeg]: Scirocco, 1997. 11–16.

———. and Alison Sealy Smith. "The Nike Method." *CTR* 97 (Winter 1998): 24–30.

———, et al. "Writing Through Race: Black Writers on Being Edited, Published, and Reviewed in Canada." *Quill & Quire* 66 (May 2000): 1, 18–19.

Tompkins, Joanne. "Infinitely Rehearsing Performance and Identity: *Afrika Solo* and *The Book of Jessica*." *CTR* 74 (Spring 1993): 35–39.

———. "'The Story of Rehearsal Never Ends': Rehearsal, Performance, Identity in Settler-Culture Drama." *Canadian Literature* 144 (Spring 1995): 142–61.

Yhap, Beverly. "On Their Own Terms." *CTR* 56 (Fall 1988): 25–30.

B. **HARLEM DUET**: SELECTED REVIEWS

Chapman, Geoff. "A Brittle Celebration of Race and Gender." *Toronto Star*, 2 November 1997, C6.

Colbourn, John. "Harlem Rendered in Vivid Colour." *Toronto Sun*, 26 April 1997.

Knowles, Richard P. "Letters in Canada 1997: Drama." *University of Toronto Quarterly* 68 (Winter 1998/99): 320.

Nolan, Yvette. "*Harlem Duet*." *Prairie Fire* 19 (Summer 1998): 199–200.

Taylor, Kate. "Characters Lost in Political Lessons." *Globe and Mail*, 28 April 1997, C3.

Wagner, Vit. "Theatre as It Should Be." *Toronto Star*, 27 April 1997, B3.

JUDITH THOMPSON

A. BIOGRAPHY AND CRITICISM

Adam, Julie. "The Implicated Audience: Judith Thompson's Anti-Naturalism in *The Crackwalker, White Biting Dog, I Am Yours* and *Lion in the Streets*." In *Women on the Canadian Stage*. Ed. Rita Much. 21–29.

Bessai, Diane. "Women Dramatists: Sharon Pollock and Judith Thompson." In *Post-Colonial English Drama*. Ed. Bruce King. NY: St. Martin's, 1992. 97–117.

Duchesne, Scott. "Our Country's Good: The Export Market Favours Walker, Tremblay and Thompson." *Theatrum* 38 (April/May 1994): 19–23.

Filewod, Alan. "Critical Mass: Assigning Value and Place in Canadian Drama." In *On-Stage and Off-Stage: English Canadian Drama in Discourse*. Ed. Albert-Reiner Glaap with Rolf Althorp. 32–50.

———, and Allan Watts, eds. *Judith Thompson Casebook*. *CTR* 89 (Winter 1996).

Grace, Sherrill. "Going North on Judith Thompson's *Sled*." *Essays in Theatre* 16 (May 1998): 153–64.

Harvie, Jennifer. "Constructing Fictions of an Essential Reality or 'This Pickshur is Niiiice': Judith Thompson's *Lion in the Streets*." *Theatre Research in Canada* 13 (Spring/Fall 1992): 81–93.

———. "(Im)Possibility: Fantasy and Judith Thompson's Drama." In *On-Stage and Off-Stage: English Canadian Drama in Discourse*. Ed. Albert-Reiner Glaap with Rolf Althorp. 240–56.

Hunt, Nigel. "In Contact with the Dark." *Books in Canada* 17 (March 1988): 10–12.

Jansen, Ann. Introduction to *White Sand* by Judith Thompson. In *Airborne: Radio Plays by Women*. Ed. Ann Jansen. Winnipeg: Blizzard, 1991. 2–5.

Knowles, Richard Paul. "Computers Keep Your Office Tidier [Interview]." *CTR* 81 (Winter 1994): 29–31.

———. "The Achievement of Grace." *Brick* 41 (Summer 1991): 33–36.

———. "The Fractured Subject of Judith Thompson." In *Lion in the Streets* by Judith Thompson. Toronto: Coach House, 1992. 7–10.

Maufort, Marc. "Poetic Realism Reinvented: Canadian Women Playwrights and the Search for a New Theatrical Idiom." *Études Canadiennes/Canadian Studies* 42 (1997): 27–38.

Nunn, Robert. "Spatial Metaphor in the Plays of Judith Thompson." *Theatre History in Canada* 10 (Spring 1989): 3–29.

Rafelman, Rachel. "'What I Show Are Simple Moments of Truth.'" *Globe and Mail*, 1 December 1990, C2.

Rudakoff, Judith. "Under the Goddess's Cloak: reCalling the Wild, enGendering the Power." In *Women on the Canadian Stage*. Ed. Rita Much. 115–30.

———, and Rita Much, eds. *Fair Play*. 87–104.

Sinclair, Gregory J. "Live from Off-stage: Playwrights Walker, Walmsley and Thompson Shout from the Street." *Canadian Forum* 66 (August/September 1986): 6–11.

Steed, Judy. "Thompson Different from Her Characters." *Globe and Mail*, 11 February 1982, E5.

Thompson, Judith. "One Twelfth." In *Language in Her Eye: Views on Writing and Gender by Canadian Women Writing in English*. Ed. Libby Scheier, Sarah Sheard and Eleanor Wachtel. Toronto: Coach House, 1990. 263–67.

———. "Why Should a Playwright Direct Her Own Plays?" In *Women on the Canadian Stage*. Ed. Rita Much. 104–08.

———, et al. "Looking to the Lady: Re-examining Women's Theatre." Ed. Soraya Peerbaye. *CTR* 84 (Fall 1995): 22–25.

Toles, George. "'Cause You're the Only One I Want': The Anatomy of Love in the Plays of Judith Thompson." *Canadian Literature* 118 (Autumn 1988): 116–35.

Tomc, Sandra. "Revisions of Probability: An Interview with Judith Thompson." *CTR* 59 (Summer 1989): 18–23.

Wachtel, Eleanor. "An Interview with Judith Thompson." *Brick* 41 (Summer 1991): 37–41.

Wilson, Ann. "The Culture of Abuse in *Under the Skin*, *This Is for You, Anna* and *Lion in the Streets*. In *Contemporary Issues in Canadian Drama*. Ed. Per Brask. 160–70.

Zimmerman, Cynthia. "A Conversation with Judith Thompson." *Canadian Drama* 16.2 (1990): 184–94.

———. *Playwriting Women: Female Voices in English Canada*. 176–209.

B. **LION IN THE STREETS**: SELECTED REVIEWS

Armstrong, John. "Sharp Cast and Razor Wit Help to Hone Tale of Animal Savagery." *Vancouver Sun*, 18 November 1991, C2.

Bemrose, John. "Lionhearted Drama." *Maclean's* (19 November 1990): 69.

Chung, Kathy. "Emotions and Facts." *Canadian Literature* 141 (Summer 1994): 132–34.

Conlogue, Ray. "Drama Succeeds by Baring Its Teeth." *Globe and Mail*, 8 November 1990, C1.

Crowder, Eleanor and Sarah B. Hood. "*Lion in the Streets*." *Theatrum* 22 (February/March 1991): 38–39.

Cushman, Robert. "Exploring a Limitless Domain of Human Misery." *Globe and Mail*, 4 June 1990, C8.

Donnelly, Pat. "The Shrill of It All." *Montreal Gazette*, 26 September 1991, D13.

Kirchhoff, H.J. "A Lion in Winnipeg." *Globe and Mail*, 19 January 1995, E2.

Levental, Igor and Jessica Levental. "Guided Tour Through Hell." *B.C. Reports*, 2 December 1991, p. 27.

Morrow, Martin. "Sage Theatre Debuts with a Lacerating Lion." *Calgary Herald*, 13 September 1998, C6.

Nightingale, Benedict. "*Lion in the Streets*." *The Times* (London), 21 April 1993.

Rosborough, Linda. "Grim Play Emotionally Draining." *Winnipeg Free Press*, 13 January 1995, D5.

Wagner, Vit. "A Strong Cast Helps Tarragon's Tame Play." *Toronto Star*, 4 June 1990, C1.

———. "Thompson's Duet a Theatre Triumph." *Toronto Star*, 15 November 1990, B5.

GUILLERMO VERDECCHIA

A. BIOGRAPHY AND CRITICISM

Coulthard, Lisa. "'The Line's Getting Mighty Blurry': Politics, Polemics, and Performance in *The Noam Chomsky Lectures*." *Studies in Canadian Literature* 20.2 (1995): 44–56.

Crook, Barbara. "Verdecchia Presents a Challenge to the Frontier Mentality." *Vancouver Sun*, 28 May 1994, B7.

Dafoe, Chris. "Someone Keeps Moving the Border." *Globe and Mail*, 16 February 1994, A18.

Friedlander, Mira. "Verdecchia Grapples with Continental Issues." *Toronto Star*, 21 January 1993, E11.

Gilbert, Helen and Joanne Tompkins. *Post-Colonial Drama: Theory, Practice, Politics*. London: Routledge, 1996. 285–88.

Gomez, Mayte. "Healing the Border Wound: *Fronteras Americanas* and the Future of Canadian Multiculturalism." *Theatre Research in Canada* 16.1–2 (1995): 26–39.

Harvie, Jennifer. "The Nth Degree: An Interview with Guillermo Verdecchia." *CTR* 92 (Fall 1997): 46–49.

Hunt, Nigel. "The Chomsky Boys." *Brick* 45 (Winter 1993): 38–43.

Kareda, Urjo. Foreword to *Fronteras Americanas* by Guillermo Verdecchia. Vancouver: Talonbooks, 1997. 9–12.

Nothof, Anne. "The Construction and Deconstruction of Border Zones in *Fronteras Americanas* by Guillermo Verdecchia and *Amigo's Blue Guitar* by Joan MacLeod." *Theatre Research in Canada* 20 (Spring 1999): 3–15.

Sherman, Jason. "The Daniel Brooks Lectures." *CTR* 67 (Summer 1991): 17–21.

Verdecchia, Guillermo. "Politics in Playwriting." *Betty Lambert Society Newsletter* (September 1992): 2–4.

———. "Spanglish." *In 2 Print* (Summer 2000): 10.

———, et al. "Culture Inc." *This Magazine* 32 (September-October 1998): 14–17.

Wilson, Ann. "Border Crossing: The Technologies of Identity in *Fronteras Americanas*." *Australasian Drama Studies* 29 (October 1996): 7–16.

B. FRONTERAS AMERICANAS: SELECTED REVIEWS

Buchholz, Garth. "Solo Performer Punctures Stereotype in Tour de Force." *Winnipeg Free Press*, 28 October 1994, D4.

Chapman, Geoff. "Argentine Canadian Lays It on Border Line." *Toronto Star*, 8 October 1993, C14.

Crook, Barbara. "Verdecchia's Two Characters Take Local Theatre to New Fronteras." *Vancouver Sun*, 14 January 1995, B6.

Kirchhoff, H.J. "Bashing Stereotypes with Stereotypes." *Globe and Mail*, 28 January 1993, C2.

———. "Verdecchia Returns, Leaner and Angrier." *Globe and Mail*, 8 October 1993, C8.

Mitchell, Elizabeth. "*Fronteras Americanas*." *Theatrum* 37 (February/March 1994): 29–30.

Reid, Robert. "*Fronteras Americanas* Fascinating, by Turns Funny, Thought Provoking." *Kitchener Record*, 21 October 1999.

Uhlyarick, Georgiana. "*Fronteras Americanas*." *Theatrum* 33 (April/May 1993): 41.

van Dijk, Maarten. "*Fronteras Americanas*." *CTR* 79/80 (Fall 1994): 157–59.

Wagner, Vit. "One Man's Show Another's Lesson." *Toronto Star*, 28 January 1993, D4.

GEORGE F. WALKER

A. BIOGRAPHY AND CRITICISM

Borkowski, Andrew. "Theatre of the Improbable: George F. Walker." *Canadian Forum* 70 (September 1991): 16–19.

Bortolotti, Dan. "Dramatic Intensity." *Books in Canada* 24 (April 1995): 24–27.

Conolly, L.W., ed. *Canadian Drama and the Critics*, 207–16, 297–301.

Corbeil, Carol. "A Conversation with George Walker." *Brick* 58 (Winter 1998): 59–67.

De Raey, Daniel. "Introduction." *Suburban Motel* by George F. Walker. Rev. ed., 4–6. Vancouver: Talonbooks, 1999.

Gass, Ken. "Introduction." In *Three Plays by George Walker*, 9–15. Toronto: Coach House, 1978.

"George F. Walker." In *Contemporary Literary Criticism: Yearbook 1989*. Vol. 61. Ed. Roger Matuz, 422–34. Detroit: Gale Research, 1990.

Hadfield, Dorothy. "The Role Power Plays in George F. Walker's Detective Trilogy." *Essays in Theatre* 16 (November 1997): 67–84.

Haff, Stephen. "The Brave Comedy of Big Emotions: An Introduction." *Shared Anxiety: Selected Plays by George F. Walker*, xi–xvii. Toronto: Coach House, 1994.

———. "Slashing the Pleasantly Vague: George F. Walker and the Word." *Essays in Theatre* 10 (November 1991): 59–69.

Hallgren, Chris. "George Walker: The Serious and the Comic." *Scene Changes* 7 (March-April 1979): 23–25.

Johnson, Chris. *Essays on George F. Walker: Playing with Anxiety*. Winnipeg: Blizzard, 1999.

———. "George F. Walker: B-Movies Beyond the Absurd." *Canadian Literature* 85 (Summer 1980): 87–103.

———. "George F. Walker Directs George F. Walker." *Theatre History in Canada* 9 (Fall 1988): 157–72.

———. "George F. Walker." *Post-Colonial English Drama: Commonwealth Drama since 1960*. Ed. Bruce King, 82–96. NY: St. Martin's, 1992.

———. "'I Put It in Terms Which Cover the Spectrum': Mixed Convention and Dramatic Strategies in George F. Walker's *Criminals in Love*." *On-Stage and Off-Stage: English Canadian Drama in Discourse*. Ed. Albert-Reiner Glaap. 257–69.

Johnston, Denis W. "George F. Walker: Liberal Idealism and the Power Plays." *Canadian Drama* 10.2 (1984): 195–206.

Knowles, Richard Paul. "The Dramaturgy of the Perverse." *Theatre Research International* 17 (Autumn 1992): 226–35.

Lane, William. "Introduction." In *The Power Plays* by George F. Walker, 9–14. Toronto: Coach House, 1984.

———. "Introduction." In *Zastrozzi: The Master of Discipline*, 3–6. Toronto: Playwrights Co-op, 1979.

Nyman, Ed. "Out with the Queers: Moral Triage and George F. Walker's *Theatre of the Film Noir*." *Australasian Drama Studies* 29 (October 1996): 57–66.

Posner, Michael. "Voices from a Strange Motel." *Globe and Mail*, 23 October 1997, A12–13.

Sinclair, Gregory J. "Live from Off-Stage." *Canadian Forum* 65 (August/September 1986): 6–11.

Usmiani, Renate. *Second Stage*. 35–38.

Wagner, Vit. "Drawing Us All into One Flea-Bag Room." *Toronto Star*, 20 June 1998, M3.

Walker, Craig. "Three Tutorial Plays: *The Lesson, The Prince of Naples* and *Oleanna*." *Modern Drama* 40 (Spring 1997): 149–62.

Wallace, Robert. "George F. Walker." In *Profiles in Canadian Literature*. 6th ser., 105–12.

———. "Looking for the Light: A Conversation with George F. Walker." *Canadian Drama* 14.1 (1988): 22–33.

———, and Cynthia Zimmerman, eds. *The Work*. 212–25.

Wasserman, Jerry. "'It's the Do-Gooders Burn My Ass': Modern Canadian Drama and the Crisis of Liberalism." *Modern Drama* 43 (Spring 2000): 32–47.

———. "'Making Things Clear': The *film noir* Plays of George F. Walker." *Canadian Drama* 8.1 (1982): 99–101.

Wynne-Jones, Tim. "Acts of Darkness." *Books in Canada* 14 (April 1985): 11–14.

B. **PROBLEM CHILD**: SELECTED REVIEWS

Barnard, Elissa. "Bizarre Action Drives Wacky *Problem Child*." *Halifax Chronicle Herald*, 8 November 1998, B5.

Birnie, Peter. "Motel Plays Get Mixed Reception." *Vancouver Sun*, 9 March 1999, C5.

Chapman, Geoff. "Walker's Dramatic Return." *Toronto Star*, 27 October 1997, E5.

Coulbourn, John. "Room with a Super, Sordid View." *Toronto Sun*, 26 October 1997.

Donnelly, Pat. "Pas de Problème Here." *Montreal Gazette*, 16 October 1998, D7.

Maufort, Marc. "A Passage to Belgium: George F. Walker's 'Problem Child' in Brussels." *CTR* 105 (Winter 2001): 20–23.

Taylor, Kate. "Motel Cycle a Gritty Triumph." *Globe and Mail*, 28 October 1997, A17.

Thomas, Colin. "A Darkly Comic Double Bill."
Georgia Straight, 11–18 March 1999, 73.

Wagner, Vit. "Playwright Walker Takes Audience
for Wild Ride." *Toronto Star,* 11 October
1998, B3.